STUDIES IN RENAISSANCE
AND BAROQUE ART
PRESENTED TO ANTHONY BLUNT

PHAIDON

Studies in Renaissance & Baroque Art

presented to

ANTHONY BLUNT

on his 60th birthday

PHAIDON LONDON · NEW YORK

GB STANDARD BOOK NUMBER 7148 1320 6

MADE IN GREAT BRITAIN 1967

PRINTED BY R & R CLARK LTD · EDINBURGH

EDITORIAL PREFACE

WITH this volume of essays we celebrate Sir Anthony Blunt's sixtieth birthday. It may fairly be said that he is a little young to receive a *Festschrift*, and that he is – happily – nowhere near retirement. But this year marks another anniversary, for it is now exactly twenty years since he was appointed as Director of the Courtauld Institute. This double event seemed to us to call for a tribute.

In deciding upon the form of this volume we found ourselves in a dilemma. Anthony's circle of friends, colleagues and former students, and the circle of his own interests in the history of art alone, were both far too wide to permit us to ask everyone to contribute who qualified on one or other of these grounds, and some principle of selection was inevitable. We decided to restrict contributions by subject-matter, believing that the coherence thus gained would produce a book of the most permanence and usefulness; we based our criterion on the area of scholarship which his name most naturally brings to mind and where many of his own most memorable contributions have been made: French and Italian art and architecture of the sixteenth and seventeenth centuries. Our invitations were therefore sent to scholars whose essays might, collectively, most closely reflect his major interests. We were well aware that this decision, like any other, would entail the omission of some of his closest friends, oldest colleagues and most outstanding students; we simply ask for their understanding, and his.

We should like to express our gratitude to the Phaidon Press for the enthusiasm with which they greeted this project, and for their tolerance and care during its fulfilment. And we are much indebted to the Directors of Courtaulds Ltd., from whom we received a generous grant towards its production. We should also like to thank Angela Benham, Susan Weatherby and Flavia Grant-Duff for secretarial and editorial assistance.

The other members of the Editorial Committee would like to add that the burden of all editorial work on this volume has fallen on the shoulders of two of their number, Michael Kitson and John Shearman. Had it not been for their devoted services, the material could never have been assembled.

Editorial Committee:

JEANNE COURTAULD   JOHN POPE-HENNESSY
MICHAEL KITSON   ELSA SCHEERER
BENEDICT NICOLSON   JOHN SHEARMAN
          GEORGE ZARNECKI

Sir Anthony Blunt, K.C.V.O.

CONTENTS

A PERSONAL PREFACE

THE arts of France have always been, I think, his native arts for Anthony, and a childhood spent largely in Paris meant that the Louvre was his first 'national gallery'. This was already clear by the time when I first remember discussing painters with him. It was in dormitory in school in 1922 that – perhaps somewhat to the disapproval of our companions – an argument occurred whether Ingres was 'better' than Giorgione. Anthony was for Ingres. Even then I think the shadow of Poussin was to be discerned on the horizon, for I left school the next year with a conviction, not altogether self-induced, that Poussin was a very great master whom one must take a good deal of trouble to understand and to love. A strong influence on this bent in him towards the arts was his eldest brother, Wilfrid Blunt, who was then more than half determined to become a painter: another was that humanest of schoolmasters, George Sargeaunt.

It was at Trinity, Cambridge, that the style of his mind was formed. The imprint of the Cambridge of that decade on her sons is something which perhaps only an Oxford man can fully savour – and that thirty years later; for, as was normal for many Oxford men of that generation, it never occurred to me to visit Cambridge. I only discerned from occasional encounters with Anthony the development of engrossing interests in Picasso and the painting of the present century, in German and Austrian Baroque, and in the central field of his Cambridge research, which flowered into *Artistic Theory in Italy*. It was from G. David's wonderful bookshop, as it was in those days, that he started forming what has become a remarkable library; and Andrew Gow, with his formidable knowledge of Italian paintings, was a great source of encouragement, for it was then thought rather eccentric to be interested in the history of art.

It was only towards the end of his Cambridge years that the film of my memory again reveals lively exposures of Anthony, when he spent some time, in 1933 and 1934, at the British School at Rome, looking especially at the Baroque. Many of the less familiar buildings of Rome are enlivened in recollection by having been visited with him. We took much trouble to explore the monuments of what we called 'the Passalacqua Period', which was as neglected then as it is fashionable today, and, at meal times in the School, the secretary would become exasperated at our conversation in a language which she called 'Blunterhouse' and which she was powerless to understand. The vividness of one's memories is not always matched by the weightiness of their content, but I remember with particular pleasure a joint visit to the Salentino. We would read aloud to one another the sillier passages in M. S. Briggs' *In the Heel of Italy* before setting out to explore the churches of Lecce and its neighbourhood: a trip to Galatina on hired bicycles of excruciating form is never to be forgotten, nor is our arrival one Sunday at Otranto to find a shop-window full of ties which appeared to date back to the Bourbon period – which was irrevocably closed. It was from Otranto that Anthony despatched a folkloristic postcard of the four hundred local martyrs to Ezra Pound, which effectively closed a tiresome disagreement and received the answer 'You win'.

It is not fashionable today to recall the thirties with approval, but there was much to be said for them. You could get a great deal of work done for what would now seem a very little money, and the bogey word 'currency' was little mentioned.

From Trinity Anthony migrated to the staff of the Warburg Institute, where the enchanting personality of Fritz Saxl and a library of a new kind provided a valuable counterpoint to the direct knowledge of buildings and works of art acquired by frequent travel in the same years. A curious interest in Blake also developed at this time. Perhaps not all our friends of that decade turned out in the end altogether as one would have wished, but they are still remembered with affection. The curtain lines for this period were spoken, if my memory is correct, on Platform 3 at Waterloo Station. Messrs. Auden and Isherwood were being seen off to the United States, and a voice I never identified said 'I suppose everyone in England worth saving is here!'

In 1939 Anthony became Reader in the History of Art and Deputy Director of the Courtauld Institute – the first step to the work of a lifetime, which was to be immediately interrupted by the war. In the Eastern Mediterranean I heard very little news of individual friends in the western theatre of war, and a veil of security hung over all our doings. Before I returned to England at the end of 1944 – to find Anthony gratifyingly unchanged – I had heard almost nothing of him except that he had been seen riding an army issue motorbike. This is a phenomenon I have yet to witness with my own eyes.

Before the war the Courtauld had something of the air of a curiosity in the London scene: by the end of the war, as a result of a change in our sense of values, it had almost insensibly become a force. The institution to which Anthony returned, and of which he became Director exactly twenty years ago, was something which had never previously existed in London. Before the war the London art scene may be said to have consisted of Museum people, the art trade, and a handful of 'amateurs' – and there was a very general mistrust between these worlds. In the last twenty years all this has changed, and changed very much for the better. The Courtauld, under Anthony's directorship, has trained recruits for the country's Museums, Universities and Art Schools, as well as for the art trade, and the various sides are now very much more concerned with the same standards than could have been said before. This year alone he has twenty-five higher degree students working under his supervision. Teaching, together with the Institute and all its activities, has become one of the most important parts of his life. But it is teaching as much by example as by precept, and the qualities of intellect and moral integrity which are the foundation of his books and lectures are conveyed to pupils willing to absorb them without pressure or any parade of doctrine.

The contributors to this volume will have their own knowledge and memories of the

Courtauld and of its Director during the last twenty years. Watching from the outside vantage point of an almost perpetual external examiner, it has seemed to me that common sense has led to many improvements during these years, and what is heartening is that these changes have been the result of profiting by experience. But the Surveyorship of the Queen's Pictures and the responsibility of being the leader of a sort of third estate in the art world has encouraged the imposition of further heavy burdens on one who has never had a great gift for saying 'No'. There are few government or official agencies seriously concerned with the promotion of the arts on which Anthony has not served or is not still serving. The National Art Collections Fund, the National Trust, the Reviewing Committee on the Export of Works of Art and other bodies owe a great deal to his conciliatory rather than crusading contribution to their committees, and have occupied a great deal of his time. But this has not interrupted a steady flow of scholarship in which the Royal Collections and Poussin and the French seventeenth century have provided the most constant basic material. As the bibliography at the end of this volume shows, the importance of his published work is so great that it is almost invidious to single out anything for special mention, but for an Englishman to have been asked to take a large part in the organization of the great Poussin exhibition in Paris in 1960 and to prepare its catalogue is something really to be proud of, and that exhibition itself still seems to me to have been the finest achievement of its kind within my memory. The three massive volumes on Poussin may be considered Anthony's own tribute to his sixtieth birthday, and the papers which fill the following pages may be thought of as clustering around them with affectionate regard.

ELLIS WATERHOUSE

LUDWIG H. HEYDENREICH

Federico da Montefeltro as a Building Patron
Some Remarks on the Ducal Palace of Urbino

THE high regard which Federico da Montefeltro enjoyed among his contemporaries was certainly due in the first place to his success on the battlefield and to his statesmanship, but it culminated in admiration for his intelligence, his knowledge and his culture. A true humaneness stamped his character and actions. The beautiful and lifelike picture of Federico drawn by Vespasiano da Bisticci has withstood all historical criticism. The tributes to his extraordinary personality, which exemplifies our ideal of the *principe umanista*, extend from Benedetto Baldi to Dennistoun, and all the evidence that has recently come to light – especially Federico's letters – confirm the judgment of these writers.[1] The Palazzo Ducale at Urbino[2] is the visible expression of this noble rule. Federico spent more than thirty years on building his residence, which, both in plan and decoration, was executed essentially according to his instructions. This great enterprise accompanied his whole life, grew, as it were, with him, and passed through such transformations on its way that it is precisely in them that we can recognize the controlling initiative of its patron.

If in this way all the various parts of the palace reflect – as we shall try to show – a quite unusual individuality of architectural planning, this culminates, however, in one group of rooms, which – in spite of its small overall size – represents the ideal centre of the whole residence, and which, by its singularity as a purely humanistic conceit,

must be considered the proper invention of its owner. This is the so-called *appartamento del Duca*. For a better understanding of its characteristics as well as of its meaning, it seems appropriate to give first a short survey of the general situation.

The moment at which Federico conceived the idea of building a new residence for himself cannot be exactly dated, yet it was probably connected with the consolidation of his authority, and with his success as a *condottiere*, which led to a growing demand for his services. That may have been about 1450. What Federico first had in mind was a spreading palazzo in the 'new style', which would incorporate parts of an older building, in a similar way to what he had seen at Mantua as a young man. Two buildings on the south hill between the Palazzo del Conte Antonio and the old Castellare were the starting-points of the new project. Between 1450 and 1465 there arose the first, already very large palace which, being a rectangular block with an interior courtyard, approximately conformed to the contemporary pattern for buildings of its kind. But in 1450 Federico in fact had very few models to go by; in Florence, the foundation-stone of the Palazzo Medici was laid in 1444; at Mantua, the Gonzaga were just beginning to remodel their residence; in Rome, such building had hardly begun. Thus in a general way the new style was only just getting into its stride, and there was very little to be seen. The conception of the palazzo must therefore be attributed largely to Federico himself. The main architect in charge during this first campaign was the Florentine Maso di Bartolomeo, with some co-workers; he was assisted later – if we accept G. Marchini's attractive arguments – for a short time by Giorgio da Sebenico, whose hand can be recognized in a number of delicately worked console-capitals.[3] And it is a fascinating idea, too – first put forward by Mario Salmi – to see in the refined style of the architectural articulation the additional influence of Piero della Francesca, in whose pictures – for instance the *Flagellation of Christ* painted for Federico – the ideal architecture looks like a prototype for the decorative scheme of the Palazzo Ducale.[4]

Be that as it may, and despite the imposing size of the first building and the great care that was lavished upon it, it

1. Francesco Filelfo, *Commentarii de vita e rebus gestis Frederici comitis urbinatis (ligae) italicae imperatoris*, ed. G. Zannoni, in *Atti e Memorie della Deputazione di Storia Patria delle Marche*, v, 1901, pp. 263 ff.; Vespasiano da Bisticci, *Vita degli uomini singolari*, ed. P. D'Ancona and E. Aeschlimann, Milan, 1950; Bernardino Baldi, *Vita e fatti di Federigo di Montefeltro*, ed. Rome, 1724; J. Dennistoun, *Memoirs of the Dukes of Urbino*, London, 1851 (2nd ed., London, 1909); R. de la Sézeranne, *Le Condottiere Federigo di Montefeltro*, Paris, 1927; *Ordini e offitii alla corte del Serenissimo signor Duca d'Urbino*, a cura della R. Acc. Raffaello, Urbino, 1932; Federigo da Montefeltro, *Lettere di stato e d'arte, 1470–1480*, ed. Paolo Alatri, Rome, 1949; G. Franceschini, *Figure del rinascimento urbinate*, Urbino, 1959.

2. C. Budenich, *Il Palazzo Ducale di Urbino*, Leipzig, 1905; Th. Hofmann, *Bauten des Herzogs Federigo da Montefeltro als erste Werke der Hochrenaissance*, Leipzig, 1905. The standard work is by P. Rotondi, *Il Palazzo Ducale di Urbino*, 2 vols., Urbino, 1950, with many plans and illustrations and a complete list of literary sources. Further: P. Zambetti, *Il Palazzo Ducale di Urbino*, Rome, 1951; G. Marchini, 'Il Palazzo Ducale di Urbino,' *Rinascimento*, IX, 1958, pp. 43 ff.; idem, 'Aggiunte al Palazzo Ducale di Urbino,' *Boll. d'arte*, XLV, 1960, pp. 73 ff.

3. G. Marchini, 'Aggiunte . . .', *op. cit.*, p. 76.

4. Mario Salmi, *Piero della Francesca ed il Palazzo Ducale di Urbino* Florence, 1945.

remained entirely bound to the formal idiom of its time. This will become clear to any visitor to Urbino who is aware of the radical change of plan which determined the second stage in the building, in which the splendour of the architectural conception offers a striking contrast to the previous parts of the palazzo.

Very little had been done up to that time to take full advantage of the unique site. True, the palazzo, like its medieval predecessors, stood on the slope of a hill and, as a compact block (with comparatively small windows distributed over large wall-surfaces), it dominated the scene. But its disposition ignored the natural setting and had no kind of direct relationship to it. The first great idea in the change of plan consisted in the studied setting of the new parts of the building against their natural background, which became the leitmotif governing all the technical problems. It gave the whole organism a new meaning and a new value. The enlargement consisted, first, of the addition of a new

wing to the still open north side of the courtyard, and this was to become the main part of the residence. Furthermore, a second, transverse wing (the Sala delle Veglie) was erected, which incorporated in the general lay-out the last medieval building still standing – the Castellare. A wall running from the Castellare to the northern tower made a space for a garden-terrace (*giardino pensile*), and thus an organic conclusion to the whole was achieved.

These alterations gave the palazzo two important fronts. To the west, the grand loggia façade, flanked by turrets and looking out over the open country, was set in perspective in such a way that anyone approaching it along the western road saw it as a single picture; to the east the town front formed, with its transverse wing, a decorative façade of a piazza, which was to be closed on the third side by the huge mass of the Duomo.

With this extension, the whole building became that grandiose complex which was so vividly described by Bal-

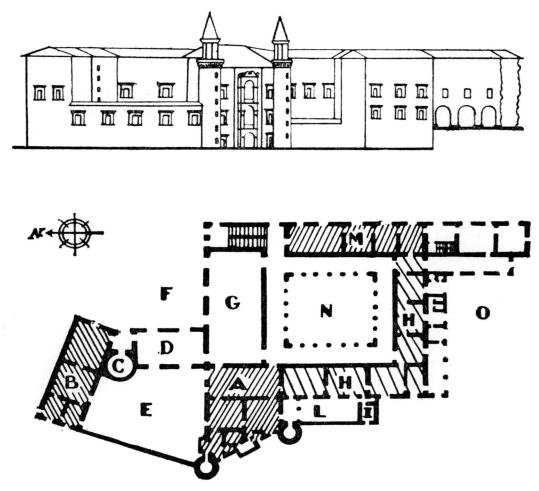

Elevation of Palazzo Ducale at Urbino, with plan at the level of the *piano nobile*. (From Rotondi, *Il Palazzo Ducale di Urbino*.)
A: Appartamento del Duca. B: Appartamento della Duchessa, in the old Castellare. D: Sala delle Veglie.
E: Giardino pensile. F: Piazza duca Federico. G: Salone del trono. N: Cortile d'onore.

dassare Castiglione: 'nel l'aspero sito d'Urbino edificò un palazzo, secondo la opinione di molti il più bello che in tutta l'Italia si ritrovi; e d'ogni cosa si ben lo fornì, che non un palazzo, ma una città in forma di palazzo pareva'.⁵
This bold project required for its realization an equally bold architect. Federico found, or rather discovered, such a man in Luciano Laurana, whom he had met at Pesaro in the service of the Sforza.⁶ As early as 1465 Laurana had prepared a model of the residence.⁷ The document of 1468, in which Federico confers plenary powers on Laurana as architect-in-chief, is one of the most instructive of the period; it bears witness, above all, to the impressive specialized knowledge of a patron who, finding no great master available in Florence at the time, recognized the foreigner's quality and took him into his service.⁸ What makes Laurana

a great architect is not only his remarkable mastery of the technique of masonry, but his extraordinary feeling for mass and proportion. This dual capacity, which combines the experience of a fortress-builder with a particularly fine sense of the architectural site, can be seen in the ingenious arrangement of the different parts of the building, in the composition of the two fronts and in the disposition of the interior. Laurana was in charge of the building until 1472, when he was succeeded by Francesco di Giorgio Martini.⁹ The most important parts of the 'second plan of Urbino' were therefore executed under the direction of Laurana, but following, I am convinced, to a great extent the instructions of Federico; if that is the case the result must be considered – using Filarete's terms – as a true fruit of the 'marriage' between architect and patron who together 'generate' the building as their child.¹⁰ All the evidence points to Federico da Montefeltro himself as the author of the new conception of the residence. In my opinion it must have been the plan of Pienza which suggested the idea to him. As is well known, Pope Pius II had carefully related the layout of the piazza at Pienza to its natural background; huge sums were spent on building a prodigious substructure for the choir of the cathedral and the palace garden – for the sole purpose of opening a view on to the Val d'Orcia and Monte Amiata. Work began in 1458 and was halted in 1464. Reading the description of the family palazzo at Pienza which Pius II gives in his *Commentari*,¹¹ we find, beyond a general resemblance between the two projects, many details akin to those at Urbino: the unusually spacious staircase, the suite of the Pope's private rooms in the second storey behind the great hall, with the chapel, bedroom and study leading into the loggia from which the view opens.¹² All

5. B. Castiglione, *Il corteggiano*, Lib. I, cap. 2, ed. V. Cian, Florence, 1908, pp. 13 ff. A large number of other contemporary appreciations are quoted by Rotondi and Franceschini, *passim*.

6. Bibliography: Thieme-Becker, 1928, vol. XXII, pp. 442 ff., with earlier literature. Also: A. Venturi, *L'arte*, XLI, 1938, p. 370; P. Rotondi, *op. cit.*, *passim*; L. Grassi, *Palladio*, IV, 1954, p. 97; G. Marchini, *Rinascimento*, *op. cit.*, p. 43; L. Babic, *Actes XIXᵉ Congrès international histoire de l'art*, Paris, 1959, p. 231. A good summary of the origins of Laurana's style appears in M. Salmi, *Piero della Francesca ed il Pal. Ducale*, *op. cit.*, pp. 100 ff.

7. Franceschini, *op. cit.*, pp. 68 ff.

8. Federicus, Montis Feretri Urbini ac Durantis Comes, Ser.me q. Lege Cap.s G(e)n(er)alis etc.
   Quelli huomini noi giudicamo dever essere honorati, et commendati, li q(u)ali si trovano esser ornati d'ingegno e di virtù et max. di quelle virtù che sempre sono state in prezzo appresso li antiqui et moderni com'è la virtù dell'Architettura fondata in l'arte dell'aritmetica e geometria, che sono, delle sette arti liberali, et delle principali, perchè sono in primo gradu certitudinis, et è arte di gran scienza et di grandi ingegno, et da noi molto extimata, et apprezzata, et havendo noi cercato per tutto, et in Toscana massime dove è la fontana delli Architettori, et non avendo trovato huomo che sia veram(en)te intendente, et ben perito, in tal mistiero, ultimam(en)te havendo per fama prima inteso et poi per esperienza veduto et conosciuto quanto l'egregio huomo Mastro Lutiano ostensore di questa sia dotto, et instrutto in quest'arte, et havendo deliberato di fare in la n(os)tra Città d'Urbino una habitatione bella, e degna, quanto si conviene alla conditione, e(t) laudabil fama delli n(os)tri progenitori, et anco alla condition n(os)tra, Noi avemo elletto et deputato il detto m.ro Lutiano per Ingegniero et Capo di tutti li m(aest)ri che lavoraranno alla dett'opera, così di murare, come de M(aest)ri d'intagliare Pietre e(t) M(aest)ri di Legnami, et fabri, et d'ogn' altra persona di qualunche grado, et di qualunche essercitio lavorasse alla detta opera, et così volemo, et commandamo a' detti M(aest)ri et operarij, et a ciascuno de n(ost)ri Uff.li, et suddite ch'havessero a provedere fare et operare alcuna cosa in la dett'opera, che al detto m.ro Lutiano debbano in ogni cosa obedire, et far quanto per lui li sarà comandato non altram(en)te che alla n(os)tra propria persona . . . Dando al detto m(aest)ro Lutiano pieno arbitrio et potestà et libera bailia, et possanza, di posser cassare, rimovere qualunche m(aest)ro, et operario che fusse alla dett'opera, che non li piacesse o non li satisfacesse a suo modo et di posser condurre altri Maestri, et operarij, et darli a lavorare a cottimo o a giornate come li piacesse et così di poter punire et condennare et ritenere del salario et provvisioni de chi

non facesse il dovere et tutte l'altre cose fare le quali s'appartiene ad un Architettore et Capo m(aest)ro deputato ad un lavoro, et quello proprio che potessimo fatto fare questa p(rese)nte patente, et sigillare del n(ost)ro maggior sigillo.
Dat. in Castello Papie die X. Junij 1468.
    Loco ✠ Sigilli.   Io ser Ant. subscripsit
First published in G. Gaye, *Carteggio*, I, 1839, p. 214. Our reprint is taken from Rotondi, *op. cit.*, I, p. 109.

9. For Francesco di Giorgio's share of the work, cf. P. Rotondi, *op. cit.*, I, pp. 289 ff. and G. Marchini's valuable statements in *Rinascimento*, *op. cit.*, pp. 60 ff.

10. Filarete, *Trattato*, Lib. II, ed. J. Spencer, New Haven and London, 1965, I, p. 16 ff. For Vespasiano da Bisticci's statements of Federico's qualities as an expert in architecture, see below, p. 6.

11. *The Commentaries of Pius II*, translated by Florence Alden Gragg, introduction and notes by Leona C. Gabel, *Smith College Studies in History*, XXII, Northampton, Mass., 1936/37, pp. 597 ff., especially pp. 599/600.

12. According to the Pope's description, each tread of the double-flight staircase should be 9 feet wide (i.e. about 3 metres); in the execution they became smaller (*c.* 2·20 m.; cf. the plan in Stegmann-Geymüller, *Die Architektur der Renaissance in Toskana*, III: *Bernardo Rossellino*, p. 6, and E. Carli, *Pienza*, 1965, p. 43). The staircase of Urbino, having a width of 3 metres for each tread and being much greater in its depth (*c.* 15 m.), far surpasses even the original project for Pienza.

these reappear, with certain modifications, in the new north wing of the palazzo of Urbino. The massive substructures that were necessary, if only for aesthetic effect, for the turreted front and garden-terrace entailed even greater difficulties than those at Pienza.[13]

The turret front as such, on the other hand, with its many-storeyed loggia, is a motif which may have been suggested to Federico, as has often been said,[14] by the triumphal arch of Castel Nuovo, Naples; the metamorphosis of the portal of a bastion into a loggia, however, is a unique and inspired adaptation.

The junction between the old and new buildings is made by the courtyard. The visitor, already attuned to grandeur by the two exterior views of the residence – the turret front from the country and the piazza front from the town – enters the palace by way of the spacious, but austere, barrel-vaulted archway,[15] and senses the great courtyard as a kind of solemn prelude to what awaits him in the interior. Unlike the steep and comparatively enclosed courts in Florentine palazzi, the courtyard of Urbino is a wide open space surrounded by arcades. While in Tuscan courts the columns, even those at the corners, are uniform throughout, at Urbino the pillars at the corners are emphatically stressed. Thus there is a feeling that this space, which is closed on all sides, is formed by the meeting of four quite independent and fully developed façades. Before the roof mezzanine was added in the sixteenth century, the original courtyard appeared still more open, spacious and airy. The choice simplicity of its structure gives it a monumental dignity. By the use of the most subtle devices of perspective – the pattern of the pavement, or the slight shift of the windows behind the arcades on the south side facing the entrance – the visitor's first general impression is directed so that he grasps the courtyard in one grandiose pictorial view.[16]

By way of the spacious and lavishly ornamented stairs – so far as I know, one of the first examples of monumental steps[17] – one arrives at the piano nobile, where the treatment of the new parts of the building bears the same personal

stamp as the exterior. We confine ourselves to those parts that contain the governmental and domestic quarters of the Duke – that is, essentially, the northern side. This contains the impressive suite of rooms which begins with the majestic Sala del Trono – by its dimensions, proportions and above all by its peculiar and ingenious barrel-shaped vault, a masterpiece of Laurana's art and one of the most beautiful halls in Quattrocento architecture;[18] next to it is a second large room for official receptions, the 'Sala degli Angeli'; passing this we enter finally the private quarter, the appartamento del Duca.

Beyond the bedroom and a connecting smaller audience-chamber lies the famous ensemble of rooms, which forms the innermost core of the whole vast building. On the smallest scale and distributed over three low storeys of the turret front, this ambiente represents Federico's most personal, most private world. From a bathroom all'antica[19] on the ground-floor (with an adjacent hall for games) one mounts by way of the spiral staircase in the turret and enters on the second floor the adjacent sanctuaries of the 'Cappella del Perdono' and the 'Tempietto delle Muse'.

Never before had such a place of 'neighbourly' worship to Ancient and Christian ideology been erected. No architect would have had an idea of this kind on his own; it is an intellectual concept that can only have originated with the patron himself, aided by some humanistic adviser.[20]

The 'Cappella del Perdono' employs no figurative decoration but is distinguished, like an early Christian sacellum, only by the use of coloured marbles and stucco ornaments – a precious casket to guard the image of the Holy Virgin. The walls of the 'Tempietto delle Muse', on the other hand, were covered with pictures of the nine goddesses, while the

13. For the colossal substructures of Urbino and their execution by Laurana and Francesco di Giorgio, see Rotondi, op. cit., pp. 213 ff. and G. Marchini in Rinascimento, op. cit., pp. 65/66.

14. G. Marchini, op. cit., pp. 51 f.

15. There existed only two other androni of similar monumental size in contemporary architecture: that of the Palazzo Pitti, built between 1456 and 1460 (later transformed by Ammanati) and that of the Palazzo Venezia at Rome, completed about 1465.

16. Cf. G. Marchini, op. cit., p. 71. The geometrical pattern of the pavement recalls again the piazza of Pienza, where a similar scheme of white stripes adds to the optical effect of perspective.

17. See above note 12. See also G. Marchini, op. cit., p. 50, and Benedetto Baldi, op. cit., p. 275. Vasari in his Life of Francesco di Giorgio (Vite, ed. Milanesi, III, p. 71) and Daniele Barbaro in his Commentary on Vitruvius (ed. Venice, 1567, p. 352) particularly praise the staircase. Leonardo da Vinci made a sketch of it in his notebook L (fol. 19).

18. The Sala del Trono has two unusual constructional features: the huge vault (Spiegelgewölbe), the ingenious masonry of which, in the true curvature of a barrel, can be well seen from above at roof-level, and the 'indirect lighting' of the hall. In the lunettes of the long wall, opposite the windows facing the piazza, there are blind windows, now completely closed, which once let in some indirect light from the courtyard side, thus illuminating the vault. This construction, too, can be observed from above in the corridor of the upper mezzanine storey. Both features, which increase the grandiose effect of this extremely large room, are characteristic inventions of Laurana, who with his technical skill fulfilled the wish of his patron for brightness in the building; this requirement had been formulated by Pius II: 'prima aedium gratia lux est'.

19. Little attention has been paid to this charming design, which is, so far as we know, one of the first examples of its kind in the Renaissance. Alberti and Filarete do not mention the bathroom in private buildings, for both of them deal in their treatises only with public baths of the type of the ancient Terme. Pliny, however, in his famous letter on his Villa Laurentinum, describes its bathroom in detail; it may be that this letter – an inspiration, as we shall see below, for the disposition of Federico's domestic quarters – was also the source which led the latter to the idea of his private bath.

20. Cf. the description of the two chapels in Rotondi, op. cit., pp. 357 ff.

apse contained a representation of Apollo.[21] Both chapels are so small as to have been intended exclusively for the Duke; only a few persons could have found room in them. Mounting the spiral staircase still further one reaches the main floor, where – accessible also from the Duke's bedroom or the Guardaroba – we come to Federico's famous *studiolo*; 3·5 × 3·5 metres in area and about 5 metres high, it is no more nor less than a retreat. On the walls, above panels in splendid intarsia-work, were Justus van Gent's well-known portraits of twenty-eight representatives of wisdom from ancient times to the present. It is clear that these had been chosen by Federico himself as his teachers and models, because the selection does not fit in with any conventional classification, but is extremely personal.[22] On the front wall of the study Federico had himself portrayed, with his son: reading a book, seated, but in full accoutrement as a general, with all his insignia and decorations. A special prominence is given to the Order of the Garter,[23] a pardonable vanity that is all the easier to understand since precisely this 'apparel' symbolically expresses the idea of the Study: the statesman has withdrawn from the cares and duties of the *vita activa* to the serene realm of the *vita contemplativa* and seeks elevation of spirit as well as counsel from his preceptors. Just as the Roman statesman, Pliny the Younger, had created for himself in his villa, Laurentinum, a private corner – a 'buon retiro' – where, shielded from all disturbance and freed from the vexations of his administrative duties, he was able to devote himself

to the *otium* of studies, so Federico had himself shown in his little study as the statesman *procul negotiis*.

There are indeed such close relations between Federico's private apartment and Pliny's *diaeta*, which he described so vividly in his famous letter on the Laurentinum, that we are inclined to assume a direct connection. The varied character given to the several *cubicula*, their tiny size and their remoteness, and finally the emphasis on the prospect over the broad countryside from a kind of balcony – all these elements in Pliny's description appear, *mutatis mutandis*, in Federico's *appartamento*. And like Pliny, Federico could say with pride and pleasure 'amores mei, re vera amores, ipse posui'.[24]

It seems probable that Leone Battista Alberti may have been the mediator in this charming *concetto*. Both he and the Duke give mutual testimony to the close friendship that existed between them. Alberti was frequently Federico's guest at Urbino in his later years, and there are good reasons for believing that he even intended to dedicate to him the *De re aedificatoria libri decem*.[25] The letters of Pliny

21. The ground plan of the Cappella del Perdono corresponds somewhat with the small private chapel of Pope Nicolas V in the Vatican (demolished in the seventeenth century and preserved only in a drawing attributed to A. da Sangallo, Florence, Uffizi 3989A), which had a similar apse framed by a pair of columns. The pictorial decoration of the Tempietto delle Muse may have had some relation to the once famous *studio* of the Villa Belfiore at Ferrara, which Federico da Montefeltro must have known well; from the Court of Ferrara, he obtained, too (about 1471), Lazarelli's *De imaginibus deorum* (*Codices Urbinates Latini*, 716). Piero della Francesca had also been at Ferrara, just when the Belfiore was painted (1450), and may have transmitted the programme (cf. Roberto Longhi, *Officina Ferrarese*, 1934, p. 24 and Rotondi, *op. cit.*, p. 335). As a whole, however, the idea of combining a Christian with a pagan *sacellum* to form this exceptional 'Doppelkapelle' is entirely new and again the result of the mutually inspiring co-operation between patron and architect, so characteristic of Urbino.

22. We must forbear to discuss here in detail the fascinating problem of the *Studiolo* programme. We owe to Rotondi the brilliant reconstruction of the room in its original state; he describes the many motives of the intarsia-work and the two-storied balcony with the 28 *uomini illustri*. By means of the inscriptions under the portraits we can recognize clearly the personal esteem which links Federico with his ideal preceptors; we read constantly 'Fed(ericus) po(suit)' or 'Fed.possi curavit'; most impressive are the words of veneration which he finds for his contemporaries Pius II, Sixtus IV and, last but not least, the beloved teacher of his youth, Vittorino da Feltre.

23. For the Garter cf. Dennistoun, *op. cit.*, I, pp. 223 ff.

24. To be precise, Pliny describes two quiet corners in his Villa Laurentinum. The first group of rooms belonged to the main building: 'adnectitur angulo (a small courtyard between the main building and the beach) cubiculum in hapsida curvatum, quod ambitum solis fenestris omnibus sequitur. Parieti eius in bybliothecae speciem armarium insertum est, quod non legendos libros, sed lectitandos capit. Adhaeret dormitorium membrum transitu interiacente, qui suspensus et tabulatus conceptum vaporem salubri temperamento huc illuc digerit et ministrat'. The second *ambiente*, the *diaeta* proper, lay at the end of the large garden, separated from the villa itself: 'in capite xysti, deinceps cryptoporticus, horti diaeta est, amores mei, re vera amores. Ipse posui . . . contra parietem medium zotheca perquam eleganter recedit, quae specularibus et velis obductis reductisve modo adicitur cubiculo, modo aufertur. Lectum et duas cathedras capit; a pedibus mare, a tergo villae, a capite silvae: tot facies locorum totidem fenestris et distinguit et miscet. Iunctum est cubiculum noctis et somni; non illud voces servolorum, non maris murmur, non tempestatum motus, non fulgurum lumen ac ne diem quidem sentit nisi fenestris apertis. Tam alti abditique secreti illa ratio, quod interiacens andron parietem cubiculi hortique distinguit atque ita omnem sonum media inanitate consumit. Adplicitum est cubiculo hypocauston perexiguum, quod angusta fenestra suppositum calorem, ut ratio exigit, aut effundit aut retinet. Procoeton inde et cubiculum porrigitur in solem, quem orientem statim exceptum ultra meridiem oblicum quidem, sed tamen servat. In hanc ego diaetam cum me recepi, abesse mihi etiam a villa mea videor magnamque eius voluptatem praecipue Saturnalibus capio, cum reliqua pars tecti licentia dierum festisque clamoribus personat; nam nec ipse meorum lusibus nec illi studiis meis obstrepunt.' (Plinius, *Epistolae*, II, 17: C. Plinius Gallo suo S., ed. K. Lehmann-Hartleben, *Plinio il Giovane. Lettere scelte con commento archaeologico*, Florence, 1936, XIX, p. 43 ff.). To the striking correspondence between Pliny's *diaeta* and Federico's *appartamento* belongs, too, the above-mentioned private library; its 'armarium insertum, quod non legendos libros, sed lectitandos capit', recalls Federigo's *studiolo* with its intarsia cupboards.

25. Baldi, *Vita di Federigo*, *op. cit.*, III, p. 55, speaks of 'testimoni di scrittori degni di fede che a lui egli dedicasse quei dieci libri che

were known to the Duke, as is clear from a fine codex, written for him (and still existing today in the Vatican *fundus* of the Codices Urbinates).[26] There is one further argument in favour of our hypothesis: in the tenth book of his treatise on architecture, while dealing with the arrangement of an undisturbed, quiet room, Alberti quotes a passage from this very letter of Pliny's.[27]

So, the apartment of the Duke with its singular and beautiful *concetto* should be understood as the result of a threefold co-operation between the patron, the humanist adviser and the executive architect, each of them contributing to the whole with his particular experience and knowledge.[28] The leading spirit, however, was the patron. Vespasiano de Bisticci gives us a memorable picture of the Duke's interest in every aspect of architecture:

> con tanta copia e maestria scrisse dell'architettura, se bene morto lui, Bernardo suo fratello, indotta a ciò dalle persuasioni d'Angelo Poliziano, lo donò a Lorenzo de'Medici'. (Cf. G. Mancini, *Vita di Leone Battista Alberti*, Florence, 1911, pp. 482–483). Concerning the close relation between Alberti and the Duke, we have the contemporary testimony of Cristoforo Landino, who, in his *Disputationes Camaldulenses*, dedicated to Federico da Montefeltro, lets Alberti say: 'per l'antica ospitalità e per la vecchia amicizia spessissimo fui testimone della temperanza di Federigo allorchè ogni anno per salute e riposo fuggendo gli autunni romani vo a diporto presso di lui, e mi sembra dalle cene di Sardanapalo capitare ai conviti d'Alcinoo ed incontrare un ospite socratico' (Cf. G. Mancini, *op. cit.*, p. 479); and Federico himself confirms his friendship in his beautiful letter to Landino: 'Delectaverunt me mirum in modum Camaldulenses disputationes tuae ac suavissima epistola quam una misisti amantissimis verbis ornatam . . . et quod imprimis delectavit me maxime, tantus fuit amor in me tuus, ut, perscrutatis diligenter personarum rationibus, vi sua animi mei affectus pulcerrime propexeris, quippe quos omnes disceptantes quos introduxeris plurimum amem, et plurimi faciam virtutem eorum. Nihil fuit familiarius neque amanticus amicitia qua Batista ed ego eramus coniuncti . . .' (Federigo da Montefeltro, *Lettere di stato e d'arte, op. cit.*, pp. 102 f. See also Dennistoun, *op. cit.*, p. 217).

26. *Bibliothecae Apostolicae Vaticanae . . . Codices Urbinates Latini*, ed. C. Stornajolo, III, Rome, 1921, p. 176, no. 1153 (ind. vet. N. 4,643). On fol. 1 are the coats of arms of the Count Federico, so the codex must have been acquired before 1474.

27. Alberti, *De re aedificatoria*, Lib. x, cap. 13. There are many proofs that Alberti's description of the country house (Lib. v, cap. 14–17) was also based on knowledge of Pliny's letters.

28. This is not the place to deal in detail with the problem concerning the shares of Luciano Laurana and Francesco di Giorgio Martini in the execution of the *appartamento del Duca*. The general layout of the northern wing of the palace and the construction of its main parts – including the turret front and its rooms – belong to the Laurana period (1464–72); on the other hand the date of the ceiling in the *studiolo* (1476) and a contemporary report, that the 'Cappella del Perdono' was finished about or just before 1480, show that the final completion of these rooms was achieved during the superintendence of Francesco di Giorgio (cf. Rotondi, *op. cit.*, pp. 219 ff., especially p. 223) But the

'[Federico da Montefeltro] aveva voluto avere notizia di architettura, della quale l'età sua, non dico signori ma di privati, non c'era chi avesse tanta notizia quanto la sua Signoria. Vedasi tutti gli edifici fatti fare da lui, l'ordine grande e le misure d'ogni cosa come l'ha osservate, e maxime il palagio suo, che in questa età non s'è fatto più degno edificio, si bene inteso, e dove siano tante degne cose quante in quello. Bene ch'egli avesse architettori appresso della sua Signoria, e pareva, a udirne ragionare, che la principale arte ch'egli avesse fatta mai fusse l'architettura; in modo ne sapeva ragionare a mettere in opera per lo suo consiglio! . . .'[29]

Our investigation of the building confirms Vespasiano's statement in detail. Federico's main intention was to relieve his palace of its previous citadel-like character and to turn it into a residence suited to a beneficent and prosperous regime. This is the most significant feature of his building project, which in its 'meaning' is the first example of its type.[30] Similar ideas already underlay Pope Pius's creation of Pienza; but the humanistic concept led, in Federico's work, to the realization of a far more profound intellectual content. Pliny's retreat for contemplative leisure receives at Federico's hands a sublimation in the direction of the ethical. The models of classical antiquity are joined to those of Christianity in a synthesis, differing essentially from that of medieval Scholasticism in its direct reference to original sources. In the continuous inter-relation of *vita activa* and *vita contemplativa* Federico sees his basic principle of conduct. From this he draws the strength to carry out the precepts of *buon governo*, the seat and visible expression of which in all its aspects is his palace at Urbino as 'Idee und Gestalt'.[31]

decisive phase of planning, in which was born the *concetto* of the *appartamento del Duca*, began in the second half of the sixties.

29. Reprinted from P. Rotondi, *op. cit.*, p. 412.

30. In the discussion after the Selwyn Brinton Lecture in 1965, delivered by Dr. Peter Murray on 'The Italian Renaissance Architect', Sir Kenneth Clark pointed out the difficulty of defining the word 'architect' in the Renaissance in so far as the great masters of building were at the same time painters or sculptors too; furthermore, some great painters became advisers in architectural planning, for example, Piero della Francesca at Urbino or Andrea Mantegna at Mantua. These manifold capabilities of the architect as designer must also be considered in direct relation to the patron, who in all periods of architectural history takes a particular and active interest in the realization of architectural ideas. The palace of Urbino offers us an illuminating example in this respect: it is a true synthesis of ingenious planning and ingenious execution. And the form and style of the building depend to a large degree on the interdependence between these two factors.

31. By kind permission of Professor Nikolaus Pevsner, editor of the Pelican History of Art, this essay includes material from the author's *Italian Architecture in the 15th Century*, to appear as Part I of the forthcoming volume, *Italian Architecture of the Renaissance*.

PETER MURRAY

Menicantonio, du Cerceau, and the Towers of St. Peter's

ON the 18th of April 1506, Julius II laid the foundation stone of New St. Peter's. Two eye-witness accounts of the ceremony have come down to us, differing only in small details, and, as both were written by officials of the Papal Court who had been responsible for the arrangements, they seem to afford primary evidence for the establishment of at least a provisional design. This design was on the reverse of a medal of Julius and examples of it were buried in the foundations. The account given by Johannes Burchard, the Master of Ceremonies, runs: 'Sabbato in albis, 18 aprilis. Ego autem adverti Pape, benedixi aquam. . . . Postquam posuit illum lapidem, muratores posuerunt in quodam vase cooperto duas aureas medalias valoris ducatorum L, et sex vel plures de metallo cum facie Pape in cappa, ab una parte, ab alia designum edificii prout in eo quod accepi. . . .'[1]

His rival, Paris de Grassis, Bishop of Pesaro, who seldom missed a chance to disagree with the Master of Ceremonies, gives a more detailed account: 'et quidam faber argentarius qui attulit XII monetas novas sive medallias latas sicut est una ostia misse communis, grossas vero sicut costa unius gladioli communis; et ab una parte erat imago Pape Julii cum his litteris, videlicet: JULIUS.LIGUR.SECUNDUS. PONTIFEX.MAXIMUS.ANNO.SUI.PONTIFICATUS.MDVI et ab alia erat forma templi sive edificii quod volebat eri-

gere, cum litteris his, videlicet: INSTAURATIO BASILICE APOSTOLORUM PETRI ET PAULI PER JUL.II.PONT.MAX. et inferius erat hoc verbum, videlicet VATICANUM. Harum autem monetarum, due erant auree . . . et alie X erant ex auricalco . . .'[2] After this he insinuates that Burchard abstracted one of the medals.

Apart from this medal – no example of which is known with the full inscription quoted by Paris de Grassis – the only truly primary evidence which remains to us is the drawing known as the Parchment Plan (Uffizi A.1: see below), which is traditionally Bramante's own original design. Unfortunately, not one of these pieces of evidence is completely authenticated. The Parchment Plan is inscribed *Sto. Pietro di mano di Bramante. Pianta di Sto. Pietro mano di Bramante che non ebbe effetto*, in what seems certainly to be the handwriting of Antonio da Sangallo the Younger. Later, the drawing belonged to Vasari who regarded it as the work of Bramante: 'fece infiniti disegni; ma fra gli altri ne fece uno che fu molto mirabile, dove egli mostrò quella intelligenza che si poteva maggiore, con dua campanili che mettono in mezzo la facciata, come si vede nelle monete che battè poi Giulio II e Leon X, fatte da Caradosso eccellentissimo orefice, che nel far conj non ebbe pari; come ancora si vede la medaglia di Bramante fatta da lui . . .'.[3] Although there can be no reasonable doubt that the drawing is by Bramante there is room for speculation on its date; and it is also possible to argue that it never really possessed the authority claimed for it by Sangallo's inscription.

The case is rather different with the medals. In spite of the description by Paris de Grassis and the attribution to Caradosso made by Vasari, there is a problem of attribution since it is not quite certain which of three possible claimants was the medal buried in the foundations and which was, on the 18th April 1506, however temporarily, the definitive design. The problem lies in the fact that there are two different medals, one of which is known in two

1. *Johannis Burchardi Diarium* (1483–1506), ed. L. Thuasne, 3 vols., Paris, 1883–85, III, pp. 422 ff.

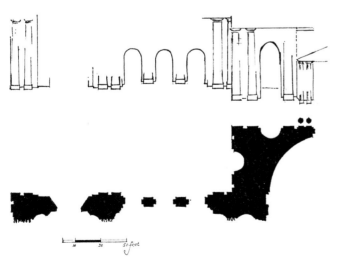

Reconstruction using the Parchment Plan, with pilaster heights based on those in the Belvedere, S.M. della Pace, and the Tempietto.

2. *Ibid.* Thuasne quotes the whole passage from Paris de Grassis as a footnote to Burchard's account. A very slightly different version is quoted from Muratori by G. F. Hill in his *Corpus of Italian Medals*, 2 vols., 1930, s.v. Caradosso. The medal by Caradosso, discussed below, bears the inscription (obverse) IVLIVS.LIGUR.PAPA.SECVNDVS.MCCCCCVI. and (reverse) TEMPLI.PETRI.INSTAVRACIO.VATICANUS.M. (i.e. Mons).

3. Vasari-Milanesi, IV, 161. The identification with the Parchment Plan is in the highest degree probable – see O. Kurz in *Old Master Drawings*, 12, Dec. 1937, 33.

separate states. The two different medals are those always known as the Caradosso (Fig. 1) and the Serbaldi (Fig. 3) and in both cases the attribution is not entirely beyond doubt. Vasari attributes the medal dated 1506 to Caradosso, and stylistic evidence supports him. Caradosso was a goldsmith active in Milan from 1475 until about 1499 – that is, at exactly the same time as Bramante. In 1505 Caradosso settled in Rome and worked for successive Popes until his death in 1526/7. In 1508 he is known to have been living in the Belvedere as a neighbour of Bramante.[4] It is intrinsically probable, therefore, that he should be the maker of a medal with the head of Bramante on the obverse (Hill 657)[5] and with *Fidelitas Labor* and a distant view of St. Peter's on the reverse. There seems to be no possible doubt that this medal is by the same hand as Hill 659 (Fig. 1), the even more famous medal of Julius II with the façade of St. Peter's and the inscription *Templi. Petri. Instauracio. Vaticanus. M(ons)* on the reverse. This inscription corresponds fairly closely with that recorded by Paris de Grassis, and the engraving produced in 1517 by Agostino Veneziano (Fig. 2) seems to confirm the Caradosso medal as the one which represented the official project of 1506. Unfortunately there exists a variant form of this medal. The engraving corresponds very closely to the form represented by Fig. 1, which is the British Museum example. The variant, which seems to have escaped the notice both of Hill and of writers on Bramante, is in fact the form reproduced by Förster in his monograph, and by Halm (see below note 9). This variant clearly shows a segmental pediment over the main doorway and a stepped half-dome immediately above it similar in type to the great dome over the crossing. It is also possible that the arcades, which are clearly visible in the British Museum example on the inner sides of each of the towers, may have been turned into colonnades with straight entablatures. (I have not had an opportunity of examining an actual example of this form and the photographs are not clear enough.) It seems remarkable that there should be two variants of this commemorative medal since it must have been an expensive undertaking to re-cut the die. From the point of view of the history of St. Peter's, it seems to afford yet further evidence of the fluidity of the design even in the earliest stages.

The Serbaldi medal (Fig. 3: Hill 870, 871) is also attributed on grounds of style to the official engraver to the Roman Mint. Serbaldi held this post from 1499 until at least 1522 so that he would seem to be a likely candidate for the making of the official medal, or at least in a position to know what the official projects were. In fact, however,

Hill treats the reverse of the medal – the side showing St. Peter's – with a great deal of caution and seems to imply that all known examples may be made up or altered in some way. The balance of probability, therefore, seems to lie with the version of Caradosso's medal illustrated here and disseminated by the Agostino Veneziano engraving of 1517. Properly speaking, the engraving should be included in the next category of evidence, which is even more difficult to assess. If the Caradosso medal and the Parchment Plan must be regarded as primary sources, then the engraving, although produced after Bramante's death, comes very nearly into the same category. There are, however, several drawings by Peruzzi which may have been produced in Bramante's lifetime and may have been more or less supervised by him. Next, there are the plates in Serlio (which are always regarded as reproducing drawings by Peruzzi), and there are also numerous drawings and engravings, with varying claims to represent Bramante's ideas, which can be given to Menicantonio de Chiarellis, Antonio da Sangallo the Younger, J.-A. du Cerceau the Elder, and a draughtsman from the circle of Altdorfer. Possibly more important than any of these is the mention by Serlio of a model by Bramante himself – 'lascio non solamente la fabrica imperfetta, ma ancora il modello rimase imperfetto in alcune parti . . .'. This might refer to no more than a drawing, but there is a positive reference to a wooden model by the historian Onofrio Panvinio in his *De rebus antiquis*, probably written in the pontificate of Pius V (1566–72). Here he says: 'Tunc Bramantius, exemplari novi templi e ligno fabricato, admirabilis fabricae vaticanae fundamenta posuit; quibus vix inchoatis, rebus humanis eximitur, exemplari quoque ligneo imperfecto relicto, in quo conficiendo nobilissimi quique architecti concertarunt. Ea in re Raphaëlis urbinatis. . . iudicium praevaluit, qui a Bramantii vestigiis non discedendo rem totam egregie complevit. . . . Balthassar senensis . . . isque Bramantii vestigia partim sequutus, eiusdem dem (*sic*) exemplar decurtavit, ex oblongo quadratum fecit. . . .' In the same author's book on the basilicas of Rome, published in 1570, the chapter on St. Peter's contains no mention of this model.[6]

As soon as one looks at all closely at the Parchment Plan and the Caradosso medal it is evident that the medal differs in several important respects, either because of changes in the design or because the medallist was not concerned with accuracy of detail. The former seems the more likely, since the differences are both striking and of a kind likely to be due to rethinking. Thus, the Parchment Plan can be reconstructed (see p. 7) as having two insulated columns, with pilaster responds, at each side of the main doorway, presumably carrying a pediment. Beyond these, the façade is continued by larger pilasters (presumably carrying the

---

4. L. Pastor, *History of the Popes*, VI, 461.
5. It should be observed that Hill 657, the portrait medal of Bramante, shows the design of St. Peter's on the reverse in the same form as that represented in the B.M. example reproduced in Fig. 1.

6. Onofrius Panvinius, *De rebus antiquis memorabilibus, et praestantia Basilicae Sancti Petri . . . libri VII*, printed in Mai, *Spicilegium Romanum*, IX, 1843, pp. 365–366.

entablature above the pediment, as in both Caradosso's and Serbaldi's medals). Next, there is a niche, of considerable size by comparison with the paired columns, and then a pair of pilasters to close the end of the main, projecting, façade. At a depth equal to half the width of the main front the main side walls can be reconstructed: they have a pair of pilasters at the extreme outside edge, matching those on the entrance front, then there is a break back in the wall-surface, presumably of the panelled type Bramante employed at Sant' Ambrogio in Milan and elsewhere. There is next a large opening, much wider at its mouth than even the main doorway, but narrowing to the same width as the latter at the entrance to the sacristies in the towers: this alone makes the opening unlikely to be a window-space, as has sometimes been suggested. The break forward and the pair of pilasters are then repeated to complete the tower unit, which is about two-thirds the width of the main front. This element is followed by an open arcade of three bays, each pier being faced by a pilaster of the same size as those on the towers. The design is then completed, at the angle with the front projection, by one complete pilaster and one bent round the angle.

Further, since we have a very good idea of the size of the whole basilica as originally projected,[7] as well as of the size as built, it is possible to make a plausible guess at the sizes of all these elements. Such a reconstruction is here offered, based on the Parchment Plan and the width (approximately 150 m.) of the existing building. The figure of 500 feet for the overall measurement of Bramante's plan will be near enough for the present purpose, and the proportions of the orders can be reconstructed from Bramante's own practice at the Belvedere, the Tempietto and Sta Maria della Pace. The Caradosso medal (Fig. 1) differs in several respects, though it must be emphasized that the basic design corresponds very closely with the Parchment Plan, so that it is possible to infer such features as the pediment from one to the other. The Caradosso medal shows a central doorway with a pediment, but with no indication of the coupled columns supporting it (incidentally, such a use of coupled columns is antique, but would be difficult to parallel in the early Renaissance). The next major difference between the medal and the Parchment Plan is that the medal shows paired pilasters where the drawing has only one, and, after the niche which is common to both, the drawing has a pair of pilasters to close the angle and the medal shows nothing at all. Both then have the three-arch arcade, although the scale of the medal is really too small to see the end pilasters (they are not shown in Agostino Veneziano's engraving). The medal has an effect of perspective to indicate the depth of the towers, which are quite different from those indicated in the Parchment Plan. They have neither pilasters nor opening, but only a large square panel incised in the wall-surface, emphasizing the cube of the lowest storey: the cube accords with the description of a tower given by Alberti (Book VIII, c. 5). In particular, the woodcut in the first illustrated edition (1550) of Alberti's *De re aedificatoria* (Fig. 4) is so close to the type employed by Bramante that there must surely be a connection between the two.

The engraving of 1517 by Agostino Veneziano (Fig. 2) corresponds very closely to the Caradosso medal and was almost certainly made from it. The towers and arcades are identical, but the main entrance in the engraving shows angle pilasters (or half-columns) – i.e. six elements against the four in the medal – while the side niches have triangular pediments added to the round-headed arches clearly visible in the medal. The Serbaldi medal (Fig. 3) differs from the Parchment Plan, the Caradosso medal, and the Agostino Veneziano engraving in several respects. The towers are capped by hemispherical domes, very like those in the Alberti illustration, and quite different from all the other versions. The towers themselves are also more satisfactory in design. The arcades seem to have straight entablatures, and there are six pilasters on the main front; but the side niches have now disappeared. The door pediment appears to be supported on single, not double, columns or pilasters. So far, the two towers seem to be confined to the front and there is no evidence that they were intended to be repeated in each corner, even though this is the case at San Lorenzo in Milan, perhaps the most important prototype for the early stages of the design of New St. Peter's. So far as I know, the first representation of four towers is the engraving by J.-A. du Cerceau, both in the unique impression in Basle – first connected with St. Peter's by Geymüller[8] – and in the variant of it published in his *Temples* of 1550. What is more interesting, the du Cerceau engraving seems clearly to derive from a drawing in the Foulc Sketchbook, attributed by Geymüller to du Cerceau. This drawing is inscribed *Templum Cereris*, and a copy of it, with the same inscription, was published by Geymüller from the Destailleur collection. Another copy, inscribed *Temple de Ceres deesse des blez*, is in the Fitzwilliam Museum, Cambridge (Fig. 5), and yet another variant is in Schloss Wolfegg. However, the Basle and *Temples* engravings show four towers while the Foulc-Destailleur-Fitzwilliam drawings have only one (i.e. intended to show two, one at each side of the entrance). The Wolfegg drawing comes from the Altdorfer circle, and was recently published by the late Peter Halm.[9] It shows the whole façade, but the two halves

7. E.g. from Serlio, Book III: 'Il detto Tempio è misurato a palmo Romano antico . . . & l'ambulatione di mezo è larga palmi novantadue, & quelle dalle bande sono per la metà di questa'. Later he adds 'dall' un pilastro all' altro è palmi cento & quattro, il diametro della cupola di mezo è palmi cento ottantaotto . . .'.

8. H. de Geymüller, *Les Du Cerceau . . .*, Paris and London, 1887, fig. 5 and p. 22. The *Templum Cereris* drawings are figs. 3 and 4, pp. 16–23. The Fitzwilliam drawing, fig. 6, is here published for the first time.

9. P. Halm in *Münchener Jahrbuch*, II, 1951, pp. 143 ff.

differ slightly – most significantly in the indication of a front and a back tower on the left half, and only a single, front, tower on the right. It seems most likely that the Wolfegg drawing was based on a print of the Agostino Veneziano engraving, but, since this does not show the four-tower arrangement, the draughtsman may also have known and used one of the du Cerceau engravings or even a drawing such as the *Portail de temple* (Vat. lat. 4398).

As Geymüller pointed out, the drawings by du Cerceau are quite close to St. Peter's as represented by the Caradosso medal or the Agostino Veneziano engraving, and much closer to it than the du Cerceau engravings, which obviously represent a fantasia on the St. Peter's–ancient Temple theme. Geymüller also pointed out the possibility that there was an actual model of St. Peter's, which was used by the draughtsman of a sketchbook in Munich: he identified this draughtsman, too, with J.-A. du Cerceau,[10] but Sir Anthony Blunt has proposed Philibert de l'Orme as a more likely author.[11] It is possible, therefore, that Philibert made some drawings from an existing model of St. Peter's and these drawings – some of which have survived in the Munich sketchbook – may have been copied by other French draughtsmen. In other words, du Cerceau's drawings and engravings are based on a drawing which goes back to Philibert, but which was combined by du Cerceau with some of the features of the model and engraving by Antonio da Sangallo the Younger (Fig. 8), which would have been more up-to-date in the late 1540's.

By far the most important event in Bramante studies in recent years has been the emergence on the New York art market of a sketchbook (now in the collection of Mr. Paul Mellon) containing drawings by Menicantonio de Chiarellis. This man, a Roman, was first recorded as working at the Vatican in 1505, and was at St. Peter's ('Menico Antonio di Jacopo') in August 1507, when he was carving capitals to Bramante's designs; after that his name occurs sufficiently often for us to know that he had a position in the Fabbrica which gave him access to Bramante's projects. His sketchbook carries the date 1513, just before Bramante's death, but several of the drawings in it must date from the twenties.

On ff. 80v and 81 there are two drawings of the façade and section of St. Peter's (Fig. 6), which, in view of their provenance, must be considered as carrying considerable authority. In fact, it seems likely that a comparison between the Menicantonio section and, on the one hand the Parchment Plan and the Caradosso and Serbaldi medals, and, on the other, the drawings by Peruzzi, the Serlio woodcuts, the model by Sangallo and the Madonna di San Biagio by his uncle, the elder Antonio da Sangallo, will afford grounds for the hypothesis that the Menicantonio drawing is the most accurate surviving record of Bramante's intentions,

although at a later stage in the evolution of the design than that represented by the medals. The date is a matter for speculation, but it may well be that the Menicantonio drawing was taken from the lost model recorded by Serlio, Panvinius, and, perhaps, Philibert de l'Orme.

To begin with, the Menicantonio drawing differs from the Parchment Plan and the Caradosso/Serbaldi medals in having a cube for the lowest storey of the tower, but it is a cube divided by an order and entablature at about two-thirds of its height. The order, reduced in size, now has six pilasters spread across the width of the tower, where the Parchment Plan has only four, and none are visible on the medals. The new arrangement is 2–1–1–2, with three niches, so that the rhythm is far more complex than in the Plan or medals, a fact which makes it likely that the Menicantonio drawing represents a redaction some time later than 1506.

Between the tower and the portico the Menicantonio drawing shows a more complex arrangement, and one that seems to take account of the fact that the scale is enormous. Thus, the arcade is now done away with, in favour of an open screen of columns, with a straight entablature. Above this, the Roman window is now transformed into another, Ionic, screen surmounted by an exceptionally shallow segmental pediment. As in the earlier designs, this has a hemispherical cupola above and behind it, rising to the level of the transept roof-line. The main frontispiece now has a huge pair of coupled pilasters[12] with niches between them and a great triangular pediment. These pilasters and their entablature would have risen something like 130 feet from the ground. The actual entrance is now through a screen of columns (each about 50 feet high), with a similar screen above containing the Benediction Loggia in a great central window. This window has a segmental pediment and is incorporated into the colonnade in a way reminiscent of Raphael's Palazzo Branconio and Palazzo Pandolfini: again, this seems to indicate the last years of Bramante's career. Stylistically, the most important feature of this design is the way in which the order is made to run, whether columns or pilasters, as a unifying feature of the whole of the lower part. In the Parchment Plan the 2–2–1–1–2 . . . ordonnance is rather simple, but the medals are merely awkward in their arrangement. Again, therefore, the Menicantonio drawing must be regarded as a representation of Bramante's thought at an advanced stage of the evolution of the design.

The base of the tower now consists of a high storey – higher than it is wide – divided into a lower stage consisting of

10. *Les Du Cerceau*, pp. 14–18.
11. A. Blunt, *Philibert de l'Orme*, London, 1958, pp. 15 ff.

12. The drawing does not, of course, indicate whether these are pilasters or half-columns, or even attached columns. On the analogy of Bramante's work at the Pace and his feeling for the continuity of wall-surface and pilaster elements I think it more likely that these were pilasters. Columns, on the other hand, would have been used for both the screens.

two pilasters, a blind niche, a single pilaster on either side of a window (or an elaborate niche) and then an exact repeat of the pilasters and niche. Above this is an attic with elaborate panels, mouldings and swags reminiscent of an antique altar. This disposition is repeated three times for each of the upper storeys, but the final stage consists of a more open arrangement with a central Palladian motive (perhaps the earliest known), and, finally, a sort of obelisk, the top of which is level with the ball of the lantern of the dome itself. This curious form may well have been inspired by the Vatican obelisk, which is known to have interested Bramante on account of its supposed connection with Julius Caesar.

It is an odd fact that the Cambridge draughtsman (Fig. 5) seems to repeat this feature of the Menicantonio drawing rather more accurately than du Cerceau in the Foulc Sketchbook (if it be by him) or the Destailleur draughtsman. In the same way, the Cambridge draughtsman shows an effect of perspective in the columnar screen which seems to show that he was not copying an elevation, such as Menicantonio's, but was perhaps working from a three-dimensional model. Taking everything into account, it seems that a single prototype, in three dimensions, lies behind the Menicantonio drawings and also the drawings and engravings from the du Cerceau circle. Philibert de l'Orme may well have been the original source for all the French versions, but he was using the same prototype as Menicantonio and that was something preserved in the Fabbrica itself.

Finally, the section given by Menicantonio makes it clear that the towers were confined to the front, with smaller, domical structures at the back. The very close correspondence between the great dome as drawn by Menicantonio and that published by Serlio[13] is a further corroboration of the general reliability of Menicantonio. A little-known drawing by Peruzzi (Fig. 7: Uffizi A. 106) shows a tower which, in its general configuration, is so close to Menicantonio's version that one is forced to the conclusion that there is a common source.

The Madonna di San Biagio at Montepulciano was begun by Antonio da Sangallo the Elder in 1518, some years after Bramante's death, but it is so Bramantesque in character, and is so superior in quality to anything else associable with Antonio that it has always been recognized as something to be taken into account when considering the design of St. Peter's. This façade is probably the nearest approximation known to us of the intended effect of St. Peter's as it would have appeared in three dimensions, but, at the same time, it is probable that the elaborate and ugly model made by Labacco for the younger Sangallo (Fig. 8), while he was Capomaestro of St. Peter's, may have more of Bramante's original ideas in it than one would, at first sight, care to admit.

13. In Book III, 1540.

JOHN SHEARMAN

Raphael . . . 'Fa il Bramante'

In the historiography of Renaissance architecture there is no odder case than that of Raphael. Opinion as to the extent and significance of his architectural practice varies astonishingly. It is said, for example, that 'Raffaello non fece mai . . . professione vera e propria di architetto',[1] and then there are the opposite extremists (like myself) who believe that for the last six years of his life Raphael was the greatest living and practising architect. Obviously, one of the factors permitting this range of opinion is the almost total absence of studies by Raphael for buildings. But it may fairly be said that this scarcity is no more remarkable than that of Giulio's architectural drawings. Nor is it so peculiar that the hazards of survival should have dealt harshly with them, for they must have seemed of much less interest than the figure drawings to the early collectors, who are the ones that determine survival.

The evidence derived from drawings for Raphael's practice is indeed limited. The architectural drawings, as distinct from those for architecture in paintings, may be divided into three groups, the first of which has nothing to do with the invention of buildings – these are the archeological studies, represented by two proto-Palladian studies of motifs from the Pantheon.[2] Second, there are a number of rather obscure experiments, typical of which are the elevation and plan of (apparently) a mausoleum on the study at Lille for the *Madonna Alba*, which are unlikely to be connected with any commission. And then, finally, there are studies which clearly were made for a building to be erected. These are exemplified by a somewhat unrevealing ground-plan for the Chigi Chapel,[3] and a fascinating but inscrutable study with three site-plans, a staircase and section and elevation of a pilaster order.[4]

In this paper I propose to discuss four neglected drawings in the Ashmolean Museum belonging to the second and third categories. The first of these is on the *verso* of a familiar drawing for the *Madonna del Cardellino*;[5] the sheet is stuck down, and being fragile cannot be lifted, so the black chalk drawings on the back can only be seen against the light (Fig. I, *recto* view reversed). What is then revealed is at first sight not unnaturally confusing, but five distinct patterns of lines may be isolated. Two of these I cannot interpret: a group of three broadly curving lines passing through the centre from top to bottom, and a group of nearly transversal lines just below the centre which converge at the right edge to enclose a small circle. The other three sketches are intelligible and interrelated. The clearest, and in some ways the most interesting, is the small ground-plan on the right, just above the centre. It is fragmentary, but appears to represent a chapel – which could be centrally-planned – or the crossing of a small church. The two visible apses both appear to contain altars and in the lower one a line across its entrance may mark a step. Remarkable above all is the placing of thick free-standing columns on bases in the corners of the square central space.

The ideas in this plan are related both to antiquity and to recent practice. It resembles a rare type of Roman tomb, recorded in Renaissance drawings; and its direct source of inspiration is likely to be either San Bernardino at Urbino (1482–91) or Cronaca's Cappella Tanai de' Nerli (*c.* 1500) in the right transept of San Francesco al Monte, just outside Florence – or possibly both. The former was more similar, before rebuilding of the choir, in the regular pattern of apses (but with a nave, which Raphael may or may not have intended); and, while both buildings have corner-columns, Cronaca's are proportionally larger and approach the emphasis selected by Raphael, and his chapel is more similar in scale – if we correctly read altars on Raphael's

1. Renato Lefevre, 'Note sulla "Vigna" del cardinale Giulio', *Studi Romani*, IX, 1961, p. 396.
2. R.I.B.A., XIII, fol. I r. and v.; see Giangiorgio Zorzi, 'Due schizzi archeologici di Raffaello fra i disegni palladiani di Londra', *Palladio*, N.S., I, 1951, p. 171, who argues convincingly their influence upon Palladio's drawing method; to his bibliography should be added: H. Geymüller, *Raffaello Sanzio studiato come architetto*, Milan, 1884, p. 71, to whom is due their introduction to Raphael literature. The purpose of two earlier views of the Pantheon on Uffizi 164ᴬ r. and v. (Fischel 216, 217) may be somewhat different; see H. Geymüller, 'Trois dessins d'architecture de Raphaël', *GBA*, 2ᵉ pér., III, 1870, p. 79, and Wolfgang Lotz, 'Das Raumbild in der italienischen Architektur-Zeichnung der Renaissance', *Mitteilungen des Kunsthistorischen Institutes in Florenz*, VII, 1953–56, p. 218.
3. Uffizi, 165ᴬ; Geymüller, 1884, pl. III.
4. Uffizi, 1474ᴱv.; J. D. Passavant, *Rafael von Urbino*, II, Leipzig,

1839, p. 486; G. Frizzoni, *I disegni . . . degli Uffizi*, Ser. III, fasc. 2, *Disegni di Raffaello*, Florence, 1914, No. 16; Konrad Oberhuber, in *Master Drawings*, I, 1963, p. 46 (repr.); connected by Frizzoni with the Farnesina, by Oberhuber more specifically with the *stalle* – the dimensions of the pilaster order are right for this solution but the purpose of the other studies remains obscure.
5. *Verso* of Fischel 114; K. T. Parker, *Catalogue of the Collection of Drawings in the Ashmolean Museum*, II, Oxford, 1956, no. 517v.; Parker, unlike Fischel, observed these *verso* studies but did not comment or commit himself to an attribution. I would like to thank Hugh Macandrew for his repeated kindness at the Ashmolean Museum and the exceptional care he took in obtaining for me the new photographs reproduced here.

plan.[6] The dense plasticity of Raphael's design, however, greatly exceeds that of all remote and recent prototypes, and even exceeds that of Giuliano da Sangallo's *ricetto* to the sacristy of Santo Spirito.

The question at once poses itself: since such full-bodied forms are characteristic of Raphael's painted architecture at about the time of the *Expulsion of Heliodorus* (1512), are these studies of the same date (about 1506) as the *recto*? Certainly there are instances of drawings by Raphael of different dates appearing on the same sheet; and the absence of a considerable corpus of architectural drawings, together with the hazards of comparing those that survive with figure drawings,[7] makes the judgment of date on grounds of graphic style an exercise of limited credibility – more especially when we cannot see the drawing itself. Nevertheless there is in our obscured view of these sketches no sign of inconsistency with Raphael's black-chalk style just before the journey to Rome, and it seems to me probable that their appearance will prove extremely close to that of another little-known architectural sketch at Oxford, also in black chalk and also on the *verso* of a study for the *Madonna del Cardellino* (Fig. 2).[8] This, which appears to be an idea for, or perhaps after, the end-wall of a barrel-vaulted church or chapel, is so simple in its motifs and composition that a late date is improbable. And it would, in any case, be a remarkable coincidence if both these architectural drawings were later yet both on the *versos* of studies – in effect virtually consecutive – for the same work of about 1506.

To return to the 'chapel plan' (Fig. 1): to its left, in the centre of the sheet, is a perspective interior view of an approximately similar architectural space, which is to be read with the reproduction turned on its left side. A corner-column supports an entablature angled over it, and the walls facing and to the left each have arched openings, one of which is provided with impost-capital and supporting pilaster; the arched openings are not necessarily niches, but probably so since that to the left is closed off below, perhaps by an altar-table.

If the ideas of the 'chapel plan' are visualized in perspective here, they are more strikingly and rather differently developed in the fifth and last of these studies, the ground-plan along the bottom. This is part of a latin-cross church. In what remains of the crossing the essentially square space with apsidal openings and the thick corner columns reappear – but on these a dome is now superimposed. Raphael, it seems, could hardly have intended pendentives, since the thickening of the columns would not allow the system used in San Bernardino, and it is probable that he already envisaged here the astonishingly inventive solution painted in the *Expulsion of Heliodorus*, where the rings of the domes of the Temple rest directly on the columns to form their entablatures.[9] The radius of the lightly-drawn dome indicates that the sketch shows most of the width of the nave, and hence that the two free-standing columns on the façade flank a central door and no more were intended. If these sketches were made about 1506 it seems improbable, from our admittedly limited knowledge of Raphael's architectural career, that they were made in response to a specific commission.[10] I think it is more likely that they are the day-dreams of a man born to be an architect, and a more or less subconscious preparation for a career. But if that is all they are, they nevertheless provide evidence of a hitherto unsuspected inventive activity and – perhaps more important – of an ambition to be an architect even while, around 1506, his professional status as a major painter was scarcely securely established.

At Oxford there is another architectural study which is at once of far greater significance for the study of Raphael, and one of the most beautiful of all Renaissance architectural drawings (Figs. 5, 6).[11] Since Robinson first doubted the traditional attribution to Raphael it has passed out of all – or almost all – reckoning of his architectural activity. And yet there can be no doubt of the answer when the question is raised once more. Its quality, both as design and as architectural draughtsmanship, is more than sufficient, entailing even a reassessment of our ideas of Raphael's capacity in

6. The projections in Cronaca's chapel, however, are not apsidal but rectangular and those at the side are little more than recesses. For the drawings after related Roman tombs, see R.I.B.A., Palladio XI, fol. 21v. (Giangiorgio Zorzi, *I disegni delle antichità di Andrea Palladio*, Venice, 1959, fig. 271), and another among the Albani volumes at Windsor, CLXXXVI, fol. 17v. (inv. 10370v.). For the reconstruction of San Bernardino, see now Antonio Terzaghi, 'Indirizzi del classicismo nell'architettura del tardo quattrocento nelle Marche', *Atti del XI Congresso di Storia di Architettura* (1959), Rome, 1965, p. 329, but for the date: Pasquale Rotondi, 'Quando fu costruita la chiesa di San Bernardino in Urbino?', *Belle Arti*, 1949, p. 191.

7. Such a comparison need not, however, be entirely fruitless – for example with the black chalk head-studies of 1506–7 on the *verso* of Oxford 527 (repr. Fischel, *R.Z.*, Cat. fig. 116).

8. Parker, 1956, No. 516v., who first noticed this study but again made no specific attribution to Raphael, except perhaps by inference.

9. Further discussion in John Shearman, 'Raphael's unexecuted projects for the Stanze', *Walter Friedlaender zum 90. Geburtstag*, Berlin, 1965, p. 169.

10. The years around 1506 were by no means the Florentine Period of conventional history; it is most probable that if Raphael was working here on a real project, its source was the court at Urbino, a city which is, of course, of great importance in the formation of Raphael the architect; the connection of these studies with San Bernardino, even more obvious in the church-plan, is a case in point.

11. Parker, 1956, no. 579; to his bibliography may be added: Woodburn's inventory of Lawrence's house, *c.* 1830, as Raphael, no. 95 ('Design for a Church with some architectural studies on the back, pen, lightly washed'), and Raffaelle Ojetti, 'Discorso su Raffaello Sanzio', *Atti del Collegio degli ingegneri ed architetti di Roma*, 1883, p. 22 (*recto* only, as a design by Raphael for an unidentified villa). It was exhibited with other Raphael drawings from Oxford at the South Kensington Museum in 1859.

both respects. And more specifically it does exactly resemble the style of his few later architectural studies. In
Fig. 3, for example, we may compare a detail with another
from the throne in his study of 1516 for the *Monteluce
Coronation*.[12] Or we may compare the distinctive notation
of structural elements with that on the two detail-studies
from the Pantheon in the Palladio volumes at the R.I.B.A.;[13]
the indications of column or pilaster bases, for instance,
form an interchangeable series. The less finished drafts on
the *verso* (Fig. 4), certainly by the same hand as those on the
recto, include dimensions in Raphael's hand,[14] and their
style in general should be confronted with an important
sketch by Raphael for St. Peter's recently discovered by
Konrad Oberhuber.[15]

The large drawing on the *recto* (Figs. 5, 6) differs from the
available comparative material in its formality (there is no
other elevation) and in the inclusion of modelling in a
light bistre wash. For both reasons it is the most complete
of his architectural studies, and the effect of the wash in
particular is marvellous in the original, not only for its
delicate definition of volumes of form and of space but
also – typically for Raphael's later drawings – for its no less
delicate description of the passage of light.

The elevation, even so, is not easy to interpret in its present
state. Providentially there survives a photograph made in
1859 (Fig. 5)[16] which shows it before restoration and crop-
ping on all sides. The old photograph is more complete
and stronger in line, while the new one (Fig. 6) is less confused by foxing, and the greater sensitivity of its film to the
light bistre wash more than offsets the fading of the latter
over a hundred years.

The original as it now stands, when supplemented by the
old print, shows a perfectly comprehensible elevation of a
villa of unusual though not unique design. The low wings,
with sloping tiled roofs and window-tabernacles, flank a
tall central body composed of towers joined by an arch and
column-screen.[17] The topmost profile is distinctively that
of a Tuscan villa, with machicolation and pitched roofs.
From this main body projects a majestic doric loggia,[18] of

three balustraded, arched openings, a frontispiece with
segmental pediment, and a balustraded terrace on top, on
the level of the space enclosed by the column-screen and
towers. The loggia shares with the wings a common
entablature, a moulding at the level of column-bases and
window-sills, and a broad protruding band of masonry as a
base. This is not the ground-level, but in turn rests upon a
basement, of uncertain height, with a sloping fortress-like
profile under the wings. Access to the loggia is intended
only from within, and the basement profile below this
section is vertical, which suggests that it may have been
meant to carry a *portone* to afford entrance to the whole
villa at ground-level. The central balustrade of the *loggia
pensile* projects once more and is supported on consoles
rising from the basement.

On the *verso* five studies may be distinguished (Fig. 4). The
first plan is the fragmentary one top left. Around a central
salone is a suite of seven rooms, the one to the right probably a loggia, and a short entrance-passage from a door
flanked by columns. In the second plan, immediately to the
right, this simple scheme is abandoned for one of less
regularity, the axis of which is, however, unclear; this plan
has dimensions, including a total depth of 15 – that is about
33·5 metres if the units are *canne*. Next follows the most
coherent plan, in the centre, in which the asymmetry of the
second is clarified. The *salone* has disappeared and now a
small central room is the centre of a swastika-like sequence,
regular except that the unit top left is divided; now the
loggia is the unit lower right, and this looks onto a hemicycle marked with columns.[19] The entrance is in the
bottom wall of this plan.

Corresponding to the wall facing the hemicycle in this plan
is the elevation on the right of the sheet. This again is
remarkable for its eccentricity; the offsetting of the 'serliana' loggia to the left is balanced by the echo of its central
arch in a pediment over the wall-space to the right, and
symmetry is reasserted in the upper profile of sloping roofs
and machicolated tower, perhaps an *altana*. To the right
of this sketch are converging lines which may indicate a
wall receding towards the façade. This elevation makes it
clear that the loggia is raised above ground-level, and this
suggests that the hemicycle in front on the related plan is
not a garden but a fish-pond, and the circular object in it is
probably a fountain. Thus the sequence of raised, rhythmic-
ally-ordered loggia, fish-pond and exedra anticipates in
miniature that of Palazzo del Tè.

The fifth study, overlapping the third but drawn on a
larger scale, is confused further by lines showing through
from the *recto*; it may be read, however, as the revising of
a repetition of the third plan, incorporating a staircase and

12. Ashmolean Museum, Parker, 1956, no. 565; for the date and
    purpose see John Shearman, 'The Chigi Chapel in S. Maria del
    Popolo', *JWCI*, XXIV, 1961, pp. 149, 159.

13. See above, n. 2.

14. Compare those in pen on the R.I.B.A. drawings, or on the
    Chigi Chapel plan, repr. Geymüller, 1884, pl. III.

15. Uffizi 1973[F]; Oberhuber was kind enough to show me his dis-
    covery before publication; see now *Mitteilungen des Kunsthis-
    torischen Institutes in Florenz*, XII, 1966, p. 225. This pen-style may
    also be found in the small staircase-study on Uffizi 1474[E]v. (see
    above, note 4).

16. Courtauld Institute, Conway Library; another print in the
    Raphael Collection at Windsor (Ruland, p. 300, no. I, 1) is itself
    very faded.

17. The opening seems too large for a window; the motif is derived
    from Roman thermae.

18. The shadow cast by this loggia on the right suggests a consider-

able projection – probably to the extent of an arch equal to those
    along the front.

19. Beyond the hemicycle is half an oval, which may represent
    excavation into a hillside.

experimenting with replacing the offset loggia by a centralized re-entrant semicircular one, obviously designed to harmonize with the hemicycle in front.

It is uncertain and perhaps unlikely that the studies on *recto* and *verso* are for the same building. The scale of the elevation on the *recto* may be guessed using the height of the balusters as a guide, and its length may not be very different from the 15 *canne* indicated on the *verso* plan; but still it seems intended for a more imposing building. The façade cannot be related to any developed in the plans, and the sloping basement suggests a very different kind of structure. The building on the *verso* is an urbane *casino*, not unlike an anticipation of those at Bagnaia; the elevation on the *recto* shows a seigneurial *vigna*, with the scale and significance of Michelozzo's Villa Medici at Fiesole.[20] Certainly these projects are related (by motifs, like the *serliana* and machicolation) but in a way to be expected in those that sprang from Raphael's mind contemporaneously. Should it turn out that they are for the same building, then the project changed unrecognizably in kind as well as in form.

For what purpose were the drawings made? In the case of the *recto* elevation Parker was the first to observe one clue: a Medici emblem, ring-and-diamond, crowning the frontispiece. But there is another, for the six *palle* are laid out punningly along the balustrade.[21] Late in the 1930's a press-cutting photograph of Villa Madama was pasted into the Ashmolean copy of Robinson's *Critical Account* next to his entry on this drawing; the hint was taken by Parker, but rejected along with Raphael's authorship, in spite of his observation of the emblem. But it may have been correct. Our knowledge and theories about the genesis of Villa Madama are both very confused, and in need of clarification brought by new material. As the material stands (though not as theories stand), it may be argued that the project grew from a relatively compact beginning;[22] and it would

be reasonable if Villa Madama was initially conceived on the scale of Michelozzo's Villa Medici at Fiesole, which is so clearly – even at the most advanced stages – the overriding precedent for planning the villa-block in relation to gardens, site-inclination, river, view and ancillaries such as stables.[23] The hypothesis would then be as follows. The elevation on the *recto* of the Oxford drawing is intended for the façade towards the river (east), not towards the *giardino segreto* (north) where the famous painted loggia was built; this will explain why the drawn loggia is a hanging one very like that of the *casino* at Caprarola, for the site-slope would leave the main rooms on this side above ground-level, with an entrance in the basement. If the building is approximately square in plan, then it is easy to imagine projecting logge on the façades to left (south) and right (north), providing for entrance from the direction of Rome and the *giardino segreto* respectively.[24] In other words, the elevation belongs to a stage in the evolution of the villa-block of the Villa Medici type before it was opened out around the cortile that is shown in the surviving plans – before, that is, the full influence of classical antiquity.

There is no conclusive evidence for this view. But it is a fact that in the two mature plans for Villa Madama, Uffizi 314[A] and 273[A], the three-opening hanging loggia reappears on the river-façade, and in the second of these (at the very least a record of Raphaelesque ideas for the villa) the balustrade of the central frontispiece projects as it does in the Oxford drawing. The thermae-motifs of arch and column-screen reappear on the definitive, partly-erected, river-façade, though differently distributed. Then it is noteworthy that the design of the window-tabernacles in the elevation is identical to that of the door-case between Bandinelli's *giganti* in the *giardino segreto*, which was among the earliest parts executed (about 1519).[25] On morphological and technical grounds the drawing should be dated to the period, about 1517 to 1520, that included the conception of Villa Madama.[26] And, finally, this *is* a Medici

20. Or the project in Serlio's Book VII, chap. 2.

21. Such punning with the *palle* was always a temptation; compare Michelozzo's capitals at Bosco ai Frati, or the Orsini bear who juggles with them in a freize at Bracciano.

22. This is not the place for a discussion of these problems, the following are at present the known ground-plans of the villa proper: (i) Uffizi 1054[A] (compact nearly square block with corner *torrioni* and circular court; Geymüller, 1884, fig. 63, or T. Hofmann, *Raffael als Architekt*, I, Leipzig, 1911, pl. xxvi (b)). (ii) Uffizi 179[A] (on which the plan differs not by change of scale or principle in the central block but by the moving of the *torrioni* to enclose on the south side an entrance court; the place of these *torrioni* is till subject to revision here; Hofmann, I, pl. xxvi (a)). (iii) Uffizi 314[A] (the complete project with the enclosed *giardino segreto* extended northwards to balance the entrance court, making a long rectangle enclosed by *torrioni*; Geymüller, 1884, pls. IV, VI). All these drawings are by Antonio da Sangallo the younger, but in my view there is sufficient evidence that the ideas were in origin Raphael's. The large plan by Battista Sangallo, Uffizi 273[A] (project extended as 314[A] but with rectangular central court; Geymüller, 1884, pl. IV), is usually held

to represent the earliest stage in design, and this may be the case; but in my view it is not possible to accept both (i) and (iv) in a logical sequence of development with the other two, and on present evidence it is not clear which should be excluded. However, it is certain that (ii) precedes (iii).

23. This connection has not passed unnoticed (for instance by C. L. Frommel, *Die Farnesina und Peruzzis architektonisches Frühwerk*, Berlin, 1961, pp. 86–88), but it remains to be exploited further.

24. It has been suggested, I think with some reason, that the elevation of the garden loggia in Serlio's Book III – with the three arches centred on the villa-block and symmetrically flanked by niches – was based upon an actual early design. In that case this façade would initially have been more consonant with the Oxford drawing than appears possible in the asymmetrical executed version.

25. Detlef Heikamp, 'In margine alla "Vita" di Baccio Bandinelli del Vasari', *Paragone*, CLXXXXI, 1966, p. 52.

26. Progress on the site was reported in a letter from Castiglione to Isabella d'Este, 16th June 1519; the relevant passage is omitted

project, but not of Leo X for in that case the papal symbol would surely crown the frontispiece; Villa Madama was at first the *vigna* of Cardinal Giulio. The project is no day-dream, so there is a simple choice of hypotheses: that it was for Villa Madama, or that it was for some other Medici (but almost certainly not Florentine) villa-commission of the same date that is otherwise unrecorded.[27] Certainly there are obstacles to the acceptance of the first hypothesis; nevertheless I find it more credible than the alternative.

The purpose of the sketches on the *verso*, if it is not the same, is even more a matter for speculation for there is no indication of the patron. The deliberate asymmetry of the tiny elevation is striking, and suggests the possibility that the building was not self-sufficient. Was the *casino* to go in the enormously extensive gardens of Villa Madama, for which grottoes and nymphaea were planned?

The *recto* elevation has one interesting aspect that will not be apparent in reproduction: an underlying modular construction drawn with the stylus. Multiples of a basic unit marked off along the floor-line of the loggia determine the spacing of columns, pilasters and the widths of the arches.[28] A semi-circle centred on the base-line and tangential to the top of the architrave of the frontispiece provides the centres for the side arches where it intersects their vertical axes, provided by the modulus. This technique of construction contributes a certain perceptible harmony and order to the loggia. Moreover its demonstrable employment here supports the methodological validity of an analytical technique in modern architectural history which – it must be admitted – leads sometimes to diagrams that most naturally provoke derision. The simplicity of Raphael's apparatus and aims should perhaps be taken as a useful guide to what may be accepted along these lines without scepticism.

The villa conceived here has an arresting shape that demands comment; in some of its aspects it is not unprece-

dented. The combination of the rustic and mediaeval flavour above with the noble classicism of the lower part is reminiscent, for example, of the Belvedere of Innocent VIII or the medal-design for Bramante's Palazzo dei Tribunali.[29] It arises very naturally in this case because Raphael's design has its roots not only in such a building as Michelozzo's Villa Medici (contributing the triple-arch loggia flanked by single windows) but also in the preceding Tuscan tradition of the fortified villa. When the loggia is subtracted, rather close prototypes can be found for the block-form with dramatic towers linked together.[30] Raphael's elevation, however, does not tell us whether his intention was to have two or four towers, and if it was the latter then he recalled the type of villa-rocca that also lay behind Poggio Reale at Naples.[31] From this type, too, Leonardo had evolved about 1505 a villa design with a profile not unlike Raphael's, if it had four towers.[32] There may be some connection here, for I believe it can be shown that Raphael had access to Leonardo's architectural studies.[33] This general type, at all events, is in different ways classicized – in the upper part by the insertion of the arch and column-screen and the application of the *serliana* windows as decoratively as the machicolation, but in the lower part by the total characterization of the structure itself, *all'antica*. Raphael was not, of course, the first to revive the segmental pediment, but here and elsewhere he endowed it with a very personal emphasis and

29. A similar conjunction is found in another palace design from the circle of Bramante and Raphael in the Menicantonio sketchbook in the Mellon Collection, fol. 8r.
30. An example is reproduced by Bernhard Patzak, *Palast und Villa in Toscana*, I, Leipzig, 1912, pl. 86; an even closer parallel (twin towers, linking arcade, sloping basement) is reproduced in A. Grandjean de Montigny and A. Famin, *Architecture toscane*, ed. New York, 1923, pl. 23, with the description: 'Petit palais, via dei Guicciardini' (Florence); these illustrations are to be treated with circumspection, though they are not normally fanciful in structural outlines, and I have not identified the building; almost none of the old Via de' Guicciardini survives.
31. For example the Castello delle quattro torri, Siena (Patzak, 1912, pl. 154).
32. Windsor 12591r.; Carlo Pedretti, *A Chronology of Leonardo da Vinci's Architectural Studies after 1500*, Geneva, 1962, p. 49, and Luigi Firpo, *Leonardo architetto e urbanista*, Turin, 1962, p. 118, both loosely connected it with a palace for Charles d'Amboise. This design is connected with the earliest surviving Villa Madama ground-plan (Uffizi 1054ᴬ – cf. the *torrioni*) and with the Oxford drawing (cf. the mediaeval central cluster rising from a classically ordered *piano nobile*).
33. For example the newly discovered drawings after the Chigi *stalle* (Metropolitan Museum, 49.92.44/50) show an interior arrangement remarkably similar to that of the model stables designed by Leonardo c. 1490 (Cod. Triv. 21v.; Firpo, 1962, p. 88). The Metropolitan drawings also elucidate an interesting detail: that the *portone* of the *stalle* had full columns recessed in the wall rather than half-columns, as had been thought; again the inspiration may be Leonardesque (cf. Firpo, 1936, p. 109), but in this case an antique prototype may apply better (cf. the façade recorded in the *Codex Barberini*, fol. 70v., drawn in more detail in Albani CLXXXVI at Windsor, fol. 6, inv. 10359).

by Vincenzo Golzio, *Raffaello nei documenti*, Vatican City, 1936, p. 100, but is given by J. A. Crowe and G. B. Cavalcaselle, *Raphael*, II, London, 1885, p. 468, and by Renato Lefevre in *Studi Romani*, IX, 1961, p. 399. Lefevre, p. 395, suggests convincingly that Raphael's lost letter describing the villa (see Golzio, 1936, p. 147) was also of 1519. The preliminary planning, therefore, is likely to have been in 1517–18.
27. The basement-profile, among other things, excludes any connection with contemporary modifications to the Papal villa at La Magliana. The state of the Medici dynasty 1516–20 virtually precludes the possibility that it could have been commissioned by them for Florence where – in any case – another villa was scarcely a necessity; at that moment Cardinal Giulio was supervising the completion of Poggio a Caiano.
28. It is interesting to compare the passage describing the laying out of elevation-drawings (without, however, the modular principle) in Raphael's letter to Leo X, 1519 (Golzio, 1936, pp. 89–90); Francis Huemer, 'Raphael and the Villa Madama', *Essays in honor of Walter Friedlaender*, New York, 1965, p. 97, argues persuasively that Raphael at this point in his discussion of the types of architectural drawing has in mind those he has made for Villa Madama.

gravitas. These qualities in his frontispiece are those of the monumental tabernacles of the Pantheon, like the one that contains his own tomb, accentuated by the translation to doric; to them he adds tension and movement, as if the pediment were a strip of the cornice bent into a bow.

I believe that this design, like the other earliest stages of the evolution of Villa Madama, was well known in the sixteenth century and exercised its due influence upon Giulio Romano, Jacopo Sansovino, Vignola, Palladio and other architects.[34] But it seems to me that there is yet another aspect of this drawing that is more important than its purpose, its sources or its influence. Naturally, if it is for Villa Madama then it affects profoundly the debate upon the responsibility of Raphael or Antonio da Sangallo for that building's invention. There is, however, another conclusion to be drawn which is subject only to the concession that the drawing is Raphael's. The studies on *recto* and *verso* demonstrate, more convincingly and more eloquently than any other known drawing by Raphael, his *intimate* involvement in all stages of architectural design. They show him at work from the invention to the resolu-

34. The elevation clearly influenced that of the loggia-façade of Villa Lante on the Janiculum; and what may be the earliest plan for Villa Madama, Uffizi 1054A, is related to two copied in the Berlin Heemskerck sketchbook (II, fol. 13r.) that seem to have been starting-points for the Palazzo del Tè; Uffizi 1054A also seems to be causally connected with the Palace of Charles V at Granada, and with Serlio's projects for the Louvre – and, of course, with Caprarola. Raphael's balcony projecting on consoles, in the Oxford elevation, may be compared with the one on Jacopo Sansovino's Palazzo Gaddi (which may be very close in date, if it is, indeed, original); for Vignola, compare the loggia façade of the *casino* at Caprarola, and for Palladio, Villa Marcello near Vicenza. Other buildings that seem to be influenced by this elevation are Villa di S. Colomba, Siena, and Villa Piccolomini, Frascati.

tion, groping from the incoherent to the articulate, and as deeply committed in this art as his more familiar drawings show him committed to painting. On this evidence he was not, for example, the kind of architect who needed supposedly more professional help in the manipulation of the orders; this conclusion is one of the unique contributions of the elevation on the *recto*. No less revealing are the drafts on the *verso*, for these provide us with examples of that kind of drawing, the existence of which had hitherto to be assumed and was sometimes not admitted, which formed (if we so conceive the situation) the basis of fair-copies by his assistants, such as the three plans for Villa Madama by Antonio da Sangallo. It cannot, then, be doubted that Raphael *was* the complete professional architect; and thus matured the ambition, so evident about 1506 (Fig. 1) when opportunity had not yet arisen.

The literary evidence concurs. Art-history has scarcely recovered from Vasari's underestimation of Raphael's architectural practice. Raphael's own contemporaries saw its reality. Celio Calcagnini describes him in a letter of 1519–1520: 'Architectus vero tantae industriae, ut ea *inveniat ac perficiat*, quae solertissima ingenia fieri posse desperarunt'.[35] The title of this paper was taken from a letter from Alfonso Paolucci, agent of the Duke of Ferrara in Rome, dated 17th September 1519: Raphael cannot be bullied, he says, 'perchè invero li homini de questa excellentia sentono tutti del melencolico. Et tanto più questo si sente, per essersi posto in questa architectura, *et fa il Bramante* . . .'; that very morning he had met him supervising the re-erection of pilasters in fortifications near the Vatican. . . .[36] It is true that Paolucci's remark *fa il Bramante* has a caustic dimension – but it was also meant as a statement of fact.

35. Golzio, 1936, p. 282.
36. Golzio, 1936, p. 97.

c

JOHN WHITE

Raphael: The Relationship between Failure and Success

RAPHAEL's unclouded personality, the swiftness of his rise to fame, and the magnitude of his achievement by the time of his death in 1520 at the age of thirty-seven, too often lead to the assumption that his artistic life was effortless. Where weakness is acknowledged, particularly in his early works, it tends to be the purely negative aspects, the lingering of flaccid Peruginesque workshop patterns in heads or limbs or draperies, that are noted. Because even his partial failures are in many cases finer works of art than his contemporaries' complete successes, the significance of the way in which, throughout his career, he partly fails in a particular painting to achieve the goal towards which he seems demonstrably to have been working is often not well understood. Nevertheless, the very speed of Raphael's development can only be fully comprehended in the light of certain kinds of partial failure. Just as falling is an integral part of learning to walk or to jump, failure is normally essential to success in all forms of learning, and it is not only in the work of Raphael that this is easily forgotten. The more sensitive an artist is the more likely he is to eliminate his failures in some way before they become part of his public output. In Raphael's case, his determination to advance at all costs, and the number of his surviving drawings, make the processes of trial and error, of self-criticism and of artistic self-improvement easy to follow.

Perugino's highly organized and thoroughly successful workshop, and the constant struggle to transcend the limitations implicit in that success, provide the background to the whole of Raphael's early career. Perugino invariably tended to compose his altarpieces through the permutation of a relatively small number of ready-made figure poses themselves composed of standard, interchangeable elements.[1] Observation only played an important part during the initial process of establishing a given pose. Similarly, he had reduced the problem of the relationship between pictorial surface-pattern and pictorial depth to a simple formula. Largely ignoring the Florentine struggle to integrate the two and to set the figures within, and indeed as far as possible throughout, the pictorial space, Perugino normally creates a foreground screen of figures which maintains the surface tension of his design. In extreme cases such as the *Madonna in Glory* from Vallombrosa, now in the Uffizi (Fig. 1) the minimal overlapping within the network of clearly silhouetted figures almost gives the effect of a stained-glass window with its leaded contours.[2] Behind this screen he then develops uninhabited architectural and landscape spaces stretching far into the depths, and often of great bareness and great beauty.

As has long been recognized, Raphael's determination to escape the limitations of such a formula conditions every aspect of his *Coronation of the Virgin* of c. 1502–3, now in the Vatican (Fig. 2). Above all it explains both his creation and his continuing acceptance of the most extraordinary, and for him uncharacteristic, element in his design; namely the great central hiatus which slashes across the composition, cutting it in two. The diagonal setting of the sharply lit sarcophagus, contrasting with the depth-annihilating frontality and low viewpoint of that in Perugino's *Resurrection* in the Vatican is used to force a realistic three-dimensionality upon a still uncertain figure group.[3] Whereas the silhouettes of Perugino's depthless line of Saints in his *Madonna in Glory* break comparatively casually across the line of the horizon, those in Raphael's design are close-knit to the distant line of hills beyond the indefinite middleground. In the upper half of the composition the semicircle of the music-making angels and the strongly diagonal setting and heavy draperies both of Christ and of the Virgin denote a similar determination to replace a flat screen by a firmly three-dimensional, space-defining group. Indeed, it is very noticeable that if either half of Raphael's *Coronation* is considered by itself the impression of three-dimensionality is far more compelling than that created by the composition as a whole.

It is this very success in creating three-dimensionality in both of its main components which forces Raphael to cut his whole design in two. In Perugino's *Madonna in Glory* it is immaterial that the Saints who gaze so reverently

---

1. For the sake of brevity only, for it is capable of almost indefinite extension, a typical sequence may be represented by the *Madonna and Saints* in San Domenico in Fiesole, the *Madonna and Saints* of 1493 in Vienna, and the *Madonna and Saints* of 1494 in Cremona. In them the St. John the Baptist becomes successively St. Peter and St. James simply by change of dress and attributes, and between the latter two even the dress hardly varies. The same pose exactly, but reversed except for the head, then also serves for St. Paul and St. Augustine in the Vienna and Cremona paintings. The Virgin is identical in pose in all three, and the Christ Child is only varied in the Vienna picture as regards the position of the head and of one hand.

2. See O. Fischel, *Raphael*, London, 1948, p. 18; on p. 21 the left central music-making angel is attributed to Raphael.

3. In Perugino's painting the careful diagonal disposition of the lid diminishes even further the impression of depth given by the body of the sarcophagus, whilst also informing the enquiring mind that the latter is indeed a long rectangular object stretching back six feet or so into pictorial space.

upwards can, in physical terms, see nothing of the scene at which they are supposedly looking. No truly spatial relationships are involved at any point. The earthly and heavenly zones are joined together not by the physical connections of the real, three-dimensional world but by the interlocking jig-saw of the surface-pattern by which the standing Saints and the heavenly symbols are indissolubly connected. If Raphael had attempted any similar linkage of the upper and lower parts of his design, the outcome would not have been compositional unity but compositional disaster. Because of his insistence on the three-dimensional reality of both the earthly and the heavenly groups, the spatial illogicality of the total situation would have been obtrusively underlined. If he had established connections between the upper and lower zones which clearly showed that the standing figures were underneath or behind the coronation group, it would also have become painfully obvious that these same worshipping apostles could see only clouds at best or backsides at the worst. If, to avoid this undesirable result the coronation had been clearly set back, with the apostles in a nearer spatial zone, it would have been no less apparent that, in gazing forwards and upwards, space, and completely empty space at that, was all that they would see. It is precisely the latter, physically ridiculous situation which is so painstakingly established with the aid of a semi-circular figure grouping and boldly squared pavement by the follower of Giovanni Bellini who painted what is, in many respects, the extremely beautiful *Madonna in Glory* in S. Pietro Martire at Murano. It is just this danger which Raphael, as yet unable to escape completely from his Peruginesque precedents, sought to avoid by isolating the two spatially incompatible elements of his design and by insulating them from all unnecessary contact even at the cost of a great central gap.

The entire range of Raphael's early works, and notably such major paintings as the *Spozalizio* of 1504 with its many subtle devices for ensuring the unity of foreground and background, shows that the dramatic element implicit in his formal solution for the *Coronation* was an incidental outcome of the nature of the problem with which he faced himself, and not a primary objective. This is confirmed by the struggle for increased spatial coherence which takes place in all three of the predella panels of the *Coronation* itself. The extent to which the starting-point for this predella is a typically Peruginesque manipulation of the component elements of Perugino's own altarpiece of the *Madonna and Six Saints* at Fano on which it is, at the same time, a kind of critical commentary, is well known. How, in the *Annunciation* (Fig. 3), Perugino's completely logical and severely tripartite architectural setting, in which the Angel Gabriel is isolated in one compartment, the Virgin in another, and the last, accounting for not quite one third of the entire space, is empty, has been replaced with a structurally hard to read but far more unitary space, has

been analysed in detail.[4] It is important to remember that even at the height of his career Raphael never confused the logic of pictorial architecture with that of real architecture. This is shown, in the *School of Athens*, by the structural impossibility of the relationship between the piers of the great crossing and the drum which they supposedly support.[5] In the present context the interesting thing about the early *Annunciation* is that, like the main panel above, it contains an unresolved conflict of a purely visual kind.

In setting the figures of the *Annunciation* firmly within the pictorial space Raphael has also been concerned, in the Florentine manner, to unify the dual action. Perugino, in his version of the scene, painted in 1497, was content to direct the act of annunciation entirely across the picture plane, whilst the Descent of the Paraclete appears as a visually unrelated phenomenon occurring wholly at right angles to it. Raphael, by placing God the Father between Gabriel and the Virgin, creates instead a diagonal that harmonises the two elements of a single significant event. He also replaces Perugino's kneeling, static Gabriel by a swiftly moving figure whose motion is the physical embodiment of the spiritual drama. However, because he is still dependent upon Perugino for the whole basis of his design, he has only been able to break down the architectural barrier, implicit even in the modified tripartite structure with its far wider centre-section, by placing Gabriel in front of the foremost of the left-hand columns. The visual consequence, already apparent in the pricked, preparatory cartoon,[6] is that the column is thrust back into the pictorial space. The overlapping of one object by another is physiologically one of the most powerful of all depth-indicators. Any object that is partly masked by one immediately in front of it always appears to lie in a much deeper plane than a similar, equally distant object which is not so masked. Donatello made positive use of this phenomenon in his relief of the *Miracle of the Miser's Heart* on the altar at Padua. In order to keep his three-dimensional and surface patterns in balance he deliberately left the further pier of the foremost structure on the left unmasked, whilst the nearer is heavily overlaid by figures. The structural relationship remains clear, but the visual effect is to make the two forms seem to lie in almost the same plane.[7]

Such compositional sophistication was as yet beyond the

---

4. See M. Ermers, *Die Architekturen Raffaels in seinen Fresken, Tafelbildern und Teppichen*, Strassburg, 1909, pp. 5 ff.

5. The architectural plan is discussed in Ermers, *op. cit.*, p. 34 ff., but the reconstruction in his pl. IXa does not appear to be correct as regards the main crossing. Below the pendentives in the fresco itself there appear to be no diagonal or other structurally suitable supporting elements.

6. O. Fischel, *Raphaels Zeichnungen*, Berlin, 1913, I, no. 28, p. 53 and pl. 28.

7. This phenomenon is discussed in the general context of Donatello's spatial designs in J. White, *The Birth and Rebirth of Pictorial Space*, London, 1957, p. 159.

reach of the young Raphael. In his design the consequences are startling in an evidently quite uncalculated way. He has carefully allowed the base of the left-hand column to remain visible between the angel Gabriel's legs. Its precise position in pictorial space is then established with absolute clarity by the transverse band of the squared pavement which links it to its opposite number, the unmasked column beside the Virgin on the right. In spite of all this, it is visually speaking quite impossible, when looking at the main body of the column itself, to tell that it lies in the same plane as the foremost column on the right. It seems instead to float uncertainly in an indeterminate position deeper in pictorial space somewhere between the planes denoted by the first and second columns on the right. Again, as in the main panel, though in a rather different way, Raphael's determination to achieve a certain kind of spatial and dramatic realism has carried him out of his compositional depth.

It is precisely because of his achievements as a designer of pictorial space, which, as Vasari makes clear, were from the first amongst his main claims to fame, that it is important to see how very real, and at the time apparently insurmountable in certain cases, were the problems which Raphael faced. They were problems which he himself set for himself and which he could not and would not shirk by the normal and extremely simple process of avoidance. The difficulties and partial failures which are an inseperable ingredient of the major triumphs of his early years should not be thought of merely as a symptom of youthful endeavours rapidly outgrown. The *Entombment* in the Borghese Gallery seems no less clearly to be just such another major work and just such another partial failure in certain respects. It is also every bit as obviously a criticism of the nature of his own Florentine output as the *Coronation* was a commentary on what were to him the deficiencies of Perugino's typical creations. By 1507 he had clearly become aware that whilst he himself was a thoroughly successful Madonna painter, Leonardo and Michelangelo were something quite different. The *Entombment* is, moreover, a key to the understanding of the swift succession of Raphael's early Roman triumphs, much in the same way as the revolutionary but only partially successful fresco of the *Repulse of Attila* is a key to the processes which lead to the finest achievements of his last years.

A similar determination to burst the bonds of his artistic education and to advance at almost any incidental cost; a similar concentration on some major problem which he has set himself is often visible in Raphael's drawings, and particularly in his approach to anatomical problems.

In the studies in Oxford and Lille for two of the music-making angels for the *Coronation*,[8] in which he is concen-

trating on general problems of pose and movement, Raphael shows, as in the majority of his early drawings, his mastery of parallel hatching and of simple systems of cross-hatching as a means of evoking smoothly idealized and generalized forms. Where, as in the brilliant *Study for St. Thomas* also in Lille,[9] in which the entire essence of the pose is summed up in the disembodied head and hands, he is content to establish two main planes of chin and cheek without descent to any kind of detail, there is complete sureness and clarity in the straightforward parallel hatching system that is used. The limitations of Raphael's control over the method at this point are, however, made particularly obvious when an unavoidably complex problem such as the description of the junction of the foreshortened palm and wrist of the figure's left hand has to be faced. The organizational clarity of the stroke can then only be maintained by a thoroughly arbitrary reorganization of the anatomical facts. The difficulty of setting up a coherent and flexible stroke organization capable of being made to cope with any situation which arises without breaking down[10] is seen again in a slightly different form in the *Study for the head of St. James* in the British Museum (Fig. 4). Here Raphael attacks the detailed problems of anatomical description which he had not needed to face in the purely pose-fixing compositional *Study for St. Thomas*. The problem is no longer merely to establish the basic column of the neck and the general planes of chin and cheek, but to describe the precise surface movement of the flesh as the Saint's head strains back. Everywhere on the neck, but particularly in the region of the adam's apple it is evident that Raphael is feeling his way into uncharted territory. At every point he is struggling to find some sort of *ad hoc* solution for the particular, detailed problem with which he is immediately faced. As a result, the potentially homogeneous and flexible system of cross-hatching, which he has chosen to use as being most appropriate to the nature of the task in hand, loses all coherence. It ceases to be, or rather it never becomes, a regular and supple organizational network, and takes on the appearance of a choppy sea with wind and tide running across each other. No sooner does one hatching pattern gain a semblance of coherence over some area of a fraction of a square centimetre or so than it is over-run and interrupted by the need to find some means of describing an adjacent dip or swelling in the flesh. The confused cross-currents of the strokes are everywhere

8. Fischel, *op. cit.*, I, no. 18, p. 49, pl. 18, and K. T. Parker, *Catalogue of the Drawings in the Ashmolean Museum*, II, Oxford, 1956, p. 261; also Fischel, *op. cit.*, I, no. 21, p. 50 and pl. 21 (Musée Wicar, No. 444).

9. Musée Wicar, no. 440; Fischal, *op. cit.*, I, no. 16, p. 49 and pl. 16.
10. The problems involved in developing an organization of brush- or pen-stroke capable of standing up to the demands placed on it by his vision, or indeed of contributing to the creation of that vision inasmuch as a work of art is expressible only in terms of its concrete existence, is faced by every artist. One of the best analyses of some of these problems with reference to a particular artist, especially in relation to draughtsmanship, is E. Panofsky, *Albrecht Dürer*, Princeton, 1945.

indicative of struggle and uncertainty.[11] In Renaissance painting there is a general tendency for the finished work to show a certain simplification and suppression of detail in comparison with the life-studies which precede it. Nevertheless, the impression that Raphael's difficulty was to him no minor matter seems to be confirmed by the way in which the knob of the adam's apple has been almost entirely suppressed, and the difficult passage where the point of the chin and the contour of the cheek converge considerably simplified, in the painted head for which this drawing is seemingly the final preparation.

A different aspect of the conflict between Raphael's highly developed sense of pattern and of line and his ignorance of anatomical detail at this stage in his career is apparent in the splendid study of a *Nude Man seen from Behind* which represents one of his earliest surviving attempts to repair the deficiency.[12] The magnificent slatted pattern of the right leg is especially revealing. Like the reticulation of the back it creates a wonderfully decorative analogy or substitute for the physical forms involved. It is, however, one which can withstand no very close comparison with the detail of the muscular systems which it purports to describe. Indeed, in the sensitivity to decorative interval and repetition and to geometric pattern which they so clearly reveal,[13]

Raphael's early drawings in many respects underline the extent to which medieval ways of thinking and methods of design live on to provide the basis for so much of the Renaissance revolution. Much in the same way, the organization of Perugino's very workshop remains purely medieval in its apparent structure despite the Renaissance characteristics of its output.

The way in which, under the impact of experiment and observation, Renaissance geometry grows out of medieval geometry, and highly simplified ideals of form give way to new forms which in many ways are no less idealized, but which are more complex in themselves and in their relationship to observable reality, is epitomized on the two sides of the sheet of studies (Figs. 5–6) for the *Belle Jardinière* preserved in the Ashmolean.

If the first great struggle of Raphael's artistic career was the one involved in his break-away from the trammels of Perugino's workshop, the second was his fight to withstand and to absorb the impact of the move to Florence *c.*1504–5. By *c.* 1507, when he was working on the *Belle Jardinière*, the initial period of excited shock in the face of the towering achievements of Leonardo and Michelangelo which is represented by paintings such as the *Terranuova Madonna* was far behind him. Then, in the classic pattern of artistic first reaction to fundamentally new and profound experiences, he had been able only to take over certain superficialities of style such as a lower general tone, or to incorporate, as a wholly meaningless and incongruous connective

11. Uncertainty in his use of cross-hatching is found in a number of Raphael's early drawings. One of the best examples occurs in the beautiful study of the head and shoulders of a young woman in the British Museum (1895-9-15-611, P. Pouncey and J. A. Gere, *Italian Drawings in the Department of Prints and Drawings, Raphael and His Circle*, London, 1962, no. 3, p. 4 and frontispiece). Here nothing in the anatomical structure seems to explain the precise form taken and the area covered by the broadly cross-hatched passage half to two-thirds of the way up the left cheek. The transition to simple parallel hatching is particularly abrupt at the lower end, and makes it difficult to accept the whole as an area of light reflected from the veil. Nevertheless it may well be that Raphael is here stretching his technical powers in order to try to catch just such a subtle light-effect on the surface of a basically smooth form.

12. No. 1860-6-16-94; Pouncey and Gere, *op. cit.*, no. 1, p. 2, pl. 2.

13. One of the most interesting examples of Raphael's methods is provided by the study for the *Madonna del Granduca* (Uffizi 505; Fischel, *op. cit.*, II, no. 105, p. 131 and pl. 105). Raphael's original intention was to have a circular format, and he was at great pains to relate the narrow vertical of the figures as closely as possible to the geometry of the frame. The tilting of the two heads, and the long, slow curve of the head-dress, accelerating into the swift, swinging curves that unite the Virgin's free hand to the Christ Child's feet, are all calculated to this end. The outcome is a near-oval, set within the circle, and running through the two heads, the Virgin's free arm and hand, and finally through the forward foot of the Child and the Virgin's supporting hand and its associated swirl of drapery. The pull of this form, combined with a wish to reduce the large areas of disassociated landscape on either side of the figures, was evidently such that Raphael decided to substitute a framing oval for the original circle. A series of faint, and not so faint, traces then show that, still not satisfied with the degree of concentration thus achieved, he experimented with a series of progressively narrower rect-

angles until he had finally established a tall, narrow format closely approaching that of the eventual painting.

At this point the landscape, originally needed in order to provide a series of steadying horizontals for the circle with which he started, became superfluous, and every remaining form was modified to fit the new geometry. In the painting the tilt of the heads is much reduced. The horizontal at the Virgin's neck is strongly emphasized by a tonal contrast absent in the drawing. The curve in the cloak is flattened out, and the lower system of curves abolished by bringing the Virgin's free hand up and by altering the drapery-pattern. The Christ Child's feet are drawn closer together, and for the pool of shadow which originally broke the vertical of his body, allowing it to harmonize as much as possible with the contained oval, Raphael substitutes an intensified highlight of white drapery. The outcome is a series of accentuated horizontals and verticals which fit the Child's forms to the geometry of the enclosing rectangle to which each and every element of the design is now so beautifully adapted.

In many of Raphael's works, from the very beginning of his career to the very end, his starting point is largely geometrical. In some cases, as in that of the *Madonna of the Meadow*, the initial geometry, which is there that of the triangle established in the sheet of studies in the Albertina (S.R. 248; Fischel, *op. cit.*, II, no. 115, p. 140 and pl. 115), controls the final design. In others it does not. In that of the *Bridgewater Madonna*, for example, the stark triangular form which he obtained by abstracting the Virgin and Child from Michelangelo's marble tondo, now in the Royal Academy, and then drawing in and greatly accentuating the Virgin's originally invisible arm (Louvre 03,856; Fischel, *op. cit.*, no. 108, p. 136 and pl. 108) had to be completely reorganized before a satisfactory final result could be achieved.

element in the pattern of an otherwise almost entirely planar painting, some startling foreshortening such as the Virgin's outstretched hand which, in Leonardo's *Virgin of the Rocks*, had held deep psychological and iconographic as well as formal meaning.[14] Now, in the Oxford studies for the infant Christ of the *Belle Jardinière*, after so many drawings from the *Battle Cartoons*, from the sculpture of Donatello and Michelangelo, and from Leonardo's finished and unfinished works, he is again faced with a problem of detailed anatomical description similar in principle to the one which had proved so baffling in his *Study for the Head of St. James*.

The Oxford sheet of studies (Fig. 5) seems to radiate self-confidence and control. The large, firm curves of the standing figure, the confident attack upon its twisting pose, the idealized beauty of the forms, are matched at every point in the uppermost, and apparently final, study of the detailed problems of the pressures acting upon chubby, infant feet and ankles. At first glance the absorption of detail and the particularization of form recalls such drawings made by Leonardo in the late 'seventies as that of the *Virgin and Child with a Bowl of Cherries* now in the Louvre.[15] Yet it is hardly less immediately apparent that, for all his study of Leonardo's drawings as well as of his paintings, Raphael's by now well-established methods are almost wholly different. They have little or nothing to do with the constant, meaningful irregularities of the Pollaiuolesque, swift, broken, form-following, form-creating, swelling and diminishing contour-line with which Leonardo, even at so early a stage in his career, unconsciously expresses the depth of his anatomical understanding. On the contrary, the seeming particularizations of form in Raphael's contour-line in this apparently detailed study from the life are created by the intersection of a series of geometrically regular curves. The geometrical idealization of carefully observed forms is as clear here, in the end-product of a series of studies from the life, as is the pure geometry of triangle and circle which provides the starting point in so many of his composition studies for projected paintings.

It is precisely at this moment of seemingly confident achievement, when he had learnt so much and put it to such personal and effective use, that Raphael seems suddenly to have realized to the full the fundamental nature of his ignorance in the face of the now established Florentine artistic discipline. Raphael's vigorous and, as drawings, beautiful variations on the theme of the *Bathers* readily show how little he knew of the details of anatomical fact

when compared with Michelangelo.[16] It is indeed, almost at the end of his Florentine period, that Raphael himself seems to have understood that he could go no further; that he could never hope to stand against the Florentines until he too had learnt the structural fundamentals of the human figure. Already in the mid-fourteen-sixties men such as Pollaiuolo had seen that further advance was impossible without the knowledge obtained from dissections. All that could be done by observation of the fleshy outer envelope of the human form had seemingly been achieved. Only through an understanding of the exact nature of the forces which conditioned the shapes taken up by man's external skin could further possibilities be opened up. Now, c. 1507, Raphael, at the moment seemingly, in the *Belle Jardinière*, of achieving all that he had set himself to do in the already long line of his Florentine Madonnas, finally comes to the same realization.

It is on the back of the same Oxford sheet on which he made his studies for the Christ Child that Raphael drew the famous and pathetic 'skeleton' (Fig. 6) which may have been a study for a *Pietà* or *Man of Sorrows* or even represent part of a chain of thought arising from the preliminaries for the *Entombment*, signed and dated 1507, and now in the Borghese Gallery. It is pathetic in every sense, and not in subject matter only. Its very badness is what makes it so significant. As with the very similar drawing of skeletal figures for the *Entombment* which is in the British Museum,[17] it is clearly not a drawing of a skeleton at all. It is Raphael contemplating a slightly unusual pose and wondering what a figure in this position would look like if it were a skeleton. This is a very different matter. As with the female supporting figure in the drawing for the *Entombment*, Raphael begins with a normal, though less plump, external view of the head and neck. From these admittedly emaciated forms he gradually works down towards the skeleton. In doing so he reveals the extreme limitations of his knowledge.[18] Even the drawing of the pelvis, the most fully realized bone structure in both studies, tells as much in terms of ignorance of specific detail as of general knowledge

14. Apart from its compositional function in emphasizing the Christ Child, it expresses the sudden pang of sorrow and the instinctive desire to protect her Son as the Virgin has an intuition of the Passion, implicit in the figure of St. John and made explicit by his reed-cross in the later version in the National Gallery in London.

15. A. E. Popham, *The Drawings of Leonardo da Vinci*, London, 1946, no. 25, pl. 25.

16. The most significant of these studies is possibly British Museum 1895-9-15-624 (Pouncey and Gere, *op. cit.*, no. 20 *recto*, p. 17, pl. 25). Comparison of the right shoulder and upper arm of the top left-hand figure, which is probably directly derived from the *Bathers*, or of the similar elements of the lower, central figure, with such of Michelangelo's own studies for his cartoon as those in the Ashmolean (Parker, *op. cit.*, no. 296, pp. 139–40, pl. LXXI) and in the British Museum (1877-5-2-116; J. Wilde, *Italian Drawings in the Department of Prints and Drawings, Michelangelo and his Studio*, London, 1953, no. 6 *recto*, pp. 14 ff. and pl. XII) vividly demonstrates the width of the gulf.

17. No. 1895-9-15-617; Pouncey and Gere, *op. cit.*, no. 11, pp. 9–10, pl. 13. Both these drawings of skeletons have been doubted, but are now generally accepted as being by Raphael himself.

18. Even the head of the skeletal, supported figure in the *Entombment* study is not a true skull. It has, for example, a nose instead of a nasal cavity.

of the structural situation.[19] Elsewhere vague travesties of bony structure tail dejectedly away.

Nevertheless, just as an awareness of the significance of Raphael's compositional difficulties in his early years leads to a better understanding of the nature and mechanics of his meteoric rise in these respects, so a sympathetic realization of just how bad these wish-fulfilment skeletons are as skeletons gives a further insight into Raphael's stature both as an artist and as a man. These drawings seem indeed to represent a moment of intense artistic self-awareness and of sweeping self-criticism. How sweeping is shown by the fact that within two or three years at the most he was producing drawings like the magnificent study for the Apollo of the *Parnassus*, now in Lille.[20] Such drawings epitomize the wholly different quality and range of anatomical understanding on which Raphael's Roman style is founded, and which is apparent from the period of the preparations for the Stanza della Segnatura onwards. It is also interesting that it is just at the moment when the *Entombment*, which began as a static Peruginesque tableau for the contemplation of the pious, is being slowly transformed into Raphael's first, and only partially successful, attempt to challenge Leonardo and Michelangelo on their own, securely held high ground of the dramatic narrative that Raphael seems to reveal his dawning awareness of the hopelessness of the enterprise in his existing state of knowledge.[21] Typically, and most significantly for his future achievements, Raphael did not, as would certainly have been the case with Leonardo in a similar situation, shrink from completion of the painting.

If the 'skeletons' of 1506–7 do represent an intense moment of truth for Raphael, and if they were, in consequence, the immediate prelude to a period of concentrated anatomical study, it is at least a little easier to see how Raphael came to make such full and instantaneous use of his introduction to Michelangelo's Roman style, and could so rapidly complete yet one more revolution in his own stylistic development. With Raphael, the tranquil golden boy of the Renaissance, it seems that an awareness of the part which failure and self-criticism played in his artistic life is essential for some understanding of the speed of his artistic growth and of the constant, swift succession of his triumphs.

19. The pelvis in the Oxford drawing is particularly weak. Even the outline as a whole has only a very vague relationship to reality. The British Museum study shows much better appreciation of the structure of the head of the femur, of the disposition of the iliac crest and fossa, and of the pubic arch and obturator foramen. The actual shapes, however, and particularly the relationship between the hip-socket and the obturator foramen, are grossly distorted.

20. Musée Wicar, no. 542–543; Fischel, *op. cit.*, v, no. 245, p. 262 and pl. 245. From this time onwards even the less detailed action studies carry a new conviction anatomically speaking.

The sheet with four anatomical studies in the Musée Bonnat in Bayonne (Inv. 683 *verso*; J. Bean, *Les Dessins italiens de la collection Bonnat*, Paris, 1960, no. 132), none of which involves an actual skeleton, would, if it is indeed by Raphael, confirm the advance of his knowledge. The effort to achieve anatomical accuracy in the left-hand torso is extreme, as also is the case in parts of the one next to it. The two right-hand figures then provide a complete and characteristic contrast in approach, being extremely simplified and stylized exercises in the geometry of the human form in action.

21. Raphael's first idea is reminiscent in general structure of Perugino's *Entombment* of 1495 from S. Chiara in Florence, now in the Palazzo Pitti.

KENNETH CLARK

Francesco Melzi as Preserver of Leonardo da Vinci's Drawings

BY his will of 23rd April 1519 Leonardo made Francesco Melzi the heir of all his belongings, including 'tutti e ciaschaduno li libri che il dicto testatore ha da presente, et altri instrumenti e portracti circa l'arte sua et industria de pictori'. Melzi had joined him as a pupil soon after his return to Milan in 1508, and remained with him for the rest of his life, not simply as a pupil, but as a friend and, latterly, as a loving adopted son. In the spring and summer of 1513 Leonardo stayed in Melzi's villa at Vaprio d'Adda, where he did the exquisite drawings of rivers now at Windsor, 12398–12400; and, as Professor Pedretti has shown, Leonardo made a number of architectural drawings for the rebuilding of the villa, which were probably never carried out. Melzi is recorded as accompanying Leonardo to Rome, and to Amboise, and he is mentioned in the well known account of Antonio de Beatis' visit to Leonardo at Cloux. It was he who wrote to Leonardo's mother announcing his death, and referring to him as 'mio quanto optimo padre, per la cui morte sarebbe impossibile che io potesse esprimere il dolore che io ho preso'.

Soon after Leonardo's death he returned to his villa at Vaprio d'Adda near Milan, and we know that various people visited him there to look at his treasures, including, in 1523, the Duke of Ferrara's Agent and presumably Vasari, who records in the 1550 edition of the Vite, 'Di queste carte della notamia degli uomini n'è gran parte nelle mani di messer Francesco da Melzo gentiluomo milanese, che nel tempo di Lionardo era bellissimo fanciullo e molto amato da lui, cosi come oggi è bello e gentile vecchio, che le ha care e tiene come per reliquie tal carte'.

Melzi lived on till 1570, and seems to have devoted most of his time to looking after his great legacy. He attempted to arrange Leonardo's manuscripts and it has been argued[1] that he actually copied out with his own hand the notes on painting which now form the Codex Urbinas Vaticanus, and are known to us as the *Trattato della pittura*. For this reason it seems fair to assume that the numerous copies of Leonardo's drawings in the Windsor Collection, all obviously by the same hand, are the work of Francesco Melzi. This general inference is confirmed by the well-known sheet in the Ambrosiana (Fig. 5) of a man's head in profile, signed by Francesco Melzi and dated the 14th August 1510; one inscription on the drawing tells us that he was aged

seventeen, another that he was aged nineteen. The style of this drawing is exactly that of a large number of the Windsor copies. Basically it is the style of Leonardo, but it differs in that the modelling is smoother and more opaque, the outline dead and even. We have no difficulty in recognizing the same hand in such a drawing as the grotesque head of woman ('the ugly duchess') '492, the caricature heads '493, the man with flowing hair '494, the seated man in profile '584 (Figs. 1–4), or the horses legs on '298. Most of Melzi's copies are in the same medium, red chalk on white paper, but when the occasion demanded it he could use other media. The Dantesque monster (Barbariccia) on '371 is on red paper, with touches of black chalk and white, as well as red; and the copy of a 'Deluge' drawing '381 is in black chalk on yellowish paper, and recognizable as Melzi only when one examines closely the character of the line. The quality of Melzi's copies varies considerably; '299 is a much better copy than '298, and the study of a dog on '361 is of such high quality that Mr. Popham believed it to be genuine. But these variations are such as could be accounted for by circumstances, the interest that Melzi felt in his task and perhaps the urgency with which the copy had to be made.

It is usually supposed that Melzi, who looked after Leonardo's drawings for over fifty years, made these copies during his long period of custodianship. But I am inclined to believe that Melzi's copies and retouchings were done in Leonardo's lifetime and on his instructions. We know that drawings by admired artists were carefully collected in the early sixteenth century. The Neptune that Leonardo did for his friend Antonio Segni was one of the earliest of 'presentation drawings';[2] and we cannot doubt that after 1510, when his output as an artist had dwindled but his fame had increased, he must have been constantly requested for 'something from his hand'. This theory is supported by the character of the actual drawings copied. They are exactly what Leonardo's patrons would have wanted from him. The ugly Duchess, '492, is the most 'poussée' of all the grotesques; the man with wavy hair '494 and the seated

1. Cf. Carlo Pedretti, *Leonardo da Vinci on Painting. A lost Book (Libro A)*, University of California Press, 1964, pp. 98 ff.

2. Leonardo seems also to have been the originator of the 'woman in profile all'antica' as the subject of such presentation drawings, cf. the drawing in Windsor 12508 (which has never been adequately photographed), dateable 1510–13 and the engraving in the British Museum, Hind, *Early Italian Engraving*, vol. VI, 1948, pl. 620, which seems to reproduce a somewhat earlier drawing by Leonardo.

man '584 have the somewhat self-conscious character of 'presentation drawings'. They are Leonardo at his most recognizable: and it is interesting to see that the idea of the Leonardesque, which was to survive till the middle of the nineteenth century, had been formed in Leonardo's lifetime.

These drawings are not particularly attractive to us; but we can be sure that Melzi's copies do not greatly misrepresent the originals, because in several instances the originals have survived. One of them is the head in the top right-hand corner of '493, which has been cut out of its context and is now in the Kunsthalle at Hamburg; another is the study of horses legs '299, an exceptionally good copy, which might have been accepted as authentic were it not shaded from right to left. The original is in Budapest. Most instructive of all is the study of horses legs '302, of which Leonardo's original (or part of it) is at Windsor '301, and has been placed beside it in the same mount (Figs. 7, 8). Melzi's copy is shaded from left to right, and in a small reproduction might easily pass as authentic. But comparison with the original shows how wooden is Melzi's outline compared to the vital, nervous touch of Leonardo. It is by constantly referring back to these two drawings that we can settle such difficult cases as the dog on '361.

These 'replacement copies' present no problems; but when we come to the drawings that Melzi retouched we are on more difficult ground. Here, too, I believe that Melzi was working on his master's instructions. Leonardo used two drawing techniques that grew extremely faint. One of them, on white unprepared paper, was a hard black chalk or lead point, which has become almost invisible; the other was red chalk used on a red prepared paper of almost the same colour. A drawing in this technique that has not been retouched is the head and shoulders of an elderly man, '598, and it proves how faint the drawings were allowed to become before it was thought necessary to rescue them. That they had begun to vanish in Leonardo's lifetime is shown by the fact that many of them have been retouched by Leonardo himself; and it is this, of course, that presents the connoisseur with a delicate problem. In some cases we can be sure. The head of a man with a turban ('Dante') on '580 has certainly been strengthened by a pupil, and the head of St. Anne, '534 has been so completely 'gone over' that very little of Leonardo's original line is visible. On the other hand, I have little doubt Leonardo himself added the pen outlines to red chalk studies of legs such as '620, 629, etc. Between these two extremes are several drawings that still leave one in doubt. An artist's hand will be less lively when retouching one of his earlier drawings to save it from annihilation than when responding to the pressure of creative excitement, and some 'inking in' that is almost cer-

tainly by Leonardo is surprisingly tame, for example the small figures of men in action on '644. When the retouching is in chalk the problem is more delicate, as in the study of horses legs, '333. Even in reproduction (Fig. 9) the outlines reveal the lifeless touch of Melzi, who was no doubt working over a drawing of the same type as '314. But whether he also worked up the shading I cannot say. An insoluble puzzle is the sheet of cats '363 (Fig. 6). The black chalk with which it was first drawn must have grown very faint in Leonardo's time, and it has been inked over with a wooden touch. Can Leonardo's hand be responsible for the dreary outlines of the central cats? I ask myself the same kind of question before an even more famous drawing, the study of flowers in the Venice Academy, where the stalks have exactly the same dull, lifeless quality as the cats' tails. On the whole I incline to think that they are by Leonardo, but that they were inked in very late in his life, long after the impulse of the original studies had faded. The same insensitive line is to be found in some of the later anatomical drawings, in which Leonardo was concerned only with demonstrating a theory, and probably the cats on '363 and the horses on '331 were intended as illustrations to a treatise on the movement of animals, and belong to a period when Leonardo, perhaps with Melzi's influence, was attempting to give some theoretical order to his vast collection of data. I should add that, in addition to his 'replacement copies' and restorations, the Leone volume contained a few of Melzi's original drawings which happened to be on the backs of Leonardos. Such is the pen and ink scribble of two figures embracing on '641 *recto*, which also contains a scrap of Melzi's writing and a landscape that might be preparatory to the picture in Berlin of Vertumnus and Pomona which is attributed to him by a reliable tradition; and such, I believe, are the red chalk heads of women, '639 *verso*, '654 *recto* and '663 *verso*. Finally, the drawing of a Columbine which disappeared from the collection during the summer of 1907, seems from a photograph[3] to have provided a connecting link between Melzi as a copyist and Melzi as an independent artist. The outlines and modelling are exactly in the style of the 'replacement drawings', but the flowers seem to be preparatory studies for Melzi's picture in the Hermitage of a lady with a columbine. Probably it was a copy of an original drawing by Leonardo which Melzi was allowed to use as the central motif in one of his rare attempts at painting.

3. The best accessible reproduction is in *Leonardo da Vinci, La vita di Giorgio Vasari*, a cura di Giovanni Poggi, Firenze, 1919, pl. CXXXVIII. The former assistant in the Windsor Castle library used to maintain that the drawing was destroyed by Müller Walde at the time when that great scholar was going out of his mind.

A. E. POPHAM

The Baiardo Inventory

THE late Prof. Attilio Rapetti of Piacenza published in 1940[1] an inventory of pictures, drawings, prints and other objects which bore the headings 'Inventario delle Pitture del q. s. Cavagliere Bayardo' and 'Inventario delli disegni del q. s. Cavaglier Bayardo'. Professor Rapetti claimed that the Cavaliere Baiardo in question was the owner of Parmigianino's famous painting of *Cupid shaping his Bow* now at Vienna and that this painting was the first item in the inventory: 'Un' Cupido colorito finito di mano del Parmesanino alto B2 e più'.[2] This claim seems to me to be justified.

According to Padre Ireneo Affò,[3] Francesco Baiardo died on 30th September 1561, and there is every reason to suppose that the inventory was drawn up on or about that date. This branch of the Baiardo family apparently became extinct in the male line with the death of Francesco, as his heir was a grandson, Marcantonio Cavalca. Vasari, when he visited Parma in 1566, almost certainly saw the *Cupid*, which he describes with enthusiasm 'nello studio del signor Marc'Antonio Cavalca, erede del cavalier Baiardo; con molti disegni che ha raccolti, di mano del medesimo [Parmigianino], bellissimi e ben finiti d'ogni sorte. . . .'[4]

The inventory, even if the handwriting points to the early seventeenth, rather than to the sixteenth, century, is no doubt a faithful copy of the original manuscript.[5] It must be one of the earliest, if not the earliest, detailed record of a collection of drawings to have reached us and is a document of no little interest in the history of collecting as well as of importance to the student of Parmigianino's drawings. The attributions to Parmigianino of any drawings or pictures contained in it must carry great weight.[6]

Baiardo's taste as a collector was far from catholic. His pictures, with very few exceptions, were the work of Parmese artists. Out of 63 items listed as the contents of three 'camerine', all presumably framed and hung, 17 were prints by Marcantonio and Dürer. Of the remaining pictures and drawings, 24 were by Parmigianino, four by Mazzola Bedoli (three reproducing drawings by Parmigianino[7]), one by Correggio, and two by Giorgio da Parma (Giorgio Gandini del Grano, who died in Parma in 1536). There were only two paintings by named artists of other schools, one of Christ in chiaroscuro by Don Giulio, presumably Giulio Clovio, and a *Venus and Adonis* by Titian. The description of this picture (no. 47) 'Un' quadro d'Adone e Venere co' uno cupido che dorme e duoi cani colorito finito alto B 2 largo B 2½ di mano di Ticiano' makes it virtually certain that it was a copy of the painting in the Prado made for Philip II in 1554. There were also four 'paesi fiamenghi' and fourteen pictures or drawings either entirely unattributed or with the not very helpful indication 'di buon mano' or 'd'un valent'huomo'.

As a collector of drawings the Cavaliere's taste was even more specialized, not to say parochial. Of the 558 drawings listed, only a single one is given to any artist other than Parmigianino, no. 120 'Un' disegno d'uno huomo co' un' panno intorno, et una Gamba ignuda di lapis rosso quasi finito di Mastro Ant.º da Correggio alto o. 5'. The 'Gamba ignuda' suggests St. Roch as the subject of the drawing and the possibility that it was a study for the saint in the *Madonna of St. Sebastian* at Dresden, but this is pure sur-

1. Attilio Rapetti, *Un inventario di opere del Parmigianino. Archivio Storico per le Provincie Parmensi*, v, 1940. In using Prof. Rapetti's transcription the reader should note that in the case of the drawings the sign preceding the measurements should in every case be read as o. for 'oncie' not B (for bracci) as it is interpreted by him. The items in the inventory are unnumbered and those quoted were supplied by Prof. Rapetti, who gave separate numbers to *recto and verso* of the same sheet, when these are described in the inventory. This was acquired after Prof. Rapetti's death by the Biblioteca Comunale at Piacenza. I am much indebted to Prof. Conte Emilio Nasalli Rocca, director of the library, for arranging to have the manuscript microfilmed on my behalf.
2. The height of the picture is 65·3 cm., of which, according to the 1965 Vienna catalogue, 11 cm. are later additions.
3. *Vita del graziosissimo pittore . . . il Parmigianino*. Parma, 1764. p. 83, note 3.
4. Vasari-Milanesi, v, p. 230.
5. Prof. Rapetti held that the paper and the writing were characteristic of the sixteenth century (introductory note), but my impression, reinforced by the opinion of the Department of Manuscripts of the British Museum, is that the writing is rather of the early seventeenth century.

6. Prof. Freedberg (*Parmigianino, His Works in Painting*, Cambridge, Mass., 1950, pp. 239–240) quotes the entries regarding pictures by Parmigianino in the inventory. He complains of the vagueness of the descriptions and measurements which 'make it impossible to check the few items which may perhaps be identifiable with surviving works: there is thus no way of determining the extent of the credibility of the other attributions in the inventory'. This scepticism is, as we shall see, hardly justified.
7. Of one (no. 5) 'Un' Presepio colorito è finito di man di M. Gironimo Mazollo ritrato da un' disegno del Parmesanino Longo B. I alto o. 10', Baiardo also possessed Parmigianino's drawing (no. 37) 'Un quadretto co' uno presepio in disegno di chiaro e scuro finito alto B. I largo o. 10 di mano dil Parmesanino dal quale il Mazollo ha tolto il colorito', though we must assume that in one or other of the entries the measurements were inadvertently transposed.

mise. There was in addition a series of the costumes of 36 nations 'di buona mano' (nos. 567 to 649).

The Cavaliere Baiardo, together with Damiano de Pleta, the architect, went surety for Parmigianino in the considerable sum of 200 scudi d'oro on 27th September 1535, when a new contract for the decoration of the Steccata was drawn up,[8] the artist having failed to carry out the stipulations of the original contract of 1531. Parmigianino of course never finished the work or refunded the money before his death in 1540 and the two guarantors were legally bound to pay the Steccata the 200 scudi in full. It appears, however, that the officials of the Steccata agreed on 19th September 1544,[9] to a valuation of the work which Parmigianino had completed and that the heirs should only be responsible for paying the difference between this valuation and the money advanced to the deceased artist, 200 scudi d'oro plus an extra 50 which had subsequently been paid to him. As the agreed valuation was 224 scudi d'oro this difference only amounted to 26 scudi and it is probable that Parmigianino's heirs were in a position to pay up and that the guarantors were not called upon, but no documents recording the outcome of this tangled affair have, as far as I know, been published.

It would, however, have been natural that when the Cavaliere Baiardo agreed to act as guarantor, he should have demanded some security and that this would have taken the form of paintings and drawings and been the origin of his extensive collection of Parmigianino's works. Whether Damiano de Pleta may equally have demanded some such security is of course unknown. In a 'ricordo' on the back of a drawing at Windsor[10] Parmigianino noted the payment to Damiano of two scudi d'oro on 22nd December 1537, but gives no explanation of the transaction.

In any case the relations between the Baiardo family, Damiano de Pleta and Parmigianino must have been close. It was the Cavaliere's sister, Elena Baiardo, widow of Francesco Tagliaferri, who had commissioned the *Madonna del collo lungo* from Parmigianino on 23rd December 1534, as the altarpiece for the church of the Servites in Parma. Damiano de Pleta had supplied a drawing of the decoration of this chapel. Parmigianino was paid in advance for the picture and as security for completing it by the following Pentecost gave his house 'in vicinio Sancti Pauli pro burgo Assidum'. The picture was left unfinished at his death, but there is, as far as I know, no record of Elena Tagliaferri's having foreclosed on the property. Indeed in his will the artist directed that his heirs should pay his sister 100 scudi

d'oro from the proceeds of the sale of his house in Parma, presumably the same.

The drawings by Parmigianino were mounted in seven albums, but only a proportion of the contents of these is separately described and measurements given in 'oncie'. The 'oncia' is a twelfth part of the 'braccio di Legname' as used in Parma at this period and is roughly equivalent to 4·5 cm. The compiler of the inventory confines himself to 'oncie' and occasionally half 'oncie', so that his measurements are obviously only approximate. Normally, moreover, he gives only the height and this seems to be that of the principal figure rather than that of the whole sheet, as we shall see.

The number of entries in the inventory which can be brought into relation with existing drawings is disappointingly small. In fact there are only three about which no possible doubt can exist, though there is a strong probability that a number of others are those described. It will be best to deal with the three certain drawings first, so that we can form an idea of the compiler's methods.

Nos. 231 and 232. 'Un' disegno di doi puttini, in scurto di lapis rosso, finito dil parmesanino nel riverso dil quale e una Madona col puttino in brazzo, un' Angelo in piedi co' tre altre teste bozzate ben[mo] dil Parmesanino alto o. 3 [=13·5 cm.]'. This exactly describes a sheet in the Louvre[11] with drawings on both sides (Figs. 1 and 2). The two *putti* seen foreshortened are drawn in red chalk and finished; the Madonna holds the Child in her arms, there is a standing angel, three heads in the background and the whole is 'bozzato' not 'finito' like the other side. The height of the sheet is 18·7 cm., which does not, it is true, correspond with the three 'oncie' of the inventory. These must refer either to the height of one of the *putti* or to that of the Madonna.

Nos. 235 and 236. 'Un' disegno d'una serva[12] vestita, co' le brazza ignude di lapis rosso finita dil parmesanino alta o. 4 nel riverso dil quale son due donne ignude di lapis rosso, una della quali e finita, et l'altra no' dil Parmesanino alto o. 4 [=18 cm.]'. This must be a sheet at Budapest,[13] which answers perfectly to this description (Figs. 3 and 4). Its present height is 18·3 cm. but it appears to have been cut down and the measurements must again be those of the figures.

Nos. 305 and 306. 'Un' disegno d'uno Giovine vestito in parte tocco d'acquarella e di penna, lumatto di biacca, e finito alto o. 3 [=13·5 cm.] ed tre altre gambe della medema inventione et uno schizzo di pena della medema inventione, ogni cosa dil Parmesanino, nel riverso dil qual'e

8. The contract is printed by A. O. Quintavalle, *Il Parmigianino*, Milan, 1948, pp. 165–167.

9. A document now illegible, but of which a summary by Affò is printed by Quintavalle, *op. cit.*, pp. 169–170.

10. A. E. Popham and Johannes Wilde, *The Italian Drawings of the XV and XVI centuries . . . at Windsor Castle*, London, 1949, no. 601.

11. No. 6417. The present *verso* (treated as the *recto* in the inventory) of two *putti* is illustrated in my book on *The Drawings of Parmigianino*, London, 1953, pl. VIIIA.

12. Rapetti reads 'sema', a word not to be found in the dictionaries.

13. No. 2138. Published and illustrated by Dr. Ivan Fenyö in the *Burl M.*, CV, 1963, p. 149 and figs. 13 and 11.

un san Gironimo d'acquarella, et di pena come finito alto o. 2 [=9 cm.] et dui altri schizzi, uno di lapis rosso l'altro d'acquarella dil Parmesanino'. This careful and detailed description leaves no doubt that this is the drawing in the British Museum[14] (Figs. 5 and 6). The measurements must be either those of the actual figures or of the framing lines which contain them.

Having established the connection between these three sheets and entries in the inventory, we can examine the compiler's methods and terminology, in the hope that we may be able to identify other drawings. He seems to be accurate and consistent in his description of techniques, as is shown by the entry for the British Museum drawing. 'Acquarella' is of course the term habitually employed for a drawing shaded in brown or bistre. He seems particular in using the term 'finito', as in the *recto* of the Louvre drawing, contrasted with 'bozzato' for the *verso* of the same sheet. He does not rather surprisingly confine himself to describing in detail the more elaborate and complete drawings as the careful entry for the British Museum drawing demonstrates as well as the 'bozzato ben^{mo} '– one of his very rare qualitative comments – referring to the *verso* of the Louvre sheet. The measurements are the least satisfactory part of his entries as in these cases they must refer to the figures and not to the sheets on which these are drawn. There seems to have been no consistent chronological or other arrangement of the drawings in the albums. Of the three sheets identified, that in the Louvre (nos. 231 and 232 of Rapetti's numeration) is the second item in the third volume, though it dates from Parmigianino's first period in Parma and the Virgin and Child with the angel on the *verso* is almost certainly a study for the painting at Madrid, believed to be one of the works which Vasari tells us he took with him to Rome in 1523–24. The Budapest drawing, on the other hand (nos. 235 and 236), the fifth drawing in the same album belongs to the period after the artist's return to Parma about 1531, as the unfinished nude on the *verso* is related to the Virgins of the Steccata. The British Museum drawing (nos. 305 and 306), no. 5 in the fourth book, the *recto* of which represents the preaching of St. John the Baptist and the *verso* St. Jerome, must have some connection with the National Gallery altarpiece of 1527.

If the three drawings I have discussed are the only ones, the identification of which is beyond all doubt, there are a number of others which it is tempting to relate to entries in the inventory. Among these are some only known from old facsimiles, which can however generally be relied on as accurate.

In the 'Primo Libro grande' no. 72 'Un' disegno di san Gironimo nel deserto co' certi camelli tocco di pena e finito dal Parmesanino alto o. 5 largo o. 7 [=22·5×31·5 cm.]' is almost certainly the lost drawing of which Rosa-

spina made an etching,[15] when it belonged to Giovanni Antonio Armano shortly before 1788 (Fig. 7). The original was subsequently in the collection of Sir Thomas Lawrence and is described in the catalogue of the fourth exhibition of his drawings held in 1836, no. 11, as having formed part of the Arundel and Zanetti collections. The measurements given there are equivalent to 20·2×31·7 cm., which correspond with those of the inventory as to width, but are less by about two centimetres as to height. It may well have been cut at the top or bottom. This must have been one of Parmigianino's largest and most elaborately finished drawings.

No. 73, 'Un disegno di Venere col cupido che gli vuole levare l'archo di chiaro e scuro finito dal Parmesanino alto o. 3 largo o. 2½ [13·5 × 11·2 cm.]', is likely to be either the drawing at Budapest[16] or a very similar one in the collection of Major E. S. Robb in London. Both are drawn on natural blue paper, washed and heightened with white, and are of approximately the same size, 18·8×14·3 and 17·1 × 14·6 cm. respectively.

No. 74, 'Un' disegno di Vulcano che vuole battere sopra l'incugine co' Venere col cupido a collo, tocco di penna finito dil Parmesanino alto o. 4 largo 4 [=18×18 cm.]', is presumably the drawing which was etched by Hendrick van den Borcht when it formed part of the Arundel collection, then by G. A. Faldoni when it belonged to Zanetti (Weigel 5607) and finally by Rosaspina after G. A. Armano had acquired it. It too was absorbed into the Lawrence collection and figures as no. 47 in the exhibition catalogue, where its dimensions are given as equivalent to 17·1 × 15·8 cm., showing a considerable difference from those given in the inventory. There is no doubt, however, that the drawing, even before it entered the Arundel collection, had been trimmed at any rate at the sides, as is shown by an old copy.

No. 98, 'Un' disegno d'uno giovine in piede tocco di penna et finito che tien' a mano un' asino, bozzato del Parmesanino alto o. 3 [=13·5 cm.]', can with probability be identified as the drawing in a private collection (Fig. 8), assuming again that the three 'oncie' refer to the figure and not to the whole sheet, which now measures 19·6 × 19 cm.

No. 108, 'Un' disegno di Giove che siede col fulmine in mano tocco di penna, e finito dil Parmesanino alto o. 2½ [=11·2 cm.]', may probably be identified with the drawing now in the Hermitage.[17] This was etched by Lucas Vorsterman when in the Arundel collection and subsequently belonged to Mariette. Again the dimensions must be those of the figure, not of the whole sheet, which now measures 14 × 11 cm.

---

14. Pp. 2–131. No. 82 in the new British Museum Catalogue of drawings by artists working in Parma.

15. Undescribed. Impression in British Museum 1919-4-15-188.

16. Ill. *Bulletin du Musée National Hongrois des Beaux-Arts*, XIX, 1961, p. 47, fig. 33.

17. Illustrated in M. Dobroklonsky, *Drawings of the Italian School of the XV and XVI centuries in the Hermitage*, Moscow, 1940, no. 267.

No. 115. 'Un disegno di nove figurine di Moysé diferenti l'uno dal'altro, di chiaro e scuro finito in parte dil Parmesanino alto o. 2 l'uno [=9 cm.).' Though it is tempting to identify this as the drawing now in the Metropolitan Museum,[18] which in fact contains nine studies for the Moses in the Steccata, there are objections to such an identification. In the first place there are also studies of the Eve on the *verso* and as we have seen in other cases the compiler of the inventory is careful to note when a sheet has drawings on both sides. In the second place one would expect him to describe the New York drawing as 'tocco d'acquarella e di penna', as in the case of the British Museum drawing of the Baptist preaching, not as 'di chiaro et scuro', which rather suggests a drawing on coloured paper washed and heightened with white, like those of Venus taking Cupid's bow away referred to above. The measurements 'o. 2 l'uno' agree fairly well with those of the two largest figures on the New York sheet, but on a strict reading all the nine figures should be of the same size.

The second volume only contained 20 drawings of which 12 are separately described. Of these 6 were studies for the Steccata Virgins, one was for the Adam and another for the Eve, presumably also the figures in the Steccata. The descriptions are insufficiently precise to allow of their identification with any of the numerous existing drawings. The third volume contained 47 drawings of which 14 are separately inventoried. Among these are some which may tentatively be recognized among existing drawings.

No. 230, 'Un disegno di Ganymede ignudo, co' due coppe in mano di chiaro e scuro, co' un' gruppo di figure di un' lato et un' altro dal' altro et un fiume abasso tutto finito dil Parmesanino alto o. 4 largo 4 [=18 × 18 cm.]', might well be the drawing formerly belonging to Lord Northampton and now in the collection of Mr. Embiricos in London,[19] but again there are objections. The sheet now measures 18 × 14·8 cm., so that we should have to suppose it considerably cut at the sides, which is possible, and again we

should expect it to be described as 'a l'acquarella' rather than 'di chiaro e scuro', as it is drawn in pen and ink and washed.

No. 238, 'Un'disegno d'un' Ganimede ignudo co' una coppa in mano et un' fiume a piedi finito d'acquarella di Parmesanino alto o. 3 [=13·5 cm.]', is probably the drawing now in the Louvre,[20] which measures 14·8 cm. in height, that is about 1·3 cm. higher than the dimensions given in the inventory.

No. 310, 'Un' disegno d'uno Pastore tocco d'Acquarella co' due pecore, come finito del Parmesanino alto o. 3 [=13·5 cm.]', might well be the drawing of an old shepherd now in the Art Institute at Chicago,[21] which measures 14·2 in height.

The fifth book contained 57 drawings, of which only 4 are separately described and none of which is identifiable.

The sixth book contained 56 drawings, of which 13 are listed separately. It is possible that no. 453, 'Un disegno di san Cristoforo, tocco d'acquarella, lumatto di biacca, finito dil Parmesanino alto o. 4 [=18 cm.]', is the carefully finished drawing now in the École des Beaux-Arts, Paris.[22] None of the 63 drawings in the eighth book is listed separately, though the subjects of 17 of them are summarily described, subjects many of which are to be found among existing drawings by Parmigianino. 'Un aquila', for example, might be the red chalk drawing in the British Museum.[23] It should, however, be borne in mind that there are many examples among existing drawings of the same subject being many times repeated – the Adam, the Eve, the Virgins in the Steccata, Venus taking Cupid's bow away, a woman crowning a horse, for example – and that it is impossible in many cases to feel certain that a drawing summarily described in the inventory is one of the same subject which survives.

18. No. 62.135. Both *recto* and *verso* illustrated in my book cited above pls. LVI and LVII. The *recto* illustrated in Jacob Bean, *100 European Drawings in the Metropolitan Museum*, New York, 1964, pl. 21.

19. Illustrated in my book, pl. LXI.

20. No. R. F. 580. Also illustrated in my book pl. LXII.

21. Illustrated by Bertha M. Wiles, Art Institute of Chicago *Museum Studies*, I, 1966, p. 100, fig. 6.

22. Masson Bequest, No. 2367. From the Arundel collection, when it was etched by Hendrick van den Borcht. It subsequently belonged to Everard Jabach and to the Earl of Dartmouth. There is a copy of it in the Louvre, which was published as the original, in *L'Arte*, XXX, 1927, p. 265.

23. 1905-11-10-45. No. 65 in the new British Museum Catalogue.

MICHAEL LEVEY

Sacred and Profane Significance in
Two Paintings by Bronzino

THE cold marble paintings of Bronzino are polished surfaces from which one's glance may too easily and rapidly slip off, with an impression received well before the artist has finished conveying his intention. One never reads of the tempo which pictures should be looked at; yet it is obvious that sophisticated styles of painting may require the eye to move at first with deliberate slowness over the composition, savouring its meaning rather than seizing it at a mere *coup d'œil* and hastening on. With Bronzino the very sophistication has perhaps worked against him, leading to a vague sense that his pictures do not mean a great deal; such elaborate beautifully-wrought form might seem in some modern eyes to imply trivial or almost non-existent content. And there is also apparent a melancholy reserve, a suppression of the exuberant or the excited, which Henry James expressed in describing the wonderful Bronzino which resembled Milly Theale, the portrait of 'a very great personage – only unaccompanied by a joy'. Bronzino is a master of complex *maniera*, a highly conscious artist both in paint and in words, who could be said almost to have fused two talents in his poem 'Sopra una Pittura d'una Venere'[1] – in itself a testimony to his interest in giving special significance to what is shown in a picture.

Two pictures by Bronzino in the National Gallery are worth re-examination, partly because the sheer familiarity of their subject-matter discourages one from looking too carefully. They take the staple human theme of mother and child, shown in the small-scale religious picture (Fig. 1) and the large-scale mythological picture (Fig. 3) which is probably the finest of all Bronzino's subject-pictures.[2] The *Venus and Cupid* has usually been supposed to be an abstruse allegory, probably of lechery, and the *Virgin and Child* has usually been treated as just a simple devotional group. What is depicted in the *Virgin and Child* can be shown to be rather deeper and more poignant than that title would suggest. For the *Venus and Cupid* what is proposed here is

a new interpretation, radically different from previously accepted theories. Bronzino himself would have been the first to realize in both cases that his subject matter was not new; what was needed was first to present some refined aspect, novel perhaps in its treatment, an *invenzione* with echoes, conscious echoes of the great Florentine tradition. Behind the *Virgin and Child* is ultimately to be detected Leonardo; behind the allegory of *Venus and Cupid* there is patently present the active genius of Michelangelo.

Two ideas are united in the *Virgin and Child*, both already stated in the work of Leonardo. One concerns the Child's recognition of his destiny, the Cross; the other is connected with the related role of the Infant Baptist. Bronzino's starting-point seems to lie in the *Madonna of the Yarnwinder*, one of Leonardo's most popular and copied compositions, where the Child makes a cross for himself from the Virgin's spindles. The second theme receives its most memorable expression in the *Madonna of the Rocks*; the setting of that, and the protective gesture of the Virgin towards the Infant Baptist, both find some recollection in Bronzino's composition. The fusion of the two motifs, whereby the Passion theme is introduced by the Baptist, probably already occurred to Leonardo[3] but had been most obviously expressed in several paintings by Raphael. In the *Madonna in the Meadow* and the *Alba Madonna* the Christ Child is shown on the point of taking the Cross from the Baptist. Bronzino's treatment of that motif is shown in a picture at Washington, one version of a composition that was once claimed to be Raphael's.[4] In the London picture the action is carried a stage further. Any possible ambiguity over whether the cross is taken or given is removed by the quite marked seizure of the cross by the Child; and Bronzino adds a further, tautly elegant touch which enhances the emotional effect of this childhood recognition of the future Passion. Some earlier sixteenth-century Florentine treatments had already shown the Christ Child holding the

---

1. A convenient edition of the poems is *Sonetti di Angiolo Allori detto il Bronzino . . .*, 1823, where this poem is on p. 5; this edition also includes several poems addressed *to* Bronzino and indirectly provides useful indications of some now missing or unidentified portraits.

2. For further details and discussion about these two pictures, cf. Cecil Gould, *National Gallery Catalogues: the Sixteenth-Century Italian Schools (excluding the Venetian)*, 1962, pp. 21 ff.; for the *Venus and Cupid*, also cf. A. Emiliani, *Il Bronzino*, Milan, 1960, text accompanying pls. 46–50.

3. The painted composition, existing in several versions (Oxford, Florence, etc.) is called *The Madonna with the Children at Play*, a title which obscures the subject's significance; Michelangelo's *Taddei Tondo* is, of course, relevant to any wider discussion of this theme.

4. The Washington picture is reproduced by Emiliani, *op. cit.*, pl. 89. The composition, with the figures shown full length, is claimed to be a Raphael by F. Steinchen, *Raphaels seit 1508 verschollene, in St. Petersburg aufgefundene Madonna di Siena*, St. Petersburg, 1894.

Cross taken out of the Baptist's hands, the mood being more playful than intense: Pontormo shows him thus in the S. Michele Visdomini altarpiece, and there are variant examples in the work of Bugiardini and Piero di Cosimo.5 Bronzino's setting is a strange rocky defile, hard enough to detect in the original and liable to be invisible in photographs, with suggestions of cave-like formation in the right background – symbolizing the desert into which the Baptist had withdrawn. It is a return to Leonardesque mystery after the daylight of Raphael's settings of the subject. The Baptist's role is emphasized by his prominence at the front of the composition, and by the high-lit tapering hand of the Madonna that binds him into the group. The mood seems to have quickened in contrast to the adagio rhythms of Raphael. The Christ Child is posed in a dramatic attitude that could hardly be held even for a moment, but presumably genuflecting as he raises his eyes in dedication to the Cross. The theme of self-dedication is expressed by a further motif, obvious in itself but very unusual and perhaps invented by Bronzino. Here it is made part of the virtuoso balancing act the Child performs. With a hand bent back in tense grace he begins to lift from his head the garland of varied flowers. The symbolism of this *concetto* seems clear enough: the flowers must represent innocence, or perhaps childish pleasure; and perhaps there is also meant to be a tremor of awareness that the head that wore them will later wear a crown of thorns. A garland of joy is now exchanged for a cross – a cross which, though brought by the Baptist, is rightly appropriated by the Christ Child. Nevertheless, it is the Baptist who remains instrumental in the revelation of the Child's destiny to suffer and redeem: '*Tu, puer, Propheta Altissimi vocaberis*'.6 An additional symbol is held up by the Baptist, a handful of strawberries, which probably refer here to the fruitful, righteous life of Christ (or possibly to that of the Baptist himself). The strawberry usually appears in painting with this significance but perhaps it has some specific application to the present theme;7

a strawberry plant is very prominent growing beside the Infant Baptist in the *Alba Madonna*. The fourth figure in Bronzino's picture, an old female saint who grasps a staff and looks over the Virgin's shoulder, seems much more likely to be St. Elizabeth than St. Anne, given the role played by the Baptist and the legend of his mother hiding him in the wilderness.

It has often been suggested, but remains unproven, that the London picture is one of the two Madonna paintings, '*belli a maraviglia*', executed for Bartolomeo Panciatichi. The painting which definitely belonged to Panciatichi is the Uffizi *Holy Family* (Fig. 2) with the Panciatichi arms on a banner in the background. This too is more than just a simple devotional group. The setting is a similar rocky countryside, and again the Infant Baptist plays a prominent part, though the Christ Child now passively sleeps. A clue to the action is contained in the object that props the Child's pillow; this is not another pillow but St. Joseph's sack, here symbolizing probably not the flight into Egypt but the return from Egypt.8 St. John the Baptist greets the Holy Family on their return; the kiss he gives the Child combines homage with affection, a recognition made clear by his scroll placed so that the spectator can read the words AGNUS DEI. Bronzino's use of the motif of St. Joseph's sack, combined with the presence of the Baptist, is not unique. It occurs, for example, in Fra Bartolommeo's *Virgin adoring the Child, with S. Joseph* in the National Gallery (3914), where the Baptist appears as a small figure in the background. In his own picture Bronzino again emphasises the Baptist's role; S. Joseph remains an onlooker, and the Uffizi composition treats in effect the same theme as the London one, expressing an earlier moment in the relationship of the two holy children. First the Baptist recognizes the Child as the Saviour; then the Child recognizes his own destiny. Christ's passivity in one contrasts with his exaltation and action in the other. Any stylistic comparison between the two paintings is very difficult, because that in London is damaged and extensively repainted. However, a definite affinity exists in subject matter, and even in compositional arrangement. It may therefore be worthwhile considering again, for fresh reasons, whether the London picture could indeed be the second of the two painted for Panciatichi.

5. For reproductions of relevant work by these two artists, cf. S. J. Freedberg, *Painting of the High Renaissance in Rome and Florence*, II, Cambridge, Mass., 1961, ills. 271, 273, 295. A Sarto composition, with both Children holding the Cross, is dealt with by J. Shearman, *Andrea del Sarto*, I, Oxford, 1965, p. 91 (repr. pl. 99a), II, cat. no. 62.

6. *Luke*, I, 76; the text is included in the mass for St. John's Day.

7. The strawberry has an interesting history as a symbol. Its double significance is well brought out by L. J. Ross, 'The Meaning of Strawberries in Shakespeare', *Studies in the Renaissance*, VII, New York, 1960, pp. 225–240. In discussing its symbolic meaning as the fruit of righteousness, he cites the present painting by Bronzino (p. 236). Further general comments are in E. Haig, *Floral Symbolism of the Great Masters*, London, 1913, pp. 268–271; some useful indications are given by L. Behling, *Die Pflanze in der mittelalterlichen Tafelmalerei*, Weimar, 1957; there is a German legend connecting it with children's souls and even a mention of St. John's Day (Behling, *op. cit.*, p. 19, with further bibliographical references).

8. For some comment on this rare theme in art, cf. A. Masseron, *Saint Jean-Baptiste dans l'art*, Grenoble, 1957, p. 72; the subject derives from the *Meditationis Vitae Christi* (cf. the English edition of the very fully illustrated Paris MS., by I. Ragusa & R. B. Green, Princeton, 1961, p. 80), and was treated by Ghirlandaio (Masseron, *op. cit.*, fig. 65) and by Signorelli (Masseron, fig. 61) where the two united families are shown with both Children still very young. Although the subject is rare, it may occur unrecognized in several sixteenth-century pictures, e.g. Bugiardini's *Holy Family* in the Uffizi (Freedberg, *op. cit.*, ill. 590) and the Granacci *Holy Family* (Freedberg, ill. 601) in the collection of the Duke of Buccleuch.

In the *Venus and Cupid* (Fig. 3) where he deals with another mother and 'santo *figlio*' (his own words for Cupid in the already cited poem), Bronzino is equally concerned with expressing new aspects of a familiar theme.9 Here his *concetti* flower most beautifully, but unfortunately in a way that has misled modern commentators on the picture. Some of the personifications in it were correctly identified by Vasari,10 whose words have not been taken quite as seriously as they deserve. And the whole composition seems to argue an awareness in the spectator, as well as in the artist, of at least one Michelangelo composition.

To Bronzino Michelangelo stands as artistic grandfather, while Pontormo emotionally and artistically represents a father. This relationship is borne out in the *Venus and Cupid* which has, as it were, descended in that line to Bronzino, who makes the final and most elaborate statement of the subject. It was for a Florentine friend, the banker Bartolomeo Bettini, that around 1532–33 Michelangelo executed a cartoon of a nude *Venus Kissing Cupid*.11 With Michelangelo's agreement, this was to serve for a painting by Pontormo; Bettini intended to set up the painting in a room where it would be accompanied by portraits of the Tuscan lyric poets, to be painted by Bronzino. Thus the three artists were already brought into connection with the theme. Pontormo executed his painting but, to Michelangelo's annoyance, allowed it to pass to Duke Alessandro de' Medici; it is later recorded in the *guardaroba* of Cosimo I12 and would of course be familiar to Bronzino. Even though it is now difficult to know which surviving version of this design was executed by Pontormo himself, the composition itself is established (Fig. 5).13 And Vasari records the existence of the portraits of the poets by Bronzino: '*il ritratto di Dante, Petrarca, e Boccaccio, figure dal mezzo in su, bellissime*'.14

From all this it seems immediately clear that neither Bettini nor Michelangelo had intended to create an allegory of lechery or luxury. That the erotic power of Venus was more relevant we might guess from the appearance of the central composition alone. The trio of poets were probably present as witnesses to the power of beauty and the force of love. But there is also supporting evidence in a contemporary poem addressed to Michelangelo on this very cartoon; there Venus is apostrophized as the force which can bring Cupid to her lips:

> *di te piagato il core,*
> *Si sforza, quant' ei puo, baciarti Amore.*15

What Venus needs to do is to seduce Cupid, either to equip herself with his powers or – virtually the same thing – to take away his powers. Michelangelo depicts her slyly drawing an arrow from his quiver even while she kisses him. An engraving after Goltzius (Fig. 6)16 shows a similar sort of subject, and the lines underneath the composition make it quite explicit. When Venus conquers Cupid she has nothing else to fear; herself beauty, she has disarmed love. And it is in similar terms, as a triumph of Venus, that we may turn back to consider in detail Bronzino's painting. Perhaps the first thing to note is a flaw in the usual theory, learnedly proposed and discussed by Panofsky, that the painting is an allegory of the exposure of luxury: those who indulge in sensual love doing so at their peril, as revealed by Time and Truth.17 The profile at the upper left-hand corner (Fig. 4) is not, however, Truth; nor is it Night 'attempting to obstruct the process of "unveiling"'.18 This head can clearly be seen to be a mask, and symbolizes *la Fraude*, as Vasari said, noting that she appeared on the same side of the picture as *la Gelosia* who is indeed visible below, tearing her hair. Strictly speaking, it is a hollow mask attached to a neck; that it extends no further back is apparent in the original where leaves fill the space where the back of the head should be; the hair is only a tuft at the top of the mask, and, though the eye-sockets are modelled and shadowed, they definitely lack pupils. It is perhaps part of Bronzino's concept of *la Fraude* that, at first sight, this mask should *seem* convincing; only closer examination reveals the emptiness behind. It is further obvious that

9. The subject was treated by Bronzino himself in two other pictures, at Budapest and in the Galleria Colonna, Rome (Emiliani, *op. cit.* pls. 84 and 85). These variants of the theme relate respectively to the London composition and to the Michelangelo-Pontormo design to be discussed further in the text. It should be noted that in the Budapest picture Venus already holds one of Cupid's arrows; in the Rome picture she has teasingly taken his bow which she keeps out of his reach. At first the London composition seems to have shown Venus merely kissing Cupid and clasping his head (cf. Gould, *op. cit.*, p. 21 for the evidence of X-rays).

10. Vasari-Milanesi, VII, 598–599.

11. Cf. C. de Tolnay, *Michelangelo*, III, Princeton, New Jersey, 1948, pp. 194–196, for the lost cartoon and copies of it.

12. Recorded there in the inventory of 1553; cf. C. Conti, *La prima reggia di Cosimo I de' Medici*, Florence, 1893, p. 81.

13. This version, in the Accademia, Florence, exhibited in the *Mostra del Pontormo*, Florence, 1956, no. 66; some further discussion of Pontormo and Michelangelo in this connection is in J. Cox Rearick, *The Drawings of Pontormo*, I, Cambridge, Mass., 1964, p. 294 (no. 325), and *passim*.

14. Vasari-Milanesi, VII, 595.

15. The poem printed by K. Frey, *Die Dichtungen des Michelangiolo Buonarotti*, 1897, p. 271 (no. CLXXIX).

16. F. W. H. Hollstein, *Dutch and Flemish Etchings, Engravings and Woodcuts*, VIII, Amsterdam, n.d., J. Saenredam after Goltzius, no. 353.

17. For full discussion see E. Panofsky, *Studies in Iconology*, New York, 1962, ed., pp. 86 ff., including the suggestion that the design was conceived as a contrasting companion to the *Innocence* tapestry.

18. Panofsky, *ed. cit.*, p. vii, recording this addendum contributed by W. Friedlaender to his original identifications. It may further be supposed that Vasari would recognize a personification of Night which, it is true, might be shown with masks as a symbol. One of Vasari's own frescoes in the Palazzo Vecchio depicts Night with masks, a lamp and bats; he makes Prince Francesco de' Medici praise this depiction in the *Ragionamenti* (cf. Vasari-Milanesi, VIII, 24).

Time is quite unconcerned with either Venus or Cupid; it is at *la Fraude* that he glares, and whose drapery he attempts to tear off, to reveal her deceitful vacuity. To some extent, he is doing the same office as Venus: Time reveals Falsehood, and Beauty conquers Love. It was on the opposite side of the picture to *la Fraude* that Vasari identified *il Piacere*; and the girl in a green dress who holds a honeycomb in one hand, and the sting of her tail in the other, represents that double aspect of Pleasure. There is a moral here – not for us but for Cupid. Even while he enjoys the honeyed kiss offered so seductively by his mother, he is being robbed of his arrow (the picture is exact in its physiological symbolism too, it should be noted). The motif of honeycomb and sting to symbolize Cupid's own pleasure followed by pain goes back to an idyll by Theocritus (XIX), and it provided a popular Northern Renaissance subject for that Northern Bronzino, Cranach.[19] In such pictures Venus is markedly superior in her attitude, amused, didactic – and untouched. In Bronzino's composition, the rose-throwing putto who is *Giuoco* (Folly perhaps rather than Jest) aims at Cupid, and thus reinforces the presence beside him of *Pleasure*. These are, in Vasari's words, '*passioni d'amore*', quite literally, because they are the emotions that Cupid is going to feel when pleasure's sting, his own folly, even perhaps his mother's deceit, are all experienced by him; Time will show.

'Armed by winged Cupid, Venus has great powers . . .': the tag under the Goltzius composition is apposite also for the figure of Venus who is the central, triumphant, motif of Bronzino's picture. A dominant but fully reclining figure in Michelangelo's design, she is made even more dominant in the upright zigzag pose which Bronzino gives her. As a result, her figure fills a large portion of the picture area, and her pose recalls in several ways (including the upraised arm) the Virgin's pose in the *Doni Tondo*. A double homage is thus paid to Michelangelo: as inspirer of the theme and as inventor of the pose adapted for Venus. In one hand the goddess clasps what has been called merely 'an apple', although it is in fact the golden apple awarded her by Paris. In classical statues of her as *Venus Victrix* she usually holds this; here it seems a further hint of her triumphant appearance as queen of beauty (an aspect enhanced by her elaborate diadem). While she raises her face to Cupid's for the kiss, with lips parted and her tongue beguilingly visible, she holds up behind his head the symbol of her new triumph, the arrow drawn from his quiver. It is part of Bronzino's concept that here Cupid should not yet be aware that she has taken it. But the theme of Cupid disarmed by Venus is as old as antique gems and is found as late as Fragonard. Other sixteenth-century Italian treatments of it offer contrasts and comparison to

Bronzino. An unattributed engraving in Mannerist style (Fig. 7) is not so far from Bronzino's composition; Venus holds both bow and arrow, and Cupid endeavours to recover his bow. The subject was also treated by Cambiaso in rather similar style, showing Cupid trying to recover sometimes his bow, sometimes an arrow, held out of his reach by Venus.[20] Such treatments are obvious and explicit when compared to Bronzino's – but then they offer no difficulty in comprehension. He has achieved something more intricate and subtle: his Venus conquers Cupid by sweetness, not force. Nevertheless, she does conquer, and her doing so is the picture's subject.

Although what is proposed here is a new interpretation, it should be noted that doubts were long ago expressed about some of the identifications proposed by Panofsky – and indeed about his interpretation of the picture as an indictment of luxury. In reviewing the first edition of *Studies in Iconology*, Professor A. H. Gilbert, as well as doubting the identification of the upper left-hand figure as Truth, drew attention to the fact that a pillow is given the significance of flattery by Vincent of Beauvais. Cupid is shown by Bronzino kneeling on one, and the suggestion accords well with other indications that Cupid is being beguiled by his mother. In a note accompanying Gilbert's review, Professor H. W. Janson expressed his doubts also about 'Truth' and pertinently wrote: 'If . . . the picture really represents a moralistic indictment of Luxury in the spirit of the Counter-Reformation, it would appear strange that there is no hint of such a significance in Vasari's account of it.'[21]
A final point concerns the commissioning of the picture. Vasari says that it was sent into France to Francis I (died 1547),[22] though he does not imply that it was commissioned for that purpose. It might be tempting at first to wonder if the original commissioner was Bettini, since he had the room with the Bronzino 'portraits' and had lost the relevant Pontormo painting. It would, however, be remarkably bad luck if he lost this Bronzino as well. More conceivably, Cosimo I, the owner of the Pontormo-Michelangelo, might well have been instigated by such possession to have his painter execute an elaborate variation on it – perhaps originally with no specific destination in mind. The subject is not one to appeal very much within Cosimo's narrow, dynastically-obsessed circle. Without the prestige of having served for Michelangelo, it might have proved unacceptable. From Bronzino Cosimo usually commissioned portraits or religious pictures; and whoever owned this masterpiece seems to have been prepared speedily to part with it. For Francis I it was certainly an ideal gift.

19. Examples of Cranach's treatment of the theme, with moral overtones, are in M. J. Friedländer and J. Rosenberg, *Die Gemälde von Lucas Cranach*, Berlin, 1932, nos. 202, 203, 319, 320, 321; further on this point, cf. G. Bauch in *Repertorium für Kunstwissenschaft*, 1894, pp. 434–435.

20. For a typical treatment of the subject by Cambiaso, cf. B. Suida Manning and W. Suida, *Luca Cambiaso*, Milan, 1958, p. 153 and fig. 268.

21. Reviews by A. H. Gilbert and H. W. Janson in the *Art Bulletin*, XXII, 1940, pp. 172–175; Dr. J. Shearman kindly drew my attention to these references.

22. The date is given incorrectly by Emiliani, *op. cit.*, text for his pl. 84.

D

MICHAEL HIRST

Salviati's Two Apostles in the Oratorio of
S. Giovanni Decollato

WHEN members of the Arciconfraternità of S. Giovanni Decollato first began the project of decorating the walls of their Oratorio with fresco scenes of the Baptist's life, it is unlikely that they envisaged that the work would be as protracted as it was, in fact, to prove. The programme of mural painting began soon after the completion of the Oratorio's actual construction, in about 1536; it ended only in the early 1550's.

A substantial share of the responsibility for the delays which dogged the project was Francesco Salviati's. He left Rome soon after the completion of his first work in the Oratorio – the *Visitation* of 1538, the second scene of the cycle. He was not back in Rome until 1541, and left again in the autumn of 1543 without resuming activity for the Confraternity. He seems to have settled for the third time in Rome only in 1548; and it is a striking tribute to the patience of the members of the Confraternity that they reserved for their missing painter the third scene of the series, *The Nativity of the Baptist*, for the space of thirteen years, and in the meantime proceeded to commission other artists for subsequent episodes in the cycle.[1] Perhaps the fact that these episodes, painted in the Oratorio during Salviati's absences, did not equal what he had achieved in the *Visitation* helped confirm their decision to await his return. Salviati did not always encounter such patience on the part of frustrated patrons.[2]

His contribution to the decoration of the Oratorio in this later phase was three-fold: he painted the scene of the *Nativity of the Baptist* in the space left empty since 1538; he executed a remarkable *trompe-l'œil* window and adjacent strip of landscape to the right of the *Nativity*; and he added a frescoed *Apostle* on each side of Jacopino del Conte's *Deposition* on the altar-wall (Fig. 1). The *Nativity* is dated 1551 on the painted architrave forming the top frame of the fresco, and we might expect the flanking window and the two *Apostles* (Figs. 5-6) to be of the same phase of activity. With regard to the two saints, this expectation can be confirmed; for an unpublished payment made in August 1550 for the dismantling of the scaffolding erected for the execution of the *Apostles* exists in one of the Confraternity's surviving account books.[3]

Vasari's reference to the *Nativity* and to *SS. Bartholomew* and *Andrew* follows his account of Salviati's decoration of the Cappella del Pallio in the Cancelleria for Cardinal Alessandro Farnese.[4] He tells us that the *Apostles* were commissioned by Bartolommeo Bussotti. This man is more than just a name. We know that Bussotti, or Bussotto, was an eminent banker and merchant in Rome in the early 1550's, who helped finance projects of the family of Julius III and who had extensive dealings with Florence. Karl Frey even suggested that he may have been a relation of Vasari's; letters show that the two men were close friends for over twenty years.[5] Almost exactly two decades after

---

1. For Salviati's two narrative frescoes in the Oratorio, see A. Venturi, *Storia . . .*, IX, 6, figs. 83 and 104; also H. Voss in *Die Malerei der Spätrenaissance in Rom und Florenz*, Berlin, 1920, I, pp. 233–234 and 254–256, and the present writer in the *Burl M.*, June 1961, pp. 236–240.

2. The turbulent nature of Salviati's relations with those he served is illustrated with graphic vividness in the letter written to him by Annibale Caro in February 1544, remonstrating with the painter over his abrupt departure from Rome and Pier Luigi Farnese's service without leave. The latter, reports Caro, 'venne molto in colera contro di voi', and he begs the artist to return to Rome and to act with greater circumspection. Other, less direct evidence exists which suggests that Salviati could behave with equal recklessness towards Pier Luigi's son, Cardinal Alessandro (For Caro's letter, see *Lettere familiari di Annibal Caro*, ed. Aulo Greco, I, Florence, 1957, pp. 294–296.)

3. Archivio of the Arciconfraternità of S. Giovanni Decollato, Entrata e Uscita 1550–1556, c. 74 *verso*. The entry runs: 'E addi 26 detto (August) b. 5 p diffare el palcho del oratorio che aveva fatto f^co salviatj p dipignere li apostolj ———— b. 5'. There exists in the same account book a payment relating to the scene of the *Nativity of the Baptist* which suggests that most of this scene had also been painted in 1550 (c. 31 *verso*, 5th September 1550): 'A choncimi di nostra compagnia ▽ ventitre di m^ta paghatj alli bondini del bancho p resto di ▽ 33 – si paghono a f^co salviatj p resto della pittura del quadro della nativita di san giovannj batista———————▽ 23'. A third payment, with no precise context mentioned, was made to Salviati in May 1551 (c. 34): 'A ms. franc^o salviati pittore ▽ cinque'. (I owe a great debt to the kindness of Prince Sigismondo Chigi and to Marchese Italo Pucci who allowed me, in 1961, access to the Confraternity's archives.) The hitherto unpublished photographs of the two *Apostles* reproduced here show Salviati's figures after the restoration of the Oratorio frescoes, in 1954. It is a curious fact that, while Salviati's narrative frescoes in the Oratorio have been reproduced and discussed on a number of occasions, the two *Apostles* have scarcely ever received any comment – they are unmentioned even in Voss's excellent chapter on Salviati. So far as I know, Venturi's tiny reproduction of the *St. Andrew* is the only one ever to have been published (in *Storia . . .*, IX, 6, fig. 105).

4. Vasari-Milanese, VII, 31.

5. K. Frey, *Der literarische Nachlass Giorgio Vasaris*, I, Munich, 1923, p. 340.

Bussotti had provided the funds for the Oratorio *Apostles*, he ordered a painting of St. Bartholomew, his name-saint, from Vasari himself.[6] The choice of St. Bartholomew for one of the figures for the Oratorio altar-wall is, therefore, scarcely surprising, although his companion St. Andrew had better claims to representation in a building dedicated to the Baptist.[7]

It is likely that the areas on each side of Jacopino's altar-piece were the penultimate part of the Oratorio's wall-surface to be frescoed; once most of the other three walls had been completed, the need to provide also for those two vertical rectangular areas must have seemed insistent.[8] The decision to have the single frescoed figure of a saint each side of a panel altarpiece was in no sense an innovation; there are many Roman precedents for such an altar-wall arrangement. But there are few figures in this particular context which parallel those painted by Salviati. For him, the task of designing flanking figures of this kind was a new one and he brought to bear on the problems it raised the boldness of conception which characterizes so much of his work in this, his richest and most prolific period as a fresco painter. Perhaps most remarkable is the figure-scale he adopted, which eclipses completely not only that in Jaco-pino's altarpiece but also that of the figures in the neigh-bouring frescoes; as painted, both Apostles are over seven feet high.[9] The two are also, in a very real sense, a com-positional unity. Their movements are no more exactly complementary than are, for example, those of Donatello's paired figures in his reliefs on the doors in the Old Sacristy of S. Lorenzo, but neither is formally complete without the other. Both look inward, St. Bartholomew with a sharp turn of the body axis, St. Andrew in *contrapposto* almost Seicentesque in its sway and breadth. The massive forms, clearly conceived as a unit by the artist, are bound together, despite the intervening space, as are the figures who crowd on the farther sides of Christ and His Mother in Michel-angelo's *Last Judgement*.

Salviati painted the *Apostles* when he was forty-one years old and when his fresco style was undergoing a recogniz-able change of character. In the immediately preceding frescoes in the chapel of the Cancelleria, there is already evident a move away from the style of the middle 1540's, as exemplified in the works in the Sala dell'Udienza in Palazzo Vecchio in Florence. Surfaces of the Cancelleria forms are less brilliant than those in the Florentine frescoes, the treatment of paint seems heavier and denser (with a marked reduction in *al secco* additions), and the colour is deeper and more sombre. These characteristics are en-countered also in the Oratorio *Apostles* and the *Nativity* scene, where the colour anticipates that in the frescoes of the *Salone* of Palazzo Farnese.[10]

As if emphasizing the fact that they were painted at the turn of the half-century of the Cinquecento, different aspects of the two *Apostles* point towards the future and draw inspiration from the past. Moschini, in one of the very few references to either figure to have been published, noticed how the movement of the stooping, turning *St. Bartholomew* anticipates the ideals of movement of Tin-toretto, and, it might be added, of the mature rather than the early Tintoretto.[11] For *St. Andrew*, parallels in later sixteenth-century painting are more difficult to find; an image of such assertiveness was alien to the ideals of a majority of the succeeding generation of painters in Rome. The figure exemplifies as clearly as any which Salviati ever painted that alliance of plastic modelling and play of line which is one of the most striking features of his art. The unbroken curves of the saint's cloak show well how developed this sense of line was. But they are not gratui-tous. Utterly unlike Baroque drapery in its morphology, St. Andrew's cloak has this in common with it, that it is an indispensable part of the formal pattern and also contri-butes to the characterization of heroic vitality of its wearer. However remote such a prototype may seem at first glance, I think that the *St. Andrew* can also be regarded as a token of Salviati's admiration for Michelangelo's *Christ* in S. Maria sopra Minerva (Fig. 2). There is a good deal of evi-dence that artists in Rome in the 1540's found more to appreciate in the Minerva *Christ* than have many modern

6. K. Frey, *Der literarische Nachlass . . .*, II, Munich, 1930, p. 679.

7. St. Andrew was one of the two disciples of the Baptist who be-came disciples of Christ; see John, I, 35–42.

8. Most, though not all, of the narrative scenes have dates in the painted cartouches of the crowning entablature – there are blank cartouches above both *Apostle* figures. For a number of reasons it seems to me likely that the only part of the Oratorio decoration to have followed the painting of the two *Apostles* was the final narrative scene which adjoins *St. Andrew* and which is dated 1553. The frescoed architectural framework of the areas where Salviati painted his two figures was, I believe, already executed before he began work there; under good light one can see the lines of the pre-existing corner pier beneath the overlapping end of St. Andrew's protruding cross. I do not believe this framework is the work of Salviati; rather, I suspect it may be by Jacopino del Conte who painted the panel altarpiece.

9. Or about 2·20 metres.

10. I cannot concur with a recent suggestion that two of the three narrative frescoes of the Cancelleria chapel date from the early 1540's, with its implication that the work there was carried out by Salviati in two distinct stages and with a further implication that Vasari's statement about the commission is wrong. The decoration of the Cancelleria chapel – rarely discussed because scarcely ever accessible – does raise some problems but these are not, it seems to me, primarily chronological ones. (For the suggestion of a break in Salviati's activity there, see Iris H. Cheney, in the *Art Bulletin*, 1963, p. 341, note 30.)

11. See V. Moschini, *S. Giovanni Decollato*, Rome, 1926, p. 45. Compare *St. Bartholomew* with, for example, the figure twice repeated in Tintoretto's drawing, Uffizi no. 12999[F], made for the latter's picture of *Christ washing the Apostles' Feet*, in S. Stefano, Venice; reproduced in D. von Hadeln, *Zeichnungen des Giacomo Tintoretto*, Berlin, 1922, pl. 15, or in G. Delogu, *Tintoretto*, Milan, 1953, pl. 13.

critics. It is well known that Michelangelo's figure was planned for a tabernacle, but it is rarely emphasized that, because of this, the *Christ* was planned essentially as a frontal figure alone. Perhaps Cinquecento artists were more sensitive to Michelangelo's intentions, even when they emended his ideal; it is a fact that copies after the *Christ*, and variations derived from it, seem almost universally faithful to the figure's frontal view. Salviati had included a reference to the *Christ* in a work just prior to the Oratorio *Apostles*, the fresco of the *Beheading of the Baptist* in the chapel in the Cancelleria, in the figure of the young soldier who holds – in place of Michelangelo's cross – a banner (Fig. 3). There, the proportions are still fairly faithful to the prototype.[12] But in a drawing after the Minerva *Christ* by another artist, traditionally identified as Daniele da Volterra, the form has undergone changes which help to prepare us for the metamorphosis of Salviati's *St. Andrew* (Fig. 4). The proportions of the figure on this sheet, which is in the Uffizi, have been significantly broadened – compare even the head in the copy with that of the model; the form in the drawing could be called a *critique* of the earlier work in the light of the ideals of the *Last Judgement*.[13]

Michelangelo's *Christ*, as set up, flanks the high altar of S. Maria sopra Minerva, and Salviati's *St. Andrew* is similarly placed in relation to the altar of the Oratorio of S. Giovanni Decollato: the appropriateness of the inspiration of the former is obvious. But the echo of the Minerva figure is not *St. Andrew*'s only claim to affiliation with sculpture, even if, for its three-dimensional realization, a block of quite extraordinary width would be required for figure and cross. The areas each side of Jacopino's altarpiece may be compared to those of giant niches or rather, given the pre-existing painted framework of the Oratorio wall, to tabernacles trabeated like the one which originally housed Jacopo Sansovino's *St. James* in S. Giacomo degli Spagnuoli. St. Andrew's right foot rests on a kind of pedestal block just as St. Bartholomew's rests on a pile of one of his attributes – the books, Both figures emerge from the painted wall plane, St. Andrew's cross breaking the frescoed corner pier with a violence of foreshortening very different from the gentle inclination of the cross of the Minerva *Christ*. Behind both figures Salviati painted a pale pinkish-grey open sky, in colour similar to that in the fresco of the *Visitation*. But many of both figures' contours are heavily shadowed, so that, whilst the relationship of white marble before a dark bay is reversed, the tonal contrast and with it the plastic intensity of the forms is preserved.

Salviati's figures do not aspire to the appearance of marble, as do some of those in the later frescoes and panel paintings of Daniele da Volterra; still less did he abandon painting for sculpture, as did the latter. His genius was essentially pictorial – we need surely look no further than the treatment of the play of light over *St. Andrew* to recognize this fact. But the study of sculpture demonstrably began early in his life and he does not seem to have abandoned it as he grew older.[14] Salviati made no contribution to Varchi's symposium on the rival merits of painting and sculpture, published just one year before he painted the Oratorio *Apostles*. It is at least possible that he regarded such a debate as futile. Nevertheless, his *St. Andrew* could be regarded as an implicit restatement of a view which had been so recently disavowed in Varchi's little book, that sculpture could serve as 'la lanterna della pittura'.

12. Salviati, although changing the role of the hands, retained the particularly emphatic stress on the right hand's extended index finger, a detail we find elsewhere in the Cancelleria frescoes and which is echoed in the right hand of *St. Andrew* in the Oratorio. For a rather similar employment of the Minerva *Christ*'s design for a young Roman soldier by Parmigianino earlier, see Antonio da Trento's chiaroscuro print of the *Martyrdom of SS. Peter and Paul*, Bartsch, XII, p. 79, no. 28 (repr. in M. Pittaluga, *L'incisione italiana nel cinquecento*, Milan, 1928, fig. 179, or in G. Copertini, *Il Parmigianino*, Parma, 1932, II, pl. CXXX).

13. The drawing is Uffizi, Santarelli 215, red chalk over traces of black chalk, measuring 32·3 by 19·8 cm. It seems to have been first published, as by Daniele, by G. Briganti without any comment in his *Il manierismo e Pellegrino Tibaldi*, Rome, 1948, pl. 74. The drawing's attribution is problematic. Its style is not comparable to that of the more familiar kind of Daniele sheet, with dense and highly finished modelling. If by Daniele, it must be a drawing done by him just after he had arrived in Rome, and his early chalk drawing style is still very much a matter for speculation.

14. Some of his earliest surviving drawings record this study of sculpture; see, for example, J. Wilde, *Italian Drawings in the Department of Prints and Drawings in the British Museum: Michelangelo and his Studio*, London, 1953, no. 100, *recto* and *verso*. For another, later example, *ibid.*, no. 101, and also the present writer in *Zeitschrift für Kunstgeschichte*, 1963, p. 156. Salviati's appreciation of sculpture is only one of many aspects of his work and outlook which deserve discussion, but it is an important one, with great relevance to the development of his own conception of form.

GEORG KAUFFMANN

Das Forum von Florenz

ALS 1560 der Baubeginn der Uffizien bevorstand, gab es eine Kontroverse.[1] Sie entzündete sich am Gebälk des neuen Gebäudes. Vasari, dem der Auftrag übergeben worden war, hatte es sich gerade durchlaufend gedacht, während Ammanati es gern durch Bogen unterbrochen hätte: "mia viddi el modello suo, schizai questa come piu ragione darchitetura".[2] Die Kritik erhob sich also aus Gründen der architektonischen Vernunft.

Ammanatis Alternativvorschlag entwickelt ein ganzes Wandfeld. Sein aufsteigender Bogen übergreift das Mezzanin, rührt an das Hauptgeschoss und zielt über das gestreckte Fenster in die Mittelsenkrechte, das Ganze einem kompositorischen Zug und zugleich einer formalen Syntax unterwerfend, die – dorisch unten, jonisch oben – ihre Logik aus Vitruvs Superposition bezieht. Vasari konzentriert sich dagegen nur auf das Dorische. Er studiert vornehmlich Säulen und Gebälk, die eigentlichen Träger des dorischen Charakters. Zwar hält sich alles darüber Aufgehende auch durchaus im dorischen Klima, aber es bleibt doch der unten so ausgeprägten Ordnung gegenüber, z.B. auch durch das Fehlen von Kapitellen, sehr viel indifferenter, sozusagen geschlechtslos. Der Unterschied liegt in zwei völlig entgegengesetzten Auffassungen von "Ordnung". Bei Vasari ist speziell die "Säulenordnung" gemeint, Vitruvs "genus". Ammanati dagegen hat das Zusammenwirken des dorischen und jonischen Ornamentmusters im Auge und damit die Stimmigkeit im Ganzen, von der Vitruv als "ordinatio" spricht. Sie leitet sich noch aus der "klassischen" Baupraxis her, die sie als Produkt jener "architektonischen Vernunft" entwickelt hatte, von der Ammanati spricht.

Vasaris Plan ist un-klassisch. Peruzzis römischer Palazzo Massimo, Vignolas Villa Giulia, Michelangelos Laurenzianavorhalle verschieben gleichfalls das Gewicht von der "ordinatio" auf das "genus" der dorischen Ordnung. Besonders eng sind die Verbindungen zum Palazzo Massimo. Nicht nur der vielzitierten, durch das Gewölbe brechenden Mezzaninfenster im Hof, sondern auch der überschlanken Proportionen von Säulen und Gebälk an der Fassade wegen. In ihrer Streckung von mehr als 8 unteren Durchmessern sind die Säulen des Palazzo Massimo wie der Uffizien erst durch Palladio kanonisch geworden. Nach Wurm leitete sich das Geschlecht der Massimo mythischerweise von Herkules her – darum das Dorische. In Florenz wurde diese Ordnung von Cosimo I gewünscht; vielleicht in Parallele zu Serlio, der zuerst die bestimmten Gottheiten gewidmeten Ordnungen aufs Profane orientiert und die Dorica dem Herrscher zugewiesen hat.

Gegenüber Ammanati bleibt Vasaris Lösung aber auch die "theoretischere". Forderte Serlio die Dorica für den Herrscher, so wünscht Alberti das gerade Gebälk für hervorragende Personen. Vasari war dies gut bekannt. Spricht nämlich Alberti über das Problem des Brechens von geradem Gebälk bei weiter Säulenstellung, so greift Vasari diese Frage im Kapitel über die Architektur im Vorspann der "Viten" auf und erläutert dann den eigenen Lösungsvorschlag an seinem Uffiziengebälk, bei dem er tragende Strukturen eingezogen hatte, wie Lando Bartolis – im Einzelnen allerdings nicht ganz korrektes – Schnittbild zeigen kann.[3] Damit gewinnen wir eine charakteristische Reihe: wir sehen die Idee des Gebälks sich zusammen mit der Idee eines Baus für den Herrscher entwickeln, sehen dann die technische Realisierung im Schatten eines alberti'schen Problems, und finden schliesslich das Endergebnis in Vasaris Kapitel "Dell'Architectura" wieder in den Bereich des Theorems zurückgeführt. Ein reflektives Verfahren.

Es wird zu berücksichtigen sein. Denn es gebietet Vorsicht, sobald man dieser Kunst von der ästhetisch-formalen Seite her beizukommen sucht. Wer die Uffizien mit ihrem geraden Gebälk, das den Blick wie an einer Schiene dem zentrierenden Fluchtpunkt in der Tiefe zueilen lässt, mit Worten wie "Unstabilität" oder "fliehender Raum" stilistisch greifen zu können glaubt, sagt wohl nichts Falsches.

1. Die gebotene Begrenzung erlaubt an dieser Stelle keine Dokumentation. Da mit gehörigen Anmerkungen der Umfang das gesetzte Mass überschritten hätte, wird der Text – etwas gekürzt – so geboten, wie er am 2.8.1966 auf der Eröffnungssitzung des Zehnten Deutschen Kunsthistorikertages in Münster vorgetragen worden ist. – Besondere Anregung verdanke ich A. Blunt, *Artistic Theory in Italy, 1450–1600*, Oxford, 1940 (II. ed. 1956).

2. So vermerkt Ammanati auf seinem Entwurf. E. Vodoz, in *Mitteilungen des Kunsthistorischen Institutes in Florenz*, VI, 1941, s. 67.

3. L. Bartoli, *Galleria degli Uffizi, Firenze*; *Introduzione all'Architettura*, Firenze, 1946, fig. 1. – Schon früher hat man versucht, die von Vasari geschilderte Gebälkkonstruktion der Uffizien zu rekonstruieren: B. Brown, *Vasari on Technique*, London, 1907, s. 71. – 1959 wurde die Konstruktion anlässlich einer Restaurierung kurz freigelegt. Dabei zeigte sich, dass Bartolis Rekonstruktion insofern zu berichtigen ist, als die hinteren gedrängten Backsteinlagen nicht waagerecht, sondern im Bogen geführt sind. Leider war keine photographische Aufnahme zu erhalten. Das Verfahren selbst könnte vom Baptisterium angeregt sein, wo hinter dem Innengebälk verhehlte Stützbogen liegen. Brunelleschi arbeitet in der Pazzikapelle ähnlich; vgl. P. Sanpaolesi, *Brunelleschi*, Milano, 1962, Textabb. F.

Aber er sagt auch nichts Wesentliches. Denn dieses charakteristische Gebälk z.B. lehrt, dass der Schwerpunkt der Planung ganz woanders gelegen hat.

★

Die Uffizien wurden im Zuge einer sehr viel weiter ausgreifenden Umgestaltung des ganzen Signorienbezirks errichtet. Schrittweise hatte der seit 1537 regierende Herzog Cosimo I die Gewalt über Toscana an sich gebracht. Es galt, den Titel des Herzogs zu bewahren und den des Grossherzogs zu erringen. Vorausschauend wurde die Ehe zwischen dem Erbprinzen Francesco mit Johanna von Österreich, einer Schwester Maximilians II, angestrebt. 1565 feierte man die glanzvolle Hochzeit. Die meisten Veränderungen im Signorienbezirk stehen mit ihr in direktem oder indirektem Zusammenhang.

Der herrscherliche Gesichtspunkt ist also ein ganz zentraler. Nun braucht aber ein Herrscher einen Herrschersitz. Als alte Bürgerstadt konnte Florenz auf diesen Anspruch nicht vorbereitet sein. Und so entstand etwas Neues. Es bot keine Analogie zu oberitalienischen Tyrannensitzen, stand vielmehr der Antike nahe. Anlässlich des Uffiziengebälks spricht Vasari vom "vero modo che usarono gli antichi". Allerdings ist hier ein ideales Altertum gemeint. Sollte Florenz z.B. nunmehr ein "Forum" erhalten, so nicht etwa das römische Forum, sondern jenen Mittelpunkt, der seit Vitruv zu einem gedachten Zentrum städtebaulicher Spekulation geworden war.

Die einzelnen Bemerkungen, kleinere wie grössere, fügen sich zwanglos. Unter dem Portikus der Uffizien stehen Sitzbänke. Keine der florentiner Loggien oder Vorhallen seit dem Trecento hatte sie. Vitruv fordert Bänke am Forum, in der Palästra.[4] – Ein Grundrissentwurf zeigt einen langgestreckten Block, der einen Hof umschliesst, Abb. 1. Aussen wie innen ist er von Kolonnaden umzogen. Nachdem Stegmann und Geymüller zunächst an Vasari gedacht hatten, gibt man den Plan heute dem Neffen Giorgio.[5] Das Blatt liegt im florentiner Kabinett zusammen mit anderen, die allesamt für die Uffizien bestimmt waren und auch dieses trägt die zeitgenössische Beischrift "Questa pianta fu fatta per fare i Magistrati di Firenze"; – so wurden die Uffizien damals genannt. Wenn dieser Plan aber zu den Uffizienentwürfen gehört, kann er kaum etwas anderes als einen Gedanken des älteren Vasari reproduzieren. Dass er so nicht zustande kam, lässt sich verstehen; denn wo wäre ohne robusten Eingriff in die Substanz im Umkreis des Palazzo Vecchio Raum für das wirksame In-Erscheinung-Treten dieses ja auch mit der Aussenansicht

rechnenden Baublocks zu schaffen gewesen![6] Der Idee haftet etwas utopisch-filaretehaftes an. Deshalb braucht sie nicht aus der Luft gegriffen zu sein. Sehen wir sie einmal mit einer Illustration aus Caporalis Vitruvausgabe von 1533 zusammen, Abb. 2. Dort zeigt man einen Bau, der als "forum" bezeichnet wird (genauer gesagt handelt es sich wohl um die Basilika am Forum), und zwar sowohl nach Art der Griechen als quadratischen wie auch "al costume de Latini" als gestreckten Baublock, aussen wie innen von Kolonnaden umzogen und mit einem Einbau in der Mitte, analog der von Vasari an entsprechender Stelle konzipierten kleinen Rundkirche.

Im Endeffekt begnügte man sich mit der schon 1546 neben der Loggia dei Lanzi zum Arno hin durchgebrochenen Gasse, die rechts wie links mit einem Mantelbau verkleidet wurde. So findet sich der heutige Beschauer mit dem Bau nicht von aussen konfrontiert, sondern quasi nach innen versetzt, als stehe er im Hof der rechtwinklig vom Hauptplatz abgehenden Basilika, nicht unähnlich der Disposition des pompejanischen Forums. Dass dabei die Mitte zwischen dem Portikus wie eine seichte Wanne um einige Stufen vertieft ist, entspricht erneut Vitruv, der eine Säulenhalle gelegentlich in der Mitte um 2 Stufen versenkt wissen will.

Damit ist die Grundvorstellung umrissen. Schon der Gedanke, die 13 "magistrati", die Zünfte, auf einem öffentlichen Platz zu vereinen, entspricht ihr. Denn die Träger der öffentlichen Geschäfte gehörten in der Antike aufs Forum. Andererseits vertreibt die "forensis dignitas" – ein Ausdruck des Aristoteles – die Krämer. Axel Boethius hat bemerkt, die Ansiedlung von Goldschmieden und Juwelieren anstelle der Metzger auf dem Ponte Vecchio hinge mit der Aktivierung des Gedankens einer Forums-Imunität zusammen.[7] – Unter Cosimo I nahm die Antike wieder zunehmend den Charakter eines Musters an. Der Herzog wünschte sich und die Seinen auf einer Art Kaiserkameo abgebildet und wenn Montaigne 1581 berichtet, die Medici kühlten ihren Wein nach Weise der Alten mit Schnee, so ist das nicht ein Zug gespreizter Art, sondern berechnete Handlungsweise. Sicher gab es dabei auch modische Spielerei. Wenn man aber findet, dass das Operntheater in den Uffizien untergebracht wird und Vitruv im Forum ein Theater verlangt, möchte man sich angesichts der Grundvorstellung doch fragen, wo anders

4. Vitruv v, 11, 2. – Alberti wiederholt die Forderung nach Sitzgelegenheit an öffentlichen Orten v, 8.

5. Uffizi 4881ᴬ. Zuletzt: *Mostra documentaria e iconografica della fabbrica degli Uffizi*, ASF, Firenze, 1958, Nr. 49. – Als Giorgio Vasari d. Ä. publiziert von Stegmann-Geymüller, *Toscanawerk*, x, fig. 1.

6. Siehe K. Frey, *Der literarische Nachlass Giorgio Vasaris*, München, 1923, s. 537. Die dort erwähnte Quelle, derzufolge der Abriss von 300 Häusern für den Bau der Uffizien nötig sei, wird von U. Dorini (*Rivista Storica degli Archivi Toscani*, XI, 1933) als Settimannis Memorie Fiorentine präzisiert. Am 10.3.1560 wundert sich der Duca über die grosse Zahl abzureissender Häuser und vermutet "se già voi (Vasari) non haveste pensato di fare altra strada o altra fantasia" (Frey a.a.O., s. 538). Könnte sich das auf Uffizi 4881ᴬ beziehen?

7. A. Boethius, *The Golden House of Nero*, Ann Arbor, 1960, s. 70.

sonst in Florenz ein angemessener Platz für das Theater zu finden gewesen wäre.

★

Herz und Mittelpunkt der neuen Gestaltung war der Palazzo Vecchio. Sein Umbau zog sich in zahlreichen Einzelaktionen über Jahre hin, so dass ich nur einiges herausgreifen kann.

Die alte Treppe verlief im Hof gradlinig an der Fassadeninnenseite. Vasari errichtete jenseits des Hofes in vielen Mühen, eingreifend in einen zweiten, den "Dogana"-Hof, eine neue, doppelläufige Treppenanlage. Damit wurde der erste Hof, Kern des alten Palastes, zum Vorhof degradiert, zum Atrium, oder – genauer (da Vasari auch den Porphyrbrunnen mit Verocchios Putto installieren liess) – zum "cavum". Das ist Vitruvs Ausdruck für einen solchen Vorhof mit Brunnen. Dann erst folgte die neue Treppe und der zweite Hof. Auf diese Weise wurde der alten Stadtfestung ein neuer Haustyp oktroyiert, die "Casa degli antichi Romani", wie Vitruv sie nennt, Palladio sie in Barbaros Ausgabe illustriert und in eigenen Entwürfen variiert hat, z.B. beim Palazzo Porto Festa. Mit ziemlich geringen Korrekturen verlieh Vasari mit seiner neuen Treppe dem wuchtigen Palast den auch stilistisch neuen Zug zur Tiefe und zugleich eine ikonographisch fassbare Grundrissdisposition antiker Herkunft, aber modernen Zuschnitts. Eine Leistung von berninihafter Geschicklichkeit.

Im Einzelnen erschöpft seine Stilgebung sich nicht im Geist der Antikenrezeption, sondern weiss auf intuitive Art eine florentinisch-venezianisch-römische Cinquecentoatmosphäre in den Komplex von Architektur, Malerei und Plastik aufzunehmen und ihn damit zu durchdringen; was zu erkennen gibt, wie sehr Vasari in einer überlokalen, gesamtitalienischen Sphäre beheimatet ist. So tragen seine Arbeiten auch an keiner Stelle einen archäologischen Zug. Auf dem Wege zur Antike spielt die Architekturtheorie eine wichtige Rolle. Der Architekt holt seine Kenntnisse über das Altertum aus Vitruv und Alberti. Dabei wirkt die Theorie nicht nur vermittelnd, sondern auch filternd. Das bewirkt zweifellos eine Entfärbung vom Historischen, ermöglicht diesem Teil des vasarischen Schaffens freilich auch Momente, wo nur noch die Architekturtheorie und die Antike garnicht mehr spricht.

1562 war die Decke des Salone dei Cinquecento um mehr als 7 m auf eine Höhe von 18 m angehoben worden. Eine technisch sehr komplizierte Korrektur. Michelangelo hatte sie befürwortet und wir haben den Grund wahrscheinlich in einem neuen Sinn für Proportionen zu suchen, der freilich durch Theorie provoziert worden sein kann. Nach Vitruvs numerischer Raumproportion war Alberti der erste, der das Prinzip der Harmonie einführte, was Palladios Traktat übernommen hat. – Der Riesensaal leidet unter einem verzogenen Grundriss. Deshalb hatte sich

schon Baccio d'Agnolo an der nördlichen Schmalwand mit einer Verschleierungsarchitektur plagen müssen, die handwerklich Vasaris Beifall fand, sachlich aber seine Kritik herausforderte, besser hätte man – seiner Meinung nach – durch einen rechten Winkel begradigen und das sich abspaltende spitzwinklige Dreieck wie einen Rest beiseite lassen sollen. In seiner Deckeneinteilung ist Vasari dann auch so verfahren und man kann konstatieren, dass auf gleiche Weise Serlio schiefwinklige Grundrisse systematisiert haben will.

Zur Hochzeit von 1565 malte Vasari den zum "cavum" gewordenen Vorhof mit Städtebildern und Grotesken aus und versah Michelozzos Säulen mit prächtigen Stuckmänteln. Vitruv hat die Grotesken nicht geschätzt. Der Charakter ist hier also weniger vitruvianisch als humanistisch. Städtebilder gab es schon im Vatican. Landschaften mit Grotesken kombiniert kommen vorher im Odeon Cornaro zu Padua vor.[8] Merkwürdig "nordisch" die Idee der Stuckgrotesken an den Säulen. Sehe ich recht, liegen die Vorlagen dieses vielfach bewegten Motivbestandes aus der Bacchus- und Venussphäre weniger in der florentiner Feltrini-Überlieferung als in den vitalen Druckblättern des Agostino Veneziano. Vasari hat sich gern an Druckgraphik orientiert. Die aufgesetzten Stäbe am Säulenschuh, ein nicht minder merkwürdiges Motiv, können Vredeman de Vries abgeschaut sein, dessen entsprechende Blätter seit 1563 bekannt gewesen sind. Damit kommen wir erneut der Architekturtheorie nahe.

★

Der ganze Prozess der Modernisierung des Palazzo Vecchio liegt im Zeitgeist. Serlio macht Idealvorschläge für stilistische Auffrischung gotischer Gebäude. Auch beim Ausbau des Palazzo Pitti handelt es sich um Aktualisierung eines älteren Baues, diesmal des Quattrocento.

Die Oberleitung war Ammanati übertragen. Seine Tätigkeit gehört in den Zusammenhang von Vasaris Arbeiten am "Forum". Seit 1565 sind Palazzo Vecchio und Pitti über den Arno hinweg durch einen Gang verbunden. Als man 1550 den alten Bau des Luca Pitti erwarb, sollte der Herzogin zu einer luftigen Bleibe verholfen werden. Zum ersten Male bekam Florenz ein "Schloss" für die Gemahlin des regierenden Herrn. "Das Anwesen der Fürstin" – so lesen wir bei Alberti – "wird auf besonders würdiger Stelle erbaut werden. Getrennt vom Hause des Gemahls."[9] Wichtig ist der Begriff der "Fürstin", denn er deutet seinerseits auf das herrscherliche Ziel, dem alle damals projektierten Unternehmungen in dieser oder jener Weise zu dienen hatten.

Insofern war Ammanatis Ausgangslage derjenigen Vasaris nicht unähnlich, als auch er einen schon vorhandenen Bau berücksichtigen musste. Allerdings führte seine Bindung

8. E. Forssman, *Palladios Lehrgebäude*, Stockholm, 1965, s. 74. Den Gedanken Forssmans verdanke ich vielfältige Anregungen.
9. Alberti v, 2.

an die "ragione d'architettura" zu Spannungen zwischen
einem traditionellen Bauverhalten und der neuartigen Disposition im Ganzen. Sein Stil ist konservativer. Die Ordnungen in ihrer Verbindung mit Rustika folgen einer
mindestens 20 Jahre alten venezianisch-veronesischen Tradition, die Idee des "vertieften Hofes" nach Art der Villa
Giulia oder der Villa Imperiale nördlich Pesaro ist noch
älter. Die Gesamtanlage gehört dagegen in einen aktuel-
leren Prozess.

Ammanatis Grundriss des Hofbaus geht mit palladian-
ischen Entwürfen zusammen. Man braucht nur anstelle der
Hofgrotte einen ovalen Saal zu setzen. – Im zweiten Arbeits-
gang wurden in der Querachse Flügel zugefügt. Auch
dafür hat Palladio Beispiele. Allerdings beschrieb schon
Alberti einen solchen Flügelbau als Villa, nur wurde
dergleichen zu seiner Zeit nicht gebaut. James Ackerman
hat erläutert, wie die von Alberti oder Francesco di Giorgio
entworfenen Idealvillen erst im 16. Jahrhundert hatten
realisiert werden können, nachdem die mittelalterlichen,
sich bis zur Hochrenaissance behauptenden Typen aus-
gestorben waren.[10] Nun begann also der Villenbau in aller
Breite, sei es in Rom, in den Marken, im Veneto oder in
Florenz. Vasari war es bei seiner Umgestaltung des Arreals
um den Palazzo Vecchio um Realisierung eines ursprünglich ideal gedachten städtischen Mittelpunktes gegangen.
Beim Pitti handelt es sich ganz ähnlich um einen länd-
lichen Aufenthalt, der sich aus einem nicht minder idealen
Bezirk der Frührenaissance entwickelte. Und so kommt
denn auch bei Ammanati die Architekturtheorie ins Spiel.
Jeder Besucher der imponierenden Anlage spürt das
"Städtische", vor allem in dem grossen "römischen" Hof.
Hager spricht von der "abgeschlossenen Kastenform", die
der Bau mit der Villa Imperiale bei Pesaro teilt, als sei
man noch gehemmt gewesen, sich der Natur auf schlichte
Weise hinzugeben. Womöglich hat auch Vitruv bremsend
gewirkt, der ja die Villa weitgehend vernachlässigt und nur
als deplaciertes Stadthaus gelten lässt. Erst Palladio hat die
Fesseln abgestreift und zum genuinen Landhaus hinge-
funden. Offenbar gelang dies aus der glücklichen Stunde
venezianisch-veronesischer Bautradition heraus. Welche
Rolle die Theorie dabei spielt, ist kürzlich von Forssman
erläutert worden. Es war eine gewisse Gleichzeitigkeit von
Bauen und Denken, wunderbar sich ergänzend in Palladio.
Ammanati war kein Denker, andererseits Serlio kein
grosser Realisateur. Ammanati und Serlio aber stehen
zueinander in etwa dem Verhältnis wie Bau und Gedanke
in dem einzigen Palladio.

Um nochmals auf die Rustika über den Ordnungen zu
kommen: Serlio hat sie als erster theoretisch legitimiert.
Ihm sind viele weitere Einzelformen verpflichtet, das
Mittelfenster der Hoffassade ist Schulbeispiel der "Ser-

liana". Auch die Vorliebe der Pittianlage für Grotten geht
mit Serlio zusammen.

An der "grotta grande" des Boboligartens ist beinahe 40
Jahre lang, von 1556 bis 1592 gearbeitet worden. Innen
entfaltet sich ein kurioses Material von Tropfstein, Muscheln und Kieseln, aus dem sich in felsiger Landschaft nach
der Sintflut ein neues Menschengeschlecht erhebt. Michel-
angelos Sklaven winden sich in den Ecken aus Schlamm
und Stein einem neuen Leben entgegen. Die Thematik ist
kürzlich von Heikamp klargelegt worden.[11] Der Deutung
des Ganzen als Parodie der klassischen Architektur vermag
ich freilich nicht zu folgen. Dergleichen passte besser in die
40-er Jahre, in die Nachfolge des Giulio Romano, der in
seinen Grotten ein Kräftemessen zwischen geregelter Kunst-
welt und destruktivem Wucher veranstaltet hat. Höchstens
die Fassade, mit der die Arbeit begann, hat noch etwas
davon. Auch wird man den Innenraum schwerlich mit
Heikamp mit einem neuen Drang zu den Geheimnissen
der Natur in Verbindung bringen können. Dazu ist die
Attitüde zu bizarr. Warum nicht nun auch für dieses
Kunststück Serlio befragen?

In Serlios Traktat entspricht das illustrierende Bild nicht
immer dem erklärenden Text. Das trifft z.B. zu für die
"satirische Szene". Das Bild zeigt den bekannten Hänsel-
und-Gretel-Wald. Der zugehörige Text ist aber nicht nur
ausführlicher, sofern er auch von Personen berichtet, er
schildert überhaupt ein ganz anderes Milieu. Dies Milieu
aber ist das der Boboligrotte. Zwischen Bäumen, Felsen,
Hügeln, Gebirgen, Blumen und Brunnen – so heisst es im
Text – leben freizügig durch keine Konvention Verbildete,
"che licentiosamente vivono", so etwa wie de Rossis
Liebesgruppe in der zweiten Kammer. Habe man nun für
diese Szene kein echtes Gras, keine wirklichen Blumen, so
nehme man doch künstliches Material, imitiere durch
Malerei (wie dies in der Grotte Pocetti getan hat). Je teurer,
desto besser, die Besteller hätten Geld und wollten unter-
halten sein. Serlio selbst habe dergleichen schon einmal
gesehen, gemacht von Girolamo Genga, "ad instantia del
suo Padrone Francesco Maria Duca di Urbino", ausgeführt in Meergestein, Muscheln, Schneckenhäusern, Korallen, Perlmutter und Krebsschalen. Dies Material kommt
auch in der Grotte vor, nebst den von Serlio geforderten
Sirenen, Nymphen, seltsamen Tieren – wir sehen Panther,
Luchs, Bär, Affe, Papagei etc. Und als 1592 als letztes Aus-
stattungsstück schliesslich Giovanni Bolognas Brunnen
errichtet wurde, da war auch Venus in die Szene getreten,
jene Göttin, die am ehesten die Herren des Ortes, eben die
Satyrn in dieser "satirischen Szene" hervorzulocken weiss.
Das Entscheidende der "satirischen Szene" ist ihr artifi-
zieller Charakter. Serlio lobt an ihr das Künstliche als das
Natürliche. So wird die "grotta grande" zur dauerhaften
Theaterdekoration, wie auch Vasaris Hochzeitsdekoration
des "cavum" im Palazzo Vecchio oder der aus gleichem

10. J. Ackerman, "Sources of the Renaissance Villa", *XXth International Congress of the History of Art*, New York, 1961, II,
s. 6–18.

11. *Antichità viva*, Nr. 4, 1965.

Anlass errichtete "Biancone" Bandinellis bis zu unseren Tagen hin überdauert haben.

Insofern auch Buontalenti an dieser Grotte beteiligt war, der genialste "Maschinenmeister" des Jahrhunderts, finden wir ihn hier also zum ersten Male an einer "Bühne" beschäftigt. Genga wurde von Serlio erwähnt. Er war der Architekt jener Villa Imperiale bei Pesaro, die – mit Craig Smyth[12] – als das dem Pitti am nächsten kommende Beispiel zu nennen wäre und um 1530 für jenen Francesco Maria della Rovere errichtet wurde, für den – nach Serlio – Genga auch die "satirische Szene" gemacht hatte. Die Beziehungen liegen damit klar vor unseren Augen. Vasari, der die Villa Imperiale bereits 1550 in seinen Viten erwähnt, war mit Genga gut bekannt, dieser hatte in den späten 30-er Jahren, zur Bauzeit der Villa Imperiale, seinen Sohn Bartolomeo zu Vasari und Ammanati nach Florenz geschickt.

So leitet sich also diese Grotte nicht etwa direkt aus Rom her, sondern aus den Marken und Buontalenti führt sich als Gengaschüler ein. Serlio, der Theoretiker, steht mit im Bunde, sofern er das Geschaffene alsbald rationalisiert.

Wirkt hier die Theorie als Bestandteil einer ungeteilten künstlerischen Welt, so hat Ammanati in späteren Jahren den theoretischen Anteil isoliert. Die Idealstadtentwürfe, die ich mir am besten unter Vasaris Einfluss um 1565 entstanden denken kann, sind kühle Produkte eines Rechners. Der Umschlag zur Intellektualität düfte sich parallel der spekulativen Arbeit an Vasaris "Forums"-Konzeption – um diese Bezeichnung für das Gesamtunternehmen beizubehalten – vollzogen haben und so war ich dem Zufall dankbar, der mir im Florentiner Staatsarchiv eine Rechnung in die Hand spielte, in der Ammanati seinem Buchhändler ein Paket theoretischer Literatur quittiert: "Bartolomeo Ammanati de dare di 18 dicembre 35 sono per una Architetura di Leone Battista Alberti, di Piero Cataneo, Sebastiano Serlio e Cosimo Bartoli".[13] Eine so umfangreiche Akquisition auf einen Schlag ist nur als entschiedene Hinwendung zur Gedanklichkeit zu verstehen. Sie wurde in der Tat zum erwarteten Zeitpunkt vollzogen, denn die Rechnung ist datiert. Wir lesen auf ihrem Kopf das Jahr 1564.

★

Verfolgen wir auf solche Weise den Weg von Kunst zu Theorie, darf andererseits nicht jener Weg übersehen werden, der von der historischen Theorie zur Kunst führt und zur Vervollständigung des Bildes beiträgt.

Vasaris Arbeiten in und um den Palazzo Vecchio stehen vor dem Hintergrund der Tatsache, dass die Stadt im Altertum ein antikes Forum nicht besessen hat. Zwar

suchte man nach, fand aber nur das schon von Bruni als "Parlagio" bezeichnete Amphitheater in Richtung auf Sta. Croce. Im 16. Jahrhundert entdeckte man weitere Fundamente, auch Statuen, die Vincenzo Borghini zu einer Rekonstruktion ermunterten, welche bis ins 18. Jahrhundert Grundlage aller Angaben über den antiken Bau bleiben sollte. Borghini aber war einer der engsten Freunde Vasaris.

Unter Cosimo I nahmen derartige Forschungen eine bestimmte Richtung. Die ältere Überlieferung sah in Florenz eine antike Gründung, war jedoch der Überzeugung, die Stadt sei unter Attila zerstört und erst von Karl dem Grossen neu begründet worden. Das jetzige Florenz wäre demnach karolingischen Ursprungs. Im Zusammenhang seiner herrscherlichen Ansprüche wäre es dem Herzog lieber gewesen, er hätte eine antike Stadt regieren können, und so erhielt Borghini den Auftrag, der Frage nachzugehen.

In einem Manuskriptband Borghinis, dessen Kenntnis ich der Freundlichkeit Nicolai Rubinsteins verdanke und aus dem der "Parlagio" Grundriss stammt, finden wir die Untersuchungen zur karolingischen Toscana, darin eine Übertragung der Schriften Einhards ins Italienische, sowie auch Karls des Grossen Horoskop.[14] Schliesslich fand Borghini heraus, es sei, wie der Herzog hoffte, Karl habe die Stadt nur erweitert, diese selbst sei römischen Ursprungs, gegründet von den Triumvirn Antonius, Lepidus und Octavius, dem späteren Augustus. Cosimo konnte sich nunmehr als Nachfahre eines Kaisers fühlen. Sogleich ergriff er die sich bietenden Möglichkeiten. Nicht nur übernahm er des Augustus Sternbild, den Capricorn, sondern setzte auch den Widder in die Reihe seiner Zeichen, denn unter diesem Sternbild sollte Florenz am 25. März gegründet worden sein. Deshalb beginnt auch das Florentiner Jahr mit diesem Datum und da durch himmlische Fügung an einem 25. März der Erbprinz Francesco geboren wurde, bestand kein Zweifel, die Dynastie entwickelte sich unter günstigem Stern.

★

Vitruv und Alberti dienten Vasari als Mittler des Wissens über die Antike.[15] Der wissenschaftliche Bestandteil war also von vornherein künstlerisch gefärbt. Ebensowenig verfuhr Borghini als "reiner" Historiker. In seinen Papieren finden sich von Malern kopierte Inschriften, von Francesco Morandini, gen. "Il Poppi", liess er sich Teile des Baptisteriums zeichnen, Wappen deuten, die ältesten Dokumente von Sta. Croce kopieren.

12. C. H. Smyth, "The Sunken Courts of the Villa Giulia and the Villa Imperiale", in *Essays in Memory of Karl Lehmann*, New York, 1964, s. 304–13.

13. ASF, *Conventi Gesuiti* F 1037, fz 241.

14. BNF, *Carte Strozziane*, xxv, 551. – Da Herr Rubinstein demnächst eine Publikation über dieses Manuskript plant, versage ich mir weiteres Eingehen auf die kunsthistorische Bedeutung desselben.

15. Der Vasari wahrscheinlich am nächsten kommende Theoretiker ist Cataneo. Bei ihm findet sich expressis verbis die Gleichsetzung von "piazza" mit "forum".

Eine dieser Zeichnungen studiert das Liegen zu Tische, Abb. 3. Bedenkt man das Datum, wohl um 1565, so stehen wir vor einem der frühesten, wenn nicht überhaupt dem frühest bekannten Beispiel dieser Version des Gastmahls seit der Antike.[16] – Eine andere Zeichnung bringt den florentiner Dom nach Andrea da Firenzes Fresko in der Spanischen Kapelle. – Eine weitere zeigt das florentiner Stadtbild des Mittelalters. Wer würde in diesen Arbeiten Zeichnungen des späteren Cinquecento vermuten, aus der Zeit der Uffizien? Entzückend die Bleistiftskizze eines knieenden Stifterkindes, Abb. 4. Welch liebevolles Auge für den Stil des Trecento! Diese Studien sind mehr als Bestandsaufnahmen. Sie verraten eine Interessiertheit, die über ihren Gegenstand hinausweist. Ihr "Historismus" entspricht dem Verhältnis zur Geschichte, auf dem Vasaris Viten ebenso aufbauen wie seine berühmte Sammlung alter Graphik; Ordnung von Fakten der Vergangenheit nicht auf dem Wege einer rein literarischen Konstruktion, sondern auf der Basis eines unmittelbar einfühlsamen, intuitiv sich des Stiles bemächtigenden Kunstverständnisses. Vasari steht also nicht allein. Seine historische Leistung reflektiert bei Borghini und den für diesen tätigen Künstlern und empfängt auch ihrerseits von dort ihr Licht.

★

Mit umso grösserem Recht dürfen wir nun von einer Kunst der Vasarizeit sprechen. Sie wird im allgemeinen als eine "manieristische" Phase bezeichnet. Wollten wir ihren "Stil" näher beschreiben, hätten wir nach unseren bisherigen Beobachtungen in erster Linie festzuhalten, dass sie sich vorwiegend an Modellen orientiert, weniger an "Natur", oder an "Wirklichkeit", sodass wir von einer Verhaltensweise zu sprechen haben, die mit dem Wort "concettismo" umschrieben wird.
Nicht nur die schöpferische Leistung, der ganze kulturelle Hintergrund ist damals vom "concettismo" geprägt gewesen. So ergab sich der flüchtige Augenblick einer einmalig homogenen Verhaltensweise zwischen Künstler und Auftraggeber. Es besteht ja kein grundsätzlicher Unterschied zwischen Cosimo I, der sich als Augustus fühlt, und Vasari als dem Baumeister eines "Forum". 1564 dankte Cosimo in einem merkwürdigen Augenblick ab, um die Herrschaft dem Sohn Francesco zu übertragen. Formal kann man hier eine Art von Weltflucht nach dem tragischen Tode der Gattin in Jahre 1562 sehen. Der tiefer in die Zusammenhänge dringende Blick sieht in Wahrheit das analogische Verhalten zum Rücktritt Karls V, der 1556 in gleicher Weise zu Lebzeiten dem Tronerben die Zügel des Staates übergeben hatte. – Die Leichenfeier für Michelangelo wurde – wie kürzlich Wittkower betonte – analog der Leichenfeier für Karl V in Brüssel ausgerichtet. Erst wenn man das verstanden hat, vermag man den unge-

heuren Rang zu ermessen, den Michelangelo am Ende im Bewusstsein der Florentiner erklommen hatte.[17] – Nehmen wir ein ganz anderes Beispiel. Der erwähnte Verbindungsgang zwischen Palazzo Vecchio und Palazzo Pitti ist ganz offensichtlich formal nur ein reines Zweckgebilde, ohne künstlerische Dimension. Aber gerade der Zweck bleibt im Dunkeln. Es scheint keine einleuchtende Definition dieses Zwecks zu geben. Die Version, Cosimo habe seinen statthaltenden Sohn durch diesen Gang "überwachen" wollen, ist viel zu vordergründig. Kunstgeschichtlich sehen wir uns in ganz andere Richtung verwiesen. Ein solcher Gang kommt in Pfalzen vor, im Süden wie im Norden, in Palermo wie in Aachen, um von einander abgelegene zusammengehörende Baulichkeiten kommunizieren zu lassen. Er weist gleichfalls in die "herrscherliche" Sphäre. Wir finden also im Alltag wie in Politik wieder, was uns als Merkmal künstlerischen Verhaltens entgegengetreten war. Wollen wir dieses Merkmal abschliessend charakterisieren, könnten wir zunächst – mit Wölfflin – von einer "innerlich weiterarbeitenden Formengeschichte" sprechen. Allerdings werden mit den "concetti" Formen einbezogen, die nur Denkwert, keinen Kunstwert besitzen. Dass sie zu Bestandteilen des internen künstlerischen Prozesses werden, verdanken sie dem mimetischen Rückgriff eines Gestaltungswillens, der das "concetto" in den Planungsvorgang einführt, um es dann zum Bestandteil einer kohärenten Struktur zu machen. Diese Struktur ist die Metapher. Die Kunst der Vasarizeit ist ihrem Wesen nach metaphorisch.[18] Aus diesem ihrem Charakter lassen sich nun ihre wichtigen Züge, die Züge also des sogenannten florentiner Manierismus ableiten. Hugo Friedrich hat vor einigen Jahren dem metaphorischen Stil eindringliche Worte gewidmet. Metaphern besorgen eine Verähnlichung zwischen Entferntem. Sie schaffen in einem Bilde Verwandtschaften zwischen einem Einzigartigen und einem anderen Einzigartigen. Verbindet man den Hof des Palazzo Vecchio mit dem concetto des vitruvischen "cavum", werden die Massen der Wirklichkeit verrückt, was wiederum eine direkte Ursache zu sein scheint des Fiktiven aller Äusserungen, des Anschauungsfeindlichen, des Un-klassischen bei Vasari, des Un-naiven, alles dessen also, was wir an diesem Stil gelegentlich beklagen und gründlich als un-künstlerisch missverstehen. Oder eine andere Konsequenz: seiner Metaphorik nach ist dieser Stil auf Vorbilder angewiesen. Nun besteht aber ein Unterschied zwischen der rückgreifenden Bezugnahme auf ein Vorbild, weil es als Modellfall schlechthin unentbehrlich ist, – und dem Rückgriff auf ein Vorbild, weil in ihm eine andere Kunstleistung anklingen soll. Eine

16. Vgl. A. Blunt, "The Triclinium in Religious Art", *JWCI*, II, 1938–39, ss. 271–276.

17. E. Borsook, "Art and Politics at the Medici Court – 1: The Funeral of Cosimo I de' Medici", *Mitteilungen des Kunsthistorischen Institutes in Florenz*, XII, 1965, s. 34.

18. Anregungen für das Folgende verdanke ich H. Friedrich, *Epochen der italienischen Lyrik*, Frankfurt a. Main, 1964, ss. 636 ff.

Untersuchung dieses metaphorischen Stiles würde wahrscheinlich ein Vorwiegen des Letzteren nachweisen können, sodass wir alsdann generell den Umgang nicht bloss mit *antikem Gedankengut*, sondern mit *Kunstwerken der Vergangenheit*, sei es, wie es in Vasaris Viten geschieht, sei es in Borghinis Studienblättern, als zum Stilbild gehörig und in dieser speziellen Art von Metaphorik wurzelnd verstehen müssen. – Und schliesslich: "Concettismo ist keine Technik, sondern eine Optik" (Friedrich). Stets drängt er zur formulierten Aussage. Schon sein Vorhandensein hebt die Kunst über das bloss Wirkliche ihrer Gegenstände in die Verstehbarkeit.

Es leuchtet ein, wie sehr gerade der Charakter des Intelligiblen die damals sich bildenden Ansätze der Kunstgeschichte befördern musste. Andererseits aber weitete der wachsende kunstgeschichtliche Überblick den Radius des Feldes, aus dem *concetti* gewonnen werden konnten. Wir werden deshalb mit Gewissheit in der Zukunft sehr weitreichende Verbindungen zu knüpfen haben. Vom bloss italienischen Kunstkreis her – und dies bezeichnet vielleicht eine gewisse Schwäche neuerer Vasariarbeiten – ist diesem Künstler kaum beizukommen. Die Rolle der Fontainebleaustecher wäre zu prüfen. Oder blicken wir auf Vasaris letztes Werk, das Studiolo für Francesco I im Palazzo Vecchio. Als *zweigeschossiger* Bau (er hat ja noch einen zugehörigen Oberstock über sich!) gehört dieser sicher kostbarste Innenraum der Medici in die Traditionslinie doppelgeschossiger Palastkapellen. Das kleine Interieur lädt zum Meditieren und zu "höheren" Gedanken ein. Von der Komposition her aus dem sakralen Bereich der Delmonte-Gräber gespeist, huldigt die Dekoration einem naturhaften Pantheismus. Die Ausstattung operiert wie bei einem gotischen Innenraum mit Statuen. Die Kombination von Architektur und Metallarbeit, in der westlichen Welt alt und konstant, ist allgemeines und immer wiederkehrendes Merkmal des "Hofstils". Auch, dass man das Obergeschoss als "Tesoro" bezeichnet ist erheblich, wird doch im Mittelalter der *Schatz* vielfach mit der Hofkapelle verbunden. Bei der Ste-Chapelle in Paris befand er sich nördlich der Apsis. Die Glasfenster dieses französischen Beispiels wecken übrigens die Assoziation zu der lückenlosen Ausstattung des Studiolo mit Gemälden, diese sind natürlich nicht transparent, aber wozu auch in einem Raum, der nur mit künstlicher Innenbeleuchtung rechnet, als feiere man in ihm den Ritus einer humanistischen Religion. Es würde jetzt zuweit führen, die Belege einer sakralen Tönung weltlicher Kunstgebilde dieser Zeit zu mehren; aber gewiss sind die Stuckgrotesken an den Säulen im Hof des Palazzo Vecchio mit ihrer waagerechten Teilung, den Putten, und dem Weinlaub *auch* mit den frühchristlichen Säulen aus Alt-St. Peter zusammen zu sehen. Uns fällt dabei wieder die Rundkirche im Hof des utopischen Vasari-Grundrisses für die Uffizien ein. Buontalentis Tribuna für die mediceischen Kunstwerke bietet ein weiteres Beispiel, wird dieses

Gehäuse für weltliche Schätze doch wie eine frühchristliche Kirche mit Perlmuttranken und einer Kuppel wie im Baptisterium sowie einem "Altarraum" versehen, der eigene seitliche Beleuchtung besitzt und in dem Michelangelos Madonnenbild über Hainhofers Kunstschrank wie über einem Altaraufbau Platz gefunden hatte.

Die Vasari unmittelbar voraufgehende Periode zeigte etwas Eigentümliches. Die florentiner Frührenaissance entfaltete einen neuen magischen Glanz und wurde für kurze Zeit wieder attraktiv. Bandinellis Petrus der Domtribuna ist eine Nachbildung von Donatellos Petrus an Or San Michele.[19] Cellinis Liegefiguren am Sockel des Salzfasses für Franz I in ihren gerundeten Buchten und den einzelnen Köpfen dazwischen nehmen Ghibertis Liegefiguren nebst seinen Einzelköpfen von der Paradiesestüre auf. Als habe die Stadt, der eine eigene Hochrenaissance versagt geblieben ist, nicht von der Faszination ihrer lokalen Frühstufe loskommen können.

Nur vor diesem Hintergrund wird man den Umschwung begreifen. Der Blick weitet sich über Florenz hinaus auf ganz Europa, die Leistung wird nicht mehr nur im Formalen, sondern auch in der treffenden Fassung des Inhaltlichen gesehen. Versetzt man Vasari in die weite Landschaft der europäischen Kunst, wird er zu einer stilprägenden Kraft des Jahrhunderts, zu einer Gründungsfigur des Barock. In einer ersten Version für die Schmalwand des Studiolo für Francesco I hatte er das Lünettenbild mit den Jahreszeiten entworfen. Die endgültige Ausführung weicht von dieser Fassung ab. Inmitten das Bildnis des nunmehr verstorbenen Cosimo I, umgeben vom Kreis des Zodiakus, rechts wie links Putten mit Flügeln, Abb 5. Thematisch hat sich nichts verändert, es ist bei den Jahreszeiten geblieben. Nur wurde das Thema jetzt nach einer antiken Prägung formuliert, nach dem damals in Rom, heute in Dumbarton Oaks befindlichen Jahreszeitensarkophag, Abb. 6.[20] Ihm verdankt Vasari auch die Idee, das Bildnis der Gemahlin Eleonora von Toledo mit einzubeziehen, es befindet sich in entsprechender Dekoration an der Lünette gegenüber. Abgesehen von dem neuerlichen Beispiel "all'antica", abgesehen auch von dem neuerlichen Beispiel einer sakralen Anspielung im profanen Raum lehrt die Verwerfung der eigenen Erfindung, wie sehr der "concettismo" die Überlieferung respektierte, das den Kern der Metapher ausmachende Bild lieber dem Schatz überkommener Gestaltungen als der eigenen Willkür anvertrauen wollte.

Vasari – um dies schliesslich noch hervorzuheben – wird mit recht einer der Väter der Kunstgeschichte genannt. Nur ist er mehr als bloss der Begründer einer "Stil"-Kunstgeschichte. Nach allem Gesagten dürfte klar sein, dass er gleichzeitig ein Wegbereiter ikonographischen Denkens gewesen ist.

19. Diese Beziehung zuerst gesehen von H. Kauffmann, *Donatello*, Berlin, 1935, s. 198, Anm. 31.
20. Diese Beziehung ist von M. Rinehart, *Burl M.*, 1964, s. 74, übersehen.

JUERGEN SCHULZ

Pordenone's Cupolas

It has been observed several times since the 1920's that Pordenone's painted cupolas in Treviso and Cortemaggiore are remarkably early examples of an almost baroque illusionism. Painted figures and architecture seemingly replace the entire dome, and cross-relations are established with representations elsewhere in the same room, in a manner that breaches the limits of the self-contained work of art.[1] What is true of these two fresco cycles, however, is true of all his dome decorations that survive. Pordenone's œuvre of painted cupolas is remarkable in its entirety.

The decoration of the later 1520's at Cortemaggiore can serve as the type. Since it is impossible to photograph the cycle as a whole in its restricted site,[2] and the town of Cortemaggiore is hard to reach, a description may not be out of place.

The frescoes decorate a chapel in the south-east corner of the Franciscan monastery church of the SS. Annunziata, opening off a space in the south aisle that at one time served as the mausoleum of the Pallavicino family (the founders and rulers of Cortemaggiore and the builders of the church). Presumably also the chapel was their foundation, for the Pallavicino arms appear on each side of the entrance.[3]

The only plastic forms in the octagonal room are the altar, directly opposite the entrance, and a stucco cornice. A deep window recess is located in the centre bay on the right. All other architectural forms are imaginary. They serve as the framework for a complex cycle of representations on the theme of the Immaculate Conception. On the bottom of the walls is a painted marble sockle. Above it, on the level of the altar is a fictive shelf supporting four imaginary niches. In each niche stands the figure of an authority for the doctrine of the Immaculate Conception, exhibiting a passage from his writings on a scroll. They are (left to right); Origen,[4] Solomon, St. Cyril of Jerusalem and St. Cyprian of Carthage. Between the last two figures lies the altar, the altarpiece of which was let into the wall and enclosed by a painted frame (Fig. 2).[5] It shows the four Fathers of the Church grouped around the Immaculata, and two cherubs bringing down to earth the soul of Christ.[6] The bay to the right of St. Cyprian contains the window, framed by another painted niche. The last bay, between window and entrance, contains a representation of *St. Jerome in the Wilderness*, enclosed in a rectangular painted frame. Set in an ample landscape, it looks like a scene glimpsed through a window.[7]

Atop of the painted niches lies the real stucco cornice.

1. The point was first made by K. Schwarzweller in a University of Göttingen dissertation of 1935, *Giovanni Antonio da Pordenone*, n. p. or d., pp. 50, 84 (cited as Schwarzweller throughout these notes). It has been made a number of times independently since then: by the present writer in a Courtauld Institute thesis of 1958 (*Venetian Ceiling Painting of the 16th Century*), J. Shearman, in 'The Chigi Chapel in S. Maria del Popolo', *JWCI*, XXIV, 1961, p. 145, and W. Timofiewitsch, in Reclams Kunstführer, *Italien*, II, *Oberitalien Ost*, Stuttgart, 1965, p. 494.
2. Individual portions of the scheme are illus. by G. Fiocco, *G. A. Pordenone*, Padua, ²1943, pls. 141–145 (cited as Fiocco, *Pordenone*, throughout these notes), and Venturi, *Storia*, IX, 3, figs. 483–487.
3. Schwarzweller, Cat. no. 6. The fullest accounts of the church and chapel to date are resp., L. Dodi, *L'architettura quattrocentesca nella Val d'Arda* (*Biblioteca storica piacentina*, XVIII), Piacenza, 1934, pp. 84 f., and A. Pettorelli, 'La Capp. dei Pallavicino a Cortemaggiore', *Bollettino storico piacentino*, XVII, 1922, pp. 74 f.
   There is little external evidence for dating the frescoes. Cortemaggiore was ruled in Pordenone's time by Gian Lodovico II Pallavicino (1509–27) and Gerolamo Pallavicino (1527–57). The former was active during the foreign wars on the French side, and was on missions or imprisoned during most of 1521–27. Cf. P. Litta, *Celebri famiglie italiane*, Milan, 1819–83, IV, fasc. xli, tav. 22; F. Guicciardini, *Storia d'Italia*, Bk. xv, ch. xiv, ed. C. Panigada, Bari, 1929, IV, p. 256, and E. Seletti, *La città di Busseto, capitale dello stato Pallavicino*, Milan, 1883, II, p. 324. The latter is unknown before the 1540's. Cf. Litta, *loc. cit.*
   On the grounds of style one would put the frescoes in the later

1520's. Venturi, *vol. cit.*, p. 713, has suggested a date in the mid-1530's, but this has not found acceptance.
4. Pettorelli, *op. cit.*, p. 78, calls the figure 'S. Giovanni', but it is labelled Origen on its scroll.
5. The original was appropriated by the Farnese and is now in Naples; Schwarzweller, Cat. no. 14. The copy that replaced it was moved in 1759 to a position in front of the wall and put in a frame that is far too large for the site. At the same time an enlarged altar was made that destroyed a portion of the neighboring, painted niches. (The date of these works is given by Flaminio di Parma, *Memorie istoriche . . . dell'osservante provincia di Bologna*, I, Parma, 1760–61, p. 243.)
6. Only St. Jerome is recognizably characterized, but the four saints are probably the Latin Fathers, who were a common element in Immaculist imagery since the fifteenth century; cf. M. Levi d'Ancona, *The Iconography of the Immaculate Conception*, n. p. (*Monographs on Archaeology and Fine Arts*, VII), 1957, p. 11. For the motive of the Christ Child, which is drawn from Annunciation scenes, see D. M. Robb, 'The Iconography of the Annunciation', *Art Bulletin*, XVIII, 1936, pp. 523 f.
7. The departure from the scheme of the rest of the chapel may be partly explained by the fact that this wall can only be seen with one's back to the room. But it remains puzzling, as does the fact that St. Jerome, counting the fresco and the altarpiece, appears twice. Perhaps the fresco was painted before the larger decoration had been decided upon, and was spared when the latter came to be made.

Above it, in the bottom of the vault, is a series of painted lunettes containing foreshortened busts of prophets and sibyls, seen against open sky. Painted corbels rise between the lunettes and support a second, false cornice that frames an imaginary opening in the vault. God the Father and a host of cherubs enter through it and rush toward the altar (Fig. 1). Not only do all these representations bear on the one subject of the Immaculate Conception, but they are also closely concerted to reinforce each other. The authorities in the niches look either toward the spectator entering the chapel (Sts. Cyprian and Cyril), toward God (Solomon), or toward the altarpiece (Origen). One of the sibyls fixes her eyes upon the spectator while pointing toward God. A prophet stares at the spectator while pointing toward the altar; the other prophets and sibyls look either at the altar or the dome. The group of cherubs in the altarpiece who bear the soul of Christ come from a point directly beneath the outstretched hand of God. It is He Who is the author of the Incarnation and of its vehicle. The dome and altarpiece are the focal points around which everything else in the decoration revolves.

The scheme is striking on two counts. The opening of the entire vault to a group of heavenly figures, seen as if from below, is a considerable step beyond any illusions practiced in fifteenth- and earlier sixteenth-century vault painting. And the close interrelation of all the elements of the fresco cycle is greater than any degree of such integration seen before. In developing the vault composition Pordenone seems to have drawn on the sum total of Italian experience in dome painting up to that time. Illusionism had been an ingredient of it since Mantegna's Camera degli Sposi at Mantua and Melozzo's Cappella del Tesoro at Loreto and Cappella Feo at Forlì.[8] But these decorations and those derived from them incorporated the painted figures in a painted architectural setting that replaced the forms of the real architecture. Suppression of almost all architecture, real or painted, could be seen on the other hand in certain vault decorations in the Romagna by followers of Melozzo.[9] It is common

also since the earliest times in half-dome representations.[10] Both of these latter classes of decoration, however, lacked the illusionistic consistency that marked the former group of works. Some forms are foreshortened while others are not, and a dramatic unity between the representations' and the spectator's space fails to come into being.[11] Pordenone's dome fuses these two currents.

Mantegna is also the ultimate source, as J. Shearman has pointed out, for the association across space and in one action of different zones of a chapel decoration.[12] The former's fresco of The Assumption in the Eremitani at Padua shows the Virgin looking and rising toward a figure of God that was painted by another artist, in the vault directly above.[13] Raphael gave the motive its High Renaissance formulation when he designed the Chigi Chapel in S. Maria del Popolo in c. 1515. He planned an Assumption for the altarpiece, and for the apex of the dome he designed a figure of God the Father that would have linked with the altarpiece not only ideally but also visually, in that it was illusionistically foreshortened[14].

The stimuli which led Pordenone to develop his own scheme must have been obtained on his trip to Central Italy in 1518–19.[15] He had made only sparing and conventional use of illusionistic motives before this time. But the

8. For what follows, cf. Shearman, op. cit., pp. 138 f. The book by S. Sanström, Levels of Unreality, Uppsala (Figura, N.S. IV), 1963, adds nothing to the subject.
Mantegna's frescoes are illus. by E. Tietze Conrat, Mantegna, London, 1955, pl. 78; there too a detail of the dome of his burial chapel, pl. 152, and references for his decoration in the chapel of Pope Innocent VIII in the Villa Belvedere, p. 23. The latter no longer survives, but was reflected in the Mantegnesque dome decoration of S. Francesco at Mantua, now itself destroyed but illus. in E. Marani and C. Perino, Mantova: Le arti, II, Dall'inizio del sec. XV alla metà del XVI, Mantua, Istituto C. d'Arco, 1961, II, pl. 95. Melozzo's domes are illus. by R. Buscaroli, Melozzo da Forlì, Rome, 1938, pp. 84, 104. His cupola at Loreto was imitated in Verona by Gianmaria Falconetto; illus. G. Fiocco, 'Le architetture di G. M. Falconetto', Dedalo, XI, 1930/31, p.1204.
9. They were the domes of the Sepolcreto degli Sforza, in S. Francesco, Cotignola, and of the third chapel on the right in S. Biagio, Forlì, both destroyed in World War II. The first was

attributed to Francesco and Bernardino Zaganelli, the second to Marco Palmezzano. Cf. R. Buscaroli, 'Opere inedite di influsso melozziano . . .', Melozzo da Forlì, no. VI, January 1939, pp. 286 f., illus., and C. Grigioni, Marco Palmezzano, Faenza, 1956, pp. 599 f.
10. It is true already of Early Christian apse mosaics. In the fifteenth century in Italy, The Assumption or Coronation of the Virgin was commonly represented in half domes, without any suggestion of supporting architecture, but only a strip of ground of some kind at cornice level; cf. the Coronation by Filippo Lippi and his studio in the Cathedral of Spoleto (M. Pittaluga, Filippo Lippi, Florence, 1949, pl. 181).
11. Melozzo may have been an exception in this case. His fresco of the Ascension of Christ, formerly in the half dome of SS. Apostoli at Rome and removed in 1711, appears from surviving fragments to have been at least an attempt to show a half-dome scene in consistent perspective. Illus. Buscaroli, Melozzi da Forlì, Rome, 1938, pp. 62 f.
12. For what follows, see Shearman, op. cit., p. 145.
13. The vault frescoes were destroyed in World War II. Illus., G. Fiocco, L'arte di A. Mantegna (Saggi e studi di storia dell'arte, I), Venice, 1959, pls. 105, 133.
14. Illus., Raffael: Des Meisters Gemälde, Stuttgart/Berlin (Klassiker der Kunst, I), 5th ed., 1923, p. 152.
15. W. Arslan (in Thieme-Becker, XXVII, p. 270) and Fiocco (Pordenone, p. 38) would place the artist's visit to Central Italy in the year 1516, together with his fresco in Alviano (near Orvieto), the only concrete evidence for such a trip. Schwarzweller gives cogent reasons (pp. 43 f.) for preferring a date of 1518–19 for both the visit and the painting. Fiocco's suggestion (p. 44) that the artist made a second trip at the latter time is a needless complication. In fact, Pordenone painted nothing before the Trevisan frescoes that demanded a first-hand knowledge of the Sistine Ceiling or Raphael's ultima maniera, and Schwarzweller's thesis is to be preferred.

dome he painted directly after his return, in the Malchio-stro Chapel of the Cathedral of Treviso,[16] was boldly conceived as an imaginary extension of the chapel's real space. The dome is now destroyed, but the real vault was entirely painted away. In its place one saw a fictive balustrade, open sky, and God the Father amidst a crowd of cherubs. Representations of Fathers of the Church survive in the pendentives. The figures lean out of their circular niches to gaze at the beholder or the dome. One stares at the spectator and points into the dome. The apparition in the dome was shown moving toward Titian's altarpiece of *The Annunciation* and supplied the figure of God the Father that was lacking in the painting itself.[17] While the cherubs in Pordenone's dome were inspired by the *putti* in Titian's *Assunta* at Venice, his figure of God was an amalgam of the different forms under which Michelangelo had painted Him in the Sistine Ceiling. And the illusionistic conceit was similar to that planned by Raphael in the Chigi Chapel.

The development seems to have been entirely independent of Correggio, whose cupola in the church of S. Giovanni Evangelista at Parma similarly showed nothing but foreshortened figures and open sky, and incorporated figural motives inspired by the Sistine Ceiling. Correggio's fresco was begun only in the summer of 1520 by which time Pordenone's dome must have been finished.[18]

Pordenone re-used the figure group and the illusionistic metaphor of the Trevisan dome in one form or another at Cortemaggiore, Venice and Piacenza. In the case of the church of S. Rocco at Venice, the frescoes he painted in the tribune during 1528–29 have been replaced.[19] But their subjects and arrangement followed the same pattern. In the dome Pordenone painted God the Father amidst angels. Directly beneath, in the half dome of the apse, he represented *The Transfiguration*. Although the iconography was novel (the presence of God at the Transfiguration was normally indicated by a ray of light or an inscription), the group in the dome must have been meant to link with the scene in the apse.

The Piacenzan decorations consist of three mural cycles in the church of S. Maria di Campagna. The latter is a greek-cross church with a central, octagonal dome and small domed chapels in the corners of the cross. Pordenone's paintings decorate the main dome and the walls and domes of two of the chapels.[20] (He also painted a figure of *St. Augustine* in the entrance of the nave.) They have been mentioned by all writers on the artist, but they have not been fully published up to now, nor have they been correctly dated. A close examination of the documents, attempted in the appendix below, shows that the top of the main dome was painted by Pordenone in 1530–32, the Chapel of St. Catherine at the same time, and the Chapel of the Virgin sometime between 1532 and 1535 (except for its pilasters, which also date from 1530–32). All three cycles are of interest.

The main dome consists of eight triangular picture fields separated by broad raised ribs and truncated at the apex by

16. Schwarzweller, Cat. no. 24. Construction of the chapel was in hand in April of 1518 (G. Liberali, *Lotto, Pordenone e Tiziano a Treviso*, Venice [Istituto veneto di science, lettere ed arti, *Memorie di classe scienze morali e lettere*, XXXIII, iii], 1963, p. 45). By October of 1519 the fabric was finished and by August of the following year Pordenone had signed a fresco in the bottom register of the decoration and taken up residence in Cremona to begin an even larger fresco cycle (L. Coletti, 'Intorno ad un nuovo ritratto del vescovo Bernardo de' Rossi', *Rassegna d'Arte*, XXI, 1921, p. 414; Schwarzweller, Cat. no. 7).
For illus., see Fiocco, *Pordenone*, pls. 72–77. The dome was destroyed in World War II.

17. Illus., H. Tietze, *Titian: The Paintings and Drawings*, London, ²1950, fig. 65. The documents published by Liberali, *op. cit.*, indicate a possibility that Titain's painting was already ordered in 1517 and finished in 1519 (pp. 46 f., 61). The interdependence of the dome and altarpiece, in any case, suggests that the two were conceived in one moment, when the two artists were able actively to collaborate in working out the decoration of the chapel.

18. Correggio received his first payment for the fresco in July 1520 (P. L. Pungileoni, *Memorie istoriche di Antonio Allegri detto il Correggio*, II, Parma, 1817–21, p. 171). For illus., see A. Ghidiglia Quintavalle, *Gli affreschi del Correggio in San Giovanni Evangelista a Parma*, Milan, 1962.

19. Schwarzweller, Cat. no. 32. Most writers have wrongly given 1527 as the date of the decision to proceed with painting the church's tribune. The document (last published by G. Ludwig,

'Archivalische Beiträge z. Gesch. d. venezianischen Malerei', *Jahrbuch d. K. preussischen Kunstsammlungen*, XXVI, 1905, *Beiheft*, pp. 124 f.) is actually of 1528, being dated February 1527 *more veneto*.
Pordenone's frescoes were said to be in a 'stato di total distruzione' as early as the 1680's (G. Nicoletti, *Illustrazione della chiesa e scuola di S. Rocco in Venezia*, Venice [Deputazione veneta di storia patria, *Miscellanea*, III], 1885, p. 20, n. 1). They were entirely replaced shortly before 1733 by the Piazzetta follower, Giuseppe Angeli (the renovation is first mentioned by A. M. Zanetti, *Descrizione di tutte le pubbliche pitture della città di Venezia*, Venice, 1733, p. 301). It has been generally assumed that Angeli followed Pordenone's original frescoes closely, but this seems not to have been the case. The large scale and Veronesian figure types of some of the angels in the dome, the continuous spiral pattern of their movement, and the dazzling streaks of light are all characteristic of *Settecento* vault painting rather than of Pordenone. Furthermore (something which escaped Schwarzweller's notice) the subjects of the seven Old Testament scenes in the drum of the dome no longer correspond in every case with those that were originally there. M. Boschini listed the following: *The Sacrifice of Abraham, Triumph of David, Judith and Holofernes, Moses Receiving the Law, Joshua Halting the Sun, Noah's Sleep* and *Samson Drinking from the Jawbone of an Ass* (*La carta del navegar pitoresco*, Venice, 1660, p. 92). Angeli's frescoes include the first four subjects, but otherwise show: *Jael Driving the Nail through Sisara's Head, Hagar and the Angel* and *Elijah and the Angel*. His *Sacrifice of Abraham*, moreover, is based on Titian's painting now in S. Maria della Salute, which was painted many years after Pordenone's frescoes. It follows from all this, that we cannot reconstruct the individual compositions, or judge the style of the latter from the paintings by Angeli.

20. Schwarzweller, Cat. no. 15.

a raised band that frames the opening to the lantern (Fig. 6). The ribs are covered with putti, trophies, and grisaille scenes from the Old Testament. The picture fields are imagined open to the sky and show foreshortened figures of men and women upon clouds and clusters of putti.[21] A figure of God the Father accompanied by three cherubs appears in the lantern. The theme of the dome is unclear. The principal figures include a prophet, a hero, and a king of the Old Testament, the twelve Sibyls and St. Jerome.[22] Two of the grisaille scenes are from the Creation. The remainder illustrate the survival of those who have faith in the Lord.[23]

It has been suggested that the figure of the Almighty was meant to link with the *Assumption* in the cycle of Marian scenes around the drum.[24] The relationship is not as direct and theatrical as is the case in Pordenone's other decorations (the figures in the *Assumption* are unforeshortened and rather small in scale), but the Virgin and God do look toward each other. However, the Marian cycle was painted by a different artist more than ten years after completion of the dome, and Pordenone himself represented *The Assumption* elsewhere in the church. It seems likely therefore that the link was introduced by the later artist and was not part of the original scheme.

God the Father none the less is the centre of the representation and the excitement of the figures in the dome refers to Him. Several point to Him, others have their eyes fixed on Him, still others point to Him and look out at the beholder. The subject seems to be something like God in Glory acclaimed by his witnesses. The content is analogous to that of Correggio's cupola at S. Giovanni Evangelista in Parma, which represents Christ in Glory acclaimed by the Apostles. Correggio's frescoes were certainly known to Pordenone by this time. The standing and seated figures in the picture fields contain echoes of Apostles in the latter dome and of Apostles and ephebi in the dome of the Cathedral of Parma.

The influence of the Parmesan cupolas is apparent furthermore in the subject matter of the two chapel domes. A notice in a nineteenth-century guide book, that 'the supports of the arches' in these chapels were painted by a minor seventeenth-century artist, Benedetto Marini, can be disregarded.[25] Although the frescoes have been restored in the past, it is unmistakable from their style that the decorations of both the Chapel of the Virgin and the Chapel of St. Catherine were entirely invented by Pordenone and executed by him and his assistants.

The chapel domes are octagonal, like the main dome. They are supported by tall drums articulated by pilasters and arches, some blind, others containing round-headed windows. The domes themselves, like the main dome, are made of eight ribs, eight picture fields and a lantern. The frescoes in the dome of the Chapel of St. Catherine are the least well preserved of all of Pordenone's decorations in the church. Large areas of the original paint have flaked away, and what remains is darkened with dirt and streaked with water stains. But the representations are still largely recognizable. *Virtues* are painted on the pilasters of the drum and female saints in the arched recesses.[26] Single and paired figures of kneeling men appear alternately in the picture fields of the dome (Fig. 3). Putti and grisaille scenes from the Passion of Christ are painted on the ribs. The lantern is empty today, but the upturned faces of the twelve kneeling men in the dome show that originally some figure or object, purporting to exist in the same space as they, was represented there. It seems reasonable, in view of the subject matter of the grisailles, to assume that it was a figure of Christ. In that case, the subject of the dome as a whole was probably Christ in Glory acclaimed by the Apostles – the same subject as that of Correggio's dome in San Giovanni Evangelista at Parma. Such a representation would have

21. Illus., A. Corna, *Storia ed arte di Santa Maria di Campagna*, Bergamo, 1908, at pp. 90, 92, and, G. Ferrari, *Piacenza*, Bergamo (Italia artistica, cvi), 1931, pp. 90 f. Copies at Chatsworth of four of the groups of *putti* were mistaken by Fiocco for studies by Pordenone for the dome of S. Rocco (*Pordenone*, pp. 65, 87).

22. Early writers give no title to these frescoes (e.g. G. Ridolfi, *Le maraviglie dell'arte*, i, Venice, 1648, p. 107; ed. D. von Hadeln, i, Berlin, 1914–24, p. 125: 'historie sacre'). Modern guidebooks and critics call them prophets and sibyls.
    Among the twenty male figures (not nineteen, as Schwarzweller writes, p. 137) four can be identified: *Samson* (his wrists shackled) on the north-east; *St. Jerome* (with a lion) on the south; *Habakkuk* (carrying a basket) on the south-east; and *David* (a lyre at his feet) on the west. (The lyre is more clearly visible in the drawing; K. T. Parker, *Catalogue of the Collection of Drawings in the Ashmolean Museum*, ii, Italian Schools, Oxford, 1956, no. 490, illus.)
    Among the twelve female figures, four bear recognizable attributes that match the descriptions in the popular catalogue of sibyls by F. Barbieri (É. Mâle, *L'Art religieux de la fin du moyen age . . .*, Paris, ³1925, pp. 258 f.). They are: *Lybica*, *Hellespontica*, *Erythraea* and *Delphica*, on resp. the south-east, south, south-west, and north-west sides of the dome.

23. The scenes are: *The Creation, Creation of Man, Noah, Sacrifice of Abraham, Joseph Sold by his Brothers, Moses Receiving the Law, David and Goliath* and *Judith and Holofernes*.

24. Shearman, *op. cit.*, p. 145, n. 75.

25. The report originates with L. Cerri, *Guida di Piacenza*, Piacenza, n.d. [1894], pp. 72 f. It has been repeated by Corna, *op. cit.*, pp. 85, 88, 159, and G. Fiocco, *Santa Maria di Campagna* (Itinerari piacentini, iii), Piacenza, 1960, pp. 58, 62. Cerri and Corna use the word 'peduccio' (console, support), while Fiocco uses the word 'pennacchio' (pendentive), but the change of sense seems to be inadvertent. The published documents give no basis for asigning Marini any work in either chapel. According to Corna p. 160, n. 1) the artist was paid in 1623 and 1627 for certain 'figure fatte sotto larchitrave maggiore del cornicione'. This must mean the paintings by him in the high frieze of the nave, which are still there today.

26. Schwarzweller, Cat. no. 15, part 2, confuses the location of these representations. Four of the allegories on the pilasters can still be recognized: *Faith, Hope, Charity* and *Justice*. None of the saints in the recesses remains identifiable.

linked directly with the fresco of the *Disputation of St. Catherine* on the north wall of the chapel (Fig. 4). The saint is shown looking neither at the disputants nor at the emperor who ordered the debate, but straight toward the beholder, her right hand raised to point up into the dome. According to the *Golden Legend*, her words at this moment were, 'God, Jesu Christ shall be only with me, and He shall be my reward, for He is the crown and hope of them that fight for Him.'[27]

In the Chapel of the Virgin the dome decoration does not interact as dramatically with the representations below. Figures of saints are shown on the pilasters and in the arched recesses of the drum. The dome's picture fields are painted with pairs of musician angels (Fig. 5). The ribs are covered with the familiar putti, together with grisaille allegories that are today partially effaced. In the lantern is represented a female figure floating with her arms outspread. Ridolfi identified her with St. Catherine,[28] but it seems more likely that the subject was meant for *The Assumption of the Virgin*. The subject is the same as that of the Cathedral dome at Parma, and the figure of the Virgin seems distantly related to the floating figure of the welcoming Archangel in that fresco.[29]

Pordenone painted still one other cupola, in the church of San Giovanni Elimosinario at Venice. It no longer survives and we do not know what it looked like or what, if any, illusionistic effects it made use of.[30] But the six cupolas that still survive or were adequately photographed or described before they were destroyed are sufficient to gauge his importance in the field of vault decoration.

The motive of God the Father amidst cherubs which he used so consistently was taken as a model for ceiling representations of the Almighty by many North Italian artists of the sixteenth century. We find it not only as one might expect in the fresco cycles of his pupils,[31] but also in the work of more independent artists. Camillo Boccaccino used it for the figure of Christ in the representation of *Christ Appearing to the Evangelists*, in the apse of S. Sigismondo, outside Cremona.[32] Lorenzo Lotto was inspired by

it for the figure of God the Father in the vault of the Chapel of the Virgin of S. Michele al Pozzo Bianco, in Bergamo.[33] Even Tintoretto did not hesitate to incorporate it into the well-known *Apotheosis of St. Roch* which he gave to the Scuola di S. Rocco in Venice in 1564 for the centrepiece of their Albergo's ceiling.[34]

The illusionistic conceit of Pordenone's cupolas, whereby the representation in the dome relates directly to other elements of the decoration elsewhere in the same room, was likewise adopted by various North Italians. G. B. Zelotti made use of it in his decoration of the early 1560's in the crossing of the abbey church of Praglia, near Padua. For the free-standing high altar beneath the dome he painted an *Assumption of the Virgin*. In the drum of the dome he frescoed four scenes from the infancy and youth of Christ, and in the dome itself open sky, a foreshortened balustrade and Pordenonesque figures of angels surrounding a glory of light. The frescoes in the dome completed not only the *Assumption*, but also Domenico Campagnola's slightly earlier fresco of *The Ascension of Christ* in the half dome of the apse.[35]

Giulio Campi exploited the device even more systematically in the east end of SS. Margherita e Pelagia at Cremona. On the rear wall of the small oval sanctuary (which cannot be photographed because a tall baroque altar stands in the way) he painted three groups of foreshortened figures: a Holy Family in the centre, adoring shepherds on the left and three kings with a train of attendants on the right. Some kind of imaginary architecture divided and framed these scenes and tied them to the real pilasters and entablature of the room. Both the shepherds and kings and the architecture have been drastically restored, but the scheme originated with Giulio[36]. Above the real and painted architecture rises the oval dome in which are painted a fictive balustrade and a figure of God the Father surrounded by cherubs, being borne past the balustrade and into the chapel on a cloud. At the summit of the dome, in a glory, appears the Holy Ghost (Fig. 7).[37] Despite the Parmigian-

---

27. Jacobus da Voragine, *Legenda Aurea*, ed. T. Graesse, Leipzig, [2]1850, p. 792. The translation here used is Caxton's: *The Golden Legend*, VII, London, 1900, p. 20.

28. Ridolfi, *loc. cit.*

29. Illus., C. Ricci, *Correggio*, Rome, n.d. [1929], pl. CCXI.

30. It is listed by M. Boschini, *Le minere della pittura*, Venice, 1664, p. 262, D. Martinelli, *Il ritratto di Venezia*, Venice, [2]1705, p. 365, and A. M. Zanetti, *Descrizione di tutte le pubbliche pitture . . . di Venezia*, Venice, 1733, p. 275. After that it is no longer mentioned.

31. E.g. the vault decoration by Pomponio Amalteo in S. Maria dei Battuti at S. Vito al Tagliamento (illus., A. Moschetti, *I danni ai monumenti e alle opere d'arte delle Venezie nella guerra mondiale*, Venice, 1932, p. 412, fig. 350).

32. Illus., Venturi, IX, 6, fig. 491. The seated and standing figures below Christ seem to have been inspired by the main dome at Piacenza.

33. Illus., B. Berenson, *Lorenzo Lotto*, London, [2]1956, pl. 164.

34. Illus., E. von der Bercken, *Die Gemälde des Jacopo Tintoretto*, Munich, 1942, pl. 234.

35. There are no photographs of this complex. Zelotti's altarpiece, furthermore, was removed from the high altar early in this century and now hangs over the entrance to the church. The scheme may have been influenced by Veronese's frescoes of after 1559 in S. Sebastiano, for which see below. Cf. further, D. von Hadeln, 'Veronese und Zelotti', II, *Jahrbuch d. K. preussischen Kunstsammlungen*, XXXVI, 1915, pp. 122 f., and, R. Colpi, 'Domenico Campagnola', *Bollettino del Museo Civico di Padova*, XXXI/XLIII, 1942/54, pp. 102 f.

36. The murals were completely repainted in a restoration of 1733 that is reported by G. B. Zaist, *Notizie istoriche de' pittori . . . cremonesi*, I, Cremona, 1774, pp. 120 f.
A date of 1547 is usually given for these frescoes, but that is the date of the dedicatory inscription on the front of the church which presumably refers to the fabric, not the decoration.

37. C. Sorte, *Osservationi nella pittura*, Venice, 1581, p. 14 v. (ed. P.

esque elegance of some of the cherubs, the figure group clearly derives from Pordenone, and the organization of the decoration as a whole as well.

At Venice, the presbytery of S. Sebastiano was decorated in a similar fashion by Veronese. His frescoes do not survive, but from descriptions we know that they represented the *Assumption of the Virgin* in the half dome of the apse, a balustrade with music-making angels in the drum of the dome, and God the Father in the dome itself.[38]

> Barocchi, *Trattati d'arte del cinquecento*, I, Bari, 1960–62, p. 295) called the representation a Trinity. Many guide-books have repeated this, and so has A. Perotti, *I pittori Campi da Cremona*, Milan, n.d. [1932], p. 30. However, the appellation fits only if one includes the Christ Child in the *Holy Family* on the wall. There is no figure of Christ in the vault, nor room for one.
>
> 38. The fullest description in Ridolfi, *op. cit.*, I, p. 288 (ed. von Hadeln, I, p. 301). Cf. further, T. Pignatti, *Le pitture di Paolo*

Veronese's general predeliction for illusionism in wall decoration was owed no doubt in large part to the influence of Giulio Romano. Certainly he was familiar with Giulio's elaborately illusionistic representation of the *Assumption* in the Cathedral of Verona, which likewise distributes the action over several wall surfaces.[39] But in the presbytery of S. Sebastiano the program was so similar to the cupolas by and after Pordenone as to suggest the latter were his source.

> *Veronese nella chiesa di S. Sebastiano in Venezia*, Milan, 1966, pp. 90 f. Pignatti plausibly connects with these frescoes a payment record of 1559 concerning alterations to the presbytery windows, but postpones the date of the paintings to 1561 for unexplained reasons.
>
> 39. The frescoes were designed by Giulio and executed by Torbido in 1534; illus., F. Hartt, *Giulio Romano*, II, New Haven, 1958, figs. 425–430.

APPENDIX

The church of Santa Maria di Campagna at Piacenza was built to house a miraculous image of the Virgin kept previously in a shrine on the same spot.[1] Its fabric was completed in 1528 and in February 1530 (not 1529, as is everywhere written) the rectors of the church concluded a contract with Pordenone for painting of the cupola over the crossing. That contract does not survive, but is mentioned in a later document.[2] Painting began soon afterwards and by March 1532 considerably more than had been contracted for was completed. At that time (not March 1531, as is everywhere written), the artist had received 620 scudi for work on the dome. He had also worked elsewhere in the church, for which 400 scudi were owing him. He was now given leave to absent himself from Piacenza for a period of up to four months, with the understanding that he would return to complete the dome. The rectors agreed to reserve the entire Easter offering, to be collected three weeks hence, to cover future payments to him. They also

1. A. Corna, *Storia ed arte in Santa Maria di Campagna*, Bergamo, 1908, p. 57 f.
2. In an undated draft agreement for completion of the main dome, the date of the original contract is given as, 'Anno ab Incarnatione Domini Nostri Jesu Christi 1529 die quinto decimo mensis Febbruarij' (V. Joppi, *Contributo terzo alla storia dell'arte in Friuli*, Venice [Deputazione veneta di storia patria, *Miscellanea*, XII], 1892, p. 50 f., doc. XV).
Reckoning the years by the Incarnation, or Florentine style, meant, beginning the new year on 25th March, the Feast of the Annunciation. It was the usual way of reckoning time at Piacenza until 1749 (cf. A. Cappelli, *Cronologia e calendario perpetuo*, Milan, 1906, pp. xi f., xvi; H. Grotefend, *Taschenbuch der Zeitrechnung*, Hannover, [10]1960, p. 13). Hence, 15th February 1529 *stilus Incarnationis* corresponds to 15th February 1530 *stilus Circumcisionis*, the modern way of reckoning time.

agreed to assume the debt of 400 scudi for his other work in the church.

'... dicto Magistro Ioan Antonio habia pincto parte del dicto Tiburio, et recepute parte del precio promisso per dicta opera, cioè scuti seicento venti ... Conciosia cosa anchora che dicto Magistro Ioan Antonio se volia absentare da questa Cita anchora de voluntà de dicti Signori Rectori, per dui over tri mesi, et volendo li prefati Signori Rectori provedere, che sia finita dicta opera, ed ad ciò che dicto Magistro Ioan Antonio possa ritornare de bono aequo ad perficere dicta Opera ... [therefore] Dicti Signori Rectori promettano a dicto Magistro Io. Antonio, che qui presente, et che accepta, che tutti li dinari de la Offerta grande se ha ad farse par la Pascha de la resurrectione proxime ad venire, et de la Cassa, siano in tutto d'epso Magistro Io. Antonio, et siano depositati in mane del Thesaurario de dicta fabrica, et de li quali ne epsi Signori Rectori, soi successori, ne altra Persona ne possa disponere in altra Persona ne ad altro effetto, ma ala ritornata d'epso Magistro Io. Antonio ad fornir l'opra ut infra li siano exbursati per dicto texoriero ut supra la Mercede sua de dicta Pictura. Dicto Magistro Io. Antonio promette a li dicti Signori Rectori presenti, et che acceptano retornare in termino de mesi quatri proxime ad venire et fornire, et perficere dicta Opera del Tiburio ...

Item, che epso Magistro Io. Antonio è creditore de la predicta fabrica ultra la sua Mercede, del Tiburio quando [sic] per la pictura de la Capella del signor Cavalero Messer Francesco Pavaro de libre quatre cente Imperiali, et ultra ciò quelle quattre colunne angulare che sono dentro dela Capella secunde dice dicto Magistro Io.

E

Antonio, epsi Signori Fabricieri promectano dicte libre quatre cente Imperiali, et de piu per quelle Colunne angulare. . . .'3

The 'parte del Tiburio' finished at that time was almost certainly the entirety of that portion of the main dome which Pordenone actually executed (i.e. the dome proper, exclusive of the window zone and drum). The chapel of Francesco Pavaro was that of St. Catherine.4 The 'Capella secunde' was very likely that of the Virgin, owned by the Rollieri family.5 It is the only other chapel in the church besides that of St. Catherine where Pordenone painted the pilasters and arch soffits with figures of wrestling putti and trophies.

There is no record of when or whether Pordenone returned.6 By the Summer of 1535 the rectors were vainly soliciting his presence from the government of Venice, in whose employ he was then and remained for two years more.7 In December 1536 they decided that solicitations were useless and appointed one of their number to act as attorney and settle with Pordenone as best he could. The decision makes it clear that by 1536 the artist was no longer a creditor but a debtor of the church.8 It follows that in the interval between March 1532 and the summer of 1535 Pordenone had received the 400 lire owing him and more. Hence it follows also that sometime between 1532 and 1535 Pordenone had actually returned to Piacenza. The works by him that now exist in the church but are not listed in the agreement of March 1532, presumably were added at this later moment.

The above argument yields the following chronology: 1530–32, the main dome, the Chapel of St. Catherine, pilasters of the Chapel of the Virgin; between 1532 and 1535, remainder of the Chapel of the Virgin, *St. Augustine*. As is known, Pordenone did not return a third time to Piacenza, and the 'opera del Tiburio' was not finished by him. The upper frieze, window zone, drum proper and pendentives of the dome were painted instead by Bernardino Gatti, called 'il Soiaro', who signed the work and dated it 1543.9

3. Joppi, *loc. cit.*, p. 53 f., doc. XVII. The document begins, 'In Nomine Domini amen. Anno ab incarnatione ejusdem millesimo quingentesimo trigesimo primo. Indictione quinta, die undecimo mensis Martii.' The year is 1532 our style, as can be controlled by the mention of the Indiction. Piacenza used the *indictio Bedana*, or *cesarea*, which counted the years in every indiction from 24th September. In the 1530's the fifth indiction fell in 1531/32, and in Piacenza covered the period September 1531–September 1532. March of the fifth indiction therefore was March 1532. (Cf. Cappelli, *op. cit.*, pp. viii, 81; Grotefend, *op. cit.*, pp. 8, 140.)

4. Thus Corna, *op. cit.*, p. 79.

5. Corna, *op. cit.*, p. 82.

6. As mentioned above, there survives an undated draft agreement for completion of the main dome (Joppi, *op. cit.*, pp. 50 f., doc. XV). The work is to be done by a set date, left blank in the draft. The Rectors agree to post bond in the city of Venice for the eventual sum that will be owing Pordenone for completion of the dome. Pordenone agrees to make bond in Venice of 200 scudi that he will forfeit to the church as an indemnity in the event of non-performance on his part. The draft is unfinished and may never have been used in an executed agreement. It probably dates from 1536 when the Rectors were trying to obtain a legal settlement with Pordenone, by then resident in Venice (see below).

7. Shortly after July 1535 the rectors were informed by the Council of Ten that Pordenone could not return to Piacenza because, 'hora si attrovi qui de ordine nostro per compir una sala che facemo nel palazo nostro'. (G. Ludwig, 'Archivalische Beiträge z. Gesch. d. venezianischen Malerei', *Jahrbuch d. K. preussischen Kunstsammlungen*, XXVI, 1905, *Beiheft*, p. 126.) The room was the old Sala dello Scrutinio in the Ducal Palace where Pordenone painted the ceiling (cf. C. Ridolfi, *Le maraviglie dell'arte*, ed. D. von Hadeln, I, Berlin, 1914–24, p. 123).

8. The decision is reported by Joppi (*op. cit.*, p. 35) and reprinted in part by Corna (*op. cit.*, pp. 92–93).

9. The four zones show respectively: mythological processions and medallions; *St. John the Baptist*, *St. Paul* and six apostles; eight scenes from the life of the Virgin; and the Evangelists. They are signed beneath the *Annunciation*, BERNARDINI DE GATTIS PAPIENSIS OPVS M.D. XXXXIII.

Some of the Marian scenes are illustrated by G. Ferrari, *Piacenza*, Bergamo (Italia artistica, CVI), 1931, p. 91.

WALTER FRIEDLAENDER †

The Domestication of Cupid

A PAINTING which was exhibited many years ago at the 1939 World's Fair (Fig. 1) interested me because of its curious subject-matter. It illustrates the *Domestication of Cupid*. Stylistically, the painting shows the characteristics of the late Mannerist school of Fontainebleau, and is close to the work of Niccolò dell'Abbate, who came to France as a companion of Primaticcio in 1552. It probably belongs to Niccolò's later development or, more likely, to his school. The painting consists of two parts: a main section with seven figures – Cupid and the usual six Vestals – in relief against a dark wall; and, at the far left, a narrow strip of background important to an explanation of the subject. One sees a small round temple which can be nothing else but a sanctuary of Vesta, the goddess of the hearth and of domestic chastity. Its architecture closely resembles that of a temple of Vesta illustrated in Cartari (Fig. 4).[1] Vesta is one personification of Juno, who was worshipped as protectress of matrimony as well as Queen of the gods.[2] The peacock, Juno's favourite bird, perches on the portico of the temple in the painting. Small figures of the maidens of Vesta, the Vestals, going to and from the *tempietto* in a kind of torch-dance, carry and extinguish the torches which they have ignited at the sacred fire.

The action in the main part of the painting is concentrated on the disarmament of Cupid. In a Michelangelesque pose, he slumbers quietly unaware that all the weapons with which he can disrupt the peaceful harmony of the household are being taken from him. At the left, holding Cupid's bow, stands the first Vestal, a tall figure clad in the loose garb typical of her station. Behind her appears another of Vesta's servants bearing two torches (as Hymenaeus usually carries). The two center Vestals, with a rather complicated involvement of limbs, kneel and bend over Cupid, surreptitiously blindfolding him. They loop a scarf about his curls, ready to pull it tight. One of these two figures has torn a handful of feathers from Cupid's wing, so that he cannot use it. The next figure, standing in a very contrived pose with her back to us, holds his quiver of arrows. The last Vestal, surprisingly quite nude, carries a javelin, an attribute of Vesta herself. In this way, the maidens have utterly domesticated Cupid. He can no longer shoot or fly at liberty, and the world is protected by the goddess from the whims of the lascivious boy.[3]

The Fontainebleau *Domestication of Cupid* is a key to our understanding of two famous paintings by Titian, whose content and meaning have been badly misinterpreted. These are the '*Allegory of Alfonso d'Avalos*' in the Louvre, from about 1530, and the *Blindfolding of Cupid* in the Borghese Gallery, *c.* 1565. Both pictures illustrate that the power of Cupid can be imprisoned within the confines of domesticity, and, as in the 'Abbate' painting, the taming proceeds under the guardianship of Vesta.

The earlier so-called *Allegory of Alfonso d'Avalos* (Fig. 2) is entitled simply an *Allegory* in the latest catalogue of the Louvre.[4] Alfonso d'Avalos, Marchese del Vasto, was a general employed by Charles V to fight the Turks. He was a member of Titian's circle, and was married to the beautiful and virtuous Mary of Aragon.[5] Panofsky has followed most modern scholars in denying the presence of Avalos in the Louvre painting, because the figure bears no definite resemblance to the known portraits of Avalos, namely the *Allocution* in the Prado and the portrait in the Ganay collection, Paris.[6] Nevertheless, there is some possibility that the sentimental tradition which associates the famous general Avalos with the painting, and which goes relatively far back – to van der Doort's catalogue in manuscript (*c.* 1637) of the pictures of Charles I[7] – had some foundation. It is not altogether impossible that so public a personality as the Marchese might have wished to own a private allegory in which his features were deliberately obscured – especially since the subject is so intimate.[8]

At any rate, the name of the gentleman depicted is not important to the meaning of the picture. In his precious armor, seriously and with dignity, he makes a possessive gesture to his lady, who receives it in the same contemplative, slightly melancholy spirit. Her bosom bared, she sits

Petrarch's Laura, tames Love (see M. Davies, *National Gallery Catalogues: The Earlier Italian Schools*, 1961, p. 472).

4. L. Hautecœur, *Catalogue des peintures*, 1926, II, p. 134.

5. See Aretino, *Lettere sull'arte*, ed. Milan, 1957, Letter LXXXV.

6. E. Panofsky, *Studies in Iconology*, 1939, p. 160.

7. See *Abraham van der Doort's Catalogue of the Collection of Charles I*, ed. O. Millar, vol. XXVII of the *Journal of the Walpole Society*, 1960, p. 16.

8. In this connection, I would draw attention to the portrait in the Gemäldegalerie, Kassel, also formerly associated with the Marchese del Vasto. It is usually dated quite late, about 1550. The hero, with his supercilious air, his grotesquely ornamented helmet and his enormous dog, strikes me as a kind of *Miles Gloriosus*, leading me even to suggest that the Kassel painting might be a parody aimed at the general, who was an intimate of the Titian circle.

1. V. Cartari, *Imagini de gli dei*, Padua, 1615 edition, p. 200.

2. *Ibid.*, Venice, 1647 ed., p. 106.

3. Similar theme and motifs appear in a Signorelli fresco (London, National Gallery) of *c.* 1509, where Chastity, personified as

holding a crystal sphere – a rather transparent symbol for the uncertainties of fate. Similar examples of seated women with spheres include Giovanni Bellini's allegory of *Fortuna Amoris* or *Incostanza*, in the Accademia, Venice, and a woodcut among the annotations to Cartari (Fig. 5).[9] The sphere, because of its fragility, suggests the possibility of danger to the stability of their marriage.

The other side of the painting illustrates the means of averting this danger. The rather austere lady at right cannot be, as she has been identified in previous interpretations, a Venus or a symbol affiliated with earthly love. Nor can she be a 'Faith', a 'Victory' or any other bloodless allegorical personification, of a kind Titian would never have used voluntarily. In general he favored mythological situations and figures more easily recognizable, and more immediately a part of sensual reality.

The protectress of undisturbed domestic peace is the goddess Vesta, and in the painting it is she who, anxious to secure the harmony of the couple, attends to their union. Venus by her nature can wear no crown, but it is the right of Vesta, as a member of the royal family, as sister and substitute for the Queen Juno, to wear one. In an illustration of Vesta in annotations to Cartari (Fig. 3), she wears a similar coronet of foliage.[10] Here she approaches breathlessly, her hand to her throat. As in the Fontainebleau work, it is her function to watch over the behavior of Cupid. She recommends him in his act of homage to the seated lady. Originally, her gesture of presentation was more exaggerated, as photographs of the underdrawing after relining of the canvas show.[11] Cupid has already been domesticated, and submits good-naturedly by presenting his bundle of arrows, made innocuous because they are tied together, to the 'bride'. The third advancing figure, jubilantly raising high a large, shallow basket of flowers is, as has already been suggested, Hymen.[12] His introductory blessing is necessary for any successful marriage.[13] A visual parallel for this youth with flowers is found in the Cartari woodcut previously mentioned (Fig. 5), where four putti bear little baskets of flowers as congratulatory offerings to the seated woman.

On the basis again of the Fontainebleau painting, the explanation of the much later Borghese *Blindfolding of Cupid* (Fig. 6) seems still more obvious. A seated woman, clad in a simple white gown with a blue mantle, binds the eyes of the Cupid in her lap with a golden scarf. Her expression is rather reserved. Once again she is quite surely not a Venus, but the disciplinarian Vesta. On the back of her head she wears a prominent crown with a single pendant stone.[14] She gives thoughtful attention to the whispered advice of her small ally Anteros. She seems almost to stop tying the knot in mid-action, hesitating to deprive the amiable little genius of his powerful faculty. Opposite Vesta on the right, two rather androgynous, strong-limbed figures in red cloaks watch the goddess as if waiting for further directions. They hold the weapons of which they have just deprived Cupid. The one seen in profile has his quiver and arrows. This maiden is a formal and psychological descendant of the 'Vesta' figure in the earlier *Allegory*. The maiden hovering behind her has taken Cupid's rather tall bow. Both are surely Vestals, as before, helping the chaste goddess to execute her will.

The personal and romantic overtones which enrich the Avalos *Allegory* have disappeared in the late Borghese painting. In the *Allegory* Titian's strongly subjective feeling and the light and shadow placed it in a distinctly *malerisch-tönisch* sphere, still deriving from Giorgionism. The *Blindfolding of Cupid*, on the other hand, has an overall tonality and a conception that is 'philosophically mythological'. That is to say, an intellectual abstraction has been distilled from the instructive *exempla* of the gods. Certainly the *Allegory* served as prototype for Titian's *Blindfolding of Cupid*. Although some motifs, like the magnificent female profile at the right, the pose and general importance of the seated woman at the left, and even the placement of her arm-bracelet are retained, Titian's emphasis on an emotional interplay has vanished. The figures are now monumental and impersonal, remote from life in the manner characteristic of Titian's late style. The Vestals of the Borghese painting closely resemble the massive female nudes, with their splendid, opalescent skins, of the Prado *Spain Succouring Religion* and of the Vienna *Nymph and Shepherd*. In this painting, so rigidly structured yet so suffused with color, Titian's genius synthesized what, in seventeenth-century art, would emerge as contraries: classicistic order and *bravura* color.

9. *Ed. cit.* in note 1, p. 527.

10. *Ibid.*, p. 523.

11. I am very grateful to M. Pierre Rosenberg of the Louvre for this and other technical information about the Avalos *Allegory*. Titian made several such changes between the underdrawing and the painting as it is known today, but they do not significantly alter our conclusions.

12. Crowe and Cavalcaselle, *The Life and Times of Titian*, 1881, I, p. 374, and others.

13. For Hymen see W. Friedlaender, 'Hymenaea', *Essays in Honor of Erwin Panofsky*, 1961, I, pp. 153–156.

14. The stone is an elaboration of the solitary jewel which Juno wears in her role as protectress of marriage. Cartari, *Imagini de gli dei*, Venice, 1647 ed., p. 106.
[This article was completed by Professor Friedlaender a few days before his death on 6 September 1966 and was his last work.]

JAMES S. ACKERMAN

Palladio's Vicenza: A Bird's-eye Plan of *c.* 1571

ONE of the largest, most accurate and most handsome bird's-eye city plans of the Renaissance, showing the town of Vicenza from the north, is preserved in the Biblioteca Angelica in Rome, as item 81 of a cartographical collection numbered B. 22. 11 (Fig. 1).[1] Measuring *c.* 1·36 × 1·52 m., it is drawn in pen with bistre ink on six strips of characteristic drawing-paper of the period (without watermarks) pasted together to form the single oversized sheet. The author squared his sheet with black chalk, using squares of 8 × 8 cms., and finished by painting in the waterways with blue aquarelle mixed with white. The plan is well preserved, considering that it was bound with many folds into a volume of maps until 1965, when the Directress, D.ssa Giorgetti Vichi, generously volunteered to have it restored and mounted on canvas to prevent further damage and to make it possible to take the photographs published here.[2] The edges had been cropped on all sides, cutting off some of the lettering and an indeterminate amount of the suburban area.

The elegance and freedom of the drawing and the skill in presenting each building in the most revealing possible aspect without making the perspective distortions disturbing suggest that the author was a proficient figural artist and not a cartographer. The plan is remarkably similar in style and technique to the manuscript plan of Rome dated 1562 in the Burlington collection in the Library of the Royal Institute of British Architects in London, which has been attributed to Giovanni Antonio Dosio.[3] The distinc-

tiveness of the hand suggests that the plan was not made for reproduction in a print; conventions are personal and not chosen for the convenience of an engraver. Possibly the drawing was a study for a civic mural: the squaring of the sheet seems to have been intended to facilitate enlargement after the drawing was finished rather than to establish scale or a system of co-ordinates.

In accordance with the Vitruvian description of city design,[4] the plan is oriented to the eight major winds, the names of which appear in Roman capitals at the four corners and in the center of each side. The north wind (*Tramontana*) appears at the lower left and, following clockwise, *Greco* (also called Grego, or Aquilo), *Levante* (east), *Sirocco* (south), *Ostro*, *Gabino* (also Garbino), *Ponente* (west), and *Maistro* (also Maestro).

The plan shows Vicenza divided into a central core with its own system of fortifications and gates, and walled suburbs to the north (Borgo di Pusterla, incompletely fortified), east, south and west (probably called, after their principal gates, Borgo S. Piero, Borgo del Monte and Borgo Nuovo, respectively). The form of the domestic buildings and the history of the churches suggest that the major suburban development occurred in the period between the late fourteenth and the late fifteenth centuries, the earliest being the northern portion (bottom center in Fig. 1) of the western suburb, outside the porta Nuova. In addition to the two rivers encircling Vicenza, the Bacchiglione on the north and east, and the Retrone on the west and south, the plan shows a system of canal-moats encircling the fortifications, which has since been filled in. The route to Padua appears in the upper left, the Verona road in the lower right, and the Campo Marzo and Monte Berico in the upper right.

The following description is in two parts; the first reproduces with historical notes the topographical information provided in the author's hand, which is concerned primarily with religious establishments, streets and city gates, and the second discusses the plan as a record of Palladio's activity in Vicenza.[5]

1. The plan was discovered by Roberto Almagià, who cited it without a description in *Le pitture murali della Galleria delle carte geografiche* (*Monumenta Cartografica Vaticana, III*), Vatican City, 1952, p. 69, no. 7.

   A proper topographical and historical study of this plan could be made only in Vicenza; my intention is to sketch the essentials briefly enough to encourage a more qualified scholar to go farther. I am indebted to Prof. Antonio Dalla Pozza, Director of the Biblioteca Bertoliana in Vicenza, for assistance in studying the plan, and to the American Council of Learned Societies and the American Academy in Rome for the opportunity to pursue studies on Palladio in Italy.

2. A previous restoration had protected the edges of the plan by pasted reinforcements of paper with eighteenth (?) century writing. There is rubbing and some obliteration along the former folds and especially at their corners.

3. Reproduced in H. Egger, *Römische Veduten*, II, Vienna, 1932, pls. 118–122. On the attribution, see L. Wachler, 'Giovannantonio Dosio', *Röm. Jb. für Kunstgeschichte*, IV, 1940, pp. 232 ff. and Fig. 169. The plan is inscribed: 'LA CITTÀ DI ROMA DELINEATA NEL PONTIFICATO DI PIO IV. L'ANNO MDLXII. 1562.'

4. Vitruvius, *On Architecture*, I, vi. For the Italian nomenclature of this time and locale, see *I dieci libri dell'Architettura di M. Vitruvio*, ed. Daniele Barbaro, Venice, 1567, pp. 58 ff.

5. Historical data on the monuments (given in parentheses) are taken from W. Arslan, *Catalogo delle cose d'arte e d'antichità d'Italia: Vicenza, I, Le chiese*, Rome, 1956, and from F. Barbieri, R. Cevese and L. Magagnato, *Guida di Vicenza*, 2ª ediz., Vicenza, 1956, except where otherwise noted. Names appearing in italics are transcribed from the plan without corrections.

CENTRAL SECTION (Fig. 2)

The area within the inner circle of fortifications walls is divided into northern and southern halves by the *Strada maggior* (che) *va al Castel* (now Corso Andrea Palladio), extending from the *Isola dove* (si) *fal marcato di Animali e di legne* (now Piazza Giacomo Matteotti) near the *Ponte di S. Piero* on the east (Fig. 4, right center) to the *Castello* with its high Gothic tower and *Porta* on the west. At the point where this street is crossed at a right angle by the street (now Via C. Battisti and Corso Fogazzaro) leading to *il Domo* (Duomo) appears a circular plaque of a kind often used in the middle ages to indicate the intersection of the Roman Cardo and Decumanus. Only two other streets in the central section are identified: the *strada di S. Apostolo* (Fig. 2, top center; now Contrà SS. Apostoli) and the *strada del Palla magio* (Fig. 2, right center to upper right; now Contrà More Pallamaio); the same name is indicated for the street just within the fortifications in this area.

The southwest segment of the inner town is dominated by *il Domo* (Early Christian and subsequent medieval buildings were replaced starting in the fourteenth century; the façade is inscribed 1467; the choir was begun by Lorenzo da Bologna in 1487;[6] the dome on designs of Palladio in 1567; the façade spires shown in the plan collapsed in 1581). In the neighboring area:

S. *Antonio* (the church is destroyed;[7] the name survives in the Strada di S. Antonio alongside)

Piazza del Domo (the buildings shown to the rear of the square were replaced by the Oratorio del Gonfalone and the Palazzetto Roma in 1596 and 1599)

Vescovada (showing the Loggia Zeno in the court, of 1494–95; the piazza façade was replaced in 1819)

Pescaria, between the Cathedral and the Basilica.

Toward the walls (Fig. 2, upper right; Fig. 5, center)

S. *Maria di gratia* (delle Grazie; church of 1494, demolished in *c.* 1580 and rebuilt)

Giardini di Mons.or Arcidia(co)*no* (destroyed; a Renaissance parterre garden of the same style as the Valmarana garden, lower right corner of Fig. 2, with a gate on the *Strada del Palla magio* that appears to be Palladian and a central casino

Ponte furo, spanning the Retrone; a large house appears to be built on the bridge.

The southeast segment is dominated by the *Piazza Maggiore* (now dei Signori), the *Piazza delle Biade* and the Basilica (see below), and contains to the south of this group:

S. *Maria di servi*, beyond the *Piazza delle Biade* (church

6. See G. Lorenzoni, *Lorenzo da Bologna*, Venice, 1963, pp. 29 ff. and figs. 21–26.

7. Anon. (E. Arnaldi, O. Vecchia, L. Buffetti), *Descrizione delle architettura, pitture e scolture di Vicenza*, Vicenza, 1779, pp. 16 f. I have not found the date of the original church.

and cloister started in the early fourteenth century; the church, rebuilt in 1407, was extended toward the façade in 1490; portal of 1531; façade, eighteenth century)

Ponte di S. Michele and *Ponte delle Becharie* (now Ponte S. Paolo), crossing the Retrone; note the numerous millwheels by the bridges.

Between the Retrone and the walls:

S. *Michele* (church of 1264, destroyed 1810)

Between the *Piazza Maggiore* and the *Strada Maggiore*:

S. *Vicenzo* (church of before 1388, remodeled 1499–1500; a façade toward the Piazza was added in 1614–1617).

Between S. *Vicenzo* and the *Isola*:

A small church with an illegible inscription just to the left of S. Vincenzo near the Piazza

S. *Fusto* (SS. Faustino e Giovita, medieval church remodeled in the early eighteenth century; Palladian façade by Bertotti Scamozzi, 1774; deconsecrated).

The northeast segment is without inscriptions except for the area adjacent to the *Ponte di S. Piero* (Fig. 4, right center), which contains:

S. *Maria di Angioli*, along the walls by the gate destroyed; church founded in 1463, with eighteenth-century façade)

Pregione vecchie and *Munition* (the Venetian arsenal), on the future site of the Teatro Olimpico (see below)

S. *Corona* (thirteenth-century church with cloister of 1477).

In the northwest segment, along the walls, appear two inscriptions (Fig. 2, bottom center):

S. *Lorenzo* (church and campanile begun 1281; cloister 1492)

Hospital di S. Marcello (twelfth-century structure remodeled in the eighteenth century and destroyed in 1810).

NORTHERN QUARTER (Fig. 3)

The two major arteries of the northern suburb are the *Strada del Borgo di Pusterla* (now Contrà San Marco), extending from the *Porta Pusterla* over the *Fiume Bachiglione* to the *Porta di S. Bortolamio* in the outer ring of fortifications, and the *Strada delle Convertite* (now Contrà della Misericordia), which intersects it at a right angle.

Along the *Borgo di Pusterla*:

S. *Marco* (destroyed Romanesque church; the name later passed to S. Girolamo)

S. *Geronimo* (S. Girolamo degli Scalzi or San Marco, 1481–91, replaced by an eighteenth-century church)

S. *francesco* (destroyed early sixteenth-century church and convent of Clares; the name is preserved in the present Contrà S. Francesco)

S. *Bortolamio* (S. Bortolo, Gothic church and cloister remodeled in 1420 and 1447; destroyed 1838)

Porta di San Bortolamio (partly destroyed gate of 1435).
Along the *Strada delle Convertite*:
   La Misericordia (Santa Maria or Ospizio della Miseri-
      cordia, church of 1414–28; the remodeling of 1584–
      1594 is not shown in the plan)
   Santuario delle Convertite (now Santa Maria Maddalena,
      with an eighteenth-century façade).
Along *Strada di S. Biasio* (now Contrà Pedemuro, Contrà
S. Biagio) between the *Fiume Bachiglione* and the inner walls:
   S. Biasio (largely destroyed church and cloister of 1522–
      1533; three semicircular side chapels are indicated).
East of *Borgo di Pusterla* and a canal, now filled in, on the
site of the present Giardino Querini:
   chiodare (blacksmith or nail-factory?).
Southeast of the *chiodare* at the bend of the river (lower
center in Fig. 4), alongside the fortifications of the eastern
quarter:
   Monasterio della Aricella (Santa Maria Araceli, a vulgar-
      ization of Ad Cellam, church and cloister of 1214, re-
      built in 1675–80 on designs of Carlo Borella).

EASTERN QUARTER (Fig. 4)

This quarter of the city is joined to the center by the
Ponte di S. Piero, which leads to a piazza (now XX Set-
tembre) from which five streets radiate. The first to the
right, running due south, is the *Strada di S. Piero*. The
second, *Strada de fontana di S. Domenico*, extends southwest
to a fountain with a tabernacle and continues east, while the
Strada della Porta di Padova forks to the southwest, terminating in the *Porta di Padova* and its suburb.
   S. Piero (S. Pietro) with its large cloister and campanile
      appears to the west of the Porta (church and cloister
      consecrated 1495; the simple façade shown here with
      a lean-to porch was replaced in 1597)
   San Domenico, its cloister, orchard and gardens with
      pergolas, appears in the block at the terminus of the
      Strada de fontana (church and cloister of 1483; choir,
      1537; campanile, 1556).
The name of the street extending east of the piazza and
along the garden walls of S. Domenico, partly obliterated,
may be *Strada di Angiolini* (now Via XX Novembre), in
association with *S. Maria di Angioli*, on the city side of the
bridge. The *Strada di S. lucia*, extending northeast from the
piazza, leads to the *Porta* and church of the same name.
   S. lucia, on the extreme edge of the plan (fourteenth-
      century, remodeled in the seventeenth century).
Outside the northern fortification wall of the eastern
quarter is a strip inscribed *Tiro de' Bombardieri*.

SOUTHERN QUARTER (Fig. 5)

The plan shows this quarter, at the foot of Monte Berico,
as having developed along only three streets; the major

one, *Strada dal monte* (now Contrà S. Tomaso; Contrà
Sta. Caterina), starting at the *Porta di mezzo* in the inner
ring of fortifications and terminating at the *Porta da monte*
(top left in Fig. 5); the *Strada della lupa* (now Via Valmer-
lara; Via Generale Chinotto), which terminates at the
Porta della lupa, intersects it at a Y marked by a circular
plaque or fountain; and the *Strada di S. Silvestro* crossing at
a right angle marked by a wellhead.
Moving along the *Strada del monte* from the center there
are four churches on the left:
   S. Bernardino (now Oratorio di Sta. Chiara; an early
      fifteenth-century chapel with a large octagonal church
      alongside begun in 1451)
   S. Thomaso (thirteenth-century church and cloister re-
      modeled about 1430; deconsecrated and partly de-
      stroyed)
   S. Catarina (a modest church and cloister begun in 1292
      and rebuilt on a larger scale in 1625, with a façade of
      1672)
   Ogni Santi (church and cloister begun in 1292; the
      cloister was rebuilt in 1698, and the church was
      destroyed).
At the end of the *Strada di S. Silvestro* along the walls:
   S. Silvestro (a twelfth-century church remodeled in 1568;
      it is not clear whether the façade shown in the plan is
      the original or the Renaissance one. The campanile
      shown here was destroyed in 1809).

CAMPO MARZO (Fig. 1)

The area of the *Campo Marzo dove si fanno la fiera* to the
southwest was kept free of buildings. Access is by a ruined
arch (Roman?) at the Castello, and the Campo itself con-
tains only a monumental column topped by a cross and a
structure that can be identified with the since destroyed
'Cavallerizza', the stables of an aristocratic equestrian
society.[8]
West of the Campo Marzo, outside the bend of the
Retrone river:
   Lazaretto S. Lazaro (destroyed); judging from the posi-
      tion, a hospital for communicable diseases.
Above the road south from the hospital:
   Sasso di (illegible)[9]; a grotto.
On the hill (Monte Berico) overlooking the Campo
Marzo:
   S. Maria del Monte (Gothic church of 1428 with additions
      of 1479–80 by Lorenzo da Bologna, overshadowed in
      1688–1703 by the monumental Santuario of Carlo
      Borrella, which replaced a basilica designed in 1576 by
      Palladio, of which nothing appears here).

8. Arnaldi, *et al.*, *op. cit.*, pp. 43 f. and unnumbered plate.
9. The name is decipherable on the original, but I neglected to
   transcribe it in Rome.

On the *Strada che va a Verona*, just north of the Campo Marzo (Figs. 1, 6):

Porta del Castello

Giardino del Valmarana, a large formal Renaissance garden divided into parterres, with a central tempietto, since destroyed, that might have been designed by Palladio (now Giardino Salvi; designed for Count Giacomo Valmarana in 1552; the loggia built for Leonardo Valmarana in *c*. 1592 is not shown)

S. Buovo (Bovo; Fig. 6, top center; fourteenth-century, deconsecrated in 1774)

S. Nicola (oratorio built in 1505, remodeled 1617–18; façade of 1676)

S. Martino (destroyed).

South of the Verona road, the large monastic complex of:

S. Felice (SS. Felice e Fortunato, an important fourth- and fifth-century martyrium rebuilt in the Romanesque period with a portal of 1158 and a campanile of 1166 crowned in the fourteenth century. The three-arched Renaissance portico shown on the plan was removed for the construction of a Baroque façade that was destroyed in turn during the restoration of 1935–1939).[10]

The church of San Valentino, erected on the Verona road in 1584, does not appear.

WESTERN QUARTER (Fig. 6)

The quarter is bounded by the Bacchiglione river on the east and by a moat and fortifications extending from the river at a right angle at the huge medieval *Rochetta* to parallel the Verona road.

The quarter is divided into blocks by five-plus streets running east and west, and two north and south. Starting at the east-west wall parallel to the Verona road, the street within the wall is unnamed; the next to the north is *Cantarana* (now Contrà del Quartiere and Via G. Bonotto; a name preserved in the modern Contrà Cantarane, which replaces the moat outside the inner city walls, now destroyed). The next street to the north is the *Borgo di Porta nova* (now Contrà Lodi), the western half of which becomes *Strada di S. Maria nova*. At the foot of this street:

S. Maria nova (cloister begun in 1539; the church shown here [of the same date?] was rebuilt starting in 1585 and consecrated in 1606 or 1616).

The next street, *Strada di S. Rocho* (now Contrà S. Rocco) terminates at the wall in:

S. Rocho (church started in 1485, possibly by Lorenzo da Bologna; cloister in 1479; still under construction in 1530; façade of 1530, apparently on an earlier design; the crown of the campanile is of the later sixteenth century).

Paralleling the westernmost portion of this street is the *Strada del Corpo di Xp̄o* (now Contrà Corpus Domini), terminating in:

Corpo di Xp̄o (remodeled in 1584, since destroyed).

The northernmost street, which splits into three branches in the westernmost portion, is the *Strada del Carmine che va a S. Croce* (now Corso Fogazzaro and Contrà Porta Sta Croce) which terminates at:

S. Croce (a large monastic complex of the twelfth century, rebuilt in the eighteenth century).

Adjoining the northern fortifications of the quarter near the bend of the Bacchiglione (Fig. 3, far right):

S. Maria di Carmine (church and cloister founded in 1372 with fifteenth-century additions, reduced in size in the eighteenth century and regothicized in 1862–67).

The broad street running north and south in the center of the western quarter is the *Strada della porta di S. felice* (now Contrà Porta Nova; S. Ambrogio; Giovanni Busaro). The street parallel to it, joining Sta. Croce to the *Rochetta* (now Contrà Mura S. Rocco; Mura Corpus Domini), is not named.

SUMMARY

An analysis of the history of the identified buildings provides a preliminary basis for dating the plan. A *terminus post quem* is established by the appearance of the Cathedral cupola and lantern, designed in 1567.[11] The *terminus ante* is established by the absence of the new Santuario di Monte Berico, begun in 1576, and of San Valentino, 1584, Supporting this evidence are buildings appearing here that were destroyed in the 1580's: Santa Maria delle Grazie, replaced in 1580; the Ospizio della Misericordia, remodeled 1584–1594; and Santa Maria Nuova, rebuilt in 1585. Finally, the crowning pinnacles of the Cathedral, shown here, collapsed in 1581. The period of the plan, then, appears to be limited to the span 1567–1576/80; it can be reduced greatly by the study of the representation of Palladio's buildings in the following section.

The date matches the only document of the period relating to the preparation of a city plan of Vicenza. On 6th April 1580, a secretary of Pope Gregory XIII wrote to the government of Vicenza to request a plan to be used as a model for one of the topographical frescoes being planned by Egnatio Danti for the Galleria delle Carte Geografiche in the Vatican.[12] Since the city plans in this series all were bird's-eye views, it was understood that this kind of a drawing was

---

10. G. Lorenzon, *La basilica di SS. Felice e Fortunato in Vicenza*, Vicenza, 1937. The portico is represented in an intarsia panel in the church of Sta. Corona.

11. This evidence is affected by the draughtsman's readiness to complete buildings that were in progress at the time, such as the Basilica; but the cupola, whether finished or not, cannot have been pictured before it was designed.

12. G. Fasolo has published the relevant documents in a discussion of sixteenth-century plans of Vicenza and its province ('Notizie di arte e di storia vicentina', *Archivio veneto*, XXII, 1938, pp. 294 ff., cited by Almagià, *loc. cit.*).

required. The request from Rome was preceded by an earlier one, since a document of 1579 indicates that the plan requested already had been prepared:

> Adì X Dicembre 1579 diedi un scudo a maestro Batista Pittoni miniatore a bon conto della copia del disegno della città nostra essendomi così stato ordinato dalli Mag. Sig. Deputati per mandarlo a Roma.[13]

That the plan in the Angelica is the one sent in 1580 is probable. The rough frescoed plan in the Galleria is a poor copy,[14] either of this drawing or of another version taken from the same source. Its orientation is identical, as well as its format and coverage. All the differences in the Galleria plan are due to careless copying or a misunderstanding of the original (e.g. the Campo Marzo is represented as if it were the lower slope of Monte Berico). The fact that the Angelica plan is squared for enlargement reinforces the impression that it was the one employed by Danti, as does its presence in a Roman ecclesiastical library. Finally, the stature of the copyist, Pittoni, would explain the high quality of the draftsmanship.

If this conclusion is correct, the Angelica plan must have been drawn before 1579; this is not to say, however, that it was prepared specifically for the papal commission, because the document refers to the plan sent to Rome as a copy of an existing plan.

THE BUILDINGS OF PALLADIO

One of the most valuable aspects of the plan for Renaissance scholars is its documentation on Palladio's career in Vicenza. The buildings he designed prior to his departure for Venice in 1570/71 not only are clearly delineated in their original form, but are given special attention by the draftsman, who drew them larger than life, and in greater detail than any other non-religious structures.

CASA CIVENA (Figs. 2, 7: no. 1). Palladio's earliest urban work (1540–46),[15] appears in the south corner of the inner town, just to the left of the bridge designated *ponte furo*, overlooking the Retrone river. It is shown from the rear, rising higher than its neighbors. The two-storey elevation has three arches on piers facing an ample formal garden with parterres, broader than the house itself, and a window over each arch; there are chimneys at the ends of the gable roof.

The elevation does not conform closely to the existing house, which has a three-arched columnar portico bay at

the center flanked by two projecting wall bays on either side, one of which projects farther than the other. Yet the drawing has documentary value. It suggests that the original garden façade was narrower by two bays than the existing one, and this impression is strengthened by the modern plan,[16] which shows the projecting outer bays as structurally independent from the core (there is not even a connection between the southern one and the rest of the house), and entirely unpalladian in design. Probably Palladio planned a T-shaped building with a five-bay street façade the two outer bays of which were to be only one room in depth, and a three-bay garden façade to which the present projecting outer bays were added at a later date by another architect.[17]

PALAZZO THIENE (designed 1545–50; Figs. 7, 8: no. 2)[18] appears on the plan two blocks north of the *Piazza Maggiore*, substantially in its present form. Only one corner of the grandiose project illustrated in the *Quattro libri* was completed: four of the seven court bays on the north and east, the corresponding portion of the street façade on the east, and the projecting corner block of the northern façade. The northern wing encompasses a late fifteenth-century palace by Lorenzo da Bologna, the façade of which shows clearly on the plan.

There are inscriptions celebrating the completion of the eastern block in 1556 and of the northern block in 1558. The plan, however, gives the impression that the latter is still unfinished: the draftsman shows the roof of the northern block one-half storey lower than that of the eastern block; its peak is at the level of the second-story arches of the court. Either the arches on the north had not been executed at this time (the 1558 inscription is on the course separating the groundfloor court arcade from the second story) or the artist lowered the roof simply to clarify his description by revealing the court.

THE BASILICA (1549–; Figs. 7, 8: no. 3),[19] on the south edge of the *Piazza Maggiore*, appears in its present form, though the artist cannot have seen it as he drew it. The arches of the upper story were started only in 1564, after a new model by Palladio, and only four were finished by 1570 when the war against the Turks halted construction.

13. *Ibid.*, p. 295, from the Vicenza archive, *Libro provigioni*, 1575–80, c. 687; the writer is Filippo Pigafetta. Giovanni Battista Pittoni (1520–83) was a distinguished Vicentine engraver and miniaturist who published a book on Roman antiquities in 1561 and was therefore in Rome at the time when the technique of the bird's-eye plan was being perfected there (see note 3).

14. *Ibid.*, pl. VIII; Almagià, *op. cit.*, pl. XXXIX.

15. G. G. Zorzi, *Le opere pubbliche e i palazzi privati di Andrea Palladio*, Venice, 1965, pp. 183 ff. (hereafter cited as 'Zorzi 1965').

16. Zorzi 1965, pl. III (from a survey of 1940).

17. The later builder may have known that Palladio considered projecting outer bays in his preparatory drawings (Zorzi 1965, figs. 145–148).

18. A contract of 1542 (referring to Palladio as a mason) for the building of the palace, and the interior decorations by Vittoria, who left Vicenza in 1553, are the grounds for dating the design (Zorzi 1965, pp. 204–213). I share Zorzi's opinion that the palace contracted for in 1542 was not started, and that the family commissioned a new design somewhat later; R. Cevese supports the early date (*I palazzi dei Thiene sede della Banca Popolare di Vicenza*, Vicenza, 1952).

19. Zorzi 1965, pp. 43–75, esp. p. 50. An excellent monograph by F. Barbieri is awaiting publication by the Centro internazionale di storia dell'Architettura in Vicenza.

The contract for a second group of four arches was signed in 1572, but they were not completed by 1585, when another contract was signed. The façade on the *Piazza Maggiore* must have been completed as we see it here by *c.* 1590, a decade after Palladio's death. The building was completed in 1617.

Sixteenth-century cartographers frequently completed structures in progress when this could be done simply by carrying on motives already initiated. The draftsman here finished the Basilica because there was no question of how construction would continue, and because it would be impossible at this scale convincingly to draw partly-built arches and vaults hidden by scaffolding. He chose not to do the same for Palazzo Thiene and other palaces because they were not in progress; construction had been permanently abandoned.

THE PALAZZO CHIERICATI (1550–; Figs. 7, 8: no. 4),[20] facing the *Isola dove fal marcato di Animali e di legne*, is shown in the truncated condition in which it remained prior to the late-seventeenth century, when the major part was completed according to Palladio's design. An inscription discovered during the recent restoration indicates that by 1552 the three columnar bays comprising the south wing of the façade were almost finished. In 1570 Valerio, the son of the original owner Girolamo Chiericati, was living in the completed portion; an inventory made at his death in 1609 shows that in addition to the southern façade loggia only a part of one bay of the central block had been finished, including one window of the central *salone* of the upper story. A temporary gallery connected the unfinished *salone* with the rooms on the south side (which were finished on both stories) and with the old houses on the nothern end of the property, which had not yet been demolished, and which appear in our plan. Inigo Jones, when he visited Vicenza, confirmed the fact that only the southern wing had risen much above the foundations.[21]

The documents are confirmed by our plan, which shows a tower-like block representing the loggia of the southern wing. Behind the loggia, however, the construction has reached only the height of one story, which is roofed. At this time, then, Valerio Chiericati had only three new rooms in his palace; these were decorated during the 1550's, notably by the painter Zelotti and the sculptor Ridolfi. It would be interesting to know how the decorations were protected when the roof was removed to raise the upper story.

There is one anomaly in the drawing: the north front of the loggia as shown in the plan is drawn with arches on both stories, a balcony and crowning obelisks (later re-placed by statues) designed for the completed lateral façade; but this front, which was to abut the central block of the façade, should appear as a party-wall with columns carrying a lintel on the ground floor and a doorway in a plain wall above. Undoubtedly the artist, wishing to give an impression of Palladio's design, transferred to the north the completed *southern* front of the loggia, which looks just as it appears here.[22]

It is important for the criticism of Palladio's design and siting of the palace that it was not conceived as a unit in an enclosed square as we see it today, but on a formless market-place, and that the upper loggia would have provided a view over the fortifications onto the river.

THE PALAZZO ISEPPO PORTO (before 1552–; Figs. 7, 8: no. 5),[23] on Contrà Porti, the street running north from the center of the Basilica to the *Porta Pusterla*, is shown from the rear, with its northern and court façades. Palladio completed only the front block of this palace; he had intended to place an identical block on the street behind, and to join the two by a court in the form of a Roman peristyle with colossal columns. The court façade appears on the plan as it is today,[24] seven bays wide with a large central arch on the ground floor (the draftsman omitted one window on either side of the arch, and the row of smaller mezzanine windows at the level of the keystone). At some later time (nineteenth century?), the court was framed by a low arcade on either side, abutting the outer-most groundfloor windows. There is no garden behind the palace; perhaps the family still hoped to realize Palladio's scheme.

THE PALAZZO VALMARANA (1555/6–; Figs. 7, 8: no. 7)[25] unfortunately appears at an angle that reveals nothing of interest. Only the street front, the court façade behind it, and a portion of the southern wing was completed. We see the roof and the side façade on the northwest and the upper story of the street façade, on which the artist had room to sketch only three of the seven windows. A view of the court is blocked by an intervening dwelling; the tower of the church of S. Giacomo appears at the rear of the court.

THE PALAZZO SCHIO-ANGARAN (before 1566; Figs. 3, 7 no. 8)[26] appears on the *Borgo di Pusterla* as the second building on the west side of the street between the river and the church of S. Marco. It is drawn from the rear, with a four-arched loggia alongside the garden or court. As Palladio appears in the documents as the author only of a design for the street façade of an existing house (probably mid-sixteenth century), the view is of peripheral interest.

20. F. Barbieri, 'Il palazzo Chiericati sede del Museo Civico di Vicenza', *Il Museo Civico di Vicenza*, Vicenza, 1961, I, pp. 9–62; Zorzi 1965, pp. 196–204, and figs. 188–202.
21. Quoted by Zorzi 1965, p. 200, from Jones' notes on Palladio's *Quattro libri* (still unpublished).
22. Zorzi, 1965, fig. 200. The artist has put a recessed panel above the arch of the upper loggia which does not exist.
23. Zorzi 1965, pp. 187–195.
24. *Ibid.*, fig. 174.
25. *Ibid.*, pp. 247–253, figs. 298–312.
26. *Ibid.*, pp. 290–294, figs. 361–367.

THE PALAZZO MONTANO BARBARAN (1569/70-; Figs. 7, 8: no. 9)[27] appears at the corner of Contrà Porti and Contrà Riale, facing the fifteenth-century rear façade of Palazzo Thiene. Only the two bays of the northern façade with their two orders of half-columns now facing the Contrà Riale are shown. The viewpoint reveals the southern and western limits of the court; the loggias with two orders of free-standing columns that now border the court on the southern and part of the eastern side do not appear; apparently they were not yet built. This is not surprising, since they are not a feature of Palladio's project published in the *Quattro libri* (Book II, pp. 22 f.) or of the earlier drawings for the palace in London.[28] None of these plans shows construction on the south side of the court because, as Palladio says, the client was unable to buy the requisite property. He adds, however, that the property was finally purchased in time to revise the plan to provide 'l'istesso ordine in tutte e due le parti', but not in time to change the woodcut plan prepared for the publication of the *Quattro libri* in 1570, and he says that the foundations were laid at the time of writing (1569?). In a document of 31st March 1570, Montano Barbaran asks the Consiglio Maggiore for permission to close the *strata comunis Rialis* during the construction of the 'fabricam quam facere intendit'.

The construction must have proceeded rapidly, because there is no evidence in the Angelica plan of Palladian or other structures started after 1570. But given the fact that the artist altered the views of the Basilica and of Pal. Chiericati to give a better image of Palladio's intention, it is possible that the Barbaran façade, which appears finished, was actually in an earlier stage of construction. The possibility that the artist 'completed' an unfinished elevation is strengthened by the fact that he made mistakes in the upper portion, omitting the low attic story and showing the slanting hip roof as if it terminated in a gable on the plane of the façade.

THE SITES OF FUTURE BUILDINGS
BY PALLADIO

On the site of the LOGGIA DEL CAPITANIATO (1571-72; Figs. 7, 8: no. 10) the plan shows a tower belonging to the palace of the Capitano (the governor appointed by the Venetian Republic) and, beyond it, structures with sloping roofs. Alongside appears an arch, since dismantled, spanning the present Via Cavour. Whether the sloping roofs are part of the palace or the earlier, fourteenth-century *lodia magna* remodeled before 1521 by Scarpagnino is uncertain; in any event, Palladio's loggia is not shown.[29]

The decision to build a new loggia was made by the city Council in January 1565, but no action was taken; in April 1571 the Council considered the testimony of experts that the old loggia was in danger of imminent collapse, and appropriated 300 Ducats to be used either for restoration or for a new structure. Documents of August 1571 refer to work on the Palladian building; it was reported to be nearly finished in October, but public funds were diverted to further construction in May 1572.[30] There is no record of how much longer the work continued. By the winter of 1571-72, then, the Loggia would have advanced far enough to be represented if the plan had been drawn after this date. Thus the Loggia offers decisive negative evidence for dating the plan prior to this time.

The site of the TEATRO OLIMPICO (1580-; Figs. 7, 8: no. 11) is a block of structures facing the *Isola* behind Santa Corona. The portion facing the Isola is labled *Pregion vecchie* and that to the rear *Munition*; the high wall surrounding the compound has arched portals on the south and west.

The land for the theatre was ceded by the city to the Accademia Olimpica in February 1580.[31] Palladio placed the theatre at the northern end of the site, within the arsenal, and used the structures on the side toward the river for anterooms and an entrance. Much of the prison court was preserved in the rebuilding.

On the site of the unfinished PAL. (Alessandro) PORTO-BREGANZE (posthumous; Figs. 2, 7: no. 12) on the Piazza di Castello, there is an unprepossessing two-story house. This palace and Palladio's authorship is undocumented, except that Vincenzo Scamozzi listed it among the buildings he had 'finished' with some alteration.[32] But the

that Palladio altered the design of the lateral façade to celebrate the victory of Lepanto after October 1571.

30. The claim in a document of October 1571 that the 'fabrica della loggia . . . è ridotta talmente a buoni termini . . . che alla festa di S. Martino (11 Nov.) sarà in coperta' (Zorzi, document 9) is difficult to credit; buildings of this size were not completed in three months in the Renaissance; furthermore, construction was still in progress in May 1572, after which there is a gap of a decade in the records. But the work must have been nearly finished in that year, because the painter Giovanni Antonio Fasolo, who died in 1572, was called to do the interior frescoes.

31. L. Puppi, *Il Teatro Olimpico*, Vicenza, 1963, pp. 44 f.

32. V. Scamozzi, *Idea dell'architettura universale*, Venice, 1615, I, iii, p. 266; Scamozzi's failure to mention Palladio is not significant; he was so envious of his predecessor that the name does not appear in his book, and he went so far as to attribute the design of Villa Barbaro in Maser to its owner, Daniele Barbaro (Zorzi 1965, pp. 287 f.).

The court of the palace was to have terminated in a unique hemicycle, evidence of which still is preserved in the slight curvature of the southernmost of the five surviving half columns The hemicycle is reconstructed by Bertotti Scamozzi in his plates of 1786 (Zorzi, fig. 359), but the evidence for it was missed by Muttoni when he sketched the remains (Zorzi, fig. 358) and even by the modern surveyor (Zorzi, pl. XII). The survey plans are concerned only with the interior disposition, and Zorzi was

27. *Ibid.*, pp. 253-260, figs. 313-315; 318-332.
28. *Ibid.*, fig. 313.
29. *Ibid.*, pp. 109-124. R. Wittkower (*Architectural Principles in the Age of Humanism*, rev. ed., London, 1962, pp. 88 f.) proposes

conception is so much in harmony with Palladio's work of the 1570's that the traditional attribution has been accepted by most modern critics. The Angelica plan supports the impression based on evidence of style that the palace is at least as late as the Loggia del Capitaniato.

EVIDENCE ON BUILDINGS ATTRIBUTED TO PALLADIO

The CASA COGOLLO (1559-; Figs. 7, 8: no. 6), misnamed the 'House of Palladio', is difficult to identify on the plan. The existing house faces the *strada Maggiore* across from the Pal. Chiericati at a point where the plan shows a low gable-roofed structure on the corner across from the *Pregion vecchie* (Fig. 8: no. 11) and alongside it, the high wall of the cemetery of Sta. Corona. The draftsman may have meant the gabled building to represent the Casa Cogollo, which now is not at the corner of the block but is flanked on the east by a structure of indeterminate date;[33] or he may have overlooked it. In this case the evidence of the plan is inconclusive.

The construction of the house can be followed in documents; it was under way in 1559 but not yet complete in 1566/67.[34] In the record of 1559, Pietro Cogollo is required to erect a façade on his house within three years as a condition of retaining his Vicentine citizenship conferred in the same act. But there is no evidence that the requirement was fulfilled.[35] The façade of the present house is the only element of the design attributed to Palladio. The traditional attribution has been accepted by a majority of critics; I

share the opinion of Magagnato and Cevese that it is a school work; the proportions, detailing and overall composition do not measure up to the Palladian canon.[36]

The future site of the PAL. THIENE-BONIN LONGARE (Fig. 2,: A) opposite the Castello at the west end of the *strada Maggiore* appears surrounded by a wall on three sides and by small houses on the fourth (north) side. This situation accords nicely with a document of 1562[37] in which the owner, Orazio Thiene, asks the maggior consilio 'di serar un certo mio vacuo che è vicino alla mura del Castello et fin hora circumdatolo in bona parte'. At the same time, he asks permission to repair some of his houses along the moat 'sul canton di Stra', and to be given nine feet of the public street within the walls 'per poter tirar il muro dritto al triangolo che va a retta linea a pontar nel mio muro'. The 'triangolo' appears to be the angle (the canton di Stra?) of fortification just to the east of the Castello tower, and the houses referred to must be those flanking the tower. Orazio's purpose is 'lo abellimento della facciata del Cantone'.[38]

The date and attribution of the palace erected in the 'vacuo' is contested. Pane and Zorzi have given it to Palladio; Barbieri and Cevese to Scamozzi, placing it in the first decade of the seventeenth century, an opinion which I share.[39] Zorzi dates the palace 1571-72 on the grounds that Orazio Thiene returned to Vicenza from a mission in 1570. He also publishes without comment a document of 1572 concerning the division of property between Orazio and Francesco Thiene, which mentions a house assigned to Orazio 'apud viam comunis principalem' on the south and 'apud viam qua itur ad pontem nuncupatum delle belle ed ad hospetale san Marcelli' (the street flanking the *Hospital di S. Marcello*) on the north – a description that takes in the entire block by the Castle. There are two reasons for believing that the document does not refer to the present Pal. Thiene: first, the house is designated 'cum curte de ante et de retro et viridario veteri muris clauso' (the present palace has no forecourt); and second, another house, assigned to Francesco, is described with a 'viam publicam

---

misled by these errors into rejecting Bertotti's reconstruction. The error is noted also in R. Cevese's review (*Bollettino del Centro Internazionale di Storia dell'Architettura*, VI, 1964, p. 356).

33. The details are eighteenth-century, but the structure could be earlier.

34. Zorzi 1965, pp. 232-239.

35. *Ibid.* (pp. 233 f. and document 5) makes the assumption that Cogollo already had a house on this site in May 1559 on which the new façade was to be added, and that the construction referred to from June 1559 through 1567 was an addition to this house. However, the documents do not mention additions; that of June 1559 (doc. 3) begins: 'Intendendo io Pietro Cogollo voler fabricare una mia casa . . . in la contrà de S.ta Corona apresso la via comune et apresso la scola di S. Maria de la Misericordia di S. Corona . . .' (the following statements show that construction had begun). Possibly the house to be embellished by a façade in three years 'contractae Sanctae Coronae contra domum q. Augustini de Colzade', was another in which Cogollo lived while building the new one; though it was in the same block, it is designated as being alongside the Colzade house, while further documents refer to the house being built alongside the School of the Misericordia (the structure the roof of which appears on the east side of the cemetery?). Zorzi's proposal that the façade was completed by 1564, when litigation occurred over the estimates for stone-cutting (doc. 4, from A. dalla Pozza, *Palladio*, Vicenza, 1943, p. 150, doc. xiv) is unacceptable; the document does not specify either how the stones were to be used, or that they had been used at the time.

36. L. Magagnato, in *Guida*, pp. 158 f.; R. Cevese, *op. cit.*, in note 32, pp. 351 f.

37. Zorzi 1965, pp. 277 f. and document 1.

38. Our plan permits a correction of Zorzi's interpretation of the document (*loc. cit.*) in which the 'Canton di Strà' is identified as the *strada maggiore* (Corso Palladio) and the 'façade and angle to be beautified' as a cluster of houses on the site of the present Pal. Thiene. There were no houses on the site prior to the construction of the palace.

39. R. Pane, *Andrea Palladio*, Turin, 1961, pp. 359 f.; Zorzi 1965, *loc. cit.* (based on his 'Due rivendicazioni palladiani', *Arte veneta*, VI, 1952, pp. 130-135; he attributed only the side façade to Scamozzi); F. Barbieri in *Guida*, 1956, pp. 19 f.; R. Cevese, *op. cit.*, pp. 354 f. Scamozzi, who lists the palace among those he 'finished according to my design', indicated that he took over a building that had been started for Francesco Thiene and finished for Enea, Orazio's son (*op. cit.*, I, iii, p. 266).

versus septentrionem supradictum cum viridario novo muris circumdato', very likely the 'vacuo' walled in after 1562 (hence 'novo'). If my analysis is correct, the palace would have been commissioned by Francesco Thiene, as Scamozzi said, at some time before his death in 1593, and have passed to Orazio's son Enea, who completed it before Scamozzi wrote in 1613. Zorzi's arguments for the date 1571–72 and for Palladio's authorship, based on documents indicating close contacts between the architect and Orazio, are therefore open to question.[40]

CONCLUSION

The evidence of Palladio's buildings is decisive for dating the plan, which shows all the buildings designed before,

and none after the publication of the *Quattro libri* in 1570. It post-dates the design if not the full realization of the Pal. Montano Barbaran in 1569/70, and predates the completion of the Loggia del Capitaniato in 1571/72.[41] Nothing in the representation of the other buildings in Vicenza appears to contradict this conclusion.

For the study of Palladio's Vicentine work, the principal function of the plan is in substantiating a number of conclusions that previously had been only inferred. It demands no changes in the established chronology, and it sustains doubts about Palladio's authorship of the lateral wings of the rear façade of Casa Civena, the court loggia of the Pal. Barbaran and the Pal. Thiene–Bonin Longare. But because it vividly brings to life the ambience of Cinquecento Vicenza, its documentary function is overshadowed by its value as an image of a complete urban organism – perhaps the finest existing record of its kind of a provincial Renaissance town.

40. Zorzi (1965, pp. 282 ff.) has attempted to add to Palladio's *œuvre* a palace for Giuliano and Guido Piovene (built in the early 1570's; destroyed in 1818) that faced the Isola on one side and the banks of the Bacchiglione on the other, and may have replaced or have adjoined the group of buildings on this site in our plan (Fig. 4, right center). The basis of the attribution is the presumed similarity of Palladio's design for a palace façade in the Museo Civico in Vicenza to two eighteenth-century representations of the palace: the dell'Acqua plan and an anonymous engraving of 1711. Although both designs employ the colossal order, I do not find the parallels convincing (not does Cevese,

op. cit., p. 356, who even questions the authorship of the drawing, which I believe to be autograph).

41. In the extremely unlikely event that a structure as important as the Loggia was inadvertently omitted by the artist, or allowed to be obscured by intervening structures, the date of the plan could still be determined within the decade preceding 1579 according to the evidence cited on pp. 56 f.

E. H. GOMBRICH

Celebrations in Venice of the Holy League and of the Victory of Lepanto

IN his article on El Greco's *Dream of Philip II*, one of his first major contributions to the *Journal of the Warburg and Courtauld Institutes*,[1] Anthony Blunt had occasion to occupy himself with the works of art celebrating the Holy League and its sadly impermanent achievement, the Victory of Lepanto. I therefore hope that this little offering may be acceptable to him, though it does not add much to what was known at the time when he wrote. The main interest to art historians of the five texts to which I want to draw attention[2] lies less, perhaps, in the iconography of the pageants themselves, than in the role assigned to paintings in two of them. But beyond this historical evidence, the general question of the relation between the iconography of pageants and that of painting may prove of potential interest.

I

Il Bellissimo et Sontuoso Trionfo fatto nella Magnifica Città di Venetia nella publicatione della Lega; . . . et appresso alcuni avisi di Famagosta, e di Candia, 1571.[3]

This famous procession on the occasion of the announcement of the formation of the League was much publicized. There exists both a French and a German translation of the pamphlet;[4] there is also an anonymous print (Fig. 1) claiming to show the procession.[5] It is true that on closer scrutiny this print does not inspire much confidence. Not only is the Palazzo Ducale represented – with remarkable licence – as a Romanesque building, but two processions are shown wending their way through the crowd of on-lookers in a manner which would certainly have resulted in a traffic jam. One procession issues from the Palazzo Ducale and returns to the Basilica of San Marco, the other is leaving San Marco to march towards the Merceria. But it is possible to make out in the foreground some of the allegorical representations which are described in our pamphlet, which is dated 6th July 1571.

Its first part describes the procession after the service at San Marco:

> Tutte le scole grandi, una à gara dell'altra, si sono sforzate di fare bellissima, e ricca mostra di argentarie et ori, ma io ne dirò de una sola, la quale oltra le argentarie, ha fatto molti tribunali, sopra de quali erano diversi giovani, che facevano diverse cose.

Unfortunately we are not told which of the *Scuole* arranged these dumbshows, which simply and effectively explained and anticipated the purpose of the League. The first platform (*tribunale*) showed the *Gran Turco* as a huge dragon with a crescent on its head, which three richly clad youths pierced with their swords; it is possible to make out the dragon in the bottom left foreground of the print where, apparently, the three youths are shown on the platform in front. It is easier to recognize the second *tableau*, in which three youths were dressed as the three Theological Virtues, Faith, Hope and Charity, alluding no doubt also to the three members of the League. According to the description, the next three *tribunali* showed these members – the Pope, King Philip II and the Doge – singly. Judging by the print, these rulers were accompanied by other figures paying homage. Perhaps Neptune, so clearly visible here, personified Venice. The print does not show clearly what is described as the fifth *tableau*, which adds the most interesting touch to an otherwise fairly conventional display. It showed the three members of the League together:

> cioè il Papa in habito Pontificale, il Re Filippo in habito Regale, et il Doge in habito Dogale; et questi tre giovani havevano le mascare fatte a similitudine di quel tale che rappresentavano.

The introduction of 'live portraits' strongly suggests the participation of an artist. If only we had a right to surmise that the *Scuola* concerned was that of San Rocco, we could let our imagination run further. It would not be hard to

1. Vol. III, 1939–40, pp. 58–69.
2. Four of them (my I, III, IV and V) are to be found in a miscellaneous volume in the Library of Printed Books of the British Museum (1071.g.7) entitled, somewhat inaccurately, *Poemetti varii*, 1549–1656. Some 24 of its 96 numbers are pamphlets concerned with events before and after the battle of Lepanto, including some not listed in Emmanueli Antonio Cicogna, *Saggio di Bibliografia Veneziana*, Venice, 1847 which does, however, list those discussed here except no. IV.
3. Brit. Mus. 1071.g.7/9.
4. The French translation, published in Lyons in 1571, is in the British Museum Library (C.128.e.4). What is obviously a German translation of the same pamphlet is listed in Katalog 70, of the J. Halle Antiquariat, Munich, 1929 (*Neue Zeitungen*) no. 426.
5. I should like to thank Miss Jennifer Fletcher, who traced for me a copy of this print (which is listed in Cicogna, *loc. cit.*) in the Museo Correr. She also found that it was copied in an amended and generalized form in the series *Habiti d'homini et donne veneziane con la processione della Serma Signoria et altri particolari* etc., by Giacomo Franco.

imagine the additional *tribunali* in terms of Tintoretto's imagery, for one showed a mountain in which arms were forged (faintly visible on the print), while in the next coins were struck. More obscure was a reed hut (*uno tigurio fatto de canelli*) with two turning wheels outside, which seemed to pull the hut along as if it were a cart.[6] One large wheel can just be seen on the print where the procession turns the corner. On the print these three had been overtaken by the group which is described as the last one, displaying a bark rowed by a naked moor with wings and horns to signify Charon carrying off a Turk. The remaining description of the splendid procession which followed is too general to merit quotation. And greater splendours were to follow when, three months later, after the fearful slaughter of Lepanto, victory seemed a reality.

II

Ragguaglio delle Allegrezze, Solennità, e feste, fatte in Venetia per la felice Vittoria, al Clariss. Sig. Girolamo Diedo, digniss. Consigliere di Corfù (signed by Rocco Benedetti), Venice, 1571.[7]

This pamphlet (which has been used by historians of Venice, but somewhat inaccurately as far as its art historical information is concerned),[8] is by a writer of some skill[9] who witnessed the arrival of the good tidings in Venice on 9th October, two days after the battle, and who covers the events up to 20th November, the date of his letter. He vividly describes the solemn thanksgiving services in San Marco with their beautiful music, the official speeches in honour of the fallen, and the public rejoicings which followed.

The initiative for independent celebrations came from the German merchants who were given permission to celebrate, '*fatte che fussero le solennità spirituali*'. The interpretation of this restriction was obviously fairly lax, for what they did was to decorate the *Fondaco dei Tedeschi* with tapestries and to illuminate it with torches and lights, playing music and letting off fireworks for three nights in succession. Their example caught on, and a competition developed between various quarters in arranging celebrations, one for instance being held in Canareggio under the very eyes of the Turks in order to annoy them. But the main body of Benedetti's letter is concerned with the wonders and splendours of the celebrations organized by the *Drappieri* on the island and bridge of the Rialto.

The bridge, of course, was then still a wooden structure, and the street markets and wooden booths which filled the area on the northern bank were considered rather an eyesore, a situation which Sansovino's *Fabriche Nuove* were intended to alleviate.[10] It must have been all the more impressive, though, to see this busy quarter transformed into the proverbial fairy palace by relatively simple, though surely expensive means, with the help of tapestries, buntings, standards, canopies and lanterns. Benedetti, understandably, is more concerned with the psychological effect of these displays than with their accurate description. He is touching and amusing in his enthusiastic account of the throngs of beautiful women and of the good-natured crowds who came to see the illuminations. No one was too morose to feel joy, no husband was too jealous to take his wife to see the show, no dignitary so grand as to feel it a dishonour to show himself there. Even pickpockets, we are told, abstained from plying their trade. The really interesting part for the art historian in the factual description is Benedetti's account of the open air exhibition of masterpieces which formed part of this display:

> Il portico della Drapperia è di tramito dritto cento e più passa, e le Botteghe seguono per ordine una dietro l'altra. Stesero da un capo all'altro un cielo di panni turchini con stelle, et altri ornamenti. V'appesero sotto molti honorevoli lanternoni, ò diciamo fanali dorati. Le Botteghe, i muri, i banchi, e le colonne del portico furono tutte acconciate di sontuose tappezzarie. Ad ogni volto fù messo un festone. A torno tutte le fabriche nove della piazza dal ponte sino all'imboccar della Ruga de' Orefici, e cosi da l'altra parte si tirorono panni fini scarlati, e vi s'attacarono sopra con equali distantie bellissime pitture d'imprese, di Dei marini, e d'altri Dei favolosi. S'adornò poi ciascuna bottega d'armi, di spoglie, e di trofei di nemici presi nella battaglia, e di quadri maravigliosi di Giovan Bellino, di Giorgion da Castel Franco, di Raffael d'Urbino, del Pordenone, di Sebastianello, di Titiano, del Bassanese miracoloso in pingere cose pastorali, e di molti altri eccellentissimi pittori.
>
> S'adornò parimente il parangone con le sue botteghe, ch'è come V.S. Clarissima sa, un calle poco manco lungo del portico. S'adornarono anco tutte le botteghe del ponte da una banda, e da l'altra, e tutte l'altre botteghe d'intorno la piazza. Drizzossi à pe del ponte un'eminente portone, e da l'altro capo verso i Orefici un'altro, sopra i quali erano le armi di Collegati, cioè quella di sua Santità nel mezzo, quella della Maestà del Re Catholico alla destra, e quella di San Marco alla sinistra. Si spiegaro

6. Reed huts were sometimes shown as the dwellings of the first inhabitants of Venice.

7. Brit Mus. 1313.c.47.

8. It is the main source of the account in Francesco Sansovino, *Venetia città nobilissima*, Book X (Venice, 1663, p. 415). This was used, in its turn, by P. Molmenti, *La storia di Venezia nella vita privata*, 4th ed., vol. II, Bergamo, 1906, p. 86. The pamphlet is also cited in Stirling Maxwell, *Don John of Austria*, London, 1883.

9. For Rocco Benedetti's other works see G. Mazzuchelli, *Gli scrittori d'Italia*, I, Brescia, 1753, s.v.

10. Roberto Cessi and Annibale Alberti, *Rialto*, Bologna, 1934, esp. pp. 122 ff.

in gran numero a tutti i volti, e balconi bandiere honoratissime, et in mezzo della piazza furono appesi alquanti stendardi di San Marco. Durò la festa tre giorni, e tre notti continue.

One would love to know whether the paintings displayed in this setting came from the collections of cloth merchants, or whether they were borrowed for the occasion. In any case the episode shows that by 1571 a painting by one of these masters would rank with golden vessels and other treasures as a luxury object, a proud possession which it was a privilege to own, and to be shown. The inclusion in this list of Giovanni Bellini's name suggests that the great ancestor of Venetian painting was part of the *canon*. The way, finally, *il Bassanese* is singled out for a special laudatory sentence is interesting, since it may indicate that his name was not expected to be as familiar to readers as that of the other great masters with whom he is coupled.[11] In addition, of course, the characterization of his skill in painting pastoral themes confirms, what is anyhow clear from the context, that these paintings by great masters were here exhibited not for the sake of their subject matter – religious or patriotic – but simply as treasure to enhance the splendour of the occasion.

Benedetti appears to have been so impressed by what may have been one of the first public exhibitions of great paintings that he does not mention any of the paintings done *ad hoc* for the occasion. Obviously there could have been very little time to produce such works, but if we are to believe another description of the same celebrations some paintings were commissioned to form part of the decorations – perhaps in connection with the triumphal arches flanking the bridge. They were possibly only in monochrome, as one of them is described in the next pamphlet as *una pittura in bianco e rosso*, recalling an under-painting.

III

Il vero e Mirabilissimo apparato over Conciero con il glorioso trionfo nell'inclita Città di Venetia, in Rivoalto celebrato, per i dignissimi, e integerrimi Merchanti Drappieri, in essaltatione de la Santa Fede. . . .[12]

This pamphlet of seven pages is unfortunately written in verse, by a poetaster who finds it hard enough to subject his panegyric to the discipline of his twenty-nine *stanze* in *ottave rime*. His tendency to fall into Venetian dialect and the frequency of misprints present the reader with problems of interpretation and emendation, possibly worthy of a better cause.[13] But we should not be too hard on our author. After all he wrote for people who had seen the display, rather than for posterity, and his readers were probably more eager for praise than for sober facts. Thus we are told predictably (and probably truthfully) that Apelles and Zeuxis would have been dumbfounded at the sight of the paintings shown, but it is not clear whether this praise refers to the exhibition (not otherwise mentioned), or to the decorations.

What we can gather is that crude satire of the type of popular woodcuts played its conspicuous part in the programme. On mounting the bridge one saw on the right the representation of a scene which also occurs in some of the other pamphlets published at the time – the renegade Karakosh who fought on the side of the Turks[14] is shown being received into hell where Charon (whom we have met before) refuses to ferry him across, for he would need a worse inferno for this *bestia*:[15]

12. Nel montar alla dritta si scopriva
     Quel manigoldo rinegato cane
     Caracossa, ché 'l ciel tanto abhoriva,
     E il mondo l'opre sue, tanto profane,
     Che da un che 'l mirava si stupiva
     Di modo tal, che le sue membra insane
     Eran rimase tronche in varii pezzi
     Nel mar, acciò mai più non se ne avezzi.

13. Pallido smorto e brutto un diavol pare,
     Proprio in vederlo par facci paura
     Chi vien si al vero vivo assimigliare
     Creggio ben che l'inferno e la natura
     Un'altro simil si peggior non fare
     Il pò; una si brutta creatura
     Pallido e smorto venne, e si stupiva
     Caronte in faccia, e d'odio il cor bolliva.

14. 'Chi è costui (ahimè) si empio ladro'
     Grida, e con furor la barcha caccia
     A l'altra riva in se 'si ben lo squadro'
     Disse costui, 'che ben l'ho visto in faccia

11. It may be significant that Francesco Sansovino, *op. cit.*, replaces his name on the list by that of Michelangelo, a most unlikely artist to figure in an exhibition of this kind. Consequently this relatively early reference to Jacopo Bassano has escaped the specialists. Jacopo's skill in painting animals had been mentioned by Vasari in 1568, but by 1571 he had not yet had more than two public commissions in Venice. Titian bought his large picture of the animals entering the ark (Madrid, Prado, No. 22) about that time. I am much indebted to Professor Roger Rearick who is preparing a study on the Bassanos for the above information.

12. Brit. Mus. 1071.g.7/87.

13. I confess to having troubled no fewer than six of my colleagues, all specialists in Renaissance studies, with these problems. If I do not mention them singly it is not for lack of gratitude but because I found that their opinions were so divergent that in the end I had to accept responsibility for the interpretation here presented.

14. Stirling Maxwell, *op. cit.*, I, 399, 408, 409, 416.

15. *Dialogo di Caracosa e Caronte, il quale gli nega il passo della sua barca, con due Barzelette nove sopra la vittoria de' Christiani* (No. 91 of the British Museum Miscellany); a *Sonetto in dialogo de Caracossa e Plutone* is contained in No. 83; another news bulletin from hell was apparently contained in the incomplete pamphlet No. 85 which has on its cover a crude woodcut of a devil carrying off a soul and of a man impaled.

E quel Giotton[16] che dal suo Athil abadro
Risona il traditor[17] o vil cagnaccia
Bestia, non menter sù, ch'un altro inferno
Peggior per te bisogna e fuoco eterno'.

15. Il miser con furor si crucia grida
Che l'eterna giustizia gli tormenta.
Caronta di passarlo non si fida,
Onde tra se ne geme, e si lamenta
'Anima ladra, tu sei tanto infida'
Disse, poi con furor al collo centa
S'attrova ardente tutta una cathena,
De ferro e fuoco, al fondo il caccia e mena.

On the left, probably opposite, one could see the picture of another renegade enemy, one who had actually got away with his contingent and who was still at large: the Turkish commander Ouloudji Ali, whom the Spaniards called Uchi Ali, and the Venetians nicknamed *Occhiali*.[18] The satirical picture was obviously based on his nickname for it showed him with staring eyes and with spectacles on his nose peering at 'that other heir of Christ'. Since the poet uses the same epithet in an earlier stanza for the Lion of St. Mark, that is for Venice, we may assume that the lion was shown and between the two figures a representation of Venice. However, the description here is again confused, and possibly garbled. Indeed the second stanza would be even harder to interpret, were it not for the fact that its motif also occurs in one of the contemporary pamphlets, '*Il grandissimo lamento che ha fatto Occhiali, nel scampo della sanguinosa guerra*'.[19] As in our description, the lament sounds serious enough, but it could only be put into the mouth of the enemy, for officially there was only rejoicing on the Christian side. Thus it must be Occhiali who was shown praying to his Mohammed to give him Argus eyes, to make his final getaway from the Christians.

16. Tal ivi alla sinistra appare in forma
Del ponte in alto L'occhiali, si vede
Gli occhi a sborriti, che non par che dorma,
Gli occhiali al naso e mira questa herede
Quella altra di Giesù, e la sua forma
Canina e giusta[20] – e tra se questa sede
Di Venetia, si degna, e si famosa,
Ch'al mondo sopra a l'altre e gloriosa.

17. Vede alle volte gli occhi allocio[21] gira
Di si brutta figura, par spavente
Dopo ripieno e acceso di tant'ira
Ch'el petto, il core, e gli occhi se ne sente

16. Giotton-Ghiottone, a glutton, a word of abuse.
17. This line is obscure.
18. Stirling Maxwell, I, 397.
19. No. 82 of the Miscellany.
20. I read: '*è la sua forma canina e giusta*', he is represented like a dog and rightly so.
21. '*Al luogo*'?

F

Poi pian ne geme, e piange, e ne suspira,
Che per un can sia morta tanta gente,[22]
Poi prega il suo Macon,[23] che gli occhi d'argo
Gli dia che a christian possa far largo.

If this description remains rather obscure the *stanze* devoted to the central image are unfortunately even more elusive and tantalizing. As far as one can penetrate through the rhetoric this was a painting in red and white representing the personification of Venice as Queen of the Seas. We are familiar with this type of allegorical composition from the ceiling paintings of the Palazzo Ducale, but the famous works by Paolo Veronese and Tintoretto which come to mind were all painted about ten years later, after the fire. It seems that *Venezia* as a personification first made her appearance in painting on the ceiling cycle of 1553/54,[24] but there she still lacked the religious connotations which the later programme developed with such fervour. Maybe the painting here apostrophized represented a stage along this road of apotheosis; admittedly it is not easy to disentangle in the *stanze* the author's praise of his city from his description of the way she was represented. But very probably the author took his cue from the painting where he describes her as a Being sent from heaven, and as the Queen of the Seas.

21. L'ornamento del velo e di natura
Qui gloriosamente allarga e spande
La magna nobiltà. Al suo ciel fura
Tutto il suo bello ch'ei hà ne suo bande.
Di l'una più di l'altra creatura
Gentil Donna si vede, che par mande
Iddio dal cielo in terra qui frà noi
Da non mancar giamai ne tempi suoi.[25]

22. Li adorni maranzar[26] con somma gloria
Han di lor data al mondo honor e fama
Allegrezza di si alta vittoria

22. Occhiali can hardly have referred to himself as to a dog but we must apparently read this line as a reflection of the onlooker who sees him groaning, since so many people have died 'because of this dog'.
23. Macon is Mohammed.
24. Konrad Escher, 'Die grossen Gemäldefolgen im Dogenpalast in Venedig und ihre inhaltliche Bedeutung für den Barock', *Repertorium für Kunstwissenschaft*, XLI (1918), pp. 87–125.
25. I translate with Prof. N. Rubinstein: 'Here the beauty of the decorations (*il velo* being the canopy over the streets) and of nature gloriously spread their great nobility. It robs the heavens of all the beauty it has within its compass. A beautiful woman is seen who is more the creature of the one (heaven) than of the other (nature) and who appears to have been sent to earth by God. . . .
26. '*Maranzar*' appears to be a misprint possibly due to contamination with the word *mancar* in the line above. I assume it to be some derivation from *mercanti*, the merchants or mercers who arranged the pageant. It is they who will have left the permanent memorial to their fame when God will have called them to heaven one after the other, having wreathed their place (*luoghi*) with festoons where all the Muses seem to dwell.

Ch'uno a può l'altro, ed dio nel ciel gli chiama
Quanta di lor poi lassaran memoria!
E sempre verde è la sua Aurea rama
E cinti de feston suoi lochi adorni
Dove ogni Musa par ch'indi soggiorni.

23. Tutti in honor di Dio, sempre laudando
Suo alto nome, e sua divina essenza
Con tutti i Santi suoi glorificando
Di l'un, e l'altro sua alta prudenza,
Il gran Santo Leon cui sempre amando
Vien sua fiola, ne pò un'hora senza
In cor tenerla, e prega il sommo Iddio
La guardi e salvi da tormento rio.

24. Questa è colei ch'el gran scettro gemmato
Ha cinto in fronte alla christiana croce
Questa è colei da ogni gran pirratro
Ha'l gran mare Adriatico, e sua foce,
Tutto netto indi, e tutto ben purgato;
E chiamata da iddio con viva voce
Pe'l gran sostegno suo, e chiave fatta
Di quella sempre immaculata, e intatta.

25. Del mar Regina, e resto nunque posso
Cacciar la vela in mille viva carte.[27]
La veggio eterna in ciò mio cuor e mosso
D'affecion ripieno, hor fatta à arte
Hò visto una pittura in bianco e rosso
Depinta e mover gli occhi d'ogni parte
Tal in vederla un gran stupor parea
Simil a quella della gente hebrea.[28]

It is a relief to turn from these cloudy lines to the comparatively sober next stanza from which we learn that 'inside the barrier' there was a painting of the Holy Virgin on a golden canvas, presumably one of the church standards mentioned by Benedetti:

26. Dentro del palco poscia, la Regina
Del cielo e terra, stella e chiara luce
Ho vista in tela d'or, tanto divina
Quanto esser pò, come signora e duce
Del tutto e vaga stella matutina.
Beato è quel ch'appresso à lor conduce
Suo netto cor, e tanto adorna e bella
Più che non è nel ciel ciascuna stella.

IV

When Rocco Benedetti had published his *Ragguaglio* on 20th November, of the celebrations he had seen, he men-

tioned in conclusion that the Tuscan silk merchants had announced another celebration on which he would report in due course. He does not appear to have done so, but the lacuna is filled by another poetic description of that event, which does not seem to have been recorded before, entitled

Le Feste et Trionfi de li honorati Mercanti della seta, con il superbo apparato fatto in Rialto nuovo. Per l'allegrezza della Vittoria. . . .[29]

Its dedication to Benedetto Ferro and other heads of the guild is signed by one Raffaello Thoscano and dated 8th December 1571. The poem consists of sixteen *stanze* in *ottave rime* and a concluding Sonnet to the League calling upon its members not to allow the enemy any breathing space – a piece of advice which was notoriously not taken. The poet's skill is not much superior to that of his Venetian predecessor, but at least it is always clear what he wants to say. Indeed his poem, which largely concentrates on the praise of the five main organizers, pleasantly confirms the existence of that spirit of competition which Benedetti had described:

3. Se ricchi e gran trofei fero i Germani,
E maggior pompa, di panno i Merchanti,
Più superbo apparecchio hoggi i Toschani
Con suoni han fatto, e suntuosi canti. . . .

Once more the main elements of the decoration were precious fabrics, while the celebrations were probably also measured in decibels.

9. Il gran romor di piffari e tamburi
E di trombe s'udiva insino al cielo;
Fracasso di bombarde, che gli oscuri
Fumini facean per l'aria un folto velo.
Di seta e d'oro adorni erano i muri,
Che quanto più or penso, di più zelo
M'accendo di cantare in belle carte,
Quanta sia degna de la seta l'arte.

But at least we learn from this doggerel that the Tuscans, too, displayed paintings which are unlikely to have been made for the occasion. They were portraits of the leading generals, Barbarigo, who had been killed in the battle,[30] Sebastiano Venier, the Venetian commander, represented in armour, sceptre in hand,[31] and, in addition two Tuscans, who were not actually involved in the battle. The first,

27. 'I stop here for a I cannot embark on a description even if I have a thousand glowing pages'?
28. The image attracts the eye from everywhere. The comparison with the Jewish people refers to the erection of the brazen serpent (Numbers XXI, 8). I am indebted for this interpretation to Professor Otto Kurz.
29. Brit. Mus. 1071.g.7/12. The pamphlet is misbound but the pages are easily arranged.
30. The portrait by Tintoretto of a Venetian Admiral in the Uffizi is identified as Barbarigo by Hans Tietze, *Tintoretto*, London, 1948, p. 351.
31. For portraits of Venier see P. Molmenti, *Sebastiano Veniero e la battaglia di Lepanto*, Florence, 1899. There is a portrait by Tintoretto answering our description in the Kunsthistorisches Museum in Vienna, which may, however, be only a copy, cf. Hans Tietze, *op cit.*, p. 380.

'whom all Europe honours', is evidently Filippo Strozzi, who was at least active in the fight against the Turks, having been a naval commander during the defence of Malta in 1566; the other, Cosimo I de' Medici, could not of course be omitted in a festival arranged by the Tuscans.

> 10. Di Santo Andrea quel glorioso giorno
>   La Messa e 'l Vespro si cantò solenne,
>   Con tante torcie et altri lumi intorno
>   Che tuta la cittade à veder venne.
>   Quindi si vedde in un bel quadro adorno
>   Il Barbarigo, che morte sostenne
>   Per mantener la fè del Redentore,
>   Ch'or vive in ciel con più felice honore.
>
> 11. Del gran Veniero il bel ritratto anchora
>   Armato vidi con lo settro in mano,
>   Lo Strozzi poi, che tutta Europa honora
>   E vidi in tela il gran Duca Thoscano.
>   Altari e tempi ne gli hospitii e fora
>   Si ricchi si vedeano, ch'ogni humano
>   Amirato restava, anzi conquiso
>   Vedendo in terra un novo Paradiso.

But the *pièce de résistance*, apparently, was an illuminated pyramid which turned round on its axis, with statues or paintings of four divinities:

> 13. Poi v'era una Piramida ch'intorno
>   Girava accesa con mirabile arte,
>   Ch'un altra, dove parte e torna il giorno,
>   Mai non si vidde, ne si scrisse in carte.
>   Quindi Nettuno all'hor facea soggiorno
>   Giove, Saturno, e 'l bellicoso Marte,
>   Che non solo à veder tanti trofei
>   Gli homin venivan, ma gli eccelsi Dei. . .

V

Ordine, et Dechiaratione di tutta la Mascherata, fatta nella Città di Venetia la Domenica di Carnevale, 1571, per la gloriosa Vittoria contra Turchi, Venice, 1572.[32]
The preface to this anonymous pamphlet of fifteen pages stresses the demand for information about this great procession, of which the writer lists the exact number of participants, totalling 340 of which 140 were dressed up as Turkish slaves and 189 were musicians of one kind or another. The first part, consisting of five triumphal chariots, was a plain political allegory. Faith was in the van, trampling on the Turkish serpent, her chariot being preceded by youths in *habito Ninfale* representing Hope and Charity and accompanied by two warriors with mottoes. The chariot was followed by the four Cardinal Virtues which, as we read, inspired the leaders of the armies. Men

32. Brit. Mus. 1071.g.7/14. The pamphlet is completely misbound and the sequence of the pages had first to be unscrambled.

dressed as Turkish prisoners in chains filled the intervals between the floats. The next one carried the personification of Rome, followed by Spain on '*uno carro Trionfante con prospettive del Stretto di Gibilterra et monti Pirenei*', and by Venice on a sea chariot '*vestita con carpetta d'oro, vesta di brocado, et manto Ducal cremesino, adornata di perle, zoglie, et cadene d'oro, et havea un Leone di stucco in seno*'. Finally the three members of the League were followed by the chariot of Victory, a woman in red velvet with a palm branch in her left and in her right three laurel wreaths, under her feet '*era legato uno schiavetto, vestito honoratamente*', the chariot itself providing the bleeding serpent, cut in two.
These five, we learn, referred to the Victory, but there were seven others more in accord with Venetian custom, signifying good auguries for the future; they all represented feast days, accompanied by children but also by Turkish prisoners. The first of these may be worth quoting as a sample, for its association with Father Christmas:

> Uno carro trionfante fatto a scartozzi, dipinto a mascheroni, con una sedia: sopra la quale vi era uno vestito con un rubon di Damasco fodrato di zebelini, saglio, e baretta di veluto: qual contava danari in uno bacil d'argento, per significar il PRIMO giorno dell'anno chiamato 'Giorno di Buona Man', nel qual giorno si suol dar alli putti dinari, mandar presenti alli amici et parenti de marzapanni, crostolli, et confettioni de più sorte, però seguivano
>> Due da putti con il precettore, che facevano festa di tal giorno per la buona mano, over manza ricevuta. Due vestiti di veluto con marzapanni in bacili d'argento. Due altri vestiti honoratamente con pignocade in piatti d'argento.
>> Et due altri vestiti al modo soprascritto con crostolli in piatti d'argento . . .

There followed '*uno corpolente, vestito all'antiga, figurato per CARNEVALE*', succeeded by musicians whose song is recorded; an emaciated old woman in black representing *Lent*, her suite carrying lenten food; a personification of *Easter* with cows and dairymaids 'to show that Easter comes between fish and meat'; then a richly bejewelled woman representing *La SENSA* (Ascension), the day of the main fair of Venice, with children blowing glass trumpets and merchants showing their wares of jewels and cloth. The next feast, the *First of August*, was represented by Bacchus, for on that day *se suole mandar a donar meloni et malvasie*. Five Germans with beakers and bottles followed singing a drinking song; and a child with a torch represented St. Martin's Day, '*per cio che vanno la notte con detti torzi di pegola accesi, sonando con gnachere et cantando, ali quali vien donato delli frutti*', the children singing a song of triumph for the victory and expressing hopes for a new one soon. Finally, the popular theme merged with the Petrarchan tradition, the last two chariots being those of *Father Time* with a white beard, wings and a clock in his hand, and a *Triumph of Death*, 'per dimostrare che in questa Vittoria anchor lei ha trionfato . . .'

What provides food for thought for the art historian in such a description is not only the identity of certain themes which are shared by painting and pageantry, but also the resistance of painting to other subjects. In 1918 Konrad Escher published an important article on the decorative cycles of the Palazzo Ducale[33] which he considered the source of the Iconography of Fame in the official art of the Baroque. There is no doubt that this iconography and its technique of political rhetoric is much indebted to the tradition of pageants which consumed so much of the energy of the time. This must be true of Venice, no less than of other centres. But while certain motifs and symbols

33. See note 24 on p. 65 above.

first seen in the improvised decorations of festivals were easily absorbed into the mainstream of art, the embodiment of others into an oil painting or a fresco might have been felt a breach of decorum by any artist trained in the classical tradition. The undisguised attack on individual enemies such as Karakosh and Uchi Ali, as they appeared in the celebrations of the *Drappieri*, might be a subject for woodcuts or popular engravings, but not for the brush; even the homely personifications of popular feast days shown in the carnival procession were outside the range of serious artists in Italy. In the north, of course, these divisions were less rigid, but even there the hierarchy of *genres* overlapped with the hierarchy of media. This is an aspect of iconography on which little work has been done so far. Perhaps the investigation of pageants could throw some light on this problem as well.

JAN BIAŁOSTOCKI

The Sea-Thiasos in Renaissance Sepulchral Art

ART-HISTORICAL studies published by Andreas Rumpf, Sir Kenneth Clark and Mrs. Phyllis Pray Bober have shown that Roman sarcophagi with representations of *Sea-Thiasos* – showing nereids, tritons, dolphins and other sea creatures – served as a stock of images for artists of the Middle Ages and Renaissance, furnishing them with a pattern of the beautiful, pliant young female body.[1] We recognize nereids in Dosio's drawings after Roman antiquities; in a miniature by Attavante; in a relief by Giuliano da San Gallo; in Mantegna engravings; in Riccio's reliefs on the Paschal candlestick of the Paduan Santo; in Leopardi's decorations of the banner-holders in Piazza San Marco at Venice; in pictures by Raphael, Lotto, Titian, Agostino Carracci, Rubens and Poussin.[2] A sixteenth-century Venetian *cassone* in the Cleveland Museum of Art is an example of the adaptation of the whole composition of a sarcophagus with nereids and tritons to the front of a marriage chest.[3] Echoes of the beautiful nudes which appear in the nereid-sarcophagi resound in the North in the works of Memling, Dürer and the later Netherlandish Mannerists.[4]

It is often difficult to decide whether classical motifs which were applied to decoration in the late Quattrocento and early Cinquecento retained their original meaning. Sometimes an understanding of the classical motif may be present; sometimes the dynamism of the motif may be used by the artist to produce what Warburg called *Pathosformel*; sometimes the only meaning of a classical motif used in a modern context may have been to bring into the composition an association with antiquity and to give it in this way a framework of dignity, inherent in the style *all'antica*.[5] In classical art nereids appeared in various contexts,[6] but their best known – although not completely explained – function is likely to have been that of appearing – together with hippocamps and tritons – on Roman sarcophagi in those lively and rich pageants known as *Sea-Thiasoi*.[7] Most nereids in Renaissance art were derived from these sarcophagi. Were they considered by Renaissance artists as suitable for tomb decoration?

Some examples of nereids and tritons may indeed be found in sepulchral iconography. One is a rather damaged tomb of Angelo Balsamo, by Antonello Freri, now in the Museo Nazionale at Messina (Fig. 1).[8] It was erected originally in

1. Andreas Rumpf, *Die Meerwesen auf den antiken Sarkophagreliefs* (Robert and Rodenwaldt's Corpus, v, 1), Berlin, 1939; Kenneth Clark, 'Transformations of Nereids in the Renaissance', *Burl M.*, XCVII, 1955, pp. 214–217; Phyllis Pray Bober, 'An Antique Sea-Thiasos in The Renaissance', in *Essays in Memory of Karl Lehmann*, New York, 1964, pp. 43–48.
2. See literature quoted above; for Mantegna, see studies by R. Förster in Prussian *Jahrbuch*, XXIII, 1902, pp. 205 ff. and recently Fritz Eichler, 'Mantegnas Seekentauren und die Antike. Ein römischer Fries mit Meerthiasos', *Festschrift K. M. Swoboda*, Vienna, Wiesbaden, 1959, pp. 91–96. For Riccio, see Leo Planiscig, *Andrea Riccio*, Vienna, 1927, p. 266; for Agostino Carracci, J. R. Martin, *The Farnese Gallery*, Princeton, N.J., 1965, p. 108; for Poussin, the discussion in the *JWCI*, i.e. Frank H. Sommer (XXIV, 1961, pp. 323–327), Michael Levey (XXVI, 1963, pp. 359–360) and Charles Dempsey (XXVIII, 1965, pp. 338–343).
3. *Cassone* with the coat of arms of the Masino family; Venetian, mid-sixteenth century, Cleveland Museum of Art, no. 42.607.
4. See the female nude in the first plane of the central panel of the *Last Judgement* triptych by Memling in the Muzeum Pomorskie at Gdańsk (cf. the present author's *Corpus des primitifs flamands*, *9: Les Musées de Pologne*, Brussels, 1966, pl. CXIII). For Dürer: Engraving, B.71. One can find several examples in the work of Wttewael and Bloemaert.
5. For this problem, see Aby Warburg's *Gesammelte Schriften*, Berlin-Leipzig, 1932; André Chastel, *Art et humanisme à Florence au temps de Laurent le Magnifique*, Paris, 1959; E. H. Gombrich, 'The Style *all'antica*: Imitation and Assimilation', *Studies in Western Art*, II: *The Renaissance and Mannerism*, Princeton, N.J., 1963, pp. 31–41.
6. For early examples, see Katharine Shepard, *The Fish-Tailed Monster in Greek and Etruscan Art*, New York, 1940. For the Despoina group by Damofontes, see G. Dickins in the *BSA*, 1906–7, pp. 357–384 and G. Guidi, 'La decorazione del manto di Despoina nel gruppo di Damofonte di Messene', *Annuario della Reale Scuola Archeologica di Atene . . .*, IV/V, 1921–22 (ed. 1924), pp. 97–115. Nereids appeared, for instance, on the decoration of the ritual pool in Baalbek (Erwin Goodenough, *Jewish Symbols in the Greco-Roman Period*, VIII, New York, 1958, p. 99) and the so-called 'base of Domitius Ahenobarbus' (Karl Schefold, 'Zur Basis des Domitius Ahenobarbus', *Essays Lehmann*, op. cit. in note 1, pp. 279–287). 'Skopas was probably the first artist to use the Nereid riders in an imposing work' (Shepard, op. cit. above, p. 52), i.e. the famous and certainly influential lost group known from Pliny's description (*Nat. hist.*, XXXVI, 26). Nereids also appeared in classical art in representations of Achilles' funeral (Fritz Eichler, 'Thetis und Nereiden mit den Waffen Achills', *Essays Lehmann*, op. cit., pp. 100–102).
7. General information in Roscher's *Ausführlicher Lexikon der griechischen und römischen Mythologie*, III, Leipzig, 1897–1909, pp. 207–237 (Weizsäcker, s.v. Nereid), and v, 1916–24, pp. 1150–1207 (R. Dressler, s.v. Triton); also in Pauly-Wissowa, *Realenzyklopaedie der klassischen Altertumswissenschaft*, II Series, XIII half-vol., Stuttgart, 1939 (reprint 1958), pp. 245–304 (H. Herter, s.v. Triton), especially pp. 278–286.
8. G. La Corte-Cailler, 'La ricostruzione del monumento Balsamo', *Archivio Storico Messinese*, VI, 1905, pp. 157–161; Enrico Mauceri, 'Antonello Freri scultore messinese del Rinascimento', *BdA*, XIX, 1925/26, pp. 385–398.

1507 and then reconstructed in San Francesco d'Assisi in Messina before being damaged in the earthquake of 1908. Enrico Mauceri has recomposed the monument in the Messina Museum. The front of the sarcophagus on which Angelo Balsamo is kneeling is adorned with a large relief, representing a *Sea-Thiasos*, in which, however, few figures take part; although not of very high quality, this relief has been considered by La Corte Caillier to be a Greek original. The form of the nude female figure riding on the sea-horse is obviously inspired by the classical nereids. Mauceri has interpreted the girl as Amphitrite, since Neptune clearly appears to the right. She is, however, too far separated from him to be Amphitrite, who is normally represented together with him in one chariot or shell in images of their Triumph or Wedding. This relief should therefore perhaps be interpreted as a representation of Venus-Marina, as in the case of Poussin's picture. A putto with laurel leaves and a burning torch introduces an obvious funerary symbolism.

However the main figures are finally interpreted, it cannot be excluded that this example of the *Sea-Thiasos*, which was no doubt inspired by classical nereid-sarcophagi to be found in Sicily,[9] was intended to suggest the achievements of the deceased in some maritime role. We know only that Angelo Balsamo was a Messinese citizen of an old family and that in 1499–1500 he was a senator of the city. Since Neptune often appears in the town monuments of Messina – he appears already in classical times on the coins of South Italian (or Sicilian Greek) cities[10] – it is, I think, plausible to explain the *Sea-Thiasos* on the Balsamo monument at least partly in a secular way. Such is also probably the meaning of the nereids, tritons and putti with dolphins, connected with the representation of Alphonso of Aragon and his court, attributed to Luciano Laurana, on the Gateway of the Castel Nuovo at Naples,[11] or on the northern portal of Catania Cathedral, attributed to G. D. Mazzola (1577). It must be admitted that, even if the sculptor's intention was to stress in a metaphorical way Angelo Balsamo's links with the sea, the use of classical, mythological and completely nude figures on a tomb situated in a church was a new thing. On the other hand, classical mythology and classical forms were symbolic of a new concept of

dignity, and the integration of the deceased into the world of classical tradition would have been felt to be sufficient to counterbalance the unorthodox nudity and the appearance of monstrous and pagan creatures in the framework of a Christian tomb. Or perhaps the classical motifs were chosen so as to convey a Christian message in the fashionable language of the style *all'antica*.

We know that not long before, at the very heart of the classical Renaissance, in Florence, Francesco Sassetti chose to decorate his and his wife's tombs, erected between 1485 and 1491 in their chapel in SS. Trinita, Florence, with mythological motifs.[12] These tombs are among the most important examples of the application of new, pagan motifs in a religious context, as Warburg has shown. Not only do they contain centaurs, which had a very personal meaning for Sassetti, and which were conceived – according to Warburg – as symbols of energy; we also find a nereid riding a triton in a roundel on the framing arch of Nera Sassetti's tomb (Fig. 2). Such a motif appears also on one of the marble panels in the Sanctuary of S. Gennaro in the choir of Naples Cathedral (by T. Malvito, 1508). We also know – and this is fairly important – that at least one classical nereid sarcophagus was re-used during the Renaissance.[13] Such a readaptation shows that the classical iconography of this monument was found compatible with the new, Christian content of the altered sarcophagus.

It is strange indeed that the richest programme including nereids in a sepulchral context is to be met with very far

9. For sarcophagi in Sicily, some not known to Rumpf (see note 1 above), see Vincenzo Tusa, *I sarcophagi romani in Sicilia*, Palermo, 1957. There is a similar publication, also supplementing Rumpf, for Sardinia: Gennaro Pesce, *Sarcofagi romani di Sardegna*, Roma, 1957.

10. An example from Paestum: Leo and Maria Lanckoroński, *Mythen und Münzen. Griechisches Geld im Zeichen griechischen Glaubens. Die Heiligung des Profanen*, München, 1958, fig. 4.

11. John Pope-Hennessy, *Italian High Renaissance and Baroque Sculpture*, II, London, 1963, pl. 107; Eileen R. Driscoll, 'Alfonso of Aragon as a Patron of Art', *Essays Lehmann, op. cit.*, pp. 87–96, figs. 4–5. Representations of the *Sea-Thiasos* are also to be found on the portal of the Castle at La Calahorra, Spain; see Diego Angulo Iñiguez, *La mitología y el arte español del Renacimiento*, Madrid, 1952, fig. 1.

12. Frida Schottmüller, *Repertorium für Kunstwissenschaft*, XXV, 1902, pp. 401 ff.; Aby Warburg, 'Francesco Sassettis letztwillige Verfügung' in *Gesammelte Schriften*, Berlin–Leipzig, 1932, I, pp. 127–158; Adolfo Venturi, 'Le sculture dei sarcofagi di Francesco e di Nera Sassetti in Santa Trinita a Firenze', *L'Arte*, XIII, 1910, pp. 385–389; E. and W. Paatz, *Die Kirchen von Florenz*, V, Frankfurt, 1953, pp. 295 ff., 362; Erwin Panofsky, *Tomb Sculpture*, New York, 1964, p. 73, fig. 314. Various sea creatures appear also in the decoration of the tomb of Cardinal Scarampo in San Lorenzo in Damaso, Rome, dating in its present form from about 1515 (see Gerald S. Davies, *Renascence. The Sculptured Tombs of the Fifteenth Century in Rome*, London, 1910, fig. 24), as well as in the tomb of Beatrice and Lavinia Ponzetti (1505) in Santa Maria della Pace, Rome (reproduced in the same book, fig. 72). A nereid on a hippocamp is represented on the base to the left of the Vendramin tomb by Tullio Lombardo in SS. Giovanni e Paolo, Venice.

13. Palermo, Church of S. Francesco. The portrait in the *clipeus* was changed about the middle of the fifteenth century, when the sarcophagus was adapted for Riccarda Filangieri (whose name is also carved in the *clipeus*); cf. Tusa, *op. cit.* in note 9, No. 61, fig. 138, pp. 132–133. He dates the sarcophagus in the third century A.D. For an early Christian example (a nereid sarcophagus of the second century, Christianized in the fifth century by the addition of an inscription and the cross, found at S. Lorenzo, Rome), see Visconti, *Bulletino della Commissione Archeologica Municipale di Roma*, I, 1872–73, pp. 192–200 and C. M. Kauffmann, *Die sepulcralen jenseits Denkmäler der Antike und des Urchristentums. Beiträge zur Vita-Beata-Vorstellung der römischen Kaiserzeit . . .*, Mainz, 1900, p. 28.

from classical soil – as well as very far from the sea, which might have provided a secular explanation for its appearance – in the Royal Funerary Chapel built in Cracow Cathedral in the years 1517–33, in which the tomb of the Polish king Sigismund I, and later that of Sigismund II August, were placed.[14] This Royal mausoleum, built to the order of Sigismund I by an Italian team of artists under the direction of the Florentine Bartholo Berrecci, took the place of one of the Gothic chapels on the southern side of the Cathedral. It was erected as a completely new structure and its importance for Polish art was momentous, since it introduced into the Late Gothic scene the fully developed language of the High Renaissance. The interior of the chapel has the plan of a Greek cross with very short arms, although from the outside its shape is cubic. Against the south wall opposite the entrance arch a royal throne is situated; against the east wall is the altar and opposite that, the tomb. When the son and successor of the founder of the mausoleum, Sigismund II August, approached old age, he ordered his own sarcophagus to be placed in the Chapel. Thus in the 1570's the tomb structure was remodelled; both sarcophagi were now placed in the same niche – that of the elder king being raised to the second storey, that of the younger one being on the lower.

The lower zone of all four walls is composed according to a triumphal arch pattern (Fig. 3).[15] This composition is crowned by a cornice, above which large lunettes form the transition to the drum of the dome. While the lower zone is decorated with large marble statues of saints – the patrons of the King, of Poland and of Cracow – together with circular reliefs representing Evangelists and Prophets, and while the marble panelling of the walls and pilasters include rather restrained classical ornament, the upper zone above the main cornice is full of dramatic, lively and plastic reliefs. The surface of each lunette is divided into five fields. Their exterior limits are formed by arches supported by the outer pilasters of the wall. An interior arch supported by the pilasters situated in the middle part of the wall delimits a smaller tympanum in the middle of the lunette, the surface of which is divided into three fields by two vertical strips. In the resulting five irregular fields an abundant sculptural decoration is provided, which draws heavily on classical models and which combines ornamental plants and fantastic animals (chiefly situated in the central tympanum) with figurative scenes representing nereids, tritons and other more or less identifiable classical figures (chiefly situated in the irregular spaces to the left and right). The Cracow Royal Chapel has been studied thoroughly by

Polish – and some foreign – art historians. Recently an excellent comprehensive study of its architectural forms and symbolic meaning was published by Professor Lech Kalinowski.[16] In all studies of this monument known to me, the decoration of the upper zone is characterized as an expression of the almost pagan joy of life associated with the Renaissance, and as far removed from the sacred character of a church, not connected with religious ideas or the symbolism of death.[17] In these studies the obviously erotic character of some of the triton and nereid scenes is stressed. Professor Kalinowski mentions the similarity of some of these scenes to the classical nereid sarcophagi, but in his interpretation the upper zone – considered as that in which the artist was allowed to give his imagination free rein – is opposed to the lower one, where figures of saints and prophets had to be placed according to a programme approved by the king and invented by his advisors or even by himself. I agree with that interpretation, but I should like to suggest that the sculptor, Berrecci, used the freedom given to him, not to oppose the religious programme in the lower zone, but to complement the basic religious idea of the chapel by using classical motifs of related meaning.

When we look at the reliefs decorating the upper zone of the Sigismund Chapel with the tradition of the sepulchral function of nereids and tritons in mind, we may find, if not a comprehensive iconographic programme, at least a message suggestive of the sepulchral and eschatological meaning of the Chapel as a whole which – in terms borrowed from classical tradition – expressed religious ideas concerning the immortality of the soul.

1. In the tympanum above the entrance arch, intertwined with the leaves of ornamental acanthus, are two figures, Adam and Eve, bound to the Tree of Knowledge.[18] In the same panel, putti with tridents are fighting dragons. Birds – which may be only ornamental motifs but might also be regarded as emblems of the soul – pick grapes, perhaps connected with Eucharistic symbolism. The remaining four fields are decorated with ornamental grotesque decoration, with flowers and sphinxes – motifs often recurring on Roman sarcophagi.

2. In the upper zone of the west wall, above the niche containing the royal sarcophagi and statues, three fields in the middle are decorated with ornamental grotesques. In the field on the extreme right a triton appears carrying a nude nereid on his back, among dolphins and satyrs. A cupid with his bow, and another nereid, are present. The last field to the left includes a winged female with satyr legs, bearing a basket of fruit on her head. She seems to be a

14. For the documented history of the construction of the tomb, see Stefan Komornicki, 'Kaplica Zygmuntowska w katedrze na Wawelu: 1517–1533', *Rocznik Krakowski*, XXIII, 1931.

15. The place of the chapel in the development of this theme in Renaissance architecture was recently studied by L. Kalinowski in his essay mentioned in the following note.

16. Lech Kalinowski, 'Treści artystyczne i ideowe Kaplicy Zygmuntowskiej', *Studia do Dziejów Wawelu*, Kraków, II, 1961, pp. 1–117.

17. So, for instance, Adam Bochnak, *Kaplica Zygmuntowska*, 1953.

18. Kalinowski assumes they are not Adam and Eve but representations of earthly love (*op. cit.* in note 16, p. 104); I think it is possible to retain the traditional interpretation.

personification of Plenty and she may suggest the classical idea of Paradise, or the Islands of the Blessed.

3. In the lunette above the wall with the royal throne, opposite the entrance arch, three fields in the middle are filled with motifs suggestive of plenty; fruit, flowers, amorini and ornamental dragons fill up these fields. An ornamental dragon is also to be found in the field at the far left. But to the right again (Fig. 6) a powerful triton, with head transformed into an acanthus plant, is shown carrying away a nereid, whose hair and billowing drapery suggest the violence of the movement, while her gestures show her resistance to the rape. A putto, or youth, who attacks the triton as if in defence of the abducted nereid, accompanies the group.

4. On the last (east) wall, above the altar (Fig. 4), a similar nereid and triton scene is shown in the field to the left, while in the field to the right a group of fighting tritons appears, associated with whom is a male human figure. This group may be reminiscent of the fight of the gods with the giants, or perhaps of the fight of Hercules with the triton. Above this group a huge monster hovers in which it is possible to recognize Scylla – as suggested by Kalinowski. In the middle arch, in the central panel between the two fields filled with ornamental plants (Fig. 5), a woman whom I believe to be a Venus Anadyomene is revealed, her hair still wet with water. She appears between her two companions (Cupid and Himerus?) and holds the winding leaves of acanthus. Above her, three more putti appear among the grotesque decorations.

The scenes just described are situated above the projecting cornice, which contains the following inscription (partly restored, with a mistake – DAT for DAS – in the nineteenth century) running round the chapel:

CONFITEANTVR TIBI DOMINE OMNES GENTES. / QVI DAS SALVTEM REGIBVS. / DEVS IVDICIVM TVVM REGI DA. / BEATI QVI IN DOMINO MORIVNTVR.

The meaning of this inscription, composed as it is of quotations from the Psalms, together with one from the Revelation, may include some political and dynastic allusions, and it is studied in this respect by Kalinowski in his article. Whatever the truth of this, the inscription clearly announces faith in salvation.

It would be difficult to believe that, above a text expressive of the King's strong religious feelings and his hope in salvation, a simple decorative montage of classical motifs would have been placed. The obvious erotic character of these motifs must have been motivated, or justified, by a specific meaning suited to the dignity of a royal mausoleum. Even in the Sassetti tombs in Florence the appearance of pagan motifs was justified by their symbolic significance and their relation to Christian ideas.

It seems to me that the upper zone of the Sigismund Chapel contains a – perhaps not completely coherent and explicit – message, but one which is still quite intelligible, if it is

approached with that meaning in mind which the classical motifs used in it are believed to have had in Antiquity. I shall argue that the upper zone develops in a humanistic language the hope of salvation expressed by the inscription in the religious zone below it.

Although there are always sceptics to discount the spiritual meaning of tritons with nereids on their backs – Rumpf, Nock and Stern among the most important – the majority of classical scholars – Cumont, Walter, Matz and, most recently, Andreae – seem to have returned to the opinion of the older school of archaeologists and to agree that tritons and nereids in classical art expressed the idea of the journey of the soul to the paradise of the ancients – the Islands of the Blessed.[19] There is no space here to recapitulate this classical eschatological doctrine. However, it seems plausible to assume that at least some artists of the Renaissance, confronted with numerous examples of the classical triton and nereid motif in a sepulchral context, did interpret it as a death image. The patterns of movement inherent in it could hardly fail to appeal to Renaissance artists, and it is not improbable that they interpreted these movements as expressive of the journey of the human soul to the after-life. The very manner, so dramatic and violent, in which tritons abduct nereids in the Cracow Chapel decorations may be expressive of such an idea.

The dolphins, whose supple forms fill the framing fields of the round windows in the drum and which appear in some of the spandrels above the central arches of the lower zone, were almost omnipresent on funerary monuments in Antiquity: they were regarded as bearers of the souls of the deceased and as symbols of salvation.[20] The fantastic world of sea creatures, of violently fighting tritons, of monsters and of beautiful women was probably intended to convey the classical ideas of the after-life.

Finally, above the altar niche, in a daring counterpart to the

19. For arguments against the allegorical interpretation of Sea-Thiasos, see Rumpf, op. cit. in note 1; A. D. Nock, 'Sarcophagi and Symbolism', American Journal of Archaeology, L, 1946, pp. 166 ff.; H. Stern, Dumbarton Oaks Papers, XII, 1958, p. 191. Opinions favourable to such an interpretation have been expressed by, among others, Eugénie Sellers-Strong (Apotheosis and After-Life, New York, 1915, p. 153); Franz Cumont (After-Life in Roman Paganism, New Haven, 1923, p. 155; Recherches sur le symbolisme funéraire des Romains, Paris, 1942, pp. 166, 306; Lux Perpetua, Paris, 1949, p. 286); Otto Walter ('Darstellung von Meerwesen auf römischen Sarkophagen', Archaiologike Ephemeris, 1953–54 [ed. 1955], pp. 81–86); F. Matz (Gnomon, XXXIII, 1961, p. 63); Karl Schefold ('La force créatrice du symbolisme funéraire des Romains', Revue archéologique, II, 1961, p. 186); Bernhard Andreae (Studien zur römischen Grabkunst, Heidelberg, 1963, pp. 133–135, 166–167); and H. Sichtermann (Enciclopedia dell'arte antica, V, p. 422.)

20. Hermann Usener, Die Sintfluthsagen, Bonn, 1899; Eunice Burr Stebbins, The Dolphin in the Literature and Art of Greece and Rome, Menasha, Wisc., 1929; Cumont, Lux Perpetua, op. cit. in note 19, p. 286; Goodenough, Jewish Symbols . . ., op. cit. in note 6, V, pp. 22–27.

Christian idea of salvation, the personification of the classical one is displayed: Venus Anadyomene. I have little doubt that it is she who is represented by this nude female figure. Anadyomene appeared on classical sarcophagi as a focal point, supported in her shell by tritons.[21] She 'speaks of Birth and Re-birth, of Generation and Re-Generation, of Love and Triumph, of Purification and Salvation'.[22]

For the humanists, Venus stood for the highest spiritual values. She was called *Sancta Venere* by Boccaccio, and *sacrata e vera dea* by Giovanni di Francesco Nesi.[23] Gombrich has shown how many spiritual and religious ideas were inherent in Botticelli's famous picture.[24] In Antiquity Venus was also considered among other things as a leader of the souls of the departed.[25] Finally the amorini in the pageant of Venus and the erotic element in the *Sea-Thiasos* scenes were expressive in Late Classical times of the ideas of generation, rebirth and salvation.[26]

It is difficult to believe that a nude female pagan deity – however small – could have been represented above the altar of the sepulchral chapel of the king of one of the most important Catholic countries, were she not intended as a humanistic expression *all'antica* of the basically Christian idea of eternal life and salvation.

The tradition of tombs decorated inside with nereids and other sea creatures suggesting a long journey of the soul to the place of eternal happiness is significant, if limited to Antiquity. In Etruscan art such tomb decorations are found;[27] they also appear among the stucco reliefs on the Valerii tomb on the Via Latina, Rome.[28] They are to be found again in the so-called Pythagorean basilica close to Porta Maggiore in Rome, which is considered by some scholars to be a funerary structure.[29] Carcopino's analysis of its decoration could be applied to the Cracow mausoleum as well: 'Isolated, these types of banal decoration could not perhaps pretend to have any specific meaning. But represented with that insistence, situated close to one another and deliberately repeated, they acquire in such a place the value of a religious sign; and all of them converge toward the desired shore, the memory of which they evoke just as the legends from which they originated had as their common scene the shores of the Ocean, from which men embark for the Islands of the Blessed.'[30]

That a spiritual meaning may be attached to erotic subject matter is known from even later times than the sixteenth century, since Ovidian *erotica* had been accorded divine and ethical associations in *Ovide moralisé*.[13] It is, to be sure, a little unexpected to find such symbolism far away from Neoplatonic centres, in a Northern European capital, where, although humanism in literature and scholarship was in a flourishing state of development, we lack any comparative material and where there was no classical tradition in the fine arts. We have to admit that this transplantation of Renaissance mythological symbolism from Italy to Poland must have been the work of the Florentine architect, Bartholo Berrecci. He could have known Botticelli's *Venus* and the other works of the Neoplatonic movement. He borrowed, for instance, one of the triton and nereid motifs from Raphael's *Galatea* fresco, as was observed by a Polish scholar.[32] It is also possible that Berrecci was encouraged in his projects by the king and his humanistic court. With his Tuscan and possibly Lombard collaborators, the artist created a masterpiece, not only because he transplanted under a Northern sky the forms of the Italian High Renaissance, but also because he created a decoration which conveyed a basically Christian content through classical imagery and associations.

21. See the sarcophagi in Rumpf, *op. cit.* in note 1, nos. 91–95, pp. 36–39.

22. William S. Heckscher, 'The Anadyomene in the Mediaeval Tradition (Pelagia-Cleopatra-Aphrodite). A Prelude to Botticelli's *Birth of Venus*', *Nederlands Kunsthistorisch Jaarboek*, VII, 1956, p. 3.

23. Heckscher, *op. cit.*, p. 7.

24. E. H. Gombrich, 'Botticelli's Mythologies', *JWCI*, VIII, 1945, pp. 7–60. Ficino conceived Anadyomene as 'Humanitas, born of Heaven and more than others beloved of God All Highest' (quoted by Gombrich, pp. 16 ff.).

25. Cf. Alfred C. Rush, *Death and Burial in Christian Antiquity*, Washington, D.C., 1941, p. 28; Tibullus, *Carmina*, I, III, vv. 57 f.: 'ipsa Venus campos ducet in Elysios' (quoted by Heckscher, *op. cit.* in note 22, p. 21).

26. Goodenough, *op. cit.* in note 6, v, p. 26. He describes a Christian Coptic object, which seems to be a eucharistic paten, representing Aphrodite Anadyomene with her dolphins holding a cross in a wreath over her head; cf. his fig. 35: Coptic Museum, Cairo.

27. Shepard, *op. cit.* in note 6, pp. 33, 50. Rumpf, *op. cit.* in note 1. For the wall decorations at Albanella, close to Salerno, see Minervini, 'Brevi osservazioni su' dipinti di alcune tombe di Albanella', *Bullettino Archeologico Napolitano*, N.S., III, 1855, no. 67 (17), pp. 132–136, pl. 11. The most famous sepulchral monument decorated with nereids was of course that of Xantos, where, however, they were represented outside. The meaning of the monument is not wholly explained. See Charles Picard, 'Les Néréides funéraires du monument de Xanthos', *Revue de l'histoire des religions*, LII (vol. CIII), 1931, pp. 5–28; also Panofsky, *op. cit.*, p. 22.

28. Guidi, *op cit.* in note 6, p. 107, fig. 5.

29. Franz Cumont, 'La Basilique souterraine de la Porta Maggiore', *Revue Archéologique*, v, sér., VII–VIII, 1918, pp. 52–73; Jérôme Carcopino, *Études romaines. I. La Basilique pythagoricienne de la porte majeure*, Paris, 1944.

30. Carcopino, *op. cit.*, p. 297.

31. C. de Boer, 'Ovide moralisé', *Verhandelingen der koninklijk Akademie van Wetenschapen te Amsterdam*, Afd. Letterkunde, N.S., XV, 1915; XXI, 1920; XXX, 1931–32. J. R. Martin, *op. cit.* in note 2, p. 86, has found in Annibale Carracci's *Farnese Gallery*, 'the revelation of the spiritual through the medium of the sensual' and he sees in the *Triumph of Bacchus and Ariadne* the expression of the power of divine love to exalt and transfigure the human soul. See, however, Donald Posner's review: *Art Bulletin*, XLVIII, 1966, pp. 109–114.

32. Julian Pagaczewski, 'Jan Michałowicz z Urzędowa', *Rocznik Krakowski*, XXVIII, 1937, p. 66 f. Mentioned also by Kalinowski, *op. cit.* in note 16.

On his lost epitaph Berrecci was described as 'multis virtutibus, litteris et variis artibus mechanicis ornatus' and as 'philosophiae amator'.[33] He must have felt like a pioneer of the style *all'antica* not only in the field of form but also in that of thought. As he worked in a world which must have seemed to him still to belong to the mediaeval past, he probably felt he was fulfilling a mission and this enhanced his self-esteem. He has left a document of his new-found pride in a form not to be met with in Italy. He has situated his signature at a most unusual place: in the highest ring of the lantern above the dome. There, between the crown composed of angels' heads and the central seraphim, a beautiful inscription in Roman characters records the name: BARTHOLO FLORENTINO ORIFICE.

33. Kalinowski, *op. cit.*, p. 108.

The Origins of the Sculptor, Juan de Juni

ALTHOUGH the art of the sculptor, Juan de Juni, who died in Valladolid in 1577, has been discussed by various writers, his origins have hitherto remained obscure.[1] Neither the contracts for his works nor the lawsuits to which they gave rise yield much information on this point. However, during one case – that over an altarpiece by Juni for the church of Santa Maria la Antigua in Valladolid – two witnesses, the sculptor, Miguel de Barreda, and Gerónimo Vázquez, declared that he had learnt his art in France.[2] This has been interpreted as an underhand criticism of Juni since it implied contempt for the 'modern' sources of his style; that is, he had not received the classical Italian training expected by current fashion.[3] Taking their cue from this, scholars have suspected from the Spanish pronunciation and spelling of Juni's name that he was born at Joigny (Yonne) in France.[4] Otherwise, all the documents relating to his life and work refer exclusively to the period between his arrival in León in north-western Spain in 1533 and his death in Valladolid.

Nevertheless, it is sufficiently clear from his style that he had visited Italy and that he was attracted there more to the art of Jacopo della Quercia than to Michelangelo. Juni infused solemnity and pathos into the former's artistic vocabulary, converting it into a suitable medium for the expression of exalted religious feeling. His groupings and figures are consciously thought out and are always grandiose. They reveal a marked personal idiom, in which the style of the High Renaissance and its transmutation into Mannerism appear superimposed on older forms.

There exists, however, a sixteenth-century text that does, to my mind, clarify Juni's origins. In it a 'maestro Janni franzese' is described as fully expert in his craft on his arrival in Florence. There he achieved fame for himself on account of the perfection of his wood-carving. The text also serves to identify one of this sculptor's earliest works, still fortunately surviving, and thus offers a pointer to his sources. If, as I think, 'maestro Janni' and Juan de Juni are one and the same sculptor, this text is doubly important, since it confirms Barreda's and Vázquez's statements that Juni was trained in France; that is, in an ambience in which Gothic forms were still a living force. Possibly out of spite, neither of these witnesses mentioned Juni's stay in Florence, but the fact that he must have stayed there is demonstrated by his sculptures executed in Spain.

The text itself is a very familiar one. Indeed, it is astonishing that it has not previously been pointed out, either by Spanish or French scholars. Although Juni can properly be considered Spanish, because of the many years he lived in Spain and because he learnt to interpret the profound religious feeling characteristic of Castile, the fact emerges that he was born in France. In this he was not unique, since there were a number of French artists working in Spain at the time, although none was equal to him in quality.

The text is the second edition of Vasari's *Lives* (1568), *sc.* one of the chapters on sculpture in the Introduction (ed. Milanesi, I, p. 166): chapter VII – '*Como si conducono le figure di legno.*' After discussing the best type of wood for carving and the difficulties of the craft, Vasari writes:

'E sebbene e' non hanno gli stranieri quel perfetto disegno che nelle cose loro dimostrano gl'Italiani, hanno niente-dimeno operato ed operano continuamente in guisa, che riducono le cose a tanta sottigliezza, che elle fanno stupire il mondo: come si può vedere in un'opera, o per

---

1. Juan José Martín Gonzalez, *Juan de Juni*, Madrid, 1954, and J. M. de Azcarate, *Escultura del siglo XVI (Ars Hispanae*, vol. XII), Madrid, 1958, recapitulate all that is known to date. Nothing significant has been added since. As to his age and biography, Juni declared in 1577 that he was sixty years old 'more or less', but he must have been much older as he appeared in León in 1533 and died in Valladolid in 1577.
2. The lawsuit was between Juni and the sculptor, Francisco Gilarte. Answering questions put by Gilarte, Miguel de Barreda stated: 'Francisco Giralte es de más cienza y más fundada que el dicho Juni, porque sabe este testigo quel dicho Giralte lo deprendió de Berruguete y de otros maestros muy entendidos en Ytalia y sus obras dél dan testimonio dello y el dicho Juni deprendió en Franzia y su arte dél da a entender . . . que no es de tanta arte ny zienzia . . .' Gerónimo Vásquez's evidence included the phrase: '. . . la obra y arte del dicho Juan de Juny es francesa. . . .' Both witnesses appeared on behalf of Gilarte. See Martín Monsó, *Estudios histórico-artísticos*, Valladolid, 1901, p. 333.
3. Barreda also declared on the same occasion: 'la . . ., traza del dicho Juny no muestra ser oficial perfeto en escultura ny brutescos, ny arquitectura, porque antes parescen sus obras ser a lo moderno que a lo Romano, que agora se usa . . .'
4. The first to hold this view were Bertaux (in Michel's *Histoire de l'art*, vol. IV, 2, p. 978) and Gómez Moreno (*Catálogo monumental de la provincia de León*, written in 1906–8 although not published until 1925). The suggestion was widely adopted; see J. J. Martín Gonzalez, *op. cit.*, in note 1, p. 7. Like other scholars, the latter considers that the name Juni, by which the sculptor was known in Castile, was or became a patronymic. Various members of his family were known by it; for example, his natural son, Isaac de Juni, also a sculptor, and a son by his first marriage, Pablo Juni de Montoya. The children of his third marriage, Ana María and José y Simeón, also appear to have used the name. See Agapito y Revilla, 'Un testamento inédito de Juan de Juni', *Boletino del Museo Provincial de Bellas Artes de Valladolid*, 1927, p. 148.

meglio dire un miracolo di legno, di mano di maestro
Janni franzese; il quale habitando nella città di Firenze, la
quale egli si aveva eletta per patria, prese in modo nelle
cose del disegno, del quale gli dilettò sempre, la maniera
italiana, che, con la pratica che aveva nel lavorare il
legno, fece di tiglio una figura d'un San Rocco, grande
quanto il naturale; e condusse con sottilissimo intaglio
tanto morbidi e traforati in panni che la vestono, ed in
modo cartosi, e con bello andare l'ordine delle pieghe,
che non si può veder cosa più maravigliosa. Similmente
condusse la testa, la barba, le mani e le gambe di quel
Santo con tanta perfezione, che ella ha meritato e merita
sempre lode infinita da tutti gli uomini; e, che è più,
acciò si veggia in tutte le sue parti l'eccellenza del-
l'artefice, è stata conservata insino a oggi questa figura
nella Nunziata di Firenze, sotto il pergamo, senza alcuna
coperta di colori o di pitture, nello stesso color del-
lengname, e con la solita pulitezza e perfezione che
maestro Janni le diede, bellissima sopra tutte l'altre che si
veggia intagliata in legno.'

The statue of *St. Roch* (Fig. 1) is still in the church of the SS.
Annunziata in Florence. It agrees exactly with Vasari's
description. Its size, the treatment of the wood and the
minor details such as the saint's leg all correspond to the
text.

With regard to the identification of Janni with Juni, it
should be remembered that, in the sixteenth century, the
letter 'J' in Spanish was not the hard and aspirated sound it
has since become but would have been pronounced in
Castile as a soft j, more as in French. In addition, Juni is
referred to in some Castilian documents as 'de Juanin' or
'de Joni'.⁵ Moreover, certain details of the *St. Roch* recall a
number of the early Spanish works by Juni. This is especially true of his first sculptures executed in León, such as the
gigantic heads at St. Marcos in León.

The *St. Roch* has previously been attributed to both a
'maestro Gian' (perhaps Jean Chavier, or Chavenier, of
Rouen), who worked in San Luigi dei Francesi in Rome,⁶
and Veit Stoss, a Nuremberg sculptor who spent most of
his career in Poland,⁷ but these names have since been

discarded and no convincing substitute has been proposed.

Scholars who have suggested Veit Stoss have rested their
case on the statue's formal characteristics. However, Stoss's
typical folds, known in German as *Ohrenfalten* – that is to
say, convoluted curves in the shape of an ear, into which
heavy clothing falls – are not unique, despite the fact that
he used them frequently and in his own distinctive way.⁸
In fact they can be paralleled in the work of earlier Rhenish
sculptors, such as Leinberger; and these folds were imitated
not only by sculptors influenced by Stoss but also, independently, by other Rhenish and Burgundian artists. However, this is not the place to go further into this problem or
to give specific examples.

If additional confirmation were needed that Juni is a strong
candidate for the authorship of the *St. Roch*, one might
quote Marcel Raymond, an old and respected authority
on Florentine sculpture, who, in reply to an enquiry,
wrote⁹ that the statue could, on stylistic grounds, be from
the hand of a French sculptor and that it exhibited traditional formulas used by sculptors in Burgundy and
Champagne.

As we have seen, Vasari describes Janni as French, and even
the most superficial look at sculptures known to be Burgundian or by artists working under Burgundian influence
reveals a relationship in sculptural treatment to the *St.
Roch*. We need search no further than the Louvre, which
contains a well-known statue possessing the necessary char-

to give reasons for it. However, Vasari states that Janni produced
his statue in Florence and that he chose this city as his place of
residence. This means that he must have lived there for some time.
What is known of the career of Veit Stoss does not seem to allow
of his having spent any considerable period in Florence.

8. I am not acquainted with recent publications on Stoss in Poland,
nor do I know if any document has been found that alters the
previous chronology. In one of the latest books (Oltarz Krà-
kowski, *Wit Stwosz*, 1964) I was unable to discover anything
new.
   The sculptor was born about 1445. In 1480 he had already finished
the altar of Cracow Cathedral and he remained in Poland for
several more years, since various of his works exist, or have existed,
there, dated 1492 and 1493. In 1496 he returned to Nuremberg
but was compelled to leave the city in 1503 as he became bankrupt.
In 1504 he was in Munmerstadt. In 1505 a pardon was granted to
him by the Emperor, whereupon he returned to his native city,
where he died, aged about eighty-five, in 1533. Many works
from the last years of his life which survive in the Rhine Valley
suggest that he did not leave his homeland again.
   More than this, if his work is considered as a whole, a clear
development between the sculptures of the Cracow and Bamberg
altars can be seen – a development in which the figure of *St. Roch*
is hard to include. For this reason, Professor Pinder, who dated
the *St. Roch* in 1516 – in one of his most eloquent books – found
some difficulty in placing this figure among Stoss's works and
used an unconvincing argument to sustain the attribution (*Werden
deutscher Form*, III, *Die deutsche Kunst der Dürerzeit*, 1940, p. 190).
9. Quoted by G. Baldwin Brown, *Vasari on Technique*, 1907 (reprinted 1960), p. 175.

5. The spelling varies according to the documents, i.e. Joni, Juny
(with and without accents), Juani and, in a lawsuit over the altarpiece of the church of Santiago in Cáceres (Martín Monsó, *op. cit.*
in note 2, p. 162), Juan de Xuni (statement of Miguel de Cyeça).
What is more, in a lawsuit in 1570 over the painting for St.
Andrew in Valladolid (Agapito y Revilla, *op. cit.* in previous note,
p. 152), his natural son clearly signed his name Isaac de Juññí
(with a double n, written ñ, and with a clear accent over the i),
which seems to imply a strong pronunciation of the n and the i.
6. According to Vasari (Milanesi, I, p. 122), 'maestro Gian' was the
author of a relief in this church. Although he was a Renaissance
artist, there appears to be no connection whatever between his
work and that of the sculptor of the *St. Roch* in Florence.
7. This attribution was due to Professor H. Voss (Prussian *Jahrbuch*,
1908, p. 20) and has since been accepted by historians of German
art, above all by Pinder, who not only insisted on it but also tried

acteristics, the *Virgin of Isenheim*. The folds of the broad and heavy tunic of this figure suggest to me that it is by a master whose sources were similar to those of Janni.

These forms – the *Ohrenfalten* and the angular folds – were used in the *St. Roch*, although they were interpreted there in terms of the classical style Juni had learnt in Italy. Similar sculptural conventions, mixed with reminiscences of della Quercia, Michelangelo and the *Laocoön*, reappear in his sculptures executed in Spain. His works were achieved in a complex formal language in which the different volumes were united by enveloping curves. This was one of the main characteristics of his style.

ANDRÉ CHASTEL

La Demeure Royale au XVIe siècle et le Nouveau Louvre

ON a de bonnes raisons de penser que le Louvre de Pierre Lescot a fait sensation dans le royaume et même dans toute l'Europe.[1] Il intéressait les diplomates: il est bien connu que le rapport de l'ambassadeur vénitien Lippomano fournit en 1557 des indications précieuses pour l'histoire du palais.[2]

Pour bien mesurer la portée de cette réussite, il convient donc de la considérer non seulement du point de vue habituel du développement interne, si l'on peut dire, de l'architecture française, mais aussi dans la perspective élargie de la demeure royale en occident.[3] Le même souci de prestige artistique anime alors les protagonistes de la politique: Charles-Quint, François Ier, Henri VIII. Le principe d'ostentation, propre à l'architecture "royale", acquiert une force nouvelle avec le double souci de culture et de grandeur, qui marque tous ces règnes. Une sorte de concurrence intellectuelle et artistique double, prolonge et parfois infléchit la politique de puissance. Les princes rivaux se surveillent et tiennent à répondre à toute initiative notable par un effort du même ordre.

Pendant trente ans, François Ier, le plus ambitieux des Valois, ne cessa de mener le jeu. La liste de ses entreprises est impressionnante et donne au premier abord une impression d'incohérence et de prodigalité comme toute l'activité de ce prince. Mais de 1516 au nouveau Louvre – décidé en 1546, c'est-à-dire quelques mois avant sa mort –, il y a un développement dans les projets royaux. Leur succession fait apparaître comme la maturation d'une idée: tous les types de plans sont essayés tour à tour, on oscille de

la création entièrement neuve, comme Chambord, le château de Madrid .., à la transformation plus ou moins radicale des anciennes demeures: Blois, Saint-Germain-en-Laye, le Louvre. Le problème est de soutenir aux yeux d'une cour que fréquente l'aristocratie de l'Europe entière, la supériorité spécifique du palais français, en tenant compte de tout ce qui, ailleurs, a été produit de remarquable dans le même genre.

Ce fut sans doute une première fois le cas avec Chambord, dont la construction décidée de bonne heure et interrompue par la malheureuse campagne de 1525 ne se ralentit sérieusement qu'après 1534: ce devait être l'une de ces démonstrations calculées de la nouvelle architecture de "cour" avec son extraordinaire donjon – escalier.[4]

4. Sur Chambord: F. Gébelin, *Les Châteaux de la Renaissance*, Paris, 1925. Sur le passage des *Quattro libri* (1570) de Palladio, voir notre essai: "Palladio et l'escalier", *Bollettino del Centro Internazionale di Storia dell'Architettura*, VII, 1966.

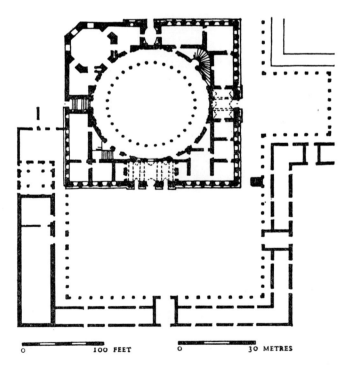

Pedro Machuca: Grenade, Palais de Charles-Quint, 1527–1568. Plan. (D'après G. Kubler et M. Soria, *Art and Architecture in Spain and Portugal. . . . 1500–1800*, Penguin Books, 1959, p. 11, fig. 6.)

1. Voir Anthony Blunt, *Art and Architecture in France*, Londres, 1953, p. 51 et s.
Sur le Louvre de François Ier et de Henri II, on doit toujours s'appuyer sur les travaux de L. Hautecœur, *Histoire du Louvre*, Paris, 1927, "Le Louvre de Pierre Lescot", *GBA*, 1927 (suivi d'une discussion par L. Batiffol, "Les premières constructions de Pierre Lescot au Louvre d'après de nouveaux documents," *GBA*, 1930) et les compléments apportés dans l'*Histoire de l'architecture classique en France*, nouv. éd., tome VII, 'La Formation de l'idèal classique', I, Paris, 1965, p. 273 et s. Nombreux documents réunis par A. Berty et H. Legrand, *Topographie historique du vieux Paris*, 2 vol., 1867 et 1885.
2. *Relations des ambassadeurs vénitiens*, tome II, souvent citées par les auteurs. Nous n'entrons pas ici dans la discussion de l'interprétation à donner à la phrase: "il n'y en a qu'un quart de fait", qui concerne soit l'aile ouest d'un quadrilatère égal à celui de l'ancien Louvre, soit l'angle sud-ouest tout entier, représentant un quart du nouveau Louvre.
3. Ce point de vue est amorcé dans N. Pevsner, *An Outline of European Architecture*, Londres, 1943 (nouv. éd. 1962).

On est moins surpris de son parti singulier quand on voit Palladio lui-même mentionner avec admiration l'escalier à double vis, si complexe et si parfaitement approprié au spectacle que doit se donner à elle-même une société fondée sur le faste. Nous suivons mal les modalités de l'influence qu'a pu exercer le parti même de Chambord. Mais tout le monde s'accorde à en saisir l'écho dans l'entreprise de Nonsuch, où se retrouvent la liaison étroite avec le site, le jardin des "antiques", la façade ouverte sur la nature et le système à quatre tours d'angle. L'effet d'ensemble a dû être assez proche, bien que les représentations qui subsistent ne concernent que la façade d'entrée proprement Tudor, et non le front sur le parc.⁵

Il serait surprenant de ne trouver aucune contrepartie à ces préoccupations du côté de l'Espagne. Charles-Quint, rival heureux de François Iᵉʳ à l'Empire, avait entrepris à Grenade un château grandiose qui devait couronner avec une insistance bien compréhensible chez l'héritier des souverains catholiques, le plateau fortifié des Almoravides. Cet ouvrage (p. 78), moins célèbre que la cathédrale, et resté d'ailleurs inachevé, apparaît comme une remarquable innovation dans le type de la demeure "royale".⁶ Le style est infiniment plus sévère qu'à Chambord ou à Nonsuch, qui étaient avant tout des châteaux de plaisance et l'affirmaient avec éclat. De pure dérivation "romaine", le château inscrit dans un plan carré une cour parfaitement circulaire, dotée d'un portique continu. On peut se croire en présence de l'adaptation "séculière" (et sans le Tempietto) du plan prévu par Bramante pour la cour de San Pietro in Montorio que nous a transmis Serlio. Conformément à une évolution qui se dessinait depuis longtemps dans l'architecture "noble", la cour intérieure, pourvue d'une galerie courant au-dessus d'un portique, est traitée en lieu de fête et de représentations. Mais on peut aussi observer dans ce parti la reprise d'une vieille formule attestée dans le royaume de Majorque dès le début du XIVᵉ siècle. Tout se passe comme si l'Empereur avait demandé à l'architecte Machuca, comme François Iᵉʳ au constructeur de Chambord et Henri VIII à celui de Nonsuch, une interprétation "moderne" de l'architecture, intégrant certains traits spécifiques du pays.⁷

Le château de Grenade avait été commencé en 1527. Cette date est importante aussi pour la France. Elle correspond à l'orientation nouvelle des préoccupations de François Iᵉʳ vers Paris et l'Ile de France. A Paris tout était à faire. La destruction sensationnelle du donjon de Charles V, les travaux de 1532, semblaient bien annoncer un grand changement. Le problème de la "demeure royale" revient avec insistance à cette phase du règne comme à la précédente. On peut être un peu surpris que les choses aient été si difficiles et si lentes. Il y eut sans doute une hésitation prolongée entre l'idée de transformer les bâtiments anciens, comme à Fontainebleau et à Saint-Germain, et celle d'édifier un ouvrage entièrement neuf et "moderne", moderne signifiant maintenant quelque chose de bien différent de Chambord, qui vers 1535-40 apparaissait comme dépassé.

Les revers et les crises de la fin du règne ne suffisent pas à expliquer les délais d'une réalisation fort attendue. Les difficultés d'ordre topographique, nées du fait que le Louvre était proprement enrobé dans la zone occidentale de la ville, ont dû avoir leur importance. Un grand parti était nécessaire; mais on ne pouvait étendre le terrain disponible qu'au prix de négociations interminables et en brisant des résistances du type de celles qui, après 1630, ne cesseront de gêner l'établissement d'un accès digne du palais à travers la ville.⁸ Comment rebâtir dignement le Louvre sur place? Dès le départ il existait une contradiction entre la conception de l'entreprise et les possibilités de réalisation.

Nous serions portés à attribuer de l'importance à la venue de Charles-Quint qui fut amené, par des circonstances quelques peu paradoxales, à traverser la France et à visiter Paris dans l'hiver 1538-39. On connaît les efforts accomplis par le prince Valois pour briller aux yeux de son adversaire en le conduisant de fête en fête, de splendeur en splendeur. La rencontre rappelle la joute de luxe et de grandeur du Camp du Drap d'Or. Sauval a signalé comment le Louvre fut hâtivement aménagé pour la venue de la cour. Son insuffisance était devenue éclatante.⁹ On peut donc situer

5. L'intérieur, comme le confirme la relation de l'ambassadeur Sir John Wallop (1540), était en liaison directe avec celui de Fontainebleau. Le même rapport indique, d'ailleurs, combien François Iᵉʳ était, de son côté, intéressé par les particularités de Hampton Court, et en particulier, l'emploi général des dorures dans les ornements.
Sur Nonsuch, disparu au XVIIᵉ siècle, la documentation a été récemment renouvelée par les fouilles, dont J. Dent, *The Quest for Nonsuch*, Londres, 1962, a exposé les résultats. Voir aussi Ian Dunlop, *Palaces and Progresses of Elizabeth I*, Londres, 1962, où l'on trouve citée, p. 111, la lettre de Sir John Wallop (17 novembre 1540).

6. Il n'existe pas d'étude d'ensemble récente sur le château impérial de Grenade. Plutôt que de rappeler des références dispersées, il peut suffire de renvoyer au vol. XI de *Ars Hispaniae*. Dans son étude sur la cathédrale voisine de Grenade, E. Rosenthal, *The Cathedral of Granada*, Princeton, 1961, a bien montré l'action de l'idéologie "impériale" sur l'évolution de l'architecture.

7. Nous pensons, en particulier, au curieux château à plan circulaire de Bellves, dont les travaux sont entrepris en 1300. M. Durliat, *L'Art dans le royaume de Majorque*, Toulouse, 1962, p. 206 et s., envisage comme probable le lien avec Castel del Monte, autre demeure impériale.

8. Sur cette difficulté au cours des âges, déjà bien marquée par L. Hautecœur, *op. cit.*, nous serons amené à revenir dans une enquête sur l'architecture et l'urbanisme du quartier des Halles. Voir l'étude que nous publions avec J. Pérouse de Montclos, "L'aménagement de l'accès oriental du Louvre", *Les Monuments historiques de la France*, XII, 3, 1966, pp. 176-232.

9. Sauval, *Histoire et recherche des antiquités de la ville de Paris*, Paris, 1714, II, p. 49: "Le Louvre était en si mauvais état que du temps de François Iᵉʳ pour y loger Charles-Quint en 1539 il

aux environs de 1539–1540, le moment où l'on devait trouver insupportable l'absence d'un vrai palais royal à Paris, après tant d'expériences novatrices sur la Loire et dans le périphérie de l'Ile de France.

Le temps n'était plus où l'on pouvait confier à des entrepreneurs français de second ordre la conduite d'opérations, fondées sur des dessins ou des maquettes d'italiens.

Fontainebleau n'avait vraiment démarré qu'avec la venue du Rosso, puis du Primatice, en 1530–31. Or, le Rosso disparaît précisément en 1540 et le Primatice reste attaché au chantier décoratif de Fontainebleau. Les "architecteurs" français de la nouvelle génération ne sont pas encore formés; on peut donc se demander s'il ne convient pas de relier dans une large mesure à ces préoccupations l'invitation adressée coup sur aux deux Bolonais, Sebastiano Serlio et Vignole et leur venue en France à la fin de 1540 ou au tout début de 1541.

Pour Vignole, son premier biographe P. Danti, dans *Due regole di prospettiva* (1587) affirme que François Ier avait demandé à l'architecte "le plan d'un palais".[10] Nous connaissons assez les préoccupations du Roi pour en accepter l'idée; la date et les circonstances du voyage peuvent inviter à penser que ce projet concernait le nouveau Louvre. Mais, jusqu'à nouvel ordre, nous ne savons rien de plus.

Il n'en est pas tout à fait de même pour Serlio. Sa venue en France a été rapprochée des projets royaux pour le Louvre une première fois par Claude Perrault lui-même, qui dans la préface à sa traduction de Vitruve a déclaré expressément: "Lorsque le Roi françois I fit venir d'italie Seb. Serlio, à qui il donna la conduite des bâtiments de Fontainebleau, nos architectes profitèrent si bien de ses instructions que, pour le projet du Louvre, le dessin d'un Français, l'abbé de Clagny, fut préféré au dessin de Serlio" (Préface de *l'Architecture générale de Vitruve*, réduite en abrégé, Paris, 1674). Tout semble dit en quelques mots: l'affectation de Sébastien à Fontainebleau, que confirment les Lettres patentes du 27 décembre 1541 et les Comptes des Bâtiments, mais aussi la portée des enseignements de Serlio et le fait qu'il ait concouru pour le Louvre. Ce dernier point a été repris expressément par Germain Brice en 1684:

> fallut faire quantité de réparations. On dora toutes les girouettes. Les armes de France, en plusieurs endroits furent peintes et arborées. On attacha contre le mur, tant des escaliers que des salles et des antichambres des chandeliers de laiton. La plupart des croisées furent agrandies et les vitres peintes. On augmenta le nombre des appartements. On fit des lices: il y eut des joutes et des tournois. En un mot on n'oublia ni n'épargna rien, afin d'y mieux recevoir l'Empereur et le régaler magnifiquement. Et de fait on rendit ce château si logeable que Charles-Quint, Le Roi, la Reine, le Dauphin, la Dauphine, le Roi et la Reine de Navarre, les enfants de France, le cardinal de Tournon, le Connétable et même la Duchesse d'Étampes, maîtresse de François Ier, y eurent chacun des appartements proportionnés a leur qualité."

10. Sorbelli, *Memorie e studi intorno a Jacopo Barozzi*, Vignola, 1908.

"Pour conduire ce bâtiment avec plus de soins et pour le rendre plus régulier, il fit venir exprès d'Italie un des plus renommés architectes, & celui qui a le mieux écrit sur l'art de bâtir, nommé Sébastien Serlio, dont cependant les desseins, quoique très beaux, ne furent pas suivis; ceux de Pierre Lescot, Seigneur de Clagny qu'on appelait ordinairement l'abbé de Clagny, d'une famille de Paris considérable dans la robe, ayant été trouvés infiniment plus réguliers & plus magnifiques. Ce ne fut pas sans raison, puisque le peu de choses que l'on voit de cet habile maître peut passer sans contredit pour la plus belle et la plus correcte architecture que l'on connaisse, si l'on en croit les personnes les plus capables d'en juger."[11]

Cette affirmation a été considérée avec suspicion, et l'on s'est généralement gardé d'en tirer trop vite parti pour éclairer l'histoire du Louvre.[12] C'est vers Fontainebleau et non vers Paris qu'a été orienté Serlio quand, déjà âgé

11. Germain Brice, *Nouvelle description de la ville de Paris*, 8e édition, 1725, I, p. 47. Le passage a été déjà commenté de près par Berty, *Topographie historique du vieux Paris*, 1876, VII, p. 206: "La résolution de bâtir le Louvre étant définitivement adoptée par le Roi, quelque grandes qu'aient été les embarras financiers qui traversèrent ses desseins; ils le préoccupèrent peut-être moins que le choix d'un architecte capable de réaliser dignement sa pensée. Son engouement pour les artistes italiens était tel, qu'on doit s'étonner de la préférence qu'il donna à un français. Il est vrai que ce français dressa ses plans d'après les idées les plus avancées, et qu'il pourrait bien n'avoir fait que succéder à un Bolonais, dont la médiocre capacité s'était trop clairement révélée." – Ici vient la citation de Brice – "Il n'entrait point dans les usages de Brice de citer les autorités, de sorte qu'on est réduit à se demander où il avait puisé cette anecdote, qui ne paraît point avoir été connue de Sauval, et dont nous ne sachions pas qu'il soit fait mention antérieurement. Mais on a fort enchéri depuis sur le récit de G. Brice, en ajoutant que Serlio reconnut lui-même la supériorité de son concurrent. L'historiette ressemble beaucoup à un de ces enjolivements qu'il a été trop longtemps de mode de broder sur le fond des choses vraies. Les artistes italiens appelés en France ne péchaient point par excès de modestie; bien au contraire; ils étaient pleins de morgue . . . Quant à cette circonstance que des dessins furent demandés à Serlio en même temps qu'à LESCOT, elle peut avoir été apprise à Brice par un de ces 'curieux' qu'il fréquentait, et n'est point invraisemblable; mais il reste à prouver qu'elle a pour fondement autre chose qu'une tradition sans valeur. Ce dont nous avons la certitude morale, c'est que Serlio ne fut pas appelé d'Italie en vue d'une reconstitution du Louvre."

12. Dans sa précieuse *Histoire du Louvre*, L. Hautecœur, *op. cit.*, p. 15, n'a pas cru devoir retenir ce témoignage: "On a raconté que François Ier avait à cet effet (et ce pour fournir les plans du nouveau palais) mandé Serlio, mais que les plans de cet étranger avaient été jugés inférieurs à ceux de Lescot. Aucun document ne confirme ce fait." Dans la nouvelle édition (1965) de sa grande *Histoire de l'architecture classique en France*, tome I, *La Formation de l'idéal classique*, II, p. 122, où il analyse avec pénétration l'enseignement de Serlio et son immense influence, Hautecœur est amené à constater: "il (Serlio) traça dans son livre VI les plans d'un palais royal; il s'agit, semble-t-il, d'un projet de palais idéal et non pas, comme on l'a dit, d'un projet pour le Louvre." La convergence des faits, des dates et de la "tradition", nous ont orienté vers une conclusion différente.

(soixante-cinq ans passés), il est arrivé en France. Toutefois la réapparition du VIᵉ livre, resté inédit, de Serlio nous semble profondément modifier les données du problème et inviter à quelques réflexions nouvelles.[13] C'est sans nul doute le prestige dû à ses publications qui a éveillé l'intérêt du cardinal d'Armagnac puis du roi François pour maître Sébastien. Les volumes édités en 1537 et 1540 à Venise furent suivis de trois autres en 1545 et 1547 à Paris. Le livre VI consacré à la demeure était annoncé dès 1545 et devait offrir un cahier de modèles, fort attendu, à l'architecture française. Il a, comme on le sait, été remplacé, d'une manière qui semble improvisée, en 1551 à Lyon par le *libro extraordinario* (c'est-à-dire: hors série) consacré à des types de portes monumentales, qui se révélèrent d'ailleurs d'une très grande importance.

Mais enfin, il reste assez surprenant que le recueil prévu n'ait finalement pas été publié, car il est le couronnement de l'œuvre de Serlio et le fruit d'un travail d'adaptation des partis italiens aux usages français conduit avec une conscience assez exemplaire en tenant compte, selon ses propres paroles *"delle commodità di Franza le quali veramente ho trovato buone"*.[14] Mais, ce qui n'est pas moins digne d'attention, c'est la présentation qu'on y trouve des types hiérarchisés, comme le requerait la société française, *"incomminciendo dalla minima casipola del povero contadino et seguitando di grado in grado fin alla casa del principe"*. De ces demeures royales Serlio étudie les deux types fondamentaux: *"le maggiori fuori della città. Di poi di parte in parte si dirà di quelle dentro di essa città ..."* Ces études pour les châteaux à la campagne d'une part, et les palais de ville d'autre part, occupent une portion notable du manuscrit dans chacune des deux versions conservées, et les commentaires de Serlio impliquent nettement que ces projets ont été conçus pour le prince et soumis à son attention. Leur examen détaillé déborderait le cadre de cet article, où nous devons seulement souligner le fait qu'on y voit clairement se dégager pour la première fois les deux solutions qui apparaissent finalement comme les seules possibles, c'est-à-dire adaptées à la Majesté d'un grand roi: l'édifice de plan centré clairement de'fini dans le jeu des masses et l'ensemble complexe de cours et de portiques.

La *casa di un re* explicite le premier parti (Fig. 1): un quadrilatère pourvu de pavillons d'angle enveloppe une plate-forme surélevée, où se dresse un édifice de plan massé, fortement articulé (Fig. 2). De plan carré, il élève au-dessus de quatre pavillons d'angle reliés par des portiques – sur un plan qui rappelle le château de Madrid et ses précédents italiens – une rotonde intérieure nettement surélevée. L'organisation complexe de la structure semble traduire directement aux yeux comme un symbole plastique de la réalité monarchique. Le parti peut passer, grâce à certains détails, comme les escaliers droits qui coupent la plateforme et la rotonde intérieure, pour une anticipation de certaines solutions palladiennes. Il est typique d'une orientation d'avenir.

Quant à l'*habitatione regale*, dont le titre même indique qu'elle est directement conçue pour François Iᵉʳ, elle est l'occasion d'une suite de variations sur l'organisation de *cortili* de plan varié. Serlio a d'abord explicité sa pensée dans la surprenante conception des fᵒˢ 45–47, où la *reggia*, la demeure royale, reçoit la forme d'un amphithéâtre ovale (Fig. 3); il prévoit deux façades concentriques, et la plus animée est celle qui se trouve tournée vers l'intérieur de l'arène. Après cette démonstration – si surprenante et neuve – de ce qu'on pourrait appeler le palais-amphithéâtre, Serlio dans une nouvelle série de projets étudie l'intégration du *cortile* circulaire ou ovale à un vaste organisme, qui lui paraît nécessaire pour deux raisons: l'une de majesté royale, l'autre de convenance administrative. *"La casa del re deve essere sopra tutta le altre magnifica et grande et richissima di ornamenti"*; cette magnificence s'exprime par un système complexe de *cortili* co-ordonnés par des ailes longitudinales et horizontales qui découpent une sorte de réseau régulier, et c'est là une grande commodité pour la distribution des services, idée neuve et importante de concentration gouvernementale: *"hora"*, dit Serlio, *"mi convien trattare del principe absoluto al quale si conviene più che ad ognaltro administrare la giusticia"* (MS. Munich, fᵒ 64), en commentant l'un de ces ensembles géants (Fig. 4).

Les cours s'y comportent comme autant de cellules articulées selon un parti extrêmement régulier; les plus importantes sont mises en valeur par un portique qui souligne leur configuration. Le schéma le plus typique est celui qui présente une suite de cours successivement carrée, octogonale et circulaire (MS. Columbia fᵒ 71, MS. Munich 72), la cour médiane accompagnée de quatre salles d'angle à plan centré, dont deux au moins ont la destination de chapelles, ce qui ramène en élévation au parti à quatre tours, mais avec un accompagnement spectaculaire d'ailes et de passages. Une immense façade se trouve ainsi dégagée vers un jardin encadré, lui aussi de portiques, et comprenant dans l'axe une forme en exèdre qui ne peut pas ne

13. Il existe – comme on sait – en deux versions, l'une au cabinet des estampes de Munich, l'autre à l'Avery Library, Université Columbia, New York. La publication du second MS. a été annoncée par W. Dinsmoor, dans un copieux article préliminaire "The Literary Remains of Sebastiano Serlio", *Art Bulletin*, XXIV, 1942, mais n'a toujours pas vu le jour. P. du Colombier et P. d'Espezel, "Le VIᵉ livre retrouvé de Serlio et l'architecture française de la Renaissance", *GBA*, 1934, II, p. 42 et s., avaient souligné l'intérêt exceptionnel de l'ouvrage. Voir aussi M. H. Huber, "Sebastiano Serlio: sur une architecture civile *alla parisiana*", *L'Information d'Histoire de l'Art*, X, 1965, no. 1, p. 9. Le Doct. M. Rosci (Université de Milan) vient d'en publier une édition critique, dont il n'a pas été possible de tenir compte ici.
14. Ce qu'ont souligné P. du Colombier et P. d'Espezel, *art. cit.* Sur la "leçon" de Serlio, voir A. Blunt, *op. cit.*, p. 44 et s.; L. Hautecœur, nouvelle éd., 1965, p. 119 et s.

pas rappeller la terminaison du parc du palais du Té à Mantoue.[15]

Dans une variante qui n'apparaît que dans le MS. de Munich (Fig. 4), le plan, couvrant deux feuillets, traite la cellule centrale comme une cour ovale, en la faisant précéder et suivre d'une cour carrée à portiques. L'ensemble, également pris dans un rectangle, comporte douze *cortili*; mais à l'extrémité supérieure, ils s'ouvrent comme des cours d'entrée, et à l'extrémité sud se développe une façade ambitieuse, avec un léger ressaut et un escalier monumental. Dans ce plan, manifestement très étudié, se résume la conception nouvelle de la "demeure royale", et on peut le considérer comme le dernier mot de Serlio en ce domaine. Or, il se trouve reproduit dans une gravure anonyme de l'Institut de France (Fig. 5) que M. Hautecœur a tout naturellement rapproché des compositions d'Androuet du Cerceau.[16] Il serait important de savoir quand et à quelle occasion le plan a eu les honneurs de la gravure. Ce document nous atteste, en tout cas, l'intérêt porté au projet de Serlio dans les milieux de la cour. Certaines analogies apparaissent avec le superbe plan des Tuileries de Philibert de l'Orme, publié par du Cerceau, qui nous présente un développement génial des idées énoncées par Serlio: le système des cours perd de sa naïveté grâce à l'extension de la grande aile centrale et à la subordination des cours secondaires; le changement d'orientation qui donne pour axe au château le petit côté, permet le déploiement de deux façades rythmées par les saillies du pavillon. Serlio n'a fait qu'esquisser – assez laborieusement – ce que la nouvelle génération allait mieux concevoir, mais les préoccupations de grandeur et de traitement monumental sont les mêmes. On en revient donc à se demander si Claude Perrault et Germain Brice n'ont pas eu raison de parler de la participation de Serlio au "concours" du Louvre des Valois.

La cour circulaire instituant un véritable amphithéâtre au cours de l'édifice pouvait – en raison du précédent proche du palais de Grenade – apparaître comme indispensable à la formule moderne de la demeure royale. Son intégration au parti déjà acclimaté et francisé du château à quatre pavillons d'angle, à la faveur d'un réseau régulier de *cortili*, offrait une sorte de conclusion originale et nécessaire aux exigences du programme. Les textes d'accompagnement de maître Sébastien ne cessent de répéter que tous ces projets ont été étudiés pour François Ier et, en particulier, le grand ensemble destiné *"al gran Re Francesco l'ingegno e l'animo e il potere del quale si vede in molti edificii da sua maiestà ordinati e in gran parte finiti"*. Allusion à ce qui a été fait: Chambord, Madrid, mais bien vraisemblablement aussi à ce qui reste à faire, c'est-à-dire au Louvre. Car *la casa del Re in città* était, on ne peut en douter, après 1540 l'une des hantises de la fin du règne.

Aucun des projets de Serlio ne fut retenu. Et l'on ne pourrait s'en étonner que si C. Perrault et G. Brice, en nous signalant leur existence, ne donnaient une raison décisive du choix final et tardif de François Ier: la qualité supérieure du plan de Lescot. Il est seulement malheureux que nous ne connaissions pas la conception d'ensemble de l'abbé de Clagny: outre les mérites éclatants de son élévation de façade, il put bénéficier aussi de la prudence avec laquelle il abordait le problème, en épousant purement et simplement les contours de la vieille forteresse de Charles V. Le remplacement de l'aile ouest par un corps de bâtiment de volumes, en gros, identique, avait sans doute l'avantage de ne pas trop préjuger de l'avenir.

Les projets de Serlio pour *la casa del Re in città*, à moins de démolitions incroyables à l'ouest de Saint-Germain-l'Auxerrois, n'étaient concevables qu'*extra muros* à l'emplacement des Tuileries de Philibert. Les circonstances dans lesquelles a été décidé le nouveau Louvre, continuent à nous échapper dans une trop large mesure. Mais si l'on doit, comme nous le croyons à notre tour, faire intervenir le diligent – et modeste – Serlio, à un certain moment du problème, plusieurs particularités de la situation des années 1550–60 peuvent s'éclairer. D'abord la retraite impécunieuse du vieil architecte, qui n'a pas réalisé son chef-d'œuvre et s'attache à la publication de son traité, en continuant à perfectionner son livre VI. Et d'autre part le ton de gratitude et de révérence avec lequel tous les architectes français notoires ont parlé de lui. Philibert et Jean Goujon l'ont traité comme leur maître, et la manière dont ses projets ont fructifié, apparaît comme la revanche posthume de celui qui avait su proposer à la demeure bourgeoise et rurale française des schémas féconds, mais qui, malgré des propositions ingénieuses, variées et stimulantes, avait finalement échoué devant le thème majeur de la "demeure royale".

15. On observe aussi que cette composition "axée" est contemporaine des "perspectives dynamiques" de Michel-Ange, sur lesquelles a insisté judicieusement J. Ackerman, *The Architecture of Michelangelo*, 2 vol., Londres, 1961. Il nous paraît forcé d'en faire un trait spécifique de l'architecture française, comme dans la courte note de B. Lowry, "High Renaissance Architecture", *College Art Journal*, XVII, 1957, p. 115.

16. L. Hautecœur, *Histoire de l'architecture classique*, nouv. éd., tome II, vol. I, fig. 171, p. 441. La prédilection de Du Cerceau pour les compositions à plan central, annulaire, tréflé ou cruciforme, est frappante. Il paraît difficile de ne pas établir un rapport de filiation entre les deux "thèmes" de l'amphithéâtre et du quadrilatère et le singulier projet du *Livre d'architecture*, 1582, XX, où, sur un socle bastionné, s'élève un vaste édifice cruciforme, dont le centre s'ouvre sur une immense cour circulaire à portique, un second anneau contenant quatre systèmes rigoureusement symétriques d'escaliers accédant à l'étage; voir Hautecœur, *ibid.*, p. 438.

MICHEL LACLOTTE

Quelques tableaux bourguignons du XVIᵉ siècle

Si l'activité des peintres italiens et français à Fontainebleau fait l'objet d'incessantes hypothèses, si le catalogue des portraitistes de la Cour s'appuie toujours, pour une bonne part, sur les bases établies par L. Dimier et E. Moreau-Nélaton, un examen d'ensemble des autres sources de production picturale du XVIᵉ siècle français, celle des provinces, n'a pas encore été tenté. La plupart des histoires générales de notre peinture ignorent même jusqu'à l'existence d'ateliers ou d'artistes travaillant loin de la Cour et dont les recherches de Chennevières et d'autres érudits du XIXᵉ siècle, celles, plus récentes, de L. H. Labande sur la Provence, de R. Mesuret sur le Languedoc, des organisateurs de l'exposition troyenne de 1953 sur la Champagne, de J. Thuillier sur le Pseudo Félix-Chrestien ont pourtant permis d'entrevoir l'importance. Il faudra bien un jour rassembler les pièces documentaires du dossier, identifier les nombreux tableaux qui, sous attributions italienne, flamande ou germanique attendent leur naturalisation française dans les églises, les châteaux et les musées de nos provinces, et dresser enfin un bilan. Refaire en somme pour le XVIᵉ siècle ce qui fut fait, il y a soixante ans, pour les "Primitifs" français.[1]

Dans son maître-ouvrage consacré à l'art français de 1500 à 1700, A. F. Blunt indique déjà une première voie de recherches lorsqu'il souligne l'intérêt de certaines peintures religieuses de l'Est de la France. C'est en effet, semble-t-il, dans ces régions que la quête risque d'être la plus fructueuse. Le propos de cette modeste note n'est certes pas d'apporter des conclusions générales sur la peinture provinciale au XVIᵉ siècle, mais, en attendant les recensements systématiques qui s'imposent, d'attirer simplement l'attention sur quelques tableaux encore trop peu connus.

On s'étonne ainsi que le monumental *Triptyque de l'Eucharistie* (Figs. 1–2), anonyme mais daté 1515, du Musée d'Autun, publié par L. Réau et cité par A. F. Blunt,[2] n'ait pas acquis la notoriété qu'il mérite. Il révèle pourtant une personnalité exceptionnelle, qui tout en s'inspirant de la manière italianisante des Flandres et surtout des Pays-Bas du Nord, aboutit à une robuste stylisation plastique dont aucun Néerlandais contemporain ne fournit d'exemple aussi net et qui paraît présager les simplifications d'un

Scorel.[3] Certes le peintre bourguignon ignore la cohérence spatiale enseignée par les italiens au maître d'Utrecht. Mais la force insolite de son art ne tient-elle pas précisément à la juxtaposition assez anarchique de morceaux franchement "cubistes" (tel le crâne de saint Pierre dans la *Cène* du triptyque) et de détails vrais (l'admirable portrait de l'apôtre au premier plan à gauche de la même composition ou la nature morte d'*Abraham et Melchisédech*), de déformations un peu absurdes et d'effets de trompe-l'œil (les reflets eyckiens dans l'armure de Melchisédech) révélant un désir ostentatoire d'objectivité réaliste?

Aucune des peintures actuellement repérées en Bourgogne et dans les régions voisines et datant du premier tiers du siècle ne recèle de qualités aussi neuves. Plusieurs cependant sont dignes de mieux retenir l'attention. C'est le cas d'un groupe d'œuvres dont la plus ancienne, datée de 1521, est une *Présentation de la Vierge au Temple* (musée de Dijon) naguère attribuée à Pontormo puis à un maître allemand et que nous avons suggéré de restituer à un peintre travaillant en Bourgogne.[4] Il nous semble légitime de rapprocher de ce tableau les *Saintes Femmes au Tombeau* (Fig. 3) de l'Hospice de Cluny et un remarquable triptyque, avec la *Déploration du Christ* (Fig. 4) (Hôtel de Ville de Châtillon-sur-Chalaronne dans l'Ain), qui date de 1527. Cette dernière peinture offre à son tour d'étroites analogies avec deux panneaux de retable (Figs. 5–6) (au recto: la *Montée au Calvaire* et la *Mise au Tombeau*) conservés à l'église Notre-Dame de Bourg-en-Bresse et datés de 1523.[5]

De mérite inégal, ces quatre œuvres nous paraissent – outre d'évidentes parentés typologiques (visages, mains, draperies, tissus, paysages) – recourir à un style commun: compositions sobres et monumentales, solidement construites et groupant les figures sur un seul plan comme pour un haut-relief (la verticale étant souvent accusée par le profil pur d'un ou de plusieurs personnages), modelé simplifié déterminant de larges aplats, coloris clair. Ce sont précisément

---

1. L'exposition de 1904 présentait bien quelques tableaux du XVIᵉ s., mais sans rien de systématique dans leur groupement.
2. L. Réau, *Les Richesses d'art: la Bourgogne, la peinture*, 1929, pls. 22–24; A. Blunt, *Art and Architecture in France, 1550–1700*, 2ᵉ éd., 1957, p. 237.

3. La comparaison avec des œuvres contemporaines françaises, telles que la *Mise au Tombeau* de Marly-le-Roy (1516) ou la *Déposition du Christ* datée de 1515 (Springfield) et la *Mise au Tombeau* (coll. Mrs. Hart), ces dernières dûes au Monogrammist M͞m (cf. *Connoisseur*, oct. 1961, repr. et *Bulletin* du musée de Springfield, juin-juillet 1960, repr.), œuvres encore toute "médiévales", accuse le "modernisme" du peintre d'Autun. Ce dernier a-t-il connu la *Cène* gravée par Marc-Antoine? L'hypothèse, soulevée par John Shearman, n'est pas absurde.
4. Exposition du *XVIᵉ s. européen dans les collections publiques françaises*, Paris, Petit-Palais, 1965, catal. no. 332, repr.
5. A. Germain, in *GBA*, 1923, I, p. 114 sq.

les traits qui définissent la manière du peintre de l'*Eucharistie* d'Autun. Informé par une culture artistique moins provinciale, celui-ci met évidemment ces moyens techniques au service d'une imagination poétique plus inventive que celle des peintres de Bourg, de Châtillon ou de Cluny. Il nous paraît cependant raisonnable de considérer que ces tableaux et quelques autres[6] témoignent de l'existence en Bourgogne et dans la Bresse, durant le premier tiers du XVIe siècle, d'un courant pictural, provincial à coup sûr, mais original, et qui prolonge l'école régionale du XVe siècle en "francisant" comme elle la manière flamande. Que, pour ce faire, les peintres du XVIe siècle, animés d'un souci constant de sobre élégance et de dignité expressive, aient eu recours à l'enseignement traditionnel des grandes techniques médiévales alors toujours en vigueur, la sculpture – qui soutient leur volonté de simplicité monumentale et de force plastique – et le vitrail – qui explique la clarté de leur coloris posé en aplats –, est une nouvelle preuve de cette continuité: n'est-ce pas ainsi que les meilleurs peintres français du XVe siècle avaient conquis leur indépendance et échappé à l'emprise flamande?

Fortement liés ainsi à la tradition picturale française, ces peintres, faute d'imagination iconographique, ont pourtant souvent recours à des modèles étrangers "modernes". La *Présentation* de Dijon démarque celle de Dürer (*Vie de la Vierge*, publiée en 1511). De leur côté, l'auteur des panneaux de Bourg et celui du triptyque de Châtillon-sur-Chalaronne, tout en se souvenant des grandes *Mises au Tombeau* de la sculpture gothique, ont certainement eu entre les mains les planches de la *Petite* et de la *Grande Passion* du même maître, parues aussi en 1511. On ne s'en étonne pas lorsqu'on sait le succès européen de ces suites de gravures. Il est plus surprenant de reconnaître dans le triptyque (Fig. 7)[7] de Saint-Pantaléon (Saône-et-Loire), encadrée de volets et derrière un parapet à la flamande, la *Vierge aux Rochers* de Léonard, non pas celle aujourd'hui au Louvre – ce qui aurait prouvé la présence du tableau en France dès 1520, preuve si souvent cherchée! –, mais celle de Londres peinte

pour San Francesco Grande de Milan et alors en place. Il s'agit donc de la traduction, à la mode bourguignonne telle que nous l'avons décrite, d'une copie de ce dernier tableau, l'un de ceux de Léonard qui suscita le plus grand nombre d'imitations. Le musée de Budapest conserve, attribués à un peintre flamand, deux volets figurant, comme ceux de Saint-Pantaléon, Sainte Catherine et Sainte Barbe (Figs. 8–9) et qui paraissent bien provenir d'un triptyque identique. On remarquera d'ailleurs que le visage de Sainte Barbe s'inspire de celui de l'Ange de la *Vierge aux Rochers*. Ces analogies et aussi la facture des panneaux hongrois, supérieure à celle du retable de Saint-Pantaléon mais si proche par exemple de celle du panneau de Cluny, nous autorisent à proposer leur annexion à l'"école" bourguignonne.[8]

Nous n'avons pas à suivre ici la destinée des ateliers bourguignons après 1530. Contentons-nous d'observer que la tradition locale y fut assez forte pour imprégner profondément l'œuvre du plus grand peintre travaillant dans la région au XVIe siècle, le pseudo Félix-Chrestien, sans doute d'origine nordique pourtant et lié aux courants nouveaux. On sait que la province voisine, la Champagne, donna naissance au XVIe siècle à une école prolifique; les églises de Troyes et de la région sont encore pleines de retables ou de panneaux peints, plus d'une centaine, datant du XVIe siècle. A vrai dire la qualité moyenne de ces œuvres, reflets souvent rustiques de poncifs flamands ou germaniques, est passablement artisanale et nous suivons F. Mathey lorsqu'il avance que l'école troyenne de peinture au XIVe siècle est avant tout celle des verriers.[9] Or il se trouve que les deux peintures champenoises qui, à notre avis, dépassent le niveau moyen de la production locale, l'*Assomption* (1522; au revers: *Sainte Élisabeth*) et le *Songe de saint Joseph* portant au revers *Jésus parmi les Docteurs* (1541), toutes deux au musée de Vauluisant à Troyes, offrent de réelles analogies d'esprit et de manière avec des tableaux bourguignons. L'*Assomption* constitue presque un pendant à la *Presentation de la Vierge* de Dijon citée plus haut et le *Songé de saint Joseph* – selon nous l'un des chefs-d'œuvre de la peinture française du XVIe siècle – rappelle de troublante façon le style du pseudo Félix-Chrestien.[10] Est-il dès lors imprudent de suggérer, grâce aux témoignages rares mais

6. Citons par exemple: le Retable de Saint Jérôme (1518), provenant de Notre-Dame de Bourg-en-Bresse, au musée de cette ville (A. Germain, *Le Musée de Bourg*, s.d., fig. 33–38), le Retable de Saint Laurent (1522) à Saint-Léger-sur-Dheune (Saône-et-Loire), le Retable de Girard de Vienne et Bénigne de Dinteville (1526) au château de Commarin (Côte-d'Or) exposé avec "*Les Plus Belles Œuvres des coll. de la Côte-d'Or*" au musée de Dijon en 1958 (catal. no. 1–4, repr.), le Triptyque de l'*Adoration des Bergers* (1526) de l'église de Saint-Trivier-de-Courtes (Ain) qui viendrait de Senosans (Saône-et-Loire) et fut exposé (ainsi que les panneaux de Notre-Dame de Bourg et le Retable de Châtillon-sur-Chalaronne) au musée de Bourg en 1958 (*Marguerite d'Autriche*; catal. no. 143, repr.). Un *Saint Georges délivrant la princesse* du Louvre, panneau en grisaille, paraît de même origine.
Le Triptyque de la Vierge provenant de Beaune et aujourd'hui à Auxey (exposé en 1950 au Petit-Palais (*La Vierge dans l'art français*, no. 59) est d'un style différent, simple adaptation provinciale de Dürer et des flamands.
7. E. Castelnuovo, in *Paragone*, no. 39, 1953, p. 59, fig. 30.

8. Les panneaux seraient datés 1520, comme le triptyque de Saint-Pantaléon. Attribués aujourd'hui à l'école flamande, ils furent jadis considérés comme français par G. von Terey et à ce titre exposés à l'exposition de Primitifs de 1904 (no. 372).
9. F. Mathey in catal. de l'exposition *Les Trésors d'art de l'école troyenne* (Musée de Vauluisant, Troyes, 1953) et in *Combat-Art*, no. 3, 1 janvier 1954.
10. Cf. catal. expos. Petit-Palais, 1965, *cit.*, nos. 332, 333 et 232 et 335. Ces analogies, rendues sensibles par la confrontation des œuvres à cette exposition, ont frappé les spécialistes; par ailleurs le caractère "français" du Retable de Sainte Eugénie du pseudo Félix-Chrestien (no. 232) est clairement apparu à bon nombre d'entre eux.

remarquables qui en subsistent,[11] la permanence d'une véritable école de peinture en Bourgogne durant la première moitié du XVIᵉ siècle, assez originale pour enrichir tout en la poursuivant la tradition du XVᵉ siècle, assez forte pour étendre son rayonnement sur la Bresse et marquer de son influence la Champagne?

11. La rareté des peintures subsistant en Bourgogne par rapport à celles conservées en Champagne peut s'expliquer en partie par le fait que la première province, plus prospère que la seconde aux XVIIᵉ et XVIIIᵉ siècles, a notablement enrichi ses églises au cours de ces deux siècles, donc renouvelé le décor de ces églises et pratiqué d'abondantes destructions d'œuvres reputées "gothiques". Le hasard des hécatombes révolutionnaires peut aussi expliquer cette disparité.

CHARLES STERLING

Un Portrait inconnu par Jean Clouet

EN 1925, le City Art Museum de Saint Louis faisait l'acquisition d'un fort beau portrait d'*Homme aux pièces d'or* (Fig. 8).[1] Représenté à mi-corps, sur un fond noir, debout ou assis derrière un comptoir couvert d'une étoffe verte, vêtu d'une cotte rouge orangé et d'un pourpoint noir, l'homme tient dans sa gauche une plume d'oie qu'il appuie sur un papier portant l'inscription: LAN.1522 FAIT A 35; il était donc né en 1487. Les doigts de l'autre main touchent, comme s'ils les comptaient, des pièces d'or parmi lesquelles on distingue des écus français du début du XVIᵉ siècle.[2] Le tableau provenait de la collection du comte de la Rochefoucauld, duc de Brisaccia, au Château d'Eschemont. Il était alors traditionnellement attribué à un peintre anonyme français et fort bien caractérisé dans une note du Bulletin du Musée: "That it is a French painting of the period there can be little doubt although it has been ascribed to various contemporary Flemish masters".[3]

Pris isolément, le costume, la langue de l'inscription, les pièces d'or, la provenance, bien que tous français n'auraient pas suffi pour exclure un peintre flamand portraiturant un personnage français soit en France soit aux Pays-Bas. Car dans le premier quart du XVIᵉ siècle, on parlait toujours le français à Bruxelles et à Malines, à la cour de Marguerite d'Autriche, et la circulation de la monnaie d'or était internationale. Pourtant, le concours de ces circonstances militait en faveur de l'attribution traditionnelle. Mais le progrès n'est pas toujours de ce monde et l'attribution fut promptement changée. On donna d'abord le tableau à Jan Mostaert, thèse insoutenable. On le qualifia ensuite de "franco-flamand", catégorie foncièrement justifiée par les caractères stylistiques, mais, au début du XVIᵉ siècle, historiquement vide de sens. En 1930, un critique allemand proposa le nom de Barthel Bruyn; et, en 1952 encore, un autre critique allemand pensa à un peintre d'Augsbourg ou de Bâle. En 1944, j'ai écrit au Musée que l'œuvre me paraissait suffisamment proche de Jean Clouet pour qu'on puisse songer à la lui rendre.[4] La vague désignation

"franco-flamand", qui continua à lui être appliquée, s'avéra néfaste pour la réputation du tableau; elle l'a enfoncé dans l'obscurité. Il n'a même pas été mentionné dans un guide du Musée réimprimé en 1954, alors qu'une médiocre copie du portrait de François Iᵉʳ par Joos van Clève y recevait les honneurs d'une reproduction. Il n'a pas été choisi pour figurer dans l'exposition des cinquante meilleures peintures du Musée, en 1958, où des œuvres de moindre intérêt l'ont supplanté.[5] Il semble donc utile de justifier une attribution proposé il y a vingt ans, d'autant plus qu'on ne connaissait jusqu'à présent que sept portraits sur panneau certains de Jean Clouet. Celui de Saint Louis est l'un des meilleurs et, seul portant une date, il contribue à éclairer l'évolution et les habitudes d'atelier de l'artiste.

Les œuvres de Jean Clouet portraitiste[2] nous sont aujourd'hui connues de façon incontestable. Depuis longtemps, on a remarqué la parfaite unité de style d'un vaste groupe de têtes dessinées – 130 "crayons" environ, la majorité à Chantilly. On s'est aperçu en même temps que plusieurs de ces têtes ont servi de préparation à des portraits en miniature ou sur panneau qui subsistent. Leurs modèles identifiés et leurs costumes indiquent la période de 1515 à 1540 environ; ce sont là les dates entre lesquelles s'étend la partie documentée de la carrière française de Jean Clouet dit Janet ou Genet, peintre arrivé des Pays-Bas (1516 à 1540 ou 1541, le temps de sa mort). Or, l'un de ces portraits sur panneau, celui de Guillaume Budé (Metropolitan Museum, New York),[7] est attesté, vers 1536, par le grand humaniste lui-même comme une œuvre de "Maître Genet Clouet"; et le dessin préliminaire de sa tête fait précisément partie du groupe de Chantilly. Ainsi se trouve solidement fondée l'attribution à Jean Clouet de tout ce groupe de dessins, de huit miniatures et de sept panneaux dont la plupart sont

Rauh, conservateur, et Mr. Clements L. Robertson, restaurateur du Musée, de m'avoir communiqué ces renseignements et d'autres, d'ordre technique, qui m'ont été très utiles.

5. *City Art Museum of Saint Louis, Handbook* (sans date, 1954); catalogue de l'exposition *Fifty Masterworks from the City Art Museum of Saint Louis*, New York, Wildenstein Gall., 1958.

6. Il ne convient pas, en effet, d'oublier que Jean Clouet a fait également des compositions religieuses dont on ignore tout. Ce ne devait être cependant qu'une activité accessoire: par les contemporains, par Budé, par exemple, il était considéré et apprécié comme un spécialiste du portrait: "pictor iconicus".

7. On trouve de ce tableau fort endommagé et restauré, mais toujours impressionnant, une assez bonne reproduction en couleur (malheureusement coupée dans le bas et à gauche, ce qui change sa composition) in *La Peinture française de Fouquet à Poussin*, Skira, 1963, p. 120.

---

1. Panneau de chêne. 42·5 × 32·5 cm. (16¾ × 12¾ in.).
2. En 1955, Mr. Herbert A. Cahn a reconnu dans ces pièces, où la fleur de lys se distingue clairement, des écus français de la seconde moitié du XVᵉ siècle. Il semble cependant que ce soient plutôt des pièces du règne de Louis XII et de François Iᵉʳ (cf. H. Hoffmann, *Les Monnaies royales de France*, II, Paris, 1878, pl. LIV).
3. *Bulletin of the City Art Museum of Saint Louis*, XI, January 1926, p. 3. Note non signée.
4. Toutes ces opinions sont consignées au dossier du tableau dans les archives du Musée de Saint Louis. Je remercie Miss Emily

authentifiées par des crayons correspondants et les autres –
ceux dont les crayons sont perdus – par une parenté
stylistique évidente.[8]

C'est également le cas du portrait de Saint Louis, le crayon
sur le vif qui a servi à peindre dans l'atelier la tête du
modèle ne paraît pas conservé. Je ne crois pas qu'il y ait
grande chance à le jamais retrouver. Car les crayons qui
ont survécu sont ceux des membres de la famille royale, des
personnages de la cour et de quelques grands intellectuels
dont la réputation s'imposa à la cour; ce sont eux que les
contemporains collectionnaient. L'homme de Saint Louis
n'appartenait pas à ce milieu, c'était un bourgeois. Mais,
comme dans tous les tableaux de Jean Clouet la tête peinte
suit de près le crayon, il suffit de comparer la tête à Saint
Louis à un crayon de l'artiste des alentours de 1520 (Fig. 8
et Fig. 4), pour y retrouver le même dessin du nez et de la
bouche, les mêmes accents sur le menton, les mêmes légères
poches sous les yeux (très nettes dans la peinture et toujours
perceptibles dans la reproduction). La parenté est si étroite
qu'à première vue on croirait à l'identité du modèle. Il n'en
est rien, il s'agit de portraits de deux hommes différents
portant des chapeaux et des coiffures analogues.[9] Mais cette
parenté est la meilleure preuve de l'identité du dessinateur
qui a construit ces visages. Quant à la facture picturale, elle
se retrouve également dans les panneaux certains de Jean
Clouet: les manches de la petite *Charlotte de France* (vers
1524; coll. Mrs. J. Epstein, Chicago) et les manches de
l'homme de Saint Louis sont froissées en plis luisants et
sinueux d'une similitude frappante (Fig. 8 et Fig. 5). Les
mains dans ces deux tableaux, sans être d'un dessin et d'un
modelé identiques peuvent être d'un même artiste travaillant à deux ans d'intervalle; elles sont soumises à une
stylisation amplifiante analogue.[10] L'attribution du portrait
de Saint Louis à Jean Clouet paraît donc assurée.

Il n'en est malheureusement pas de même de l'identité du
modèle qui demeure anonyme. Toutes les recherches res-
tèrent jusqu'à présent infructueuses. Ceci, en dépit de nombreuses données fournies par le peintre lui-même et mises en
évidence: un écu d'armes sur la bague de la main gauche,
très petit mais très net, qui se lit: *d'argent à deux bandes
d'azur accompagnées de trois roses de gueules posées deux et un*;
le bouton du pourpoint qui porte un monogramme com-

plexe mais également fort clair, donnant soit le nom du
personnage soit sa devise; enfin, sa date de naissance, 1487.
La présence de l'argent a fait penser qu'il s'agit d'un
banquier. Mais la plume jointe à l'argent conviendrait
aussi bien, peut-être même mieux, à un marchand, comme
c'est le cas dans plusieurs portraits de Holbein. Ces deux
attributs pourraient également caractériser un fonction-
naire de finances, qui manie l'argent et tient des comptes en
même temps, receveur de finances ou trésorier. Les portraits de marchands ne sont pas connus en France au XVIe
siècle. Ceux de grands bourgeois, fonctionnaires de
finances, pouvaient par contre être traditionnels à Tours
depuis que Fouquet en a donné l'exemple en représentant
Étienne Chevalier. Il paraît vraisemblable que Clouet ait pu
peindre à Tours, où il est mentionné entre 1516 et 1529 et,
spécifiquement, en 1522,[11] un trésorier (de la ville ou du roi,
dont il était déjà "valet de chambre ordinaire") qui aurait
pu lui faire des paiements pour ses travaux.[12]

La date de 1522 permet de se rendre mieux compte de l'art
de Jean Clouet: elle prouve que sa conception de portrait
n'évolua pas de façon constante de la tradition gothique
flamande vers la nouveauté italienne de la Renaissance;
qu'elle fut plutôt hésitante et timide. On a déjà observée le
peu de nuances dans le style de ses crayons qui s'étendent
pourtant sur un quart de siècle. Les têtes peintes qui correspondent aux crayons conservés, si elles varient en plasticité,
ne forment pas non plus une suite chronologique témoi-
gnant d'une progression délibérée.

Il en est de même de la composition des portraits à mi-
corps. Pour que nous puissions parler d'un développement
logique de la composition dans le sens de l'évolution du
portrait septentrional contemporain – celui de Quentin
Massys, de Gossaert, de Joos van Clève ou de Holbein – il
aurait fallu qu'on trouve chez Jean Clouet l'évocation d'un
espace de plus en plus profond et une monumentalité
croissante; en un mot, une distance grandissante, à la fois
plastique et psychologique, entre nous et le modèle. A un
type de portrait archaïque, hérité du XVe siècle, devrait succéder un type marqué de la recherche d'une amplification,

8. Bien que le nombre de sept panneaux soit le même que chez
Dimier (*Hist. de la peinture du portrait en France*, II, Paris, 1925,
pp. 33–34), ma liste ne comporte pas les mêmes tableaux. Elle
en exclut le *Petit portrait de François Ier*, au Louvre, que je tiens
pour une copie et que je remplace par *Madame de Canaples*
d'Édimbourg.

9. La coiffure de l'homme à Saint Louis montre un repentir exactement semblable à celui du crayon de Chantilly repr. pl. CXII du
grand recueil de Moreau-Nélaton. Ce repentir qui forme une
tache brune sur la joue est maintenant très gênant.

10. La date du tableau de Chicago que Dimier situe vers 1520 doit
en effet être avancée. Charlotte mourut le 8 septembre 1524 à
l'âge de sept ans et huit mois. Il est évident que son âge apparent
dans le tableau indique au moins sept ans.

11. Le 10 mai 1522, il s'engage à peindre un *Saint Jérôme*. Le 6 juin
suivant, dans un acte d'achat, il est dit "présent" (Ch. L. Grand-
maison, *Les Arts en Touraine*, 1870, p. 64).

12. Dans le monogramme du bouton on distingue nettement les
lettres MTRAVENI et un S qui les *traverse* toutes. Les archives de
Tours contiennent des paiements à des artistes employés à l'entrée
de François Ier qui furent effectués, en 1516 et 1520, par le
receveur de la ville du nom de Martin Travers, échevin et
membre d'une famille tourangelle éminente. Cette belle coincidence, agrémentée d'un jeu de mots bien dans l'esprit du temps,
m'avait fait espérer l'identification du personnage. Mais les
armes de la famille Travers, telles du moins qu'on a pu les
retrouver jusqu'à présent, ne correspondent pas à l'écu du portrait. Je remercie beaucoup le prof. Bernard Chevalier et Madame
N. Reynaud, Chargée de Mission au Musée du Louvre, d'avoir
bien voulu entreprendre sur ma demande, à Paris et à Tours,
des recherches au sujet de Martin Travers.

d'un anoblissement du modèle, à l'italienne. Après les personnages placés tout à l'avant-plan du tableau et à l'étroit dans le cadre, tournés entièrement, tête et buste, de trois quarts, et ainsi se laissant comme suprendre et s'offrant passivement à notre investigation, nous devrions rencontrer des personnages déployés frontalement, situés contre un fond plus vaste et souvent derrière une table où quelques objets servant d'attribut trouvent de la place, des individus qui nous imposent leur personnalité et qui se laissent contempler dans un froid éloignement. Or, ces deux types de compositions existent effectivement chez Clouet, mais ils ne se présentent presque jamais dans leur pureté et ne se suivent pas chronologiquement. Leurs traits constitutifs sont toujours mêlés et ils sont synchroniques. En 1522, l'*Homme aux pièces d'or* est bien plus avancé que ne le sera *Charlotte de France* deux ans plus tard. Vers 1535, *Guillaume Budé* représente le type le plus évolué parmi les portraits connus de Clouet, mais à la même époque l'*Inconnu au Pétrarque* (Fig. 1), bien que monumental par son buste déployé, est archaïque par sa mise en page étroite et son manque d'espace profond.

Non seulement la composition mais certaines parties significatives des portraits de Jean Clouet telles que les mains appartiennent à deux types bien distincts et cependant contemporains. Les unes sont directement réalistes, aux doigts souples, d'un contour plutôt sinueux (Claude de Guise, vers 1525-30, Fig. 6; *Madame de Canaples*, vers 1525, Édimbourg; *Louis de Nevers*, vers 1535, Bergame; *Budé*, vers 1535); elles sont disposées à l'avant-plan selon l'antique tradition remontant à Roger van der Weyden. Les autres mains sont, au contraire, calmes et amples, aux doigts plutôt rectilignes et cylindriques, stylisés à l'italienne, comparables aux doigts de Holbein. Telles sont les mains de la petite Charlotte (Fig. 5) et celles de l'*Inconnu au Pétrarque* (vers 1535; Fig. 1).[13] On ne saurait en douter, il y a là à l'œuvre deux artistes différents; et l'auteur des mains stylisées appartient à une génération plus jeune, il assimile aisément l'esprit volumétrique italien. Qui peuvent être ces deux peintres dans l'atelier de Jean Clouet? La haute qualité du dessin et du modelé interdisent de voir en eux des aides subalternes. En effet, nous possédons des indices qui permettent de croire qu'il s'agit d'une collaboration des deux maîtres: les mains "gothiques", à la flamande, sont du vieux Jean Clouet; les mains "à l'italienne", de son jeune fils, François.

Pour les premières, la preuve nous est fournie par les crayons originaux de Jean, ceux qui, exceptionnellement, comportent des mains. Voici un *Inconnu* (vers 1535-40; Fig. 7) qui, tout comme Claude de Guise (Fig. 6), repose sa

main droite dans les plis de son manteau drapé comme une toge; geste imité des statues et des bustes de patriciens romains et employé non seulement par Holbein (1533, Berlin) mais aussi en France par Perréal.[14] Les deux mains sont d'un caractère tout à fait similaire, dans les deux le pouce est recourbé. Pour les mains de type italianisant, nous n'avons qu'à les comparer à celles des tableaux signés de François Clouet, de la célèbre *Dame au bain* par exemple (Fig. 3): ce sont les doigts de Charlotte de France (Fig. 5) ou de l'*Inconnu au Pétrarque* (Fig. 1), pliés anguleusement, rectilignes, cylindriques et seulement à peine plus allongés, plus élégants comme il convient à une œuvre de beaucoup postérieure et marquée par l'influence accrue de Florence et de Fontainebleau.

Mais si François a pu peindre dans l'atelier de son père, vers 1524, les mains de Charlotte de France, il aurait fallu qu'il ait eu à cette époque entre 15 et 20 ans – l'âge où la formation encore médiévale permettait aux talents de mûrir, témoin Lucas de Leyde. Il faudrait situer sa naissance entre 1505 et 1510 environ. Cela n'est point invraisemblable et Anthony Blunt est arrivé à la même conclusion: "his birth must be placed not later than 1510 and probably rather earlier".[15] Il est en effet certain que son père a dû s'établir en France tout au début du siècle. S'il n'est pas exact que Lemaire de Belges le cite dans sa *Plainte du désiré* (rédigée déjà en 1503),[16] nous avons le témoignage d'un texte de François Ier daté de 1541 qui parle du séjour en France de Clouet le père sous "nos prédécesseurs roys"; ce qui indique pour le moins le règne de Louis XII: 1498-1515. Il est plus que probable que l'apprentissage de François auprès de son père l'ait conduit de bonne heure à une collaboration intime: son style personnel émerge directement de celui de Jean et les contemporains, étendant au fils le surnom du père, en confondant les deux sous l'appellation de Janet, exprimèrent clairement la continuité de leur art. Le texte de 1541 qui déclare que François "a jà si bien ymyté" le talent de son père est fort significatif à cet égard.

On est en droit de penser que les débuts personnels de François consistaient à exécuter des parties de certains portraits, telles que les mains ou le costume, que son père lui confiait. Mai il y a un cas où sa part paraît prépondérante, où la composition serait de lui tandis que la part de Jean serait limitée au crayon qui a servi à peindre la tête. C'est le cas du *Grand portrait de François Ier* au Louvre, (Fig. 2).

Je n'ai jamais pu comprendre pourquoi l'attribution de ce tableau à "Janet", adoptée dans la collection royale fran-

13. Les mains de l'homme de Saint Louis combinent un contour encore curviligne avec les doigts déjà géométrisés. Comme elles sont de deux ans antérieures à celles de *Charlotte* (voir note 10), elles pourraient bien représenter la première intervention du collaborateur de Jean Clouet, que je crois être son fils François.

14. Reprod. in Charles Sterling, "Une peinture certaine de Perréal enfin retrouvée", *L'Œil*, juillet-août 1963, p. 8, fig. 16.
15. *Art and Architecture in France 1500 to 1700*, Londres, 1953, p. 69.
16. Lemaire ne parle que de Jean Hay, et Moreau-Nélaton suivi encore par Blunt (*op. cit.*, p. 38) crut à une transcription phonétique de Janet (Jehannet). Mais nous savons que Jean Hay exista it et qu'il est l'auteur du remarquable *Ecce Homo* du Musée de Bruxelles authentifié par une inscription et daté de 1494.

çaise en 1642, a été rejetée par la critique moderne en faveur d'une attribution à un peintre italien ou même à un peintre suisse ou allemand. Rien dans ce panneau n'autorise son exclusion du domaine de la peinture française; ni le style, plus plan que celui des Italiens et plus linéaire que celui des Allemands; ni l'exécution plus mince, plus unie que chez les uns et les autres. En revanche, il se relie de près aux deux Clouet. La tête – on est d'accord là-dessus depuis longtemps – répète un crayon de Jean. La main gauche du roi n'est qu'une répétition presque textuelle de la main de l'*Inconnu au Pétrarque* (vers 1535; Fig. 1). Les plis tourmentés et scintillants, ceux de *Claude de Guise* (vers 1525–30; Fig. 6), François en emporte l'habitude de l'atelier paternel et les emploiera à peine simplifiés, "dégothicisés", dans ses œuvres certaines, dans les manches d'*Odet de Coligny* (1548, Chantilly),[17] dans le rideau de *Pierre Quthe* (1562; Louvre), dans la *Dame au bain* (vers 1570? Fig. 3); et ce sont ces plis-là, précisément, qu'on trouve dans le grand portrait de François Ier (Fig. 2). Qu'est-ce donc qui paraît insolite dans ce tableau? C'est tout d'abord le fait incontestable – Anthony Blunt y a déjà insisté[18] – que la conception d'ensemble d'un tel portrait ne peut être de Jean Clouet. Cette figure monumentale et stylisée n'a pu être conçue que par un artiste qui profite déjà des portraits maniéristes toscans. Ensuite, ce qui gêne et diminue l'effet du tableau c'est la contradiction que l'on sent entre, d'une part, la tête, pâle, plate, modelée sous un éclairage égal, et, d'autre part, le corps et les mains, nettement ombrés et, de ce fait, plus volumineux. C'est précisément le contraste entre l'art de Jean et l'art de François.

On l'a déjà observé avec raison, l'idée même de cette effigie officielle, imposante et décorative, et l'attitude des mains – la droite tenant des gants, la gauche posée sur la poignée de l'épée – vient des portraits de Holbein, de celui de Charles de Solier, seigneur de Morette, ambassadeur de France, peint à Londres en 1534–35 (Dresde).[19] Mais elle a pu également refléter la première version du portrait d'Henry VIII datant de la seconde moitié de l'année 1535 (Coll. Thyssen, Lugano).[20] La cour de France était fort au courant de l'œuvre de Holbein en Angleterre. Les ambassadeurs français qui ont précédé Morette, Jean de Dinteville et George de Selve, se sont fait peindre par lui, en 1533, en un tableau magistral. Son ambassade terminée en juillet 1535, Morette a dû ramener son portrait en France. Il y a bien des chances pour qu'il l'ait montré à François Ier et pour qu'il ait raconté que son rival anglais s'est fait représenter dans une composition semblable. Mais déjà un peu plus tôt les échos des grandioses effigies frontales de Holbein (inaugurées en 1527 par le portrait de Guildford, à Windsor) ont dû pénétrer en France: car c'est ainsi que, lorsqu'il séjourna à la cour de François Ier, entre 1530 et 1535, Joos van Clève peignit ce roi (Coll. Johnson, Philadelphie).[21]

Il le représenta exactement comme il apparaît dans le grand portrait du Louvre, à mi-corps, derrière un parapet couvert d'un drap, le buste largement déployé de face, la tête de trois-quarts, la main gauche tenant des gants, la droite sur l'épée, avec l'index détaché et posé sur le pommeau. Cette concordance est frappante. Il semble donc vraisemblable que le roi de France ait demandé, en 1535 ou 1536, à son peintre en titre, Jean Clouet, de faire son portrait en une sorte de compétition avec Holbein et avec Joos van Clève. Mais Jean était déjà trop âgé pour s'attaquer à une telle effigie monumentale, trop moderne pour lui, bien étrangère à ses habitudes. Ce fut son fils qui dût s'en charger, en utilisant pour la tête du roi un crayon du père et en respectant son style. Le tableau sortirait donc de l'atelier de Jean mais sa conception et son exécution seraient de François Clouet.

Ce qui distingue l'art du vieux maître de celui de son fils le distingue également de Holbein et de ses contemporains flamands, Massys, Gossaert ou Joos van Clève: un lien profond avec ses crayons, un style qui tend à préserver dans l'émail de la peinture la pâle plasticité du dessin. Holbein, lorsqu'il peint une tête d'après son dessin, il la solidifie par un modelé supplémentaire, lui donne une fermeté minérale, une expression durcie: il continue à rechercher dans ses

17. Ce très beau portrait (repr. in Moreau-Nélaton, *Les Clouet et leurs émules*, I, Paris, 1924, fig. 27), montre, à mon avis, tous les traits caractéristiques de l'art de François Clouet.

18. *Op. cit.*, p. 41 note 35.

19. *Ibid.*

20. Ainsi que l'indique Glaser (*Thieme-Becker*, XVII, p. 350), Nicolas Bourbon de Vandœuvre appelle Holbein "peintre royal" comme si celui-ci était déjà au service d'Henry VIII (ou simplement l'auteur d'un portrait du roi?) à l'époque où le poète français séjourna à Londres, en 1535. En effet, la première version connue du portrait d'Henry VIII par Holbein (Coll. Thyssen, Lugano) pourrait très bien dater de cette année-là: le roi y porte la barbe qu'il adopta en mai 1535, en imitant François Ier, et il abandonna peu de temps après le col haut. (Cf. *Catalogue of the Exhibition of Pictures from the Thyssen-Bornemisza Collection*, National Gallery, Londres, 1959, no. 65). Ce tableau, dont la composition surprend par son archaïsme, a été sans doute réduit, peut-être pour faire

un pendant à un portrait postérieur, peint après mai 1536, de sa troisième femme, Jane Seymour. Avant la réduction, avec un fond plus important et les mains entièrement visibles, sa composition devait ressembler beaucoup à celle du grand portrait de François Ier au Louvre.

21. Repr. Max. J. Friedlaender, *Altniederlaendische Malerei*, XI, Berlin, 1931, pl. XLIII. Le séjour de Joos van Clève en France, documenté par Guicciardini (1567) ne saurait se placer, comme l'a montré Friedlaender, qu'après 1530 et avant 1535. Guicciardini dit que le Flamand a peint en France non seulement le roi et la reine (dont les portraits subsistent) mais aussi "altri principi". Il a donc pu peindre encore le vieux Guillaume de Montmorency qui mourut en 1531. Car le portrait de celui-ci au Musée de Lyon ne semble être qu'une dérivation française d'une œuvre de Joos van Clève: il suffit de le comparer aux portraits du Prado et de Cassel (Friedlaender, pl. XLVI et pl. LV). Le portrait de Montmorency au Louvre en serait une autre dérivation française, avec des variantes.

personnages cette volonté de puissance qui animait le portrait allemand tout au long du XVe siècle. Clouet, élevé dans la moëlleuse vision flamande, la rendit en France moins charnelle, délicatement modulée plutôt que palpable. Même quand ses modèles respirent une virile énergie, ils sont dépourvus de cette concentration expressive qui frise l'aggressivité sous un pinceau allemand ou flamand. Ce style tranquille et égal, il le doit au contact avec les crayons français dont il trouva la pratique en Touraine depuis Fouquet. Aux alentours de 1500, ces portraits dessinés étaient déjà très fréquents en France. Jean Perréal dont nous connaissons maintenant des œuvres certaines, l'aîné de Jean Clouet et son confrère sur la liste des peintres du roi, en avait l'habitude.[22] Ses crayons et d'autres, anonymes, conservés à l'Ermitage, du temps de Charles VIII (mort en 1498), montrent une technique des hachures parallèles employées pour les parties ombrées. Cette technique ne vient donc pas chez Clouet de Léonard, tout au plus s'affirma-t-elle, après 1516, sous l'influence lombarde en faisant fondre les traits parallèles en zones d'ombres suaves. Solario (en France, dès 1507),[23] Perréal (dès 1510 environ,

après ses longs séjours lombards), Léonard lui-même (en France, dès 1516) furent autant de sources qui ont pu nourrir les portraits de Jean Clouet d'éléments variés de l'esthétique de la Renaissance. Mais dans le contexte historique du portrait français des alentours de 1500, Clouet ne fait que renforcer une tendance vers la solidité et vers l'ampleur qu'on observe déjà dans les œuvres tardives du Maître de Moulins (*Dauphin Charles Orland*, au Louvre; le *Donateur avec saint Maurice*, à Glasgow) et dans celles de Perréal (*Portrait d'une dame anglaise*, 1514, National Portrait Gallery, Londres; *Monsieur de Bellefourrière*, 1521, New York). Bien qu'un peu plus avancé, il reste l'un de ceux qui aménagent la transition. C'est seulement son fils François, toujours fidèle aux traditions flamandes,[24] mais s'ouvrant également et dès ses débuts aux leçons italiennes, qui donnera dans le grand portrait de François Ier le premier véritable portrait français de la Renaissance.

L'auteur, qui ignorait l'étude de 1929, n'a pas fourni d'éléments convaincants, surtout en ce qui concerne les dessins.

24. Il est curieux d'observer que dans la *Dame au bain* qui ne daterait peut-être que des dernières de François Clouet, vers 1570, la nature morte est d'une similitude de style frappante avec celle qu'on voit dans la *Réunion galante avec la vue de Notre-Dame* (Musée Carnavalet et Musée de Budapest), œuvre d'un Flamand qui passa par Paris, vers 1535-40 (attribué à tort au Monogrammiste de Brunswick, Cat. Exp. *Le Siècle de Brueghel*, no. 252, fig. 135).

22. Dès avant 1500. Cf. *L'Œil*, juillet-août 1963, fig. 11.
23. Après l'intéressant travail d'Irène Adler (Vienna *Jahrbuch*, 1929), Luise Cogliati Arano (*Arte Lombarda*, 1963, pp. 147-156) est revenue sur les rapports possibles entre Solario et Jean Clouet.

SYLVIE BÉGUIN

Guillaume Dumée, disciple de Dubreuil

L'EXPOSITION du "XVIᵉ siècle européen" au Petit Palais[1] fut une heureuse occasion pour montrer de nouveau à Paris[2] un beau dessin (Fig. 1) de Besançon qui provient de la collection Gigoux: le premier inventaire des dessins de Besançon, rédigé par Fernand Mercier en 1933, l'attribuait à Poussin:[3] c'est Lavallée qui le donna à Dubreuil, attribution qui m'avait paru très vraisemblable et que j'avais suivie.[4] Cependant la confrontation de ce dessin avec les autres dessins du Louvre de Dubreuil présentés à la Galerie Mollien lors des manifestations parisiennes de 1965–66,[5] m'amena à réviser cette attribution, tant le dessin me parut différent de ses œuvres certaines.

En effet, le trait y est un peu plus lâché et plus approximatif que chez Dubreuil; l'emploi du lavis, le modelé, par hâchures, ne ressemblent pas à ceux qu'il adopte généralement. Dubreuil esquisse autrement ses paysages et ses personnages n'ont jamais sur le visage un air aussi caricatural; ses drapés ne présentent pas cette lourdeur ni ces ombres accusées. Le rythme vertical du dessin de Besançon contraste avec le rythme toujours très varié des dessins de Dubreuil au Louvre. Les figures y sont groupées en un bloc à peine animé par les poses des têtes: seul le geste des bras amorce un mouvement, procédé repris de Dubreuil mais moins dynamique que chez lui parce que sans écho dans le reste de la composition. Les raccourcis peu habiles des personnages, la pose systématique des pieds, l'espace assez gauchement indiqué et qui "remonte" ne suggérant pas une véritable profondeur, tous ces traits ne font que rappeler d'assez loin, sans jamais l'égaler, Dubreuil toujours si maître de ses moyens . . .[6]

Par contre, les analogies qui m'avaient déjà frappée entre le dessin de Besançon et un dessin de Dumée à l'École des Beaux-Arts *Olinde et Sophronie délivrés du bûcher* (Fig. 2), me parurent telles en confrontant les deux dessins que j'acquis bientôt la conviction qu'il fallait les attribuer tous deux au même artiste, Dumée.

On ne connaît plus guère Guillaume Dumée dont le nom est cité par Félibien parmi les noms des artistes les plus célèbres et les mieux connus de tous les temps.[7] Quelques rares mentions le sauvent encore de l'oubli: on ne sait quand il mourut après avoir mené une carrière officielle puisqu'il fut peintre du Roi, chargé de décorer les résidences royales, en particulier Saint-Germain et le Louvre, "peintre pour les tapisseries".[8] Son activité se situe essentiellement dans la première moitié du XVIIᵉ siècle.

Il travailla certainement avec Dubreuil aux décorations du château de Saint-Germain entreprises avant 1602, et le dessin de l'École des Beaux-Arts montre qu'il a subi son influence: des liens d'amitié unissaient les deux artistes;[9] sans doute Dumée fut-il chargé, à la mort de Dubreuil, de continuer les travaux de Saint-Germain et, plus tard, de veiller à leur conservation comme le prouvent certains textes[10].

d'anges que Catherine Monbeig-Goguel me signale parmi les dessins de Vasari (2119); *Thétis plongeant Achille dans l'eau du Styx* (8753), très belle étude classée parmi les Anonymes de l'École de Fontainebleau; enfin un projet décoratif (pour une cheminée?) (33554) classé parmi les Anonymes français XVIᵉ siècle que Roselyne Bacou, conservateur des Dessins, et moi-même, avons récemment retrouvé.

7. A. Félibien, *Noms des peintres les plus célèbres et les plus connus anciens et modernes*, Paris, 1679, p. 36.

8. La bibliographie essentielle sur Guillaume Dumée reste celle indiquée par *Thieme-Becker*, x, 1914 (article de H. Vollmer). Il faut y ajouter pour les tapisseries la référence au livre de H. Göbel, *Wandteppiche, Die romanischen Länder. Die Wandteppiche und Manufakturen in Frankreich, Italien, Spanien und Portugal*, Leipzig, 1928, 2 volumes.

9. En effet Toussaint Dubreuil (avec Ambroise Dubois) est parrain de son fils Toussaint (Comte de Laborde, *La Renaissance des arts à la cour de France*, Paris, 1855, p. 686). Ces liens d'amitié survécurent à la mort de Dubreuil: la fille de Dubreuil, Marie, est, le 7 novembre 1605, marraine d'un autre enfant de Guillaume Dumée, Louis (A. Jal, *Dictionnaire critique de biographie et d'histoire*, éd. de 1867, Paris, p. 854).

10. Document du 3 février 1605 publié dans les *Archives de l'Art français* (Document III): "Aujourd'hui 3ème jour de Février 1605 le Roy étant à Paris averti de l'expérience et la suffisance de Guillaume Dumée en l'art de peinture, ayant travaillé aux ouvrages de Peinture que sa dite Majesté a fait commencer les bâtiments de ses châteaux du Louvre et de St. Germain en Laye, qu'elle désire faire continuer et parachever . . .". Guillaume Dumée

1. *Le Seizième Siècle européen: peintures et dessins dans les collections publiques françaises*, Paris, Petit Palais, octobre 1965–janvier 1966.

2. *Besançon, le plus ancien musée de France*, Paris, Musée des Arts décoratifs, 1957, no. 134.

3. Je dois ces précisions à Mlle Cornillot, conservateur des Musées de Besançon.

4. P. Lavallée, *Les Techniques du dessin*, Paris, 1943, p. 5, no. 1; S. Béguin, "Toussaint Dubreuil peintre d'Henri IV", *Art de France*, IV, 1964, pp. 100–103, fig. p. 102, et *Catalogue du XVIᵉ siècle européen*, no. 121. Ne croyant pas que ce dessin représente *Diane et ses nymphes*, ni qu'il puisse se rapporter aux cartons de l'*Histoire de Diane*, j'avais proposé de le rapprocher des décorations du château de Saint-Germain.

5. *Le Seizième Siècle européen: dessins du Louvre*, Paris, Musée du Louvre, octobre-décembre 1965, no. 157 à 162; 258 à 260 (notices de Geneviève Monier, assistante au Cabinet des Dessins).

6. Comparer avec les dessins exposés à la galerie Mollien ou avec ceux reproduits dans *Art de France*, 1964 (op. cit., note 4) auxquels il faut ajouter au Louvre: trois petites *Études d'anges* (5841), à tort attribuées à Niccolo dell'Abbate, et une quatrième *Étude*

91

Le Louvre possède un dessin de Dumée, copie d'après *le Sacrifice* de Dubreuil, tableau provenant du décor perdu de Saint-Germain, copie bien intéressante à comparer au dessin préparatoire de Dubreuil pour le même tableau également au Louvre.[11] L'attribution de cette copie est basée sur la mention ancienne "Dumée" au revers: elle n'est pas contredite par le style si on la compare avec *l'Olinde et Sophronie délivrés du bûcher* de l'École des Beaux-Arts. L'École des Beaux-Arts conserve, en outre, sous le nom de Dumée, une *Cène* au luminisme très accentué aux notations pittoresques et un peu caricaturales[12] dont le verso et le recto présentent deux interprétations différentes. Enfin deux tableaux lui ont parfois été attribués que nous examinerons plus loin.

Le dessin de l'École des Beaux-Arts, *Olinde et Sophronie délivrés du bûcher* (Fig. 2),[13] est une pièce très sûre pour caractériser Guillaume Dumée, figure de peintre et de dessinateur encore très obscure; en effet non seulement ce dessin porte une inscription ancienne, "Dumée", en bas à gauche, mais son sujet correspond de plus exactement à une composition peinte par Dumée pour le Cabinet de la Reine au Louvre qui nous est décrit par Félibien. On retrouve dans l'*Olinde et Sophronie délivrés du bûcher* le même usage du lavis que dans le dessin de Besançon, le même modelé par hachures obliques; le trait est aussi très comparable. Les personnages y ont la même pose hanchée; la même façon de placer les pieds (identiques dans le dessin de

Besançon), légèrement en retrait l'un de l'autre; les mains, les raccourcis des bras sont vraiment tout à fait semblables. Le côté un peu sommaire des indications est encore plus accentué dans le dessin des Beaux-Arts que dans le dessin de Besançon, mais le rythme vertical est bien le même ainsi que la manière de grouper les figures. Ce qui semble caractéristique (et que nous avons précisément relevé dans le dessin de Besançon) c'est le statisme des figures, le mouvement n'étant suggéré que par l'inclinaison opposée des têtes et les gestes des bras, et aussi la manière d'étaler largement les rehauts de gouache blanche dans les lumières.

Si l'on accepte ce rapprochement, il faudrait donc rendre à Dumée le beau dessin de Besançon: serait-il alors toujours en rapport avec le décor de Saint-Germain comme je l'avais pensé – lorsque je croyais encore ce dessin de Dubreuil? Cela n'est pas impossible mais reste à établir, car nous n'avons aucun document qui nous permette de considérer Dumée comme l'inventeur des décorations de Saint-Germain qui ont été toujours traditionnellement attribuées à Dubreuil. Comme le dessin d'après le *Sacrifice antique* (Louvre) le dessin de Besançon est peut être inspiré d'une composition de Dubreuil: mais son caractère spontané semble écarter cette hypothèse; ce pourrait être aussi une étude originale de Dumée en vue d'un autre ensemble. . . .

L'*Olinde et Sophronie délivrés du bûcher* (École des Beaux-Arts) de Dumée est un projet pour l'un des sujets tirés de la *Jérusalem délivrée* du Tasse qui ornaient au Louvre le Cabinet de la Reine décoré vers 1610–14 sous la régence de Marie de Médicis:[14] Félibien[15] nous donne le nom des

se serait démis de cette charge en 1610 lors de sa nomination de "peintre pour les tapisseries" mais l'aurait reprise le 3 avril 1626 avec son fils Toussaint (cf. Jal, *op. cit.*, note 9, p. 854). Le document du 3 février 1605 établit le rôle prépondérant de Dumée dans les travaux de Saint-Germain, auxquels participa aussi Louis Poisson, comme on peut le déduire d'un autre document publié dans le même volume (p. 243) concernant le Brevet du 5 septembre 1613 de son fils Pierre Poisson.

11. Cette copie de Dumée (RF.29895) est mentionnée par Ph. de Chennevières, *Essai sur l'histoire de la peinture française*, Paris, 1894, pp. 49–50; par L. Dimier, *Critique et controverse*, Paris, 1909, pp. 45–46. Cf. S. Béguin, *Art de France, op. cit.*, note 128, p. 104, où elle est comparée au 3693 de Guiffrey, dessin original de Dubreuil pour le tableau du *Sacrifice antique* (Louvre). On y voit nettement apparaître les caractéristiques de Dumée: un graphisme lâché et un peu approximatif, un style beaucoup plus caricatural que celui de Dubreuil, une certaine difficulté à suggérer l'espace.

12. *La Cène* (Paris, École des Beaux-Arts, collection Masson), à la plume et lavis de bistre, repris de gouache sur papier bistré, 22·4 × 37 cm.; attribué à Dumée dans l'inventaire de la collection Masson, no. 916. Cette attribution n'est pas appuyée par une mention ancienne comme pour les autres dessins. Elle me paraît cependant très vraisemblable: le lavis, les types, la lumière contrastée rappellent nettement (parfois en les exagérant) les autres dessins.

13. *Olinde et Sophronie délivrés du bûcher* (Paris, École des Beaux-Arts, collections: Chennevières; Mander; Masson), à la plume lavis de bistre et gouache sur papier bistré; 26 × 33·7 cm.; en bas à droite inscription ancienne "Dumée". Exposé à *La Renaissance italienne et ses prolongements européens*, Paris, École des Beaux-Arts, 1958, no. 76.

14. L'histoire des appartements royaux di Louvre est loin d'être claire. Si les compositions décrites par Félibien furent exécutées sous la régence à l'appartement de la Reine mère, elles doivent se rapporter à l'appartement du rez-de-chaussée de l'aile méridionale donnant sur le jardin, en bordure du quai, traditionnellement réservé aux Reines mères et que Marie de Médicis fit améliorer et embellir avant l'arrivée d'Anne d'Autriche afin de lui céder l'appartement de l'étage. Ces travaux et embellissements eurent lieu vers 1613, ils n'étaient pas encore terminés en 1616 (cf. C. Aulanier, *Le Pavillon du roi: les appartements de la reine*, Paris, 1958, p. 39, et *La Salle des Cariatides et les salles grecques*, Paris, 1955, pp. 80–81). Si l'on admet, avec Sauval, l'existence dans ce Cabinet de peintures relatives à l'histoire des Médicis, peintures mentionnées par Bailly (*Inventaire des tableaux du roy*, rédigé en 1709 par Nicolas Bailly, publié par F. Engerand, Paris, 1899, pp. 285–286 et pp. 569–571), huit sous le nom de Clouet au Luxembourg et dix autres anonymes au "vieux Louvre, appartement de la Reyne mère", la localisation de la décoration dans l'appartement du rez-de-chaussée devient certaine. (Au sujet de ces tableaux voir la note 18.) C'est ce qui paraît aussi se dégager du texte de L. Hautecœur, *Histoire du Louvre*, ed. 1953, Paris, p. 37) qui rapproche la décoration (qu'il attribue, en suivant Sauval, à Bunel, Dubois, Fréminet) des travaux entrepris à cet appartement en 1613. Cependant, E. J. Ciprut et L. H. Collard (*Nouveaux Documents sur le Louvre*, Paris, 1963, p. 32, notes 1 à 3), font état d'un marché du 12 janvier 1610 concernant deux chambres situées "au dessous du Cabinet de la Reine" au nom de Nicolas Pontheron, artiste figurant encore en 1624 dans les Comptes de Dépenses du Louvre

artistes qui y travaillèrent et le sujet des peintures; à côté de Dumée il cite Honnet, Bunel et Dubois. Sauval[16] dont le comte de Clarac[17] note justement la préférence pour les nouveaux appartements d'Anne d'Autriche au Louvre, ne décrit pas le Cabinet de la Reine et de plus se trompe sur les artistes qui participèrent à sa décoration: il ne parle pas de Dumée ni d'Honnet, sans doute déjà oubliés, les remplaçant par les noms plus fameux de Fréminet et d'Évrard (pour Errard) citant en outre comme Félibien, Bunel et Dubois. Ces erreurs de Sauval sont intéressantes: elles prouvent la qualité de tout l'ensemble qui justifiait l'attribution aux artistes les plus célèbres de l'époque qui rivalisèrent "autant par émulation entre eux que pour faire quelque chose qui plût à cette Princesse [Marie de Médicis] . . ." (Sauval).

Le décor du Cabinet de la Reine comprenait, selon Félibien, au-dessus du lambris doré dix compositions ainsi réparties: trois tableaux de Honnet, deux de Bunel, deux de Dubois et trois de Dumée.[18] On ne les connaît plus aujourd'hui que grâce à quelques dessins: deux à l'École des Beaux-Arts

(dont le dessin de Dumée que nous venons de mentionner, ainsi qu'un autre attribué à Dubois) et un dessin du Louvre attribué à Honnet.

Félibien commence par décrire les tableaux d'Honnet pour cet ensemble: "dans le premier il peignit le magicien Ismène qui persuade le Roi Aladin de prendre l'image de la Vierge qui était dans une chapelle des chrétiens afin de s'en servir dans ses enchantements"; "dans le deuxième on voit Aladin qui enlève cette image". On n'a pas jusqu'ici retrouvé de dessins préparatoires pour ces deux tableaux: par contre, pour le troisième tableau, "Sophronie qui pour sauver les chrétiens s'excuse d'avoir ôté l'image du lieu où Aladin l'avait transporté", on connaît au Louvre un beau projet attribué autrefois au Primatice et que Dimier a justement rendu à Honnet (Fig. 3),[19] en se basant sur la description de Félibien: proche de Dumée, mais plus nerveux et plus baroque, Honnet, dans ce joli dessin, offre quelque rapport avec Dubois dont il se distingue par un faire plus schématique, un trait moins souple, moins d'aisance à disposer ses figures, des architectures très lourdes bien différentes des fonds si légèrement indiqués de Dubois.

Félibien mentionne ensuite les compositions malheureusement perdues de Bunel: "le magicien faisant des enchantements en présence d'Aladin" et "le Roi qui commande que l'on mette les chrétiens à mort", puis les compositions de Dubois: "Olinde qui se présente devant Aladin pour mourir au lieu de Sophronie", sujet jusqu'ici inconnu, et "Sophronie qui soutient au Roi que c'est elle qui a dérobé l'image". On a rapproché de cette dernière composition un beau dessin de l'École des Beaux-Arts (Fig. 4)[20] qui est

---

pour la charge de l'entretien "de toutes les peintures et lambris du logis bas du Louvre". Ces documents prouvent donc que les travaux à l'appartement du rez-de-chaussée et l'annexion par la Reine de certaines pièces du palais pour son usage personnel sont antérieurs aux dates admises jusqu'ici. Cependant ils paraissent se référer à un ensemble différent de celui qui nous intéresse. La participation de Bunel et de Dubois, tous deux morts en 1614, postule cette date extrême pour la décoration et les écarte évidemment des travaux entrepris en 1627 au "Cabinet de la Reine" dont les paiements ont été retrouvés par Ciprut (*Bulletin de la société de l'histoire de l'art français*, Paris, 1954, p. 182). Les dates de 1610–14 sont vraisemblables pour les dessins de Dumée et d'Honnet, malgré la forte influence de Dubreuil (mort en 1602) car cette influence marque aussi la suite du *Pastor Fido* (concours de 1609). La date de 1610–14 n'est pas sans poser, d'autre part, certains problèmes pour Errard (mentionné par Sauval et Félibien) au décor du plafond du Cabinet car, si l'on en croit un document publié par Batiffol ("Les Travaux du Louvre sous Henri IV", *GBA*, Période IV, VII, 1912, p. 173), Errard ne semble s'être venu de Nantes à Paris qu'en 1618.

15. A. Félibien, *Entretiens sur les vies et ouvrages des plus excellents peintres anciens et modernes*, III, éd. de 1725, Trévoux, pp. 127–129.

16. H. Sauval, *Histoire et recherches des antiquités de la ville de Paris*, II, p. 34. Cf. L. Hautecœur, *op. cit.* en note 14, p. 37.

17. Comte de Clarac, *Description historique et géographique du Louvre et des Tuileries*, Paris, 1853, p. 498.

18. Cf. Félibien et Clarac, *op. cit.*; à ce sujet voir aussi Laborde, (*op. cit.* en note 9, pp. 99–110) qui mentionne en outre la série des peintures en partie attribuées à Clouet dans l'inventaire de Bailly dont certaines ornèrent plus tard le Cabinet Doré de Marie de Médicis au Luxembourg. J. Adhémar (*Burl M.*, LXXXX, 1948, pp. 145–146) avait mentionné cette série, à propos d'un tableau déposé par le Louvre à Dijon, proposant de l'identifier avec l'une des peintures autrefois à Meudon, attribuée à G. Boba. Ces peintures ont été aussi étudiées par Sir Anthony Blunt dans une conférence donnée à l'Institut Courtauld le 19 novembre 1963 (*The Paintings which decorated the Cabinet Doré of Marie de Médicis at the Palais du Luxembourg*), répétée à Paris, à l'École du Louvre, le 13 janvier 1964 (*Les Tableaux du Cabinet Doré de Marie de Médicis au Palais du Luxembourg*).

19. Gabriel Honnet, *Scène de la Jérusalem délivrée* (Musée du Louvre, Cabinet des Dessins, no. 33.563); à la pierre noire lavis d'encre de chine, rehaussé de blanc; 25·9 × 28·9 cm.; attribution de Dimier au revers qui a plusieurs fois mentionné ce dessin dans ses ouvrages. Le dessin porte une attribution ancienne à Primatice; attribué ensuite à un Anonyme français du XVIe siècle.

20. Cf. *La Renaissance italienne et ses prolongements européens*, Paris, École des Beaux-Arts, 1958, no. 74 (comme "*Sophronie devant Aladin*") et mis correctement en rapport avec le Cabinet de la Reine; Collections Ph. de Chennevières et Masson; pierre noire, lavis de bistre et rehauts de gouache sur papier bistré; 24·4 × 31 cm. L'attribution à Dubois a été, en particulier, soutenue par J. Adhémar (*Le Dessin français*, Genève, 1954, p. 138, pl. 90), qui rapproche ce dessin de la décoration du château de Saint-Germain à laquelle Dubois ne semble pas, en réalité, avoir jamais participé, ce qui semble confirmé par le fait qu'à la mort de Dubreuil les travaux furent confiés à Dumée (qu'on aurait sans doute préféré à Dubois, si celui-ci plus célèbre avait effectivement joué un rôle à Saint-Germain . . .). J. Adhémar, tout en remarquant que le sujet du dessin de l'École des Beaux-Arts n'apparaît pas parmi les sujets décrits par Bailly au château de Saint-Germain, l'appelle *La Belle Chariclée devant le Roi d'Éthiopie* (sans doute par confusion avec l'*Histoire de Théagène et Chariclée* peinte par Dubois au château de Fontainebleau). Dimier ne cite pas ce dessin. Même en admettant, à cause de la date (avant 1614), que ce soit là une expression extrême de l'art de Dubois, il y a un tel écart avec ses types, ses compositions, son graphisme, ses drapés, sa manière d'indiquer les

cependant très différent de tout ce que nous connaissons jusqu'ici de Dubois. Le style de Dubois dessinateur vers cette date nous est, en effet, assez bien connu, par plusieurs exemples sûrs qui révèlent une tout autre manière.[21] Si le dessin de l'École des Beaux-Arts était bien le projet de Dubois pour le Cabinet de la Reine, il devrait représenter *Sophronie qui soutient au Roi que c'est elle qui a dérobé l'image*"; mais la belle figure drapée, aux voiles opulents, ne ressemble guère à la Sophronie en courte tunique que nous voyons apparaître dans le dessin de Dumée à l'École des Beaux-Arts ou dans celui de Honnet, au Louvre. Fière et magnifiquement vêtue, la jeune femme debout, face à Aladin, n'a guère l'attitude de la pauvre captive Sophronie . . .

Ces remarques, d'ordre iconographique, viennent appuyer les considérations basées sur le style du dessin et parlent contre son rapprochement avec le tableau perdu de Dubois. Par contre la jeune femme du dessin évoque la femme de profil à droite dans *l'Olinde et Sophronie délivrés du bûcher* de Dumée, figure drapée dans de larges voiles, qui parle avec Aladin (reconnaissable à son turban). Ne serait-ce pas là, dans les deux dessins le même personnage, c'est-à-dire Clorinde? Si le style du dessin attribué à Dubois diffère en effet sensiblement de ce maître, il rappelle, par contre, beaucoup Honnet ou Dumée. Il offre, en effet, ces contrastes d'ombre et de lumière si typiques de Dumée dans *l'Olinde et Sophronie délivrés du bûcher* et dans *la Cène*, ainsi que les profils caricaturaux de la *Cène*, traits que l'on retrouve aussi, mais moins accentués, chez Honnet mais aucun sujet traité par Honnet ne peut correspondre à cette scène dans le décor du Cabinet de la Reine: par contre, nous allons voir, un sujet peint par Dumée pourrait très bien y correspondre.

Félibien décrit finalement les trois compositions peintes par Dumée pour cet ensemble. Le sujet du premier tableau

nous est représenté de façon précise dans un dessin de la Bibliothèque municipale de Rouen attribué à Dubois: *Clorinde à cheval en habits de cavalier arrive à Jérusalem où elle aperçoit Sophronie et Olinde attachés sur le bûcher* (Fig. 5).[22] Clorinde sur le dessin de Rouen est à droite: elle se penche vers Aladin dont on distingue de profil la tête enturbannée; au centre le bûcher où sont attachés Olinde et Sophronie. Le dessin est à la plume, au lavis et à la sépia. On distingue au fond les architectures simplement esquissées: ces indications, très légères par rapport aux personnages, contribuent à déséquilibrer la composition qui semble se détacher sur un fond neutre alors qu'elle est, en fait, balancée, à droite et à gauche, par les masses des architectures.

Ce dessin est à tort attribué à Dubois dont il ne rappelle ni la composition ni le style. Pourrait-il être attribué à Dumée à cause de son rapport évident avec le sujet du tableau perdu du Cabinet de la Reine? Le nom de Dubois aurait pu être substitué à celui moins célèbre de Dumée d'autant plus aisément que Dubois participa lui-même à ce cycle décoratif . . . Tout en étant beaucoup moins beau que *l'Olinde et Sophronie délivrés du bûcher* de l'École des Beaux-Arts le dessin de Rouen rappelle, cependant, l'harmonie de ses contrastes accusés, son modelé par hachures parallèles: ses personnages font penser aux types caricaturaux de la *Cène* et à la façon dont Dumée esquisse les architectures. Cependant son exécution très inférieure indique sans doute qu'il s'agit d'une copie du tableau de Dumée pour le Cabinet de la Reine ou peut-être encore d'une esquisse originale au crayon de Dumée qui aurait été repassée maladroitement à la plume par un autre artiste, plus médiocre que lui.

Dans le deuxième tableau peint par Dumée, écrit Félibien, "Clorinde paraît qui demande au roi Aladin la grâce d'Olinde et de Sophronie": c'est à cette composition que nous pensions tout à l'heure à propos du dessin (Fig. 4) de l'École des Beaux-Arts que nous croyons improprement attribué à Dubois: si, dans le premier tableau de Dumée, Félibien prend bien soin de préciser que "Clorinde est en habits de cavalier" il ne dit rien de sa toilette dans le deuxième et le troisième tableau; nous savons que dans ce troisième tableau "où l'on voit les deux amants qu'on délivre du supplice" que nous connaissons grâce au dessin de l'École des Beaux-Arts (*Olinde et Sophronie délivrés du*

raccourcis, d'user du lavis et de placer les lumières, que cette attribution me paraît vraiment très difficile à soutenir. Par contre les rehauts de gouache sont tout à fait comparables avec ceux de *l'Olinde et Sophronie* de l'École des Beaux-Arts, assez lourds, écrasés, très différents de Dubreuil et de Dubois. Il est aussi intéressant de confronter la silhouette de la prétendue Sophronie avec les figures féminines de *Sylvius et son chien* du *Pastor Fido* (repr. in Göbel, *op. cit.* en note 8, II, pl. 40) ou du *Songe de Montan* (*ibid.*, pl. 41), types qui sortent évidemment de Dubreuil et non de Dubois.

21. S. Béguin, "Les Dessins d'Ambroise Dubois", *Œil*, mars 1966; auxquels il faut ajouter un beau dessin provenant de la collection Chennevières dans une collection privée parisienne, projet sans doute pour l'un des cycles romanesques de Fontainebleau et une très jolie étude de la collection Rothschild (Musée du Louvre, no. 3493), variante de celle du Louvre reproduite dans *l'Œil* pour *Théagène et Chariclée dans la Caverne*. Dans l'article de *l'Œil*, le dessin de l'École des Beaux-Arts attribué à Dubois est mentionné comme Dumée (en note 4). Dimier a attribué à Dumée non pas ce dessin (comme je l'écris par erreur dans cette note) mais *l'Olinde et Sophronie délivrés du bûcher*, les deux dessins provenant de la collection Masson, ce qui a facilité la confusion.

22. Bibliothèque municipale de Rouen (legs Jules Hedou), attribué à F. Dubois; à la plume lavis de bistre et de sépia; 25·6 × 36·7 cm.; titre donné sur le montage, sans doute de la main de Jules Hedou; à l'angle opposé, un autre collectionneur, L. Deglatigny, a écrit "Dubois, mais lequel?"; au recto du dessin, d'une écriture plus ancienne, "Dubois F.", qui peut être aussi bien interprété comme "Dubois fecit" ou Dubois François. L'attribution à ce dernier paraît curieuse étant donné le style des tableaux qu'on lui attribue. Le fait que le sujet rappelle la composition perdue de Dumée au Cabinet de la Reine incite plutôt à le rapprocher d'Ambroise Dubois (confondu avec Dumée) qui collabora, selon Félibien, à cet ensemble. Ce dessin m'a été aimablement signalé par P. Rosenberg, Assistant au Musée du Louvre.

bûcher), Clorinde, parlant avec Aladin, a retrouvé ses vêtements de femme. Elle peut donc déjà très bien être représentée ainsi dans le deuxième tableau: auprès d'Aladin attentif, elle plaide la cause des chrétiens, provoquant l'étonnement des assistants et même leurs prières; derrière elle trois personnages s'inclinent avec des poses suppliantes . . . mimique qui s'accorde bien avec la démarche de Clorinde[23] et guère avec celle de Sophronie.

Si l'iconographie du dessin de l'École des Beaux-Arts peut correspondre à la scène peinte par Dumée, le style, comme nous l'avons déjà remarqué, ne contredit pas ce rapprochement: nous avons noté qu'il faut aussi penser à Honnet, mais Honnet peint des draperies plus fluides et plus légères, ses types sont moins caricaturaux; Dumée, au contraire, aime ces lourdes étoffes aux plis profonds, ces profils grotesques, ces architectures massives, ce vigoureux emploi du lavis: nous proposons donc d'attribuer plutôt à Dumée le dessin de l'École des Beaux-Arts attribué jusqu'ici à Dubois et d'y reconnaître le projet du second tableau que Dumée peignit pour le Cabinet de la Reine.

Ces différentes attributions à Dumée précisent un peu l'idée que l'on pouvait se faire jusqu'ici de lui et permettent de mieux comprendre les charges officielles qui lui furent confiées. Les compositions du Cabinet de la Reine révèlent un talent souple et assez varié: un rôle important fut d'ailleurs dévolu à l'artiste dans ce décor puisque outre les trois grands tableaux il fut chargé de peindre "sur les lambris et sur les guichets du même Cabinet plusieurs petites figures représentant des Divinitez".[24] Un dessin représentant un *Bacchus* à Cambridge me paraît, sur photographie, présenter quelques rapports avec le style de Dumée. Serait-ce une étude pour l'une des figures de "Divinitez" dont parle Félibien?[25]

De tous ces projets se dégage le style propre de Dumée: certes il rappelle beaucoup Dubreuil et Dubois, mais son accent est moins classique que le premier et moins maniériste que le second. Ses attaches avec Fontainebleau semblent déjà plus libres que les leurs: cependant son luminisme, comme l'animation des figures, reste très maniériste, en dépit d'une emphase, d'ailleurs typique des artistes de sa génération, et d'une certaine rhétorique qui annoncent le baroque.

Il y a, de plus, chez Dumée un goût pour le bizarre, voire le grotesque, qui est d'un contemporain de Lallemand: ce n'est pas un hasard que l'un des rares tableaux qui ait été attribué à Dumée, *Le Portrait du prévôt des Marchands et des Échevins de Paris* de 1614 (Fig. 6) du Musée Carnavalet, soit actuellement plutôt considéré comme une œuvre de Lallemand.[26] Il faut dire que l'attribution de cette peinture à Guillaume Dumée est basée sur la mention d'un paiement de 500 livres à Dumée en 1612 rapportée par Champeaux pour un portrait de ce type destiné à l'Hôtel de Ville de Paris, mention qui semble aujourd'hui invérifiable. Elle ne laisse pas, cependant, d'être troublante. En effet, il est étrange que Champeaux ait avancé le nom d'un peintre alors complètement oublié, mêlé aux noms d'artistes (Francken, Beaubrun, Pourbus, Elle . . .) qui ont bien effectivement peint des tableaux pour l'Hôtel de Ville de Paris. Sans doute, Champeaux a-t-il recopié une liste qu'on ne connaît plus mentionnant tous les artistes qui travaillèrent pour l'Hôtel de Ville;[27] il serait vraiment extraordinaire qu'il ait pu inventer le nom et la date d'un paiement à Dumée, d'autant plus, d'ailleurs, que cette date n'est pas sans soulever quelques difficultés. Dumée aujourd'hui oublié, mais célèbre de son temps, aurait très bien pu recevoir une telle commande; cependant peut-on faire

---

23. Le geste de la jeune femme qui pose la main sur sa poitrine est en effet équivoque; il peut être pris pour un geste d'accusation mais peut aussi correspondre au moment où Clorinde réclame la grâce des deux jeunes gens. Dans la foule qui l'entoure ne s'esquisse, en tous cas, aucun mouvement agressif, comme on le voit, par exemple, dans la *Sophronie qui s'accuse pour sauver les chrétiens* d'Honnet. Il est surprenant aussi qu'Olinde ne figure pas à côté de Sophronie dans la scène où elle s'accuse pour mourir à sa place . . . mais il est normal, au contraire, que Clorinde soit représentée seule.

24. Félibien, *op. cit.* en note 15.

25. Cambridge, Fitzwilliam Museum. Attribué à Rosso.

26. Le tableau appartient au Musée de Versailles (Eud. Soulié, *Notice du musée national de Versailles*, Paris, 1881, no. 4165), provenant de la collection Aguado, acquis en 1845 comme Pourbus le jeune, attribué à l'École française. La notice donne l'identification des personnages et cite le paiement de 500 livres "fait le 1er août 1612 à Guillaume Dumée, maître peintre à Paris pour avoir peint le portrait des magistrats et des échevins dans un tableau unique et de plus pour avoir fait 8 portraits séparés des magistrats de la ville" (p. 315 d'après le "Registre de Recettes et dépenses de l'Hôtel de Ville de Paris déposé aux Archives impériales"; malheureusement il y a une lacune dans le registre entre 1615 et 1623); tableau déposé au Musée Carnavalet par échange en 1949. A. Champeaux (*l'Art décoratif dans le vieux Paris*, Paris, 1898, p. 205) soutient l'attribution à Dumée, sur laquelle G. Brière (*BSHAF*, 1911, p. 420) fait des réserves, répétés par G. Brière, M. Dumolin et P. Jarry dans "Les tableaux de l'hôtel de ville de Paris et de l'abbaye de Saint-Germain", *Bulletin de la société d'iconographie parisienne*, Paris, 1937, pp. 13–14; cf. aussi J. Wilhelm, "Supplément à l'ouvrage de Brière, Dumolin et Jarry sur les tableaux de l'hôtel de Ville de Paris", *BSHAF*, 1956, p. 25; Dimier, *Le Portrait français au XVIe siècle*, II, 1925, p. 201, cite le nom de Dumée parmi les noms de peintres ayant exécuté des portraits collectifs de magistrats. Le tableau est reproduit par Brière comme Dumée dans *L'Histoire de l'art* d'André Michel, V, 2, Paris, 1913, p. 789, et mentionné sous ce nom par Hautecœur, *Histoire de l'art*, II, Paris, 1959, p. 443; Ch. Sterling, "Quelques œuvres inédites des peintres Millereau, Lallemand, Vignon, Sacquespée et Simon François", *BSHAF*, 1954, p. 4 du tiré à part, le rapproche de Lallemand comme F. G. Pariset, "Documents sur Georges Lallemand", *BSHAF*, 1953, p. 171, note 1.

27. Champeaux est cité par Brière, Dumolin et Jarry, *op. cit.*, avec une allusion à de Piles qui peut faire croire, à tort, que de Piles cite lui aussi le document mentionné par Champeaux; en fait de Piles, *Abrégé de la vie des peintres*, éd. de 1699, Paris, p. 461, se contente de citer avec dédain le nom de Dumée parmi d'autres à propos des décorations des châteaux royaux.

correspondre au tableau de Carnavalet la mention rapportée par Champeaux? C'est, je crois, un problème que nous ne sommes pas vraiment en mesure de résoudre dans l'état actuel de nos connaissances. En tous cas, au point de vue de la date, comme on l'a établi, le tableau de Carnavalet correspond bien à la période (sinon à la date précise) d'exécution du tableau mentionné par Champeaux sous le nom de Dumée;[28] quant au style il est impossible de se prononcer faute d'autres œuvres peintes attribuables avec certitude à Dumée.[29] Les dessins que nous venons d'examiner n'offrent, évidemment, que peu de rapports avec le tableau de Carnavalet: les analogies que l'on peut y relever et qui paraissent rendre possible son attribution ne sont, sans doute, pas vraiment décisives, car il ne s'agit peut-être que de traits communs aux artistes de cette époque . . . Cependant, je ne crois pas que l'on puisse écarter complètement l'attribution de la peinture à Dumée, tant que l'on n'aura pas prouvé la fausseté de la mention rapportée par Champeaux ou qu'on aura pas réussi à l'élucider. L'attribution du tableau à Lallemand[30] me paraît en tous cas à exclure: la confrontation à Carnavalet du tableau attribué à Dumée avec le *Portrait du Prévôt des Échevins* de 1614 dont l'attribution à Lallemand n'a jamais été mise en doute est vraiment éclairante. Même en tenant compte du fait que les deux tableaux ont beaucoup souffert et qu'ils sont considérablement repris, il est impossible de les attribuer à la même main, tant leur style diffère à peu d'années de distance. Par rapport au tableau de Lallemand, le tableau attribué à Dumée accuse toutes ses faiblesses de dessin et de perspective, mais révèle, toutefois, des qualités de portraitiste. Son coloris très frais ne manque pas d'agrément. Il y a du charme dans l'*Adoration des Mages* peinte au fond sur le maître-autel de la chapelle, tableau dont la composition rappelle beaucoup Vignon et, par certains traits, des maîtres encore mystérieux comme le peintre de l'*Adoration des Mages* de Lille.[31] Ce qui semble aussi typique du peintre de Carnavalet c'est cet esprit d'observation un peu anecdotique révélé par certains détails, par exemple la présence des hallebardiers et des autres personnages silhouettés sous les arcades de la chapelle au second plan. Certes, ce n'est pas du grand art et l'on comprend la remarque de Sauval sur les tableaux qui décoraient la Salle de l'Hôtel de Ville: "quantité d'autres portraits peints en concurrence par les plus célèbres peintres de notre temps et qui pourtant auprès des deux Pourbus ne paraissent que des peintures de village ou du Pont Notre-Dame".[32]

Le tableau de 1614 à Carnavalet reste encore un mystère; ce n'est donc pas sur lui que nous nous baserons pour proposer d'attribuer une peinture à Dumée, mais bien sur les projets que nous avons essayé de grouper plus haut: le rapport si étroit qui les unit au *Repas* (Fig. 7) du Louvre provenant du décor de Saint-Germain,[33] permet, je crois, de proposer Dumée sinon comme "inventeur" de la peinture mais du moins comme exécutant d'un motif imaginé par Dubreuil; on retrouve vraiment dans le tableau toutes les caractéristiques des dessins de Dumée, sa manière d'esquisser les têtes et ses gestes si particuliers. Ceci est, je crois, très sensible sur le détail que nous reproduisons, de préférence à la composition entière dans l'ensemble moins lisible et en mauvais état . . .

Déjà Chennevières,[34] se basant sur un dessin de sa collection qui porte le nom de Dumée (dessin aujourd'hui au Louvre), avait proposé de donner à Dumée le tableau du *Sacrifice antique* du Louvre prenant à tort, d'ailleurs, ce dessin pour l'étude préparatoire et négligeant l'existence d'un dessin autographe de Dubreuil au Louvre pour cette même composition. L'hypothèse de Chennevières mérite-t-elle, mal-

28. Le livre de Brière, Dumolin et Jarry, 1937, *op. cit.*, résume tout ce que l'on peut savoir des tableaux de l'Hôtel de Ville et rappelle que les paiements connus ont été faits vers le mois d'août et septembre: c'est donc à la fin de l'échevinat de deux ans, coincidant souvent avec la fin d'une prévôté, que les officiers municipaux se faisaient peindre. Donc, étant donné les magistrats représentés (Gaston de Grieu, Pierre Perrot, Guillaume Clément) et les échevins (Pierre Desprez, Claude Mirault, Israël Desneux, Pierre Clapisson), le tableau attribué à Dumée, à Carnavalet, n'a pu être exécuté qu'en juillet–août 1614, fin de l'échevinage de Desprez et de Mirault. Le paiement de 1612 ne peut donc correspondre à cette œuvre, comme l'écrit justement Brière, *op. cit.*, à moins d'admettre qu'il y ait eu une erreur de chiffre qui me semble plus facile à supposer, en tous cas, que l'invention du nom de Dumée.

29. Pour le tableau du Louvre qui lui a été attribué, voir plus loin et note 34. Peut-être son style est-il exactement reflété par les tapisseries du *Pastor Fido*; mais comment y distinguer précisément Dumée de son beau-frère Laurent Guyot, qui gagna le concours avec lui et partagea sa charge de peintre pour les tapisseries?

30. Je crois que Charles Sterling écrit avec raison: "il est d'un art très voisin de Lallemand", sans le donner à ce peintre (*op. cit.* en note 26, 1954. p. 4).

31. On a aussi évoqué Lallemand à propos du tableau au fond sur le maître-autel de la chapelle. Selon Brière (*op. cit.*, 1937, p. 14) la chapelle représentée sur le portrait de 1614 serait peut-être celle de l'hôpital du Saint-Esprit attenant à l'Hôtel-Dieu où avaient lieu la plupart des cérémonies religieuses prescrites par le Bureau de la Ville. On n'en possède aucune description du début du XVIIe s. et il est donc impossible d'identifier la peinture du maître-autel qui pourrait être aussi, d'ailleurs, une création imaginaire (mais cette supposition semble peu probable). Charles Sterling avait pensé à Lallemand pour l'*Adoration des Mages* de Lille, attribué au Musée à Claude Vignon (*Peinture française: XVIe siècle–XVIIe siècle*, "Collection des maîtres," éd. Braun, 1937, fig. 7); il mentionne de nouveau ce tableau dans sa communication de 1954 (*op. cit.* en note 26, p. 7), en notant ses rapports avec Lallemand et conclut "mais des comparaisons décisives manquent toujours".

32. Sauval, *op. cit.* en note 16, II, p. 483.

33. S. Béguin, *Art de France, op. cit.* en note 4, p. 104, fig. Le sujet de ce tableau, comme d'ailleurs celui du *Sacrifice antique* du Louvre, demeure mystérieux.

34. Chennevières, *op. cit.* en note 11, 1894, p. 49. Dimier a bien vu que le dessin était une copie (*Critique et controverse*, 1909, pp. 42, 46).

gré tout, d'être reprise? Les deux tableaux du Louvre diffèrent; les ressemblances avec Dumée sont surtout frappantes dans le *Repas*, tandis que le style de Dubreuil, tel que nous le connaissons à travers les dessins, me semble mieux apparaître dans le *Sacrifice*. Leurs coloris aussi diffèrent un peu: celui du *Repas* a des tons clairs et frais qui expliquent que le tableau ait pu être classé autrefois dans les Réserves du Louvre parmi l'École italienne du XVIIIe siècle: notons, sans en tirer de conclusion, que ce coloris frais rappelle celui du tableau de Carnavalet. . . . La gamme colorée du *Sacrifice* est plus chaude, l'exécution paraît aussi supérieure . . . S'agit-il d'un autre maître? On ne reconnaît pas non plus, je crois, la main de Dumée dans les autres pièces subsistantes du décor de Saint-Germain (*Le Lever et La toilette d'une Dame* (Louvre), *Cybèle chez Morphée*, *Adieux d'un Guerrier et d'une Princesse* (Fontainebleau). La diversité des mains dans les rares tableaux qui nous sont parvenus du décor de Saint-Germain est évidente, ce qui n'a rien de surprenant étant donné les habitudes de travail de Dubreuil, sa brusque disparition et l'ampleur du programme décoratif de Saint-Germain.

Si l'attribution du *Repas* du Louvre à Dumée est juste elle permettra, peut-être, d'éclairer la figure oubliée d'un peintre qui fut célèbre de son temps, disciple de Dubreuil.

Ses dessins ont un charme timide, assez personnel; ses personnages aux gestes égarés, aux regards étranges, sont, dans leur gaucherie, authentiques et touchants; le clair obscur confère à ses compositions une mélancolie poétique et mystérieuse . . .

L'artiste nous échappe, cependant, et nous ne savons pas encore le reconnaître parmi les rares témoignages de cette époque: Dumée semble avoir tenu avec une certaine distinction sa place de décorateur au début du XVIIe siècle,[35] rivalisant sans doute, comme l'avait bien noté Sauval à propos du Cabinet de la Reine, avec ses contemporains Dubois, Honnet et le mystérieux Bunel.[36]

---

35. Göbel, *op. cit.* en note 8, p. 60, a souligné avec raison les qualités de Dumée comme peintre de tapisserie.

36. J'exprime toute ma gratitude pour leur aide au cours de cette étude à: Mme C. Aulanier, Chargée de mission au Musée du Louvre; Mlle R. Bacou, Conservateur au Cabinet des Dessins du Musée du Louvre; Mme Bouleau-Rabaud, Conservateur, École Supérieure des Beaux-Arts, Paris; Mr. M. Cormack, Conservateur au Fitzwilliam Museum, Cambridge (Angleterre), Mlle M. L. Cornillot, Conservateur du Musée de Besançon, Mlle Dupic, Conservateur de la Bibliothèque Municipale de Rouen; Mr. B. de Montgolfier, Conservateur au Musée Carnavalet, Paris; Mr. P. Rosenberg, Assistant au Département des Peintures du Musée du Louvre.

APPENDICE

Cette étude était achevée lorsque Monsieur Jean Coural, Administrateur Général du Mobilier national, eut l'extrême gentillesse de me communiquer ses importantes découvertes sur Dumée: je l'en remercie bien vivement. Elles ajoutent tant à notre connaissance de l'artiste que je suis particulièrement heureuse d'en résumer l'essentiel dans cette note en attendant la publication intégrale des documents.

Grâce au testament du 5 décembre 1645 retrouvé par Jean Coural au minutier des notaires des Archives nationales (*Étude* CV, 417) où Guillaume Dumée se dit âgé de 75 ans, testament qui fut apporté au notaire par son fils Toussaint Dumée le 8 janvier 1646, on peut établir ainsi les dates de naissance et de mort, jusqu'ici inconnues, de Guillaume Dumée: Fontainebleau(?) 1571–Paris 1646, infirmant l'hypothèse de J. Guiffrey, "Les manufactures parisiennes de tapisseries au XVIIe siècle", *Mémoires de la société de l'Histoire de Paris et de l'Ile-de-France*, p. 78) selon laquelle Dumée était probablement mort en 1636 puisque Guyot, qui lui était jusqu'ici associé, figure seul à cette date sur l'état des peintres de la maison du Roi, avec des gages augmentés de 150 livres. L'inventaire

après décès de Guillaume Dumée également dressé le 8 janvier 1646 (*Étude* CV, 488) et aussi retrouvé par Jean Coural, énumère plusieurs portraits; si ces portraits sont bien attribuables à Dumée (car il pourrait s'agir d'œuvres d'autres peintres conservés dans son atelier), ils prouvent que l'artiste mena de pair une carrière de décorateur et de portraitiste. Ceci expliquerait que dès 1612 on ait pu lui commander un des portraits de l'Hôtel de Ville.

De même, depuis la rédaction de cette étude la difficile question de l'appartement de la Reine-Mère au Louvre a été remarquablement éclairée par Monsieur Alain Erlande-Brandenburg ("Les Appartements de la Reine Mère Marie de Médicis au Louvre", *BSHAF*, 1966, pp. 105–113) qui a publié un plan inédit trouvé parmi les papiers du Ministère des Travaux Publics aux Archives nationales (F. 21.3567, pièce 5). Il précise les dispositions des pièces: pour leur décoration Mr. Erlande-Brandenburg suit la description de Sauval (comme Hautecœur) et ne mentionne pas Félibien dont le témoignage, plus précis que celui de Sauval, nous paraît, cependant, préférable.

MICHAEL JAFFÉ

Rubens and Raphael

RUBENS, like Dürer, made his way first to Venice, rather than Rome. But for an Antwerp painter of his generation, who was the most brilliant and ambitious pupil of Otto van Veen and himself wishful to be accepted as a Romanist on his return home, a pilgrimage to study at first hand the metropolitan works of Raphael was still indispensible. However before he ever set out for Italy, he was conversant, and very likely as a collector, with one important aspect of Raphael's activity: the issue of prints. He could gauge the extent to which prints advertised powers of *disegno*, as well as providing supplementary income, despite their insecurity as a means of registering and protecting designs in a Europe which bound itself by no law of international copyright. He knew, and as a man born in Germany surely relished, Vasari's account of how Raphael had been inspired to emulation by the engravings of Dürer, and so 'fece studiare Marco Antonio Bolognese in questa pratica infinitamente'.[1]

Recently in London a picture has come to light (Fig. 1), which illustrates how splendidly Rubens, as a young master still markedly under the influence of van Veen in his style of painting, was able to express his admiration for Raphael in design. This is the *Fall of Man*,[2] a composition of life-size figures, based on the engraving of the subject by Marcantonio[3] (Fig. 2). Background and accessories are freely invented by Rubens. A rabbit and a bright green parakeet are introduced, these perhaps in thought of Dürer's famous engraving of 1504. By the reeds on the river bank a monkey crouches asleep. The landscape itself, its character transformed entirely from the curiously post-Fall (and post-Dürer) view supplied for Raphael's figures by Marcantonio, is an Eden receding in fresh and luminous greens from the browns of the tree boles in the foreground and from the darker greens of the vine tendrils which hide the sexes of Adam and Eve; framed by the figures, it is an accomplished exercise in the manner of Coninxloo. But the man and the woman, whilst their poses are basically faithful to Raphael's invention, show more clearly the characteristic approach of Rubens. The heads in his revision are the one more ardent, the other more tender. The bodies are fuller, at once more heroic and more voluptuous, without being drawn by any unsubtlety of pictorial taste closer to each other. However the most revealing change is in the new-found rhetoric of Adam's massive forearm and left hand, the palm no longer burdened with the temptation of two apples. Instead his index finger points upwards to the Tempter, now serpent-headed and intent on Eve (the one blemish in the picture's condition is the loss of the top few inches of the panel on which the serpent's head would have been fully displayed). Here, where Rubens elected to make his most radical departure in the spirit of the narrative, *pentimenti* witness his determination to realize his reinterpretation precisely. The treatment of Adam's hand, half open, with the finger tips emphatically filled and rounded, is strongly reminiscent of the so-called *Portrait of a Geographer*,[4] the little painting on copper which Rubens signed and dated 1597. The distinctive treatment of Adam's hair and beard and of his head turned by Rubens slightly out of profile towards us, also of his feet and legs, finds close analogies on a comparable scale with those of Christ and His tormentors in another panel painting which is filled with people of the van Veen type: *the Mocking of Christ*,[5] a documented work of the winter of 1601–2 which Rubens was allowed to spend in Rome. This *Fall of Man* fits best into the period 1597–1600, between the end of Rubens's formal apprenticeship to van Veen, and his leaving Antwerp in May 1600. Such a large panel, composite of oak boards, is not likely either to have been transported, or to have been made up for his use, south of the Alps. It is not hard to imagine it as one of the paintings which he left behind in Antwerp. These, by his mother's account, were beautiful; and, as his nephew Philip wrote to Roger de Piles,[6] 'avant son voyage d'Italie, ils avaient quelque ressemblance avec ceux d'Octave van Veen, son maistre'. Nothing that has come down to us of the classicising works of van Veen himself is so vigorous or so intense.

Perhaps during his first years in Italy, or perhaps even

1. G. Vasari, *Le vite dei più eccellenti pittori . . .*, Florence, 1568, terza parte, p. 78.
2. Private collection, London. Oil on oak panel, 71 × 54½ ins. [evidently trimmed of a few inches along the upper edge]. Collections: Earl Cowper (red wax seal on the back); Colonel W. Forbes of Callender, Falkirk (according to Colonel Forbes this picture had been in his family for several generations), sold Christie's 29.xi.1963, as by Karel van Mander. A later attribution to Hugo Golzius has also to be rejected. The picture was cleaned in 1965, and revealed to be in excellent condition. I am grateful to the present owner for permission to publish it here.
3. Bartsch, XIV, 3, 1.

4. 'Le Siècle de Rubens', *Musées Royaux des Beaux-Arts de Belgique*, Brussels, 1965, 205 (illus.).
5. 'Le Seizième Siècle européen.' *Peintures et dessins dans les collections publiques françaises*, Paris, 1965, 252 (illus.).
6. *Bulletin-Rubens*, II, Antwerp/Brussels, 1883, p. 166.

before his ride south, Rubens made a record in sanguine[7] of Marcantonio's engraving which adapted to a rectangle Raphael's scene of *God bidding Noah build the Ark*, frescoed on the ceiling of the Stanza d'Eliodoro. In this case he made no significant variations from his model. With equal fidelity, in the same medium, and presumably also at this period shortly before or after 1600, he copied a very different kind of subject,[8] the enchanting *Alexander offering the crown to Roxana*, which Jacopo Caraglio engraved after Raphael. Here Rubens used for his immediate model either an impression of the anonymous engraving, which reverses Jacopo's or a highly finished drawing by Raphael himself. For, in the sale at Paris of Pierre Crozat's collection in 1741, lot 125 amongst the impressive collection of Raphael drawings was:[9] 'Deux, *idem*, sçavoir; les Amours d'Alexandre & de Roxane; Dessein très-arrêté & du premier ordre, & la même composition, mais où les figures sont sans aucune drapperie, Raphael ayant fait ce beau Dessein pour servir d'Étude au premier; avec les Estampes qui ont été gravées d'après ces Desseins.' The beautiful composition study in sanguine with the figures envisaged nude, which indeed is manifestly drawn by Raphael's own hand, came from the Birkenstock collection to the Albertina.[10] It is catalogued there as by 'Penni[?]', and as having been brought by Rubens from Rome; that is to say, before it came into the possession of Cardinal Bentivoglio, who gave it to Claude Mellan, the engraver; and before it came into the collection of Vaurose and Crozat. Mariette in fact was the buyer of both drawings at the Crozat sale.[11] If Rubens did not own or know either drawing at the time when he copied the composition, we can only applaud the more how well he showed himself in his copy to be the man to sense, through the comparatively dry schemata of an engraver

working at second-hand, the life of Raphael's original conception.

Rubens in Antwerp could also have known, and not only through his reading of Vasari, how excellent was the engraving of the 'bellissima carta di Raffaello da Urbino, nella quale era una Lucrezia Romana, che si ucciderà', by which Marcantonio in youth had recommended himself to the Pope's[12] painter. However the remarkable copy[13] which he made of this print, once again in the form of a highly finished drawing and on the scale of the original, is unlikely from stylistic considerations to have been made until the second period of his residence in Rome, 1605–8 (Fig. 3). At first sight one might suspect that an impression of the engraving lay beneath a palimpsest of wash and gouache. But closer inspection shows that all the work is freehand. It is on paper washed brown overall, with grey and pink gouaches and some reinforcement of pen and ink to the figure's left leg and thigh. The Greek inscription, and the landscape background of trees and buildings are omitted. The sky instead is an invention which enhances the luminosity inherent in the mixed technique of wash and bodycolour. The effect of *grisaille* echoes appropriately those late works of Mantegna which were known by heart to Rubens as a successor to the former in Gonzagan service. Numerous and subtle modifications are introduced into the life and amplitude of the drapery, the form and cadence of which correspond to those developed by Rubens during his second stay in Rome. To secure, more from a Baroque than a High Renaissance point of view, the apparent stability of Lucretia's poise at the instant of aiming the dagger, he lengthened the long fall of cloth at her left side, so as to allow folds to break onto the ground in a little pile beside the foot which bears her weight. Thus he has left a drawing which is at once a centennial tribute to Marcantonio's skill in interpreting Raphael's design, and a foretaste of those *modelletti* by which he himself was to impose his wishes on his own engravers.

The fascination for Rubens of Raphael's designs recorded by Marcantonio outlasted his stay in Italy. In the British Museum there is a drawing in sanguine, used both as chalk and as a wash applied with the point of the brush (Fig. 4).[14] The authorship used not to be in doubt. But Dr. J. Müller

7. F. Lugt, *Musée du Louvre. Inventaire général des dessins des écoles du Nord. École flamande*, II, Paris, 1949 – referred to henceforth as Lugt, *Louvre* – 1036, pl. XXXIII, as 'de la main de Rubens et datant des premières années de son séjour en Italie'. L. Burchard and R.-A. d'Hulst, *Rubens Drawings*, Brussels, 1963, 22 (illus.) state that 'this carefully executed drawing was made by Rubens during his first years in Italy'.

8. Lugt, *Louvre*, 1079, pl. XLVII, as 'D'après Raphael', with the comment that, 'Les retouches de blanc rappellent les habitudes de Rubens, mais le dessin est un peu froid pour être de lui, même dans sa jeunesse'. Lugt omits mention of Bartsch XV, 95, 62, the Jacopo Caraglio engraving after Raphael; and of the anonymous engraving which copies that print in reverse, *ibid.*, p. 96. It was the latter that Rubens used in the event that he did not know the original drawing.

9. F. Lugt, *Répertoire des catalogues de ventes, 1600–1825*, the Hague, 1938 – henceforth referred to as Lugt, *Ventes* – 536. I have used the copy of this catalogue, annotated by P. J. Mariette, which is in the Victoria and Albert Museum Library.

10. F. Stix and L. Fröhlich-Bum, *Beschreibender Katalog der Handzeichnungen in der Graph. Sammlung Albertina*, III, Vienna, 1932, 118 (illus.).

11. Lugt, *Ventes*, 536. Lugt, *Louvre*, refers to Crozat's first drawing, Louvre inv. 3885, as 'de l'école de Raphael'.

12. Vasari, *op. cit.*, p. 299. Bartsch XIV, 155, 192.

13. Private collection, London. Sold Sotheby's, 1.xii.1964 (lot 12, as 'Italian 16th century'), and 22.vii.1965 (lot 54). Pen and brown ink, and white and pink gouaches on paper washed brown. 223 × 143 mm., *doublé*. J. Denucé, *De Konstkamers van Antwerpen in de 16e en 17e Eeuwen*, Antwerp, 1932, p. 235, lists in the 1686 Inventory of Joannes Philippus Happart, 'Item eene teeckeninge Lucretia van Raphael'. Conceivably an original drawing by Raphael for this treatment of the subject was earlier available in Antwerp to Rubens, or even was owned by him.

14. A. M. Hind, *Catalogue of drawings by Dutch and Flemish Artists preserved in the Department of Prints and Drawings in the British Museum*, II, 1923, 28, pl. IV, as 'Satyr and Nymph' by Rubens. Collections: P. H. Lankrink; J. Richardson senr.; Salting.

Hofstede, whilst being the first to remark a connection with a *Pan and Syrinx* design engraved after Raphael,[15] supposes the drawing to be by the Italian engraver and only reworked by Rubens. In fact it is a free interpretation in reverse of the first state of the print, retaining as in the *Lucretia* drawing the proportions of the original figures, whilst simplifying the background. Rubens is the author throughout. He reveals the full expression of Pan, lusting to the very finger tips. He gives a long, natural fall to the hair of Syrinx, avoiding repetition of the calligraphic loop made by one tress over her bent forearm. He modulates the forms afresh, investing the bodies with a distinctively heightened vitality: so that we feel that his poetic insight has enabled him to see through the constricting medium of the engraver's interpretation to the inspiration of Raphael. Morphologically his woman and satyr belong to the period of his collaboration with Jan Brueghel, about 1615, in small figures for decorative landscapes. We may think not only of a *Pan and Syrinx* which they painted together (Fig. 5),[16] but of the more famous panel of *Adam and Eve* in the Mauritshuis.[17]

Rubens in Italy naturally went whenever possible to the direct inspiration of Raphael. On his ride south from Mantua to Rome in 1601, he must have taken note at Bologna of Raphael's *St. Cecilia*, set in the beautiful Tuscan chapel of S. Giovanni ai Monti. He was aware of the sensational effect which its arrival some eighty years before had had on the provincial painters of the city. To the noble stance and the richly brocaded dress of the central saint he was soon to pay homage in the hieratic image of *St. Helena*[18] which he devised for S. Croce in Gerusalemme.

And in that same altarpiece, painted in fulfilment of his first public commission in the metropolis, there are other clear Raphaelite echoes: in the use of Salomonic columns, for example, and in the way that the hair of the angel perched on the shaft of the Cross streams decoratively sideways, as though he were in attendance on the *Galatea*. It is likely that Rubens was eager to make drawings after all the decorations designed by Raphael for the Farnesina; although the finest of these that we know, the copy of *Psyche offering the Jar of Proserpine to Venus*,[19] appears to have been drawn in the loggia during the second rather than the first Roman visit. The supple flow of drapery and the cloud formation which support Rubens's Venus do not derive from any engraving. They are characteristically Rubensian improvisations to replace the simulated trellis-work which had been the contribution of Giovanni da Udine to the festivity of the ceiling. On the other side of this sheet Rubens copied in chalk, also directly from the vault of the Loggia di Psiche, the head and arms of the bearded river gods (Fig. 11), who recline naked amongst the cloud-borne Olympians in the scene of Psyche's reception at the *Council of the Gods*. On this *verso* the hesitations in drawing the elbows, and the markedly different degrees of finish in the two figures, are further indications that the fresco itself, and not the engraving of the scene by Jacopo Caraglio,[20] was his model; although it is more than likely that he owned, perhaps even at the time, an impression of Caraglio's print as well as of engravings by Marcantonio Raimondi after the *Jupiter Kissing Cupid*, the *Mercury*, and the *Cupid with the three Graces*,[21] and by Marco da Ravenna after the *Venus leaving Ceres and Juno*.[22] He would have been interested also in Caraglio's other print from the history of Cupid and Psyche in the loggia, the reversal of the *Mercury conducting Psyche to Olympus*;[23] in the reversal of the *Psyche returning from Tartarus*, engraved by an anonymous pupil of Marcantonio;[24] and in the *Marriage Feast*, which was published in 1545 by Antonio Salamanca;[25] not to speak of the prints after the *Amorini* scenes by Agostino Veneziano[26] and others, particularly the anonymous one which shows the cupid vaulting in the sky, with the harpy in flight to the right of him.[27]

15. Bartsch, XIV, 246, 325. Attributed to Marcantonio but perhaps, as Dr. John Shearman has suggested to me, by the Master of the Die. Müller Hofstede's opinion is on the mount of the British Museum drawing.
16. E. Speelman, London. Oil on oak panel (branded by the Antwerp Guild), 22¾ × 37 ins. This may be the painting mentioned in Jan Brueghel's diary for 1626. Collections: Schönborn, Schloss Pommersfelden; Salomon Goldschmidt; Rothschild, Vienna; Bryan Jenks, Astbury Hall, Salop. M. Rooses, *L'œuvre de P. P. Rubens*, III, Antwerp, 1890, 660, reports information from W. von Bode about another Rubens-Jan Brueghel treatment of this subject, then in the collection of Comte de Ribaudeau (panel, 62 × 80 cm.). Rooses cast doubt on the identification of this picture, by Ribaudeau family tradition, with the one said to have been removed by Denon from the Cassel Museum. That panel – 15 × 22½ pouces in the Cassel Inventory of 1749 – came from the sales of the Dame de Ste-Annaland [the Hague, 1725, 400 florins], and of Adrien Bout [the Hague, 1733, 700 florins]. J. Smith, *A Catalogue Raisonné of the Works of the most eminent Dutch, Flemish, and French Painters*, II, London, 1830, 584, evidently had not seen this picture, but confuses the issue by saying, 'This is probably a sketch for the picture in His Majesty's Collection' [Rooses, *op. cit.*, 659], and by equating pouces with English inches. I am grateful to Mr. Speelman for permission to publish his painting here.
17. Klassiker der Kunst, *Rubens*, (ed. 1921), 219.
18. Kl.d.K., 1.
19. '*Drawings and Oil Sketches by P. P. Rubens from American Collections*'. *Fogg Art Museum, Harvard University and the Pierpont Morgan Library*, Harvard (1956), 7, pl. XII (*recto* only). The opinion of Prof. J. S. Held is quoted by Miss Felice Stampfle, that 'in the present instance Rubens was working from engravings'. The source of the *verso* has not been identified hitherto, nor has it been illustrated.
20. Bartsch, XV, 89, 54.
21. Bartsch, XIV, 256–257, 342–344.
22. Bartsch, XIV, 247, 327.
23. Bartsch, XV, 86, 50.
24. Bartsch, XV, 36, 5.
25. Bartsch, XV, 43, 14.
26. *E.g.* Bartsch, XIV, 179, 218.
27. Bartsch, XV, 39, 8.

Whilst Rubens was in Italy, such a considerable number of the designs of the Farnesina decorations could have been available to him through engravings. But of important figures frescoed elsewhere for Agostino Chigi to the designs of Raphael, the *Prophets and Sibyls* in S. Maria della Pace, there was only a pair of anonymous engravings of the *Sibyls*, in reverse and of rather poor quality. Neither of the splendidly finished copies by Rubens, recognizing the 'grandezza e maestà' of the *Daniel and David*[28] and of the *Sibyl of the Resurrection*,[29] could have been drawn from these. They are drawn in the sense of the frescoes, and were done in the chapel itself, on different occasions during his second sojourn in Rome.

To the Vatican *Stanze* Rubens obtained access when he was first in Rome, presumably through his introduction from Vincenzo I Gonzaga to Cardinal Montalto. His pen and wash copy of the central group of figures from the upper tier of the *Disputa*[30] (Fig. 6) was surely made in the Stanza della Segnatura itself, and not from the rare engraving of the whole scene which Giorgio Ghisi had engraved on two plates, and which Hieronymus Cock had published in 1552.[31] This drawing, catalogued at the Royal Library, Turin, as no more than retouched by Rubens, is entirely by his hand; and it is datable to his first winter in Rome. In style it is close to the copy which he made early in his Italian career from Leonardo's *Last Supper* in S. Maria della Grazie.[32]

In the Stanza della Segnatura also, and probably during his first stay in Rome, Rubens made a copy which is freer, but this time in sanguine, of *Prudence* and her attendant putto.[33] The Agostino Veneziano engraving of 1516,[34] in which a niche and a column appear, would not have served him so well as the actual fresco. The Rubens drawing is one of those which Lankrink owned: but in this case, when the sheet was extended, Lankrink was not the repairer. Rubens himself completed the putto's right buttock, foot and wing, and the right foot of Prudence where the draughtsmanship as well as the technique are highly characteristic. He de-

parted from the composition of the fresco in the direction given to this foot of Prudence, which Raphael had painted so as to project over the parapet, sandalled, and at the same time cocked up to hide the putto's right foot; in showing the left hand of Prudence, which in the fresco is hidden by draperies; and in changing the looking-glass, in the course of his own drawing, to give it a more elliptical shape and a more prominent handle.

His excerpt[35] of *Three Warriors* from the *Alexander ordering Homer's Iliad to be stored in a Persian Chest* – the scene frescoed below the *Parnassus* in the same room – shows a considerably more advanced style, both in the opulent ease of handling his chosen media, and in readiness to invent forms freely in the spirit of Raphael which are yet idiosyncratically his own. Moreover, by contrast to his early copies from Raphael designs made in Antwerp or during his first sojourn in Rome, he is confident in increasing the scale. The fact that he has worked from an anonymous copy[36] which reverses Marcantonio's engraving, rather than from the *grisaille* painting itself, suggests that he may well have made this drawing after he had finally left Rome. Conceivably this Raphaelizing exercise dates from the period of collecting his thoughts for the series of tapestries devoted to the *History of the Consul Decius Mus*.[37] In any case he had by him, in the famous Pocket-book which he kept on his travels, a note,[38] penned on this earlier occasion from Marcantonio's engraving[39] which is in the opposite sense to Raphael's fresco, of the old helmeted warrior who stands next to Alexander and raises his hand. And that note keeps company on the same folio with other rapid *ricordi* of Raphael groups; from Marco da Ravenna's engraving,[40] which reproduces the *Fire in the Borgo* in reverse; and from Agostino Veneziano's engraving[41] of *Elymas struck with Blindness*. Thus Rubens kept the stimulus to refresh his figurative ideas at the fountain of Raphael's invention ready to hand.

For his record of the *Fire in the Borgo* Rubens, it hardly needs to be said, did not rely exclusively on the Marco da Ravenna print and on his own jottings from that. He chose to copy, not at all surprisingly, the nude figure of the man dropping from the wall[42] (Fig. 7). He possibly did this from

28. Goudstikker – *Rubens tentoonstelling*, Amsterdam, 1933, 69 (illus.), dated *c.* 1601–2 by L. Burchard and J. Q. van Regteren Altena, the principal compilers of this catalogue: but 1605–8 by M. Jaffé, *Art Quarterly*, XVIII, 1955, p. 340.

29. J. Müller Hofstede, *Master Drawings*, II, 1964, no. 1, pp. 11–13, pl. 4.

30. A. Bertini, *I disegni italiani della Biblioteca Reale di Torino*, Rome, 1958, 376 (illus.) as 'copia da Raffaello', quoting Mr. A. E. Popham's opinion that the drawing was retouched by Rubens.

31. Bartsch, XV, 394, 23.

32. M. Jaffé, *Van Dyck's Antwerp Sketchbook*, London, 1966, p. 32, fig. xx.

33. National Gallery of Scotland, D.1787; reproduced in *Fifty Master Drawings in the National Gallery of Scotland*, Edinburgh, 1961, no. 29. Red chalk, accented with a wash of the same and point of brush, on white paper, 180 × 212 mm. Collection: P. H. Lankrink. This discovery of Mr. K. Andrews is referred to by Burchard-d'Hulst, *op. cit.*, 22. I am grateful to Mr. Andrews for first calling it to my attention.

34. Bartsch, XIV, 273, 357.

35. Müller Hofstede, *loc. cit.*, p. 14, pl. 5. No dating is there suggested.

36. Reproduced by H. Delaborde, *Marc-Antoine Raimondi*, Paris, n.d., p. 218, pl. opp: p. 216.

37. Kl.d.K., 142–147.

38. Jaffé, *op. cit.*, p. 18, fig. VIII. *Ibid.*, fig. IX, illustrates the *verso* of this sheet from Rubens's Pocketbook, on which he drew a free copy from *The Judgment of Solomon*, frescoed by Raphael on the vault of the Stanza della Segnatura.

39. Bartsch, XIV, 168, 207 A.

40. Bartsch, XV, 33, 6.

41. Bartsch, XIV, 48, 43.

42. Hind, *op. cit.* in note 14, 49 (not illus.). Collection: Richard Payne Knight. Hind assumes that Rubens copied from the fresco in the Stanza dell'Incendio. At the Crozat sale [Lugt, *Ventes,*

the fresco itself, omitting the piece of drapery, and giving a more intense expression to the face and hair, but more probably worked from a preparatory study – or at least a copy of one – by Raphael. The absorption by Raphael in Rome of the message of Michelangelo was recognized superbly by Rubens. Appropriately in this copy he rendered the combined grace and dynamism of the action – which figured in his inspiration when he came to sketch the *Defeat and Death of Maxentius*[43] some fifteen years later – in the rich combination of media which Michelangelo himself had used for such a finished study as that now in the British Museum for one of the *Bathers*.[44]

Of the *Acts of the Apostles Peter and Paul*, Rubens painted a series of copies, as we know from his inventory in 1640: five in one group;[45] and a sixth which is itemized separately,[46] perhaps because it was done at a recognizably different period or on a different scale. These copies are likely to have included the *Sacrifice at Lystra* as well as the *Blinding of Elymas*, and to have been made from the cartoons rather than from the Vatican or Mantuan sets of the tapestries; for if Rubens had adequate opportunity to study the cartoons – and we know from the copy which he drew about 1600[47] of *St. Paul's Sermon at Athens* that he saw during his career the cartoons as well as the tapestries – he would have preferred to make them his models. If this conjecture is correct, his painted copies would have served as a basis for Van Dyck's highly expressive studies of heads from the *Sacrifice* and the *Blinding* which are now divided between the Koch collection and the Rubens-cantoór at Copenhagen.[48]

In his pursuit of the works of Raphael's mature achievement, Rubens did not neglect to look outside Rome. In May 1603, on his mission to the court of Philip III, with a cargo including copies by Pietro Facchetti after the Raphaels in Rome, the young Fleming remarked how the Duke of Lerma had every day the opportunity to exercise his judgment on 'tante cose bellissime del Titiano e Raphaello et altri che mi hanno fatto stupire in qualità e in quantità, in casa del Re et in Escuriale et altrove'[49] – although it is not clear just what originals by Raphael he could have seen in the Habsburg collections at this date, unless it were the Leonardesque *Holy Family with the Lamb* in the Escurial, and the portrait sometimes identified as that of *Cardinal Alidosi*. *The Vision of Ezekiel* he could have seen in the Tribuna of the Uffizi on his first visit to Florence in October 1600, when he went in the suite of the Gonzaga Duke and Duchess to the marriage by proxy of the Duchess's niece. But it is much more likely that he made his copy of that fascinatingly complex configuration in 1605–8, on one of his journeys between Rome and Mantua. His drawing follows the original faithfully, in the exacting medium of red chalk. It omits only the landscape[50] (Fig. 8). It was part of lot 1022 in the Mariette Sale of 1775: 'La Vision d'Ézéchiel, d'après Raphael, à la sanguine supérieurement bien dessiné', together with 'la belle Figure de Ganimède enlevé, d'après M. Ange, dessiné à la plume & à la pierre noire: les expressions des têtes doivent être regardées comme des chefs-d'œuvre de l'art; elles ont été retouchées par Rubens, sur ce Dessin, qui

of Van Dyck's style in copying from other masters at this time when he was evolving his peculiar brand of expressionism. Close comparisons may be made with Jaffé, *op. cit.*, II, 24 *verso* (after Mantegna) and 45 *recto* (after Bandinelli), etc. Van Dyck's sets of Apostles [e.g. the five panels in the chapel at Althorp House, Northants.] and other heads painted during his first period in Antwerp are informed by these highly expressive studies after Raphael as much as they are inspired by the example of Rubens's *Apostelado* for the Duque de Lerma. Rubens himself, even where he prefers to chalks and gouache the naturally more fluid media of ink with pen or brush, which are potentially more violent in expression, never relaxes his grasp of the plasticity of form so completely in the interest of facial expression.

536], Huquier bought lot 121 [Raphael], 'L'Académie de l'homme qui est suspendu par les bras à une muraille dans le tableau de l'Incendie *del Borgo*'. Raphael's original drawing, in sanguine, is in the Albertina, although H. Dollmayr, Vienna *Jahrbuch*, XVI, 1895, p. 249, considered it a copy. I share the opinion of Dr. Konrad Oberhuber and Dr. Shearman that this drawing is by Raphael.

43. Kl.d.K., 232.
44. J. Wilde, *Italian Drawings in the Department of Prints and Drawings in the British Museum. Michelangelo and his Studio*, London, 1953, 6 *recto*, pl. XII.
45. Denucé, *op. cit.*, p. 59, 71–75.
46. *Ibid.*, 80.
47. J. Müller Hofstede, *WRJb*, XXVII, 1965, p. 275, Abb. 199, illustrates the drawing made known by J. Q. van Regteren Altena, *Burl M.*, LXXVI, 1940, pp. 194 ff., n. 6. See note 50 below.
48. Dr. Müller Hofstede published all these copies of heads, clearly drawn by the same hand: six on one integral sheet in the Koch collection [*Master Drawings*, II, no. 1, 1964, pp. 5–7, pl. 2], and thirteen divided between six scraps in the Kongel. Kobberstik-samling at Copenhagen [*WRJb*, XXVII, 1965, pp. 278–280, Abb. 192–198]. In Müller Hofstede's opinion all are by Rubens. In mine all are by the young Van Dyck, at the period when he was most closely associated with Rubens. The mannered violence of shading and hatching, taking precedence over form, and the handling of particular features (e.g. angularities and elongations in noses, calligraphic extensions of eyebrows, etc.) are eloquent

49. *Codex Diplomaticus Rubenianus*, I, Antwerp, 1887, p. 146.
50. Museo Horne, 5549. Red chalk, heightened with buff and white gouaches, on white paper, 305 × 225 mm. Collections: P. J. Mariette (L. 1854); F. Basan; Marquis de Calvière, Sale 1779; J. C. Robinson; H. Horne. In *Bulletin-Rubens*, Antwerp, 1910, p. 198, M. Rooses reports seeing in the collection of Sir Charles Robinson this drawing and another by Rubens now missing, 'La Guérison de l'aveugle Éd'lymas d'après Raphael. A la plume, lavé de bistre H. 25, L. 38·5 cm.' This may well have been of the character and date of the drawing [27·8 × 40·5 cm.] in the University Library of Uppsala, of the *Preaching of St. Paul at Athens*, first remarked by van Regteren Altena, *loc. cit.*; see note 47 above. I am grateful to dott. L. Ragghianti Collobi for permission to publish the copy of the *Vision of Ezekiel*, and to dott. Maria Fossi-Todorow for showing me the drawing on deposit at the Uffizi.

est de Don Giulio Clovio.'[50a] These two show-pieces were knocked down for l. 59.19 to Basan, who made the catalogue. The 'Vision of Ezekiel after Raphael – red Chalk' was again sold as Rubens amongst the drawings by old masters from the collection of J. C. Robinson, at Christie's on 12th May 1902. It was bought by Dresden for £9, and subsequently by Horne. It is now in the Museo Horne, where, despite this illustrious provenance, some twentieth-century vandal with a ball-point pen has written, on the Mariette mount, 'No! No!' to the attribution not hitherto in doubt.

Where no Raphael original in painting was available to him, Rubens was prepared, even so late as his second period in Rome, to follow the design from a print. We may judge this from the handsome copy which he made, retaining the scale of the figures, from the Jacopo Caraglio engraving[51] of the *Madonna and Child Jesus, with St. Elizabeth and the Child John*.[52] Here he deviates from Caraglio only in the idiomatic expression of the faces, and in the fresh inclination of the Madonna's head.

In studying the manner in which Rubens sought so determinedly to wrest from Raphael the secrets of his power, it is instructive to turn to his reactions to Raphael's last work. Not only did he make, when he first came to Rome, an elaborate copy of the group of apostles who fill the lower left corner of the *Transfiguration*—the morphology of the bearded heads is suggestive of his style at that time[53] (Fig. 9);—but he sought, as we might expect, closer acquaintance with Raphael's creative processes. Here the engraving[54] by the Master of the Die was certainly not enough to satisfy him. Somehow he got access to at least two of Raphael's working drawings, or to studio repetitions of those; and he made from them beautiful copies. In one[55] he interpreted, with outstanding sensibility to the drama of light and atmosphere, Raphael's design at the stage when the *Transfiguration* was the single subject. In the other[56] he revised, so as to engender unity by that same sensibility, the much more advanced scheme which in essentials had to be changed in the final composition only in the disposition of the apostles in the lower left corner (already made, by Rubens, the subject of a special note) and in the position of Christ and His apostles on Mount Tabor. This second copy was inscribed 'Rafael da Urbino' in Rubens's own hand, surely not because he himself might otherwise have forgotten the derivation of the composition, but as a guide to young assistants, who would be set to copy this and other choice models of *disegno* in his Antwerp studio. We may imagine that he, of all painters the most effectively conscious of the history of art, might have pointed out to these youths how Raphael in 1520, in his ideas for the attitude and drapery of Christ, had harked back to a main source of his inspiration in Florence, the reliefs in enamelled terracotta by Luca della Robbia: in this case, to the lunette of the *Ascension*[57] over the entry to the south sacristy in S. Maria dei Fiori. Rubens himself in 1604 was to paint the *Transfiguration*[58] in fulfilment of the Gonzaga commission for the *cappella maggiore* of the Jesuit church in Mantua. On that vast stretch of canvas the outburst of radiance from the figure of Christ, the flaring light in the trees, the fringes of illumination which dramatically darken by contrast the excited silhouettes in the crowd of figures, the murky and the livid colours, all these are eloquent of his enthusiastic studies in the Scuola di S. Rocco. But the stance of Christ, the attitudes of many of those who are caught up in the miraculous happenings, the very challenge offered by the occasion to maintain the doubly laden narrative in his own treatment of the subject, show how Rubens already felt the strength to invite comparisons with Raphael. No evidence has been brought forward that Duke Vincenzo or Duchess Eleonora, or any member of their court, was able to appreciate the significance of this prodigious assertion by the young foreigner of his artistic power. Within a few years of the consecration of the chapel in SS. Trinita, the first *principe* of the Accademia di S. Luca was on his tour of North Italy. But Federico Zuccaro, intoxicated by his invitation to join a ducal hunting-party, could only just take note in passing of the decorations by

50a. M. Carlos van Hasselt has kindly drawn my attention to Don Giulio Clovio's copy of the *Rape of Ganymede*, now in a private collection in Paris. Black chalk; retouched by Rubens lightly in pen and ink, with slight touches of white gouache, 285 × 241 mm. Collections: P. P. Rubens; P. J. Muriette (L. 1854); Sir T. Lawrence (L. 2445); S. Woodburn; E. Galichon (L. 856), sale 10–14 May 1875, Lot 18; L. G. Galichon (L. 1060), sale 4–9 March 1894, Lot 12. See Vasari, *op. cit.*, p. 853. I hope to illustrate this drawing on a future occasion.

51. Bartsch, xv, 69, 5.

52. Lugt, *Louvre*, 1057, pl. XLI. Lugt states: 'Du tableau de Raphael, connu comme "La petite Sainte Famille", on connaît plusieurs repliques, dont une se trouve au Musée du Louvre . . . Rubens a sans doute copié l'exemplaire du tableau qui se trouvait à Mantoue, dans la collection des Gonzague et qui n'est pas identique à l'exemplaire du Louvre.' This misconception was repeated by Müller Hofstede, *Master Drawings*, II, no. 1, 1964, p. 14, in discussing the *Madonna Piccola Gonzaga*, rather than Caraglio's engraving, as the model used by Rubens. Lugt, *Louvre*, 1038, also fails to note that the immediate model used by Rubens for that was almost certainly an engraving (Bartsch, xv, 10, 8) by Agostino Veneziano after Raphael. This engraving, *The Manna*, is illustrated by Jaffé, *op. cit.*, fig. LXXXVII.

53. Lugt, *Louvre*, 1061 (not illus.). There is heightening in yellow as well as the white described, *ibid*. Lugt, referring to his 1060 ['Le dessin, quoique dans la manière de Rubens, n'a pas partout la fermeté de sa main'], states 'Même remarque que pour le dessin précédent; celui-ci est encore plus faible'.

54. Bartsch, xv, 188, 7.

55. K. Oberhuber, *Jahrbuch der Berliner Museen*, IV, 1962, pp. 116–149, Abb. 1.

56. *Ibid.*, abb. 3.

57. J. Pope-Hennessy, *Italian Renaissance Sculpture*, London, 1958, pl. 45.

58. Kl.d.K., 15.

Giulio, who had been officially one of the artistic heirs of Raphael. He had not a word for the recent work of Rubens.

At the time when Rubens was being promoted by Monsignor Jacomo Serra for the Oratorian commission at the Chiesa Nuova, nobody in Rome appears to have taken account of what he painted in Mantua. But Rubens, once he gained the coveted commission in the metropolis, did not shed his attachment to Raphael. In his pen sketch for the composition at an early stage, in the way in which he projects the amplitude and dignity of St. Gregory,[59] there is an unmistakable echo of the Aristotle in the *School of Athens*. Indeed recollections of single figures from Raphael's Roman works continue to reappear in vivid revisions to suit fresh contexts during the two decades following Rubens's return to Antwerp. About 1612 the crippled beggar of his *modello* of the *Miracle of St. Bavo*[60] was inspired by the equivalent figure in the *Healing of the Lame*. The blinded Elymas of the tapestry cartoon suggested the pose of the blind man in the *Miracle of St. Francis Xavier*[61] about 1619. A memory of the harpy in flight, which he had seen frescoed in the Farnesina Loggia, or an engraving,[62] provoked the drawing of the harpy[63] (Fig. 10) who was to wing her way (as we can see clearly from a fragmentary copy at Weimar[64]) through the lower zone of *The Duke of Buckingham assisted by Minerva, triumphing over Envy and Anger*.[65] And Rubens drew extensively on the education which he had won so patiently from Raphael, when he came to plan groups of figures for his first tapestry cycle on a theme of Roman history, the *Life of the Consul Decius Mus*. His recourse to Raphael, both to the *Sala di Costantino* and to the Tapestry Cartoons, is even more obvious when he undertook to design tapestries to the order of Louis XIII for his reinterpretation of the *History of Constantine*.[66]

In portraiture Rubens owed to Raphael scarcely less than he owed to Titian. His inventory in 1640 included 'Un

pourtrait, jugé pour estre de *Raphael d'Urbin*'.[67] Years before, in order to provide a setting splendid enough for his portrayal in Genoa of the Marchesa Brigida Spinola Doria, seated in an arm chair, he had turned to the concept of space and of the spread of stiff draperies which Raphael had presented in his portrait of Julius II in the guise of *Gregory IX giving the Decretals*. Behind the senatorial dignity of *Rogier Clarisse*, which he was commissioned to paint in Antwerp, lies the Papal dignity of *Julius II*.[68] And, about 1620, when he was at home painting on oak panels his copies after portraits by Holbein and by Matsys, he chose to copy also the most Venetian of Raphael's portraits, the *Baldassare Castiglione*, which he could have known in the original in the Casa Castiglione at Mantua. Whether he developed this portrait on the basis of a careful drawing which he himself made at that time, or from some old and reliable copy of the painting which was available to him in Antwerp, we do not know. Certainly his tribute to Raphael's conception ranks as a masterpiece in its own right. In the words of the present owner, 'Raphael's Castiglione is a type of the Renaissance portrait, stable, balanced and self-contained; Rubens by completing the hands and imparting a slight twist to the body, created a figure which is free in space and instinct with 'presence': in short, it is a Baroque portrait'.[69]

Rubens turned to Raphael not only for ideas in portraiture, for figures and groups in his compositions, and for pictorial devices such as Salomonic columns or the simulated effect of tapestry. Traces of these sorts of borrowing effectively disappear from his painting, after he went in 1628 to Spain for his second encounter with the Titians of the Habsburg collection.[70] What lasted in his career from the day at Verona in 1602, when he promised to his friend Jan van der Wouvere the dedication of the first engraving after one of his compositions, until 1638, that last *annus mirabilis* of print-making from his designs, was his post-Raphaelite sense of the importance of this disseminatory activity. For it was through the prints of Marcantonio and his pupils and following that he had had in his formative years his first access to Raphael. The promulgation of his own work through prints presented more difficult problems than any which had appeared for reproductive media,

59. Burchard-d'Hulst, *op. cit.*, 26 recto.
60. Kl.d.K., 272.
61. Kl.d.K., 205.
62. Bartsch, XV, 39, 8.
63. Hind, *op. cit.*, 20 (not illus.), compares this subject to 'the Evil Spirits in the picture of the *Miracle of St. Ignatius Loyola* in Vienna'. Black chalk on white paper, 263 × 366 mm. Presented to the British Museum in 1918 by Lord Glenconner.
64. Goethe Nationalmuseum, Weimar, as 'Gruppe zu einem Sturz der Verdammten. Rötelzeichnung in der Art des Peter Paul Rubens. 17. Jahrhundert.' Red chalk on white paper, 285 × 44 mm. This drawing is of the character of many in the Rubens-cantoór at Copenhagen, and may be by Willem Panneels. It refers to the composition in its circular form.
65. G. Martin, *Burl M*, CVII, 1966, pp. 613–618, gives the latest discussion. His fig. 21 illustrates the ceiling piece as it was at Osterley Park.
66. John Coolidge, *GBA*, 6e pér., LXV, 1966, pp. 271–290, provides the latest and most illuminating discussion of the Constantine series.

67. Denucé, *op. cit.*, p. 57, 19.
68. M. Jaffé, *Burl M*, XCV, 1953, pp. 387–390.
69. A. Seilern, *Flemish Paintings and Drawings at 56 Princes Gate, London*, London, 1955, 24, pls. LVII–LVIII. That the Raphael original was in the Casa Castiglione at Mantua is clearly implied, if not explicitly stated, by Beffa Negrini in *Elogi historici alcuni personaggi della famiglia Castiglione . . .*, Mantua, 1606, p. 432. I am indebted to Dr. Shearman for this valuable reference.
70. Mr. Gregory Martin has kindly called my attention to the putto painted out by Rubens in the National Gallery *Judgement of Paris* (Kl.d.K., 344), between Venus and Juno which more or less reverses the putto clinging to Hebe in Raphael's *Council of the Gods*. This pentiment of the 1630s would seem to reinforce, rather than weaken my general contention.

at least up to the time of Raphael's very last style in painting. The skill to produce through the essentially linear schemata of engraving satisfactory equivalents for the painterly style at its full development in Rubens required a graphic artist of exceptional gifts. From Lucas Vorsterman outstandingly, and later from Vorsterman's most gifted pupil Paul du Pont, Rubens demanded and got interpretative skill of an order quite beyond the powers and old-fashioned talents of such a craftsman as Philip Galle, with whose services he had earlier to be content.

The rigour and rate of these demands drove Vorsterman in 1621 to a mental breakdown of an aggressively dangerous sort. Rubens had to drive men harder than had Raphael, whose working life had been considerably shorter and less peripatetic. He got his best service when Van Dyck in the late teens of the century, or he himself in the thirties, was on the spot to provide a *modelletto* which relieved the printmaker of uncertainties in adjustment of scale or in redistribution of lights. No such refinement of working method seems to have been called for in Raphael's organization. However, the good fortune of Rubens in finding a man of Christoffel Jegher's talents in woodcutting, and his exploitation of those talents from 1632 onwards, reflects in a general way the relationship between Raphael and Ugo da Carpi. Significantly it was by a *chiaroscuro* woodcut of 'Giovanni Cornaro'[71] based on a Rubens copy[72] of a Tintoretto portrait, that Jegher recommended himself to Rubens's notice. This was surely an historically self-conscious reattachment of the technique, practised by a specialist, to the service of a major painter. For in the Low Countries during the sixteenth century, the leading practitioners of *chiaroscuro*, Bloemaert, Floris and Golzius, had each of them been creative artists in their own right; and they had used the technique essentially as an independent means of expressing their graphic ideas. Had Rubens lived to employ Jegher longer, it seems probable that the two of them would have combined further to investigate the market amongst connoisseurs for woodcuts. In earnest of this we have, on the reverse of an impression of the *Rest on the Flight*, in black and white, a trial proof in black and orange of the same print, corrected by Rubens in white gouache and oil;[73] and a black and white impression of the *Garden of Love*, washed in a greyish brown and heightened with white by Jegher, in order to try the effect in *chiaroscuro*.[74] Unfortunately we know nothing beyond Vasari's account of the working relations between Raphael and Ugo da Carpi, or between Raphael and his engravers, to

allow us to suggest more precise parallels or contrasts with the Rubens organization in this aspect.

Besides 'Un pourtrait faict après Raphael de *Baltazar de Castillion*', 'Cinq pièces des actes des Apostres faicts après *Raphael d'Urbin*', and 'une pièce des actes des Apostres faicte après *Raphael*', there was in Rubens's house at his death another of his copies painted after Raphael: item 77 'Une teste de S. Jean après *Raphael*'. This has disappeared. However there was also, item 76, 'Un Psyché après *Raphael d'Urbin*'.[75] And on 30th December 1653 in the inventory of Jeremias Wildens, the painter, item 31 was 'Een Epchige geshildert van Rubbens naer Raphael Urbine'.[76] It would be unreasonable not to identify these entries with the picture which Mr. Bryan bought for his client the 3rd and last Duke of Bridgewater at the sale of Jan Gildemeester Jansz. in 1800,[77] and which has descended through the Earls of Ellesmere to the present Duke of Sutherland[78] (Fig. 12). This panel[79] was manifestly painted by Rubens for his own pleasure, both in the groups of figures, which are essentially reassortments of those which

75. Denucé, *op. cit.*, p. 59.
76. *Ibid.*, p. 155.
77. Lugt, *Ventes*, 6102. At the same sale Bryan bought for the Duke of Bridgewater (1736–1803) the so-called *Portrait of a Burgomaster*, the canvas signed by Rembrandt and dated 1637, and Jacob Ruisdael's *View of the Old Gate of Amsterdam*. Both these Dutch paintings are still with the Rubens *Psyche* at Mertoun House [nos. 173 and 197]; and all three pictures are recognizable in the Rijksmuseum painting by A. de Lelie, dated 1794/5 of Gildemeester's gallery at Herengracht 475. See C. J. Bruyn Kops, *Bulletin van het Rijksmuseum*, 1965, no. 3, pp. 79–114.
78. *Catalogue of the Collections of Pictures and Statuary of the Rt. Honble. John Francis Glanville Scrope, Earl of Ellesmere at Bridgewater House*, London, 1926, 174. See also Smith, *op. cit.*, 587 and Supplement, 226; *Stafford Gallery*, III, London (1818), 12; and *Stafford Gallery*, London (1825), 102 (as on canvas!). I am grateful to the Duke of Sutherland for permission to publish his painting.
79. Mertoun House, Berwickshire. Oil on oak panel, planed down fine, and rebacked with three boards, probably in the eighteenth century, 38 × 29 ins. Described in the 1st Earl of Ellesmere's MSS. Note Books etc., I, p. 125: 'This will be recognized by Roman travellers as a Flemish desecration of Raphael's fresco of Psyche in the Farnesina. In one of Hogarth's prints he has placed a flowing wig on the head of Apollo of Belvedere. The profanation of expanding Raphael's classical contours into the tumefaction and flaccidity of Flemish female development is scarce less, but Rubens had thrown some of his finest colours upon the canvas, and the landscape is in his best manner.' Despite the neoclassical prejudices of the 1st Earl, the British Gallery of Pictures, 54 New Bond St., published a *Catalogue of an Exhibition containing an extensive selection of the finest specimens of the Old Masters in the cabinets and galleries of the United Kingdom, Painted in watercolours for a grand national work, now publishing, under the title of the British Gallery of Pictures*, London, 1812, including '205 Rubens – Story of Psyche. Notwithstanding this great artist made the graces of colouring too frequently the first objects of his attention, this little picture, formed of some of the most beautiful groups of the story of Cupid and Psyche, painted by Raffaello, sufficiently shows that he was not blind to the higher excellencies of the Roman school. *Marquis of Stafford's collection*.' This copy

71. C. van Hasselt, '*Gravures sur bois. Clairs-Obscurs de 1500 à 1800*'. *Exposition Paris et Rotterdam 1965–1966*, Paris, 1965, 255.
72. *Bulletin-Rubens*, V, Antwerp (1897–1910), p. 89, M. Rooses signalled the Rubens copy on panel, 59 × 48 cm., in the collection of M. Rousselli in Brussels. This painting was sold by the late F. Matthiesen in London, after the Second World War.
73. Van Hasselt, *loc. cit.*, 251.
74. M. Jaffé, *Burl M*, CVII, 1965, p. 381.

he had seen in the Loggia di Psyche, and in his own beautiful invention of the landscape of Tartarus above which they rise or soar. Before the Gildemeester sale in Amsterdam the picture appeared twice[80] during the eighteenth century at auctions in Brussels: for the first time on 10th July 1738, eighty-five years after it had left the heirs of Wildens, in the collection of the late Comte de Fraula; and, for the second time, on 18th July 1775 in the house Op de Platte-Steen of the Mesdemoiselles Regaus. In that second Brussels sale it was lot 1, described fully and accurately as, 'L'Enlèvement de Psiché par Mercure, derrière qui l'on voit Vénus dans un char, & sur la droite les trois Grâces, plus haut Cupidon semble implorer Jupiter de vouloir, en présence de plusieurs Divinités, rendre Psiché immortelle. Toutes ces figures forment par leur dégagement un coup d'œil admirable, tout à cause des belles carnations, que par rapport à la vérité de leur expression, aussi peut-on se flatter que c'est une des belles pièces de P. P. Rubens. 2 pieds 8 lignes par 3 pieds 1 ligne.' The 'belles carnations', superlatively so on Venus and on the Graces, the broken colours of Psyche's dress – mauve broken with rose and pale gold – and the ease with which the generally more voluminous draperies and bodily forms are given a freedom and flow of movement, all indicate a date not far from the National Gallery *modello* for the *Buckingham* ceiling. And the hardly less Raphaelesque group of the Graces in that, to say nothing of the winged harpy which Rubens introduced in the definitive composition, are distinct echoes of his experience twenty or so years beforehand in the Farnesina. The *Psyche* from Bridgewater House is unlikely to antedate by much the meeting between Rubens and Buckingham in Paris in 1625, out of which grew the commission for the Duke's ceiling; and it must precede, rather than follow, the years of his diplomatic voyages in Spain and England, and the renewal of his passionate interest in Titian. So the most acceptable dating for the *Psyche* is 1625–28; a most remarkable tribute by a painter in his fifties to the decorative and narrative achievement of the master whose work in Rome he had so deeply revered. The baroque movement is achieved, characteristically, not only through contrasts of repose with energetic action, but through a *degradazione* of figure scale enhanced by a lightening of tonality and a heightening of the colour key. A whole series of incidents is unified by a dramatic illumination, rich in *chiaroscuro*. These are the qualities of mastery

in oil painting which Raphael himself anticipated by the final altarpiece of his career. And Rubens did not forget the grand object lesson of the *Transfiguration* any more than the gaiety and luxury of the Loggia di Psiche. His own telling of the Psyche story is rendered with scarcely a hesitation: the left wing of Cupid with the Graces was higher and more extended; above them at first was a winged putto head puffing wind, like the one below them; there are signs of drapery which Rubens painted out below the hands of Cupid in the same scene; and he has had to feel for the silhouette of Mercury's left calf. For the elements of his figure groups Rubens did not have to rely exclusively on his own drawings of twenty years before. He can be assumed to have known two engravings by Jacopo Caraglio: one which reverses the *Mercury conducting Psyche to Olympus*, which he chose for his central incident, the other that which reproduces *the Council of the Gods*. From the latter Rubens has selected almost all the figures which he required for redeployment in the upper zone of his painting – changing Raphael's Juno into a Ceres, who would be less offended by the sight of *Jupiter kissing Cupid*, an incident conflated by him with the remains of Raphael's Council scene; and making considerable modifications to the attitudes or attributes of Pluto and Neptune as well as of Diana and Minerva. For the *Jupiter kissing Cupid* and for the *Cupid with the Three Graces*[81] (Fig. 13), Rubens could have refreshed his memory with engravings by Marcantonio; although in the latter group he felt entirely free to transform the character of Raphael's design, both physiognomically and in the more lavish display of the roundings of the black-haired Grace at the right. An engraving by Cherubino Alberti could have furnished Rubens with a convenient model, although in reverse, for the *Venus ascending to Olympus*;[82] and since this print is dated 1628, we have another pointer to the likely date of his painting. A further indication that Rubens had a fairly comprehensive collection of prints to hand when planning his composition is the way in which his Apollo is seated with the lyre fully displayed. This, unlike the poses of the Hercules and the Bacchus, does not follow the pattern of the fresco, nor that of the Caraglio print: but that of an engraving by the Master of the Die[83] after Coxie's adaptation of the Raphael theme.

was painted by W. M. Craig, Painter in Watercolours to Her Majesty. See Smith, *op. cit.*, 358 and Supplement, 164, for another, presumably late seventeenth-century copy still at Sanssouci, canvas 136×173 cm., with extensive changes in the landscape and in the drapery of Ceres. The winged putto head above the landscape is omitted, as is the goddess next Minerva. Groups [? from yet another, dismembered, copy] are at Burghley House, no. 260, 29½×25 ins., and in the collection of the late Prof. Charles Seltman at Cambridge. The picture was also engraved (1818) by Finden, as *Mercury and Hebe*.
80. Lugt, *Ventes*, 488 and 2438.

81. J. Kusnetsow, *Rubens Drawings in the State Collections of the U.S.S.R.*, Leningrad, 1966, I, claims that the drawing is a free copy by Rubens from the Farnesina fresco, clumsily reworked by another hand. It is in fact a studio copy after the group in the Sutherland picture. That it is not a preparatory drawing by Rubens for this group is evident not only from its quality, but from the prosaic *ricordo* of the position of Cupid's leg below the armpit of the left hand Grace.
82. Bartsch, XVII, 85, 107.
83. Bartsch, XV, 223, 68. The impression of this engraving at Chatsworth bears the collectors' marks of both Lely and Lankrink. It could be the actual one to which Rubens referred. Illustrated by Jaffé, *op. cit.*, fig. CXIV.

Rubens like Raphael collected engravings by Mantegna and by Dürer for their intrinsic beauty and interest, and for the edification of assistants as well as himself. For at least thirty years of his life as a painter he paid close attention to prints after Raphael, most of which he is likely to have come to possess. He made highly idiosyncratic *ricordi*, not only in drawings, but also, at either end of this period, in fully finished works in paintings: the *Fall of Man* of *c.* 1598, and the *Psyche* of *c.* 1628. The extent and importance of print-making in Raphael's organization became the paradigm for his own. He drew after Raphael's preparatory studies as well as after Raphael's definitive works; and he may himself have owned Raphael drawings, besides a painting believed to be autograph. Such unidentifiable items as 'twee teeckeningen van Rubbens naer Raphael', in the inventory of Canon Jan Philip Happart in 1686, are tantalizing.

Rubens was actively sensitive to the nature and scope of Raphael's achievement in both religious and secular art: as a narrator, as a decorator, as a portraitist, and as a designer of a vast range of works, from small devotional paintings to cartoons for tapestry. To match the grandeur of the frescoes in the Vatican, the special glory of High Renaissance painting in Rome, he produced huge triptychs on panel for St. Walpurga's, and for the Cathedral in Antwerp; and he planned a third for St. Bavo's at Ghent. In these ways he placed himself as the heir of Raphael, both as a master of *disegno*, and as a *caposcuola*.[84] In the history of western painting they rank together as the supreme impresarios.

84. It is at least noteworthy that both Raphael and Rubens, when dealing with clients, insisted on the distinction between work of their own hands and that of assistants. See V. Golzio, *Raffaello nei documenti* . . ., Vatican, 1936, p. 76; and R Magurn, *The Letters of Peter Paul Rubens*, Harvard, 1955, pp. 60–61.
As the Duke of Mantua's painter, Rubens was also required, in July 1606, to vet for possible purchase a "quadro di mano di Raffaello da Urbino", offered by Giuliano Deciaiuti's friend in Rome; see *Cod. Dipl. Rubenianus*, I, p. 336. Connoisseurship was one aspect of his study of Raphael's studio organisation.

BENEDICT NICOLSON

Bartolommeo Manfredi

OF all Italian seventeenth-century painters who were famous in their day and are once again receiving reverent attention, the Mantuan Bartolommeo Manfredi (c. 1587–1620/21),[1] the most faithful follower of the Roman Caravaggio, remains the most enigmatic. For him alone it is not permissible to construct even the semblance of a chronology, since there are no fixed points nor any obvious development, and he died young without apparently realizing, as Caravaggio did, that his life was in danger of being cut short, and so without finding any reason for stepping up the pace to compensate for its threatened brevity. We can guess that he was steeped in Giulio Romano as a youth, and on reaching Rome may have passed through an early Roncalli-like phase as Baglione implies, but all we know of his activity is confined to the years c. 1606–10 onwards when Caravaggio had him in thrall. We are unclear about his style despite a handful of semi-documented pictures (now that the Ashmolean and Albertina studies have been struck out, there are no drawings left), and this has had the effect that he has attracted to himself a number of Caravaggesque works of some quality which do not obviously belong anywhere else, but they do not form a coherent group. He is the refuse bin into which scholars chuck what puzzles them. With some temerity I am attempting in this article to clarify the situation by distinguishing between what we know, and what we think we can deduce.

Unlike Caravaggio he had no aptitude or inclination for large-scale religious works suitable for church altarpieces, but liked his religious subjects more or less to masquerade as genre, with the result that there was never anything by him, according to the sources, in public places; but he was well patronized by leading collectors, and it is to the great Roman and Florentine *palazzi* that his pictures found their way late in his life where they were admired and imitated by young artists from all over Europe. Indeed by his down-to-earth style he made the too lofty Caravaggio accessible to these young foreigners. Manfredi may have been unable to respond to the spirituality of his great revolutionary

predecessor. But he must be given the credit for sensing in Caravaggio the possibilities of an art based on ordinary real life, for extracting hints that Caravaggio only incidentally let fall, that art could be fashioned out of the trivial and licentious occupations of men as well as out of their tribulations. It was this idea, new to Rome, that he managed to pass on to his foreign imitators who, because of their local traditions, were ripe for it, but who might never have hit on it if left to themselves. Manfredi was a go-between, the setter of a fashion which, if it did not dominate the Roman scene, remained one of the miracles of those miraculous Roman years from about 1615 to the death of Valentin.

If we are to make any sense out of his style, we must first be clear as to which surviving pictures or derivations from them can be traced back to early collections. Vincenzo Giustianini acquired from him, as we might expect from what we know of this patron who was more interested in the religious work of the *Caravaggisti* than in their genre: '*un quadro di Christo, che apparisce alla Madonna, dopo la Resurrettione*', about which we know precisely nothing.[2] Cardinal Ludovico Ludovisi possessed by the early 1630's a large picture by him showing a gipsy woman telling a young man's fortune with five other half-length figures.[3] The Ludovisi picture is most likely to be the large one which passed to the Mazarin Collection showing soldiers playing draughts and a gipsy woman telling someone's fortune.[4] The Duke of Buckingham also had a picture of this subject in the late 1620's, also with seven figures.[5] Whether the

1. His birth certificate of 25th August 1582 is said by Tullio Bellomi (I, *Cremona*, 1929, pp. 796–798) to be preserved in the parish registers of Ostiano, near Mantua, but no one has ever believed in this 'document', and it is more likely that he was born a few years later, about 1587, largely because Mancini (*Considerazioni sulla pittura* . . ., I, ed. 1956, p. 251) gives his age about 1620 as 33 or 34. That he died in 1620 or early the following year is indicated by the fact that Baglione (ed. 1649, p. 159) gives his biography among those who died under Paul V (see R. Longhi, *Proporzioni*, I, 1943, p. 48 – referred to from now onwards as Longhi, 1943).

2. Recorded in Giustiniani inventory of 1638, I, no. 135 (see L. Salerno, *Burl M.*, CII, 1960, p. 101). A *Christ at Emmaus* reproduced by Landon, *Annales du Musée . . . Galerie Giustiniani*, Paris, 1812, pl. 16, as Manfredi is now in Potsdam, sensibly ascribed to Renieri (see Salerno, *loc. cit.*, no. 3). Mancini numbers Giustiniani among Manfredi's patrons, which means that he was already acquiring the artist's works during his lifetime. This is not necessarily the case with another of Manfredi's patrons, the Chigi of Siena, since Mancini's reference (*loc. cit.*) to '*Cavalier Chigi*' is a *postilla*. We are uncertain of the character of the work that passed to the Chigis.

3. Recorded in Ludovisi inventory of 1633 (see C. Garas, *Burl M.*, CIX, June 1967, no. 2).

4. Recorded in inventory of Mazarin's Collection published (1661) after his death (see Comte de Cosnac, *Les Richesses du Palais Mazarin*, 2nd ed., Paris, 1885, no. 1261, as Manfredi). Cosnac identifies it with a picture in the Louvre, but no such work exists. Could he have been confusing it with Louvre Catalogue, 1926, no. 1368, now given to Rombouts (see A. von Schneider, *Caravaggio und die Niederländer*, Marburg, 1933, pl. 41b)?

5. Recorded at York House in 1635 as 'Manfredi. An Egiptian telling Fortunes' (see R. Davies, *Burl M.*, X, 1907, pp. 376 ff.) and

108

Buckingham picture is the one now in Dresden (No. 412) we cannot be sure. But the Dresden *Fortune Teller* conforms to the descriptions of both Ludovisi and Buckingham pictures, and it sounds as though Manfredi did at least two replicas of the subject.

In the Verospi Collection, Rome, there were two Manfredis in the later seventeenth century. One, a *Christ driving the Money-Changers out of the Temple*, showed one man protecting his money with his hands for fear of losing it in a scuffle. Though Bellori's description of it[6] in 1672 corresponds to a Manfredi of this subject which passed to Mazarin[7] and thence to the French Royal Collection, where a man at a table is engaged in making precisely this unsympathetic gesture, it cannot be the same, since Bellori implies it was still in Rome when he was writing. Nor for obvious reasons can it be the one in the collection of the Duke of Savoy by 1635 (see below). It seems as though the artist, as in the case of the *Fortune Teller*, did more than one version – this time three – and that they were replicas. Two are quite unknown and the third, the one that went to France, was burnt at Strasbourg in 1870[8] and survives only in a sad engraving (Fig. 1).[9] It is hard to say what relationship it bore to the famous Checco del Caravaggio of this subject formerly in Berlin. The composition in both cases is conceived as a frieze in a setting of classical architecture. But we have no idea which came first. The other Verospi picture was a *Denial of St. Peter* showing, according to Bellori, the maid pointing St. Peter out to a dice-player who turns round towards them. The only known Manfredi composition answering to this description is a poor copy of a lost work in a Madrid Collection,[10] the original of which may well have been the picture in question.

Mancini and Bellori tell us he painted for '*L'Altezza di Toscana*', and later Lanzi also speaks of paintings '*per la Casa Medicea*', but there are no documented pictures by him in Florence. Moving northwards, we find two half-length figures of *Drinkers* in the museum at Modena which are cited as Manfredis in an inventory of 1624.[11] One

might have thought it was inconceivable that a distinguished Modenese collector should be mistaken about an attribution to a leading Italian painter who had only been dead three or four years; yet Manfredi's authorship of the two *Drinkers* has with some justification been called in question.[12] Before the mid-1630's, Manfredis were reaching Turin in large quantities. In an inventory of 1635 of the Duke of Savoy[13] which lists a handsome group of semi-Caravaggesque pictures by artists (some of whom had been living in close proximity to Manfredi in the parish of S. Lorenzo in Lucina in the 1610's[14]) such as Vouet, Gentileschi, Saraceni, Grammatica, Baglione, Checco del Caravaggio, no less than six Manfredis appear, none of which has yet been identified: the *Christ driving out the Money Changers* mentioned above, described as having eleven figures, '*e testa d'agnello*', the same number as in the Mazarin version which also includes a lamb; a *Denial of St. Peter* with half-length figures where the maid lays her hand on the shoulder of a soldier, which makes one think it was the same composition as that in Brunswick;[15] an upright *Cimon and Pero* and a *David and Goliath*,[16] two subjects, as we shall see, acquired by Buckingham about the time of Manfredi's death; a *King Midas*; and a picture showing a woman, an old man and three shepherds with pipes (a *Bacchanal*?). It is a depressing occupation, listing pictures which nobody knows, but it has this limited value: the Manfredis in Turin reinforce what we suspected from other indications, that he was in the habit of doing replicas for different patrons.

His works crossed the Alps with astonishing rapidity. Besides the *Fortune Teller* already discussed which could be the picture now in Dresden, there were four by him in Buckingham's collection at York House by the late 1620's: a *Judith and Holofernes* which appears to have passed to the French Royal Collection;[17] a scene of card-playing

---

sold as Manfredi in Antwerp in 1649 as 'A gipsy, with six other figures' (see *A Catalogue of the Curious Collection of George Villiers, Duke of Buckingham . . .*, London, 1758, p. 12).

6. Ed. 1672, p. 215.

7. Cosnac, *op. cit.*, no. 1001, as Manfredi. Later (as so often) it turned into a Valentin.

8. See C. Schneegens, *Revue Alsacienne Illustrée*, XVI, April 1914, pp. 37 ff.

9. By Haussart; see *Recueil d'estampes d'après les beaux tableaux . . . qui sont en France dans le Cabinet du Roy . . .*, II, Paris, 1742, p. 37, under no. 95.

10. As pointed out by J. Ainaud, *Anales y Boletín de los Museos de Barcelona*, V, July–December 1947, p. 399. (Ainaud reproduces the copy of the lost Manfredi between pp. 388 and 389.)

11. Inventory of Cardinal Alessandro d'Este dated 1624, see G. Campori, *Raccolta di cataloghi ed inventarii inediti . . .*, Modena, 1870, p. 67 as '. . . dui Tedeschi un che vuol bere in un fiasco, l'altro tiene un bicchiere di vino in mano, di Bartolomeo Manfredi'.

12. See R. Pallucchini, *I dipinti della Galleria di Modena*, Rome, 1949, p. 17 where Longhi is quoted as ascribing them to Tournier.

13. See A. Vesme, *Le gallerie nazionali italiane*, III, 1897, pp. 35 ff. The six Manfredis (in the order in which they are here mentioned) are nos. 206, 207, 209, 259, 323, 326. There are also tantalizing entries describing pictures by followers of Manfredi about whom we know virtually nothing, called Bartolomeo della Leonessa (nos. 186, 200, 626), 'Maltese' (nos. 212, 257) and 'Balduino il fiamingo' (no. 254). An engraving signed by a Balduino of Nice, close in style to Boetto and Molineri (as Dott.ssa Andreina Griseri kindly points out to me) was shown at the *Mostra del Barocco Piemontese*, Turin, 1963, vol. III, fig. 1, among the section devoted to books and bindings; but could a Niçois be described even in the seventeenth century as a Fleming?

14. See J. Bousquet, *Mélanges d'Archéologie et d'Histoire*, LXIV, 1952, p. 289.

15. Caravaggio Exhibition, Milan, 1951 (134), illus.

16. The inventory claims the head is by another hand.

17. Listed at York House, 1635, as Manfredi, see Davies, *Burl M.*, X, pp. 376 ff., as well as the other three mentioned below. A picture of this subject (which could be another) is in Villot's catalogue

and feasting in which soldiers and women take part;[18] and two pictures which may even have been acquired by Buckingham through Gerbier during the artist's lifetime: a *Cimon and Pero* and a *David and Goliath*.[19] It is tempting to argue that they were duplicates of the uprights acquired by the House of Savoy. None can be positively identified. 'Two fellowes playing with a wench at cards' was in Charles I's Collection as Manfredi, and is described so conscientiously by Van der Doort that it can be confidently linked with a picture in Baron Grundherr's collection in the 1940's,[20] or with a replica. Another Mazarin picture, a *Card Players*, is too vaguely described to be identifiable, though the subject is familiar enough.[21]

We are more fortunate in the case of two Manfredis which entered the collection of Leopold Wilhelm, Archduke of the Netherlands: a *Capture of Christ* and a card-playing scene. Both are lost, but the first survives in an engraving in the *Theatrum Pictorium* (1658) as well as (more conveniently) in a painting by Teniers of the Archducal Gallery[22] where it hangs on the wall (Fig. 2) surrounded by masterpieces. (The Corsini *Bacchus and Drinker* – another Manfredi which, though not documented, could not nowadays conceivably be disputed – similarly hangs in distinguished company on the walls of a picture gallery by Panini.[23]) The

Archduke himself, in Teniers' picture, graces the gallery with his presence. The other, the *Card Players*,[24] survives in various copies in Caen, Aix and elsewhere, sometimes in the company of the Uffizi *Concert Party*, which makes one think that the latter was also known as a Manfredi in the seventeenth century;[25] though we have not treated it as a documented work, like the *Bacchus and Drinker* its attribution to Manfredi is no longer open to question.

The time has now come to draw up a balance sheet. If one did not know what they looked like, one would treat as the only firmly documented pictures the two Modena *Drinkers*, but in fact, though strictly Manfredian, they are a little insipid in style, and it is possible that they are copies of lost Manfredis by an unidentified (?French) follower. Longhi (1943 and elsewhere) has transferred them to Tournier. The Grundherr *Card Players* is certainly an original and may be the one that belonged to Charles I. Several undisputed works survive in the form of copies or engravings, and in the absence of the originals must serve their limited purpose: an outline engraving reflecting the Mazarin *Christ driving out the Money-Changers*; the Archduke's *Capture of Christ* surviving in an engraving and a small Teniers copy; and his *Card Players* surviving in various copies. It is reasonable to accept the picture in Madrid as a copy of the Verospi *Denial of St. Peter*. Though it may seem self-evident that four further pictures are also by Manfredi – the Uffizi *Concert Party*, the Corsini *Bacchus and Drinker*, the Brunswick *Denial of St. Peter*, and the Dresden *Fortune Teller* – they are none of them securely documented. And that is all. No wonder art historians have shied away from this unmanageable subject.

All the same this group does make stylistic sense, and art historians have gone on from there to add others to it. The attribution to Manfredi of a *Soldier with the Head of St. John the Baptist* in the Prado[26] where the dull, prosaic description of the armour is not contradicted by the evidence of the soldiers in the Archduke's lost *Capture of Christ*, is nevertheless a borderline case. The vast *Mars, Venus and Love* in Chicago[27] has entered his œuvre without

as Manfredi under no. 248; sent to Compiègne 1874. No. 278 of Le Brun inventory (1683). I know nothing of its fate.

18. York House list, 1635 as 'A Banquett'. Sold at Antwerp 1649 (*A Catalogue . . .*, for ref. see note 5).

19. The pictures are first mentioned in an account submitted by Gerbier in 1621 of his expenditure in Italy for Buckingham, see I. G. Philip, *Burl M.*, LXXXXIX, May 1957, p. 156. Prompted by Dr. Grossmann I have attempted to establish an early attribution to Manfredi of the Vienna *David*, Exh. Milan, 1951 (38) as Caravaggio, but without success. Whether this picture which could well be by Manfredi is the one that belonged to Buckingham must remain an open question. The *Cimon and Pero* is perhaps the one in the inventory of Abraham Peronneau, Amsterdam, 6th January 1692 (see Bredius: *Künstlerinventare*, III, p. 54) with the entry: '1. Daer de doghter de Vader de borst geeft van Manfredo . . . f. 250'. We know from Sandrart that Koymann of Amsterdam was a keen collector of the artist's work, so perhaps he had a hand in its acquisition.

20. See O. Millar, *Walpole Society*, XXXVII, 1960, p. 37. Millar sensibly thinks it may be the Grundherr picture, which was in the Rutland Sale, Christie's, 16th April 1926 (21), passed to Berlin, and was exhibited in 'Italienische Malerei 17. und 18. Jahrhunderts', Wertheim, Berlin, 1927 (97), illus., as Manfredi, lent by Dr. Rothmann.

21. Mazarin inventory, 1661, no. 1052: '*Plusieurs Figures au naturel qui jouent aux cartes . . .*'

22. *Theatrum Pictorium*, no. 234. Teniers' picture showing the interior of Coudenberg Palace is in Munich. The *Capture of Christ* is listed in the inventory of the Archduke's Collection in 1659 (see A. Berger, Vienna *Jahrbuch*, I, 1883, pp. lxxix ff., under no. 92). The measurements are given with frame, but in Teniers' copy it is shown about the same height as the Giorgione *Philosophers* (121 cm.).

23. Signed and dated 1749; Wadsworth Atheneum (Hartford, Conn.). The gallery, said to be that of Cardinal Valenti Gonzaga

(1690–1756), though containing a number of Corsini pictures, is probably imaginary.

24. Archduke's inventory (see note 22), no. 364. *Theatrum Pictorium*, no. 235. Included among the plates in the *Podromus* of 1735 by F. v. Stampart and A. v. Prenner (see H. Zimerman, Vienna *Jahrbuch*, VII, 1888, where the plates are reproduced).

25. The significance of the copies was first brought out by Longhi, 1943, p. 49. See also his article in *La Revue des Arts*, VIII, 1958, p. 62.

26. Prado no. 247. Accepted by Ainaud, *Anales y Boletín de los Museos de Barcelona*, V, 1947. A reproduction will be found in A. E. Pérez Sánchez, *Pintura italiana del siglo XVII en España*, Madrid, 1965, pl. 81. An 'allegory' in the Museo Cerralbo, Madrid, listed by Pérez Sánchez, p. 291, as a possible Manfredi appears from his reproduction (pl. 80) to be a typical Pietro Paolini.

27. Longhi, 1943, pl. 53 as Manfredi.

protest. One might have expected this imposing picture to have been mentioned in the sources, but a possible explanation of the silence surrounding it is that it is an early work,[28] reminiscent not only and most obviously of Caravaggio but of the early Baglione in Berlin. Nobody is likely to quarrel, either, with the label of Manfredi for an upright fragment of a landscape-shaped composition showing *Musicians* in a London private collection.[29] The points of comparison here are the two pictures of *Card Players* formerly in the Archduke's and in Baron Grundherr's collection where one finds the same rugged types, the delicate gesture of a raised hand, and the tendency to reduce the contours of a face to geometry. Manfredi was one of those artists (Caravaggio was not) who could suffer the indignity of having his pictures truncated, and continue to make sense: for he had a habit of dividing the composition down the middle and building up groups on either side of a gap. One does not need to embark on Morellian comparisons to realize that the *Seasons* formerly in the collection of the singer Chaliapin[30] and a *Tambourine Player* in a Florentine private collection[31] are also his; and as for the Dresden *Denial of St. Peter*, in spite of the inadequacy of the only available photographs, this also introduces nothing that cannot be paralleled in other works. The man on the extreme right of the Uffizi *Tribute Money* (Fig. 6) rests his hand on his sword hilt exactly as the corresponding figure does in the Archduke's *Card Players*. This picture, although bearing a traditional attribution to Caravaggio, praised as such by Cochin,[32] hanging in Cochin's day in the Tribuna, and selected by Zoffany to represent the Caravaggesque school on the walls of his *Tribuna* (early to mid-1770's) half-hidden by the Medici *Venus*, is also an obvious Manfredi, along with its pendant, a *Christ among the Doctors* (Fig. 7).[33] And he has been credited with other works, no doubt in some cases reasonably, but my ignorance of them is such that I would be better advised to keep off them.[34]

To this list I can add some tentative suggestions. Two pictures in my own collection representing *Autumn* and *Winter*[35] (Figs. 3, 4) have stood the test of my long critical appraisal, and indeed have gained in dignity with the years. They fit best in style with the ex-Chaliapin *Seasons* but if it is claimed that this is not a documented work and therefore cannot be taken as an argument in Manfredi's favour, then we must point to the heavily lidded eyes of the card player on the right of the Grundherr picture, and to the fur hat in the ex-Mazarin *Christ driving out the Money Changers*. I used to debate whether they might not be fragments of vast compositions with full-length figures, but though elbows may appear to be 'cut', hands curve back into the lower borders with such logic and persistence that they must always have been this shape, and were once intended, along with the lost *Spring* and *Summer*, as four over-doors in the *Salone* of some Roman *palazzo*. That they have never been cut down is in fact proved by the existence of a picture in a private collection in Rome[36] (Fig. 5) representing *Summer and Autumn* and therefore presumably one of a pair of overdoors, partly based on my own picture of *Autumn*. It is by a close follower of Manfredi who has also looked attentively at Gentileschi, and possibly by a Frenchman – but we only say this because France has a monopoly of Caravaggesque sweetness which it may turn out she does not deserve, when we learn more about the organization of these Roman studios. At present we know precious little. I have come across only one other picture by the same hand as that in the Roman collection: this is a drinking and musical party in the Museum at Le Mans, of which unfortunately no photograph is available.[37] It is thoroughly French in feeling, though the influence of Gentileschi is not so marked. The figure of the boy in the background drinking from a flask – absent from the *Autumn* in my collection – appears in both compositions.

A no less complicated problem is raised by an unknown

28. A. Moir, *Los Angeles County Museum Bulletin*, XIII, 1961, p. 13 is also inclined to regard it as an early work.

29. See M. Waddingham, *Arte antica e moderna*, 1961, pp. 313 ff., as Manfredi.

30. Longhi, 1943, pl. 52 as Manfredi. He cites (p. 25) an autograph replica in a Florentine collection. The picture in Dayton Art Institute is a copy.

31. Longhi, 1943, p. 49 as Manfredi. Exh. 'Tesori segreti . . .', Florence, 1960 (63). An autograph replica is in the Museum at Lovere.

32. *Voyage d'Italie . . .*, II, Paris, ed. 1758, pp. 30–31.

33. They were both engraved as Caravaggio in the eighteenth century by, respectively, Masquelier and Dennel. I am much indebted to John Fleming for taking so much trouble in having these pictures specially photographed for me in the Uffizi storerooms. It involved several months' work.

34. I must, however, mention with approval the fine Brussels *Christ and Adulteress* which could well be by Manfredi, as Voss (*Malerei des Barock in Rom*, Berlin, 1924, p. 453) suggests. I agree with Thuillier (*Saggi e Memorie di Storia dell'Arte*, IV, 1965, p. 51) in

having doubts about the Vouet-like *Fortune Tellers* in the Pitti and the Galleria Nazionale, Rome. The *Joseph and Potiphar's Wife* in a Lempertz sale, Cologne, 14th November 1963 (64) as Manfredi strikes me as belonging to the 'Tournier' group. (I have put the name in inverted commas because it is still by no means certain that he is responsible for the well-known series of Italian-period pictures given to him.)

35. Christie's, 17th February 1956 (both lot 72), as Renieri.

36. Formerly in the Drury-Lowe Collection, see J. P. Richter, *Catalogue of the Pictures at Locko Park*, London, 1901, no. 228, as Italian seventeenth century. It is the same size as my picture (22 by 65 ins.).

37. A version passed through the Hessel Sale, Cercle Royal Artistique, Antwerp, May/June 1933 (81) as Caravaggio, and a cutting from the catalogue is preserved in one of the Caravaggio boxes in the Witt Library. The Le Mans picture is engraved as Manfredi by Haussart, 1742 in the *Recueil d'estampes . . . dans le Cabinet du Roy*; Le Brun Inventory, 1683; at Fontainebleau, 1879. What I take to be a replica is mentioned by Longhi, 1943, note 42 as a Manfredi in the Marchesa Raggi Collection, Rome, but the picture is unknown to me.

Gamblers in a private collection in the Midlands[38] (Fig. 8). It is surely by the author of the Dresden *Card Players* (No. 411) and everything would be plain-sailing, were the latter universally accepted as Manfredi's work. But it has been perceptively coupled by Longhi with the Modena *Drinkers* as a work of the young Tournier, and he no doubt would give the new picture to Tournier also. This group of four (to which others have been added, and with which I would like to associate the Attingham *Dice Players*[39]) is distinct from what we think of as Manfredi's own style, more flaccid, more pedantic, and it is not easy to convince oneself that he was capable of extending himself so far in this direction. Finally, I would like to propose that an unpublished *Crowning with Thorns* in a collection in Belgium[40] (Fig. 9) stands a better chance of being Manfredi's original than the known version in the Le Mans Museum.[41]

It is certainly superior, and until a third version comes to light to knock the other two out, it can stand as a faithful record of one of Manfredi's most impressive compositions, the kind best calculated to set Valentin off on a confident course.

We have been assuming all along that foreigners like Valentin were Manfredi's imitators, not his masters, but we cannot be quite sure. They were in fact all younger than he was, but only by a handful of years, and there is no real reason why Manfredi should not have been a Pissarro among Seurats and Signacs. We are uncertain of their birth dates but it appears that the ones closest to Manfredi – Valentin, Tournier, Seghers, Baburen, and Honthorst – were none of them born before 1590 and – more important – none came to Rome before the second decade;[42] only Terbrugghen whose *Luteplayer* in Bordeaux is a Northern counterpart of Manfredi's *Bacchus and Drinker*, was born, and came to Rome, about the same time as he did. The balance of evidence favours the opinion of Sandrart who believed that the '*methodus*' was '*Manfrediana*' and not somebody else's; and we can take it that he more than anyone was responsible for giving a new lease of life to Caravaggio's realism at the moment when it was in danger of petering out.

38. Recorded by Rev. D. P. Davies: *A new historical and descriptive View of Derbyshire . . .*, Belper, 1811, pp. 277–279, as hanging at Osmaston-by-Derby, as Annibale Carracci. The picture may well have been at Osmaston in the late eighteenth century in the collection of Sir Robert Wilmot.

39. Exh. 'Portrait Groups from National Trust Collections', Arts Council, 1960 (1) illus., as school of Manfredi.

40. Exh. 'Caravaggio en de Nederlanden', Antwerp, 1952, no. 6B of Supplement II, as attributed to Manfredi. The picture was not shown at Utrecht where the exhibition had been earlier. It was lent to Antwerp by Baronesse Rengers-van Pallandt, but is now untraced.

41. M. Hoog, *Revue des Arts*, X, 1960, pp. 272–273 and note 24 thinks it may be a picture recorded in 1769 in the church of Saint-Martin at Tournai, as by Valentin, but the one here published, from a Belgian collection, is more likely to be the

one in question. Longhi, 1943, note 42, regards the Le Mans picture as either an original or an excellent old copy, but it is in fact not a very good copy.

42. The fact that Valentin, Seghers and Tournier are not referred to by Mancini, and that Baburen and Honthorst only squeeze into his pages because they had undertaken public commissions, is also significant.

WALTER VITZTHUM

Inventar eines Sammelbandes des späten Seicento mit Zeichnungen von Pietro da Cortona und Ciro Ferri

Im Besitze Herrn John Hardings in Neu-York befand sich vor kurzem ein Band mit Zeichnungen, dem Interesse sowohl durch seinen Inhalt als durch seine Herkunft zukommt. Über den Inhalt informiert die Aufschrift auf dem Rücken des dem späten siebzehnten Jahrhundert angehörenden Einbandes: "Disegni di Pietro di Cortona e Ciro Ferri". Über die Herkunft kann mit einiger Wahrscheinlichkeit die Vermutung ausgesprochen werden, dass sich der Band zu Anfang des achtzehnten Jahrhunderts in Rom im Besitz Don Livio Odescalchis befand. Im der Tat findet sich, wie mir Herr Per Bjurström freundlich mitteilt, folgender Eintrag im 1713/14 angelegten Inventar Livio Odescalchis: "Libretto legato in quarto, coperto di carta pecora nella piegatura di fuori si legge = Disegni di Pietro da Cortona, e di Ciroferri, e detto Libro è di carte settantasette, sopra quali vi sono disegni numero novanta quattro creduti essere delli sudetti Pietro da Cortona e Ciroferri." Dass es sich um den gleichen Band handelt, geht eindeutig aus der Eintragung "Carte N°. 77 = Disegni 94" auf der ersten Seite des Neu-Yorker Bandes hervor. Es besteht somit die Möglichkeit, dass die Zeichnungen ursprünglich der Sammlung Christinas von Schweden angehörten, da wir wissen, dass Christinas Kunstbesitz nach dem Übergang an die Familie ihres Erben Cardinal Azzolino durch Don Livio erworben wurde.

Der Band enthält eine Reihe bedeutender Blätter Cortonas, dabei vor allem mehrere Studien für die Fresken des Palazzo Pitti. Der weitaus grössere Teil besteht aus flüchtigen Entwürfen Ciro Ferris – meist nicht mehr als Miniskizzen – von unterschiedlicher Qualität und da auch hier Studien für die von Ferri zu Ende geführten Fresken im Palazzo Pitti überwiegen, liegt der Gedanke nahe, dass es sich um eine Sammlung handelt, die direkt auf Ferris Atelier zurückgeht, in dem Cortonas Zeichnungen – und mehr denn je zur Zeit der Vollendung der Pitti-Fresken – eine grosse Rolle spielten.

Da Klebebände dieser Art immer unter dem Schatten der Auflösung und der Zerstreuung ihres Inhaltes stehen, mag denen, die an italienischen Zeichnungen des Barock interessiert sind, ein Dienst erwiesen sein, wenn hier die Zeichnungen in der Reihenfolge der augenblicklichen, das heisst im grossen und ganzen wohl ursprünglichen Anordnung einzeln aufgeführt und – soweit dies nötig und möglich – mit einem knappen Kommentar versehen werden. Ausser der oben zitierten Aufschrift des Einbandes findet sich auf der ersten Seite nur der erwähnte kurze Hinweis auf die ursprüngliche Seitenzahl des Bandes. Zur Zeit zählt der Band 73 Seiten mit 100 Zeichnungen. Die Zeichnungen sind unmittelbar auf die Seiten des Bandes aufgeklebt. An verschiedenen Stellen wurden Zeichnungen später entfernt und in einigen Fällen Seiten des Bandes herausgeschnitten. Mikrofilmaufnahmen der hier aufgeführten Zeichnungen (mit Ausnahme der Nummern 9 und 14 verso) wurden in der Bibliothèque d'Art et d'Archéologie der Universität Paris deponiert.

Der Verfasser ist Frau Helene Munsterberger dankbar verbunden, die das Studium des Bandes in freundlichster Weise ermöglichte.

1. Cortona: *Wahl zwischen Tugend und Müssiggang.* 162 × 235. Feder, Kreidespuren. (Abb.: *Burl M.*, CVII, 1965, p. 524, Abb. 43). Studie für das Deckenfresko der Sala di Venere im Palazzo Pitti. Das Blatt zeigt die Szene des Deckenfeldes in einen sehr frühen Stadium, in dem am linken Rand unten Herkules, die Hydra tötend, der rechts erscheinenden Venus nicht nur ikonographisch sondern auch kompositionell als Antithese gegenübergestellt ist. Die Darstellung des Tugendtempels links oben auf der Zeichnung wird im Fresko durch die ganz auf den jungen Prinzen, das heisst auf den eigentlichen Mittelpunkt des Bildes konzentrierte Figur des Herkules abgelöst. Dafür erfährt das Lager im Venusberg rechts unten auf dem Fresko eine detailliert ausgebreitete Schilderung, die auf der Zeichnung noch nicht angedeutet ist.

2. Cortona: *Wappen Alexanders VII Chigi.* 160 × 200. Feder, Kreidespuren.

3a. Ferri: *Figurenstudien.* 140 × 139. Feder, Kreidespuren. Das Blatt ist, wie oft bei Ferri, eigenhändig beschriftet: *Io Ciro Romano.*

3b. Ferri: *Weibliche Figuren auf Wolken.* 97 × 142. Kreide, Feder. Möglicherweise im Zusammenhang der Arbeit an der Decke der Sala di Apollo im Palazzo Pitti entstanden.

4. Ferri: *Putten* (recto); *Figurenstudie* (verso). 180 × 200. Feder. Auf dem verso die Aufschrift: *Io Ciro Ferri.*

5. Ferri: *Frau mit Kindern.* 161 × 197. Feder, Farbspuren.

6. Ferri: *Antike Szene.* 119 × 191. Kreide, Feder.

7. Ferri: *Pendentif mit Bischof.* 178 × 170. Kreide, Feder.

8a. Ferri: *Madonna in ovalem Rahmen* (recto); *Flussgott* (verso). 150 × 140. Kreide (recto), Feder (verso). Verso Studie für die den Tiber darstellende Rahmenfigur, die seitenverkehrt links unten auf einem unbezeichneten Stich nach Ferris *Augustusopfer* erscheint (Exemplar in der Bibliothèque Nationale). Für die Gegenfigur befindet sich eine Vorstudie im Louvre (14854).

8b. Cortona-Atelier: *Religiöse Szene*. 102×100. Ölkreide.

9. Ferri: *Antike Szene*. 149×190. Feder. Mit der Aufschrift: *Tempio della fortuna s'apre di va*. . . .

10a. Ferri: *Kniender Page*. 79×56. Feder.

10b. Ferri: *Präsentationsszene*. 91×130. Feder, Kreidespuren.

10c. Ferri: *Präsentationsszene*. 130×181. Kreide, Feder. 10a, b und c stellen Studien zur Szene *Justinian als Gesetzgeber* in der Sala di Apollo im Palazzo Pitti dar. Die schrittweise Entwicklung der Komposition, wie sie an diesen drei Zeichnungen und anderen, ebenfalls von Ferris Hand stammenden Zeichnungen des gleichen Bandes (30a und 59) verfolgt werden kann, lässt darauf schliessen, dass dem Maler beim Entwurf der vier Nebenszenen unter der Decke der Sala di Apollo von Pietro da Cortona in weitem Masse freie Hand gelassen wurde. Cortonas eigene Skizzen für diese Szenen aus der Zeit der ursprünglichen Bemalung der Decke, d.h. vor 1647, wie wir sie aus einem Beispiel in der Cooper Union (1938-88-6563) für die Augustusszene und, wenn ich nicht irre, in einer Zeichnung der Uffizien (11730 F; Abb. 5) für die Justiniansszene kennen, haben offensichtlich nur ganz allgemeine Richtlinien für Ferri bedeutet, als dieser 1659 die Dekoration des Raumes zu Ende führt.

11a. Ferri: *Findung Moses*. 140×148. Feder. Bezeichnet: *Io Ciro*. Entwurf zu einer Komposition, die auf einem fälschlich Cortona zugeschriebenem Blatte der Nationalgalerie in Kapstadt (281) weiter ausgeführt wurde. Ferri stellt das gleiche Thema ähnlich auf einem Bild in Privatbesitz in Nizza dar.

11b. Ferri: *Frauenstudie*. 70 × 75. Feder, weiss gehöht.

12. Cortona-Atelier: *Bischof* (recto); *Nischenfigur, Architekturskizze* (verso). 190×120. Feder. Besondere Bedeutung kommt der Architekturskizze der Rückseite zu, da sie offensichtlich im Zusammenhang mit Cortonas Ideen zur Umgestaltung des Boboligartens steht. Der Brunnensockel im Vordergrund (d.h. die Fontana del Carciofo), der sich auf Cortonas Zeichnungen in den Uffizien ebenso findet, beweist dies eindeutig. Die auf dem vorliegenden Blatt angedeutete Konzeption sieht als Abschluss des Hemizyklus des Amphitheaters eine konkave doppelgeschossige Loggia vor.

13. Ferri: *Putten auf Wolken*. 181×131. Rötel, Feder. Auf dem Verso eine schwache Aktstudie.

14. Ferri: *Madonna und kniende Heilige* (recto); *Nero tritt seine schwangere Frau mit dem Fuss* (verso). 180×240. Kreide. Das Verso in Anlehnung an die durch den Stich Angelo Testas bekannte Komposition eines verschollenen Frühwerks Cortonas.

15. Ferri: *Antiochus und Stratonice*. 179×243. Feder. Auf dem Verso Schriftübungen Ciro Ferris. Die Komposition der Antiochusszene von Cortonas Lünette in der Sala di Venere des Palazzo Pitti abgeleitet.

16. Cortona-Atelier: *Danae* (recto und verso). 230×175. Feder.

17a. Cortona: *Danae*. 134×139. Kreide. Stilistisch aus der Zeit um 1640.

17b. Ferri: *Hlg. Philipp Neri auf Wolken kniend*. 102×94. Feder. Adaptation der Figur des Heiligen, wie er im Apsisfresko von S. Maria in Vallicella erscheint. Es ist wahrscheinlich, dass Ferris Zeichnung auf Cortonas Vorstudie zu dieser Figur in Haarlem (648; fälschlich als Lanfranco) fusst. Daneben verrät Ferris Blatt Kenntnis von Cortonas Philipp Neri-Darstellung an der Decke des Zimmers des Heiligen im Oratorianerkloster in Rom (Briganti, Abb. 275).

18a. Cortona: *Figurenskizze*. 132×133. Feder. Rechts unten alte Bezeichnung *No. 81* in derselben Hand, die sich auf einer Studie zur Barbarinidecke in Ottawa findet (A. E. Popham und K. M. Fenwick, *National Gallery of Canada Catalogue*, IV, Toronto, 1965, Abb. 80). Die vorliegende, sehr flüchtige Studie in Untersicht gehört ungefähr der selben Zeit, vor oder kurz nach 1640, an.

18b. Cortona: *Kopfstudien antiker Krieger* (recto und verso). 78×270. Rötel, Feder.

19. Ferri: *Karossenstudie*. 176×164. Feder. In der Art der durch den Stich bekannten Entwürfe Ferris für die Karossen Castlemaines.

20a. Ferri: *Sitzender Herrscher*. 132×145. Feder, weiss gehöht.

20b. Ferri: *Madonna, die Hlg. Elisabeth und ihre Kinder*. 115×125. Feder.

21a. Ferri: *Figurenstudie*. 144×183. Feder. Mit Anklängen an Figuren der Sala di Apollo im Palazzo Pitti.

21b. Cortona: *Minerva*. 93×116. Kreide. Flüchtige Skizze für die im Gigantenkampf auf der Barberinidecke erscheinende Minerva.

22a. Ferri: *Krieger auf Wolken*. 140×120. Feder.

22b. Cortona: *Antike Gefangene*. 78 × 68. Feder.

23a. Cortona: *Diana*. 122×112. Kreide, Feder. (Abb. 4). Studie zu einer Lünette der Sala di Giove im Palazzo Pitti (Briganti, Abb. 226). Ein stilistisch ähnliches Blatt, zur Dioskurenlünette des gleichen Raumes, befindet sich in Düsseldorf (387).

23b. Ferri: *Auf Wolken gelagerte Figuren*. 111 × 190. Kreide, Feder.

24. Ferri: *Thronender Herrscher*. 174×158. Feder.

25a. Ferri: *Zwei Figuren und Karikatur*. 126×130. Feder. Bezeichnet: *Io Ciro*. Weitere Karikaturen Ferris, davon eine 1684 datiert, liegen in der Farnesina vor.

25b. Ferri: *Figurenstudien*. 125×122. Feder. Bezeichnet: *Ferri*.

26a. Cortona: *Auf Wolken lagernde Figuren*. 124 × 133. Kreide. (Abb. 3). Aus der Zeit um 1640.

26b. Cortona: *Windgötter*. 130×93. Feder.

27. Ferri: *Triumph des Bacchus* (recto); *Figuren- und Architekturstudien* (verso). 160×200. Feder. Recto Studie für das aus Lorenzis Stich bekannte Bild, das kürzlich im Pariser Kunsthandel auftauchte.

28. Ferri: *Putten und Ignudi*. 230×172. Feder.

29. Ferri: *Der Hlg. Franz hält das Christuskind*. 225 × 170. Kreide. Die aus Cortonas Bild in der Annunziata in Arezzo bekannte Komposition, wie sie mit Variationen in einer Reihe von Stichen nach Ferri vorliegt.

30a. Ferri: *Kompositionsskizze*. 98×156. Feder. Studie für die Justiniansszene in der Sala di Apollo des Palazzo Pitti.

30b. Ferri: *Kniende Heilige*. 115×138. Rötel.

31. Cortona-Atelier: *Kniender* (recto); *Figuren- und Kopfstudien* (verso). 165×145. Kreide.

32: Ferri: *David und Abigail*. 129×259. Kreide, Feder. (Abb. 7). Studie für ein Kompartiment der Querschifffresken Ferris in S. Maria Maggiore in Bergamo (Abb. 8). Ferri schreibt im Dezember 1665 an Lorenzo Magalotti zu diesem Auftrag: 'Li siti mi sono riesciti più piccoli di quello che mi credevo . . . e di già ho fatto li disegni delle storie." Im Mai des folgenden Jahres berichtet Ferri über die Vollendung der Abigailszene (Bottari, iii, pp. 53 und 55).

33: Ferri: *Kniende Figuren*. 250×145. Kreide.

34a. Cortona: *Kartusche*. 94×160. Kreide, Feder. Durch die Medici-Imprese des Diamantringes wie sie sich auch auf einer Studie Cortonas für den Stuck der Sala di Saturno in Berlin findet (*Burl M.*, cvii, 1965, p. 254, Abb. 45), als Idee zur Dekoration der Säle des Palazzo Pitti bestimmbar.

34b. Ferri: *Mosesstudien*. 97×156. Kreide.

35a. Ferri: *Konstantin erblickt das Kreuz*. 110×160. Feder.

35b. Ferri: *Heiliger im Gebet*. 92×65. Feder.

35c. Ferri: *Heiliger im Gebet*. 92×69. Feder.

36. Ferri: *Reiterschlacht* (recto); *Putten* (verso). 179×217. Feder, Rötelspuren (recto), Kreide, Rötel (verso). Die Reiterschlacht in Anlehnung an Cortonas Sacchetti-Bild entstanden und möglicherweise eine frühe Studie zum Bild in Versailles (Briganti, Abb. 152 und 154).

37. Ferri: *Engel auf Podest*. 228×170. Feder.

38a. Ferri: *Kniender*. 170×95. Feder.

38b. Cortona: *Engel*. 58×87. Feder.

39a. Cortona: *Zwei weibliche Figuren auf Wolken*. 84×174. Kreide, Rötel. Studie für die Gruppe der eine Muschel und Korallen haltenden Personifikationen des Wassers auf der Decke der Sala di Apollo. Das Blatt geht der in der Farnesina (124347) befindlichen Studie für dieselbe Gruppe zeitlich voraus.

39b. Ferri: *Tote Krieger*. 78×151. Feder.

40a. Ferri: *Putten*. 150×80. Feder.

40b. Ferri: *Heilige Familie*. 75 × 80. Feder.

41. Ferri: *Kniende Heilige und Engel* (recto); *Antikenkopie* (verso). 182×229. Kreide.

42. Ferri: *Kyros bewässert einen Orangenbaum*. 145×143.

Kreide. Studie für die in die Lünette der Fensterseite der Sala di Saturno eingeschriebene Tondokomposition. Eine frühere Studie zur selben Szene, ebenfalls von Ferris Hand, liegt im Blatt 9604 S der Uffizien vor.

43. Ferri: Kompositionsskizzen zu Darstellungen des *Tempelgangs Mariae* und der *Wiederauferstehung*. 240×170. Kreide, Feder; Klebekorrekturen. Die Wiederauferstehungsskizze Studie zu Ferris von Bloemaert gestochener Illustration im *Missale Romanum* Alexanders VII von 1662.

44. Ferri: *Frauengruppe mit Kindern*. 212×148. Kreide. Studie zum *Moseswunder* Ferris, das uns in einer Zeichnung in Windsor (A. F. Blunt and H. L. Cooke, *The Roman Drawings of the XVII and XVIII Centuries . . . at Windsor Castle*, 1960, Abb. 43) und dem Stich Pietro Aquilas bekannt ist. Das liegende Kind rechts unten auf der Zeichnung wurde von Ferri direkt aus Cortonas *Goldenem Zeitalter* im Palazzo Pitti übernommen. In der ausgeführten Komposition wurde es durch einen Esel ersetzt.

45. Ferri: *Studien zur Figur eines knienden Heiligen*. 170 ×200. Feder. Studie zum Bild der *Vision der Hlg. Maria Maddalena de' Pazzi* in der Akademie von San Fernando (Voss, p. 556). Das Bild, von Briganti zu Unrecht Cortona zugeschrieben (p. 246), wurde inzwischen von Pérez Sánchez (p. 277) an Ferri zurückgegeben. Die vorliegende Zeichnung und eine weitere des gleichen Bandes (56) stellen die Richtigkeit von Voss ursprünglicher Zuschreibung des Bildes an Ferri ausser Frage.

46. Cortona: *Liegende Venus* (recto); *Loggia* (verso). 188 ×215. Kreide (recto), Feder (verso). Idee zur Venusdarstellung auf einer der Langseiten der Barberinidecke (Briganti, Abb. 126). Stilistisch stimmt dieses Blatt genau mit der frühen Gesamtskizze in Ottawa (Popham-Fenwick, *op. cit.*, 80) überein, auf der Venus selbst noch nicht auftritt.

47a. Ferri: *Putten mit Papstwappen*. 148×150. Kreide.

47b. Cortona: *Putten*. 110×100. Kreide.

48. Cortona-Atelier: *Europa auf dem Stier* und *Kopfstudie*. 200×224. Kreide, Feder.

49a. Ferri: *Kompositionstudie mit kniender Frau und totem Kind*. 110×145. Kreide, Feder. Bezeichnet: *Io Ciro Ferri*. Teilstudie für das *Zenobiuswunderbild* in Wien (Voss, Abb. 276), für das die Gesamtstudie in der Sammlung Blunt vorliegt (Ausstellung Courtauld Institut, 1964, 26). Das von Ferri signierte Blatt bestätigt die Richtigkeit der Voss'schen Zuschreibung des Wiener Bildes, das vorher als Werk Lazzaro Baldis galt.

49b. Cortona: *Grottenarchitektur*. 100×115. Kreide, Feder.

50. Ferri: *Landschaft und Figurenskizze*. 120×100. Feder.

51. Ferri: *Scipio begutachtet Baupläne*. 140×140 (Tondo). Kreide. Studie für ein Fresko der Sala di Apollo. Die Komposition steht der ausgeführten Fassung sehr nahe.

52. Cortona: *Bekehrung Pauli*. 225 × 145. Kreide. Vorstudie zu einer Komposition, die in einem 1954 bei Col-

naghi befindlichen Blatt weiter ausgeführt wurde (Briganti, Abb. 288, 64).

53. Ferri: *Pendentif mit Prophet und Putten* (recto); *Figurenstudie* (verso). 140×135. Kreide, Feder.

54. Bernini-Kreis: *Der Tod als geflügelter Knochenmann.* 190×130. Feder, laviert. Mit der Aufschrift: "Crederei che seanche facesse una con l'ale in questo mode non facesse male. Pero la mando a lei che ancora non la fatto accio se li parrà la facci e se li par meglio far la come prima facci quello che a più gusto" und auf einem gesonderten Papier "Al Sig.re Ercole Ferrata". Es handelt sich offenbar um einen Exequiendetailentwurf, der Ferrata unterbreitet wurde.

55a. Ferri: *Jakob ringt mit dem Engel.* 200×126. Kreide, Feder. Studie für S. Maria Maggiore in Bergamo.

55b. Ferri: *Baum- und Figurenstudie.* 125×135. Feder.

56. Ferri: *Vision der Hlg. Maria Maddalena de' Pazzi.* Gesamtskizze für das Madrider Bild (v. oben 45).

57. Ferri: *Kinder mit Windhund und Papagei* (recto); *Dekorationsstudie* (verso). 150×200. Kreide.

58. Ferri: *Sitzportrait Ferdinands II von Toskana.* 147×193. Feder.

59. Ferri: *Justinian als Gesetzgeber.* 200×183. Feder. (Abb. 6). Studie für das Fresko in der Sala di Apollo des Palazzo Pitti.

60. Ferri: *Anbetung der Hirten* (recto); *Gewandstudie* (verso). 301×245. Kreide, auf dem Verso weiss gehöht. Die Komposition der Anbetungsszene ist von Cortonas Altarbild in S. Francesco in Aversa abgeleitet.

61. Cortona: *Weibliche Rückenfigur.* 266×240. Kreide, weiss gehöht. Farbspuren. (Abb.: *Burl M.*, CVII, 1965, p. 522, Abb. 41). Studie für die Figur der Kalliope in einem der Zwickel der Sala di Apollo. Die Zeichnung schliesst sich stilistisch eng an Cortonas Figurenstudien aus seiner florentiner Zeit an. Dies bedeutet, dass die Zwickel in ihrer definitiven Form schon vor Cortonas Unterbrechung der

Ausmalung der Sala di Apollo 1647 und nicht erst bei Wiederaufnahme der Arbeit durch Ciro Ferri 1659 geplant wurden.

62. Cortona: *Kopfstudie.* 142×188. Kreide. (Abb. 1). Aus der Zeit um 1630.

63a. Ferri: *Apotheose.* 130×100. Feder. Bezeichnet: *Ciro Ferri.*

63b. Ferri: *Figurenskizze.* 85×75. Feder.

63c. Ferri: *Figuren auf Wolken.* 80×80. Feder.

64a. Ferri: *Wappen Alexanders VII Chigi.* 147×118. Kreide, Rötel.

64b. Ferri: *Figuren auf Wolken.* 120×115. Feder.

65. Ferri: *Heiliger eine Kranke heilend* (recto); *Verkündigungsmadonna* (verso). 200×189. Kreide.

66: Cortona: *Krieger und Gefangene.* 200×190. Feder. Farbspuren. (Abb. 2). Stilistisch aus der Zeit um 1640 und vermutlich eine verworfene Idee zum *Eheren Zeitaltar* in der Sala della Stufa des Palazzo Pitti.

67. Cortona: *Jacobs Segen* (recto); *Antikenkopien* (verso). 206×160: Rötel (recto), Feder, Kreide (verso).

68. Ferri: *Entwurf zur Architektur einer Altarwand.* 147×258. Feder.

69. Ferri: *Prophet.* Im Zusammenhang mit der Mosaikdekoration von St. Peter entstanden. Ähnliche Entwürfe befinden sich in der Farnesina, z.B. 124407.

70. Anonyme Hand: *Madonna und zwei Heilige.* 120×160. Kreide. Beschriftet: *P. di Cort. . . .*

71. Cortona-Atelier: *Stuckstudie.* 125×80. Feder.

72a. Anonyme Hand: *Sitzende weibliche Figur.* 100×125. Kreide, Feder.

72b. Cortona-Atelier: *Stuckstudie.* 125×80. Feder.

73. Ferri: *Apotheose.* 222×167. Kreide. Studie zum Deckenfresko der Sala di Saturno. Der Entwicklungsgang der Komposition, den wir aus den Zeichnungen Ferris in der Farnesina (124348 und 125711) kennen, wird mit dem vorliegenden Blatt zum Abschluss gebracht.

A Note on Giovanni Maria Morandi

IN that part of the Galleria Nazionale of Rome which is still exhibited in the Palazzo Corsini, the full-length portrait of *Cardinal Giulio Rospigliosi*[1] (who was to be Clement IX from 1667 to 1669) is still labelled as 'attributed to Nicolas Poussin', in spite of the fact that Henri Zerner, some five years ago, showed convincingly that it must be by Morandi[2]. That is my excuse for writing about Morandi on the present occasion. The motive – which is not quite the same thing as the 'excuse' – is that, thirty years ago, when I was exploring the region around Rome, often in Anthony Blunt's company, for the preparation of the lists in my *Baroque Painting in Rome*,[3] Morandi, and especially Morandi the portraitist, proved one of the most elusive of the artists in my lists. The reason for this was largely due to the fact that Morandi's one certainly documented early portrait, the portrait of *Mario de' Fiori* of 1659 (detail Fig. 1),[4] was missing from the room in which its companions hung in the Palazzo Chigi at Ariccia on the two occasions that I went there – although a copy of the document which recorded its existence then hung in the room. It was not until I saw this picture on a later visit in 1965 that the scales fell from my eyes. The next day I looked again at the Rospigliosi portrait in the Palazzo Corsini, and the identity of hand seemed to me obvious.

Morandi's religious pictures are hardly easier to study. Until two or three years ago the only one of them in Rome in more or less visible condition was the altarpiece painted in 1686 for the D'Elce Chapel in S. Sabina,[5] which it used to be possible to see, without much trouble, in a little chapel on the Convent stairs – but this has now been transferred to a 'Museum' in the Clausura of the Convent. Fortunately, however, the *Visitation* on the altar in the south transept in S. Maria del Popolo was cleaned about two years ago and gives a good idea of his earlier style. His other religious paintings, in S. Maria in Vallicella, in S. Maria della Pace, and in the Sacristy of S. Maria dell'Anima, still count among the blackest and most invisible pictures in Rome! So little has been written about him that a summary of the present state of our knowledge may be acceptable.

The main source of information is Pascoli,[6] who may have known him, and certainly knew his pupil Odoardo Vicinelli. Pascoli gives his date of birth at Florence as 30th April 1622,[7] and he certainly died in Rome 18th February 1717. There is no trace in any work of his that we now know that Morandi studied under Biliverti before he went to Rome in the service of the Duca Salviati, who set about training him to become a sort of artistic factotum to his household. Morandi was handsome, a good dancer and a good swordsman and rider, and he clearly always fancied himself as a gentleman. The Duke sent him on an extensive training course, which cannot have lasted less than two years, which embraced all the artistic centres of North and Central Italy. In the course of this he acquired some skill in connoisseurship (which the Duke found useful) and a deviously eclectic style, which led Goethe, in an observant but uncharitable moment, to call him 'a plagiarist of plagiarists'.[8] On his return to Rome he does not at first seem to have been encouraged to accept outside commissions for some time, and (with the exception of a pair of pictures,[9] which have disappeared) we have no information about him until his election in 1657 to the Academy of St. Luke in Rome. In 1657 also he first appears in the published documents from the Chigi archives.[10] He seems to have

1. It belongs, in theory, to the collection of the Palazzo Venezia, and its number is P.V. 6965. Canvas: 2·42 × 1·75. On the back is an 'old' inscription: *N. Poussin pinxit a. 1657*: it was acquired for the State after the Principe D. Gerolamo Rospigliosi sale, Rome, 12–24 Dec. 1932 (247). Although earlier authorities accepted the attribution, Jacques Thuillier, in the proceedings of the *Colloque Poussin*, II, Paris, 1960, p. 267, made it clear that the attribution is impossible.

2. *Burl M.*, CIII, 1961, p. 66, where the Testana engraving (which gives Morandi's authorship) of the head and the bust copy at Montpellier are also reproduced. The date 1658 is perhaps not as demonstrative as Zerner suggests, since the 1658 frontispiece for the volume of Cardinals' portraits seems to have been used for later editions until at least the death of Alexander VII in 1667. The portrait was included in the exhibition, *Christina, Queen of Sweden*, Stockholm, 1966, no. 705, as by Morandi.

3. The British School at Rome (Macmillan & Co.), 1937.

4. The document is reproduced in facsimile by Vincenzo Golzio in *L'Urbe*, XXVIII, N.S. no. 1, Jan./Feb. 1965: but was first published by Golzio in *Documenti artistici sul seicento nell'Archivio Chigi*, Rome, 1939, p. 280.

5. Photo Anderson 3632: reproduced in Hermann Voss, *Die Malerei des Barock in Rom*, Berlin, 1924, p. 334.

6. Lione Pascoli, *Vite de' pittori, scultori ed architetti moderni*, II, Rome, 1736, pp. 126–137.

7. A. M. Clark informs me that the Necrologio Romano confirms the date of death, but gives Morandi's age as 97 – which would put his birth in 1620.

8. I found this quotation many years ago, but failed to note the reference, and have been unable to find it again.

9. In the Rospigliosi sale quoted under note 1, lots 292/3 were a pair of female saints, each 0·90 × 0·70, on the back of one of which was Morandi's name and the date 1645. But inscriptions on the backs of Rospigliosi pictures are not always reliable – and the statement in the catalogue that they already show a Marattesque style gives one pause.

10. Golzio, *op. cit.*, pp. 278 ff.

concerned himself a good deal with the business of the Academy, and was elected its President in 1671 and again in 1680. He was responsible for choosing Pietro Bellori to be the Academy's Secretary,[11] and was still active in judging the Academy's competitions in the last year of his life. He seems to have been on good terms with his colleagues, and his reputation can be judged from the fact that the Director of the French Academy refers to Maratta and Morandi as 'les deux plus habiles peintres de Rome' (Letter of 13th April 1694) and couples his name later in a friendly context with Baciccia (Letter of 21st November 1696). The accounts of the Duca Salviati's estate[12] confirm, what Pascoli records, that Morandi received a pension of 15 scudi a month under the Duke's will in 1707. In addition to the three pupils listed by Pascoli, he was, at the very end of his life, the teacher also of the young Francesco Zuccarelli.[13]

Morandi's pictorial output (probably never very extensive) can be conveniently considered under four headings: frescoes, altarpieces, devotional paintings on copper and portraits.

Frescoes. The only frescoes of which we have any record are three mythological ceilings, painted fairly early in his career, for the Duca Salviati. Although it is still constantly repeated[14] that these are still visible in the Palazzo Salviati alla Lungara (now the Collegio Militare), they were in fact whitewashed over soon after 1883,[15] when the rooms were converted into dormitories, and only the stucco frames remain: one of these is square, and the other two are rectangles with semi-circular projections on both the short sides.

'Altarpieces.' Pascoli gives a list of the pictures which can, with a little latitude, be described as altarpieces, and it is a remarkable fact that – except for those painted for Florence – most of these survive today and that they can be placed in a fairly satisfactory chronological order.

> *Rome. S. Maria della Pace. Death of the Virgin.* One of the series of large paintings commissioned, about 1657, under Alexander VII, for the upper wall of the octagon; above the first altar to L,. Pascoli makes it clear this was Morandi's first public commission and that he asked everybody's advice and constantly changed the composition. It was not completed when he went to Vienna (see p. 119), but he finished it after his return.

The last payment for it (the only one from the Chigi archives which has been published) was not until 23rd July 1671,[16] but it was probably finished well before then. The design follows reasonably closely the *modello* (Fig. 3; 1·12 × 1·46) in the Borghese Gallery (1959 Catalogue, vol. II, no. 156) which is presumably that recorded in Salviati possession[17] already in 1673. The picture is today so black that it is almost the only one not photographed in the recent GFN photographic campaign in S. Maria della Pace. It is best studied in the engraving by Pietro Aquila, the plate of which still belongs to the Calcografia Nazionale.

> *Rome. S. Maria del Popolo. Visitation.* Altar in south transept. The two transept altars, of exceptional magnificence, with a frame in purple breccia, supported by two Berninesque angels, set on a large base of Sicilian jasper, have the arms of Alexander VII on the base of the frames. The date of this is 1659 (G. Cugnoni, *Archivio della R. Società di Storia patria*, VI, 1883, p. 539). A *Visitation* in the Deposito of the Uffizi, which may be related to it, is not known to me.

> *Rome. S. Maria dell'Anima. Sacristy. Annunciation: Sposalizio.* Two pictures of small altarpiece size over the two doors on the 'north' side. Dated 1682 (J. Schmidlin, *Geschichte der deutsch. Nationalkirchen in Rom . . .*, 1906, p. 513.)

> *Naples. Gerolomini.* 5 to L: side walls of the Chapel. *St. Anthony of Padua: St. Peter of Alcantara.* According to Pascoli he went to Naples immediately after finishing the Anima pictures. They survive, but are the blackest pictures in the Church.

> *Rome. Convento di S. Sabina. Museo. Madonna del Rosario.* 1686. The 1686 Titi says Morandi was then painting it for the D'Elce Chapel, where it has been replaced by a Sassoferrato.

> *Siena. Cathedral.* Altar in south transept. *S. Filippo Neri.* 1687. The *Nuova guida della città di Siena*, 1822, pp. 14-15, says this was painted in 1687 and engraved by Benedetto Farjat.

> *Siena. S. Maria della Scala.* 1 to L. *Annunciation.* Date not known: different in design from the Anima picture.

> *Belvedere Ostrense (prov. Ancona). Parrocchia di S. Pietro. St. Peter.* 3·34 × 2·22. Signed and dated 1688 (*Inventario*

11. Melchior Missirini, *Memorie per servire alla storia della Romana Accademia di S. Luca*, Rome, 1823, p. 130.
12. Paola della Pergola, *Galleria Borghese: i dipinti*, II, Rome, 1959, p. 223, doc. 89.
13. Information derived from Zuccarelli himself quoted in a note in *Serie degli uomini i più illustri in pittura, scultura*, etc., XI, Florence, 1775, p. 148.
14. E.g. by *Thieme-Becker*, and last in Giorgio Torselli, *Palazzi di Roma*, Milan, 1965, p. 248.
15. Remigio Strinati, *Palazzo Salviati alla Lungara*, 1933, p. 5 (*estratto* from the commemorative volume *Collegio Militare di Roma 1883–1933*).

16. Golzio, p. 291 (*op. cit.* in note 10).
17. G. M. Silos, *Pinacotheca . . .*, Rome, 1673, Epigramma CCXXXIX. The 1745 edition of *Roma antica e moderna*, I, 114/15, also lists in the Palazzo Salviati in Rome 'un' Istoria' and pictures of S. John Baptist and S. François de Sales. A. M. Clark tells me that a signed *modello* of *S. François de Sales preaching* (fig. 2; (1·00 × 0·75) was in that part of the Chigi collection which was at Castelfusano unil 1959. S. François de Sales was beatified in 1661 and canonized in 1665 by Alexander VII (Chigi). Chigi commissions for altarpieces of this subject, painted in the 1660's, are at Ariccia (Taruffi), and the Madonna di Galloro (Guglielmo Cortese).

degli oggetti d'arte d'Italie: VIII. *Provincie di Ancona e Ascoli Piceno*, 1936, p. 56). (It is just possible, though Fermo is not in the right province, that this is the altarpiece listed by Pascoli as painted for the Cathedral of Fermo, which is not there today.)

Viterbo. Cathedral. Altar of large chapel to R. *SS. Valentine and Hilary adoring the Sacrament* (Fig. 5). Commissioned in 1696 for 300 scudi: finished 1698. (Mario Signorelli, *Il palazzo papale di Viterbo*, Viterbo, 1962, p. 139; A. Scriattoli, *Viterbo*, 1915–20 (large edition), p. 135.)

Rome. S. Maria in Vallicella. 4 to R. *Pentecost.* An inscription on the floor of the Chapel (Forcella, IV, no. 419) gives 1728 as the date when the redecoration of the Chapel by the Giraud family was completed. It is likely that the Morandi was part of this scheme, so that it is probably very late. A. M. Clark reports a bozzetto in the Deposito of the Corsini Gallery, Rome, as O. Marinari.

Florence. S. Firenze. Sacristy (formerly). *Flagellation.* Pascoli, II, p. 34 indicates that this was one of his latest works (as were two pictures for S. Pietro in Montorio in Rome, which have disappeared). It measured 7 braccia high by 4½ braccia, and is now known only from the engraving by Gaetano Vascellini in *Etruria pittrice*, II, 1795, pl. 87. I do not know what has happened to the *S. Raniero* painted for the Grand Duke.

Devotional pictures on copper. It is clear from Pascoli that Morandi made something of a speciality of devotional pictures on copper, a fashion which had been more or less restricted to Northern painters in Rome until about the middle of the seventeenth century. A liking for the high finish of Dutch *Feinmalerei* may have infected Italian connoisseurs, and the first Italian painter in Rome to exploit this taste was Alessandro Turchi, who was settled in Rome from 1619 to his death in 1649, and used both marble and copper for fairly small pictures with a high finish. Later even the most fashionable painters occasionally used this style (there are examples by both Maratta and Trevisani in the Corsini part of the Galleria Nazionale in Rome), but one gets the impression from Pascoli that Morandi, from the beginning, made something of a feature of his *rami*. The first pictures Pascoli mentions, after the full-length portrait of Monsignor Rospigliosi, are 'due gran rami' which Rospigliosi commissioned as a present for the King of Spain, who was so pleased that he ordered two more.[18] An example of Morandi's devotional paintings on copper has lately re-emerged from obscurity and been presented by

Dr. Carlo Sestieri to the Galleria Nazionale of Rome[19] (Fig. 6). Although broader in handling, it has something of the high finish of a painter such as Van der Werff, and an attribution, unassisted by the inscription on the back, would have been very difficult. I would suppose it was perhaps later than 1700 as, in style, it seems already to anticipate to some extent the neo-classic tendencies of such a painter as Benefial. It is likely that more pictures of this type will reappear.

Portraits. Morandi's chief reputation seems, however, to have been as a portrait painter, and, above all, as a portraitist of the Papal Court. Secular portraits at present known are few, although our one certain document for his early years (Fig. 1) is the *Mario de' Fiori* of 1659. This carries with it another picture also in the Palazzo Chigi at Ariccia, the portrait of Niccolò Simonelli,[20] the Keeper of Cardinal Chigi's collections. This must be of nearly the same date. Golzio's extracts from the Chigi Archives show a good many commissions for portraits up to 1662, and, for the first half of the 1660's, there was little competition from other Italian portrait painters in Rome. This was perhaps the reason why Morandi was summoned to Vienna, probably about 1666, to paint the Emperor Leopold I and other members of the Imperial family. His visit there was certainly not of long duration,[21] but it may have been fatal to his reputation at home. In 1667[22] appear the first payments to Baciccia from the Chigi, who had hitherto been Morandi's best patrons, and they soon seem to have found that Baciccia suited them better. He was in fact a better draughtsman and a master of considerably greater elegance, as a writer in 1666 already recognised.[23] Of later secular portraits I can only point with any certainty to the *Self-portrait*[24] in the collection of *Autoritratti* in the Uffizi, of which there is a variant example in the Academy of St. Luke in Rome.

When we come to portraits of senior members of the Church, we can rely for help on a very substantial body of

18. One may be the *Three Maries at the Tomb*, 0·72 × 0·54, lent to the Museo de Castrelos at Vigo and published by Alfonso E. Pérez Sánchez in *ArchEsp*, XXXV, 1962, p. 58 (pl. IIC). Dr. Erich Schleier has reported a larger version (1·77 × 1·24) on the Roman market (Gaspanini) as Placido Costanzi.

19. I am indebted for the photograph to Professor Italo Faldi. Copper: 0·815 × 0·65. An old inscription on the back gives Morandi's name and an indication that it was once in the Casa Doria. It is perhaps worth noting that, in the 1783 catalogue of the pictures in Casa Colonna, no. 549 is *Cristo in Croce spirante*, copper, 2½ palms high.

20. Reproduced in *Catalogo della mostra di Roma secentesca*, Rome, April/May 1930, fig. XII.

21. He was summoned back to Rome by Clement IX, who was elected 20th June 1667, and he had left Vienna by 21st August 1667 (letter from Count Harrach to Conte Alfonso Gonzaga di Novellara in G. Campori, *Gli artisti italiani e stranieri negli Stati Estensi*, 1855, p. 325), from which it appears that Morandi had probably painted full-lengths of the Emperor and Empress and half-length replicas for at least Count Harrach, who presented them to Conte Alfonso Gonzaga. I have found no trace of such portraits.

22. Golzio, p. 265 (*op. cit.* in note 10).

23. R. Engass, *Baciccio*, 1964, p. 182, *Doc.* 53.

24. Engraved by both Niccolò Billi and G. B. Cecchi.

engravings. The practice of publishing engraved portraits of a uniform style of all living Cardinals began in 1658 and was the enterprise of the publishing firm of Giovanni Jacopo de Rossi (de Rubeis), who was established near the Church of S. Maria della Pace. The stock was taken over in the eighteenth century by the Calcografia 'della Rev. Cam. Apost. a Pie' di Marmo', and, in the nineteenth, by the Calcografia Nazionale. As Cardinals died the date of their death was added to the plate, and cumulative sets, which were kept up to date, were available for purchase. This may be inferred from the *Indice delle stampe . . . esistenti nella già Stamperia de i de Rossi, ora nella Calcografia . . .*, Roma, 1741, p. 102, where there is advertised a 'Libro de'ritratti degli eminentissimi signori cardinali, dall'anno MDCLVIII, nel pontificato di Alessandro VII. fino al presente . . .'.

The early volumes were issued with an engraved frontispiece by Albert Clouwet after Carlo Cesi, with the date 1658 and the title 'Effigies Nomina et Cognomina S.D.N. Alexandri Papae VII et RR. DD. S.R.E. Cardd. nunc viventium', and it is probable that this frontispiece remained in use throughout the papacy of Alexander VII (i.e. until 1667[25]). I possess a copy which can hardly have been issued later than early 1662, as the last two engravings, although inscribed with the Cardinals' names (Vidoni and D'Aragona) have blank ovals where the images ought to be (the date of creation of both is given as 5th April 1660, which doesn't agree with the official lists). A number of living Cardinals are not represented, but I think one can assume that the portraits of Cardinals created by Alexander VII (i.e. not earlier than 1657), of which engravings are found in this volume, must have been painted between 1657 and 1662. As far as I can judge the more worldly Italian Cardinals liked to have their portraits painted for engraving soon after receiving the Hat, while the smarter of them sometimes substituted a revised image for publication after a few years.

This dating is important as providing a solid core of engraved portraits after Morandi which can be dated before 1662, and it also reveals that Morandi and Baciccia, from the very outset of their careers, appear as rivals in the field of Cardinalicial portraiture – for Baciccia's portraits of Cardinal Antonio Bichi and Cardinal Jacopo Franzone can, in this way, be dated between 1657/8 and 1662. Morandi became a member of the Roman Academy of St. Luke in 1657, just at the moment when he also first appears as a protégé of Cardinal Flavio Chigi, the sixteen-year-old nephew of the new Pope, Alexander VII. The Chigi archives[26] reveal payments, between 1659 and 1662, for

various portraits of Alexander VII, Cardinal Chigi and Principe Mario Chigi: after 1667 it is Baciccia who becomes the chief protégé of the family. Pascoli makes a point of saying that Baciccia painted all the seven Popes between Alexander VII and Clement XI, but he credits Morandi only with five, viz.:

Alexander VII (Chigi), 1655–67.
    At least two portraits are documented: there are engravings after Morandi by J. Testana and F. Spierre: and at least one original in the Palazzo Chigi, Ariccia.
Clement IX (Rospigliosi). 1667–69.
    There are engravings after Morandi by J. Testana and C. Waumans.
    Since Pascoli specifically states Morandi only painted five Popes it is probable that Clement X (Altieri), 1670–76, was the one left out.
Innocent XI (Odescalchi), 1676–89.
    There is an engraving after Morandi by J. Blondeau.
Alexander VIII (Ottoboni), 1689–91.
    There is an engraving after Morandi by J. Testana.
Innocent XII (Pignatelli), 1691–1700.
    An anonymous engraving after Morandi was published by Domenico de' Rossi.

To move from Popes to Cardinals, one finds that Morandi is perhaps the most heavily employed of the portrait painters whose works were engraved, from the time of Alexander VII until shortly before 1700. Baciccia and Ferdinand Voet are his most serious rivals in the earlier years, but, within a few years of 1700, Passeri, Ludovico David, Odazzi and others are the principal names. It is reasonable to assume that, when the engraving says *G.M. Morandi pinxit* (or some abbreviation of this), an oil portrait was in fact painted – but it is surprising that so few original oil portraits should at present be known. Professor Enggass has found that the same situation obtains with engraved Baciccia portraits of Cardinals, and it may well be that an investigation of the iconography of Cardinals can only properly be undertaken by some ecclesiastical agency, since it is not unlikely that a number of the original portraits may be found to exist within the Clausura of Convents. Of all the engraved portraits after Morandi known to me, only one, that of Cardinal Luigi Capponi (created 1608: died 1659), which appears in the early editions of the 1658 volume published by de' Rossi, is inscribed *Io. Mar. Morand. del.* (rather than *pinxit*): one may assume that this was done from a drawing by Morandi (perhaps after an earlier painting) rather than from an oil portrait. In all other instances the existence of an oil portrait may be presumed. It is a curious fact that the only Cardinals listed by Pascoli (II.132) as having been painted by Morandi – Cybo, Marescotti, Spada and di Carpegna (probably Ulderico created 1633) – should have had their portraits engraved without a painter's name. It is unlikely that the portrait of Cardinal Bernardino Spada, a recent acquisition for the

25. Under Innocent XI, at any rate, there was a new engraved frontispiece, by G. Audran after Ciro Ferri. It is undated but includes a medallion portrait of Innocent XI and a revised inscription.

26. V. Golzio, *Documenti . . .* (see note 4), pp. 266 f. and 278 ff.

Galleria Spada in Rome and an original, in reverse, from the engraving by Testana, is by Morandi, as is claimed by Zeri.[27] Omitting the names listed by Pascoli, the following portraits of Cardinals engraved after Morandi paintings are known to me. I have listed them for convenience in alphabetical order; the dates after each name are those of the creation as Cardinal (as given on the inscription under each portrait) and the date of death. The date of creation is not always straightforward, as a number were created *in petto* a year or so before official promulgation, and a number of these dates do not agree with those of the most official Vatican publication;[28] but, for determining the date *a quo*, the date of creation on the engraving seems the best. After the dates of the Cardinal I have given the name of the engraver. The normal size of these engravings, when bound, is about 12 × 8 inches.

Cardinal Ottavio de Acquaviva (1654–74)   J. Testana
(Painted before 1662)

Cardinal Francesco Albizzi (1654–84)   J. Testana
(Painted before 1662)

Cardinal Dezio Azzolini (1654–89)   J. Testana
(Painted before 1662: a later engraving after F. Voet)

Cardinal Gregorio Barbarigo (1660–97)   A. Clouwet
(Painted 1660–62)

Cardinal Girolamo Buonvisi (1657–77)   J. Testana
(Painted before 1662)

Cardinal Girolamo Casanate (1673–1700)   R. van Audenaerde 1695

Cardinal Flavio Chigi (1657–93)   J. Testana
(Painted before 1662. An original in Palazzo Chigi, Ariccia)

Cardinal Leandro de Colloredo (1686–1709)   J. Blondeau

Cardinal Domenico Maria Corsi (1686–97)   J. Blondeau

Cardinal Johann Casimir Denhoff (1686–97)   J. Blondeau

Cardinal Cesare Fachinetti (1643–83)   S. Picart
(Painted before 1662)

Cardinal Girolamo Farnese (1657–68)   J. Testana
(Painted before 1662)

Cardinal Giulio Gabrielli (1641–77)   J. Testana
(Painted before 1662)

Cardinal Girolamo Gastaldi (1673–85)   Pubd. by J. J. de' Rossi

Cardinal Giovanni Battista de Luca (1681–83)   J. Blondeau

Cardinal Francesco Maria Mancini (1660–72)   J. B. Bonacina

Cardinal Francesco Maria de' Medici (1686–1709)   J. Blondeau
(Painted before Blondeau's death c. 1698)

Cardinal Camillo Melzi (1657–1659)   J. Testana

Cardinal Luigi Omodei Jr. (1690–1706)   J. C. Allet

Cardinal Francesco Paolucci di Calboli (1657–66)   J. Testana
(Painted before 1662)

Cardinal Antonio Pignatelli (created 1681)   A. van Westerhout
(Painted before he became Pope as Innocent XII, 1691)

Cardinal Giulio Rospigliosi (created 1657)   J. Testana
(Painted 1657, see p. 117: later Clement IX)

Cardinal Jacopo Rospigliosi (1667–84)   A. Clouwet
(A related portrait is in the Palazzo Rospigliosi)

Abbate (later Cardinal) Felice Rospigliosi (created 1673)   A. Clouwet
(Painted before he became a Cardinal in 1673)

Cardinal Giovanni Battista Rubini (1690–1707)   J. Blondeau
(Painted before Blondeau's death c. 1698)

Cardinal Flaminio Taia (1681–82)   J. Blondeau

Cardinal Odoardo Vecchiarelli (1658–67)   A. Clouwet
(Painted before 1662)

Of engraved portraits of secular persons I only have record of the following:

Agostino Chigi   Engraved by J. Testana

Mario Chigi   Engraved by J. Testana
(There are documents for several portraits and at least one is in the Palazzo Chigi, Ariccia.)

Andrea Palladio   Engraved by Lorenzo Zucchi
(Clearly not from life)

Camillo Rospigliosi   Engraved by A. Clouwet

I can point only to one original painting with certainty from which one of these engravings was derived, the portrait (28″ × 24″) lately discovered by Anthony M. Clark on the New York art market[29] (Fig. 4), of *Cardinal Denhoff*, perhaps painted soon after his creation as a Cardinal in 1686, as he was resident in Rome. It is an excellent likeness, but tame in comparison with any portrait by Baciccia.

It is hardly conceivable that ecclesiastical portraits by Morandi cannot be found in Rome, but I am reluctant to make attributions. There are, however, two full-lengths of real distinction which I should like to put forward as candidates – the portraits of Innocent XI and of Cardinal Luigi Omodei senior in the Ante-Sacristy of S. Carlo al Corso. It is probable that the documents are in existence which will clear up their authorship, so that it should be enough to mention them.

27. Federico Zeri, *La Galleria Spada*, Firenze, 1954, p. 99 and fig. 128. It is perhaps slightly more likely that the Cardinal painted by Morandi would have been Fabrizio Spada.

28. Conte Francesco Cristofori, *Storia dei cardinali di santa romana chiesa dal secolo V all' Anno del Signore MDCCCLXXXVIII*. Propaganda Fide, 1888.

29. It was generically ascribed to the 'French School'. I am greatly indebted to Anthony Clark for constant help and consultation in preparing this article.

Realism and Idealism in the Roman Portraits of Queen Christina of Sweden

OF all European sovereigns of the seventeenth century, Queen Christina of Sweden has been handed down to posterity in the most varied sequence of portraits.[1] In that respect she even surpasses her father, Gustavus Adolphus the Great, whose likeness was more keenly sought after in Protestant countries than that of any previous Northern king.[2] In her case a certain advantage was her longer life-span. Born in 1626 she lived for almost sixty-three years, whereas her father was killed on the battlefield at the age of thirty-eight. Her relation to art and artists was also more personal and more expert. Indeed, no one can do full justice to her history without an intimate knowledge of her iconography.

Most of the portraits which have come down to us belong to her years as Queen of Sweden and to the time immediately after her abdication in 1654. Once she had settled permanently in Rome she no longer held the prominent position in European history which she had occupied during the time when she really held some of the main threads of political manœuvre and counter-manœuvre in her hand, and the immediate effect was that her portraits became much less in demand than before. This is particularly striking in the field of the graphic arts, where the broad stream of portrait prints, featuring her as one of the marvels of the world, ceases fairly abruptly after her second journey to France in 1657/58. She also no longer had the means to maintain one or several court painters in her household or to pay the leading artists in Rome according to their deserts. Nevertheless her Roman portraits form an interesting chapter not only in her own life, but also in the history of baroque portraiture in general. At the same time, it is the most neglected area of her iconography and is so full of traditional assumptions and unsolved problems that it will need many more years of research before we can know for certain when and by whom the most relevant of her portraits were executed.

As reigning Queen of Sweden, Christina had had two foreign painters in her service, the Dutchman David Beck and the Frenchman Sébastien Bourdon; she also had two miniaturists, Pierre Signac and Alexander Cooper.[3] None of them followed her in 1654 into exile. Beck, who had already left Sweden in 1651, remained, however, at least officially her court-painter, and when, in 1655, she reached Bologna on her way to Rome, we find him there before her.[4] At Forlì there existed until the Second World War a full-length portrait of Queen Christina, which may stylistically be ascribed to Beck. It shows her dressed in black, with a crown and sceptre lying on a cushion on the floor at her feet, so there can be no doubt that the portrait was done after her abdication.[5] The same face is shown in a half-length picture in the Historical Museum at Gothenburg (Fig. 1), which may also be by Beck's own hand, and in an engraving by a French artist, François Spierre, who worked in Rome in the 1650's.[6] In the hair-style with the curls falling to the shoulder, these portraits resemble Beck's different versions of her from about 1648–50, as if he had painted them from the latter and not from life. By this time Christina had sacrificed her beautiful curls; she cut them when, on her departure from Sweden, she changed her appearance and dressed like a man, travelling on horse-

1. The basis of all research on the iconography of Queen Christina is *Svenska kungliga porträtt i Svenska porträttarkivets samlingar*, I, ed. by Sixten Strömbom (*Index över svenska porträtt*, III), Stockholm, 1943, pp. 202–249. For further material and literature, see the catalogue of the XIth Council of Europe exhibition, *Christina Queen of Sweden*, Nationalmuseum, Stockholm, 1966.

2. S. Strömbom, *Iconographia Gustavi Adolphi*, Stockholm, 1932.

3. K. E. Steneberg, *Kristinatidens måleri*, Malmö, 1955.

4. In 1652 Beck was in Holland waiting for money from Queen Christina to be sent to Italy. In June 1653 he was still in Rotterdam. Later that year he is said to have been in Rome (Steneberg, Article on *David Beck* in *Svenskt konstnärslexikon*, I, Malmö, n.d., pp. 117–119, with bibliography). From the letters written by Fra Bonaventura Bisi to the Florentine court (Archivio di Stato, *Lettere artistiche diverse*, III, fol. 278 ff.), it appears that Beck had fallen seriously ill in Bologna in August 1655. He is likely to have joined her there in November. He is also known to have followed her to France in July 1656. Shortly afterwards he was back in Holland, where he fell ill and died.

5. The portrait then belonged to Marquis Paulucci di Calboli. His father acquired it from Marquis Albicini, in whose family it had remained, according to tradition, ever since Christina donated it to his ancestor on her way to Rome in November 1655. It was completely destroyed during the last war. All that remains of it seems to be a photograph in the Svenska Porträttarkivet of the Nationalmuseum, although a good seventeenth-century copy in oil was presented by the Swedish painter, Anders Zorn, to the church of Mora in Dalecarlie. With regard to the position of the crown in this portrait, one is reminded of Christina's marginal note to Linage de Vauciennes' edition of Chanut, *Mémoires de ce qui s'est passé en Suède*, 1677: 'Aussi faisait-elle gloire d'avoir mis sous les pieds ce que le reste des rois porte sur leurs testes'.

6. *Svenska kungliga porträtt*, I, no. Kr:a 43, fig. 240. On Spierre, see Thieme-Becker.

back through Denmark, Germany and Holland to Ant-werp. The portraits painted after this, produced in Flanders by Justus van Egmont, show her head covered by a wig.[7] A similar hair-style appears in an engraving (Fig. 2) at the front of Gualdo Priorato's *Historia della Sacra Real Maesta di Cristina di Svezia*, which is a complete record of her journey from Uppsala to Rome and of her glorious recep-tion there. Of all portraits, this is perhaps the most con-vincing interpretation of the ferocious side of her character; clearly this is the very woman who a year later did not shrink from pronouncing the death sentence on Monal-deschi, whom she had found guilty of high treason, and from having it carried out without mercy.[8]

Neither the engraver nor the originator of the design has left his name on this print. Too different in character from Beck's conception of the Queen, it cannot derive from an original by him. One is tempted to suggest Theodor van der Schuer, who followed Sébastien Bourdon to Stock-holm as his assistant and later reappeared in Rome as *pittore della Regina di Svezia*.[9] But the documents are silent as to his contribution to the Queen's iconography, and his achievement as a portrait painter still escapes us.[10] The *Avisi di Roma* for 29th April 1656 inform us that Gualdo's book had just appeared; meanwhile the agent of the Duke of Modena wrote to his master on 1st April the same year, mentioning a new portrait of Queen Christina executed 'alla macchia tante semigliante'.[11] Since the agent, Guidoni, added a specimen of it to his report, it may well have been this very print.

Already during her first stay in Rome, or more probably just after she had left for France, the first sculptured por-trait of Christina as ex-Queen was ordered from a young artist from Ancona, Francesco Maria Nocchieri.[12] The Senators of the Capitol claimed the Consuls of the Roman Republic as their ancestors and therefore the right to con-verse with royal persons on equal terms when receiving them in their palace. Christina's first reaction when invited to pay them an official visit was to refuse, but, as her curiosity prevailed over her vanity, she finally accepted and agreed to be received by the Senators on their terms, that is, with her hosts seated in their chairs and with their hats on. In memory of her visit, and of their victory in this matter of etiquette, the *triumviri* – S. Petrucci, J. Annibali and F. Massimo – together with the prior, C. Piccolomini, had a commemorative stone tablet made with a long inscription in Latin, the frame of which was in the form of the six mountains crowned by a star of the arms of Pope Alexander VII.[13] In the top mountain was inserted a bust in relief of the famous visitor (Fig. 3). In this portrait a curled wig of a male type covers the Queen's head, leaving only a small knot of her own hair visible at the back. A proudly projecting nose and an energetic chin are other character-istics of this likeness. Christina came to visit the Senators on the Capitol on the 7th July 1656, and on the 20th she sailed from Palo harbour to France. Consequently, there was only a fortnight left for the artist to model her profile, and this may well account for the impression of rather summary workmanship left by the relief when looked at closely. Christina seems, however, to have been satisfied herself, since she later gave Nocchieri the commission to execute the statue of Apollo which became the centre-piece in the *Sala dei Muse* of Palazzo Riario.[14] The Swedish architect, Nicodemus Tessin the Younger, who visited the palace in 1687, speaks of Nocchieri as 'Her Majesty's former sculptor who is now dead'.[15]

The tablet in the Palazzo dei Conservatori is executed in marbles of different colours, and so is a bust, traditionally said to represent Queen Christina, in the Herzog-Anton-Ulrich Museum in Brunswick (Fig. 4).[16] This has a general

7. Justus van Egmont executed two versions, one with the Queen represented as Minerva, of which there are at least three examples known today (see the Stockholm exhibition catalogue, 1966, no. 546), and another, in two examples, as Diana hunting (*ibid.*, no. 546). The first was engraved by Pontius and is probably the one referred to by R. Montecuccoli in his Antwerp diary for 17th September 1654 (*I Viaggi*, ed. by A. Gimorri, Modena, 1924, p. 42), where he writes 'Si ritorno a casa, dove la Regina fece vedere il suo ritratto del Giusto, il quale l'ha riscontrata benissimo'. The second version was done in Brussels in 1655, according to a letter by Count Dohna to his brother published by K. J. R. Burenstam, *La Reine Christine de Suède à Anvers et Bruxelles, 1654–55*, Brussels, 1891, p. 43, no. 1.

8. The best critical account of this episode, which took place at Fontainebleau, is by C. Weibull in his *Christina och Monaldesco*, Stockholm, 1936.

9. A. Bertolotti, *Artisti francesi in Roma*, Mantua, 1886, pp. 130–131.

10. Possibly he is the author of a portrait representing Queen Christina's court-tailor and valet de chambre, Johan Holm-Leijoncrona; see B. von Bonsdorff in *Finskt Museum*, 1960, pp. 11–35. Rather different from this are his wall-paintings in Maestricht, to which Mr. T. Schreuder was kind enough to draw my attention; one of them is signed *Theodorus van der Schuer, Christinae Sueciae Reginae Pictor, depinxit anno MDCLXXI*.

11. I owe this reference to an excerpt taken by C. Bildt among his papers in the Swedish Record Office.

12. Little research has so far been done on this artist. He is mentioned as the author of Queen Christina's portrait on the tablet of the Palazzo dei Conservatori in the *Nota delle musei, librarie, galerie etc. di Roma*, published anonymously by G. P. Bellori in 1664. Prof. Pietrangeli has called my attention to the fact that in the account of the costs, *Conto per l'escenzione delle lapide capitoline*, of 1st September 1657, there is, curiously enough, no payment recorded for Nocchieri's relief. Possibly the Queen took charge of it herself.

13. The best account is still C. Bildt, *Svenska minnen och märken i Rom*, Stockholm, 1900, pp. 92 ff.

14. A bozzetto of this figure has recently been identified in the Ashmolean Museum at Oxford. The Sala dei Muse and the palace of the Queen in Rome will be fully treated by S. Vänje in his forthcoming thesis (of which a first draft, *Palazzo della Regina*, was accepted in 1655 as 'licentiat-avhandling' at the Stockholm University).

15. O. Sirén, *Nicodemus Tessin d.Y:s studieresor*, Stockholm, 1914, p. 184.

16. S. Strömbom, 'Ett Kristinaporträtt i Braunschweig', *Person-historisk tidskrift*, 1914, pp. 173–174.

similarity to the type of memorial bust commonly placed in niches or above epitaphs in Roman churches. The figure wears a black veil over her head and a pointed white cape, usually worn by widows. Christina was certainly never a widow, and it is difficult to understand why she should have ordered a tomb-sculpture of this sort while still in the prime of life. Nevertheless, the face is certainly hers. Her mourning veil can only be connected with the death of her mother in 1655, too early for this bust, or with that of her cousin and successor, King Charles X Gustavus, in 1660. We know that the news of his unexpected decease reached Christina in Rome early in April that year. On the 20th of July she hurried northward to be present at the funeral and at the Diet assembled in Stockholm.[17] This gives a firm date for the Brunswick bust, provided we are right in believing it to be an authentic portrait of the Queen. In fact the profile most of all resembles the head by Nocchieri in the tablet in the Palazzo dei Conservatori done four years before. In both works, and only in them, the Queen's protuberant nose has a sharply marked angle halfway between the eyebrows and the tip. There is also a notable agreement in the carving of the lips and chin. If one hesitates to ascribe the bust to 'Her Majesty's sculptor' from Ancona, it is because so far no documents have been found to support the attribution, and nothing is known of Nocchieri's having done other similar works. When, how and why the bust came into the collection of the Dukes of Brunswick also remains problematic.

A type of face somewhat reminiscent of that on the Brunswick bust characterizes another sculptured head of Queen Christina, this time in white marble (Fig. 5). It belongs to a German collector, Herr Kettenbach, of Schorndorf, near Stuttgart.[18] It shows the Queen as Minerva wearing a helmet crowned with a sphinx but without a crest. The fracture at the neck makes it likely that the portrait was once a bust or even a full-length figure. The motif of the sphinx on top of the helmet occurs already in an engraving by J. Falck, dated 1649, which shows a bust of the Queen between symbols of peace and erudition; the same motif is repeated, without a plumed crest as in Fig. 5, in the medal by Francesco Trevani which was made in 1665 or shortly afterwards.[19] The period between the two journeys to Hamburg and Sweden, 1662–66, is the most probable date for this head. Again, one would like to know how it found its way to Germany.

The long and pointed nose characteristic of these sculptured portraits must have been the most striking feature of the Queen's appearance at the age of thirty-five or so. It is

found also in the paintings of the Queen (Fig. 6) done in Sweden in 1660–61 by Abraham Wuchters, the Danish court painter, which she brought with her on her first return to her former kingdom in the North.[20] No doubt they are the most realistic interpretations of her physiognomy ever achieved.

With this vision of the Queen in mind, it is a contrast to look at her face in the portraits painted shortly after her return from her second journey to Hamburg and Sweden in 1666–68 by a Flemish artist then fashionable in Rome, J. Ferdinand Voet (Fig. 7).[21] Instead of the almost sublime ugliness of the Wuchters portraits, Voet shows us a pretty doll's face with a rounded nose and the hair adorned with pearls. Despite the royal insignia – an ermine mantle and an orb held with a firm grasp in her left hand – one is tempted to deny that this is a portrait of Queen Christina at all. But an engraving of 1674/5 by Petrus Aquila on the title-page of an album of engravings of Raphael's paintings in the Vatican *Loggie*, dedicated to Christina, leaves no doubt. It shows her with the same face and with the – in this case very inappropriate – inscription, *Nec falso nec alieno*.

Christina's own appearance possibly underwent certain changes in the 1660's; but these could hardly have been so great as those indicated by the new portraits. We are faced with the necessity of seeking an explanation in a fundamentally different concept of portraiture. Whereas Wuchters, when taking her likeness, certainly had the Queen to sit for him, Voet cannot be acquitted of the suspicion of having painted her from imagination, obeying not so much his eye as certain conventions of female charm then current under the overwhelming influence of French court art. We know him as the fashionable interpreter *à la* Mignard of the beautiful Mancini sisters and of other rivals of Christina in Roman society, all of them rendered with faces so similar that it is more or less impossible to tell them apart.[22] His representation of the Swedish Queen is best described as a mixture of what his model may really have looked like in her most ceremonial moments and the French *idéal de beauté féminine*, as it was personified in the ladies of high French and Roman society.

From a later period we have the Queen's own words regarding her attitude to the artist's task of depicting her likeness. Commenting upon a set of medals which the Florentine sculptor, Massimiliano Soldani Benzi, made for her in 1681, she wrote:

'La figure principale est le profil de Sa Majesté, dont la physionomie et l'air sont presque inimitables à l'art. Le

17. See C. Bildt, *Christine de Suède et le cardinal Azzolino*, Paris, 1899, p. 100.
18. I have not been able to see the original which belongs to Herr Kettenbach, who kindly showed me photographs of it.
19. C. Bildt, *Les Médailles romaines de Christine de Suède*, Rome, 1908, pp. 51 ff., pl. VII.
20. See L. Rostrup-Böyesen in *Kunstmuseets Aarsskrift*, Copenhagen, 1941, pp. 80 ff.
21. K. E. Steneberg, 'Bidrag till svensk fursteikonografi, *Tidskrift för Konstvetenskap*, XX, 1936, p. 113.
22. J. Wilhelm, 'Some Unpublished Portraits by Jacob-Ferdinand Voet or from his Atelier', *The Connoisseur*, August, 1966, pp. 251–256.

fameux Bernin en fut si persuadé qu'il n'osa se promettre d'y réussir, craignant la trop grande vivacité et l'extrême impatience de la Reine, se trouvant déjà dans un âge trop avancé pour un si grand ouvrage.

Mais un jeune homme plus heureux, quoique moins habile a fait ce portrait, et, ce qu'il y a de plus admirable, il l'a fait sans que la Reine lui ait donné un moment pour la regarder. Elle, qui a un si absolu pouvoir en toutes les autres choses sur elle-même, n'a jamais pu fixer son impatience, et c'est le seul sujet de plainte qu'elle ait donné au public, qui est privé par là du plaisir de la voir telle qu'elle est.'[23]

She continues by comparing her appearance on the medal with that of the classical gods:

'Les dieux n'ont pas de sexe. Ils ne vieillissent pas. Leur vigueur ne diminue jamais. C'est un continuel printemps que leur vie, et les années ne leur apportent que des beaux jours. C'est sur ce pied que vous la voyez dans un état si jeune et si florissant.'

At the age of fifty-five, when these lines were written, Christina certainly had every reason to imagine herself back in a mythical world of eternal youth. From the portraits painted by Voet about 1669 we see, however, that this vision had started to haunt her much earlier. She had begun to regard herself more or less as a symbol of divine perfection, and, if this were to be emphasized, a realistic representation of her face and appearance would no longer do.

No doubt there is a relation between this new idealistic conception of the Queen and the aesthetics of her antiquarian, Giovanni Pietro Bellori.[24] According to the latter, every human being suffered from certain physical defects and bad proportions, however perfect a shape the Creator had given mankind at the outset. Therefore it was the artist's duty to recreate the original beauty of all things:–'far gli uomini più belle di quelly che sono comunemente ed eleggere il perfetto'.[25]

In portraiture, however, the problem was complicated by the fact, which Bellori himself had to admit, that the painter could not follow this doctrine without losing sight of his proper purpose – to make a genuine likeness. In contrast to the 'noble' painters and sculptors, the portrait painters – li pittori icastici e facitori de' ritratti – 'non serbano Idea alcuna e sono soggetti alla bruttezza del volto e del corpo, non potendo essi aggiungere bellezza, né correggere le deformità naturali, senza torre la similtudine, altrimenti il ritratto sarebbe più bello e meno simile.'[26]

Yet, with a sitter as exalted as the Queen of Sweden, the Idea ought to have a right to influence even her terrestrial likeness. The portraits showing her more or less as she actually appeared could not be looked upon as satisfactory. Here it was up to the artist to add a higher truth – to give a likeness of the beauty of her soul. It may be supposed that this was Voet's aim.

Voet 'edited' the beautiful Queen in two major redactions, one with her seated in an arm-chair and one with her walking with a lion at her side.[27] In the Ristretto delli denari pagati dal Monte della pietà dal 24 nov. 1668 per decembre 1670 a diversi mercanti, appaltatori, artisti et altri, preserved among the Queen's papers in the Record Office in Stockholm, there is a payment by order of the Queen 'Al Voet Pittore per Ritratti di S.M. 180:–', no doubt referring to these paintings.[28] Since Voet also immortalized Cardinal Azzolino, it was probably the latter who recommended him to the Swedish Queen.[29]

Apparently the new type created by Voet was regarded as the most authentic and authoritative portrait of the Queen. In the piano nobile of her palace, where her choicest Italian paintings were on display, it occupied the place of honour in the Sala grande d'Udienza reale. A Swedish visitor Mårten Törnhielm, who saw it there, says that it represented her 'in life-size, seated, holding one hand on a lion'.[30] No portrait by Voet where she is both seated and shown with a lion at her side is known to exist. But there are several versions by or after Voet where she is seen walking with the lion, on the head of which she confidently lays her left hand, while the right holds the orb close to her hip.[31] Perhaps Törnhielm confused the two types in his memory; the walking one with the lion would have been the more important 'state' version.

The lion might, of course, in this portrait as in many others of seventeenth-century monarchs, simply be regarded as a symbol of royalty, but Christina may have attached other meanings to it as well. She had in her collection a drawing by Raphael or one of his school, showing a woman leading a lion by a string, symbolizing the wild passions bridled by

23. C. Bildt, Les Médailles romaines, pp. 98 ff.

24. E. Panofsky, Idea (Studien der Bibliothek Warburg, ed. by F. Saxl), Berlin, 1960; K. Donahue, 'Giovanni Pietro Bellori', Dizianario Biographico Italiano, VII, 1965.

25. G. P. Bellori, Le vite de pittori, scultori et architetti moderni, I, Rome, 1672, ediz. facs., Roma, 1931, pp. 3–13.

26. G. P. Bellori, op. cit.

27. The seated type is in the Uffizi (Inv. no. 1890–2810). Three versions of the other are known: one in the Museum of Budrio, one in private ownership in Palermo and one in the Royal Palace of Strömsholm, Sweden.

28. Stockholm, Riksarkivet, Azzolino-saml. vol. XXVIII (K. 421).

29. Berlin, Staatliche Museen, repr. by C. Bildt, Christine de Suède et le cardinal Azzolino, opposite pl. 48.

30. See his manuscript in the Episcopal Library of Strängnäs. (J. H. Schröder, 'Om drottning Christina och hennes konstsamlingar i Rom', Svea, XIII, 1831, pp. 414 f.) The relevant passage is quoted by O. Granberg, Svenska konstsamlingarnas historia.

31. The inventory of the estates, curiously enough, does not mention this portrait among the paintings said to be in the Camera dell'Udienza grande (Rome, Archivio di Stato A.C. 917, pp. 595 ff.). In the Casino (ibid., p. 731) there was 'Un ritratto di S.M. grande con figura al naturale con Leone', possibly also by Voet. It is also mentioned in the contract between Pompeo Azzolino and Don Livio Odescalchi: 'Il rittratto grande della Regina con sua cornige dorata'.

female wisdom.[32] The motif also occurs on Renaissance medals and cameos, and Christina herself used it on the reverse of a medal where characteristically she is seen leading not one but four lions, together with the inscription 'NEC SINIT ESSE FEROS' – 'she does not allow them to be wild'.[33] When asking Voet to give her a tamed lion at her side, she might well have wished to demonstrate not only her royal prerogative, but also her 'pouvoir absolu sur elle-même'.

The new youthful face adopted by Voet to stress the immortal significance of Queen Christina at the expense of truth and realism affected in varying degrees all the following representations of her, not only in the medals, where such idealisation was, so to speak, normal, but also in the life-size portraits. However, some modifications in the direction of realism are found. In 1674 the Queen appointed a new Swedish governor of her provinces in her former country, Count Göran Gyllenstierna, and in one of the castles owned by him there is a portrait of the Queen which, according to family tradition, was sent to him from Rome.[34] It may well have been painted there, about 1675 or later. It shows the same composition as the 'state' portraits by Voet, with the Queen walking accompanied by a lion, but the colour scheme is different and so is the face which has assumed a more realistic 'masculine' character. Have we an artist here who was able to overcome the Queen's aversion to sitting for her likeness? Probably not, since the new face is sufficiently explained by its showing the influence of a portrait which David Beck painted of Christina in 1650.[35] Nevertheless, if the portrait was a gift from Queen Christina, she must have approved of the change.

Another governor of her provinces, who succeeded Gyllenstierna in 1681, Johan Paulinus Olivecrantz (the son of the Archbishop who served at her coronation in 1650), was also given a portrait of the Queen, with a face halfway between truth and flattery, and different from that in the portraits by Voet.[36] A similar type, only much harder in the rendering of light and shade, appears in the portrait of Queen Christina which once served to recall her to the members of the *Academia degli Arcadi*.[37] There the artist

combined the new head with the pose of the Queen on Voet's portrait, with the right hand holding the globe close to her hip. None of these portraits is, however, good enough to make us very curious about their painters. Towards the end of her life, Queen Christina did, however, at least once sit for a painter. A young Swedish artist, Michael Dahl, who had emigrated to England in 1682, went on a tour abroad four years later, which took him first to Paris and then to Rome. In a letter to his mother, dated 6th October 1687, he tells her that he had intended to leave Rome much earlier but had remained because he had been allowed to paint the Swedish Queen 'not one time, but several'.[38] Vertue tells the story that the Queen, having learned of Dahl's intention to provide her with a fan, answered: 'Let me be drawn with a Lyon in my hand, that better becomes the Queen of Sweden'.[39] We do not know if Dahl complied with her wish in some lost portrait. But at Grimsthorpe Castle there is a portrait of Queen Christina by Dahl which shows that they agreed on another composition (Fig. 8).[40] The artist has represented his model seated, wearing a blue cloak lined with ermine and with clusters of three crowns embroidered on it in gold. As a special compliment to her he has fastened the cloak over her right shoulder with a brooch on which is seen a cameo of her hero, Alexander the Great. She rests her left elbow on a globe explained by a motto: NE MI BISOGNA, NE MI BASTA (Neither necessary, nor sufficient for me). This is written on a scroll which also touches the crown and the sceptre, which lies on a red cushion in front of the globe. The Queen's face resembles that in the portrait sent to Johan Olivecrantz, so it may well be that that, too, goes back to an original by Dahl.[41]

Dahl's visit to Rome coincided with that of Lord Castelmaine, James II's ambassador to the Papal court, who was there with the purpose of celebrating the advent of a Catholic sovereign to the British throne. We know that Queen Christina took a vivid interest in this new evidence of the progress of the true faith in a North European country. She joined with enthusiasm in the splendid reception given to Lord Castelmaine after his official entry to Rome, by arranging for him an *Accademia per musica* in her palace.[42] It is possible that Dahl was granted the unusual favour of being allowed to paint her portrait not only

32. J. Q. van Regteren Altena, 'Les Dessins italiens de la reine Christine de Suède', *Analecta Reginensia*, II, Stockholm, 1966, pp. 55–56.

33. C. Bildt, *Les Médailles romaines*, pp. 87 ff., fig. 49. I wish to thank Professor E. Panofsky for valuable remarks concerning the iconological problems connected with this medal and its inscription.

34. I owe this information to the kindness of Countess M. Mörner, Björksund, where this portrait is kept.

35. *Svenska kungliga porträtt*, I, fig. 218.

36. This portrait is mentioned in the inventory of the estates of Lagman Johan Cedercrantz, 5th April 1700, in the following way: 'Schillerier och Conterfey: 13. Regina Christina gjordt i Rom'. I wish to thank its present owner, Mrs. G. Lundström, Ludvika, for having given me a transcript.

37. *Christina, Queen of Sweden*, Exhibition, Cat. no. 938.

38. W. Nisser, *Michael Dahl and the Contemporary Swedish School of Painting*, Upsala, 1927, pp. 12–13.

39. Nisser, *op. cit.*, p. 12.

40. Nisser, *op. cit.*, pl. v.

41. The same portrait type was used by B. Fariat for his engraving after A. Scilla, showing Queen Christina sitting on a throne surrounded by personifications of Science, Art and Literature (see the frontispiece to 'Queen Christina of Sweden: Documents and Studies', *Analecta Reginensia*, I, Stockholm, 1966). Prof. Pietrangeli has kindly called my attention to a similar allegorical painting in a private collection at Spoleto, which seems, however, to depend upon the print just mentioned.

42. *Christina, Queen of Sweden*, Exhibition, Cat. no. 945.

because he was her compatriot, but also because he came from England. It has been said that Queen Christina persuaded Dahl to become a secret convert to catholicism, but nothing in the subsequent career of the artist makes this very probable.

In sculpture, too, we find the new idea of beauty affecting the Queen's likeness. The most important monument here is the over life-size bust in white marble which went to Spain with the Queen's collection of classical marbles and has since found a permanent home in the summer palace of La Granja at San Ildefonso, near Segovia (Fig. 9).[43] Here the mantle is fastened over her shoulder with a brooch decorated with the radiant sun – another emblem often used on the reverse of the Queen's medals. 'La Reine Soleil' would be an appropriate title for this majestic sculpture, for something resplendent has been caught in the triumphant yet benevolent expression on the face. A laurel wreath adorns her curly hair, and this detail, together with the measurements, makes it possible to identify the bust with one mentioned in the inventory of her estate as having stood in Palazzo Riario in the room between that containing the Castor and Pollux group and the bathroom on the ground floor.[44] It is this portrait which gives us the best idea of what a bust by Bernini would have looked like. We know, however, that it is the work of 'Giulio del Bernino', i.e. Giulio Cartari, Bernini's most trusted pupil, who had followed him to France and had been his chief assistant in the execution of the tomb of Pope Alexander VII.[45] Owing to the idealized conception of the Queen, it is hard to tell her age in this portrait. In certain details of the costume and the hair-style it is connected with a medal by Soldani Benzi, which is known to have been made in 1681.[46] Since it is more likely that the medal depends upon the bust than vice versa, a date around 1680 is the most probable assumption.

As we have already heard in a statement by the Queen quoted above, Bernini himself never ventured to make a portrait of her. Christina's own reason for it – that she was too lively and impatient a sitter – does not accord very well with what Baldinucci tells us of the master's methods:

> . . . que nel ritrarre alcuno non voleva ch'egli stesse fermo, ma ch'e si movesse, e ch'e parlesse; perché in tal modo, diceva egli, ch'e vedera tutto il suo bello, e lo contrafaceva com'egli era.[47]

The truth is that Christina could not afford to pay Bernini as generously as did the Popes and Cardinals – which did not prevent her from saying, when she was told that

Bernini had not left more than 40,000 scudi at his death, that she would have blushed at there not being more, had he been in her service!

In his lifetime Bernini only made one major contribution to the embellishment of Queen Christina's palace – the famous mirror, in gilded gesso with the figure of Time revealing the looking-glass itself, which had the place of honour in the Sala dei Quadri.[48] Nevertheless, this piece was a contribution in its own way to the iconography of the Swedish Queen, since every time she looked into it, she saw her own face just as it was – the most striking, but also the most fugitive, of all her portraits.

What did she behold, when at the age of about sixty she looked into Bernini's mirror? What was she really like, when age, sickness and disappointment had taken their toll? There is a small painting in a Swedish private collection which has been thought by some authorities to answer this question.[49] Its chiaroscuro and its intimate realism in the manner of Rembrandt and his school make it certain that it has a Dutch, or at least a Dutch-trained artist as its author. But, although a certain likeness to Queen Christina's features cannot be denied, it is very unlikely that it really represents her. The eardrops in the shape of large pearls, which the figure in this portrait wears, are unknown from any other portrait of her, and she is not likely to have worn a costume such as this. Christina only reached the age of a little under sixty-three, but the old lady in this portrait gives the impression of being over seventy. And, if we compare her face to that of the Queen in Dahl's portrait, it is not hard to see that they could not possibly represent the same person.

Further evidence of what Queen Christina really looked like shortly before she died is contained in a bust in bronze, which was acquired in 1938 by the Swedish National Museum, together with a magnificent marble bust of Cardinal Azzolino, from descendants of his nephew and heir, Pompeo Azzolino (Fig. 10).[50] This time we are struck by a convincing resemblance to the portrait painted by Dahl in 1687. In her old age, the face of Queen Christina seems to have acquired a certain masculine strength, which reminds us in a striking way of the portraits of her cousin, Charles Gustavus' grandson, Charles XII, from the first decade of the eighteenth century.

In this bronze bust she is seen wearing a simple dress of wrinkled silk which reveals rather than conceals her two rather full breasts. A small brooch with her emblem, the Sun, is fixed to the upper part of the garment, having been

43. It was the intention, never fulfilled of the late Professor K. E. Steneberg to publish this bust, which he was the first to discover.
44. C. Bildt, *Svenska minnen och märken i Rom*, Stockholm, 1900.
45. See *Christina Queen of Sweden*, exh. cat., Stockholm, 1966, no. 680.
46. C. Bildt, *Les Médailles romaines*, fig. 55–56.
47. Baldinucci, *Vita del Cavaliere Gio. Lorenzo Bernino*, ed. by A. Riegl, Vienna, 1912, pp. 237–238.

48. R. Josephson, 'Den avslöjade sanningen', *Svenska skulpturidéer*, I, 1952, p. 128; E. Panofsky, 'Mors vitae testimonium', *Studien zur toskanischen Kunst: Festschrift für L. H. Heydenreich*, 1964, p. 224; R. Wittkower, *Gian Lorenzo Bernini*, London, 1955, p. 204.
49. See the colour reproduction on the cover of Sven Stolpe, *DrottningKristina: Efter tronavsägelsen*, Stockholm, 1961.
50. O. Antonsson, 'Report on New Acquisitions' in *Nationalmusei Årsbok*, N.S. IX, 1939, pp. 161–163.

executed in the bronze as a separate piece. Over her forehead, her hair is combed in the form of a high curled wig,
clearly in imitation of certain Roman busts of the first
century A.D. The rest is swept backwards in massive waves
alternating with tresses, ending in two ringlets behind the
neck. This is a real masterpiece of *coiffure à la mode*, in clear
contradiction of what is generally said about the Queen's
neglect of her toilet.[51]

A German scholar, Hans Wentzel, who has had the bold
idea of suggesting Andreas Schlüter as the possible author
of this bust, has claimed that this type of hair-style would
be unlikely to have appeared much before the end of the
seventeenth century,[52] and hence the bust would be
posthumous. But the penetrating realism in the treatment
of the face seems to leave no doubt that it has at least
been modelled from life by an artist who knew the Queen
well.

Once more we can refer to a medal to support a date for
this bust shortly before 1689 (Fig. 11).[53] In the portrait on
the front we easily recognize the same face with its profile
à la Charles XII and the high hair-piece over the forehead.
It is signed F. de S.U., i.e. Ferdinand de Saint-Urbain, a
medallist from Lorraine, born in 1658, who settled in
Rome in 1685. The reverse has a quotation from Virgil
(*Aeneid*, II, 777), NON SINE NUMINE, and shows the sea
and an island with a circular chapel and a bird descending
towards it (Fig. 12). The meaning of this cryptic image has
not yet been deciphered. Since the island has a shape
reminiscent of England, it might be an allegory of the
restoration of the Catholic faith in Great Britain after
James II had succeeded his brother on the English throne in
1685.[54] The medal would then have been ordered by
Queen Christina on the occasion of Lord Castelmaine's
visit in 1687. The fact that the reign of James II came to a
sudden end in 1688 would explain why the medal is known
only in three copies.

The profile view of the bust should also be compared with
the one on the high medallion above the epitaph in memory

of the Queen which has its place in the right aisle of St.
Peter's. The history of this monument is now well known,
thanks to recent research by one of Sir Anthony Blunt's
pupils.[55] It was commissioned from Carlo Fontana in 1696
by Pope Innocent XII, and was unveiled in 1702 under
Clement XI, formerly Cardinal Giovanni Francesco Albani,
one of the Queen's personal friends. The medallion was
cast in bronze by Giovanni Giardini from a model by the
French sculptor, Jean Théodon, who also sculpted the bas-
reliefs in marble on the sarcophagus. Fontana first had the
idea of erecting a statue as distinct from a plaque of the
Queen, to serve as a pendant to Bernini's monument to
Countess Matilda of Tuscany in the same aisle. There is a
drawing by him for this *concetto* in the Royal Library at
Windsor Castle, and a document refers to a wax model *di
tutta la figura della Regina*, prepared by Giardini but presumably also modelled by Théodon.

Fontana had good reasons for employing Théodon, since
the latter was well acquainted with the dead Queen. He
had come to Rome in 1676 as one of the first twelve
pensionnaires of the French Academy founded by Colbert.
He remained in this situation until 1690, when commissions
from home more or less ceased, owing to Louis XIV's
financial difficulties.[56] Théodon lived at that time in the
Via di Lungara, not far from Palazzo Riario. He was glad
to do so, because he was in love with the famous soprano,
La Georgina, also called Angelica, who had found shelter
in the palace of the Swedish Queen, when the Pope wanted
to have her sent to a convent.[57] Since Christina was a friend
of the Director of the French Academy, Charles Errard,
who made a project for her tomb,[58] and since she also had
much to do with Cardinal d'Estrées, who was a protector
of Théodon, there are several reasons to believe that she
and the French sculptor met more than once during the
Queen's last years. Of all the sculptors living in Rome at
that period, he is more likely than any other to have had a
chance to model her portrait. There is a French element in
the Stockholm bust (Fig. 10), particularly in the sober
treatment of the draperies, which makes it hard to believe
that it could have emanated from an Italian sculptor.[59] In
addition, the profile has many features in common with

51. One of her *Maxims* reads: 'Il y a des gens assez sots pour se rendre
esclaves et martirs de leurs habits et des modes. On est bien malheureux quand l'on n'est occupé tout le temps de sa vie qu'entre
un miroir et un peigne' (*Drottning Kristina, Maximer: Les Senti-
ments héroïques*, ed. by Sven Stolpe, Stockholm, 1959, no. 320.

52. H. Wentzel, 'Eine Büste der Königin Christine', *Pantheon*, XXIV,
1939, p. 374.

53. N. L. Rasmusson, 'En Kristinamedalj', *Göteborgs Musei Årstryck*,
1942, pp. 191–194. *Ibid.*, 'Medaillen auf Christina', *Analecta
Reginensia*, I, Stockholm, 1966, pp. 316–317. The medal was first
published by Fritz Dworschak ('Der Medailleur Gianlorenzo
Bernini', Prussian *Jahrbuch*, LV., 1934, p. 31, Abb. 2), who,
however, wrongly dated it about 1660.

54. Admittedly the shape of the island does not correspond to the
map of England as faithfully as one would wish. Scotland is left
out (as being too stubbornly Protestant except in the Catholic
highlands?). Alternatively, one is tempted to think of Sicily, but
no event having any reference to the life of Queen Christina is
known from that part of Italy.

55. A. Braham, 'The Tomb of Christina', *Analecta Reginensia*, I,
Stockholm, 1966, pp. 48–58, with an Appendix by Helmut
Hager.

56. Fl. Ingersoll Smouse, 'Pierre Le Gros II et les sculpteurs français
à Rome la fin du XVIIᵉ siècle', *GBA*, LV, 1913, pp. 203–217;
G. Rosenthal, *Französische Bildhauerkunst unter dem Einfluss
römischer Barockskulptur um die Wende des 18. Jahrhunderts*,
Cologne, 1933.

57. C. Bildt, 'Drottning Kristinas sista dagar', *Ord och bild*, V,
Stockholm, 1896/97.

58. Nationalmuseum Stockholm, Inv. no. 50/1905. *Christina, Queen
of Sweden*, Exhibition, Cat. no. 813.

59. This opinion is shared by R. Wittkower and Klaus Lankheit
(both in conversation), neither of whom has found it possible to
give the bust a definite attribution.

that of the medallion in St. Peter's, although the latter admittedly looks sharper and more linear in design, possibly because it was meant to be seen high up from the ground. Until the contrary can be proved from further documents, it seems reasonable to attribute this bust to Théodon. The final likeness of Queen Christina is the death mask covering her face on her tomb (Fig. 13).[60] It was executed in silver by the Papal goldsmith, Giovanni Giardini, already known to us as a bronze founder. The thin silver

mask was covered with a coat of plaster which was then painted in colours of natural complexion. It seems to be a real death mask, originally moulded on the Queen's face, but when it was prepared for its purpose, the wrinkles and angularities were smoothed out, the eyelids were slightly opened and the whole was somewhat embellished. The idealistic concept of Bellori and Voet had the last word, even in this otherwise intimate representation of the Queen's features.

POSTSCRIPT

Besides the sculptures, paintings and engravings of Queen Christina done in Rome there are from the same period a number of literary portraits describing her appearance.
They can be divided into two groups: those favourable to the Queen and apparently sanctioned by her, and those noted down by private visitors who wanted to keep in mind the impression made on them by this extraordinary person. To the first group belong two texts translated into English in the catalogue of the Stockholm exhibition.[61] One commemorates her appearance when she was first received by the Pope after her official entry into Rome on 23rd December 1655 and corresponds fairly well with the contemporary engravings. The other was apparently written by somebody at the Queen's own court with the purpose of promoting her election to the throne of Poland in 1668.[62]
Of the second group the earliest text is a passage in the diary of Philip Skippon, describing a visit he paid to the Palazzo Riario in Rome in 1664:

We went to see the Queen of Sweden's palace, and came into a chamber (hung with indecent pictures of women) where Queen Christina sat, and Cardinal Azzolino by her, and much company in the room; for the space of two hours instrumental and vocal musick entertained them, and the Queen played with her little dog, talked sometimes with the cardinal, and sometimes with the strangers; she is crook-backed, was dressed in her hair; had a cravat about her neck, and a coat with short sleeves on, and had linnen sleeves like a half shirt about her hands.[63]

Just over twenty years later a German nobleman, Count Ferdinand Christian zur Lippe, paid a visit with his brother to the Swedish Queen and described it in his diary:

Als wir zu ihrem Palast kamen, wurden wir durch ihre Edelleute und eine Menge Lakaien empfangen, die auf den Treppenstufen standen. Oben war ihr Majordomus Marquis del Monte, der uns durch eine Menge Zimmer in römischer Art in eines führte, wo ich – wenn ich so sagen darf – eine sehr lächerliche Person erblickte. Sie überraschte mich derart, daß ich zu meinem Bruder sagte: "Wer ist das, ist das die Närrin der Königin?" Er sagte mir, ich solle still sein, das sei sie selbst!
Es war aber anders als sie zu sprechen begann, nachdem ich ihr meine Reverenz gemacht hatte . . .
. . . Sie war eine Fürstin von sehr kleinem Wuchs, mit großem Gesicht und einer Habichtnase, sie hatte bei ihrem hohen Alter noch ein ziemlich frisches, aber männliches Gesicht. Sie war unbedeckt und hatte die Haare in starken Locken ganz nach oben gebunden. Sie trug einen Mannsrock mit Kravatte, wie man später die "Steinkirche" getragen hat, und einen kurzen Frauenrock unter dem Justaucorps; alles in schwarzem Damast. Der Rock, der ihr nur bis zum halben Bein ging, ließ einen glattgezogenen Seidestrumpf sehen mit einem Männerschuh, den Absatz jedoch recht hoch. Sie saß auch stets wie ein Mann, trug Männerhandschuhe und Manschetten und gestikulierte beim sprechen, wie ein Mann es getan hätte.[64]

In reading these two texts, in many ways similar to that by François-Maximilian Misson, Nouveau Voyage d'Italie (11th April 1688), one is reminded of the portraits executed by the Danish court painter Wolfgang Heimbach after the Queen's passage through Copenhagen on her first return to Sweden in 1660 and of the caricature-like engraving of her in costume de voyage, a copy of which is inscribed "So sah man auss, in Nürnberg Ao 1662".[65] No doubt executed without the Queen's permission and from memory rather than ad vivum, these portraits, which are so different in character from those done in Rome, nevertheless certainly contain a good deal of the truth – Queen Christina not as she liked to be immortalized, but as she really was.

60. Carl-Herman Hjortsjö, 'The Opening of Queen Christina's Sarcophagus in Rome', Queen Christina of Sweden: Documents and Studies, Analecta Reginensia, I, Stockholm, 1966, pp. 138–158.
61. Christina Queen of Sweden, Stockholm, 1966, pp. 397–399.
62. The text (Stockholm, Record Office, Azzolino, vol. 8) has been corrected in the Queen's own hand. Where it says that she had one of her shoulders higher than the other, she adds "just a little higher".
63. Quoted from Hugh Honour, 'Queen Christina of Sweden as a Collector', The Connoisseur, CLXIII, 1966, pp. 9 ff.
64. Erich Kittel, Memoiren des Generals Graf Ferdinand Christian zur Lippe (1668–1724), Lemgo, 1959, pp. 51 ff. I owe the knowledge of this publication to the kindness of Dr. Sven Stolpe.
65. On these portraits see the Stockholm exhibition catalogue Nos. 859, 860, 876 and 877, and the article by Göran Lindahl, 'Tre Kristina-porträtt' (Konstrevy, Stockholm, 1957, pp. 134 ff.).

M. ALPATOV

Poussin's 'Tancred and Erminia' in the Hermitage: an Interpretation

POUSSIN's *Tancred and Erminia* in the Hermitage (Fig. 1) is well known outside the Soviet Union. During the last forty years it has twice been exhibited in Paris and has been the subject of much appreciative and penetrating comment. Yet its significance has not even now been exhausted. It is a masterpiece that deserves minute and detailed study.

In the pages devoted to it, attention has generally been focused on the poetic theme which Poussin borrowed from Tasso. Indeed, a prose exposition of the corresponding stanzas of the *Gerusalemme liberata* is not infrequently substituted for a critical study of the picture itself.[1] Many authors have been so intrigued by the fate of the heroine, overwhelmed by her sudden passion for the wounded knight, that they have ascribed to Poussin's Erminia all the feelings of fear, doubt and hope experienced by her counterpart in the poem.[2] Such emotions are, however, not noticeably evident in the painting.

Art historians have rightly detected the influence of Poussin's predecessors in the picture, especially that of an artist of the Second School of Fontainebleau, Ambroise Dubois.[3] Qualities both of Venetian 'painterliness' and seventeenth-century classicism have been observed: plastic beauty, perfection of composition, figurative grace. The picture has been linked now to one style, now to another, now to several simultaneously. Yet all this, however correct, does not help us much to understand Poussin's originality. To achieve such an understanding, it is necessary partly to adopt a new critical approach.

The first question to be examined is the relationship of the painting to the text of Tasso's poem. We know that in his youth Poussin illustrated Marino's poem, *Adonis*, and that this work earned him general acclaim. It has been suggested that the artist himself accorded the *Gerusalemme liberata* a thoughtful, thorough reading or, alternatively, that one of his friends or patrons explained its beauties to him or called his attention to certain passages in the text.

The evidence of the picture is that it does indeed render a moment described in specific lines (XIX, 109). In the painting, as in the poem, the scene is a sunset with a knight lying on the ground; beside him are his servant, Vafrin, and his discarded armour; over him bends the figure of Erminia;

and in the distance appears the body of the slain Argante. However, the painting does not correspond to the text in every detail. Poussin has not shown Tancred's dark mourning garments nor Erminia's veil. Erminia's despairing cry: 'Raccogli tu l'anima mia seguaci . . .', is not suggested by her appearance in the picture. Tancred's face shows nothing but exhaustion; he betrays no surprise at the sight of Vafrin and Erminia.

The whole character of the *Gerusalemme liberata*, with its alternating impulses of passionate piety and sensually intoxicating earthly love and happiness in the style of Ariosto, is very far from the spirit of Poussin's imagery.[4] Poussin was never a mere visual translator of Tasso's poem.[5] Although the latter certainly cannot be forgotten when looking at the picture, there can be no doubt that, basically, Tasso's lines served the artist as no more than a point of departure for the creation of an independent work of art.

To understand Poussin's *Tancred and Erminia*, it is important to consider the analogies with his own works. One such analogy is the picture depicting a similar episode from the same poem, showing Armida bending over the sleeping Rinaldo (Fig. 5).[6] Others are to be found in such mythological paintings as *The Death of Adonis mourned by Venus*[7] or, from a later period, *Pyramus and Thisbe*, based on Ovid's *Metamorphoses*, showing a woman about to take her own life beside the body of her lover.[8] Lastly, there are analogies with Poussin's representations of Christian themes, such as the Munich *Pietà*[9] or the Hermitage *Descent from the Cross*.[10] In all these paintings, the situation represented is a similar one, although the recumbent hero is not necessarily dead. Less easily explained but equally self-evident is the fact that Poussin tends to use the same situation to show not the sorrows but the delights of human existence. Examples of this are the classic *Bacchanals*, or idylls, in which women lie back in luxurious and drunken abandon while satyrs bend over their sleeping

1. V. Goerz, *Tancred and Erminia*, Leningrad, 1947 (in Russian).
2. V. Volskaja, *N. Poussin*, Moscow, 1946 (in Russian), p. 47.
3. L. Hourticq, *La Jeunesse de Poussin*, 1937, p. 87; S. Béguin, 'Dessins d'Ambroise Dubois', *L'Œil*, March 1966, p. 7.

4. F. De Sanctis, *Storia della litteratura italiana*, II, Milan, 1912, p. 127.
5. For the mistaken idea that he 'competed with' and even 'surpassed' the poet, see A. Glikman, *N. Poussin*, Leningrad-Moscow, 1964 (in Russian), p. 43.
6. W. Friedlaender, *Nicolas Poussin*, Munich, 1914, p. 115.
7. *Expostion Nicolas Poussin*, Paris, 1960, Cat. no. 25 (here abbreviated to *Exp.*).
8. R. Fry, '*Pyramus and Thisbe* by Nicolas Poussin', *Burl M*, XLIII, 1923, p. 53.
9. E. Buchner, *Die alte Pinakothek München*, Munich, 1957, pl. XL.
10. *Exp.*, Cat. no. 24.

bodies (cf. the Louvre's *Venus surprised by Satyrs*).[11]

The similarity between some of Poussin's pictures representing contrasting types of theme has already been remarked on by several authors, although without any convincing explanation of it being given.[12] It seems unlikely that the reason lies in the artist's lack of invention. Nor does it appear probable that he was deliberately 'quoting' from his own works in the manner of seventeenth and eighteenth century composers.

If it is remembered that Poussin was a thinker as well as an artist, the most satisfactory explanation seems to be that in all these variations on the same basic theme he was seeking to understand human relationships and to represent them with a clarity and explicitness only possible in the visual arts. Moreover, the knowledge that the Hermitage picture is one of a series affords a deeper insight into the significance of the story of Erminia's love as it inspired the artist. There exists another painting by Poussin on the same theme in the Barber Institute of Fine Arts, Birmingham (Fig. 2).[13] Opinions differ as to the dates of the two pictures. Some consider the Hermitage version to be the earlier, others the Birmingham one.[14] Since the latter is in the same style as two early battle scenes by Poussin (one in the Hermitage, the other in the Pushkin Museum, Moscow),[15] it seems likely that it pre-dates the Hermitage *Tancred and Erminia* by several years. On the other hand, it is difficult to pronounce definitely on the dates of Poussin's pictures to within a few years using stylistic criteria alone.

It is true that both pictures are demonstrably the product of the thought, taste and hand of the same artist. Both show the same protagonists and the same moment in the unfolding of the dramatic action. Nevertheless, they are profoundly different in treatment. It has been said that the Hermitage picture is the more pictorial, the Birmingham picture the more sculptural; the one nearer to the classical style, the other to the baroque. However, the classification of the two pictures under different stylistic headings does not exhaust their significance. They can be better understood as representatives of two different modes of art. Although it is hardly possible to identify each of them with one of the four modes mentioned by Poussin himself, it is evident that the Birmingham picture is of a heroic, tragic character while the Hermitage picture has a more idyllic and pastoral one.

11. O. Grautoff, 'Nouveaux tableaux de Nicolas Poussin', *GBA* 1932, p. 327; *Exp.*, Cat. no. 34.

12. A. Blunt, *Art and Architecture in France, 1500–1700*, London, 1953, p. 186; Ch. Sterling, *Musée de l'Ermitage: la peinture française de Poussin à nos jours*, Paris, 1957.

13. T. Bodkin, 'A Re-discovered Picture by Nicolas Poussin', *Burl M.*, LXXIV, 1939, p. 252.

14. V. Goertz, V. Volskaja and A. Glikman (*op. cit.* in notes 1, 2 and 5 respectively) consider the Birmingham picture to be the earlier work of the two. A. Blunt, *Exposition Nicolas Poussin*, p. 78, no. 88, regards the Heritamge picture as the earlier.

15. *Exp.*, Paris, 1960, Cat. no. 23.

In the Birmingham picture, objects and figures are closely packed one behind the other and fill the whole canvas. In the foreground are the *dramatis personae*, behind them are the horses and, behind the horses, trees and mountains; at the top of the picture hover typically baroque cupids. The composition is based on a diagonal line leading from the lower left to the top right corner. The forms are disposed as in a bas-relief, partly overlapping one another. In character they are fragile, the draperies falling in sharply angled folds, and Erminia appears to be toppling as though her feet had been scythed away from under her. The figures are broken into by the lighting, the upper part of Tancred's body being half in shadow. The whole picture is instinct with a violent unease which creates an impression of deep emotional upheaval not yet clearly resolved.

In the Hermitage version, Erminia is performing the same action but the outcome of the dramatic conflict has now been decided. The confused agglomeration of objects and figures in the Birmingham version is replaced by a clear and stable composition. The action takes place on an open plane, the figures balance one another, the composition is compact and is centred on the recumbent figure of the wounded Tancred. The shape of the picture itself is correspondingly longer in proportion to its height. Nothing breaks or disturbs the harmony. The clothing follows the lines of the body. The shields are placed symmetrically flanking the hero. The light falls full on the brilliant red garments of the central figure (whereas in the Birmingham picture the red clothing of Vafrin is off-centre to the left). All this lends the action an impression of inevitability. The difference between the two pictures can thus be defined in psychological terms: in the Birmingham version there is agitation; in the Hermitage one, agitation has been replaced by decision. This impression, however, is conveyed not so much by the behaviour of the figures, as by the compositional structure of the two pictures.

Although, as we have seen, Poussin's paintings cannot be classed as mere illustrations, they do contain an element of dramatic action (in this connection it is pertinent to recall Bernini's characterization: 'favoleggiatore'). The Hermitage *Tancred and Ermina* is a brilliant example of this quality in post-Renaissance painting. In ancient art the drama is usually based on some direct physical or moral conflict between the heroes (for example, *Pentheus and the Maenads*, *The Punishment of Dirce*, *Achilles and Briseis*, all at Pompeii). In medieval and, to a certain extent, Renaissance art, the prototype of the drama is Calvary: earthly sufferings lead to reward in Heaven; he who accepts suffering in a spirit of meekness becomes an object of reverence. In this context it is interesting that Poussin, as a post-Renaissance artist, shows the mainspring of the drama in his *Pietà* as the triumph of a supreme effort of will, thanks to which human beings, although subject to fate and entangled in irresolvable contradictions, attain the highest virtue.

Despite the resolution of conflict in *Tancred and Erminia*, the scene represented is fraught with tension. A warrior lies on the ground supported by his friend and servant. Over them both rises the figure of a woman. She does not weep for the stricken hero as do Mary and the holy women for the dead Christ, nor does she abandon herself to despair like Venus over the body of Adonis, nor does she resemble Thisbe preparing to stab herself over the body of her beloved. Erminia stands tall over the lying Tancred, her pose expressing anxiety; in one hand shines a sword and with the other she grasps a tress of her auburn hair. Irresistible love draws her to the wounded hero and, at the same time, ennobles and transfigures her. Like the heroes of Corneille, she is tormented by the knowledge of the inevitability of fate; her nature is divided, and the bold way in which she wields the masculine weapon in her hand contrasts with the feminity of the leg glimpsed through her parted garment.

The composition of the painting has been compared to Gothic vaulting and to the movement of a great bird.[16] (Like Polonius, we can but meekly accept such comparisons.) There has also been much said about its 'classic scheme'.[17] This designation need scarcely be argued any more than it is necessary to defend the statement that Corneille's plays are written in Alexandrines. Yet all this helps little to understand Poussin's art.

It is almost impossible to describe a pictorial composition in words. The following is thus an attempt to find an indirect solution to the problem of defining and interpreting this work. To judge from Poussin's many drawings, he often made a sketch in which he set down a rough first draft of a complex, multi-figured composition. These rough drafts were never derivative, they were entirely his own creation. A fine example of such a one is the

16. O. Grautoff, *op. cit.* in note 11, p. 108; V. Volskaja, *op. cit.* in note 2, p. 47.
17. A. Glikman, *op. cit.* in note 5, p. 29.

Scheme of disposition of the three central figures in Poussin's
Tancred and Erminia.

Louvre *Bacchanal* (Fig. 3),[18] whose crystalline clarity of form recalls the drawings of Luca Cambiaso.

No doubt a similar drawing served as the basis of the Hermitage picture (though not of the one in Birmingham). The diagram on this page showing the grouping of the three principal figures is not intended as a reconstruction of Poussin's preliminary sketch. This would of course be an impossible undertaking. Its function is simply to help the reader to think away secondary details in order to obtain a clear idea of the central 'plastic motive' of the composition. The figure stretched out on the ground is the incarnation of well-deserved rest and bliss as the reward of heroic struggle. It is reminiscent of the figure of Christ in the *Pietà* and, at the same time, of the figure of a sleeping *bacchante* (not mutually exclusive associations but ones which give the image a more complex significance). The figure is not flattened to the ground like a dead body. Both the head and the legs are slightly raised. The figure standing over it appears as its antithesis; the hands are raised which render the outline tense and unquiet; the body is slightly bent, following the impulse of the heart; the clothes stream out in the wind, suggesting passion. In both figures we see movement and we see stillness. A silent dialogue arises from the counterpoint of the two silhouettes. The third figure has much in common with the lying figure except that it has risen to its knees and bends over its master, supporting and reverencing him; it seems to reconcile the contradictions between the other two. The central concept of the picture is thus: three characters, three states of being, three silhouettes; weakness and exhaustion, friendly help, passionate love and self-sacrifice.

In the Birmingham picture, the horses in the background resemble figures in a bas-relief and serve as mere attributes.[19] It has been suggested that the foreshortening of Tancred's horse in the Hermitage picture was inspired by Caravaggio's *Conversion of St. Paul*.[20] But this horse's hindquarters do not dwarf the human figures. Both the horses in the painting shelter the group from the outside world and are at the same time a part of the action. This is particularly true of Erminia's horse.[21] The expressiveness of this animal has already attracted the attention of critics. In contrast to the charger of the Birmingham picture, which is turning away from the centre of action, the horse of the Hermitage version watches in bewilderment while his warrior-mistress bends over the body of her former enemy. He towers above the human figures with his head raised. His part in the composition is similar to that played by the sculptured herms with which Poussin often con-

18. W. Friedlaender and A. Blunt, *The Drawings of Nicolas Poussin*, London, 1939, III, no. 199.
19. Cf. the painting of *Aurora and Cephalus*, London, National Gallery; W. Friedlaender, *Nicolas Poussin*, 1914, p. 163.
20. R. Jullian, 'Poussin et le caravagisme', *Colloque Nicolas Poussin*, I, Paris, 1960, p. 230.
21. G. Jedlicka, *Französische Malerei*, Zürich–Berlin, 1938, pl. 63.

trasted his dancing bacchantes.[22] In a late picture, the Hermitage *Rest on the Flight into Egypt*, the carefully painted ass serves merely as a *genre* supplement to the majestic group of human beings.[23] The picture acquires stability from the figure of the standing woman. In the Hermitage *Tancred and Erminia*, it is the heroine's horse which fulfils this function. At the same time, the horse introduces into the strictly balanced picture something of that 'naturalness' (*le naturel*) which, at that period, was much prized in France even by the most unbending representatives of classicism. The grouping of people, horses and objects forms an enclosed unit yet also serves as a kind of 'wing' opening out onto a wider stage of sunset, sky and distant mountains, on which lies the body of the defeated Argante. Although this compositional diagonal is a stylistic feature of the Baroque, it also shows one of Poussin's characteristic peculiarities: he gives prominence to the figures and to the importance of man but, at the same time, sees man always as one element in the world of nature. This conception is particularly typical of his later works, but there are traces of it even in this early picture.[24]

Although the colours and their inter-relationships correspond to the placing of objects, they are broken and mixed and do not always follow the composition as a whole. In fact, there are three areas of red in the picture; the upper and lower parts of Tancred's tunic and the plume of Vafrin's helmet. The yellow colouring of the latter's tunic almost blends into the pink strip of the sunset. We are helped to identify various objects by their colour but, at the same time, they tend to blur together in the golden air of the evening, which suggests an immediate connection between the world of people and the stormy sky streaked with the brightness of the setting sun.[25] A precious char-

22. W. Friedlaender, *op. cit.* in note 19, pp. 172, 205, 206, 215.
23. M. Alpatov, 'Poussin peintre d'histoire', *Colloque Nicolas Poussin*, Paris, 1960, figs. 163, 177, 178.
24. M. Alpatov, 'Poussin Problems', *Art Bulletin*, XVII, 1935, p. 5.
25. F. S. Licht, *Die Entwicklung der Landschaft in den Werken von Nicolas Poussin*, Basel–Stuttgart, 1954, p. 109, affirms that the landscape of the Hermitage picture has something in common with Greco.

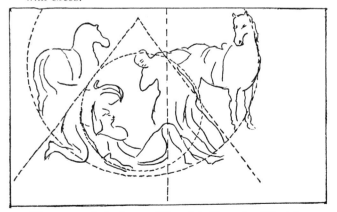

The geometrical scheme of Poussin's *Tancred and Erminia*.

acteristic (and one which we may look for in vain in many of Poussin's other works, particularly the Birmingham *Tancred and Erminia*) is that, in his desire to depict everything in visual terms, the artist knew when to stop. The fantastic beings originally conceived by his imagination are implied in the clear, distinct outlines of the forms. Charles Sterling's sensitive comparison of Erminia's horse to a mysterious creature of a dream is fully justified.[26]

The most remarkable feature of the composition is the fact that everything is conceived and executed by the artist in strict accordance with those simple rules to which the 'geometrical spirit' of the seventeenth century attached such importance. If we examine the picture from this point of view, we discover a number of regularities in these lively and expressive figures which can be reduced to geometric forms (see diagram below). Firstly, the recumbent Tancred can be included in a circle together with the bending Erminia (although the circumference will not, of course, correspond exactly to the outlines of the figures). Secondly, the three figures taken together form a wide-based pyramid. The significance of this is, however, quite other than that to be found in later pictures in which academic artists forced their figures to fit in with some preconceived geometrical shape, a procedure which they referred to as 'pyramidalising' (*pyramidaliser*). For Poussin, the pyramid, like a rhyme at the end of a line in poetry, was a happy discovery, an insight into a world of crystalline harmony.

Finally, it is noticeable that the whole group including the horses forms a great inverted arc. Strange as it may seem, this geometrical configuration has much in common with works in quite a different style, namely with French fifteenth-century paintings, particularly Quarton's *Coronation of the Virgin*, which has been aptly compared to a Gothic stained-glass window.[27] In *Tancred and Erminia*, however, the axis of the arc does not coincide with that of the composition. Tancred's raised knee marks the centre-line of the picture, which establishes a correspondence between the figure group and the total area of the canvas.

Having followed such a tortuous path in examining the composition, the question naturally arises as to how the essence of the action should be interpreted. From the viewpoint of commonsense, the answer is obvious; the picture shows a courageous female warrior overcome by love for her fallen enemy. Though not so profoundly moving as the last scene of *Romeo and Juliet*, the subject undoubtedly makes a strong appeal to our sympathies and permits us to identify with the characters. That the artist himself was not indifferent to the content of his pictures we know from his own admission as to how much feeling he put into his painting of the *Crucifixion*.[28] However, if we recall the observations we have just made about this *Tancred and*

26. Ch. Sterling, *Musée de l'Ermitage*, p. 30.
27. R. Klein, 'Art et illusion', *Art de France*, I, 1961, p. 436.
28. *Exp.*, Cat. p. 252.

Erminia as a work of art, we shall see that the essence of the action, the underlying motive of the picture, is something quite different. Superficially, the relationships between the characters are based on impressions taken from life and assimilated to their literary models, but all that has been observed or imagined by the artist is subjected to a strict set of laws dictated by reason. The Hermitage version is thus richer than the Birmingham one, since it sounds several different notes which, taken together, go to make up a harmonious chord. It is the moral effort involved in the struggle to achieve the complexity of truth which distinguishes Poussin from those illustrators or decorative artists who were always subservient to the whims of their patrons. The fact that in the Hermitage picture the dramatic scene goes to make up a harmonious and ordered whole is typical of Poussin's art. In this he was to some extent the disciple of the masters of the Renaissance, but we should beware of drawing too close a parallel between his art and Raphael's. In Poussin's painting, the artist's own way of seeing things is even more important than in that of a Renaissance artist. Behind the empirical image, we glimpse still more clearly the conviction that things are represented not as they are but as they ought to be. The charm of the visible world, the power of the artist's imagination and every impulse of fancy are subjected to the control of the mind. All this speaks against the modern tendency to look for the mainspring of Poussin's art in his literary sources.

Of course, this interpretation may well meet with scepticism, since it is founded on the master's works rather than on his recorded sayings. Perhaps the best way to check the interpretation offered is to examine other paintings by Poussin, similar in character to the *Tancred and Erminia*. Particularly useful in this connection are such pictures as the *Bacchanals* in which the artist-thinker sought to show an ideal existence.

Another example is the enchanting *Childhood of Bacchus* at Chantilly (Fig. 4). Here there is virtually no action. People are sitting, drinking and looking about them, relaxing naturally and unaffectedly and enjoying life. Taken together, the figures form a beautiful, balanced group which suggests some fundamental law of human existence. The group has its central figures flanked by others, while two infant boys recline on the ground at the feet of the grown-ups. It is typical that, while one of the figures is shown as though it were walking swiftly, it is so placed as not to disturb the general air of repose. An unspoken dialogue arises between the figures, thanks to the variety of pose and placing. Some seem to be asking questions, others answering; eyes meet and poses are repeated. Local colours dissolve in the golden, honeyed atmosphere. The picture is entirely given over to repose and peace.

The Louvre *Bacchanal with a Woman playing a Lute* is very similar in colouring to the Hermitage *Tancred and Erminia*. Again we are faced with a world in which man remains true to himself. Here we have not a complex pyramid of human relationships but the simple delight of relaxation on the bosom of the earth itself, a delight equally available to all. Only the youth with a wreath on his head raises one hand, a movement repeated by the man with his back to us. Their being corresponds to that of the tree trunks, the hills behind them and the clouds suspended in the sky. '*Une méditation plastique*' is the phrase offered by A. Châtelet and J. Thuillier to describe the creative method on which such pictures of Poussin's are founded.[29] Traces of this method are to be found in many of his other works.

The famous Louvre painting of *The Arcadian Shepherds* has afforded keen argument to scholars.[30] To compare it with Guercino's picture of the same subject helps us to understand Poussin's conception of the joyous world of Arcady and of the inevitable end of all living things. Yet discussion of the idea behind the painting has almost always been centred on the inscription engraved on the tomb. It has generally been forgotten that, independently of this fragmentary text, the artist gave his answer to the central problems of existence by means of his own pictorial art – by the positioning of the figures, by their attitudes, and in all that he chose to include in the picture.

Although the heavy stone sarcophagus is almost hidden by figures, it nevertheless forms the focal point of the composition. At the same time its shape echoes and corresponds to that of the picture itself, which gives it an added air of solidity. The living figures of the shepherds, two of which repeat each other exactly as in a mirror, are moulded against the background of the sarcophagus as in a frieze on a wall. One of them has turned away from the inscription and is gazing spell-bound at the stately woman who is walking past shepherds and sarcophagus as though, for her, they did not exist. In her aloofness from her surroundings she looks like a creature from the world of essence strayed into the world of phenomena. The sarcophagus may serve as a grim reminder of mortality even in the happy land of Arcady, but the beautiful woman, as perfect in her proportions as the columns which the artist had so admired at Nîmes, expresses a conviction of the eternal value of beauty. Poussin's picture does not make any direct statement to this effect, but it implies it. The Hermitage *Tancred and Erminia* speaks a similar language. It makes no attempt to retell Tasso's poem through the medium of colour. It is rather the result of the artist's own meditations on the sufferings of the lovers and the sweet power of love.

This characteristic of Poussin's which we have tried to

29. A. Châtelet and J. Thuillier, *La Peinture française de Fouquet à Poussin*, Geneva, 1963, p. 219.

30. E. Panofsky, 'Et in Arcadia ego', *Philosophy and History: Essays presented to Ernst Cassirer*, 1936, p. 223; J. Klein, 'An Analysis of Poussin's *Et in Arcadia ego*', *Art Bulletin*, XIX, 1937, p. 314; W. Weisbach, 'Et in Arcadia ego', *GBA*, 1937, II, p. 287; E. Panovsky, 'Et in Arcadia ego et le tombeau', *GBA*, 1938, I, p. 305.

explain is an important feature of his art. It would be a mistake, however, to think that he followed it in all his works. His rendering of another theme from Tasso, the Dulwich *Rinaldo and Armida*,[31] has much in common with the Hermitage *Tancred and Erminia*. In the Moscow *Rinaldo and Armida* (Fig. 5), however, although the execution is similar to that of the Hermitage painting, which permits us to assume that they were executed at about the same time, Poussin is very much more of an illustrator; he sparkles with erudition.[32] Some of the figures, such as the river-god and the cupid, appear to have been introduced for no better reason than decoration; and the composition lacks that unity which so enchants us in *Tancred and Erminia*. Poussin is still further from 'plastic contemplation' in the Louvre *Judgement of Solomon*, although he himself valued the picture very highly. One is tempted to describe it as a picturesque pantomime. One of the women is pleading with the King, using expressive, theatrical gestures; the other demands justice. King Solomon and the witnesses are also gesturing. These gestures are easy to interpret and to convey in words, but the picture does not provide us with an insight into that inexpressible, numinous world, into those mysteries of the human condition, on which the artist touched in his other works.

There have recently been attempts to link Poussin's method with that of the Bolognese. Reference is made to the similarity of the classic subject matter, the plastic modelling of form, the fidelity to Renaissance traditions, but the differences between Poussin and the Carracci and their followers are at least as great as the similarities. In the works of the latter, the crudely modelled figures seem to exclude space, there are no halftones and no ambience of light; the relationships of one object to another are elementary in the extreme. The preparation of the compositions *qua* compositions seems less carefully thought out.

In the works of Poussin's fellow-countrymen, even where they attempted similar themes, we once again fail to find any close analogies with his method. There is perhaps a certain similarity between Simon Vouet's *Armida seducing Rinaldo*[33] and the Birmingham version of *Tancred and Erminia*, but it bears no resemblance to the Hermitage picture. Even in the works of artists to some extent influenced by Poussin and who considered themselves at least partly his disciples, studying and annotating his works, such as Laurent de La Hyre, Sébastien Bourdon, Le Sueur and Le Brun, we fail to rediscover the great master's 'method'. Closer analogies to the essential features of Poussin's art are to be found in the works of artists who are usually contrasted with him as representatives of quite a different stylistic tradition in French art. Thus, for instance, in Watteau's *fêtes galantes*, particularly in the *Embarquement de*

Cythère, although the costumes, manners and outward appearance of the figures have nothing in common with Poussin's, they yet express certain universal human states of being, they are obedient to the same rhythms which Poussin sought after in the nude bodies of his bacchantes.[34] Chardin should also be mentioned here, although he is generally placed under a different heading in the classification of styles. The uninhibited sensuality and pliant figures of Fragonard's *Baigneuses* (Louvre) are usually compared to Boucher, yet the inevitability and harmony of the pattern which they weave, that compositional arabesque which transfigures the sense of the picture, calls to mind Poussin's *Childhood of Bacchus*.

During the period of Neo-classicism at the end of the eighteenth and the beginning of the nineteenth century, Poussin attracted considerable attention, but he was valued chiefly for his moral qualities and his ability to convey strength. In this respect, Diderot was in agreement with Buonaparte.[35] However, two great masters of the nineteenth century came very close to Poussin's method. Daumier resembled him in such pictures as his *Refugees*, where the analogy is with the generalized forms of Poussin's drawings for *The Crossing of the Red Sea*. Cézanne, as is well known, spoke of re-doing Poussin from nature, and it can justly be said that his *Baigneuse* was an attempt to understand and recreate nature by Poussin's method.

The Hermitage *Tancred and Erminia* holds its place not only in the history of the French School, but also in the history of world art. In his love of the Ancient World, Poussin was influenced by the monuments of Imperial Rome which he had permanently before him. Hence the majestic solemnity, the tension and sobriety of many of his works. In the Birmingham *Tancred and Erminia*, in particular, the sharply defined forms are reminiscent of the reliefs on Roman triumphal arches. In the Hermitage picture, however, Poussin came closer to the clear and noble simplicity of the Greeks. He could not have known the Greek Stele in the Villa Albani which was discovered only a century after his death (Fig. 6). Yet a comparison of this monument and Poussin's picture helps us to understand what he was trying to achieve. The Greek artist transforms the victory of the mounted youth over his enemy into a quintessential image of human beauty and youthful prowess. Essentially, in Poussin's Hermitage picture too, the images of the warriors, the woman and the horses are not only participants in a certain event but have also become eternal symbols of human existence.[36] Therein lies Poussin's greatness.

31. *Exp.*, Cat. no. 14.

32. Ch. Sterling, *Musée de l'Ermitage*, p. 31.

33. A. Châtelet and J. Thuillier, *op. cit.* in note 29, p. 196.

34. E. Panovsky, 'Et in Arcadia ego', p. 244: the 'Fêtes champêtres' of Watteau as allegory of transcendence.

35. M. Sauerländer, 'Die Jahreszeiten: ein Beitrag zur allegorischen Landschaft beim späten Poussin', *Münchener Jahrbuch*, 1956, p. 169; A. Chastel, 'Poussin et la postérité', *Colloque Nicolas Poussin*, I, Paris, 1960, p. 302.

36. O. Grautoff, *op. cit.*, I, p. 108, affirms that Poussin 'den Gegenstand über das Anekdotenhafte ins Allgemein-Menschliche erhebt'.

RENSSELAER W. LEE

Mola and Tasso

IN his *Inventaire des tableaux du roy* made in 1709 and 1710, Nicolas Bailly included three paintings by Pier Francesco Mola.[1] One is the famous *St. Bruno*, now in the Louvre, while the other two, the subjects of this essay, are listed with incorrect titles. The first of these (Fig. 1), says Bailly, depicts '*Tancrède qui panse un soldat blessé*', but according to the nineteenth canto of Torquato Tasso's *Gerusalemme liberata*, it is Tancred himself who is wounded and who is tended by Erminia and Vafrino. The second painting (Fig. 2), according to Bailly, portrays '*Angélique qui écrit sur un tronc d'arbre*', but while it is true that Angelica, the heroine of Ariosto's *Orlando furioso*, writes, or rather carves, on trees,[2] she does this in the company of her lover Orlando, who, in art, sometimes shares her pastime,[3] whereas the lonely figure in Mola's picture is Erminia in the guise of a shepherdess who carves the name of Tancred on a tree, from the seventh canto of Tasso's poem. Actually, the bills and receipts of 1685 when the pictures entered the Royal Collection get the titles straight and so do later inventories. Bailly, a miniaturist, was evidently not strong on his Italian literature. The two paintings were honored by being placed in the *Petit Appartement du Roi* in the flattering entourage of Paolo Veroneses, Domenichinos, Van Dycks and famous Poussins. In their modest and elegiac way they must have stood up rather well. Exactly a century later they were in the Louvre, and early in the nineteenth century were still in favor for they were reproduced in engraving with laudatory notices in the *Galerie du Musée Napoléon*.[4] In 1875, however, they left the limelight and were retired to

the Élysée Palace where they courted obscurity for many years, perhaps affording fugitive pleasure to the presidents of the Republic. The *Erminia as a Shepherdess* has now retreated even further from the public eye and shyly reposes in a small room in the Palais du Sénat. Better fortune, however, has attended the *Tancred and Erminia* which was acquired in 1955 by the De Young Museum in San Francisco.[5] The absence of both pictures from public notice for the better part of a century, still the fate of the *Erminia* in Paris, seems to have prevented their cutting any figure in Mola criticism.[6]

The taste for Tasso in France, manifested by the acquisition of these paintings in 1685 for Louis XIV, had been of long standing. Setting aside the immense popularity of the *Aminta*, the finest example in literature of what has been well called the pastoral of happiness,[7] the *Gerusalemme* was avidly read in France almost at once after its publication in 1581, the year which saw the first French edition as well.[8] During the last years of the sixteenth and throughout the seventeenth centuries it exerted a wide influence on literature, music and painting, an influence which was maintained at full tempo during the eighteenth century, and projected with added fascination for Tasso himself as a hapless romantic genius, as the 'illustre malhereux', into the nineteenth. Very early the dramatists and the writers of *romans*, chivalric or sentimental, fell under Tasso's spell, openly borrowing various episodes from the *Gerusalemme*; later, epic (such as it was) and romance assimilated them into a larger fabric. These episodes were the romantic and often pathetic stories to which the poem owes its perma-

1. Ed. F. Engerrand, Paris, 1899, pp. 213–215. The editor's notes give the history of the paintings to the end of the nineteenth century.
2. Canto XIX, stanza 36.
3. She is the sole performer, for instance, in a drawing by Ciro Ferri in Düsseldorf (Illa Budde, *Beschreibender Katalog der Hand-zeichnungen in der Staatlichen Kunstakademie Düsseldorfs*, Düsseldorf, 1930, p. 36, no. 255), in a drawing by G. B. Tiepolo in the National Gallery of Art, Washington (A. Miller, *The Drawings of Tiepolo*, London, 1956, pl. 20), and in one of his famous frescoes in the Villa Valmarana in Vicenza (R. Pallucchini, *Gli affreschi di Giambattista Tiepolo alla Villa Valmarana di Vicenza*, Bergamo, 1945, pl. 34). Occasionally both carve, as in Jacques Blanchard's painting in the Metropolitan Museum, New York, but most frequently Orlando is the performer (Laurent de la Hire, Marseilles; Michele Rocca, Walters Art Gallery, Baltimore; a drawing by G. B. Tiepolo in the Ashmolean Museum, Oxford; and other examples).
4. 10 vols., Paris, Filhol, 1804–15. For the *Erminia and Tancred*, see IV, pl. 285; for the *Erminia as a Shepherdess*, IX, pl. 586. The engravings are after drawings by A. J. F. Gregorius.

5. See *The Samuel H. Kress Collection, M. H. DeYoung Memorial Museum*, San Francisco, 1955, p. 61.
6. F. Villot, in his *Notice des tableaux exposés dans les galeries du Musée Impérial du Louvre*, I, Paris, 1865, p. 169, gives the size of the *Erminia as a Shepherdess* as 70 by 94 cm., that of the *Erminia and Tancred* as 69 by 93 cm. He calls the paintings pendants, which they are in size and subject, though there may be some difference in the date.
7. See R. Poggioli, 'The Oaten Flute', *Harvard Library Bulletin*, XI, 1957, pp. 157–158. This brilliant article deserves the attention of everyone interested in the psychology of pastoral poetry.
8. See Chandler B. Beall, *La Fortune du Tasse en France*, Eugene (Oregon), 1942, p. 14. The first seven chapters of this book contain a mine of information on Tasso's influence on French literature and criticism during the seventeenth century. A more recent book by Joyce G. Simpson, *Le Tasse et la littérature et l'art baroques en France*, Paris, 1962, propounds the interesting thesis that it was the baroque element in Tasso which brought him popularity in France and was the source of his influence on French art and letters.

nent reputation: Olindo and Sofronia tied to the stake and saved by Clorinda, the death and baptism of Clorinda at the hands of Tancred, the famous love story of Rinaldo and Armida, most popular of all, and, more rarely, Erminia's love for Tancred and her sojourn among the shepherds. As the seventeenth century advanced, indeed before it had half run its course, Tasso's theory of epic poetry was treated with respect. The *Gerusalemme* was admired by the critics as a rival of the *Iliad* and the *Aeneid* and considered with them a proper source, whether for plot, content or ornament, for those French writers who wished to attempt the noblest form of poetry.[9] And although near the century's three-quarter mark, Boileau, arch-defender of the ancients, with an eye to those inferior purveyors of the contemporary epic who looked to Tasso, could castigate the fools at court who preferred 'le clinquant de Tasse à tout l'or de Virgile',[10] people kept reading the illustrious Italian. La Fontaine esteemed him,[11] Racine and Madame de Sévigné quoted him in their letters,[12] the *Gerusalemme*, as it had earlier, provided subjects for the Royal Ballet, and Quinault, in 1685, the year in which Mola's paintings entered the Royal Collection, wrote the book for the most famous opera of the century, Lully's *Armide, tragédie en musique*.[13]

A decade and more after its publication, about the time of the first French translations in 1595, French artists, as well as writers, had begun to draw lively inspiration from the *Gerusalemme* and before 1614 two cycles of paintings illustrating the poem were executed by painters of the Second School of Fontainbleau, one by Ambroise Dubois portraying the story of the warrior maiden Clorinda in which Tancred, the wounded figure in Mola's picture, plays, as we have noted above, a prominent part;[14] the second by Dubois and others depicting the story of Olindo and Sofronia.[15] And in the course of the next twenty years Simon Vouet, a few years after his return from Italy in 1627, was to paint his famous series of twelve paintings illustrating the whole history of Rinaldo's infatuation with Armida,[16] and Nicolas Poussin, Tasso's greatest pictorial

interpreter, was also to devote four paintings to the *Gerusalemme's* most famous episode.[17] In choosing subjects from Tasso the French painters were not only in accord with the taste of their literary contemporaries; they were also following the lead of their Italian colleagues who painted Tasso subjects throughout the century. In fact, in 1683 Domenichino's beautiful *Erminia and the Shepherd* and, in 1685, his *Rinaldo and Armida*, both now in the Louvre, entered the Royal Collection.[18] These and the two paintings by Mola in which Erminia is a protagonist (Figs. 1, 2), also purchased, as we have seen, in 1685, are further testimony to Tasso's vogue in France which had lasted a full century.

The story of Erminia had less fascination than more erotic or dramatic episodes in the *Gerusalemme* for people of literary profession and taste in seventeenth-century France, probably because the great interest in the pastoral during the century was concentrated on the *Aminta*, a pastoral drama *pur sang*, whereas the first part, at least, of the story of Erminia is merely a bucolic intermezzo which breaks the serious martial action of an epic poem. The passage at the beginning of the seventh canto[19] which recounts Erminia's meeting with the shepherd and her sojourn in the country, one of the most interesting and beautiful in Italian literature, also reflects very subtly the sensitive thoughtfulness, the loneliness and the melancholy of Tasso's own soul. Erminia, a pagan princess of Antioch and the most tenderly appealing of his heroines, has fallen secretly in love with Tancred, the noblest warrior among the crusaders who are besieging Jerusalem, and this love cannot be returned because Tancred has fallen in love with Erminia's friend, the warrior maiden Clorinda. As Helen from the walls of Troy had watched the single combat of Paris and Menelaus, so Erminia from Jerusalem's ramparts watches the bloody single encounter of Tancred with the Saracen Hercules, Argante, which is halted by the coming of night. Seeking to heal Tancred's wounds she flees from Jerusalem, clad in the stolen armor of Clorinda, but is pursued by a Christian patrol and, after a perilous night when she sleeps beside the river Jordan,[20] finds her way to a shepherd's hut, at first

9. Such authors as Georges de Scudéry (*Alaric, ou Rome vaincue*, 1654) or Jean Chapelain (*La Pucelle ou la France délivrée*, 1656). See Beall, *op. cit.*, pp. 80–104; Simpson, *op. cit.*, pp. 91–95.
10. *Satire IX*, 1668, 173–176; cf. *L'Art poétique*, III, 1674, 205–216.
11. *Épître XXII*.
12. See Beall, *op. cit.*, pp. 109–110.
13. *Ibid.*, pp. 62, 120 ff.
14. See Le Père Dan, *Trésor des merveilles de la maison royale de Fontainebleau*, 1642, pp. 145–146; L. Dimier, *French Painting in the Sixteenth Century*, London, 1904, p. 269. Three of the eight paintings survive today, two still at Fontainebleau, one in the Louvre.
15. See A. Félibien, *Entretiens sur les vies . . . des plus excellents peintres anciens et modernes*, III, Trévoux, 1735, pp. 127–129. The ten paintings of this cycle are lost. Cf. Dimier, *op. cit.*, pp. 279–280.
16. See W. R. Crelly, *The Painting of Simon Vouet*, New Haven and London, 1962, pp. 105–106, 205.

17. See *The Drawings of Nicolas Poussin*, II, ed. Walter Friedlaender (in collaboration with Anthony Blunt and Rudolf Wittkower), p. 21. Cf. R. W. Lee, 'Armida's Abandonment: A Study in Tasso Iconography Before 1700', in *De Artibus opuscula XL: Essays in Honor of Erwin Panofsky*, New York, 1961, pp. 335–349 (n. 3, p. 336, lists various articles dealing with Tasso's influence on the history of painting), and A. Blunt in *Catalogue de l'Exposition Nicolas Poussin*, Paris, 1960, p. 41.
18. Bailly, *Inventaire*, ed. F. Engerrand, pp. 135–136, 165. The *Erminia and the Shepherd* was listed by Bailly as an *Armida with a Shepherd* by Annibale Carracci.
19. The first 22 stanzas. The concluding stanzas of the sixth canto are introductory to the pastoral episode in the seventh.
20. Andrea Camassei sketched the title-page for the score of an opera entitled *Erminia sul Giordano*, by Michelangelo Rossi, a pupil of Frescobaldi, which was performed in 1637. Camassei's invention, engraved by F. Greuter (Paris, Bibliothèque Nationale, Ec. 8,

frightening his children by her warlike attire. The encounter of the gentle, way-worn Erminia with the shepherd and his family in the remote and peaceful country far from the clangor of arms, a sophisticated pastoral of infinite charm and the most tender humanity, was, as historians of painting well know, a favorite subject among Italian and French artists for well over two centuries. It enlisted the talents particularly of the great Bolognese painters of the seventeenth century – Annibale Carracci, Domenichino as we have seen, Albani and Guercino – and had its worthy swan-song in Delacroix in the mid-nineteenth.[21]

The next moment in the episode which occasionally attracted the painters – notably Guercino and Pietro da Cortona – is the conversation between Erminia and the shepherd.[22] He persuades her that a tranquil, bucolic life, untroubled by the violence of war or the iniquity of courts, is the best therapy known to man, and she decides to remain with the shepherd and his family until fortune shall facilitate her return to the fitful fever of life. In the humble dress of a shepherdess she tends her flocks during the day, bringing them to the fold at night. Often in the summer heat when her lambs are resting in the shade, she follows the ancient pastoral custom, widely favored during the Renaissance and after and sanctioned by Virgil,[23] of carving the name of her beloved on trees while on others she inscribes the story of her unhappy destiny. Thus we see her in a painting of 1640 by Salvator Rosa[24] in Modena, perhaps the first example in art of this subject, in which, at the left, under a group of trees, the light striking the upper part of her body, she has carved as far as the letter N in Tancred's name, while at the right the painter deploys his genius for

landscape in a wide view over a bucolic paradise with flocks and herds and idle shepherds in the foreground. Mola's painting, probably some fifteen to twenty years later (Fig. 2), has essentially the composition of Salvator's, but where in his picture the handsome landscape steals the thunder from the action, in Mola's the firm and well-lit triangle formed by Erminia and her flock and her intent concentration as she carves Tancred's name, her arm and hand seen in clear silhouette against an aperture of light, command major attention. The picture is a fine interpretation of the characteristic union of the idyllic and the elegiac in Tasso's episode: the gentle and forlorn Erminia in the country amid the musical and sympathetic voices of nature, 'secretari del suo amore antico', inscribing the trees with Tancred's name and with the story of her unhappy plight, and bidding them preserve her memory for other lovers who may rest in their shade. Mola's own idyllic and elegiac sense which have been often remarked upon[25] must have found congenial matter in the adventures of the sensitive, star-crossed princess. The dark tonality of the richly painted landscape is in harmonious accord with the poetic mood. The composition, and elements of the landscape, recall Venice and Bologna, twin sources, as Mola's biographers tell us, of his pictorial inspiration;[26] more specifically, perhaps, the muted sumptuousness of the color recalls, at long range, Titian and the early Guercino. But in this subjective world of the Arcadian imagination, musical and melancholy, this 'tranquillity of Arcadian scenes and fairyland', to recall Sir Joshua Reynolds's famous characterization of Claude Lorrain,[27] Tasso does not permit Erminia to abide. In due course she must return to the life of action and fulfil her destiny.

This, as we read in a celebrated passage which concludes the nineteenth canto of the *Gerusalemme*,[28] is to discover Tancred desperately wounded, to give him effective first aid and to nurse him back to health. The crusader and his mortal foe, Argante, have retired to a hidden valley to finish their interrupted single combat. Vafrino, Tancred's squire, and Erminia, secretly quitting the Egyptian camp where Erminia has perforce taken refuge and in which Vafrino has undertaken a mission of espionage for the Christians, are returning to Jerusalem at sunset by remote paths when they discover, first, the dead body of Argante

64), shows Erminia armed, asleep by the Jordan; a putto holding a flaming torch and the river god are also present. See H. Goldschmidt, *Studien zur Geschichte der italienischen Oper im 17. Jahrhundert*, Leipzig, 1901, pp. 62 ff. and *Die Künstlerbiographien von Giovanni Battista Passeri*, ed. J. Hess, Leipzig and Vienna, 1934, p. 170. The scene of Erminia by the Jordan had already appeared in illustrations by Bernardo Castello for canto VII in the 1604 and 1617 editions of the *Gerusalemme* and by Antonio Tempesta in the 1607 edition.

21. Annibale's painting is in the National Gallery, London (it has been recently attributed by Professor Donald Posner of New York University, in an unpublished thesis on Annibale, to his pupil, Panico); Domenichino's in the Louvre; Albani's in the Colonna Gallery, Rome; Guercino's in the Minneapolis Institute of Arts; Delacroix's in the National Museum, Stockholm. For a discussion of the episode of Erminia in Italian painting, see R. W. Lee, 'Erminia in Minneapolis' in *Studies in Criticism and Aesthetics, 1660–1800, in honor of Samuel Holt Monk*, Minneapolis, University of Minnesota Press, 1967, pp. 36–56.

22. Guercino's painting is in City Museum and Art Gallery at Birmingham, Pietro da Cortona's in the Doria Gallery. See Lee, *ibid.*, pp. 47 ff.

23. In the *Tenth Eclogue*, 52–54, where Gallus will carve the name of Lycoris.

24. See R. Pallucchini, *I dipinti della Galleria Estense di Modena*, Rome, 1945, p. 233. The painting is reproduced in Lee, *op. cit.*, pl. IV.

25. For instance by H. Voss, in 'Di Pierfrancesco Mola, pittore e incisore comasco', *Rivista archeologica della provincia e antica diocesi di Como*, 1910, p. 189 and in *Die Malerei des Barock in Rom*, Berlin, 1924, pp. 559–560; also by R. Wittkower, *Art and Architecture in Italy*, Baltimore, 1958, p. 215.

26. See *Passeri*, ed. Hess, *op. cit.*, pp. 368–369 and L. Pascoli, *Vite de' pittori, scultori, ed architetti moderni*, I, Rome, 1730, p. 123. Cf. P. J. Mariette, *Abécédario*, IV, ed. Ph. de Chennevières et A. de Montaiglon, Paris, 1857–58, p. 3, and the remarks on the sources of Mola's style by W. Arslan, 'Opere romane di Pier Francesco Mola', *BdA*, VIII, 1928, pp. 55–80.

27. Discourse XIII.

28. Stanzas 101 ff.

and, a moment later, a Christian warrior, lying unconscious, who, when Vafrino removes his helmet, is revealed to be Tancred. This is the setting for the dramatic and pathetic episode of Erminia's discovery and care of the wounded warrior, a particular moment of which Mola illustrated in the San Francisco picture (Fig. 1). It was an episode which had already engaged the talents of several distinguished painters during the seventeenth century, not to mention others of less renown.

Evidently the painters read the story *con amore* for they followed Tasso's text with meticulous care. The exact moments which they illustrate are generally confined to four stanzas: one (104) which recounts Erminia's impassioned action when she recognizes the apparently lifeless warrior on the ground as Tancred:

> Vista la faccia scolorita e bella
>
> Non scese, no, precipitò di sella;

and a later triad of stanzas (111–113) which describe her tender and effective ministrations.[29] In the intervening passage she utters her passionate and moving lament, famous lines which, with her sorrowful invocation to the trees in the seventh canto, had already within Tasso's lifetime become the inspiration of music.[30]

It is interesting to observe with what precision each painter chooses the moment in the story which he wishes to portray. Thus the Neapolitan artist Paolo Finoglio, shortly after 1636 in a picture whose violent contrasts of light and shade are appropriate to the drama of Erminia's discovery, shows her actually in the air as she flings herself from the saddle towards the swooning Tancred whose helmet Vafrino has just removed and whose identity he reveals to Erminia with a dramatic gesture.[31] What immediately

follows was depicted by Guercino, one of the most ardent illustrators of the *Gerusalemme*, in two paintings: one, a late picture at Castle Howard[32] which shows Erminia now dismounted and rushing towards Tancred with arms outspread in the antique gesture of grief,[33] the second, a magnificent picture in his early manner, in the Doria Gallery (Fig. 3),[34] where Vafrino, kneeling at Tancred's head, uncovers his wounds while Erminia bends over him with upraised hands, a *Lamentation* in content and composition in which Erminia's gesture, which also has ancient origins, recalls the gesture of the Magdalen in religious art. These paintings all relate to the moments of discovery and recognition which precede Tasso's account of Erminia's drying and bandaging Tancred's wounds, first with her veil, then with tresses of her own hair, 'inusitate fasce', the use of which love reveals to her since her light and unsubstantial veil is insufficient. In a beautiful and poignant picture of the 1640s in Lord Methuen's collection (Fig. 5), close in its pity and passionate tenderness to the spirit of Tasso's poetry, Pietro da Cortona depicts Vafrino supporting Tancred while Erminia stanches his wounds with her veil.[35] The succeeding moment Poussin illustrated in his spacious and romantic masterpiece of about 1630 in Leningrad (Fig. XXV, 1)[36] which, it is a pleasure to remark in an essay dedicated to Sir Anthony Blunt and with all due respect to the later *Erminia and Tancred* in Birmingham,[37] must rank as the finest pictorial interpretation of this, or perhaps any, Tasso subject. This remarkable picture shows Erminia severing the locks of her hair with Tancred's sword, the scabbard of which lies nearby on the ground, while Vafrino supports the hero's body, kneeling at his head. The use of the sword,

29.   'Apre Tancredi gli occhi, e poi gli abbassa
           Torbidi e gravi: ed ella pur si lagna.
           Dice Vafrino a lei: Questi non passa;
           Curisi adunque prima, e poi si piagna.
           Egli il disarma; ella tremante e lassa
           Porge le mano a l'opere compagna;
           Mira e tratta le piaghe e, di ferute
           Guidice esperta, spera indi salute

       'Vede che il mal, da la stanchezza nasce
           E da gli umori in troppa copia sparti.
           Ma non ha, fuor ch'un velo, onde gli fasce
           Le sue ferite in sì solinghe parti.
           Amor le trova inusitate fasce,
           E di pietà le insegna insolite arti:
           Le asciugò con le chiome, e rilegolle
           Pur con le chiome, che troncar si volle;

       'Però che il velo suo bastar non puote
           Breve e sottile a le sì spesse piaghe.'

30. In the eighth book of madrigals by Giaches Wert, published in 1586, only five years after the appearance of the *Gerusalemme*. The composers of the period took a decisive step towards pathos when they turned from the *Orlando furioso* to Tasso's poem. See A. Einstein, *The Italian Madrigal*, II, Princeton, 1949, pp. 568, 574–575.

31. This is one of a highly interesting series of ten pictures, illustrat-

ing the *Gerusalemme*, still, I believe, in the Castello of Conversano near Bari. See Mario d'Orsi, 'Paolo Finoglio, pittore napoletano', *Iapigia* (Organo della R. Deputazione di Storia Patria per le Puglie), XVII, 1938, pp. 365–366, and fig. 28.

32. It was painted for Cardinal Fabrizio Savelli, but acquired and paid for in 1652 by the Archduchess of Mantua. See Lee, 'Erminia in Minneapolis' in *Studies in Criticism and Aesthetics, 1660–1800*, p. 56, note 29. Probably a good copy of the painting, not the original, was engraved by Pietro Bonato in 1805. I am indebted to Denis Mahon for this information.

33. A similar gesture and an almost identical composition are found in Guercino's *Venus and Adonis* in Dresden, painted for Cardinal Mazarin in 1647, where a putto stands at the head of Adonis who lies on the ground and Venus rushes forward, her hands raised, to kneel beside his body. See *Die Staatliche Gemäldegalerie zu Dresden, Die Romanischen Länder*, Dresden, 1929, p. 169, and the illustration, p. 170.

34. It was painted in 1618 for Marcello Provenzali and engraved by Pasqualini in 1620. See C. C. Malvasia, *Felsina pittrice*, Bologna, 1841, p. 259 (first ed. 1678).

35. See G. Briganti, *Pietro da Cortona o della pittura barocca*, Florence, 1962, pp. 224–225.

36. See Denis Mahon, *Poussiniana*, Paris and New York, 1962, pp. 27–28.

37. At the Barber Institute of Fine Arts. See A. Blunt in *Catalogue de l'Exposition Nicolas Poussin*, Paris, 1960, no. 53, pp. 87–88, and the illustration.

not mentioned by Tasso who merely says 'le chiome, che troncar si volle', is Poussin's fine invention, showing his instinct both for Aristotelian probability and poetic appropriateness.[38] The action in the dark and lonely valley, seen against the sunset sky of Tasso's poem, is cast in grave and noble rhythms, the emphatic yet fluently constructed triangle of the protagonists being grandly framed by a kind of exedra formed by the swinging curves of the great horses. In its setting, in its chivalry, in its expression of emotion, Poussin's picture guards the romantic sentiment of Tasso's episode, but also changes its passionate and sometimes rhetorical pathos into a reticent pity and tenderness. And this is characteristic of an artist who, as Reynolds said, was 'as it were, naturalized in antiquity'.[39]

These interesting interpretations of Tasso's pathetic story may serve as a background and a contrast to Mola's later painting in San Francisco (Fig. 1). Like the *Erminia* in Paris (Fig. 2), it shows, one may be bold to surmise, a mature style and may have been painted around 1655, somewhat earlier perhaps than the Paris picture where the lyrical sense for landscape, a mark of his late painting, is more profound, the tonality darker and richer, and the effect more painterly.[40] Mola's *Erminia and Tancred* is, however, a charming picture, elegiac in feeling, less passionate than Pietro da Cortona's version, less evocative and profound than Poussin's. Like the other painters, Mola had read Tasso's stanzas carefully; he illustrates a very precise moment in the narrative which we have not encountered before when Erminia, having helped Vafrino to remove Tancred's arms, 'mira e tratta le piaghe' – carefully inspects and diagnoses the extent of his wounds; this is surely the meaning of her intent gaze and of the examining touch of her fingers. The composition of the picture: masses of tree and cliff at the right with the horse's head turned towards the action, contrasted with deep space to the left, the dead Argante being seen in the middle distance, recalls Pietro da Cortona about a decade earlier (Fig. 5). In Mola, however, the action has been shifted from the right to the center of the picture and the positions of Erminia and Vafrino have been changed to form with the reclining body of Tancred a group which, while it recalls sixteenth- and seventeenth-century compositions of the *Lamentation* or *Entombment* or of other subjects of elegiac content, Christian or Pagan, cast in their mold, has the further interest of showing a clear and direct

relationship with scenes of funerary content on antique sarcophagi. In particular, Mola could have seen in Rome during the sixth and seventh decades of the seventeenth century, when he was at the height of his powers and painted the scenes from Tasso discussed in this essay, a number of sarcophagi which displayed the pathetic scene of the dying Meleager's last homecoming (Fig. 4). On these the hero is carried by a bearer who supports his head and shoulders while one or more may support his legs; standing behind him, a bearded figure – Robert calls him the pedagogue – places his left hand for support under Meleager's left wrist or forearm.[41] Such an antique group had certainly served in the early sixteenth century as a prototype for Raphael's Borghese *Entombment* where the essential arrangement is the same. The group of three figures in Mola's painting is equally indebted to the Meleager group. It also anticipates, as it were, the moment when Meleager's body will lie on his deathbed, a moment not represented on these sarcophagi which show the body carried, but portrayed on another type of sarcophagi which show the hero's death. But the closest ancient parallel to the composition of the group of Vafrino, Erminia and Tancred in Mola's picture is in the carrying scene illustrated here, exclusive, of course, of the figures supporting Meleager's legs which Tasso's story did not require. The bearer supporting Meleager's head and shoulders, the pedagogue sustaining his forearm, and the body of Meleager itself all have close counterparts in Mola's group.[42] In particular, Erminia's action in supporting the weight of Tancred's forearm, showing the limpness of the wounded warrior's hand, amounts to a signature of antiquity, especially since the relationship of the three figures in the group is so closely that of the corresponding figures on the ancient sarcophagi.[43] Thus Mola,

38. One may compare Pietro Cavallino's charming picture in Munich (Aldo de Rinaldis, *Neapolitan Painting of the Seicento*, New York, 1929, pl. 38) where, however, the painter shows scant respect for the Aristotelian proprieties for he depicts her cutting off her hair with a pair of scissors. The final moment in Erminia's care of Tancred when she bandages his wounds with her hair is conspicuous by its absence in painting: the only example I know is a damaged picture by Ottavio Vannini (1585–1643) which has been relegated to the Palazzo Pretorio in Arezzo.

39. *Discourse* XIV.

40. See Arslan, *BdA*, VIII, pp. 73 ff.

41. The detail of the sarcophagus in Fig. 5 is reproduced after a seventeenth-century drawing in the Uffizi, from C. Robert, *Die antiken Sarcophag-Reliefs*, III, Part II, Berlin, 1890, pl. XCIV, fig. 283[1]. The sarcophagus was set into a wall of the Casino, built in 1644–50, of the Villa Pamfili. For other sarcophagi visible during the seventeenth century or earlier, *ibid.*, pls. XCVI and XCVIII; for the Meleager legends, pp. 334–346, and cf. the account in the *Oxford Classical Dictionary*, Oxford, 1957, p. 554.

42. This fundamental grouping of three figures is also found on the sarcophagi which portray the dying Meleager, after his return home, reclining on his couch. Here a male figure supports the dying man's head and a female figure making a gesture of grief, but not supporting his arm as in Fig. 5, stands on the far side of the couch. This was the type of sarcophagus which served as a model for Poussin in such paintings as the *Death of Germanicus* and the *Extreme Unction* of the second series of *Sacraments*. For examples visible during Mola's activity in Rome, see Robert, *op. cit.*, III, Part II, pls. XCII–XCIII and pp. 338 ff. Cf. Walter Friedlaender, *Nicolas Poussin*, New York, 1966, pp. 19–20 and Sofie-Charlotte Emmerling, *Antikenverwendung und Antikenstudium bei Nicolas Poussin*, Würzburg, 1939, tafel I.

43. The same motif occurs again in ancient art in a scene of the *Bewailing of Actaeon* on a Roman sarcophagus in the Louvre. Here Autonoë, Actaeon's mother, sinking to her knees behind

before painting this picture, had, like Poussin throughout his life in Rome, studied the ancient reliefs and found in the representation of an elegiac subject the precise artistic model he needed for a modern subject of similar content. Indeed, Erminia's classic head and the quiet restraint of the painter's interpretation of Tasso's pathetic stanzas lend further strength to the belief that the inspiration for the grouping of his figures came from the antique rather than from those sixteenth- and seventeenth-century scenes of sorrowful content, Christian or mythological, which had, themselves, at short or long range, been influenced by these ancient renderings of the last moments of a wounded and dying warrior on Roman sarcophagi.[44]

his body, supports Actaeon's left arm, just as the pedagogue supports Meleager's. In this scene, however, no one supports Actaeon's head as he lies on the ground; his feet are held by a woman who seems to be lowering his body. For the influence of this composition and its pathos on Middle Byzantine art, see K. Weitzmann, 'The Origin of the Threnos' in *De Artibus opuscula XL: Essays in Honor of Erwin Panofsky*, New York, 1961, pp. 487 ff. and fig. 17.

44. The scenes in religious art which in a more or less precise way show the fundamental arrangement of three figures seen on the Meleager sarcophagi generally have the additional figures which the scriptural or legendary accounts require. Nevertheless, in these *Pietàs*, *Lamentations* and *Entombments*, the three figures, analogous to those in the antique group, are present in the same compositional relationship: Christ, lying on the ground or resting on the Virgin's lap, with his head and shoulders supported by John, Nicodemus or Joseph of Arimathea, while the Virgin or occasionally another figure, seated or kneeling behind Christ's body, supports his wrist or forearm in the antique manner. Thus a *Lamentation* by Ortolano (*Venturi*, IX, Part IV, p. 328, fig. 270) shows Christ supported by a bearded man while the Virgin kneels supporting his left forearm with her left hand; other figures are present including the Magdalen with upthrust hands recalling the gesture in Guercino's *Erminia and Tancred* (Fig. 3); one may compare similar compositions by Ortolano (*ibid.*, p. 335, fig. 275 and p. 337, fig. 276), also a *Lamentation* by Giovanni Paolo Rosseti and a *Pietà* by Vasari (H. Voss, *Die Malerei der Spätrenaissance in Rom und Florenz*, I, Berlin, 1920, p. 135, fig. 36 and p. 275, fig. 94). Titian's famous *Entombment* in the Louvre is highly reminiscent of the Meleager sarcophagi; the body is carried as in the ancient prototype and John supports Christ's hand in the antique manner (cf. O. Brendel, 'Borrowings from Ancient Art in Titian', *ArtB*, XXXVII, 1955, p. 119 and note 21). Very close to the antique grouping of three figures and very close to Mola's picture (Fig. 1), which it predates, is the group of three figures in another religious subject: *St. Irene Removing the Arrows from St. Sebastian's Wounds* by the Fleming Theodor Rombouts, who journeyed to Rome in 1616 (W. Bernt, *Die Niederländischen Maler des 17. Jahrhunderts*, II, Munich, 1948, fig. 685). Pagan subjects of pathetic content are also in debt to the ancient figure arrangement: a *Venus Lamenting the Death of Adonis* by Paolo Veronese (Lionel Cust, *The Bridgewater Gallery*, Westminster, 1903, pl. 14) shows a putto supporting the head and shoulders of Adonis while Venus kneels behind his reclining body supporting his left wrist with her right hand, a highly interesting and precise adaptation of the ancient grouping. Other non-religious examples showing its influence are a *Cephalus and Procris* (1657) by W. Verschoor and a *Death of Socrates* by G.

The *Erminia as a Shepherdess* and the *Erminia and Tancred* are Mola's only paintings inspired by Tasso whose habitation is known today. But according to records of French collections during the late eighteenth and early nineteenth centuries he painted others, testimony to Tasso's continuing popularity in France as well as his own.[45] These include an Erminia 'retirée chez les bergers' which might be another version of the painting in Paris (Fig. 2) and one of Erminia's conversation with the shepherd for which, as we have seen, there were already models in Guercino and Pietro da Cortona. Mola evidently read the episode of Erminia restoring her soul among the shepherds – this and the pathetic sequel of her care of Tancred – with more than usual interest and sympathy. It is, then, not improbable that Tasso's finished picture of the solitude and peace of the country, pervaded with his wholly characteristic sentiment, was a subtle influence on Mola, predisposed, as he was, to the tranquil, the idyllic and the elegiac, not only when he interpreted the *Gerusalemme*, but in other subjects – Hagar, or saints, in the wilderness, the *Rest on the Flight into Egypt* – in which he fully reveals his lyric talent as a landscape painter. Affinity between Tasso's Arcadian sentiment and a wider range of seventeenth-century landscape painting is not easy to gauge; this is the kind of relationship between poetry and painting for which the critics, otherwise acutely aware of their humanistic kinship, had no precise category. But for a century in which the *Gerusalemme* was read with enthusiasm, even to excess as Boileau thought, and alike by painters and *letterati*, it is worth keeping in mind. For in covert as well as conspicuous ways, 'nulla ars, non alterius artis, aut mater, aut propinqua est'.

Cignaroli (A. Pigler, *Barockthemen*, II, Budapest and Berlin, 1956, pp. 55 and 413); in the latter picture the figure whose hand is on Socrates' wrist is feeling his pulse, an interesting variation on the ancient motif. These and other examples, religious and mythological, leave no doubt of the profound influence of the Meleager group. For its history in Renaissance art before Titian's *Entombment* of about 1525 see A. von Salis, *Antike und Renaissance*, Erlenbach–Zürich, 1947, pp. 69 ff.

45. See H. Mireur, *Dictionnaire des ventes d'art*, V, Paris, 1911, pp. 237–238. For an account of Mola's reputation in France among distinguished collectors, as well as pertinent remarks on his style, see C. Sterling, 'Guerrier oriental par Pierfrancesco Mola', *Musées de France*, 1950, pp. 33–39.

In preparing this article I have been indebted to Rosalie Green, Jane Mull, Robert Harris, Donald Posner and Ellis Waterhouse for valuable advice.

Author's Note: After the article had gone to press, I learned through the courtesy of Ann Sutherland Harris of another painting showing Erminia carving Tancred's name which had passed through Sotheby's with the wrong title in 1963. I am indebted to Signora Bianca Riccio Baduel of Rome for lending me a photograph of this beautiful, late picture by Mola which is now in a private collection in Milan. I am also greatly indebted to Richard Cocke of Cambridge University for calling my attention recently to several drawings by Mola dealing with Tasso subjects. I shall consider these and the painting in a later article.

MICHAEL KITSON

Claude Lorrain: Two Unpublished Paintings and the Problem of Variants

THE intrinsic beauty of Claude's work is such that the publication of two unknown paintings by him would be worthwhile even if they added nothing to our knowledge of his art. On the face of it, the chance of any radically new information arising from the discovery of further paintings is small, since all 'lost' paintings except the earliest are likely to fit into a ready-made place in the *Liber Veritatis*.[1] More than this, after a slow and varied start as a painter, lasting from his return to Rome from Nancy at the end of 1626[2] until about 1633, Claude was so consistent in his aesthetic approach that any strikingly untypical picture by him is hardly to be expected. If our view of him is to be changed or enlarged by the discovery of new evidence, that evidence is more likely to turn up in the form of documents, drawings or sketches[3] than paintings.

Neither of the two paintings to be discussed here contradicts this; both are *Liber Veritatis* pictures and both are highly characteristic of the artist. Yet both, as it happens, involve a rarely mentioned problem with Claude, that of *pentimenti*. In addition, they both raise anew the difficult question of variants,[4] or 'second originals', in his work and

the bearing these might have on the function of the *Liber Veritatis*. The conclusions to be drawn from the material under review are still very uncertain; it should be said, further, that this material emphasizes an existing problem in our understanding of Claude rather than introduces a new one. Still, the artist's own variants of his paintings have never been studied as such, and it seemed worthwhile to consider the matter, draw up a list of those that are known so far and try to determine whether they conform to any system.

The larger, more beautiful and better preserved of the newly discovered paintings is a *Pastoral Landscape* (Fig. 1) now in an English private collection; it is signed and dated 'CLAVD / 1638' and is exactly recorded in *Liber Veritatis* 23 (Fig. 3).[5] According to the artist's inscription on the back of the *Liber* drawing, the patron was a 'Mr Guefié', i.e. Étienne Gueffier (1576–1660), a French diplomat in Rome who also commissioned another *Pastoral Landscape*, LV 25, from Claude, although not as a *pendant* to LV 23. By *c.* 1720, as stated in the second index of the *Liber*, the painting belonged to 'Mr Danois secretaire du roy à paris'. Its next recorded owner, mentioned by Smith in 1837,[6] was the 2nd Earl of Leitrim (1768–1854), Ireland, with whose descendants it remained until the present century.[7]

---

1. Abbreviation: LV. This famous book, now in the British Museum, is Claude's graphic record of his paintings, containing 195 drawings in chronological order from 1634 until his death in 1682. The latest account of it is in the standard monograph by Marcel Röthlisberger, *Claude Lorrain: the Paintings*, 2 vols., New Haven and London, 1961, pp. 37 f. (abbreviation: R.). The arrangement of Röthlisberger's catalogue follows the order of the *Liber Veritatis* for recorded pictures; others have a separate number. All paintings by Claude except for the few which have turned up since 1961 (see below, note 26) are reproduced in this book.

2. Following Claude's biographer, Baldinucci, this date is usually given as the 18th October 1627; see, most recently, R., p. 6. That Claude almost certainly returned a year earlier is deducible from Eckhart Knab's publication of the relevant *Stati delle Anime*, which show that the artist was in Rome at Easter 1627 ('Die Anfänge des Claude Lorrain', Vienna *Jahrbuch*, LVI, 1960, p. 162). Baldinucci states categorically that Claude arrived on St. Luke's day (18th October); if it was that day in 1626 it would fit with the expiry of his contract with Deruet at Nancy, which ran for a year from 1st October 1625 (R., p. 55).

3. One would particularly like to see further oil sketches from nature, of which hardly any survive; also the mysterious gouache sketches on panel mentioned in Félibien's diary of his visit to Rome in 1647 (Chanoine Y. Delaporte, 'André Félibien en Italie', *GBA*, 6e pér., LI, 1958, p. 206).

4. The term 'variant' rather than 'replica' is used here because, as will be seen, Claude's practice was seldom to repeat a picture

exactly but almost always to change it in some part or parts, while retaining the overall composition. O.E.D. *Variant*, sb. 1. 'A form or modification differing in some respect from other forms of the same thing. . . . 2. A variation of the original work, story, song, etc.'

5. Pen and brown wash, heightened with white, on off-white paper, 18·7 by 26·3 cm. A group of three figures corresponding to those in the centre of the Uffizi *Seaport*, LV 28, appears on the back of the drawing.
A minor problem arises here over the dates of Claude's paintings in this extremely active period of his life. LV 28 is the next dated work in the sequence of the *Liber* after the *Pastoral*, LV 23, but it is dated 1637 (see catalogue of the exhibition, *L'ideale classico* . . ., Bologna, 1962, no. 91), while LV 23 is dated 1638. A possible explanation is that the *Seaport*, Claude's most elaborate and beautiful work of its kind so far, was held back for some reason, perhaps for the addition of extra glazes and other final touches, and so was recorded and despatched to the patron several months after it was effectively complete. The probability that it was already finished before the *Pastoral* is borne out by the figures on the back of the drawing made from the latter.

6. John Smith, *Catalogue raisonné of the Most Eminent Dutch, Flemish and French Painters*, VIII, London, 1837, under no. 23.

7. I am indebted to Mr. John Quilter for this information concern-

The picture's exceptional state of preservation, revealed by recent cleaning,[8] deserves emphasis. Painted on an imperial-size canvas (39½ by 52 ins.[9]), which is larger than usual for Claude at this date although not unprecedented, this *Pastoral Landscape* is the most exquisite of his first mature period – those brilliantly productive years between about 1635 and 1640 when he first fully mastered his means of expression and gained an international reputation. Thanks to the freshness of the surface, the broad brushwork in the foliage, in the bark of the trees, in the animals and in the foreground plants stands out crisply (Fig. 5). There is a spontaneity to this brushwork, an almost bravura quality as well as a delicacy, which reminds us of the analogous use of pen, chalk and wash in the nature drawings of the same period; it was something which Claude sacrificed in his later works to an ever more painstaking elaboration. A tiny blue flower on the bank at the right of the picture by the tree-trunk creates a point of intense colour on this side; there are further less brightly coloured flowers on the same bank and in the foreground. The other colour accents in the painting appear, as we should expect, in the figures: the man in a dull-pink cap, a shot lilac and grey tunic and dull yellow-green breeches, the girl in a blue dress and a jacket of the same dull-pink. As is usual with Claude, these colours take up in concentrated form the hues distributed throughout the landscape.

The overall colour scheme of the painting is a muted grey-green, like that of the less well preserved *Landscape* (LV 8) of 1636 in the Metropolitan Museum, which likewise has trees and figures on a bank beside a mist-covered pond or stream. The thinly painted stream in the *Pastoral* – slightly worn in the middle distance, the only part of the picture not in perfect state – recedes smoothly to the background. Beneath the trees in the right foreground (Fig. 6), shadows and reflections collect and mingle in the darkened water. These shadows are continuous with those among the trees themselves, forming here a *coin de la nature* of absolute stillness, disturbed – in imagination – only by the slight rustle of deer. We are again reminded, in this passage, of the nature drawings. The ruined building on the opposite bank acts as a complementary focus of visual attraction, and it might be argued that the pale sky and misty hills in the centre are only just strong enough pictorially to hold the two sides of the composition together; in later years Claude

would have given this area greater clarity and firmness of detail. Yet he has largely overcome here the abrupt contrast between foreground and background which mars some of his still earlier works.

Compared with those after 1640, this painting is strikingly naturalistic. Apart from the architecture and the tall tree to the right, there is no grandeur to the scene, although both those motives are essential to the balance of the composition. Otherwise the painting is filled with picturesque touches: broken branches, rough edges to the foliage, a tangle of foreground plants, and goats. In few other pictures by Claude is animal life so much in evidence; goats, deer and birds are the real inhabitants of this secluded place, and in comparison with them the figures are onlookers who perform a mainly decorative function. The surface is scattered with flecks and ridges of white or near-white paint representing highlights on animals, twigs and plants. Further flashes of light break through the trees and between the columns of the ruined building – another picturesque effect which Claude abandoned later, just as he afterwards no longer separated the figures emotionally from the landscape, as he does here, but involved both in a uniformly ideal world. The overall light which enters the composition from the left is cool and subdued, although, as so often with Claude, the question whether it is a morning or evening light is hard to decide, In the centre the light has the silvery luminosity of old glass; at the edges it loses itself in shadow which absorbs the local colour,

> 'Annihilating all that's made
> To a green thought in a green shade.'[10]

The mood is one of solitude and utter tranquillity. This *Pastoral* is a rustic idyll in the exact sense of the phrase.

As has already been indicated, it is not the only version of the composition. An authentic, signed variant, identical in height but four inches narrower, belongs to the Earl of Halifax and has hitherto been accepted as the original (Fig. 2).[11] Yet there can be no doubt that Fig. 1 is the first version and the other picture the second. When both are compared with the *Liber Veritatis* drawing (Fig. 3), the former is seen to correspond almost exactly, whereas the latter shows several variations from it, namely: three figures instead of two, a pair of butting goats and a broken tree-stump in the foreground, a bridge beside the ruined building and a large boat in the middle distance. In addition, the light now falls from the right instead of from the left.[12] There is also a difference in the treatment of the building, which in the present version appears as a two-columned structure (the

ing the provenance, which is understandably confused by R., p. 143, with that of the variant belonging to Lord Halifax (see below). It was Mr. Quilter who kindly drew my attention to the painting in the first place and gave me every facility for studying it, thus making this article possible.

8. By Mr. John Brealey, who supplied the photographs and with whom I have also had long and stimulating conversations in front of the painting. It is a particular pleasure to be able to associate John Brealey's name with this tribute to Anthony Blunt.

9. 100 by 132 cm.

10. Andrew Marvell, *The Garden*.

11. See R., pp. 142–144, with provenance since 1854, when the picture was mentioned by Waagen in vol. III of *Treasures of Art in Great Britain*, p. 334. There is no earlier record than this.

12. The discrepancy in lighting between the drawing and the Halifax picture was noted, and its importance recognized, by R., *loc. cit.*

remains of a portico?) jutting out in profile, as it were. In the Halifax picture, on the other hand, the front face of the building is continued to the left, with a further section of the entablature now resting on a square pillar, leaving the 'profile' out of sight.

Now, the line of this extended entablature is clearly visible under the paint surface of the first version – one of Claude's rare known *pentimenti* (they also occur sometimes in tree-trunks and foliage). Does this mean that he might after all have painted the Halifax version first and then have started the other with the intention of repeating the architecture in the same form, afterwards changing his mind? Such a view is at first sight supported by a preparatory pen and ink drawing in the British Museum (Fig. 4),[13] which corresponds clearly to the Halifax picture and not to the present one. (No other drawings connected with the composition survive apart from that in the *Liber Veritatis*.) In fact, however, the priority of the present version seems assured, for two reasons. One, there is no evidence that Claude ever recorded a variant in preference to an original after he had started the *Liber Veritatis*; on the contrary, there is some positive evidence from his later practice that he *did* record the originals.[14] Two, despite what one might expect, it appears that a relatively detailed composition drawing, at least from his early period, is more likely to have been made for a further version of a painting than as a *première pensée* for the painting itself. Usually the 'further version' is an etching, not another painting, and there are several parallels to the British Museum drawing (Fig. 4) among the studies for etchings, the closest being that for the *Campo Vaccino* etching of 1636.[15] In both these cases, the drawings are rather crude in handling while corresponding closely in composition to the finished works for which they were made – a combination of characteristics which results in an

insensitivity not usually associated with Claude. One might even be tempted to doubt their authenticity on this ground. But any such doubt would be unjustified. These drawings are essentially different in type either from the true 'first thoughts' for paintings,[16] in which the artist is creating a fresh idea from imagination, or from the nature studies, in which he is responding to something new in the external world. It is a basic characteristic of Claude's procedure as an artist that he continued to develop the composition of a painting in his mind up to and including work on the canvas itself. Hence there are always differences between his preparatory studies for 'original' paintings (as distinct from variants) and the paintings themselves, although these differences grow less in his later years, when the preparatory work became more elaborate.[17]

The other painting to be discussed here – a *Harbour Scene*, also in an English private collection (Fig. 9) – is smaller ($29\frac{1}{4}$ by $38\frac{3}{4}$ ins.[18]) and less lyrical in feeling than the *Pastoral*, and has also recently been cleaned.[19] Some marks on a stone at the bottom right may be traces of a signature, but there is no date. However, the picture is certainly by Claude and is recorded – with one omission, to be mentioned in a moment – in *Liber Veritatis* 19 (Fig. 7).[20] The previous dated painting, a *Seaport* (LV 14), carries the date 1637; the next is the *Pastoral* (LV 23), discussed above, of 1638. The present *Harbour Scene* is therefore datable 1637/38. According to the inscription on the back of the *Liber* drawing, the patron was 'Mʳ Perochel' (1574–1659), a counsellor in Paris and Sèvres. There is then a gap in the provenance until the late eighteenth or early nineteenth century, when the picture was owned by Lord Hawke; it was acquired from the latter by the 3rd Lord Macdonald (1775–1832), from whom it descended to Sir Somerled Macdonald of Sleat.[21]]

The painting has a general grey-green tonality not unlike that of the *Pastoral*, but the lighting is more subdued and the effect more sombre; even the figures have little colour. The most impressive part is the cold light over the water in the

13. Pen and ink on off-white paper, 19·9 by 26·9 cm. *Verso*: rough outline of a landscape or harbour scene in black chalk. (See A. M. Hind, *British Museum: Catalogue of the Drawings of Claude Lorrain*, London, 1926, No. 211.) With regard to the *pentimento* in the building, John Shearman has pointed out to me that the pilaster on the left of the present version appears to be in front of the column, which suggests that it may originally have continued upwards to meet the extended entablature. If so, the building would have been painted complete as in the Halifax version. Was Claude working from the same (lost) drawing for the architecture in both cases?

14. This was the case with the *Mill* or *Marriage of Isaac and Rebecca* (LV 113), painted in 1648, of which the original is in the National Gallery, London, and the variant in the Doria Gallery, Rome. The priority of the London picture, recorded in the *Liber Veritatis*, was first demonstrated by Martin Davies, *National Gallery Catalogues: French School*, 2nd ed., London, 1957, pp. 36–42.

15. André Blum, *Les Eaux-fortes de Claude Gellée*, Paris, 1923, no. 17. This etching corresponds to the well-known painting, LV 9, in the Louvre. As in the case of the *Pastoral*, it seems to me that the drawing (Hind, *op. cit.* in note 13, no. 193) follows rather than precedes the painting.

16. Examples of these studies for paintings were shown in the exhibition, *L'ideale classico* . . ., Bologna, 1962, nos. 202 (reproduced in catalogue) and 203.

17. A distinction should perhaps be made here between composition studies and studies for figures and architectural details, which may be reproduced unaltered in the paintings.

18. 74 by 99 cm.

19. The cleaning was again carried out and the photographs provided by John Brealey; and once more I have to thank Mr. Quilter for showing me the picture.

20. Pen and brown wash, heightened with white, on blue paper, 18·7 by 26·3 cm. LV 16, *Landscape with a Picnic-party* (lost) was painted for the same patron; however, it is unlikely that they formed a pair, not only because the direction of the lighting is not complementary but also because, to judge from the *Liber* drawings, the scale of the figures did not match.

21. Lord Hawke might be the 2nd (1744–1805), 3rd (1774–1824) or 4th (1799–1869) Baron of that name.

distance and in the sky, which is well preserved and forms a strong centre to the composition, holding together the massive architecture on either side. The sun appears above the horizon almost directly over the rowing-boat, although the rays are less brilliant in the picture, at least in its present state, than in the *Liber* drawing. It seems probable that this is a sunrise rather than a sunset, but – as in the *Pastoral* – it is impossible to be sure.

The round building on the left is one of Claude's many adaptations of one of the corner towers of the Castello at Tivoli, here shorn of its masonry down one side. The square-topped arch at the right is an accurate rendering, in reverse, of the ancient Arch of the Silversmiths in Rome, which he has greatly enlarged in size and has detached from its setting against the church of San Giorgio in Velabro. In reality, the far side of the arch is built into the wall of the church; in the painting, by a typical Claudian invention, it has become the entrance to an imaginary further building situated outside the frame to the right. The detail, on the other hand, including the relief and the decoration on the pilasters, is faithfully reproduced. This fact, together with the reversal of the whole motive, suggests that Claude may have used an engraving. No detailed drawing of the arch by him is known, although he may well, of course, have made one.[22]

The *Liber* drawing (Fig. 7) corresponds closely to the painting except in one particular: the omission of an enormous man, out of proportion to the other figures, who lies asleep in the foreground. It is possible, however, that Claude began to insert this figure in the drawing but then thought better of it, realizing that he would be too big in the reduced space of the *Liber* page. In support of this theory, one can point to a staff lying on the ground (although it might have nothing to do with the man) and to a curious smudge on the drawing where the figure should be, suggesting that Claude may have started to indicate the form in brown wash and then erased it. Close inspection of the paper shows that the process cannot have gone far, yet something of this sort may have happened. If so, it would be a unique case of a *pentimento* in the *Liber Veritatis*.

At all events, the painting is much closer to drawing No. 19 than the work recently associated with it: the *Harbour Scene* in the Royal Collection at Windsor Castle (Fig. 8).[23] The latter must now be considered an autograph variant in the same way that the Halifax *Pastoral* is a variant of LV 23.

The round tower has been moved from the left to a position half hidden behind the arch on the right and is repeated in a different form in the centre distance; taller ships now appear on the left; a second portico with columns has been inserted in front of the arch; and the figures have almost all been changed, although the large sleeping man, now lying in the opposite direction, remains. By a strange coincidence, a rough outline in chalk of a composition with two arches on the right – the motive is virtually unique in Claude's work apart from the Buccleuch *Harbour Scene* of 1633, not in the *Liber Veritatis* – appears on the back of the British Museum drawing (Fig. 4) for the Halifax version of the *Pastoral*. However, the treatment is very vague and it is not certain, from indications on the left of the drawing, whether the composition was to be a harbour scene or a landscape. It may therefore be a first study for a painting that was never executed, not a draft for an alternative version of LV 19.

It is now time to consider the problem of variants as a whole in Claude's work. In Marcel Röthlisberger's comprehensive catalogue of the paintings, published in 1961, twelve pictures are listed as repetitions of known works, not counting those separately recorded in the *Liber Veritatis*, i.e., Nos. 5, 11, 13, 14, 15, 81, 107, 113, 136, 137, 154, 176.[24] A further composition, *Landscape with a Rural Dance*, not recorded in the *Liber* in any form, also exists in two versions, in the Uffizi and Westminster collections.[25] Since 1961, five further paintings by Claude have been published, three of them – the two discussed here and one other, a *Landscape with a Shepherd* in the collection of Mrs. Burns, Hertfordshire (LV 39) – being the originals of which the variants had previously been said to be recorded in the *Liber Veritatis* drawings.[26] The total number of variants on this reckoning is therefore sixteen.

Before going further, it is necessary to define more closely than has been done so far the character of a variant by Claude. First, it is a picture copied or adapted from a

22. A small early view from nature of the arch and the church, seen from the side, occurs in a drawing in the Windsor Royal Library from the Windsor–British Museum sketchbook (Anthony Blunt, *French Drawings at Windsor Castle*, Oxford and London, 1945, no. 56, pl. 87), but the treatment is far too summary to have served as a model for this painting.

23. Her Majesty the Queen, Windsor Castle; canvas 74 by 99 cm. and thus the same size as the original. For details, see R., pp. 135–138. The provenance goes back at least to George III and possibly to Frederick, Prince of Wales (died 1751).

24. I.e. the list on p. 102. I omit nos. 75 and 153 as Claude made separate *Liber* drawings of these. On the other hand, I include no. 107, the variant of which R. catalogues outside the *Liber* as no. 211.

25. R., no. 208; also mentioned on p. 102.

26. LV 39 was published by Marcel Röthlisberger in *Pantheon*, XX, 1962, pp. 167 f., repr. Strictly speaking he did not, in his book, list the other version – a *Landscape with the Rest on the Flight into Egypt* in a private collection – as the original of LV 39 and he catalogued it separately as no. 229; but he associated the picture with the drawing under LV 39.

The other two paintings to have been published recently are LV 94, *Landscape with the Judgement of Paris*, sold Sotheby's 7 July 1966 (see M. Rothlisberger, 'The Judgement of Paris by Claude', *Burl M.*, CVIII, 1966, p. 316, fig. 51) and LV 132, *Coast Scene with the Embarkation of St. Paul*, Birmingham City Art Gallery (see John Woodward, 'Paintings by Dolci and Claude for Birmingham', *Apollo*, LXXVII, 1963, pp. 250–252, repr.). Both are unique paintings, without variants, and so do not concern us here.

L

previous one, sometimes directly, sometimes by means of the *Liber* drawing, of which no separate pictorial record was made, i.e. the same drawing refers to both versions. Second, as the two paintings, LV 19 and LV 23, which have been discussed here show, Claude was unlike most artists in that he did not repeat his compositions by any means exactly but introduced considerable changes into the second version; hence the use of the term 'variants' rather than 'replicas' in this article, Third, and again unlike most artists, he did not normally paint the variant on a smaller scale but reproduced the original approximately the same size.[27] The relationship between the *Pastoral Landscape* (Fig. 1) and its variant (Fig. 2) is typical in these respects. The size is almost the same, and identifiable differences clearly distinguish the two paintings: a boat, a bridge and an extra figure are added in the variant, and the lighting and architecture are changed. Sometimes the alterations are less radical than these, as in the *Pastoral Landscape*, LV 11, where the only difference between the two versions is the omission of a goat in the variant. With the famous *Mill* or *Marriage of Isaac and Rebecca* (LV 113), the original of which is in London and the variant in Rome, the differences are smaller still.[28] Finally, in the case of the *Fight on the Bridge* (LV 137), the two versions are identical, and only the provenance indicates which of the two (it is the one now in Moscow) was the original from which the *Liber* drawing was made.[29]

At the other extreme, where the differences between original and variant are *greater* than in the case of LV 23, one is faced with an open-ended problem. How great do differences have to be before the so-called 'variant' ceases to have any connection with an 'original' and becomes a separate composition, not in the *Liber Veritatis*? The *Harbour Scene*, LV 19, would appear to mark approximately the limit in this respect; the variations between the Windsor version (Fig. 8) and the original (Fig. 9) are so considerable that they lie only just within the permissible range.[30] With the *Rest on the Flight into Egypt*, allegedly associated (see above) with the drawing of the *Pastoral Landscape*, LV 39,

the limit seems to have been passed.[31] In the last analysis this is obviously not a point on which one can be dogmatic; the distinction between 'recorded by' and 'related to' in the *Liber Veritatis* is one of degree rather than kind.

Nevertheless, some conclusions concerning Claude's practice with regard to variants and the number of them he made can, I think, be reached. It should be possible, that is to say, not only to draw up a list of those that exist in both versions but also to infer, in cases where paintings differ markedly from drawings, that the surviving paintings are variants and that originals once existed of these but have since been lost.

Again it would be a mistake to dogmatize, since variations also occur in drawings that do record originals.[32] All the same, it was Claude's habitual procedure to reproduce his paintings very accurately in the *Liber Veritatis*, in the details if not in the spatial relationships and proportions, and some reason should be found for departures from this. Moreover, since more than a dozen cases are known in which both original and variant survive, it is reasonable to assume that there must once have been more of them. Accordingly I now want to make a list of all such cases, summarizing the information where both versions exist and have been fully discussed in the literature and setting it out in more detail where new factors arise or where I believe that an original has been lost. The numbers are those of the *Liber Veritatis*.

5. *Harbour Scene*. Original (1634) in Leningrad, variant (1674) in Munich; both mentioned by Claude on the back of the *Liber* drawing; changes chiefly in the proportions, all the forms being smaller.

11. *Pastoral Landscape*. Original (1636/7) at Mellerstain, variant (same date) in a private collection, Connecticut; compositions almost identical except for omission of a goat in the centre of the variant; the variant on canvas, the original on copper.

12. *Pastoral Landscape*. The painting in Detroit (dated 1637) corresponds closely to the drawing in the details but is rectangular, whereas the drawing is cut at the corners. It is possible that a smaller original, on copper, once existed and that the Detroit painting is an enlarged variant. Against this is the fact that the painting and the drawing correspond closely in the details.

13. *Landscape with a Rural Dance*. Original (1637) belonging to the Earl of Yarborough, variant (dated 1639) in the Louvre; the two bottom corners, where the differences are greatest, are recorded in LV drawings 36 and 37.

27. An exception is the *Landscape with the Rest on the Flight into Egypt* in the Hermitage, LV 154, which Claude himself stated on the back of the *Liber* drawing that he repeated 'en petit toile' (R., p. 361); this is now lost. In another case, that of LV 13 (partly recorded in drawings 36 and 37) and its *pendant*, LV 14, the second versions (Louvre) are larger than the originals (Earl of Yarborough and Duke of Northumberland).

28. See above, note 14.

29. Strictly this should read, the painting to which the inscription on the back of the drawing ('fac. pp Allessandri', i.e. Pope Alexander VII) refers; to say that the drawing was 'made' from one or the other of two identical pictures is meaningless, although it is not in the case of LV 113, where the pictures differ slightly.

30. Until Röthlisberger, the Windsor *Harbour Scene* was not associated with LV drawing 19 at all. Yet I think he is right and that this picture is at least related to the drawing; it also belongs to the same period on stylistic grounds.

31. See above, p. 145 and note 26. The two paintings are fairly close in the arrangement of the landscape but are different in subject – a sufficient reason why Claude would not have thought of regarding LV drawing 39 as a 'record' of the *Rest on the Flight*.

32. The nature of these variations is discussed by the present writer and Marcel Röthlisberger in 'Claude Lorrain and the *Liber Veritatis* – II', *Burl M.*, CI, 1959, pp. 328 ff.

14. *Seaport*. Original (dated 1637) at Alnwick, variant (dated 1639) in the Louvre; the tree at the left omitted and a square window added above the entrance to the first palace in the variant; French arms substituted for Barberini arms on the ships and buildings.

15. *Pastoral Landscape with a Herdsman*. Original (1637) in the Pallavicini Collection, Rome, variant (same date) in the National Gallery, London; the figure moved from one side to the other in the variant and the animals and foliage at the right changed.[33]

19. *Harbour Scene*. Original (1637/38) in a private collection, London, variant (presumably same date) at Windsor; discussed in detail above.

20. *Pastoral Landscape*. The drawing differs from the painting (1637/8) at Raleigh, North Carolina, in the figures and animals (much larger), the mill in the background (smaller) and a herdsman tending goats at the right (omitted). It would seem probable that the drawing records a lost original and that the surviving painting is a variant.

21. *Landscape with a River*. Compared with the painting (1637/8) at Wildenstein's, New York, the drawing omits most of the lesser figures and the chopped tree-trunks in the foreground. It is possible that this painting is a variant of a lost original; on the other hand, the drawing is very summary throughout and was clearly done hurriedly, which may account for the missing details.

22. *Landscape with a River*. I believe that the *Liber* drawing (1637/8) almost certainly records a lost work. The 'original' is the painting in Boston, the date of which was first read (correctly) by W. G. Constable as 1631,[34] i.e. before the *Liber Veritatis* was begun. This date is confirmed by a sketch of the figure group of an artist sketching which appears on the back of a drawing for the National Gallery *View in Rome with the Trinita de' Monti* of 1632.[35] Admittedly the group is

in reverse compared with the Boston painting, but there can be little doubt concerning the connection. The *Liber* drawing omits this group together with some of the other figures, the foreground animals and some fragments of fallen columns. This is the only occasion on which Claude repeated a 'pre-*Liber*' painting in the *Liber Veritatis* itself.

23. *Pastoral Landscape*. Original (dated 1638) in an English private collection, variant (same date) belonging to the Earl of Halifax; discussed in detail above.

39. *Pastoral Landscape*. Original (1639) belonging to Mrs. Burns, Hertfordshire; whether the *Rest on the Flight into Egypt* in a private collection,[36] which differs from the former not only in subject matter but also in the landscape on the right, should be regarded as a variant or as a separate, unrecorded composition is difficult to decide.

40. *Pastoral Landscape*. The drawing differs from the painting (dated 1639) at New Bern, North Carolina, in the figures (slightly), the animals (larger in the drawing) and the trees on both sides; the hut beside the tower is on the left in the drawing, to the right of it in the painting; fragments of classical architecture at the bottom right in the painting are omitted in the drawing. These are exactly the kind of differences that occurred in the case of LV 23 and strongly suggest that the surviving painting is a variant of a lost original.

41. *Pastoral Landscape*. The painting (1639) in the Louvre shows a single figure and animals moving to the right; the drawing, three figures and animals moving to both right and left. The conclusion that the painting is a variant and that the original of LV 39 is lost is supported by the provenance; according to the *Liber* inscription, LV 39 was painted 'per Napoli', whereas the Louvre painting is known to have belonged to Louis XIV by 1683. It is possible, but surely unlikely, that this refers to the same painting.

64. *Pastoral Landscape*. Original (dated 1642) in Berlin, variant in the possession of Lord Jersey until 1945, when it was destroyed; differences in the architecture on the left, the figures, the animals and the distance on the right. The figures and animals of the variant are repeated in LV 75 (lost), which is otherwise only an approximately similar composition.

65. *Landscape with Tobias and the Angel*. A similar situation to 64, and it is possible that the two originals (i.e. LV 64 and 65), both painted for Paris, were a pair. There is evidence (see Röthlisberger) that an original exactly corresponding to the drawing (65) once existed. I believe that the *Pastoral Landscape* in the De Young Memorial Museum, San Francisco, which repeats the landscape exactly but differs in the figures, animals and

33. It has been suggested (R., p. 128) that the National Gallery version is the picture described by Baldinucci as having been painted by Claude from nature in the gardens of the Vigna Madama, in which case it would be the 'original' and the Pallavicini version, recorded in the *Liber*, the 'variant'. The priority of the two paintings is difficult to decide. There is good circumstantial evidence for the former view; on the other hand, the differences between the two paintings are consistent with those between originals and variants in the other cases mentioned, where the version which corresponds most closely to the *Liber* drawing is presumed to be the original. Despite its freshness and its resemblance to the nature drawings, there is no compelling reason to regard the National Gallery painting as a work from nature.

34. 'The Early Work of Claude Lorrain', *GBA*, 6e pér., XXVI, 1944, pp. 305 ff.

35. R., no. 214. The drawing was published by M. Dobroklonsky, 'The Drawings of Claude Lorrain in the Hermitage', *Burl M.*, CIII, 1961, p. 395, figs. 32, 33.

36. R., no. 229.

foreground, is a variant of this. Claude then repeated the composition again, with slight changes in both landscape and figures, in LV 81 (1644). This is also lost, like the original of LV 65, but a copy survives.[37]

86. *Landscape with Argus guarding Io*. The painting (1644/5) at Holkham corresponds closely to the drawing in the foreground, the figures and the animals but differs substantially in the background, which is an exact repetition of LV 79 (*Pastoral Landscape*, Grenoble). On this reasoning, the Holkham picture would be a variant, the original being lost. Against this is the evidence of the provenance, which suggests, though by no means proves, that the picture is the one painted for Cardinal Massimi, as stated in Claude's inscription on the back of the *Liber* drawing.

107. *Pastoral Landscape*. Original (1646/7) in Budapest, variant (same date) in the Hermitage; differences occur in the landscape at the right, the figures and the animals.[38]

113. *Landscape with Dancing Figures* ('*The Mill*' or *Marriage of Isaac and Rebecca*). Original (1648) in the National Gallery, London, variant (1649–50) in the Doria Gallery, Rome; almost identical except for the addition of a broken branch at the right in the variant and the raising of the bank in the centre so that it comes level with the head of the shepherd standing behind the figure group.

115. *Pastoral Landscape with the Arch of Constantine*. Original (1648) in my opinion lost; variant, dated 1651, in the Westminster Collection; differences in the variant at the right, particularly in the figures. The confused provenance also suggests that the Westminster picture may not be the one recorded in LV drawing 115.

136. *Coast Scene with the Rape of Europa*. Original (dated 1655) in Moscow, variant (dated 1667), painted from the *Liber* drawing, in the Royal Collection, Buckingham Palace; the figures and animals reduced in number in the variant and small changes made in the right background.

137. *Coast Scene with a Battle on a Bridge* (pendant to LV 136). Original (dated 1655 or 1656) in Moscow, variant (same date) in the Virginia Museum, Richmond; the two pictures are virtually identical.

154. *Landscape with the Rest on the Flight into Egypt*. Original (dated 1661) in the Hermitage; a small variant stated by Claude on the back of the *Liber* drawing to have been made in 1675 for Francesco Canser (lost).

176. *Pastoral Landscape*. Original (dated 1670) in Munich; variant stated by Claude on the back of the *Liber* drawing to have been painted for 'monsieur faché'. This variant (slightly later?) now belongs to Lord

37. R., fig. 393.
38. See above, note 24.

Fairhaven. Differences occur in the trees to the left, in the framing tree on the right and in the opening out of the space in the right centre.

Finally, two almost identical versions survive, in the Uffizi and the Westminster Collection, of an early painting not recorded in the *Liber Veritatis*: *Landscape with a Rural Dance* (c. 1635?).[39]

To summarize the position, it may be concluded from this list that at least 16, and possibly 17, paintings by Claude exist, or are known to have existed, in both original and variant forms, i.e. Nos. 5, 11, 13, 14, 15, 19, 23, 39(?), 64, 65, 107, 113, 136, 137, 154, 176 and the Uffizi/Westminster *Landscape with a Rural Dance*. This excludes variants recorded in separate drawings in the *Liber* (but includes No. 13, which was only partly recorded on the second occasion). In addition to these, I believe it can be inferred that at least another five (i.e. Nos. 20, 22, 40, 41, 115), and possibly three more (Nos. 12, 21, 86), paintings survive only as variants and that the originals are lost. There must also, of course, be a roughly equivalent number of originals of which the variants are lost.

The question is, do they conform to a system? 'System' is perhaps too strong a word but there are, I think, a few indications suggesting that Claude's method in this respect, as in others, was not haphazard. First, although they are concentrated in the early part of his career, all the variants except two – the Uffizi/Westminster picture and the Boston *Landscape with a River* – are of *Liber Veritatis* paintings. Second, Claude never made more than one variant of a painting recorded in the same drawing in the *Liber*. Where a third similar composition appears, it is recorded in a separate drawing, sometimes – as in the examples mentioned above under Nos. 64, 65 and 86 – combining elements of the two previous versions. Third, the great majority of paintings of which Claude made variants were compositions without literary subjects; they were predominantly *Pastorals*, with a scattering of *Landscapes with Rivers*, *Land-*

39. R., no. 208. There are two further cases in which the paintings differ in significant details from the drawings but which hardly lead one to expect that they are variants of lost originals. The first is LV 61, *Seaport with the Embarkation of St. Paula*, belonging to the Duke of Wellington; the drawing of this, which is unfinished, shows the figure group reversed. Yet the painting must be the one recorded in the drawing, since it has always been kept together with its *pendant*, a *Pastoral Landscape* (LV 62), which exactly corresponds to *its* drawing. The other case is that of the upright *Landscape with the Rest on the Flight into Egypt*, LV 88, now in the Cleveland Museum of Art (see *Bulletin*, XLIX, no. 10, pp. 230–235), which differs substantially from the drawing in the background. The whole composition repeats, with slight changes and a different figure subject, the *Landscape with the Finding of Moses*, LV 47, in the Prado; in fact, the painting of LV 88 repeats the background of LV 47 exactly, although the drawing does not. Theoretically there might have been three closely related versions of this composition, but this is hard to believe in practice, especially as the Cleveland picture is a very large work.

scapes with Rural Dances and *Harbour Scenes* – only a few (Nos. 65, 86, 113, 136, 137 and 154) being of religious or mythological themes. With the exception of these few, the originals – and, *a fortiori*, the variants, whose patrons are almost all unknown, were painted for unimportant patrons or possibly agents.[40]

Fourth, there are enough variants, especially if the hypothetical ones are included, to suggest that they formed a regular feature of Claude's practice as a painter, at any rate at certain periods of his career, and were not just random exceptions. From late 1636 to early 1638 – LV 11-23 – it almost seems as if *every* painting was repeated in a variant. At this moment his pictures were, of course, particularly in demand; producing the same composition twice would have saved effort; and it must be admitted that some of these compositions – originals as well as variants – lack the exquisite care of execution that characterizes the very earliest and, still more, the later paintings. Between 1638 and 1648 (LV 115) the variants become fewer and after 1648 practically cease; those made in the 1670's (Nos. 5, 154, 176) were separately noted on the backs of the *Liber* drawings.

How does all this affect our view of the role of the *Liber Veritatis*? As has already been suggested elsewhere,[41] Claude's habit of producing second versions of his compositions was the largest 'loophole' in his use of the *Liber* as

a protection against fraud. How could he authenticate a variant brought to him for checking against the book if the painting differed, as we have seen it would have done, from the drawing? The problems raised by this difficulty would take too long to discuss here; in any case, it is hard to conceive of a satisfactory answer. On the one hand, the statements made by Baldinucci as to the origin of the book[42] – that it was begun by Claude as a protection against forgery about the time that he was painting his first pictures for the King of Spain – remain confirmed by independent evidence that his pictures were being fraudulently imitated in the mid-1630's and by the date of the paintings for the King, which are now in Madrid. On the other hand, it must be asked whether the actual method of checking, as told by Claude to Baldinucci, was not perhaps a procedure adopted by him comparatively late in his career; whether, in short, the other, concealed purpose of the *Liber* – to serve as a private pattern book, enabling him to repeat his paintings and to combine and re-combine pictorial motives in ever new forms – was not uppermost at first. The concentration of the variants discussed in this article in the early part of the book and their dying away at the end conforms to a central characteristic of Claude's development – the tendency of each of his works to be treated with increasing care as a unique, finished object. But the exact function of the *Liber Veritatis* seems to be a greater enigma than before.

40. Except nos. 13 and 14, both without literary subjects, the originals of which were painted for Pope Urban VIII.

41. *Op. cit.* in note 32, pp. 333 f.

42. *Ibid.*, p. 17, note 5.

JACQUES THUILLIER

Notes sur les frères Le Nain portraitistes

I

LA gloire des frères Le Nain tient toute, à nos yeux, dans leurs tableaux paysans. Le reste de leur production vient compléter leur image sans ajouter à leur génie. Mais trop souvent l'historien d'art incline à transposer en termes historiques ce qui doit demeurer hiérarchie de valeurs. Depuis Champfleury les trois Le Nain passent généralement pour des provinciaux formés à la peinture de "genre" par un Flamand de passage,[1] puis venus, déjà forts d'une longue expérience,[2] tenter fortune dans la capitale: à leur dam, et l'incompréhension des Parisiens pour leur inspiration rustique les aurait poussés à se risquer, plus ou moins tardivement, plus ou moins adroitement, à la peinture "noble", retables et portraits. Or les documents ne confirment guère ces vues, entachées dès l'origine de quelque romantisme: et nous croyons qu'il convient d'envisager désormais une hypothèse assez différente.[3] Quand Antoine se fait recevoir maître-peintre à Saint-Germain-des-Prés, en 1629, et que s'ouvre ainsi l'atelier, les trois frères doivent avoir seulement entre vingt et trente ans.[4] Leur réputation parisienne,

qu'en fait on devine prompte, ils vont la devoir à leurs compositions religieuses et à leurs portraits. C'est par la suite qu'ils semblent faire des scènes paysannes une part essentielle de leur production: sans doute vers 1640, quand se développe dans la société parisienne la mode du grotesque et des paysanneries, quand grandit aussi la concurrence des peintres formés par Vouet, et que le goût de la capitale se porte vers un art plus délié et plus savant, rompu aux habiletés italiennes de mise en scène, pointilleux sur le chapitre des architectures et de la perspective – tout ce qu'il faut bien reconnaître le côté faible des Le Nain . . .

Répétons-le: dans ces scènes paysannes, vite appréciées si l'on en juge par le nombre des répliques, les Le Nain trouveront leur véritable originalité. Ils sauront y unir l'élégance parisienne qui fuit la vulgarité d'esprit ou d'expression (que l'on songe aux scènes familières d'un Bosse!) avec une inspiration réaliste fidèle à la province, fidèle à leur province. Alliance paradoxale, imprévisible, et réussie avec cette apparente simplicité qui est le trait le plus sûr du génie. Mais il y faut reconnaître moins le miracle du cœur chez des provinciaux naïfs que le couronnement d'un art approfondi et qui a cherché d'autres expressions. Les grands tableaux mythologiques et religieux, qui réapparaissent peu à peu,[5] occupèrent assurément dans l'activité des Le Nain une place importante: et plus encore le portrait. C'est lui qui offre sans doute la clef de leur carrière. C'est à lui qu'ils durent la meilleure part de leur succès, grâce à lui qu'ils touchèrent jusqu'à la famille royale, et probablement nouèrent ces relations qui plus tard allaient aider Matthieu à obtenir, consécration inespérée, le collier de Saint Michel.

On n'attache d'ordinaire à ces portraits qu'une importance secondaire en regard du restant de l'œuvre: pratiquement, ils n'ont guère été étudiés sérieusement jusqu'ici.[6] Pourtant

1. Cette affirmation, répétée presque partout, et censée expliquer l'intérêt des Le Nain pour le "genre" et le portrait, n'est en fait que l'extrapolation assez gratuite d'une phrase de Claude Leleu dans son *Histoire de Laon: "Ils furent formez dans cet art (la peinture) par un peintre estranger qui les instruisit, et leur monstra les regles de cet art à Laon, pendant l'espace d'un an"* (t. II, p. 592). *"Estranger"* signifie assurément *étranger au pays*: mais non pas nécessairement *de nation étrangère*, encore moins *Flamand*, encore moins *peintre de genre* . . . Au contraire un peintre s'installant pour une année à Laon avait grand chance d'y être venu exécuter quelque commande importante pour la cathédrale ou un couvent. On n'imagine guère qu'un artiste, au moins de quelque talent, fût-il protégé par la famille des d'Estrées ou des La Vieuville, ait pu trouver à Laon, pour les tableaux de genre ou les portraits, une clientèle et des occupations suffisantes pour l'y retenir une année durant.

2. Conclusion que l'on tire des dates de naissance couramment admises, comparées à celle où Antoine se fait recevoir maître-peintre à Saint-Germain-des-Prés (1629). Mais les premières se révèlent sujettes à caution (cf. *infra*). Indiquons seulement que l'on tirerait une conclusion inverse du texte de Leleu, qui aussitôt après la phrase citée plus haut (cf. note 1) enchaîne: *"de là ils passèrent à Paris, où ils se perfectionnèrent, et s'y établirent tous trois demeurant dans une mesme maison . . ." (ibid.).*

3. Nous résumons ici une démonstration que nous avons déjà esquissée dans l'introduction et les annotations à nos "Documents pour servir à l'étude des frères Le Nain", in *BSHAF*, 1963 (1964), pp. 155–284, et que nous comptons reprendre prochainement en détail.

4. Contrairement à l'opinion admise; voir *Documents . . ., op. cit.*, pp. 168–170, notes. Nous estimons raisonnable de croire que les

trois frères Le Nain naquirent, non pas en 1588, 1593 et 1607, mais entre 1598 et 1607 environ.

5. Voir notamment sur ce point Vitale Bloch, "Les frères Le Nain et leurs tableaux religieux', in *GBA*, 6e pér., XI, juin 1934, pp. 342–350; *id.* "Bacchus et Ariane by Louis Le Nain", in *AQ*, Autumn 1956, pp. 263 sq.; Jacques Thuillier, "Le Nain Studies, I. Three rediscovered Pictures", in *Burl M*, c, 1958, pp. 54–61. – Rappelons que vient de réapparaître un *Repos de la Sainte Famille en Égypte* (cf. Catalogue de Christie's, *Important Pictures by Old Masters*, vente du 1er juillet 1966, no. 34; reproduit au catalogue; 52 in. × 49 in.), qui peut être considéré comme l'une des plus émouvantes créations des frères Le Nain

6. A la confusion qui règne le plus souvent chez les auteurs ayant abordé ce sujet on opposera les précieuses indications dispensées par Charles Sterling, du catalogue de l'exposition des *Peintres*

la plupart des mentions contemporaines désignent les trois Le Nain, et Matthieu en particulier, comme portraitistes. L'un des premiers textes conservés montre Antoine recevant de la ville de Paris, dès 1632, commande du portrait des échevins.[7] En 1644 les *Galanteries de la Cour* de Du Bail[8] déclarent que l'aîné des trois frères "*reüssit mieux que peintre qui soit à Paris pour la vraye semblance des portrais qui sont fais après le naturel; car il observe si bien tous les trais & les linéamens d'un visage en sa peinture qu'il ne l'abandonne jamais que l'Art n'ayt entièrement imité la Nature*", tandis que le dernier "*sçait parfaitement bien faire ressembler ses portrais aux visages qu'il peint*". Pour le cadet, ce même roman le montre recherché de la meilleure compagnie pour l'habileté et "*la grâce*" avec lesquelles lui aussi tire le portrait. En 1646, dans le recueil poétique du *Cabinet de Mr de Scudéry*, les Le Nain figurent avec un *Portraict de Monseigneur le Cardinal Mazarin*:[9] et c'est justement un portrait de Mazarin donné par Matthieu à l'Académie en 1649 qui y conservera leur souvenir jusqu'à la Révolution.[10] Aussi bien, dans sa liste des Académiciens, Reynès cataloguera tout naturellement Matthieu comme peintre de portraits.[11] Mazarin n'était du reste pas le seul personnage illustre que Matthieu avait eu l'honneur de peindre: Leleu, consignant sans doute une tradition de famille, rapporte que "*tirant un jour la Roine Anne d'Austriche, le Roy Loüis 13. qui estoit présent dit que la Roine n'avoit jamais esté peinte dans un si beau jour*".[12] Ainsi donc, avant 1643, Matthieu avait obtenu la plus haute consécration que peintre de portrait pût obtenir en France.

D'où venait pareil succès? Assurément du talent des Le Nain à traduire avec vérité une physionomie. "*Ces trois frères excelloient à faire des têtes*", remarque Sauval à propos de la décoration exécutée à la chapelle de la Vierge de Saint-Germain-des-Prés:[13] et même devant leurs tableaux religieux, en effet, l'on sent que la main aime à particulariser les traits. Mais leur talent fut sans doute heureusement mis en valeur par leur urbanité. Fils d'un sergent royal, élevés dans un milieu relativement aisé et éclairé, ils durent faire dans Paris figure de peintres de bon ton, un peu à la manière des Beaubrun.[14] Du moins est-ce l'image que livre

d'eux le romancier Du Bail: et le goût des armes qu'affecte Matthieu, son ambition sociale, la confirment amplement. Non moins, l'accès qu'il obtint auprès d'Anne d'Autriche et de Mazarin. Reste qu'on aurait tort de sous-estimer ici un élément encore plus décisif: l'originalité de leur art.

La simplicité élégante de leurs portraits, leur manière franche, mais évitant les recherches psychologiques indiscrètes,[15] convenait au goût de la capitale vers 1635-1640. Matthieu semble y avoir tôt introduit des recherches d'éclairage capables de surprendre et de séduire.[16] Mais le trait de génie fut sans doute leur formule du "portrait de groupe". A cette société qui reprend alors une vie nouvelle, rien ne pouvait plaire davantage. De moyenne grandeur, ces tableaux étaient propres à suspendre aux murs d'une salle ou d'un cabinet; ils conservaient le souvenir de quelques amis ou parents tout en évitant l'ennui des bustes juxtaposés, et mariaient au contraire la vérité des postures naturelles avec le piquant de la scène de genre.

Or le "portrait de groupe", en France, semblait jusque-là réservé à la solennité des ex-voto ou des bureaux de ville. On ne voit pas que la formule des Le Nain se soit développée avant eux dans Paris. Au reste, entre 1630 et 1640, la trouverait-on fort répandue ailleurs, Pays-Bas exceptés?[17] Ceux-ci pouvaient offrir maint précédent, et il n'est guère plausible que les Le Nain les aient ignorés. Mais il n'est pas davantage assuré qu'il faille chercher exclusivement du côté du nord la source de cette formule.[18] Non moins que

trouvoient encore de la satisfaction dans l'entretien de ces deux habiles hommes . . ." (*Entretiens . . .*, x, éd. 1725, t. IV, p. 334-335.) Il dut en aller de même pour les frères Le Nain. Dans leur jeunesse et au début de leur carrière parisienne, sont-ils restés entièrement étrangers aux cercles des d'Estrées et des La Vieuville, les deux grandes familles de Laon, alors si haut placées à la Cour de France? On ne peut faire sur ce point que des hypothèses. Rappelons seulement que la ferme de La Jumelle, bien des Le Nain, jouxtait les propriétés des La Vieuville et payait même une redevance à ces derniers (cf. *Documents*, *op. cit.*, p. 182).

15. Par une sorte de contamination, les tableaux paysans des Le Nain ont fait souvent regarder leurs portraits comme "réalistes": en fait, du *Portrait du Marquis de Tréville* aux *Joueurs de tric-trac*, il est facile de noter que le scrupule de vérité le cède au souci d'élégance. La mise en page, ou la mise en scène, vise à créer un portrait de type *social*. Nous sommes encore bien loin des conventions mondaines d'un Nocret, puis d'un Mignard: mais déjà il s'agit d'effigies destinées à plaire.

16. Qu'il s'agisse du *Corps de garde* de 1643, avec son nocturne magistral, ou de l'éclairage aux reflets insistants dont nous parlerons plus bas (cf. III). – C'est en ce sens qu'il faut apparemment interpréter la phrase de Louis XIII rapportée par Leleu.

17. En Flandre notamment, la formule du portrait de groupe traité en scène de genre ne semble pas se développer plus tôt qu'à Paris (cf. F.-C. Legrand, *Les Peintres flamands de genre au XVII⁰ siècle*, éd. Meddens, 1963, pp. 95 sq.). C'est ainsi que certaines œuvres de Gonzales Coques (né en 1618 et par conséquent cadet des Le Nain) offrent des formules proches de celles de Matthieu: mais elles n'apparaissent pas avant 1640.

18. On l'a fait trop systématiquement à notre sens. Ainsi le catalogue de l'exposition *The Brothers Le Nain* (Toledo, octobre 1947) ne suppose-t-il pas que la *Ronde de nuit* de Rembrandt (1642)

de la *Réalité* (Musée de l'Orangerie, 1934) à celui de l'exposition *Le Nain* de Reims (Musée des Beaux-Arts, 1953) et de l'exposition *Il Seicento Europeo* (Rome, 1956).

7. *Documents . . ., op. cit.*, pp. 173-174.
8. *Ibidem*, p. 185-190. Rappelons que le témoignage de ce roman a grand chance de s'appliquer aux Le Nain. Certes, on aurait pu songer à la famille des Beaubrun, et plus précisément à Matthieu, Louis et Michel, qui pratiquèrent avec succès le portrait: mais Louis meurt dès 1627 et Michel dès 1642 . . .
9. *Ibidem*, pp. 192-193.
10. *Ibidem*, pp. 252-254.
11. *Ibidem*, pp. 256-257.
12. *Ibidem*, p. 261.
13. *Ibidem*, p. 258.
14. Parlant des deux cousins Beaubrun, Félibien remarque que leur vogue dut beaucoup à cette "*politesse*" qui faisait que les dames "*outre l'avantage qu'elles tiroient de l'agrément de leur pinceau . . .*

des exemples hollandais, il faut rapprocher la *Réunion d'amateurs* ou le *Repas de famille* des compositions antérieures ou contemporaines d'un Parisien comme Abraham Bosse. Motifs et mise en page sont semblables: Matthieu remplace seulement les visages conventionnels par des portraits. Depuis la Renaissance maint tableau de genre (et notamment les "fêtes de cour") n'avait pas manqué de mêler ainsi aux représentations l'effigie des princes: la nouveauté fut de s'emparer des scènes familières qui étaient alors fort au goût du jour – Bosse en témoigne, et la littérature du temps – et de les subordonner au portrait, à la manière des peintres hollandais. En ce sens le *Corps de garde*, la *Réunion d'amateurs* ou le *Repas de famille* tiennent dans l'histoire du portrait français une place qu'on oublie trop souvent de leur réserver.

II

Il est vrai que la plus grande partie des portraits dus aux Le Nain est détruite, ou demeure inconnue. Seuls justement les "portraits de groupe" forment encore un ensemble relativement important, et que la critique moderne a pu distribuer avec une vraisemblance satisfaisante pour l'esprit. La *Réunion de famille* de 1642 (Louvre), les *Portraits dans un intérieur* de 1647 (Louvre) ont même servi de point de départ à Paul Jamot pour caractériser la part d'Antoine dans l'œuvre des trois frères. La *Réunion d'amateurs* (Louvre) a été récemment rendue à Louis par Charles Sterling.[19] A Matthieu est donné tout un groupe qui s'organise autour du *Corps de garde* de 1643, et de la série des cinq tableaux Seyssel, aujourd'hui dispersés, dont les *Joueurs de tric-trac* (Louvre; détail, Fig. 6) et la *Leçon de danse* (Paris, coll. part.) sont les œuvres maîtresses. Le troisième frère apparait ainsi le plus brillant et le plus novateur dans ce domaine du portrait: ce qui s'accorde bien avec les témoignages conservés. En revanche les portraits isolés – qu'on imagine tout naturellement plus nombreux – sont devenus fort rares.

pourrait avoir influencé le *Corps de garde* (1643), voire que le *Syndic des drapiers* (1662) serait pour quelque chose dans la *Réunion d'amateurs* (non datée, mais que ses costumes situent clairement vers 1645)? – Il est certain que la formule des portraits organisés en conversations, musiques ou scènes champêtres se développe tôt aux Pays-Bas: or des contacts précis entre les Le Nain et la Hollande demeurent tout à fait plausibles. Matthieu, qui, nous le savons désormais, servit dans les armées du roi, n'est certes pas demeuré toute sa vie entre les clochers de Saint-Germain-des-Prés et les tours de Laon. D'autre part des tableaux comme ceux de Codde ou de Palamedesz (nés en 1599 et 1601, donc de la même génération que les Le Nain) offrent des ressemblances notables, et l'on peut croire qu'ils furent promptement connus dans Paris. – Reste qu'il faut compter aussi avec le développement français de la scène de genre, encore fort mal connu: ce qui exclut, pour l'instant, toute affirmation trop précise.

19. Cat. de l'exposition *Il Seicento Europeo*, Roma, 1956, n. 175 (pp. 163–164).

Non que les érudits et les commerçants n'aient multiplié les attributions: mais d'ordinaire aucun argument précis ne vient soutenir une intuition plus ou moins vague. Il suffit de feuilleter le recueil de Fierens pour constater l'incohérence des tableaux ainsi glissés sous ce nom avantageux: et les expositions ont souvent permis de les mettre en doute, voire de les éliminer.[20] C'est le cas, par exemple, du *Jeune homme en buste* de Laon, daté de 1646, du charmant *Jeune seigneur* de Nantes, ou encore de l'effigie élégante et grave du *Jeune garçon en buste* du Musée Calvet. La récente exposition à Paris d'œuvres des musées russes a permis pareillement d'exclure sans retour l'*Homme à la boule* de l'Ermitage,[21] d'attribution relativement récente: et tout indique qu'il faudra réserver le même sort au *Jeune homme* du Fitzwilliam Museum.[22]

Pour l'instant trois tableaux seuls offrent une entière assurance: le *Portrait du marquis de Trévilles* (coll. part.), le *Portrait de femme âgée* du Musée Calvet (Avignon), et le *Portrait d'homme* du Musée Crozatier (Le Puy) (Fig. 1). Seuls – avec les "portraits de groupe" – ils sauraient servir à l'attribution d'autres œuvres.

Le premier est signé et daté *Le Nain fecit 1644*. De grand format,[23] l'œuvre, au moins dans son état présent, apparaît décevante. L'architecture, passablement maladroite, fournit un fond de pure convention. C'est encore la mise en page du personnage, représenté en pied, qui, pour traditionnelle qu'elle soit, montre le plus d'autorité.[24] Traits qui placent cette œuvre à l'opposé de la *Réunion de famille* de 1642 et des *Portraits dans un intérieur* de 1647, avec leurs postures gauches et leur surprenante vivacité de traitement. Cette contradiction, qui a été sentie, n'a pas empêché de donner à Antoine ce portrait.[25] Il est difficile pourtant de le rapporter au seul changement d'échelle: et c'est là certainement une des obscurités, si nombreuses encore, que propose l'œuvre des trois frères.

20. Notamment l'exposition organisée en 1953 au Musée des Beaux-Arts de Reims. Plus que de la rubrique où se trouvent classés chacun des portraits, on tiendra compte de l'opinion, rapportée dans les notices du catalogue, de M. Charles Sterling.

21. Reproduit in Fierens, *Les Le Nain*, 1933, pl. LXXXV. Attribué par Serge Ernst, "Les œuvres des frères Le Nain en Russie", in *GBA*, 5e pér., XIII, 1926, t. I, p. 301 sqq.

22. Reproduit in Fierens, *op. cit.*, pl. LXXXIV.

23. *Portrait du marquis de Trévilles*, T. 2m,30 × 1m,40. Ancienne collection de la Comtesse de Mont-Réal; vendu à la Galerie Charpentier, Paris, le 12 mai 1950, no. 76 (reprod. pl. VIII).

24. Traits qui rattachent directement ce tableau à la tradition de Pourbus, à cette date déjà bien vieillie. – On les retrouve, avec assez d'insistance pour inciter à un rapprochement favorable, dans le portrait dit du *Marquis de Cinq-Mars* de l'ancienne collection Seillière (aujourd'hui au Washington County Museum of Fine Arts; 1m,92 × 1m,04; reprod. in Fierens, *op. cit.*, pl. LXXVII). Mais nous n'avons pu encore examiner directement ce tableau, dont l'attribution à Le Nain repose seulement sur la tradition, et que Champfleury jugeait pourtant l'un des plus assurés.

25. Cf. Charles Sterling, catalogue de l'exposition *Les Peintres de la réalité en France au XVIIe siècle*, *op. cit.*, no. 65, notice.

Le *Portrait de femme âgée* du Musée Calvet s'est au nettoyage révélé simple copie;[26] mais il porte une inscription, indiquant le nom des Le Nain et la date de 1644, et apparemment recopiée sur un original dont il doit livrer un souvenir assez fidèle. L'austérité de mise en page et la gravité de la psychologie le rapprochent des tableaux paysans et l'ont fait attribuer à Louis: il reste malheureusement isolé. Isolé également, le beau *Portrait d'homme* du Musée du Puy,[27] qui évoque cette fois nécessairement la part donnée à Matthieu (Fig. 1). Ni signé, ni daté, il possède seulement une attribution qui paraît remonter au XVIIIe siècle: il s'impose pourtant d'emblée comme une œuvre sûre.

Cette évidence même est bien faite pour conseiller la méfiance quand seul un vague réalisme vient recommander l'attribution. Et cependant la série des "portraits de groupe" donnés à Matthieu offre des types, des poses, des éclairages multiples: on s'étonne qu'un tel répertoire – près de cinquante figures – n'ait pas entraîné nombre d'identifications solides. Surtout quand l'inventaire après décès de Matthieu prouve qu'il avait peint quantité de portraits isolés: n'en voit-on pas mentionnés plus de cent, hommes ou femmes, personnages d'épée ou de robe, tableaux petits et grands, "tant faits que non achevez"?[28]

Comment dès lors ne pas se demander si dans l'immense quantité de portraits du XVIIe siècle qui subsistent, si mal classés, si mal étudiés, certains n'ont pas chance d'appartenir aux Le Nain? Qu'on nous permette un instant d'oublier – consciemment – les règles de la stricte prudence, et de proposer ici trois candidatures qui nous semblent appeler le nom de Matthieu. Les rapprochements de style rencontrent cette fois quelques indices extérieurs, qui ne sauraient certes valoir une bonne signature ou même une attribution ancienne, mais qui nous semblent, si faibles soient-ils, dignes d'être pris en considération. Lorsque la reconstruction de l'œuvre d'un peintre semble depuis longtemps enrayée, il peut être de bonne méthode d'avancer ainsi quelques attributions sans preuves absolues – provisoirement, et pourvu qu'on n'oublie point qu'il s'agit d'*attributions*. Aussi, laissant de côté des exemples plus simples et sûrs, choisissons-nous ces trois œuvres dans trois domaines différents, où d'ordinaire, s'agissant de Le Nain, l'on ne songe guère à pousser les investigations. Ce sont donc là des cas *extrêmes*, et que nous tenons peut-être pour moins importants en soi que par les directions de recherches qu'ils peuvent désigner.

26. Cf. Michel Laclotte, catalogue de l'exposition *Le XVIIe siècle français*, Paris, Petit Palais, mars 1958, nº 88, notice.
27. T., 0·61 m. × 0·51 m.; catalogue 1872, nº 166. Acquis avant 1866; d'après Champfleury, le vicomte de Becdelièvre l'avait acheté en 1822 à une vente faite à Paris par les experts Henry et Lebrun, et le tableau provenait d'une galerie particulière d'Angers, pillée à la Révolution (Champfleury, *Les Frères Le Nain*, Paris, 1863, p. 68).
28. *Documents, op. cit.*, p. 244.

III

L'un des traits qui distinguent d'emblée le groupe des portraits attribués avec le plus de vraisemblance à Matthieu est sa manière si particulière de modeler quelques-uns des visages en accentuant l'effet lumineux.[29] Un reflet dégage la joue du côté sombre, tandis qu'une ombre médiane s'installe le long du nez et à l'entre-deux des sourcils, parfois même envahit le front. Des accents marquent la narine, la commissure de la bouche, accusent la saillie de la lèvre inférieure et la rondeur du menton. Le visage se trouve ainsi décomposé en un jeu de valeurs insistant, qui n'épargne pas même les traits délicats des fillettes.[30] Or on retrouve avec surprise ce parti si caractéristique dans une remarquable miniature conservée au Victoria and Albert Museum:[31] comment ne pas songer aussitôt aux Le Nain?

Le médaillon (Fig. 2) est daté de 1645. On a voulu y déceler des traits hollandais:[32] mais son origine française est prouvée par l'inscription du revers, un dizain qui file assez joliment lieux communs et rimes banales,[33] faisant juger par là que le jeune défunt représenté appartenait à un cercle élégant et cultivé de Paris – tel celui où les *Galanteries de la Cour* venaient de mettre en scène les frères Le Nain, ou celui qu'évoquait deux ans auparavant le *Corps de garde* avec ses jeunes officiers à la mode.

Le portrait est traité avec une franchise nuancée de gravité qui rejette loin les conventions de la miniature. Surtout, l'œuvre tranche parmi les autres médaillons du même temps (et jusque dans la vitrine où elle est exposée) par son coloris, entièrement tenu dans les bruns, et refusant ces fraîcheurs de carnation, ces alliances de bleus et de roses alors de rigueur. S'agit-il d'une copie fidèle, par un miniaturiste parisien, d'un portrait à l'huile de Matthieu, voire

29. Ce parti se retrouve, à divers degrés, aussi bien dans le *Portrait d'homme* du Puy que dans la série de portraits de groupe dont font partie les *Joueurs de tric-trac*.
30. Ainsi dans la *Leçon de danse* de la collection Bérard, ou dans le *Jardinier* du Wallraf-Richartz Museum (fig. 3).
31. Victoria and Albert Museum, nº 39 – 1866; cf. Basil S. Long, *Victoria and Albert Museum: Hand-list of Miniature Portraits and Silhouettes*, Londres, 1930, p. 81.
32. Ainsi Basil S. Long dans le seul article qui, à notre connaissance, mentionne ce médaillon: "Quelques miniatures françaises à South Kensington", in *GBA*, 6e pér., IX, janvier 1933, pp. 10–16.
33. *Mon cœur conserve un autre objet*
Des vertus dont il eut la gloire
Gravé au fond de ma mémoire
Plus au vif que n'est ce portret
Qui represante son visage
Si dès le printems de son age
Son corps sert de pasture aux vers
La parque qui fila sa vie
Craignoit qu'un jour dans l'univers
Il ne fust trop digne d'envie
      Au mois de may l'an de
        Grace 1645.

d'un fragment de portrait collectif, qui serait de peu antérieur à la mort du modèle, soit à 1645?[34] Ou Matthieu a-t-il parfois accepté de semblables commandes? Nous inclinerions vers la première hypothèse, car en 1645 les trois frères semblent fort occupés. Mais l'œuvre est de la plus belle qualité, et la mort de ce jeune homme put être l'occasion exceptionnelle qui fit reprendre à Matthieu une technique sans doute pratiquée naguère par l'atelier.

Une seconde œuvre mérite examen. Il s'agit cette fois d'un *Portrait d'homme à mi-corps* (Fig. 4), grandeur du naturel, que possède le musée de Stockholm.[35] Par la franchise de l'observation jointe à la sobriété des moyens, ce tableau se rapproche du *Portrait d'homme* en buste du musée du Puy. Fait curieux, le nez busqué du personnage, ses lèvres bien ourlées, sa belle stature évoquent aussi le galant jardinier (Fig. 5) qui, dans la composition bien connue de Cologne, offre gravement quelques fleurs à une dame assise.[36] C'est assez pour que le nom de Le Nain, ici encore, vienne à l'esprit. Faut-il l'accepter?

La ressemblance avec le tableau du Puy est assurément trop lâche pour trancher. L'éclairage est différent, et surtout la mise en page plus large. Une main sur la hanche, le manteau jeté sur l'épaule, le personnage esquisse une pose désinvolte. La seconde main apparaît dans la lumière, la bouche s'entr'ouvre, le regard s'adresse à un interlocuteur supposé. La simplicité familière du tableau du Puy le cède à une présentation plus étudiée. Mais justement des œuvres comme le *Corps de garde* ou les *Joueurs de tric-trac* (Fig. 6) font supposer l'existence de portraits de ce type, où la recherche de la pose équilibre le réalisme de la physionomie:[37] l'élégance des "portraits de groupe", à coup sûr, se retrouvait dans les portraits isolés.

Or l'étude du détail ne contredit pas l'attribution. Le coloris, réduit aux tons gris et bruns, est d'une discrétion rare hors de l'œuvre des Le Nain. La facture offre la même sobriété. Volumes simples, draperies sans cassures anguleuses, où sont indiqués sommairement quelques creux d'ombre, linges que soulignent des rehauts de blanc posés

avec souplesse, mèches de cheveux glissant en traînées fines sur les joues ou le vêtement, sans empâtements, comme en grisaille: autant de traits qui se retrouveraient aisément du *Portrait d'homme* du Puy aux *Joueurs de tric-trac*. La main n'a pas cette finesse, ces doigts ronds aux ongles courbes et pointus que montrent les toiles attribuées à Louis; elle est curieusement modelée avec des rehauts de rouge et de bleu: mais les *Joueurs de tric-trac* ou le *Jardinier* sont justement dotés de grandes mains solidement traitées dans une facture très proche.

Le tableau est considéré au musée de Stockholm comme un portrait de Sébastien Bourdon par lui-même. Le premier point se soutient difficilement: cet homme à belle carrure, qu'aucun attribut ne désigne pour peintre, ne ressemble guère à Bourdon, méridional au visage osseux, "de taille moyenne" et "le teint pâle",[38] tel que nous le montrent plusieurs portraits irrécusables.[39] Un nez busqué, des lèvres épaisses, ne suffisent pas à établir une identité que contredit la structure même du visage large aux joues pleines.[40] Or on ne reconnaît guère plus facilement le pinceau de Bourdon que sa physionomie. Le Musée de Stockholm possède plusieurs originaux de sa main qui précisément rendent la comparaison commode. La mise en page plus alerte de Bourdon, les draperies aux cassures "cubistes", les recherches de "fondu", les effets de blanc et de noir, l'alliance des tons froids, et surtout ces bleus caractéristiques employés pour les ombres; tout s'y écarte de ce portrait, pourtant proche de date, qu'on s'est bien gardé d'accrocher à côté d'eux.[41]

Ce qui achève de rendre plausible l'hypothèse d'une attribution à Matthieu Le Nain, c'est que ce tableau fut acquis en 1914, à la suite de la vente du Marquis de Marmier, où fut dispersé le mobilier du château de Ray-sur-

34. Rappelons qu'à la vente Duclos-Dufrenoy, en 1795, figurait un médaillon à double face, représentant deux portraits d'homme et de femme, et attribué à "Petitot d'après Le Nain".

35. Toile, 102 cm. × 80 cm. Stockholm, Musée National, n. 1780. Cf. Catalogue de 1958, *Äldre utländska Mälningan och Skulpturer*, reprod. p. 25 (sous le nom de Sébastien Bourdon).

36. Nous tenons que le tableau ne saurait être interprété de façon réaliste, comme on le fait d'ordinaire à la suite de Paul Jamot ("Sur quelques œuvres de Louis et Matthieu Le Nain", in *GBA*, 5e pér., VII, 1923; publ. à part in *Nouvelles Études sur les frères Le Nain*, p. 6). Manifestement, il s'agit ici encore de portraits: aux yeux des contemporains la mise en scène familière devait ajouter quelque piquant à l'hommage galant (peut-être conjugal) que supposait le langage des fleurs.

37. Ainsi l'on retrouverait plusieurs fois l'attitude du poing sur la hanche dans le *Corps de garde* de 1643 ou dans le *Repas de famille* Choiseul, gravé par Weisbrodt en 1771 avec le nom de Le Nain.

38. L'indication est de Guillet de Saint-Georges; cf. *Mémoires inédits. . .*, 1887, t. I, p. 102.

39. Notamment l'autoportrait qu'il a glissé dans l'angle de la *Chute de Simon le Magicien* (Montpellier, cathédrale), l'*Autoportrait* en buste du Louvre et le *Portrait avec un musicien* (Coll. part., Angleterre).

40. Le nom de Bourdon paraît avoir été amené par comparaison avec le *Portrait d'un sculpteur* du Louvre, longtemps regardé comme autoportrait: identification qui n'est plus retenue aujourd'hui (cf. Michel Laclotte, catalogue de l'exposition *The Splendid Century*, Washington–Toledo–New York 1960–62, n. 75, et Pierre Rosenberg, catalogue de l'exposition *Il ritratto francese da Clouet a Degas*, Rome, 1962, n. 16. Le portrait de Bourdon gravé par Laurent Cars en 1733 d'après Rigaud offre une physionomie par certains côtés plus proche du tableau de Stockholm: mais il semble que Rigaud ait alourdi à la Louis XIV les traits de Bourdon, et l'on ne saurait se fonder sur un portrait si tardif pour identifier une effigie datant de 1645–50 – soit du moment où Bourdon n'avait que trente ans . . .

41. Rappelons que l'art de Bourdon portraitiste reste mal connu: on peut lui donner avec certitude un ensemble de portraits postérieurs à 1645–49: en revanche pour la période qui précède, un grand nombre de portraits lui sont attribués, qui apparaissent de style fort divers et de tradition très incertaine.

Saône.[42] Or en même temps que ce portrait y apparut la *Famille de paysans*, soudain reconnue pour le chef-d'œuvre des Le Nain et peu après acquise par le Louvre. Comment ne pas être tenté de penser que deux tableaux de même provenance étaient restés jusque-là réunis?[43]

L'inventaire après décès de Matthieu indique plusieurs portraits représentant de grands personnages: notamment "*unze grands portraits de mareschaux de France et autres seigneurs*", et "*douze petits tableaux representans des portraits de mareschaux de France et autres seigneurs garnis de bordures dores*".[44] Les relations du chevalier Le Nain rendent parfaitement plausible l'indication, et tout donne à penser que le peintre avait multiplié ces portraits de la haute société. N'ont-ils jamais servi de modèles aux graveurs? – On le croira difficilement si l'on songe à l'essor du portrait gravé en France vers ce moment. A partir de 1650 l'estampe commence à répandre les traits d'à peu près tous les personnages de quelque notoriété. Mais à partir de la mort de ses frères, Matthieu se montre peu soucieux de rappeler sa qualité de peintre. Il ne s'inquiète guère de faire inscrire son nom au bas des estampes – si même il ne le fait pas supprimer.[45] Et dès lors quel espoir de reconnaître, dans l'immense collection des portraits gravés du XVIIe siècle,

ceux qui peuvent s'inspirer d'un tableau peint par Matthieu? Nous voudrions pourtant désigner, à titre d'exemple, le *Portrait de Sébastien de Pontault, seigneur de Beaulieu*, gravé par Edelinck (Fig. 7).

Cette estampe fait partie du second volume des *Hommes illustres* de Charles Perrault.[46] Chaque éloge accompagne une effigie gravée, de qualité plus ou moins brillante: les meilleures sont justement celles de Gérard Edelinck, dont on sait l'habileté et la fidélité. Or sous la traduction du burin (et avec la marge d'interprétation naturelle à un graveur de la fin du siècle . . .) se retrouve quelque chose de l'éclairage contrasté que nous avons noté plus haut comme un parti caractéristique de Matthieu. Des reflets puissants dégagent la joue, éclairent par dessous la lèvre, soulignent la rondeur du visage: on devine qu'un effet de lumière animait cette effigie par ailleurs simple de mise en page et franche de psychologie. L'œuvre tranche par sa manière avec le reste du volume.

Or s'il est un personnage qu'on imagine volontiers portraituré par Matthieu, c'est justement le chevalier de Beaulieu. Mort en 1674, il appartient à la même génération que le peintre. Sans naissance ni grande fortune, il embrasse fort jeune la carrière des armes: dès le siège de la Rochelle sa bravoure lui vaut une réputation que les campagnes de la guerre de Trente ans, vers 1643–1648, portent à son comble, et que vient consacrer en 1658 l'anoblissement accordé par le roi. On lui donne rang parmi les soldats les plus glorieux du temps: mais cet ingénieur, ce contrôleur général de l'artillerie s'intéresse, sinon à la peinture, au moins au dessin, et ne semble pas détester la fréquentation des artistes.[47] Lorsque l'âge lui interdit de servir dans l'armée, il imagine ce fameux recueil des *Glorieuses conquestes de Louis-le-Grand* qui allie à la précision documentaire la qualité de l'estampe: pareille entreprise réclamait chez son auteur à la fois l'amour des armes et le goût des arts.[48] Ajoutons que Beaulieu reçut, six ans avant Matthieu, le collier de chevalier de Saint Michel.[49] Tout porte donc à

42. *Catalogue des Tableaux anciens, dessins gouaches, gravures . . . composant la collection de M. le Marquis de M(armier) et provenant du château de X . . . dont la vente aux enchères publiques aura lieu Hôtel Drouot, salle n. 10, le samedi 14 mars 1914.* N.º 35: *Bourdon, portrait de l'artiste.* Le tableau fut acquis pour 3.000 francs par Palm.
43. Il semble que les Le Nain eurent des amateurs fidèles, et leurs tableaux sont parfois restés groupés assez longtemps: vente Conti en 1777, collection Ottone Ponte di Scarnafigi, puis Seyssel. – Signalons que les *Soldats jouant aux cartes*, dits aussi *la Rixe*, tableau signé, aujourd'hui au musée de Springfield (Mass.), est signalé parfois comme provenant également de la collection de Marmier (cf. catalogue *The Brothers Le Nain, op. cit.*, p. 9): nous n'avons pu découvrir sur quelle preuve se fonde cette assertion. En revanche, ne dissimulons pas que cette collection comprenait des tableaux des XVIIe et XVIIIe siècles fort divers, dont justement un *Intérieur de Corps de garde*, dit de Sébastien Bourdon (nº 36), signé et daté de 1676 (*sic*). Or Bourdon meurt en 1671. S'agit-il d'une fausse lecture (pour 1646), ou d'une fausse signature, dissimilant peut-être, de nouveau, un Le Nain?
44. *Documents, op. cit.*, p. 244.
45. A partir de 1650, au moment où la gravure de traduction prend à Paris un développement toujours plus considérable, Matthieu ne fit certainement rien pour perpétuer par ce moyen l'art de ses frères et le sien: et ce n'est pas la moindre des raisons qui expliquent l'oubli où sombrèrent les frères Le Nain. Pratiquement le nom de Le Nain ne se trouve sous une gravure qu'au XVIIIe siècle – d'où le nombre de pièces fausses mêlées aux reproductions de leurs œuvres authentiques (cf. *Documents, op. cit.*, pp. 281–283, et part! note 11). Rappelons que peut-être y eut-il pourtant une exception: Le Blanc catalogue dans l'œuvre de Le Pautre sous le nº 14 un *Acis et Galatée d'après L. Lenain, pièce en largeur*. Malheureusement nous n'avons encore pu découvrir cette estampe, et à notre connaissance aucun des érudits qui depuis cent ans s'occupent de Le Nain n'en a signalé l'existence.
46. *Des hommes illustres qui ont paru en France pendant ce siècle, avec leur portrait au naturel, par M. Perrault*, t. II, à Paris, A. Dezollier, 1700, p. 42. Le Blanc, nº 144 de l'œuvre d'Edelinck; Weigert, nº 208.
47. On l'a dit "élève de Callot", et Beaulieu pourrait en effet avoir rencontré le graveur lorsque vers 1628–1630 celui-ci vint préparer sur place les fameuses planches du *Siège de l'île de Ré* et du *Siège de La Rochelle*: nommé tout jeune Contrôleur ordinaire de l'artillerie, Beaulieu avait précisément rempli les fonctions de cette charge au siège de La Rochelle, où Louis XIII en personne remarqua l'intrépidité de sa conduite. N'était-ce pas à lui que revenait d'indiquer les dispositions du siège à l'artiste chargé par le roi d'en perpétuer le souvenir?
48. *Les Glorieuses Conquêtes de Louis le Grand, d'après le chevalier de Beaulieu*, recueil publié après la mort du chevalier par les soins de sa nièce et demeuré célèbre sous le nom de "Grand Beaulieu". La plupart des planches sont gravées par les Cochin, les Pérelle, et J. Frosne.
49. "*Il fut nommé chevalier de l'ordre de Saint Michel le 25 may 1656 et reçu le 22 octobre suivant par le Maréchal de l'Hôpital, chevalier*

penser que Matthieu le connut, tout s'accorde à suggérer qu'il portraitura ce personnage qui devait devenir son collègue dans l'Ordre. Peut-être fut-ce déjà en ami et en honnête homme qui manie le pinceau, mais ne signe pas.[50] Et vers 1700, qui eût songé à retrouver le nom du chevalier Le Nain, sieur de la Jumelle, pour le graver au bas d'un portrait?[15]

Rien n'est plus risqué, certes, que d'attribuer le modèle d'une gravure sans la garantie de la lettre. Et nous ne nous

> *des Ordres du Roy dans l'église des Jacobins du Faubourg Saint-Honoré"* : cf. *Recueil des Chevaliers de l'ordre de Saint Michel* . . ., t. IV, fol. 408 v⁰ (Paris, Bibl. Nat., Cabinet des manuscrits, Fr. 32873). – Les tracas subis par Matthieu Le Nain lors de la révision de 1663 (voir *Documents, op. cit.*, pp. 208–219) lui furent épargnés. Fraîchement anobli, il ne possédait certes pas les quartiers nécessaires, et sa nomination était à peine moins illégitime que celle de Matthieu: mais l'estime que lui portait le roi et la considération générale que lui valaient ses hauts faits le firent dispenser par faveur spéciale des degrés qui lui manquaient.
>
> 50. Il est difficile, en tout état de cause, d'assigner une date à ce portrait. La pose semble indiquer que Beaulieu avait déjà perdu un bras (Bataille de Philippsbourg, 1643); l'âge apparent ne paraît guère pouvoir dépasser quarante-cinq ans. L'absence du collier de Saint Michel doit-elle faire penser à une date antérieure à 1656? De toute manière on ne devrait pas trop s'éloigner, semble-t-il, de 1655.
>
> 51. Il semble que pour constituer ce recueil des *Hommes illustres* on fit une recherche systématique des portraits authentiques peints

cachons pas que les trois œuvres proposées offrent entre elles, à première vue, un certain disparate. Mais les "portraits de groupe", comparés figure à figure, montreraient sans peine la même diversité: et nous jouions la difficulté en choisissant pour exemples une miniature, une peinture et une gravure. Répétons que ces attributions sont surtout destinées à en appeler d'autres, dont le nombre même fera plus facilement paraître l'exactitude ou l'erreur. Le portrait français du dix-septième siècle commence à peine à être connu: il n'y a pas longtemps que tout se résumait à Pourbus, Champaigne, Nanteuil et Rigaud. La carte demeure aujourd'hui à peine moins sommaire: mais quelques repères apparaissent enfin, les directions principales se devinent, il va falloir bientôt ordonner cet immense domaine. Notre souci était de réserver sans tarder la part des frères Le Nain. Car une fois renversée la perspective qui, depuis Champfleury et Valabrègue, fait des Le Nain, par excellence et presque par exclusive, des "peintres paysans", leur rôle en ce domaine du portrait, tout bref qu'il fut, apparaît au moins aussi remarquable que celui des Beaubrun ou d'un Nocret, tandis que leur art, si mal connu soit-il, l'emporte sans peine par la nouveauté, la diversité et la profondeur.

> ou gravés: mais on se soucia rarement d'en indiquer l'auteur. Les quelques noms que l'on rencontre sont ceux d'artistes vivants ou morts depuis peu: Rigaud, Mignard, Lefebvre . . .

OLIVER MILLAR

An Exile in Paris: The Notebooks of Richard Symonds

ON 1st January 1649 Richard Symonds left London for Paris. At the outbreak of the Civil War, when he was a young official in the Court of Chancery, he had been arrested as a delinquent to the state. In October 1643, soon after his twenty-sixth birthday, he had escaped to join the forces of Charles I at Oxford. He served in the king's troop of Life Guards under Lord Bernard Stuart, the king's cousin, and fought at Cropredy Bridge, both battles of Newbury, Naseby and the relief of Chester. When the royalist cause was finally extinguished, Symonds compounded as a delinquent, settled his affairs and prepared for a tour of the Continent.

As a young man Symonds's chief passion had been for the antiquities, the genealogy and heraldry of his native Essex; the mass of material that he collected in Essex churches before the Civil War was to prove a most valuable source for Morant in his great work on this county. During his marches with the royal armies Symonds would often hop off his horse to jot down notes of what he saw in churches past which his troop was riding; and in winter quarters in Oxford he spent many hours in the colleges, libraries and churches in the city. On the Continent he developed an insatiable interest in pictures and works of art. In Paris, and later in Italy, he filled a series of notebooks with minutely written, accurate and entirely personal descriptions, sometimes illustrated by sketches in ink, pencil and chalk, of the buildings and collections he visited. It is the purpose of this article to set on record some of his comments in Paris on contemporary and near-contemporary works of art and buildings.[1]

1. The two notebooks which Symonds kept in Paris are in the British Museum: Harl. MS. 943 and Harl. MS. 1278. The first of these is partly filled with practical matters which Symonds had to tidy up before going abroad. The second is the most orderly of all Symonds's notebooks and is entitled by him 'Description de ville de Paris. 1629 [for 1649]. par Richard Symonds Comitatus essex Gen.' He states later that the 'Description' was made 'According to ye method of Malingre in his description of it', showing that he relied for the order in which his notes were laid out on Claude Malingre's Les Antiquitez de la Ville de Paris, published in 1640.

I have not, in this short article, attempted to compile a commentary on the material collected by Symonds, but I hope to deal more worthily with him in a full edition of his travel notebooks. I have endeavoured to print Symonds's notes exactly as they were written, preserving the paragraphs into which his text is divided, but not the lines in which it is composed. I have not noted the points at which Symonds corrects himself or makes an insertion. I have indicated by square brackets an illegible word or phrase and the whereabouts in the notes of Symonds's little sketches.

Symonds left Calais on 5th January 1649. Six days later he reached Paris, having travelled through Boulogne, Montreuil, Abbeville, Beauvais and St- Denis. In the capital he stayed first with M. le Roy at 'St Cristofers' in the rue Montorgueil. Later he was at a pension, 'the 3 Mores heads' in the rue St-Jacques. He moved again, first to the rue Sept-Voyer and finally to 'ye Quatre Vents' near the Place Maubert.

In his first Parisian notebook Symonds has a short description of the Louvre:

The kings howse calld ye L'ouvre. at Paris. Next ye River is a long building of Stone. wch is ye gallery. covered wth blew Slate. [sketch]

The fore gate stands westwards where as soone as you enter you ascend some stepps of stone – wch looke into a large garden wch ascent is a stayrecase all of stone of Ovall forme ye Pillars of Black Marble

The Garden is of many walkes & knotts of box as ye garden at White hall in Essex. about ye sides are Cipresse trees about 12 in all. wch grow high. & ye body is pruned up about a mans height from ground ye boughes not tyed as ors in England. Right over agt the entrance into this Royall, Palace wch is but begun & not halfe pfected I suppose (as was intended) wthin a stone wall is a larg garden almost halfe a myle square in plano upon a flat. where at the entrance you looke thorough a walke on each side planted wth [? shee] Elmes. but ye Causeway as all other ye walkes in that garden is so troublesomely dirty that tis a labor to walke in it.

In ye middle is a grove of Cipresse, tall. & Box. make ye hedges pretty close. So that box is below & Cipresse above. in the same hedge

There is a faire pond also in this garden & 3 Crosse walkes of thick & tall box. some groves of Elmes. & some squares of box knotts.

One ye side on the right hand as you come in, is althorough out of box knotts, where ye hedges are. neately kept as this
[sketch]

Next some of the walls as in many other places of France is planted of beech wood wch growes like a hedge to defend you from ye heat refleccon of the Sun. upon those walls.

The gallery. of ye L'ouvre.

The little gallery that is as you goe from ye Qu: of Englands Cort into the long gallery. on the right side.

The pictures of the Kings of France at length. & heads round about of great officers of that time

Over ag^t on ye other side Their Queenes.

The spaces of the long gallery were p^rpard for the land-ships of all the great townes of the World

700 foot long. 10 yards broad.

2 rowes of black & White marble. the rest is paved wth brick.

Much of the Roofe is guilt – but not a q^r of it.[2]

At a slightly later date in his visit Symonds again wrote about the Louvre, in the context of a short general account of it:

The first Court is begun to be built very lofty & large: ye Front wth statues over the port, The Gallery next the Water is not halfe way rooft pavd wth brick. & 2 Row of square stones in the middle. of black & white marble.

The spaces betweene ye Windowes was designd to have ye prospects of all ye famousest Citties of the World. in painting. not one p'fected nor begun –

The Roofe has half statues & antique worke upon paint-ing of Mosaique

In a little Gallery going into ye great one are ye pictures of all the Kings of France from St Lowys. at length: & their heads of all their severall great officers about them.

Their Queenes ye other side. & their Ladyes –

Monsr Bunel was a painter in this Gallery. vide pag.332 [ie., below, page 164]

The Roofe has many storyes of men & women. At the farther end aloft sitts H.4 in a throne & his Court about him –[3]

After his first description of the Louvre, Symonds mentions the practice of writing in golden letters, over their gates, the names of the owners of the 'houses of men of honor & qualite'. This leads him on to a note on Lemercier's Palais Cardinal:

Over Cardinal Richleu's gate in golden letters cutt into black marble. Le Palais du Cardinal wch Palace is built of free stone. 2 Courts not large & a halfe Court wch lookes into the Garden. in the halfe court neare ye Pale wch is painted wth Greene. is a Tilt Rayle. The rayles of yron wch are somewhat like balconyes in this halfe Court 2 story high are guilt. The hither pt of the garden is like ye garden at the lovre of box. low. ye farther pt is groves & walkes.

about all ye house & over ye gate at the entrance is a pt of a Shipp. wth lances & speares issuing out of her & under her an anchor. his device. afore ye out gate of this palace is a square place in ye street like a market place. This palace is not far from the L'ouvre.[4]

Symonds opens his more formal Parisian notebook with a description of Notre-Dame. He includes a particularly interesting description of the paintings that decorated the interior:

The quire is adornd wth 14 faire tables, well painted that constantly hang in the arches above the seates of the Choristers.

14 Tables of painting

One well designd & painted of the Crucyfing of s^t Peter. wth his heeles upwards where the Heathen Priest is speaking to s^t Peter in his eare. pointed to the idoll wch is elevated upon a lofty pedestall. The officers about well mounted all as big as the life.

Another of bringing a Bull to Sacrifice wth musique & Triumph. whereat – – rends his Clothes. Another of St Peter. wth this written upon the frame Quod habeo hoc tibi do. healing a lame pson.

Another of a man possest bound in Chaynes. Behind ye pillars neare a great Chappel at the east end of ye Church. afore ye holy weeke did hang two very large paintings. done by. G. Lallemant. fec: 1634

In ye holy weeke & Easter in the same place was hung two faire peices of Tapistry done in Silke of the same worke: & this written in faire letters oth top.

Regnan Louis le juste dit le 13 Ces. quatre peices de Tapissre representant la Vie – & le Martyre des bien heureux Saincts. – Crepin & Crepinian des bienfaicts & liberalitez des Maistres Cordoniers de cette ville &c 1634. The Executioners tye the martyrs to a Wheele & cutt out peices of flesh out of their backs. An Angel comes from Heaven wth two Garlands one for each: Some Drowne themselves. Some have awles thrust into their heads & eyes. all rarely done in the same peices of Lalle-mant.

Right ag^t the Ladyes Altar in a long large guilt – frame & well painted for a French painter.

I suppose the best could be gotten is ye V Mary shewing the naked dead body of o^r Savio^r.

Lewis. 13. k. of F. offers his Crowne. above, as in the heavens are. a company of angels. tis designd in this manner. [sketch of it].

This was painted by Champagne a Flemand that did ye last supp at the Nunnery of Por Royal he lives in Paris. In ye space betweene this picture & ye altar of ye B.V. hang a very large Lampe of Silver, both this picture & that given to ye Church by this Qu: Regent. Ann of Austriche.

The upper pt of the Quire is often upon feast dayes hang wth new Tapistree of Greenes. & prospects, onely a small picture or two in a peice as one has o^r Savio^r & ye woman of Samaria at the Well St John baptizing of o^r Savio^r in another peice The Good Samaritane in another peice.

Easter Day. & Eve ye Quire aloft was hanged wth old large Tappistree full of persons. of the actions & suffer-ings of o^r Saviour.

. . .

2. Harl. MS. 943, ff. 37–38v.

3. Harl. MS. 1278, f. 146. Nothing survives of Jacques Bunel's work in the Louvre.

4. Harl. MS. 943, ff. 39v.–40.

The large Tables of paintings in the Quire were
Quire.   done by severall Masters. That of S? Peter putt
upon the X Crosse wᵗʰ his heeles upward was
done by Monsʳ Bordon, aupres de Palais That of S.
Going to be sawne for not worshipping the Idol. rarely
done, tis yᵉ 1 on yᵉ left hand entring West. end. done by
a Frenchman who liv'd long at Rome.

That of yᵉ Cloven tongues lesse then yᵉ life – rarely done
by Monsʳ Blanchar who is dead.⁵

In the Hôtel-Dieu Symonds saw a very recent votive
picture:

In yᵉ middle of yᵉ Hospitall is an altar rayld in. upon the
wall is a large new picture. where yᵉ Queene Regent that
now is presents her young son to yᵉ V.M. The Crosse
ladder & persons as big as the life & well done. [sketch]⁶

and in the Ste-Chapelle he was much moved by a statue by
Pilon, now in the Louvre:

Under yᵉ Organ wᶜʰ is on yᵉ North wall neare yᵉ entrance at yᵉ west end is an incomparable Statue of. Nostre
Dame De la Pitie under it cutt in stone. G PILON.f.⁷

He was particularly impressed with the convent of the
Carmelites in the rue St-Jacques:

The Altar piece is of the Anuntiation. done by Guyde
Bolyneze. sayes Malingre.
tis not altogether so big as the life.
Over it cutt into the stone in Gold letters large – A V E.
Gratia plena –
Betweene the 4 pillars. 2 flat. one of a V yᵉ other of a
Nun –
The Roofe is of stone archt over all yᵉ Dome in a Rich
glory well painted, being flat, yᵉ paintings seeme to stand
upright. as. G. the father over yᵉ altar.
The Crucifix. yᵉ 2 women standing by it.
Aaron, yᵉ children of Israel.
Elias in a fiery Chariot letting fall his mantle to one
kneeling.
Abram offring up Isaack. –
On yᵉ sides. are yᵉ pictures of a Pope. & divers Bᵖˢ
sitting upon the battlements of the Church –
The South side of the Quire is adorn'd wᵗʰ 6
Pictures.   very faire tables of Paintings. 3 lowest much
yᵉ bigger. having frames carved & guilt, &
Blew very costly in great breadth betweene the double
guilding
A Cherubim of Guilt carving betweene large Corncopias

guilt. over all either the Armes of the Donor, or. IHS
1. The Nativity
2. The Holy Ghost appearing in Cloven tongues
3. Oʳ Savior arisen from yᵉ Sepulcre, & yᵉ Assumtion
of the V. by Angels into Heaven –
4. 3. Kings of the East worshipping yᵉ Babe. rarely well
done.
5. The Presentation of the Babe in the Temple. very
large & lofty.
6. Our Savioʳ Raising of Lazarus from yᵉ Dead.
Done by Monsʳ Champagne as Mʳ Dunkomwell
sayes –
The 3 last are 10 or 12 foot broad & 16 high. as I
guesse.

I esteeme this one of the best & costliest quires in Paris. for
painting, loftines, & guilding & especially antiquity –⁸
Equally interesting, again for its description of the work of
Georges Lallemand, is Symonds's account of the interior of
Ste-Geneviève-du-Mont:

The Six Altars. in yᵉ body of yᵉ Church are well painted
by. G. Lallement. 1636
                                    1. on yᵉ North side of Lewis 13 offer-
These Altars   ing his crowne to Saint Lewis in the
are built agᵗ yᵉ   heavens.
North Wall.   2. St. Stephen a Stoning excellently
                              well done.
3. St Marie Magdalene dying among 3 Angells
South side
                                    1. Sᵗ Genovesve upon an altar of stone
These 3 agᵗ yᵉ   & yᵉ Citty of Paris in prospect
S. Wall   Divers Citizens praying to her. she
                              hath a bunch of keyes in her left hand
    & a Wax light left –
2. A Hermite.
3. Sᵗ Martyn on Horseback giving his Cloake to a
Cripple wᵗʰout clothes –
            . . .
Agᵗ yᵉ entrance into yᵉ quire left hand is painted over
that altar. S. Peter receiving yᵉ keyes of Oʳ Savioʳ. done
by G. Lallement.f.1636. Lallement was a Fr
On yᵉ right hand, over that altar is S. Paull falling from
his horse. & the light from heaven. very well painted
under is written as of most of the 6 – Lallement.fecit
Upon yᵉ top of that altar wher K. Lewis 13 offers his
Crowne to Sᵗ Lewis in the heavens. is in golden letters S.
Ludouico Regi, Proauo suo. & under yᵉ Armes of France
& Navar. Lodouicus Xiii.D⁹

5. Harl. MS. 1278, ff. 11v.–12v. The *Mays* mentioned by Symonds
include the *Crucifixion of St. Peter* by Sébastien Bourdon (1643:
Louvre); the *Sacrifice of Lystra* by Michel Corneille I (1646);
St. Paul expelling Evil Spirits by Louis Boulogne I (1646); and
Jacques Blanchard's *Descent of the Holy Spirit* (1634: Notre-
Dame). The votive picture by De Champagne is now at Caen.
On May Day 1649 Symonds records that Le Sueur's *St. Paul
at Ephesus* was exposed before the main doors of the Cathedral;
he does not give the painter's name.

6. *Ibid.*, f. 14v.   7. *Ibid.*, f. 19.

8. *Ibid.*, ff. 22–22v. The *Annunciation* by Guido is in the Louvre;
the surviving paintings from the set by De Champagne are at
Lyons, Grenoble and Dijon.

9. *Ibid.*, f. 25v., 27. None of the many paintings by Georges
Lallemand described by Symonds is known to survive. On ff.
24v.–27 is a further short note about the decoration surrounding
the principal altarpiece and a short account of a little chapel on
the south side of the cloister 'newly furnisht wᵗʰ pictures',

Symonds's very full description of pictures in the Monastery and church of the Jacobins provides valuable material on a painter, Martin de Héry, even more shadowy than Lallemand:

Many arches aloft & the sides of the South
Cloister   wall of the cloister are rarely & exquisitely
painted of the story of S. Dominique.

1. First his baptisme – many about the font, all as big as the life.
2. Next. his Confirmation by the Bp. Where yᵉ Bp is in state & great attendance. & much people all about.
3. Sᵗ Dominique stands in his habit, (wᶜʰ yᵉ Monkes now have) in the middle of the battayle: Where some are running away some shooting arrowes at the Crucifix wᶜʰ he holds in his right hand. Some lye dead behind him rarely done. In generall yᵉ description of yᵉ battaile of the – Albigeois – Vide his life in Beurrier. Upon the arch, over this painting is Written. ILLVSTRISSIMÆ. Ludovicæ Lothorenæ Principis de Conty, liberalitate, & munificentia. 1616.
   These were painted by Monsʳ de Hery a frenchman who lived 12 yeares in Italy as a painter told me dyed 3 or 4 yea: since.
4. A ship at shore. Sᵗ Dominique wants money to enter into it for to pay his passage. & 4 peices fall from – heaven. In prospect, he is casting out a divel yᵉ same painting
5. His Holines is in his Seige. accompanied wᵗʰ all yᵉ Conclave of Card: where S. Dominique comes in his habitt & receives a Patent of the Pope –

Over that painting where yᵉ ship is is this written MARIOTTVS de Vernaccinis Ciuis Florentinus primus, in Comitatu Comitis Vestiarÿ. Christianissimæ Reginæ matris. Picturam hanc ad deipiaræ Virginis Sacratissimiq Rosarÿ cultum & honorem, & beati Dominici gloriam voti memor, beneficÿq accepti gratus, posuit –
Those 5 peices of Painting afore mentiond are all of one hand. there is two more. but not so good.

. . .

In yᵉ quire are 6 large pieces. in a little piece of paper; as it were painted at the bottome of one. that is of this order holding a – gold. kind of Cup archt. Wherein is yᵉ Host a Dove whispering in his eare.

S. Thomas Aquinas Doctor angelicus – & Theologioru Princeps. 14 . . . huius Scholæ Professor publice docuit. Circa Annū Dn̄i. 1260.
A Visc: Crowne & a Miter at his feet –
Another. Beatus Albertus magnus Colomensis Sancti Thomæ Præceptor. 1260.

A large picture where S. Dominique stands behind H.4 & a Pope stands behind Qu: Marie de Medicis & before yᵐ the then Prince. these 3 kneeling to yᵉ V.M. in yᵉ Clouds. oʳ Savioʳˢ dead body in her lap. & angels flying about the Crosse. The Crowne & scepter upon the ground Sᵗ D. pointing. & shewing to. H.4.
Upon yᵉ High Altar is yᵉ picture of yᵉ Ascention A large Statue of S Dominique on one side. & . . . on the other.¹⁰

Symonds provides an equally full description of the Monastery of the Reformed Jacobins in the rue St-Honoré:

This is newly built, a faire large Court to goe to yᵉ west end of their Church. wch is so gay wᵗʰ guilding & painting as most exceeds

Each side of the Chœur are many Chappels
Quire   The walls of the quire are almost full wᵗʰ
pictures some large Tables. as storyes of S.
Dominick. & yᵉ chiefe famous fathers of this order
One is of the body of oʳ Savioʳ who descends to the Earth in a Cloud. S. Dominick wᵗʰ a sword in his head kisses his right hand. S Thomas Aquinas his left hand. Another embraces him about the middle. Two Nuns of this habit most humbly kneele & kisse his feet.
Another as big as the life, where Oʳ Savioʳ descending to the Earth in a Cloud layes his hand upon the head of one of this Order.
Another where S. Dominic receives a chaplet or paire of Beades from the hand of the V. Mary being in the Clouds.
Another where one of this order is crown'd wᵗʰ a Chaplet by Angels
Another, He being at his prayers an Angel comes from Heaven & presents him wᵗʰ a Crowne, he continuing on his knees & looking back
Another at large also of S. Thomas Aquinas yᵉ Dove at his eare. & the pictures in small of 7 Popes who were of this order, all in that frame
Many little frames besides some where Laics pray to some of this order, & he prayes to the V.
The Picture of the high Altar is oʳ Lady & the Angel. The Annuntiacon.
On the South side of the Altar is a pretty large Chappel dedicated to Sᵗ Hiacinthe built by Mary de Medicis Wife to Hen: 4ᵗʰ
The Altar picture is very large. painted, as appeares by yᵉ name thereon. I. de Letyn fecit

About 100 frames of pictures hang in this
Pictures   Chappel. being all Miracles & Cures &c the
Miracles   like done in this Chappel, & by the Intercession of this Saint
Some are where one of this order presents Children to the V.M. Ex Voto written upon. the Altar

---

apparently including pictures of SS. Julian and Thomas à Becket. On ff. 28–28v. is a description of St.-Étienne-du-Mont and on ff. 30v.–32 an account of the paintings, on the wall of the cloister of St-Germain-des-Prés, of the abbots and of the Popes of the Benedictine order.

10. Harl. MS. ff. 35–36. None of De Héry's pictures survives. In the school of the Monastery Symonds noticed paintings of famous men of the order down to 1300: 'Face & shoulders. newly done, & by some French dauber'.

Some one of this p^rsent Cavaliers to the V.

Some, wherein a Woman prayes to this Saint & he prayes to the V.M. [sketch].[11]

Symonds describes Lemercier's unfinished Sorbonne:

This stands betweene ye Rue de l'Harpe & le Rue S. Jacques.

The Chappel & colledge are new built & building. by the expence & cost of Card: Richlieu.

Nothing in all ye University like a College but this. &

chappel   The Tower of ye Chappel wch is a Cupolo. is much of it guilt. on the outside

The West end is adornd wth divers Statues of white marble. & lofty pillars: wth this in large letters cutt deepe into ye stone over the dore DEO. OPT. MAX. ARMANDVS. CARD. DE RICHELIEV.

Upon ye porch of ye North side wch is wthin the finisht great Court. to wch you ascend on 15 stone steps. & has 10 lofty strong pillars to support it under his Armes in large Character is in sculp't. ARMANDVS IOANNES CARD. DVX de Richelieu. Sorboniæ provisor. in one lyne Ædificavit Domum, et exaltavit Templum sanctum Domino. M.DC.XLII.

The Chappel is not yet finisht. wthin. there is excellent carvd worke in stone. as palme branchs hanging one over another rarely done Divers statues wthin. every window is filed wth the flourishes of ye Coate armo^r of Card. R. [sketch]

In ye chappel Windowes An Anchor B. Under all wth ye order of S. Espritt

West end on each side of the Diall wch was intended for the motion & age of the moone is S. Dionisius his head on a globe by him S Louys

The roofe of the College is of blew slate, on the ridge is lead & also at the Eeves lead

The spouts of leads wch come from the roofe are about 10 foot above ground covered wth brasse thick. at bottome of all a Dolphin gaping spitts out the water on the ground

Hall   The hall or place of   is a long square full of windowes to each of wch is divers strutts of wood. the roofe is flat of large timber colored browne

At the upper end is ye Card: picture at length as if standing in this Colledge by lofty pillars & ye North fron. of the Chappel painted in prospect.

In all ye windowes of this roome in a small glass is his Coate of armes as afore described

Garden   A little Garden behind ye hall. The wall is lyn'd wth mirtle supported by poles. besides ye walkes ye Grasse has a path cutt in workes. as at one place in Luxembourg next ye Nunnery of Mount Carmel. [sketch].

I believe ye bell here & that of Lincolns Inn. are

Bell   Unisones.

Statues   Below is ye Statue of a Woman wth a scroll in her hand treading wth her left foot on a Wolfes head And another Woman wth a Mans hart in her left hand.

Within ye body of ye Chappel are large & faire Statues in white stone rarely done of the 12 Apostles.

The Flore is Black Marble unpolisht & a Red speckled stone

a Circle in the Middle under ye Steeple –

This Chappel especially ye North stately porch is of Corinthiaque worke.[12]

Symonds's notes continue with descriptions of the Cluniac and Bernardine Colleges;[13] the notes include descriptions of paintings, but do not indicate their date or authorship. In the College of Cardinal Moyne, however, he records:

picture of Card: M.   Upon the Chimney peice is ye picture of Cardinal Moyne. in the same garbe wth Card: Richlieu's pictures. His armes. painted at bottome. His College is drawne in prospect.

H.4.   In the same hall is the picture of K.H.4 at length, drawne a proper lusty man: for bigger than he was in Trunke hose a blew Riband hanging downe his breast wth ye order of S Esprit Upon his head a black Velvet Cap. [sketch][14]

In the Monastery of the Cordeliers he saw a large recent votive picture:

In a foure square archt porch wch goes. into ye Sacristie Cloister & Church. this is painted over the dore. upon the wall, all as big as the life

[sketch]

Divers of the Order kneeling under ye Canopy praying to her.

A Multitude of ye Cord: kneeling & praying to her.

H.4 K of France a Bp behind him holding ye lyning.

A Bp & another Churchman holding the doubling up.

Si cupis optatum cæli pertingere lumen. In terras Dominā prōptus obiq cole.[15]

His account of the Augustinian church – 'Religieux Mendians nommez Augustins' – includes a description of, presumably, an important large early work by de Champagne, now in Toulouse:

The Cheifest thing observable is the Chappel de S. Esprit: where the Altar piece is ye holy ghost descending in cloven tongues. & a large new piece of. Lewis 13. & 4 officers of his Court creating Monsr de Longville of the order of S. Esprit.

---

11. *Ibid.*, ff. 39–39v. The altarpiece by Jacques Ninet de Lestin does not survive.

12. *Ibid.*, ff. 43v.–44. At least two surviving versions of De Champagne's portrait of Richelieu have the view of the Sorbonne in the background.

13. *Ibid.*, ff. 45v.–48v.

14. *Ibid.*, f. 49v.

15. *Ibid.*, f. 74.

M

Here every morning is high Masse sd for the sowle of. H.4. whose picture is also here.

. . .

The statue of S. Francois is well done in Brasse in this Cloister. wch was done by. Germ: Pilon. sayes Malingre. pag 260[16]

At the Hospital of La Charité Symonds noted two more commemorative or votive pieces:

Over ye Altar is a faire & large picture where K. Lewis 13 in his Royall Robes washes and dresses the sore of an infirme mans leg.

In another place in a large peice is painted Cardinal Richlieu giving a Patent to a father of the Order of ye Charity Very well done

In another place One of the order dead & 2 more sitting by him praying in their bookes well done[17]

Among the pictures at the Monastery of Carmes-Deschaussées, Symonds noted works by Varin and Corneille:

The picture over ye Altar is ye Purificacon of ye Autel B.V. done by. Varin. ye kings painter – Maling: p. 392

But ye paintings in ye Steeple or Cupolo wch is Circular & where divers psons looke over ye Rayles & S

Catches ye Mantle that falls from Elias in a fiery Chariot A S^t of this order A Nun of this Order lifted up in ye Clouds. All done by 2 young men of Lorraine that came from Rome, & rarely well

In ye body ag^t ye Wall hang some Tables well painted. One by Corneille. & others better. one of o^r Savio^r sitting among the Doctors – Another of ye Annuntiation. ye V. is sewing & listning very well done. – S. Joseph reading, sitting upon frames of Carpenters worke –[18]

It may be a sign of Symonds's dislike of full baroque painting that he should have omitted Rubens's name in his notice of the finest set of modern pictures then to be seen in Paris, which he saw in his visit to the Luxembourg:

The one side next ye Nunnery of Mount Calvarie is finisht & fairely guilded w^thin.

The One side is a gallery. flat Roofe but fairely guilded, & on ye sides of ye Story of the life of Marie de Medicis – Her birth. Education of all ye Graces & Arts. Her picture showne to H.4. whereat he seemes stricken. wth love. Her Mariage by an Embassado^r. for H.4. Her passage by Sea. Her Coronacon very large. Her Regency. Her. Victories. Her. Banishment. Her. Carrying up to Heaven. by Angels.

Many old little & very wel painted pieces in a little Chappel neare ye Gallery

The Antichambre is square large & the Roofe guilded.

The Cabinet de Madame is. flord wth wood wrought in little workes all severall formes pitcht in wth Silver. The Sides wansscott wth boxes of Velvet. Guilt. above Italian pictures lesse then the life of ye Mariage of this Queenes Grandfather & Father.

The Roofe is fairely guilt. A little Roome w^thin that. where ye paintings of the king's best howses are as Louvre Fontaynebleau. St Germains.

Hostel de Luxembourg

Over ye first Gate wch has many heads of fooles gaping wth hornes on their eybrows of brasse is inlayd in black marble & guilt letters cutt in Palais d'Orleans.

At each end of ye first building under an arch stand the statues in white Marble of. Hen: 4. & his Queene Sister to ye Duke of Florence. Behind each of them is a Peacock. she, in her, pride built this.[19]

Whatever his reasons for omitting Rubens's name, Symonds's admiration for classical painting was clearly developing fast. When he saw Le Sueur's pictures of the life of St. Bruno in the Chartreuse he was deeply impressed:

Had ye painting of ye life of S. Bruno bene as big as ye life as it is not, it being a 3^d pt lesse. I should have accounted it ye best I ever yet saw. And indeed that is all ye fault. Monsr De Sueur. a Parisian did it.

. . .

I had an houres discourse wth one of the Fathers, he carried me into his Cell. & wrote this, both the name of him that painted the life of St Bruno. & his owne name underneath

Monsieur Le Sueur
Dom fera[ ][20]

In his description of Port-Royal, Symonds includes a valuable note on the chapel:

The Altar is ye neatest I yet ever saw. tis bowing Altar Circular answerable to ye Wall. On each side is a large well made statue in White stone. The Picture is not very large. Tis ye last supper of o^r Saviour. rarely done. by a Flemand that lives in this Citty as a painter then coppying of it told me. one. Monsr Champagne

Not so big as the life, thats ye onely fault.

Judas wth Red haire. rarely done

Round about it a border of grape worke, guilt & exquisitely polisht

Above that in White Marble well polish't is cutt Abram offring up his son Isaack. Above which ye Host Hangs wth a costly cannopy of Needle worke drawne up by a pully of rich guilding.

A small Picture ag^t ye adjoyning of ye V.M & ye babe.

---

16. *Ibid.*, f. 76v. The *St. Francis* is apparently lost.
17. *Ibid.*, f. 83v.
18. *Ibid.*, f. 84–84v. The painting by Quentin Varin is probably the *Presentation* now in St-Joseph-des-Carmes. Michel Corneille's painting is not known to survive.

19. *Ibid.*, ff. 90–90v. Symonds continues with a detailed description of the gardens of the Luxembourg and of a very large ornamental fountain.
20. *Ibid.*, ff. 91v.–93. The paintings are now in the Louvre.

& one doing obeysance rarely done. at Rome in a costly guilt frame.

This makes a great shew being coverd wth blew shingles as Wee go into ye Carthusians.²¹

In the church of St-Honoré Symonds records another altarpiece by de Champagne:

This is ye South side of the Rue S. Honore, tis newly built w^thin. a small Church. The Altar new. & has a faire picture large done by the Dutchman Champagne. The Babe in S. Josephs Armes & the V M. standing by. Divers looking on.

In St-Martin-des-Champs Symonds noted:

The Quire is large, the Altar lofty, having a good piece of painting very large of the Circumcision & p^r sentacon of o^r Savio^r in ye Temple. painted by a frenchman that livd long time in Rome. Monsr Vignion.²²

He provides a most interesting description of the Monastery of the Célestins:

At ye West end of their neat Church is three statues large & coulourd.

On ye right hand a King & thus written on the pedestall. Karolus Quintus fundator Huius Ecclesiæ

On ye other side of the Dores a statue of a Queene & this Jehanne de Bourbon espouse de Charles quint.

Ag^t the pillar betweene the two Dores the Statue of Pope Celestine in the habit of these Religieux having in his right hand his Triple papal Crowne. in his left hand the keyes, & on that arme hangs his rich papal Cope. & this inscribed on the foot. S. Pierre Celestine

. . .

In ye middle of the Quire the lofty Deske whereon ye Booke by wch they call ye pulpitre. is of massy Brasse wth many statues of ye most excellent Statuary. Pilon.

Quire.

. . .

The Picture over ye Altar is rarely painted of the Dead body of o^r Savior. Many figures about it. done by. Michael Angelo

. . .

Here is ye most excellent piece of Painting & Sculpture in Paris

That admirable Triple statue of White speckled marble which is a guilt urne wherein is the Hart of K.H.2 See Malingre. p.587. Done by. Pilon supported by ye 3 Graces wch hold hands. Their Robes are incomparable [sketch]

They ioyne hands & one of them being Charity holds ye Urne wth her right hand.

Neare ye pillar entring in is a large Pedestall whereon stands 3 statues in Brasse. one is Justice. The other. putts out a torch. The pillar is about

Pillar

18 foot from ground Wreadthd. & curiously wrought on the summity is an Urne. wherein is the hart of Montmorency. Constable of France. see Malingre. p. 587.

One of the fathers told me that 50 Thowsand francs was offerd for it. & tis so prizd.

Another in the middle of the chappel upon a Pedestall whereon 3 little boyes putt out Torches. is the Hart of Francis. 2^d of France. V. Malingre. p.587.²³

Symonds was warm in praise of St-Paul–St-Louis:

This is accompted the choice peice of all Paris. The west end wch is in the Rue. S. Antoine is ascended by many faire stone steps. having many Statues. & faire guilt letters as you may see in Malingre. page-661.

Tis lofty, long, & very stately w^thin. ye forme of a Crosse ye East end Circular, & ye middle a Cupolo. where the pavement represents that forme, being circular & wrought like a Star in black white & Coloured stone.

Many frames of paintings well done hang upon the walls & over the Altars. S Ignace his story. Upon the East wall neare the great Altar on the north side of the Crosse is well painted. K. Lewis.13. offering One of the Order to S Lewis in the Clouds. Angels support this Chappel upon their Sholders.

The father is modest & p^rsumes not to come near the S^t but lookes toward ye left hand very modestly [sketch]

. . .

Upon one of ye paintings is thus. Mi: Corneille: inve: & fecit 1641 all are of ye same hand. He is of the order. that painted it.

The pulpit is all guilt – over every altar is in guilt letters. Unum ex septem altaribus

The high Altar has many Statues & long polisht black Marble pillars

Tis ye onely rare thing in Paris. Under ye arches. are Iron Dores where ye Jes: sitt & talke wth ye ladies & Visitors. Many stooles of Confession here.²⁴

Of the 'Maison des Religieux de La Mercy' Symonds wrote:

This is just ag^t the Hostel de Guise a small Chappel. The Altar picture is of Lallements worke. Divers shrowded under the mantle of the V. as a pope an Empero^r some of

---

21. *Ibid.*, f. 105v. The *Last Supper* is now in the Louvre.

22. *Ibid.*, ff. III, 121v.

23. *Ibid.*, ff. 126v.–128. The altarpiece by 'Michael Angelo' is now in the church of Ste-Marguerite; it was exhibited in *Le Seizième Siècle Européen*, Paris, Petit Palais, 1965–66, no. 253, as by Salviati (?), and was discussed by John Shearman in his review of the exhibition in the *Burl M.*, CVIII, 1966, pp. 60–63, fig. 2. On the basis of a document of 1548, Dr. Shearman attributed the picture to Charles Dorigny.

The *Graces* from the monument to Henry II, and the monument to Montmorency by Bullant and Prieur, are in the Louvre; the monument to Francis II, designed by Primaticcio, is now at St-Denis.

24. *Ibid.*, ff. 134v.–135.

this order, who are all white and the armes of Aragon on their breasts

2 of the order kneeling also in other frames East end towards yᵉ V. [25]

In the Franciscan Monastery of Piquepuce he noted:

The Altar peice is well painted of the 3 kings offering prsents to yᵉ babe done by Monsr Bolerye. who is dead a frenchman. Over the picture of or Savior Right side of this Altar is written. Ego sum lux mundi. & Over yᵉ picture of or L. Ego mater Lucis.

North side of the Quire over 3. Stooles of Confession wch are of stone, being pedestalls for 3 lofty Statues.

1. is an Ecce Homo. or Savior bound, & a Reed in his hand, a Body of incomparable perfections, & a face of so much sweetnes, gravity. courage, patience, & iudgmt that may be seen or imagin'd at bottome is in guilt letters Ger: Pilon. Sculptor Ævo suo incomparabilis, fecit

2. The next is, a goodly statue of or Savior in a black Garment. a Coppy of a peice of the same master

3. The 3ᵈ is or Lady sitting in a sad posture a Coppy of that under the Organs in the Chappel Sainct, Malingre calls it Nostre Dame di. La Pitie[26]

In the Hôtel de Ville Symonds recorded:

In a little Roome by the Grand Sale is a late picture of 8 officers of the Citty on their knees to this young King & the Queene mother sitting by. These Citts are in gownes right side Red, left black.[27]

Finally, in his long description of the Monastery of the Feuillants, Symonds provides more information about Bunel and Lallemand:

25. *Ibid.*, f. 141v.
26. Harl. MS. f. 143. The altarpiece was presumably by Nicolas Bollery (d. 1630).
27. *Ibid.*, f. 149.

The High Altar is all guilt. yᵉ picture is the
Altar   ascention & the Assumption of yᵉ La: painted as one of the Religieux told me by Monsr Bunel. who was yᵉ kings painter, but dead. he painted the Gallery at yᵉ Louvre.

. . .

The Quire . . . adorn'd wᵗʰ 7 large Tables of painting of yᵉ life of or Savior. done by one Frere Joseph who was of this Order. & is dead.

. . .

3 sides of this Cloister is glasd & yᵉ Walls painted wᵗʰ the life of S. Bernard Abbé. well done by G. Lallement. who did the Altars in Genovesve. One place he prayes to yᵉ Virgin M. & she presses her right breast wᵗʰ her left arme & a streame of milke falls into his Mouth.

divers looking on The Habit of S. Bernard is white

. . .

At the end of the life of S. Bernard, is as the picture in the Bernardins, or Savior descends from the Crosse to embrace him.

. . .

       One of yᵉ Rel: told me that this Lallement
painters.   was Parisien. & painted much for Monsr De Vendosme He also painted the Cloths in S. Innocents Church.

Monsr Voüet is now living & famous, he painted the Chappel for Monsr Le Chancelier.[28]

On 3rd August Symonds left Paris. Travelling via Nevers, Lyons, Chambéry and Modane, he made for Turin, where he began his tour of Italy: a tour in which he continued to make notes as full as and, to us, as absorbing, as those he had made in Paris and as those he was to make in Commonwealth London after his return home.

28. *Ibid.*, f. 151v.–152v. Nothing survives of Vouet's work in the Hôtel Séguier, carried out for the Chancellor, Pierre Séguier.

Vittone's Drawings in the Musée des Arts Décoratifs

I THINK it was about twenty years ago that I surprised Anthony Blunt by offering at the Courtauld Institute a lecture on Vittone, at that time a name that meant little or nothing to most people. Some years later he discovered and mentioned to me the two volumes of Vittone drawings in the library of the Musée des Arts Décoratifs in Paris, and I have played ever since with the idea of exploring this somewhat mysterious material. Although more recently a few scholars have been interested in these drawings, no broad analysis of the entire collection has yet been made. Such an attempt seemed to me an attractive undertaking on the occasion of this *Festschrift*.

When Bernardo Antonio Vittone died in Turin on 19th October 1770 he left behind not only a very large œuvre of most extraordinary buildings but also two printed works, the *Istruzioni elementari* of 1760 and the *Istruzioni diverse* of 1766. These treatises are now extremely rare, and this is probably one of the reasons why they have seldom been studied. I shall have to draw them into the discussion time and again in this paper. In addition to his two published works, Vittone seems to have had another manuscript ready for the press. As he himself announced in the Preface to the *Istruzioni diverse* (p. xiii), the manuscript 'che già tengo in appresto' contained a compilation of the laws set down in Justinian's *Corpus Juris Civilis* regarding buildings in town and countryside and regarding the supply of water.[1] The existence of this manuscript is attested by an inventory entry after Vittone's death which mentions five notebooks entitled: 'Leggi e Dottrine Legali concernenti gli Edificj, i Fondi, e la condotta delle acque'.[2] There was also in his estate a 'Discourse on Theatres', apparently ready for publication.[3] These manuscripts, probably of considerable

historical interest, have not yet been traced. Nor do we know what happened to the bulk of the other material to which the inventory refers.[4] But – to anticipate the result of my investigation – I believe that at least some of this material has come down to us in the Paris volumes.

The pedigree of the volumes does not go far back. In 1903 they were presented to the library of the Musée des Arts Décoratifs by the painter Albert Besnard, who had bought them in Rome, and this is virtually all we know about them. It seems that the drawings were not bound when they entered the museum. In any case, their present arrangement and binding date from 1903.[5] At that time many of the drawings were mounted on modern paper and numbered (usually with one, but sometimes with two and occasionally with three or even four sheets to a mount). The numbers in the first volume run from 1 to 132, but since Nos. 4, 11, 55 and 63 are missing, the volume contains only 128 sheets of drawings. The second volume begins with No. 133 and ends with No. 237, containing 104 sheets.[6] Thus at present there are altogether 232 old sheets with drawings in the two volumes.[7] The discrepancy between the actual number of drawings and the numbering from 1 to 237 – thus including five lacunae – is satisfactorily explained by a note on the fly-leaf, according to which the museum's librarian transferred some drawings from the Vittone volumes to a volume entitled 'Étranger XVIe au XVIIIe s.', because they were signed 'Andrea Cattaneo'.[8]

1. 'Una raccolta, che già tengo in appresto, di quelle leggi, che nel Codice, ne' Digesti, e nelle Novelle di Giustiniano disperse si trovansi, concernenti le servitù sì civili, che rustiche, gli Edifici, i fondi campestri, e la condotta dell'acque; come altresì delle sentenze più essenziali de' Giureconsoli, e specialmente del Dottore Bartolomeo Cepolla sovra le dette servitù ...' – Vittone refers in this passage to the various parts of Justinian's *Corpus*, namely the *Codex constitutionum*, the Digest or *Pandectae*, and the *Novellae constitutiones*.

2. Cf. 'Descrizione, o sia Nota delle scritture spettanti all'Eredità del fu Sig. Architetto Bernardo Vittone' in the Archivio Comunale at Carignano, published by G. Rodolfo, 'Notizie inedite dell'architetto Bernardo Vittone', in *Atti della Società Piemontese di Archeologia e Belle Arti*, xv, 1933, p. 450.

3. *Id., loc. cit.*; 'Altro quinternetto di carta pur manuscritto intitolato Discorsi Teatrali sopra la disposizione delle cose più bisognevoli

per le operazioni da farsi ne' medesimi, e del modo di praticarle'.

4. I refer here also to the very extensive inventory compiled by several lawyers in the Turin Archivio di Stato (Sez. II, libro II, vol. I, pp. 463 ff.), first excerpted by Eugenio Olivero, *Le opere di Bernardo Antonio Vittone*, Turin, 1920, p. 30, and now fully published by Paolo Portoghesi, *Bernardo Vittone*, Rome, 1966, pp. 237 ff.; see particularly Nos. 434, 761–766.

5. Height of the volumes 50·5 cm., width 36·5 cm.

6. As a rule each drawing has its own number, but the two drawings mounted on the first page of the second volume have only one number (No. 133); on the other hand, there is no No. 234.

7. The present librarian originally stated on the 'fly-leaf' of the first volume that the two volumes contain 233 drawings; but this number was crossed out and changed to 237 (corresponding to the pagination but not to the actual number of drawings).

8. The librarian noted that three sheets were transferred and, in fact, the present numbers 3433, 3434 and 3435 of the 'mixed' volume bear Cattaneo's signature. But it seems that, together with the three signed Cattaneo drawings, two other closely related drawings were removed from the Vittone volumes, viz. Nos. 3431 and 3436. It is reasonable to conclude that these five drawings were originally located in the Vittone volumes under the missing Nos. 4, 11, 55, 63, 234.

It seems that, with the exception of the Cattaneo drawings, no drawings were taken out of the material that reached the museum in 1903, but it is evident that the present arrangement played havoc with the original condition and also with the original organization of the drawings: many sheets of the original series were cut, and often carelessly cut, in order to separate, whenever possible, unconnected designs and put together similar subject matter. Even though the drawings seem originally not to have been bound, they formed a continuous series, for, in addition to the numbering of 1903, there are on many sheets two sets of older numbers, one in dark ink, the other in red crayon. The old ink numbers appear on 111 sheets[9] and the red numbers on 118 sheets,[10] but only 79 sheets carry both sets of these numbers.[11]

The number-game is worth pursuing because the older numbers offer some clues to the original character of the whole group of drawings. In the first place, both types of old numerals appear on some of the Cattaneo drawings and, since these drawings can be dated in the mid-1790's,[12] the collection cannot have been formed until after that date. Thus post-Vittone material formed part of the collection when it was ordered and numbered twice in succession at least 25 years after Vittone's death.

The old double numbering makes it likely that two different groups of material were united after 1795. This assumption finds support in the fact that the ink numbers 8, 14, 16, 19 and 28 appear twice.[13] In addition, not all the old ink numbers are by the same hand; on some sheets one finds a smaller and more spidery type of number than usual, and there are even sheets on which both types of ink numbers appear.[14] The red numbers, always centred at the top of the sheet, would appear to have superseded the ink numbers, at a time when the whole collection had come together. Now the highest old ink number is 199 and the highest red number 214, and it therefore has to be asked whether drawings were added to the collection at some time in the nineteenth century. This must be denied categorically. Where the original sheets were left more or less intact, both old numbers are regularly found.[15] Since, as I have mentioned, many old sheets were cut when preparing them for their present mounting, the old numbers were lost – sometimes the ink numbers, sometimes the red numbers and often both. Moreover, by dismembering large sheets, the number of sheets was ostensibly increased. Finally, two unconnected drawings on one large sheet, left intact, now carry two modern numbers but only one old number.[16] The discrepancy between the number of drawings in the post-1795 and the present collection is therefore fictitious rather than real.

We have seen that the Cattaneo drawings originally belonged to the present volumes and that for reasons of chronology these drawings cannot have been in Vittone's estate. This discovery invites us to inquire what the reasons are for attributing the drawings in these volumes to Vittone, as has traditionally been done. In fact, the volumes contain a great deal of extraneous material which one cannot easily associate with Vittone's name. There is a ground-plan which Michael Petzet has recognized as a project for the Kajetanerkirche at Salzburg by Kaspar Zuccalli.[17] The German inscriptions on this prove that it is an original design and, since the old numbers appear on the sheet, it cannot be a later addition to the collection. Petzet also found among the drawings a plan and section of Chiaveri's Hofkirche in Dresden; once again the old numbers guarantee the pedigree of these drawings, but Petzet is surely wrong in attributing them to Chiaveri himself.[18] They are copies after a Chiaveri project[19] and belong together with many other copies in these volumes. Hellmut Hager

9. On Nos. 8, 10, 19, 46, 66, 67, 115, 130, 166, 188, 194, 221, 236 the reading is uncertain owing to cutting; on Nos. 13 and 215 only traces are preserved.

10. On Nos. 94, 96, 162, 176 the reading is again uncertain; on Nos. 12, 13, 203 there are only traces. The 111 sheets with ink numbers correspond to 121 modern numbers and the 118 sheets with red numbers to 128 modern numbers because in some cases two unconnected drawings on one large sheet were given two modern numbers, but only one old number.

11. These numbers never coincide, e.g., red 3, 4, 5 correspond to old ink 21, 22, 12 and old ink 19, 20 to red 12, 145, etc.

12. No. 3431 is old ink 199 and red 156 (crossed out and changed into 157). No. 3434 (signed 'Cataneo 1794') is red 195. No. 3435 (signed 'Andrea Cattaneo fec. 1795') is red 194.

13. Once on copies after Carlo Fontana, corresponding to the modern Nos. 200, 219, 223, 220, 9; and once on Vittone drawings corresponding to the modern Nos. 51, 196, 29, 232, 1/2.

14. 'Spidery' numbers on Nos. 116 (old 186), 143 (old 193, crossed out in pencil and replaced by pencil No. 178; this number repeated in red, partly cut), 193 (old 185).
Two old ink numbers appear on 51 (old 8, in the normal position, centred on the long side of the sheet, and spidery 115 in the lower right hand corner); 53 (old 9 in the normal position and 10 in the top left corner); 155 (old 174 in the normal position and spidery 98 in the left bottom corner).
With the possible exception of No. 193, all the drawings mentioned in this note are original designs by Vittone. The 'spidery' ink numbers, especially those not in the 'right' position, may be serial numbers used before 1770 in Vittone's collection.

15. E.g., No. 50 – old ink 187, red 40; No. 51 – old ink 8, red 48; No. 52 – 190 and 47; No. 53 – 9 and 49; No. 54 – 140 (crossed out and replaced by 141) and 53.

16. Cf. the following large sheets: Nos. 61, 62 – old ink 7, red 39; Nos. 70, 71 – 86 and 36; Nos. 72, 73 – 87 and 34; Nos. 74, 75 – 58 and 38; Nos. 86, 87 – 89 and 123; Nos. 96, 97 – 34 and 131 (?).

17. No. 236 (old ink 171?, red 184). In a letter Dr. Petzet mentioned to me that he has handed over his discovery to E. Hubala for publication in a forthcoming paper on Zuccalli.

18. 'Ein unbekanntes Projekt Chiaveris für die Dresdener Hofkirche', *Alte und Moderne Kunst*, III, 4, 1958, p. 16 – No. 197 (old ink 144, red 205) and No. 218 (old ink 145, red 206). In this case, as in others, the rearrangement of 1903 broke up the connection between the two drawings which was preserved in the old sequence.

19. The plan corresponds to an engraving dated 1739 by Chiaveri's collaborator, Lorenzo Zucchi (E. Hempel, *Gaetano Chiaveri*,

informed me verbally that the large project of a church with an adjoining palace, of which the volumes contain the elevation and plan,[20] is copied after Pompeo Ferrari's prize-winning project in the Accademia di S. Luca, dated 1678; he also noticed that the elevation and section of a centrally planned church[21] are copied from a project of 1704 by Pietro Paolo Scaramella, the originals of which are also in the Accademia di S. Luca. Furthermore, there are copies in the volumes of the plan of S. Carlo al Corso in Rome and of the plan of S. Lorenzo in Milan.[22] I believe that more copies after miscellaneous projects are still hidden in these volumes and await identification.

The bulk of the identifiable copies were, however, made after drawings by Carlo Fontana. I have been able to trace no fewer than 70 sheets copied from Fontana drawings now in the Windsor Royal Library and the Soane Museum.[23] In addition, six sheets were copied from the Fontana volume now at Modena.[23a] The copyist used at least 138 originals, sometimes telescoping parts of three, four, five and even six originals on one sheet. In addition, 23 sheets have drawings entirely or partly derived from Fontana, the originals of which I have so far been unable to find.[24] Another 19 sheets are probably copied after Fontana.[25]

Thus Fontana originals were used for at least 99, and possibly for 118, sheets. Add to this the other 8 copies previously mentioned, the Zucalli drawing and the five certain Cattaneo drawings, originally belonging to this material, and we have 132 sheets (possibly more) out of 237 which are not original contributions by Vittone.[26] Nevertheless, Vittone's name is justifiably associated with the two volumes. Eleven drawings bear his signature,[27] 43 drawings are more or less closely related to illustrations in the *Istruzioni diverse* of 1766[28] and at least 4 (possibly 7) to the *Istruzioni elementari* of 1760.[29] Furthermore, 13 drawings can be attributed to him without reservation.[30] Thus, without counting twice Nos. 3, 50 and 206, which are signed as well as connected with his published work, 68 (71) sheets of drawings are certainly by Vittone's hand. In addition, 3 sheets with altar designs,[31] 20 sheets with portals, doors and windows and 3 sheets with towers[32] can almost certainly be given to him, while another 13 drawings may or may not be by him.[33] The Vittone group, therefore, consists of 94[34] and, more probably, 107 (110) sheets, and this number may possibly be increased to 111 (114) by the inclusion of 4 more sheets.[35]

We have now accounted for most of the numbered sheets and it so happens that the Fontana group of 118 sheets and the Vittone group of at least 107 (and perhaps 114) sheets are fairly evenly divided. But 18 sheets belong to both groups[36] and this is a phenomenon which will occupy us further.

It is these 18 sheets that provide the key to attributing the copies after Fontana to Vittone. *Prima facie*, everything militates against Vittone's authorship. Vittone, probably born in 1705, was nine years old when Fontana died in 1714. One is at first inclined to assume that the copies were made in Fontana's studio and that a late eighteenth or early nineteenth-century collector united them with a group of Vittone drawings; and the old ink numbers would seem to support such an assumption.[37] Is it imaginable that a man like Vittone, the highly strung creator of extremely

Dresden, 1955, fig. 14), but the section differs in some details from the engraved one (Hempel, fig. 20). The copyist had access to a section otherwise unrecorded. I have no doubt that the two drawings are by the copyist of the Fontana drawings (see below in text).

20. No. 146 (old ink 148, red 204); No. 148 (red 203).

21. Nos. 177 and 182 (old ink 153). I am grateful to Dr. Hager for communicating his important dicoveries to me. He intends to publish the original projects, together with the other *concorso* material in the Accademia di S. Luca.

22. S. Carlo al Corso – No. 205 (red 192); S. Lorenzo – No. 187 (red 183).

23. Nos, 8, 9, 13, 14, 15, 19, 21, 22, 30, 33, 37, 41, 48, 67, 68, 83, 84, 85, 88, 89, 93, 101, 107, 108, 109, 111, 112, 114, 117, 131, 133, 139, 140, 141, 147, 150, 153, 154, 156, 157, 158, 161, 163, 164, 166–172, 174, 175, 176, 179, 181, 183, 188, 189, 191, 200, 202, 210, 211, 212, 214, 216, 219–224, 226, 227, 228.
In his paper 'Carlo Fontanas Entwurf für das Liechtensteinpalais', in *Alte und Neue Kunst*, II, 1957, no. 5, p. 16 f., M. Petzet published No. 214, but left unmentioned the fact that Nos. 133, 139, 150, 154, 156, 157, 158, 169 also represent the same Fontana project. Nor did he know the long series of Fontana's originals at Windsor, Nos. 9552–9565, from which the 9 Paris drawings are copied.

23a. Bibl. Estense, MS. γ B.1.16; see Paris volumes Nos. 131, 179, 188, 189, 200, 202, and also No. 153 (see above, note 23). I am much indebted to Dr. Hager for this information.

24. Nos. 7, 10, 32, 34, 35, 42, 82, 86, 87, 90, 91, 92, 98, 102, 103, 105, 106, 110, 159, 180, 213, 215, 217.

25. No. 20 (altar, very Fontanesque, but with *trabucchi*, i.e. Piedmontese scale). However, the cut of this sheet indicates that it originally formed a larger sheet with No. 41, which shows an altar copied after Fontana 9498. (The plan above this altar, copied from Fontana 9739, belongs to No. 20 rather than 41). In addition, Nos. 24–28, 46, 96, 97, 134, 135, 151, 152, 178, 186, 192, 193, 201, 225.

26. This statement is a simplification. In reality some sheets combine Fontana and Vittone material; see below, p. 171.

27. Nos. 1–2 (one sheet), 3, 49, 50, 53, 54, 56, 57, 59, 81, 206.

28. Nos. 3, 5, 6, 9, 13, 16, 17, 23, 29, 32, 36, 38, 44, 50, 51, 52, 68, 90–93, 98–100, 106, 107, 110, 114, 120, 129, 138, 143, 145, 160, 165, 168 verso, 174, 181, 198, 199, 206, 206 verso, 207, 208.

29. Nos. 78, 122, 125, 132 and perhaps also 5, 7, 184.

30. Nos. 39, 40, 42, 43, 45, 60, 65, 66, 116, 155, 209, 229, 230.

31. Nos. 12, 47, 104.

32. Nos. 69–80 (for 78 see above, note 29), 94, 95, 123, 124, 126–128, 130, 162. Towers: 31, 184, 185; 184 close to *Ist. el.*, pl. LXXV.

33. Nos. 18, 61, 62, 64, 113, 136, 137, 142, 144, 190, 196, 231, 232.

34. Counting No. 78 (see notes 29 and 32) only once.

35. Of the 13 sheets not accounted for, I regard the portals and doors on Nos. 58, 118, 119, 121 as marginal Vittone drawings, while the remaining nine drawings are by different hands.

36. Nos. 7, 9, 13, 32, 42, 68, 90–93, 98, 106, 107, 110, 114, 168 verso, 174, 181. See above, notes 23, 24, 28, 29, 30.

37. Cf. above, p. 166, and notes 13, 14.

imaginative and daring dome structures, would have wanted to turn to the pedantic sobriety of Fontana's work for study and inspiration? Moreover, when and where could Vittone have copied Fontana drawings in such numbers, long after the master's death? The character of a great many sheets leaves no doubt that the copyist had full access to Fontana's drawings.[38] Bound in many volumes, the latter reached the collection of Pope Clement XI Albani (1700–21) from Fontana's estate and left Italy for good in 1762 when they were acquired by King George III.[39]

Now, unexpectedly, a number of sheets containing copies after Fontana were used by Vittone for illustrations to his treatises, particularly the *Istruzioni diverse*.[40] As to the close connection between the drawings and these engravings there cannot be any doubt; as a rule the engravings reverse, as they should, the design of the drawings. As an example I illustrate the catafalque designed by Fontana in 1707 for the memorial service for Pedro II, King of Portugal, in S. Antonio dei Portoghesi (Fig. 1; Windsor 9379), together with the Paris copy (Fig. 2; No. 114) and the engraving on plate CIII of the *Istruzioni diverse* (Fig. 3). In actual fact, the engraving is even closer – in almost every detail, including the architectural setting – to Fontana's drawing 9381 (Fig. 4). Furthermore, this engraving distinctly incorporates minor elements from Fontana 9382 and 9383. The latter Fontana drawing is copied in the centre of a composite sheet of studies in Paris (Fig. 5; No. 93),[41] while Fontana 9381 and 9382 are not among the copies. Since Vittone must have had copies of these drawings at his disposal when preparing the design for his engraving, we have definite proof that the copies preserved in the Paris volumes are only a part of a once fuller collection of copies.[41a] It may be noted that in the example under review, as elsewhere, Vittone does not mention in his text (p. 200) that his design was cribbed from Fontana.

It has become clear that, at the time of the preparation of his treatises, Vittone had in his collection copies after Fontana drawings, and the old numbers on many of these copies, which also appear on those not used for publication,

support the assumption that he owned all the copies in the Paris volumes and, as we now know, probably many more. But this in itself does not mean that he was the copyist, and my question as to when and where would he have had the opportunity to copy Fontana drawings has still to be answered. Vittone was in Rome only once, as a young man between the end of 1730 and the spring of 1733,[42] and on this occasion he might conceivably have come into possession of copies made in Fontana's studio. I believe, however, that the old tradition is correct and that it can satisfactorily be demonstrated that Vittone himself was the copyist.[43] To make this hypothesis acceptable, we have to presume, first, that in his youth he was passionately interested in Fontana's work and, second, that he had free and prolonged access to the papal collection.

Fontana's great reputation survived unabated, particularly in the circle of the Accademia di S. Luca where Vittone studied during his Roman years. Now, it is a fact to which some attention has recently been given[44] that Vittone's early work abounds with Fontanesque reminiscences. They are fully in evidence, even before his visit to Rome, in his designs for the parish church at Pecetto Torinese of 1730,[45] in his prize-winning project at the Accademia di S. Luca in 1732,[46] in his competition design for the façade of S. Giovanni in Laterano, also dated 1732,[47] and even in his later work such as the façade of SS. Vincenzo ed Anastasio at Cambiano, constructed in 1740. In the *Istituzioni elementari* (p. 285) Vittone calls Juvarra 'his master'. Insufficient attention has been paid to this claim, and it is usually maintained that he 'discovered' Juvarra only after his Roman journey. This seems, however, unlikely, not only because Vittone was an independent architect before he went to Rome, but above all because definite proof of his pre-Roman attachment to Juvarra is furnished by a hitherto unnoticed project in the Paris volumes showing the elevation, section and plan of the new *coretti* at the side of the high altar of the Oratory of the Decollazione di S. Giovanni Battista, which is dated by Vittone's own inscription 13 April 1728 (Fig. 6).[48] The Juvarresque character of this project is immediately evident and confirms Vittone's early apprenticeship with Juvarra. It is well known that the latter always held his master Carlo Fontana in the highest esteem, and it must have been he who directed Vittone's

---

38. Cf. below, p. 169, and notes 55, 56.

39. The history of the Fontana volumes will be discussed in the forthcoming Windsor Catalogue by A. Braham and H. Hager. Robert Adam negotiated the deal; see John Fleming, *Robert Adam*, Harvard Univ. Press, 1962, p. 297.

40. Cf. above, note 36.

41. The centre group with Faith and the skeleton, and the ground-plan – Fontana 9393; the two candle-holders – Fontana 9394; the armature top left – Fontana 9389 and 9403.
   There are altogether seven sheets with copies after Fontana's S. Antonio dei Portoghesi decoration. Apart from Nos. 93 and 114, Nos. 108 (F. 9396), 109 (F. 9369), 111 (F. 9370 or 9371), 112 (F. 9376 or 9377 and 9369), 181 (F. 9405).

41a. See also the tomb design, *Ist. div.*, pl. CVII top left, which is derived from Fontana 9905 (ill. in A. Braham, 'The Tomb of Christiana', *Analecta Reginensia*, I, Stockholm, 1966, fig. 11), but there is no copy after Fontana in the Paris volumes.

42. Cf. Henry A. Millon, 'Alcune osservazioni sulle opere giovanili di Bernardo Antonio Vittone', *Bollettino Piemontese della Società di Archeologia e Belle Arti*, XII–XIII, 1958–59 (offprint, p. 3).

43. Of course, none of the copies bears his signature.

44. Millon, *op. cit.*, and Paolo Portoghesi, *op. cit.*, p. 83 ff.

45. Cf. Nino Carboneri, in the catalogue of the *Mostra del Barocco Piemontese*, Turin, 1963, 'Architettura', No. 136, and Portoghesi, *loc. cit.*

46. For ill., cf. Portoghesi, figs. 1–6.

47. *Istruzioni elementari*, pl. LXXIIII. The design also contains Borrominesque elements.

48. No. 230 (old ink 163, red 177). Unfortunately, I have not been successful in finding out whether this project was executed.

attention to Fontana's work as the source and embodiment of good classical precepts in architecture. Without Juvarra's mediation, Fontana's influence on the pre-Roman Vittone (e.g., at Pecetto) would be difficult to explain. We may even go a step further and suggest that it was Juvarra who impressed on the young man the importance of a thorough study of Fontana's work, best accomplished through the established academic method of copying after drawings. Juvarra was in Rome early in 1732,[49] concurrently with Vittone; at that time the older master enjoyed an immense reputation and he – the most distinguished of Fontana's pupils – may well have intervened on behalf of his own pupil and negotiated Vittone's entry into the Albani collection,[50] which then contained the Fontana drawings. This is, of course, an unsupported speculation on my part, but it seems to me a hypothesis that makes a situation intelligible for which it would otherwise not be easy to find a plausible explanation. In any case, Vittone's authorship of the copies, which at first appeared so unlikely, is not precluded by circumstances. It remains to show that the style of the copies is his.

To determine stylistically whether a copy made after an architectural design is by one hand rather than by another is almost impossible, particularly when measured drawings are the object of study. It is true that the Paris copies after Fontana have certain idiosyncrasies in common which distinguish them clearly from Fontana's originals. Thus, in spite of close adherence to the originals, Vittone, as a rule, increased the area of shadows in his copies or even supplied shadows where there were none in the originals; in other words, he tended somewhat to dramatize Fontana's sober academic statements. His figures, too, differ slightly from the originals; they display a tendency to contraction and simplification. But all this would hardly suffice to attribute the copies to Vittone with any degree of certainty; in fact, a number of the copies look remarkably like the signed Cattaneo drawings.[51]

There exists yet another approach to the question of authorship. Many of the copies after Fontana drawings exhibit strange associatory tendencies. Parts or even fragments lifted from different original projects are often copied on a single sheet and made to run into one another; eleva-

tions and plans may be unrelated, and a sheet may present a peculiar medley of designs undecipherable without the aid of the originals. Of course, Vittone made the copies for his own education and exercise and not with an eye to art-historical analysis over two hundred years later. Nevertheless, the method he employed subconsciously seems quite his own; occasionally it calls to mind an almost schizophrenic associative mentality. A few examples may help to explain what I mean. On three sheets by Vittone are to be found copies after details of Fontana's designs for the decoration of S. Maria dell'Anima on the occasion of the memorial service to Leopold I of Austria.[52] No. 8 (red 110) combines on one sheet Fontana 9842, 9843 and 9846. No. 88 (old ink 62, red 109; Fig. 7) – a less straightforward case – shows on the left a column with hangings behind it. Fontana's original, corresponding exactly to this design, does not seem to be extant; but there is a close connection with Fontana's sketch 9837 (reversed in Vittone's design). The hanging is to be found in Fontana's sketch 9840. The column in the centre of the sheet may be based on Fontana 9836 or possibly on a less sketchy original that has not survived. The plan on the right conflates Fontana's two plans of the catafalque, 9833 and 9834. Even more obscure is the design above the plan showing a seated putto with his feet resting on a half-moon; at one side of the putto is a cannon lying on a curved wall, at the other a segmental line with a cannon next to it. The design merges the view and the plan of the same motif which appear separately on Fontana 9854.[53] Another sheet belonging to this series, No. 89 (old ink 64, red 108), is similarly based on six originals, namely (from top left to right) Fontana 9851, 9848 (bottom), 9850 (top), 9849 (bottom), 9840 and 9845. Sometimes entirely unconnected designs are united on one sheet. No. 216 (red 114) shows at the top a section and plan from the palace on the Isola Borromeo after Fontana 9751 and, underneath, the decoration of the *stanze nobili* in the same palace after Fontana 9752, while on the right of the sheet appears half of the organ, set in a rock design in the Quirinal gardens copied from Fontana 9753.[54] On the upper half of No. 147 (old ink 111, red 68) there are part of the façade of the Casa Cantonale, S. Michele a Ripa (1704), after Fontana 9730 and two plans of the same building after Fontana 9732 and 9753, the upper one irrationally turned through 180 degrees. On the lower half of the same sheet, Vittone gave in one design the elevation and section of an unidentified palace by Fontana, contracted from the two Fontana drawings 9351 and 9347. Even stranger than such conflation is the fact that the upper and lower designs are copied

49. Cf. L. Rovere, V. Viale, A. E. Brinckmann, *Filippo Juvarra*, Milan, 1937, p. 95 f.

50. Cardinal Annibale Albani had been Juvarra's patron for many years; cf. Brinckmann, *op. cit.*, p. 95 and *passim*.

51. For instance, one would not hesitate to attribute the altar drawings 21, 22, 41 to the same hand as No. 3435 (which is signed by Cattaneo), if they were not copies after Fontana's Windsor drawings 9494, 9495, 9498. Cattaneo was probably born in the mid–1760's (see below, p. 172), i.e., after the Fontana volumes had left Italy. One might also feel inclined to attribute to Cattaneo a number of drawings in Fontana's manner such as Nos. 24–28 and even the church design 198 and 199; but the latter design is in all likelihood an early project by Vittone for S. Maria Maddalena at Alba.

52. 19th October 1705. Windsor Vol. 177, Nos. 9807–59.

53. The peculiar oven at the top centre of the sheet represents the 'machina' shown on F. 9855 which absorbed the fumes produced by the eight cannons of the catafalque.

54. In this case Vittone simply turned the pages of the volume copying page after page.

from two different Fontana volumes.[55] This is not at all an uncommon occurrence[56] – a further proof, if it were needed, that the copyist was in a position to use freely the major part of Fontana's legacy of drawings.

Now a number of plates in the *Istruzioni diverse* show miscellaneous designs which are as badly co-ordinated or as crowded as the sheets of copies.[57] Indeed, it can be maintained that there exists a 'structural' similarity between some of the sheets with copies after Fontana and some of the plates in Vittone's treatises, and it is this that excludes any doubt as to the authorship of the copies. We may conclude that the copies after other architects' projects – enumerated above – are also by Vittone. They, too, were made at the time of his stay in Rome, with the exception of the copies after Chiaveri's Hofkirche project which must be dated at least ten years later.[58] The copy after S. Lorenzo at Milan probably also belongs to the later period.[59] In any case, it is revealing that the spatial complexity and sophistication of this late antique structure attracted Vittone; this copy focuses attention on a source of his mature style.

If the foregoing analysis and reconstruction of events is acceptable, there remains the surprising fact that Vittone returned to his early studies of Fontana when he began to prepare his two publications. During the interval of more than two decades he had become the acknowledged master of his generation in Piedmont. He had passed through a Rococo phase without relinquishing his attachment to classical principles, but in his late period he favoured more conventional designs with distinctly neo-classical overtones and so he moved once again closer to Carlo Fontana and to the Roman experience of his youth. It is for this reason that both publications clearly reveal Fontanesque and other Roman reminiscences.[60] However, only one

strictly architectural project, of which Vittone published the large plan and elevation, is a straightforward copy after Fontana.[61] All other cases of direct copies are to be found among the plates showing catafalques, tombs and memorials,[62] rather than buildings. Vittone had to include this material in his *Istruzioni diverse* for the sake of completeness. But as an architect in the modern sense of the word he was a stranger to this type of design, and this seems to have been the reason for his almost total reliance on his archive of drawings.

Vittone's original drawings would require a discussion of considerable length, but I can hardly do more in this paper than put down a few miscellaneous observations. The Paris volumes contain two different classes of such drawings; first, preparatory designs for actual buildings and, second, study sheets the purpose of which seems to have been to bring together a large collection of models, ultimately for publication.

A survey of the first group shows that the designs belong to all periods of Vittone's career. I have already mentioned the project of 1728 (Fig. 6); even earlier is his design for the picturesque altar, with the sculpted vision of S. Ignatius, in the Santuario di Sant'Ignazio on Monte Bastia near Lanzo, traditionally dated 1727 (Fig. 8).[63] Vittone described the altar at great length in the *Istruzioni diverse* (p. 195) and published it on pl. XCIII (Fig. 9). It is evident that the drawing served as basis for the engraving, which reverses it. Two designs for canopies, one empty, the other with the Virgin and Child, both on the same sheet (No. 3), were clearly intended for the altar of S. Chiara at Alessandria, planned before 1740, but never executed.[64] In the mid-

55. Windsor, Vols. 176 and 170.

56. E.g., No. 30 combines F. 9500 (Vol. 174) and 9717 (Vol. 176); No. 141, F. 9341 (Vol. 170) and 9735 (Vol. 176); No. 153, F. 9514, 9516 (Vol. 174) and Soane 33; No. 176, F. 9309 (Vol. 168), 9556 (Vol. 174) and Soane 23.

57. Cf., e.g., pls. XCIII (catafalques; for half of the plate see our Fig. 3) and pl. CV (tombs). On occasions the engraved designs are so closely connected that they are not easily separated, e.g., on pl. XXVIII different designs with wrought iron railings are firmly joined; other examples are on pls. X and XI.

58. See above, note 19.

59. Cf. above, note 22. The underlying pencil drawing, not entirely drawn over in pen and ink, has auxiliary lines radiating from the centre, a typical Vittone device. I have not been able to trace the drawing he copied. It may be in the Bianconi Collection, Castello Sforzesco, Milan. For similar drawings of S. Lorenzo, cf. A. Calderini, Chierici, Cecchelli, *La basilica di S. Lorenzo*, 1951, pl. LXVI.
    On the verso of Vittone's drawing there are not easily decipherable pencil sketches of characteristically Vittonesque church plans.

60. Cf., e.g., Caprarola: *Ist. el.*, pls. LXIV, LXVII, LXVIII, LXXIX; *Ist. div.*, pl. XIX. Scala Regia: *Ist. el.*, pl. LXXVIII; *Ist. div.*, pl. XX; Four Rivers Fountain, Piazza Navona: *Ist. div.*, pl. XXXV; and so forth.

61. *Ist. div.*, pl. XXXII: 'casa di campagna'. Fontana's originals of 1689: Windsor, Nos. 9706–9712. A sheet by Vittone, No. 174, shows at the top the elevation after F. 9708; in the centre a plan after F. 9710 and below it a second plan after F. 9712. The same plan appears once again on Vittone's sheet No. 69.
    It is interesting that Portoghesi, *op. cit.*, p. 171, believed this project to be an original design by Vittone.

62. A large proportion of the 26 designs on pls. CIII–CVII are derived from Fontana. Vittone used at least 19 of his copies for these plates.
    It is not astonishing that Vittone was much attracted by Fontana's decorative and 'pictorial' designs, i.e. by designs with a distinctly Baroque flavour (see Figs. 1–3). Characteristically, he copied on large sheets (corresponding to the size of the originals) Fontana's series of projects for the Fontana Trevi made in 1706 for Pope Clement XI (Windsor, Vol. 169, Nos. 9312–36). In the Paris drawings Nos. 219–224 and 226–8, he made use of 15 originals.

63. Cf. Millon, *op. cit.*, note 17. Portoghesi, *op. cit.*, p. 219, dates the altar '*c.* 1730' without giving specific reasons.
    The drawing No. 38 (Fig. 8) differs somewhat from the execution (see Portoghesi, fig. 64). The concept of the altar reveals the influence of the popular *Sacri Monti* sculpture on Vittone.

64. For the date, cf. Millon, *op. cit.* The engraving in *Ist. div.*, pl. LXXI shows a different altar design, but the connection of the drawings with S. Chiara is confirmed by a drawing in the Museo

1740's Vittone must have designed the church and college of the Chierici Regolari Ministri degli Infermi in Turin, a work that also remained unexecuted. He attached great importance to the project, for he gave it three plates in the *Istruzioni diverse* (LIII–LV) and discussed it in great detail (pp. 177 f.). The Paris volumes contain three plans of the church and adjoining building, a proof of the care he took over the preparatory stages (Nos. 138, 160, 165); No. 160 comes closest to the published plate LIII, but differs in a few minor though significant details. To the same, or possibly even a slightly earlier period, seem to belong a number of extremely important plans for S. Chiara at Vercelli (Nos. 143, 206, 206v, 207, 208). Common characteristic features leave no doubt about the identification, namely a broad sacristy with rounded-off corners and the marking of existing buildings into which the church had to be fitted.[65] The pencil sketch 206v, which returns to the plan of S. Chiara at Alessandria, appears again in the clean pen and ink drawing 207 (Fig. 10). No. 143 is reminiscent of the plan of the Santuario del Vallinotto (1738) and the church of the Chierici Regolari Ministri degli Infermi. No. 206 (Fig. 11) recalls the plan of S. Bernardino at Chieri (1740) and No. 208 is close to the published plan (*Istruzioni diverse*, pl. LXXII). Thus, in the course of developing the plan of S. Chiara at Vercelli Vittone recapitulated a number of solutions he had used around 1740.[66] A longitudinal and a cross section (Nos. 198, 199) certainly belong to an early project for S. Maria Maddalena at Alba built in 1749.[67] Very similar to the plan of this church is Vittone's project for the unexecuted parish church at Spigno Monferrato, published in the *Istruzioni diverse*, pl. LXI; No. 145 represents an annotated 'pianta abozzata' for it and should be dated about 1750. Nos. 56 and 57 show the plan and longitudinal section of S. Maria dei Servi at Alessandria with notes and the signature: 'Torino, li 17 marzo 1756 Ing.e Bernardo Vittone'. These drawings are the only surviving testimony of this unexecuted project; they are of particular interest because of their dependence on Juvarra's Chiesa del Carmine in Turin (1732–36). Finally, some designs of altars can be related to executed works: No. 12 to the two side altars in the Chiesa dello Spirito Santo at Carignano datable

1750–52;[68] No. 23 to the altar of the Cappella del Crocifisso in S. Francesco, Turin (1761);[69] No. 18 perhaps to the altar of S. Valerico in the Consolata, Turin (1764).[70] The free sketch of an altar, No. 40, so far unrelated, may be added to this list because it has on the verso the draft of a letter the date of which seems to read 'Aug. 2 - 1764'.

The drawings so far discussed belong to four decades of Vittone's professional life and it is apparent that none was made with publication in mind. Nor can it be maintained that the other class of drawings – the study sheets – were all made for this purpose. A few study sheets contain numerous miscellaneous 'notes' not destined for publication, although individual motifs could be used when the occasion arose. On Nos. 42 and 44, which originally formed a large sheet cut in two in 1903 and reunited in our Fig. 12,[71] there are assembled no less than 16 designs in pen and ink and one in crayon covering a wide range of subjects: altars, cartouches, doors and *sopraporte*, a capital, a holy-water stoup and two tabernacles. This study sheet is of particular interest because of its link both with Fontana and the *Istruzioni diverse*; the double door with the picture-frame above it is copied from the first chapel on the left in S. Maria di Montesanto in Rome,[72] while the strange door with the ram's head decoration and the realistic eagle holding an inscription-scroll in its beak and talons recurs in reverse on pl. XXIII of the *Istruzioni diverse*.[73] Other study sheets with well-arranged altars, tabernacles, windows and doors were probably made with publication in view. The example reproduced here, No. 130 (Fig. 13), shows six doors incorporating twelve alternative designs. Strangely, Vittone used in his books little of the material assembled on this type of study sheet. The possibility cannot be excluded that he planned yet another publication, apart from the two published works and the manuscripts which were ready for the press when he died.

I have mentioned above that 47 drawings are related to the illustrations in Vittone's books and that many of the engravings reverse the drawings. In spite of this, none of

Civico at Turin published by Carboneri, *op. cit.*, pl. 136 and Portoghesi, *op. cit.*, fig. 16.
65. In all the plans there appears a projecting wall next to the façade (belonging to an existing building). The engraving, *Ist. div.*, pl. LXXII, shows this situation in reverse.
66. Portoghesi, *op. cit.*, pp. 223 f., No. 21, dates the building '*c.* 1750'. If my analysis is correct, this date would be much too late. It would seem tempting to connect the plan No. 209 with the same church, but this is not possible because the building is free-standing on all sides. This interesting project, which clearly reveals its derivation from Guarini's Cappella SS. Sindone, may be dated in the late 1730's.
67. Cf. *Ist. div.*, pl. LXXIV.

68. They were designed in 1750 and executed in the following two years; cf. Portoghesi, *op. cit.*, p. 225, no. 28.
69. Ill. in Portoghesi, fig. 283 (with wrong date 1767). Engraved in *Ist. div.*, pl. XC. Although the execution dates from 1761, the design must have been made some time before that year; cf. below, note 78.
It may also be mentioned that the door design No. 129 corresponds to *Ist. div.*, pl. XXIII (below, centre), and the side doors of the façade of S. Francesco.
70. Ill. in Portoghesi, fig. 278.
71. The whole sheet originally had the red number 120 (now on 44) and the old ink No. 90. The digits '9' and '0' were separated when the sheet was cut.
72. Communicated to me by Dr. Hellmut Hager.
73. The two tabernacles on 44 have their counterparts on pls. XCV and XCVI of *Ist. div.*, but are not directly connected with any of the illustrated designs.

the drawings served the engravers directly.[74] In preparing his publications Vittone consulted his archive of drawings, lifted out what seemed to him suitable and had clean copies made for the engraver's use. In a number of cases Vittone's procedure can be reconstructed. My examples are the two tabernacle drawings, Nos. 16 and 29 (Figs. 14, 15), which served for the two tabernacles on plate XCV of the *Istruzioni diverse*. Originally, he probably designed these tabernacles as alternatives: in both drawings the altar and the angels with the Crown of Thorns and the Sudary are identical. In the engravings the altars were omitted; otherwise No. 29 was exactly followed and reversed, while the angels of No. 16 were changed to kneeling ones in the engraving.

Fortunately, the clean copy from which the engravings were made survives in the Royal Library at Turin.[75] A number of points regarding this copy are worth noting. There is a title-page that corresponds neither with that of the *Istruzioni elementari* nor with that of the *Istruzioni diverse*; the date of publication is given as 1760;[76] and, by and large, the 135 plates of the manuscript combine the illustrations of both printed works. In other words, the material Vittone had singled out for publication, including that for the *Istruzioni diverse* of 1766, was ready at the time the *Istruzioni elementari* appeared. It is for this reason that, with the exception of a very few added plates,[77] no designs of the 1760's were included in the *Istruzioni diverse*.[78] We may therefore

conclude that the bulk of the study sheets made in preparation for publication have to be dated sometime in the 1750's.

The foregoing analysis of the volumes in the Musée des Arts Décoratifs has shown that they contain four different classes of material: (1) Vittone's copies after Fontana's and other architects' works datable mainly to 1732; (2) preparatory studies for a number of Vittone's own architectural works covering the long period from 1727 to 1764; (3) study sheets, many of which were made in preparation for his publications and date from the 1750's; (4) a sprinkling of drawings by other hands, above all by Andrea Cattaneo.

Cattaneo was probably born shortly before Vittone's death. We know that in 1788 the University of Turin conferred on him the title 'architetto civile' and that he was still alive in 1831.[79] If the late eighteenth-century parish church at Favria[80] is by him, he started his career as a Vittone enthusiast. A later work, however, S. Dalmazzo at Cuorgnè (1805–10),[81] shows that he had swung towards acceptance of the prevalent neo-classical taste.

Since Cattaneo's drawings originally formed part of the collection, I am tempted to conclude that it was this somewhat obscure architect who had acquired the Vittone material from the latter's heirs. Thus, to find Cattaneo's own exercises in Vittone's manner intermingled with Vittone drawings would need no further explanation. It is likely that Cattaneo did not come into possession of all the Vittone drawings at the same moment and this would account for the inconsistencies in the numbering to which I have alluded at the beginning of this paper.

At the moment we cannot go beyond such hypothetical reconstructions. But I hope that my analysis of the two Paris volumes has solved some riddles, though many more still await clarification.[82]

74. Not a single sheet in the Paris volumes shows a layout similar to the plates of the publications.

75. Bibl. Reale, Varia 203. A bound volume of 135 pp., 44·5 × 28 cm. All the drawings are laid down on paper. Size of the drawings: 36·1 × 22·3 cm.
   The volume was exhibited at the *Mostra del Barocco Piemontese*; cf. Carboneri, *op. cit.*, p. 64, no. 176. A study of the volume announced by Carboneri had not appeared at the time of writing.

76. The title-page consists of an engraved cartouche with the following hand-written title: 'L'architetto civile volume originale delle opere del'Signor Bernardo Vitone insigne allievo dell'Accademia di Roma MDCCLX'. (The 'LX' of 1760 is superimposed upon another figure that has been erased.) Bottom left: 'Babel sculpteur'; centre: 'A Paris, chez Jacques Chéreau, rue St. Jacques au grand St. Remy'.
   Vittone's idea of publishing in Paris was abandoned and both books came out in Lugano.

77. *Ist. div.*, pls. XXIII, XXV, LIX, IC are not in the Turin volume.

78. Vittone's façade of S. Francesco at Turin and his altars inside

the church are among the Turin drawings. The date *ante quem* for these projects is therefore 1760 (see above, note 69).

79. C. Brayda, L. Coli, D. Sesia, *Ingegneri e architetti del Sei e Settecento in Piemonte*, Turin, 1963, p. 28.

80. Luigi Mallè, *Le arti figurative in Piemonte*, Turin, 1961, p. 328.

81. *Ibid.*, p. 419.

82. The watermarks, for instance, require a thorough study. This task is now made difficult because a great number of the drawings have been laid down.

FRANCIS HASKELL

Some Collectors of Venetian Art at the End of the Eighteenth Century

Della Lena's 'Esposizione istorica dello Spoglio, che di tempo in tempo si fece di Pitture in Venezia'

DON Giacomo della Lena, whose account of the 'Spoliation of pictures' from Venice is published below,[1] was himself actively engaged in the process he describes, and this gives a poignant sense of immediacy to what might otherwise be a somewhat arid document. He was one of a number of small-scale dealers, antiquarians and connoisseurs – others were his friends Sasso and Moschini – who flourished during the final years of the Republic mainly by attaching themselves to the many British consular officials who were shamelessly taking advantage of their diplomatic positions in order to indulge in profitable art dealing. These men were often themselves modest art collectors, and there is good reason to believe that it was among them that Francesco Guardi found his most sympathetic admirers: della Lena, for instance, apparently owned thirty-two *vedute* by him. Although we know almost nothing of his character, a letter from him that has survived, addressed to the famous economist G. M. Ortes, on the distinction between the arts and the sciences, shows him to have been a man of discrimination and taste. He was born in Lucca in about 1731, but from 1760 he spent most of his life in Venice as Spanish Vice-Consul, a post that he probably owed to his brother Innocenzo, who was the Ambassador's doctor. He died in June 1807, and his account here printed must have been written at most two or three years before his death.[2]

From what has been said it will be seen that della Lena was in a good position to observe the foibles of his clientèle, and some of his comments, such as those on the Russian minister Mordwinoff and the Marchese Agdolo (paragraphs 14 and 21) or on the 'primitive' pictures admired by Strange (para. 8) are exceedingly vivid and entertaining.

Indeed, the interest of the document derives partly from his portraits of now forgotten collectors, for della Lena himself admits (para. 32) – and how readily we agree with him! – that 'had he thought of it in time' it would have been a good idea to have given more details of the pictures themselves. However, though somewhat erratic where earlier collections are concerned, his account is also of considerable significance in providing us with a check-list of the principal purchasers of Venetian art during the last years of the eighteenth century and in giving us clues (which can here be only briefly indicated in the hope that they will stimulate further research) as to the provenance of many important paintings.

ESPOSIZIONE ISTORICA DELLO SPOGLIO, CHE DI TEMPO IN TEMPO SI FECE DI PITTURE IN VENEZIA

1. L'epoca dello spoglio delle Pitture di Venezia parmi, che incomincia dal Cardinale Leopoldo de' Medici,[3] che a metà del penultimo secolo, verso il 1650 teneva in Venezia un Agente di professione Pittore, il quale in compagnia di altro Pittore, il celebre Pietro Testa Lucchese,[4] che dimorava in quel tempo in Venezia, raccoglievano ambidue a gara pel Cardinale tutto il meglio, e il Buono in materia non solo di Scienze, ma delle belle Arti singolarmente; Pitture, Stampe, Disegni, Gemme, Cammei, Pietre incise, Bronzi, Scolture, & Tutto si mandava a Firenze, la di cui

1. The manuscript exists in several versions in the Biblioteca Correr in Venice (MSS. PD 767 C/17; MSS. PD 467 C.8; Raccolta Cicogna 3006/41). The earliest version – the one used here – appears to be Raccolta Cicogna 3006/9.
  It has been referred to by Haskell in *JWCI*, XXIII, 1960, p. 261 and Muraro (see Note 3), p. 74.
2. For the little that is known about him, see Haskell, *op. cit.*, pp. 261–262. We can deduce the approximate date of the document from the fact that in paras. 31 and 32 he refers, by implication, to the death of Sasso, which occurred in 1803.

3. For Cardinal Leopold's purchases of Venetian art, see Michelangelo Muraro, 'Studiosi, collezionisti e opere d'arte veneta dalle lettere al Cardinale Leopoldo de' Medici', and Lucia & Ugo Procacci, 'Il carteggio di Marco Boschini con il Cardinale Leopoldo de' Medici', both in *Saggi e memorie di storia dell'arte*, IV, Venice, 1965.
4. Were there any reason to believe this to be true, it would be of remarkable interest. However, none of the early sources refers to Testa's living in Venice and there appears to be no trace of him in the correspondence quoted by Muraro and the Procaccis. Furthermore he died in 1650. It is just conceivable that della Lena, who, like the artist, came from Lucca, had access to hitherto unexplored information in his native city.

Galleria ebbe il grande incremento dalle cose tratte da Venezia.

2. Nell'ultimo secolo venne poi Console d'Inghilterra a Venezia Giuseppe Smith.[5] Tutto il mondo sa le ricchezze ch'ei fece in questa Città col commercio de' Libri, e de' Quadri: e n'è un testimonio visibile il bel Palazzo, che si fabbricò sul Canal Grande, in oggi posseduto dal Sig. Conte Mangili, e il delizioso Luogo di Campagna a Mojano, comperato dopo sua morte dal Duca di Montallegre, e in ultimo da Ignazio Testori. Egli è noto presso i Letterati per le Buone Edizioni fatte fare col suo denaro da Giambatista Pasquali, e per la insigne Libreria da esso lui formata, che va alle stampe col titolo di Biblioteca Smithiana. La Vedova Murray Smith del fondo del Negozio Pasquali, di sua parte, o sia del defonto suo marito, vendette ai Librai Caroboli, e Pompeati per 90/m Ducati di Libri.[6] Oltre la Biblioteca è famosa la sua Raccolta di Cammei, ovvero Dittialoteca [sic] Smithiana, che va pure alle stampe. Si questa, che la Libreria furono vendute al Re d'Inghilterra per 20/m Lire sterline. Oltre ciò Smith si era riserbato i migliori Quadri della Scuola Veneziana, che la Vedova Smith si portò seco in Inghilterra.

3. Il Cognato del Console Smith, M.r Murray, che da Residente in Venezia passò Ambasciatore di S.M.B. a Costantinopoli, fece una sceltissima Raccolta di Quadri. Ne aveva tre gran Camere fornite. In occasione, che Milord Northampton fece nel Palazzo di sua Residenza il pubblico Ingresso d'Ambasciatore Straordinario Britanico, mi ricordo, che Mr. Murray mostrava ai Signori Inglesi del di lui seguito nella 3.ª Stanza i Capi Scuola, e si gloriava di contare tra essi 7 Tiziani della bella maniera di questo Autore.[7]

4. A M.r Murray succedeva Residente d'Inghilterra il Cav.re Wraight.[8] Non è credibile la sterminata quantità di Quadri, ch'egli comperò, e mandò a Londra. Il suo Palazzo a S. Giobbe pareva un Magazzino di Pitture. Non v'era angolo, nè parete, dove non ne avesse appesi. In tutte le stanze del piano superiore disabitato vi erano afastellati i Quadri, e quivi si travagliava in rifoderarli, e ristorarli. I Ristoratori a giornata erano Giammaria Sasso, e Luca Breda Veronese.

5. For the most recent documentation on Smith, see Haskell, *Patrons and Painters*, London, 1963, pp. 299–310 and pp. 391–394 and articles by Frances Vivian in *Burl M.*, CIV, 1962, pp. 330–332; 1963, pp. 157–162; and *Italian Studies*, 1963, pp. 54–66.

6. Detailed references to this transaction are to be found in the Archivio di Stato, Venice – Atti del notaio Ludovico Gabrieli, busta 7570, pp. 1215 and 1278.

7. John Murray was Resident from the end of 1754 until the middle of 1766. Nothing appears to be known about his collection.

8. Sir James Wright was Resident between 1766 and 1773. The sale catalogue of his pictures, drawn up after his death in 1803 (Christie's, 8th and 9th June 1804), contains remarkably few Venetian pictures, despite the odd 'Titian', 'Veronesse', etc., so he must have been dealing extensively if della Lena is not exaggerating.

5. L'altro Console d'Inghilterra M.r Udny, cosa non acquistò costui di superbe Pitture in Venezia, egli, che n'era intendentissimo, e sommamente avido?[9] A differenza di Diplomatici, come Console, egli avea tutta la facilità d'introdursi nelle Case Patrizie, e in tempo del famoso Ridotto profittando dello sconcerto di alcuni giuocatori, e somministrando denaro, ebbe il comodo, e la fortuna di avere alcuni pezzi di Quadri de' piu preziosi, e d'inestimabile valore. Basti il dire, che le maggiori, e piu pregiate opere della Galleria Imperiale di Russia sono di Autori della Scuola Veneziana da lui vendutivi.[10] Egli con la sua astuzia, e con la corruzione dell'oro, portò via la celebre Palla di Tiziano (sostituitovi altra Palla di nuovo fatta da Giuseppe Angeli) a S.Niccoletto de' Frari, che poscia comperò Pio VI per 12/m scudi, laddove il primo costo non fu che di 300 zecchini.[11]

6. Al tempo stesso altro Inglese capitò a Venezia per nome M.r Slade. Anche costui acquistò Quadri in gran copia. La maggior parte, e il meglio della Galleria Vetturi passò in sue mani.[12]

7. M.r Hamilton negoziante di Quadri stabilito in Roma, morto assai vecchio, finche visse comperò Quadri in

9. John Udny was Consul from 1773 to 1774. There are frequent references to his collecting in the published and unpublished literature of the period which confirm della Lena's observation that he had no inhibitions about making contact with the Venetian nobility. In 1762, for instance, he was buying from the Sagredo (Venice, Biblioteca Correr, MSS. P.D. C 2193/VII) and in 1773 he was engaged in trying to acquire a (doubtful) Veronese from one of the suppressed convents (Venice, Archivio di Stato – Inquisitori di Stato, busta 909). Two sales of pictures belonging to him are recorded – 25th April 1800 at Christie's (published W. Buchanan, *Memoirs of Painting* . . ., II, London, 1824, pp. 11–19) and 28th May 1802. There are only a few Venetian pictures among those sold by his brother Robert in May 1804.

10. The catalogues of the Hermitage Museum in Leningrad and the Pushkin Museum in Moscow show that a large number of pictures of the Venetian school came to the Russian Imperial collections from unknown sources during the last quarter of the eighteenth century, and in the light of della Lena's information we may now assume that many of these came from Udny. Among others are 7 by members of the Bassano family and school, 1 by Balestra, 2 by Paris Bordone, 4 by Veronese and school, 2 by Canaletto, 1 by Licinio, 2 by Lotto; and others by Pittoni, Tintoretto, Titian and other artists at unidentified periods. A detailed check of the Sagredo inventories (Venice, Biblioteca Correr, MSS. P.D. C 2193/I), from which we know that Udny acquired works (see previous note), might reveal the provenance of some of these pictures. For instance, the school of Bassano *Portrait of a Carthusian Monk* (inventory number 1526) might well correspond to 'Un ritratto d'un Padre Domenicano del Bassan' in the Sagredo collection; and though any conclusion must be wholly tentative at this stage, it is worth speculating whether the Lotto *Family Portrait* (inventory no. 1786) is not the same as the single item described as 'Ritratti due mezze figure di Lorenzo Lotto'.

11. The picture (*Madonna in Glory with Six Saints*) was acquired by Pope Clement XIV in 1770, and is now in the Vatican.

12. For Slade and his pictures see Buchanan, *op. cit.*, I, pp. 320–334.

Venezia.[13] Altro Inglese M[r] Hoare fece lo stesso.[14] Era commissionato di costoro il buon Sasso.[15]

8. Poi venne a Venezia il dotto Cav[re] Strange Residente d'Inghilterra.[16] Ei riempi parimente il suo Palazzo di Quadri sceltissimi: fra gli altri v'era il gran Quadro rappresentante la Resurezione di Cristo del Giorgione, figure al naturale, che Sasso fece incidere in Rame.[17] Gli riuscì di fare una raccolta singolarissima, e dirò anche unica, degli antichi Pittori Veneziani, e dello Stato. Dai primordi della Pittura essa giungeva sino ai tempi di Tiziano.[18] Il Cav[re] Strange si compiaceva oltremodo d'averla formata col mezzo dell'Intelligentissimo Sasso, e soleva dire che era la storia visibile della Pittura Veneziana. Quasi tutti que' Quadri in tavola, col nome dell'Autore, rappresentavano Madonne, e Santi, e Sante: mi spiego: alcuni la sola Madonna col Bambino, altri la Sacra Famiglia, cioè Gesù, Giuseppe, e Maria: altri finalmente la Madonna, e il Puttino con Santi, e Sante dai lati. Tra piu rimoti Pittori vi erano anche soggetti Storici, e Santi in tre comparti con la B.V. in mezzo. Mi ricordo de' tre Vivarini, del Carpaccio, di Cima, di Baxaiti, dello Squarcione, di Mantegna, e Giambellino, ognuno de' quali avea singolari pregi, ed incantava l'occhio per la bella semplicità, e verità negli accessori, e delle fabbriche, e del paesaggio; e in fine alcuni per la loro conservazione, ed altri per l'accomodatura, e ripulitura fatta dalla maestra mano del diligentissimo Sasso. In prova della copia stragrande de' Quadri da detto Cav[re] Strange acquistati a Venezia, si noti, ch'egli scrisse a Sasso di avere ricavato da suoi scarti spediti in Filadelfia 9/m zecchini.[19] Questa notizia l'ebbi dallo stesso Sasso, che mi mostrò la lettera del Cav[re] Strange, in cui gli dava tale nuova.

9. Milord Bute quando passò a Venezia, portò anch'egli non pochi quadri in Inghilterra; ma sopra tutto una quantità grande di Libri, avendo inteso dal Cav[re] Strange, che erano 26/m volumi da Milord acquistati in Venezia, la maggior parte della famosa Libreria Soranzo.[20]

10. Contemporaneamente a Milord Bute, il Marchese di Paulmy d'Argenson[21] fu Ministro di Stato, venuto Ambasciatore di Francia a Venezia, non Quadri, ma bensì Libri a josa acquistò particolarmente di Crusca, e in cio fare si valse del Servita P. Baroni Lucchese, suo amorevole, famosissimo per la sagacità, e solerzia, con cui si formò un Museo, che a detta degli Intendenti, non v'ha forse l'eguale in quanto di Medaglie d'oro, e d'argento raccolte qua, e altrove in moltifice serie delle rare, e delle rarissime. Per persuadersene bisogna averlo veduto questo Museo, come l'ho visto io.

11. Anche al Barone di Zukmantal successore nell'Ambasciata di Francia di M[r] di Paulmy venne l'uzzolo de' Quadri.[22] Questo coltissimo Cavaliere ne acquistò in [?] dato, e li spedì in piu fiate ad ornare il suo Castello in Alsacia.

12. Non si dee tralasciare il Conte Durazzo,[23] che oltre l'acquisto di alcuni superbi Quadri, potette formare in Venezia due complete Collezioni di Stampe, per l'Arciduca Alberto la prima, e per se medesimo la seconda, come si può vedere dalla Descrizione del Benincasa fatta stampare da Bodoni. Anche questa rara collezione è la Storia visibile dell'Arte. Incomincia dai Nielli, e Scuola per Scuola, sì d'Italia, che d'oltremonti, giunge sino a nostri tempi, cioè la Romana, la Fiorentina, la Veneziana, la Lombarda, la Fiaminga, la Tedesca, l'Olandese, la Francese, &c.

13. Monsignore Ranuzzi,[24] ricco Prelato, poi Cardinale, Signore di ottimo gusto, in tempo di sua Nunziatura a Venezia spese piu centinaja di Zecchini in comperare Buoni Quadri, di quei proprio che van per la maggiore, per arricchire la magnifica Galleria di sua nobilissima Famiglia in Bologna.

14. Il Ministro di Moscovia M[r] Mordwinoff[25] era proprio

13. For the most recent account of Gavin Hamilton's activities as a dealer, with many references to the sources, see David Irwin; *English Neoclassical Art*, London, 1966, and – giving a more extended treatment of the artist's dealings in old master paintings –the same writer's 'Gavin Hamilton: Archaeologist, Painter, and Dealer', *Art Bulletin*, XLIV, 1962, pp. 87–102.

14. This almost certainly refers to Henry Hoare of Stourhead (died 1785) who obtained many of his Venetian pictures from Consul Smith.

15. For Sasso, as well as para. 32 of this account, see Haskell, *Patrons and Painters*, pp. 373–375, with references to sources.

16. For Strange, who was Resident in Venice between 1774 and 1790, see Haskell, *JWCI*, XXIII, 1960, pp. 268–269.

17. In the British Museum is a print of a 'Giorgione' *Resurrection* engraved by T. van Kessel and labelled Teniers Gallery. It is clearly after a seventeenth-century picture.

18. For this aspect of Strange's collecting see the references to him in Giovanni Previtali, *La fortuna dei primitivi dal Vasari ai neoclassici*, 1964.

19. I have been unable to verify this astonishing claim. Despite the condescending tone it shows what remarkable progress American studies must have made in Italy since 1760 when Cardinal Albani had thought that Benjamin West (who began his artistic career in Philadelphia) must be a Red Indian.

20. There appears to be no publication on Bute's collections.

21. Palmy d'Argenson (1722–87) was French Ambassador in Venice between 1767 and 1768. According to Lugt, *Les Marques de collections*, Amsterdam, 1921, the print cabinet at the Bibliothèque de l'Arsenal, Paris, originated with his collection. See also *Dictionnaire de Biographie Française*.

22. François-Antoine, Baron de Zuckmantel, was French Ambassador in Venice between 1771 and 1777.

23. Count Durazzo was Ambassador of the Holy Roman Empire in Venice between 1764 and 1784. The collection of prints he assembled for the Archduke Albert (1738–1822), son of Augustus III of Saxony, laid the foundations of the Albertina print room (Lugt). His own collection was acquired by Slade (Buchanan, *op. cit.*, I, p. 331).
   See Benincasa, *Descrizione della raccolta di stampi di S.E. il sig. conte Jacopo Durazzo*, Parma, 1784.

24. Monsignor Ranuzzi was Papal Nunzio in Venice from 1776 to 1782.

25. Mordwinoff was Russian Ambassador in Venice from 1785 to 1797. The only information available about his picture-collecting

fanatico per la Pittura, al tempo stesso capriccioso, e volubile; ma siccome andava sempre in traccia del migliore, e piu perfetto, quando possedeva un Quadro se ne stufava disfacendosene, o lo cambiava giuntandovi denaro per averne altro. Non v'era mattina d'Estate, di Verno, o qualunque tempo, in cui non uscisse di Casa *en bourgeois*, e andasse ripescando quà, e là, e visitando le officine de' Pittori, e racconciatori di Quadri, in Ghetto poi, dai Rigattieri, e nelle Case dove poteva entrare incognito. La casa sua insomma parea un mercato. I Rivenditori si vedeano continuo con Quadri alla mano arrivare, uscire, e aspettarlo da basso alla riva per mostrargli Pitture. Sasso tra gli altri, che ben conosceva il genio di lui, fece vantagiosissimi negozi. Il fatto sta, che si portò in Russia una bella Galleria.

15. Tra i Compratori, ovvero Spogliatori di Quadri a Venezia dovrà annoverarsi altresi il defonto Sig. Stanislao Maria fratello maggiore di chi fa questo racconto (Dⁿ Giacomo della Lena Lucchese) uomo dotato della piu felice immaginazione, fino, e passionato conoscitore di tutto ciò che concerne la bell'Arte del Disegno, il quale ne' primi 4 in 5 anni di sua dimora in Venezia, pria di passare a Copenhagen,[26] potè raccorre da circa 300 pezzi di Quadri, e 12/m stampe da me fattegli acquistar dal vecchio Giambattista Albrizzi a S. Benetto,[27] fra le quali senza pur una da scartarne, si trovavono le piu rare freschissime Prove di Marcantonio, e de' suoi scolari Agostin Veneziano, Buonasone, Marco da Ravenna, il Mantovan, &c, &c. E tanto Pitture, che Stampe le acquistò Stanislao pel suo buon amico, e padrone, il Marchese Paolino Santini Patrizio Lucchese, assai noto presso gli amatori di Stampe per la sua grandiosa Collezione di esse, e per la bella Quadreria lasciata alla sua Famiglia, essendo anch'egli passato tra' piu.[28]

16. Io dimenticava l'ultimo Residente d'Inghilterra Cavᵉ Worsley, possessore di una copiosissima, e ricchissima Raccolta di Cammei.[29] Egli non amava il mediocre, onde

col mezzo dell'egregio Giamᵃ Sasso si fornì di non poche insigni Pitture de' classici Autori, e inoltre di Bassorilievi, Bronzi, Avorj, e Scolture. Basta dire, che detti oggetti furono assicurati per 23/m Zecchini, ben inteso non compresi i Bauletti de' Cammei, che si portò seco; e venne notizia all'Abᵗᵉ Canonici,[30] e a Sasso, che un Corsaro Francese nell'acque di Tolone predò il Bastimento su cui erano caricati.

17. Non di deve defraudare del suo luogo una Raccogliatrice di belle Pitture, la Sigᵃ Giovannina. . . . detta la Gallinara, che divenuta moglie del celebre Professore di Violino Cappucci, si diede ed abbellire delle medesime con non indifferente spesa la sua abitazione. Divorziatosi dal marito, e cangiato pensamento, o fortuna se ne son iti i suoi Quadri, e piu non esistono in Venezia.

18. Il Museo del Celebre Antonmaria Zannetti,[31] ricco di preziosi Quadri, fra quali il bel Giambellino rappresentante la Cena in Em̄aus di N.S. del quale Tiziano dipinse lo stesso sogetto, come mostra la rara stampa, cosi detta, la Nappa di Masson;[32] di disegni de' primi Maestri, di 4 dei quali del Guercino, Mʳ Denon sborsò 100 Zecchini, di copiose stampe, di preziosi Cammei; tutto è sparito, ed ha varcato i Monti, e valicato i mari.[33] Le piu belle Pitture della Galleria del Principe di Liktenstein in Vienna, come si scorge dal suo Catalogo a Stampa, l'ebbe il vecchio Principe da Venezia mediante l'amicizia di detto Zannetti.

19. L'istesso destino del prefato Museo ha avuto la cospicua Galleria del Conte Algarotti, di cui si può dire non essere rimasto che il catalogo a stampa.[34]

20. L'altra superba Galleria della Nobilissima Casa Farsetti anch'essa è sparita. Non avesse avuto altro, che l'Erodiado di Tiziano, e il Ritratto di Rembrandt, il primo per quel che ho inteso passato a Pietroburgo, e l'altro a Londra, bastavano solo questi due pezzi sublimi per abbellire la Regia di qualunque Sovrano.[35]

shows him to have been a great admirer of Francesco Maggiotto, from whom he commissioned 6 paintings between 1788 and 1790 (*ArchVeneto*, 1882, p. 305).

26. There are some references to Stanislao Maria della Lena in the 'Notizie intorno alla vita del Dottore Sig.r Innocenzo della Lena' (Lucca, Biblioteca Governativa, MS. 1685–no. 12). All the brothers seem to have owned pictures.

27. This must refer to the great publisher (for whom, see Haskell, *Patrons and Painters*, pp. 334–336). References to his vast print collection are frequently made by Moschini, but I have been unable to trace the catalogue that was compiled by Pietro Brandolese.

28. For some information about the Santini and their beautiful villa at Camigliano near Lucca, see Isa Belli Barsali, *Le Ville Lucchesi*, Rome, 1964.

29. Sir Richard Worsley was Resident from 1793 until the downfall of the Republic in 1797. In the Biblioteca Correr (Epistolario Moschini) is a letter of introduction, dated 3rd October 1793, written for him from Strange to Sasso.

30. For Canonici see Irma Merolle, 'L'abate Matteo Luigi Canonici – le sue raccolte d'arte e la sua biblioteca', *Archivum Historicum Societatis Jesu*, Jan.–Jun., 1958.

31. For Anton Maria Zanetti the Elder, see Haskell, *Patrons and Painters*, pp. 341–345, with further references.

32. For this print of Antoine Masson (1636–1700) after Titian's *Supper at Emmaus* in the Louvre, see Robert-Dumesnil, *Le Peintre-Graveur français*, I, Paris, 1835, pp. 105–106.

33. For the activities in Venice of Denon (later, as Dominique Vivant-Denon, Napoleon's celebrated director of museums), see Haskell, *Patrons and Painters*, p. 371.

34. This catalogue was compiled by G. A. Selva in 1776. For the dispersal of some of Algarotti's collection see Michael Levey in *Burl M.*, CII, 1960, p. 250.

35. For Farsetti's pictures see *Memorie della R. Accademia di Torino*, Ser. II, XXI, 1911, p. 153. The two paintings are described as follows: 'Erodiade, colla testa di San Gio. Battista Sopra un bacile, di Tiziano' (possibly one of the many versions of the picture now in the Palazzo Doria, Rome) and 'Ritratto, più di mezza figura, di Pietro Paolo Rembrandt' (a pleasant conflation of the names of two artists much admired in eighteenth-century Venice).

21. Non è da tacersi il Marchese Agdolo,[36] nativo Armeno, Agente di Sassonia, che per non so quale combinazione di Commercio dipendente da crediti, era padrone di ragguardevole quantità di Quadri, i piu de' quali della classe de' Manieristi, tutti per altro pregevoli, e della miglior maniera di que' valentuomini: v'erano de' Pietro Vecchia, de' Cav.ri Liberi, Bambini, e Celesti, de Segala, de Giulio Carpioni, e de Gregori Lazzarini: di questo valoroso Pittore due Capi d'opera, uno rappresentante Ercole, e Iole, l'altro Salomone, che incensa gli Idoli, amendue di singolare finitezz.a, e bellezza, passati in mano di Sasso, e venduti a un Negoziante, che si portò in Germania. Gli antichi poi erano stati ripasticciati, e malamente accomodati con ridipinti. Il curioso era vedere questo dabbenuomo (che sara stato intendentissimo di mussoline, e Persiane, non mai di Pittura) tutto infatuato, vano, e ambizioso per questi suoi Quadri, che ne disgravava la stessa Galleria di Dresda: v'invitiva a vederli, e quando eravate li vi conduceva per mano mostrando il tale, e tal Quadro, e poi dicea queste precise parole: "vorrei un pò sapere chi sarà quel Becco coll'effe, che non dica ch'è di Paolo, di Tiziano? & Bisognava ridere sotto le basette, e mostrare di menargliela buona tacendo. Riferisco questa particolarità perche avveniva a me stesso, e l'ho intesa istessamente da altri.

22. La Galleria del Baron Tassis[37] conteneva veramente Quadri Stimabili, e di pregio: ancor questi sono sfumati: v'erano inoltre Bronzi in rilievo, e Basso rilievo, Statuette, e Gruppi, e Busti di marmo, il tutto in copia del buon secolo XVI. Mancato l'ultimo superstite di questa nobilissima Famiglia, ho conosciuto una nubile sorella ridotta al verde, che credo sia passata a viver con altra sua Sorella maritata a Modena.

23. Passiamo alla Galleria Orsetti, sulla quale ci resta a fare poche parole poichè del merito suo siamo abbastanza istruiti dalli Scrittori delle Cose Venete, in particolare dal Cav.re Ridolfi nelle sue Vite de' Pittori Veneziani, dove cita le opere belle di que' tali [?] esistenti in Casa Orsetti:[38] Ed è tale la stima in cui si avea, che per Lascito fatto dall'ultimo della Nobile Famiglia del Cardinale Carrara di Bergamo, di un fondo di 4/m Ducati di annua rendita, da istituire in quella Città un Accademia di Pittura, ed ornarla delle migliori, e piu scelte Opere di tutte le Scuole furono deputati dalla Città i due ornatissimi Cavalieri SS.ri Conti Fratelli Marenzi, Pittore uno, e gran dilettante l'altro, a recarsi a Venezia per comperar Quadri: dopo aver essi cercato, ed esaminato quanto qui c'era di meglio, scelsero quei del Sig. Avvocato Salvatore Orsetti, col quale conchiusero il Contratto mediante un vitalizio di non so bene

se di 1000, o di 2/m Ducati all'anno. In somma tutti i Forestieri, che capitavano a Venezia per la fama di quella Galleria andavano a visitarla, anco per vedere il Ritratto del gran Raffaele, che si pretende originale.

24. Il Barone Bodisson di Famiglia originaria, non so se Tedesca, o Fiamminga avea Galleria di Quadri anch'esso: dopo la sua morte andò distrutta e dispersa.[39]

25. I Quadri di Casa Pesaro sono stati mandati, e venduti a Londra unitamente alla Libreria del Procuratore, che oltre tante belle Edizioni, racchiudeva la rara Raccolta di tutti gli Aldini (Non tutti, ma oltre la metà dei Libri impressi da que' famosi Stampatori).[40]

26. L'illustre valoroso Maffeo Pinelli alla sua insigne Libreria, di cui non c'è rimasto che il Catalogo in 6 tomi esteso dal Chiarissimo Sig. Ab.te Morelli, che è un perfetto modello di Bibliografia, aggiunse numerosa serie di belle Pitture stata essa pure venduta.[41]

27. Non rinovaremo la triste memoria de' Quadri presi nella requisizione dalli Francesi; non di quelli involuti dai Commissari, ne della superba collezione di Disegni, e Stampe alla Salute di tomi 30 altresì involuta con preziosi Codici, e Libri rarissimi di varie Biblioteche arbitrariamente tolti dalli medesimi Commissarj per non rammaricarsene maggiormente.[42]

28. Sarebbe altresì lungo discorso il volere intratenersi sulle cospicue Biblioteche sortite da Venezia. Basti solo ricordare quella del Soranzo, la Pinelliana, quella del Dottore Paitoni, del consultore Urachien [?], e piu, e piu altre alienate, e distrutte (come furono negli ultimi tempi quella dei Foscarini dei Carmini, quella del Cardinale Flangini, quella assai numerosa del Battaglia) per farsi una giusta idea, di quel che in altri tempi era Venezia.

29. Non parleremo degli Ospitaleri [?] di Quadri, voglio dire di certuni, che qui chiamansi. . . . [?], i quali con la scaltrezza, e coll'inganno hanno saputo carpire, e mandar via con poco, o nulla, eccellenti dipinture, da chi non ne conosceva il merito, o vero valore. Di costoro ne ho ancor io conosciuti, che hanno abusato dell'ignoranza degli interessati.

30. Intorno alli Speculatori, che hanno anch'essi tanto contribuito allo smercio, o sia spoglio di Quadri, di tre soli faremo cenno assai noti, un Vicentino, e due Veneziani. Privi affatto di beni di fortuna, sono diventati agiati, e ricchi col commercio de Quadri in Venezia. Il primo ha comperato poderi in sua Patria, vive di entrata, ed ha Casa in Venezia, dove tiene un emporio di Quadri, aspettando la pace, per portarseli in Russia. I principi d'uno de' due Secondi, sono stati di. . . . [?] di nave col denaro ammassato

36. Marchese Gregorio Agdollo was representative of the King of Saxony in Venice from 1750 until 1789.

37. For some information see F. M. Tassi, *Vite de' pittori, scultori e architetti bergamaschi*, Bergamo, 1793.

38. See Simona Savini Branca, *Il collezionismo veneziano nel seicento*, 1965, p. 255, and Moschini, 1806, p. 53.

39. I have been unable to trace this collector.

40. For Pesaro's pictures see the inventory published by Fiocco, *Palazzo Pesaro*, 1925, and Squibb Sale, London, 9th July 1831.

41. For Pinelli's pictures see Haskell, *Patrons and Painters*, pp. 239–240, with further references.

42. For a succinct bibliography of Napoleon's looting of Italian art see C. Gould, *Trophy of Conquest*, London, 1965.

egli ha creduto di accrescere la sua fortuna nell'acquisto di Quadri, e infatti ha formato una importante Quadreria, che va esitando. (Uno dei Speculatori di Quadri qui vivente è pur l'Avvocato Galleazzo Galeazzi, che sempre ne acquista, e al buon denaro ne vende; egli ha molta cognizione dei Pittori, ed è valentissimo a riperirli, e a nettarli. A stare con lui anche il suo Servitor piu in piccolo imparò a far lo stesso negoziato).[43]

31. Tra suddetti si dee annoverare eziando il nostro Sasso, che con la forza del genio si fece erudito, ed esperto in ogni genere di Belle Arti, e coll'industria, er specchiaa onestà di povero Tessore ch'egli era, seppe fomarsi ntel Traffico de' Quadri eredito, e stato assai considerevole. Di quest'uomo stimabile ci riserveremo a dare la notizia della sua vita; e in quanto alle belle, e pellegrine cose passate per le sue mani, diremo quello, che ne sappiamo.

32. Sarebbe stato veramente pregio dell'opera, per rendere interessanti queste notizie, che si riducono ad una sterile nomenclatura di compratori di Quadri, e Gallerie, il poter der conto dei principali nel nominare gli Autori, e riferire le opere loro; Averei pensato in tempo; questa cosa si sarebbe potuto fare agevolmente dall'abilissimo Giam[a] Sasso, la di cui sterminata memoria era un ampio repertorio in materia di Belle Arti. Quando egli avea veduto una Pittura, o una Stampa, ve ne sapeva dar contezza, magari

in capo a 10, a 15 anni notando tutte le piu minute particolarità, e facendone esattamente la storia.

33. Allorchè regnava vero Buon gusto, intelligenza, ed amore per le Arti Belle, non solo si voleano avere le produzioni di patrii Artisti, e se ne pronoveva l'emulazione, ma si procuravano ad ogni costo le forastiere. Par la qual cosa non v'era Casa Nobile, e Famiglia distinta, che non avesse la sua Galleria fornita di piu maniere di Autori singolarmente Bolognesi, Lombardi, Fiorentini, e Fiamminghi. Ne sia anche prova la magnifica Galleria Manfrin,[44] la memorisissima raccolta del Dr Pellegrini, che conta di avere 8/m pezzi:[45] e la recente dell' Ab[te] Celotti, formata in brevissimo tempo, dove si fanno ammirare i nomi maestri Veneziani, anco gli altri Italiani, e d'oltremonti.[46]

34. Qui faremo la festa di S.Fine, dicendo che malgrado la immensa incredibile quantità di Quadri usciti fuori di Paese, sembra che sia men di stupire di ciò, che di quello, che vi rimane ancora (eccettuato le Opere, che si veggono in pubblico) perche da questa dirò così, inesausta miniera, sempre se ne cavano, e vi si conservano pur tutto dì in parecchie Famiglie Nobili, e Cittadine.

43. I have unfortunately been unable to identify any of these characters.

44. For the Manfrin collection see Haskell, *Patrons and Painters*, pp. 379–381, with further references.
45. Much of the Pellegrini collection has ended up in the Museo Correr.
46. For Celotti, see Haskell, *Patrons and Painters*, p. 377.

ILLUSTRATIONS

1. Caradosso:
Foundation Medal of St. Peter's,
British Museum example.

2. Agostino Veneziano: *Engraving of St. Peter's,* 1517

3. Serbaldi: *St. Peter's Medal.*
British Museum

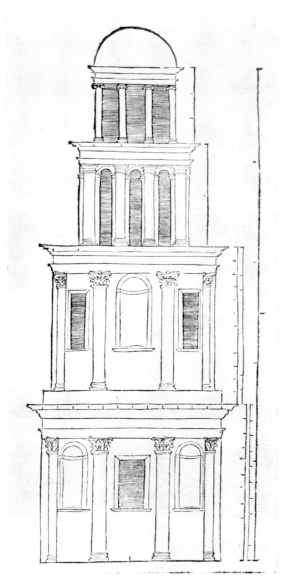

4. L. B. Alberti: *De Re Aedificatoria,* Book VIII:
Tower from the 1550 illustrated edition.

5. Anonymous French Draughtsman, Cambridge, Fitzwilliam Museum.

6. Menicantonio: Page from Sketchbook in the Collection of Mr. Paul Mellon.

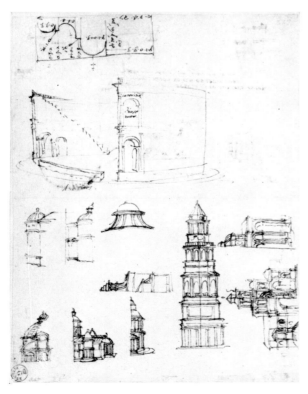

7. Baldassare Peruzzi: Drawing showing details of
St. Peter's (Florence, Uffizi A.106).

8. Antonio da Sangallo the Younger: *Model for St. Peter's.*
Rome, St. Peter's.

1. Raphael: *Architectural Studies*. Oxford, Ashmolean
Museum, No. 517 *verso* (photographed from the *recto*
against the light; reproduced by courtesy
of the Ashmolean Museum)

2. Raphael: *Study of the End Wall of a Church*.
Oxford, Ashmolean Museum, No. 516 *verso*

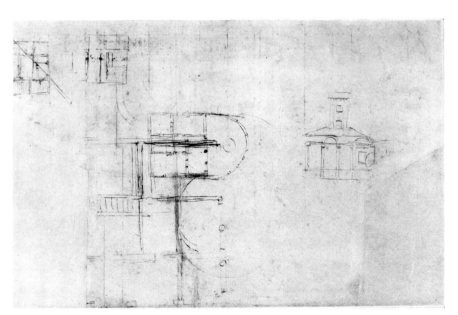

4. Raphael: *Projects for a Casino*. Oxford, Ashmolean Museum, No. 579 *verso*

3. Raphael: *Architectural Details*.
Left, detail from Ashmolean Museum, No. 565,
study for the *Monteluce Coronation*;
right, detail from Fig. 6

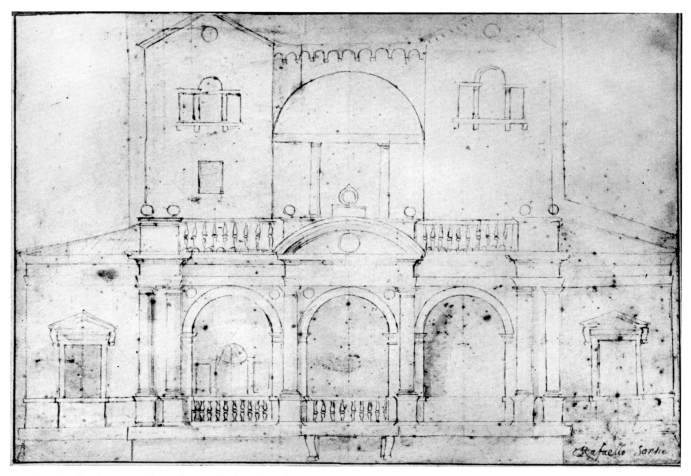

5. Raphael: *Elevation of a Villa*. Oxford, Ashmolean Museum, No. 579 *recto* (state in 1859; photo: Courtauld Institute)

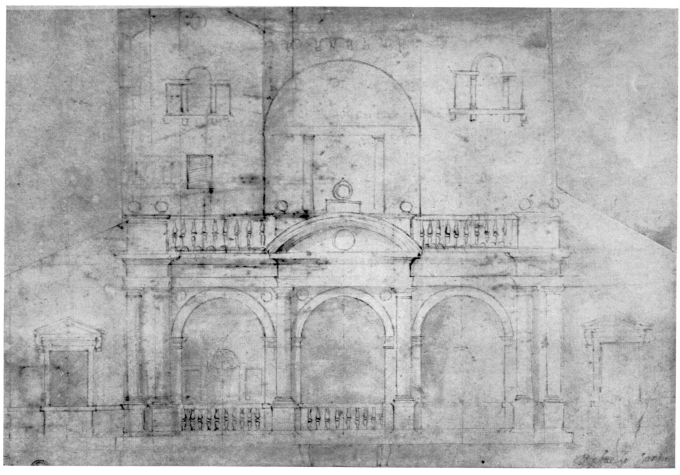

6. Raphael: *Elevation of a Villa*. Oxford, Ashmolean Museum, No. 579 *recto* (present state)

1. Perugino: *Madonna in Glory*. Florence, Uffizi

2. Raphael: *The Coronation of the Virgin*, c. 1502–3.
Rome, Vatican Gallery

3. Raphael: *The Annunciation*, part of predella of Fig. 2. Rome, Vatican Gallery

4. Raphael: *Study for the Head of St. James* in Fig. 2.
London, British Museum

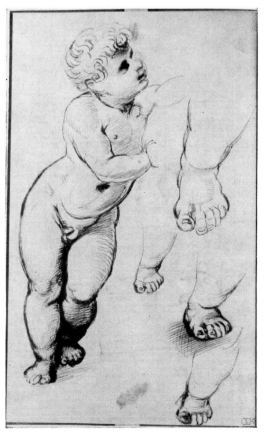

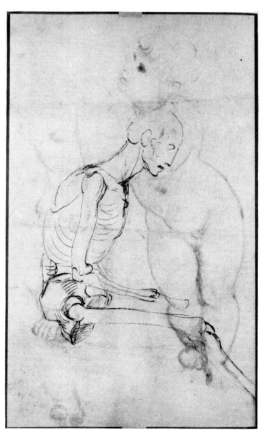

5. Raphael: *Study for the 'Belle Jardinière'*.
Oxford, Ashmolean Museum

6. Raphael: *Study of a 'Skeleton' (verso of Fig. 5).*
Oxford, Ashmolean Museum

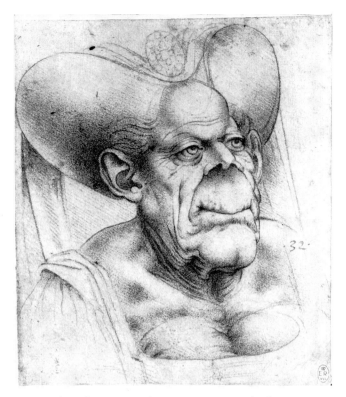

1. Melzi after Leonardo: *Grotesque Head of a Woman*.
Royal Library, 12492

2. Melzi after Leonardo: *Man with Flowing Hair*.
Royal Library, 12494

3. Melzi after Leonardo: *Four Caricature Heads*.
Royal Library, 12493

4. Melzi after Leonardo: *Seated Man in Profile*.
Royal Library, 12584

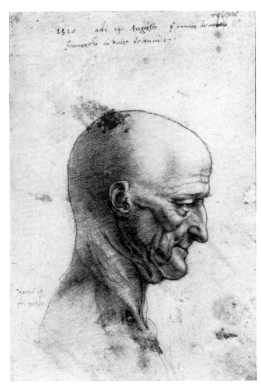

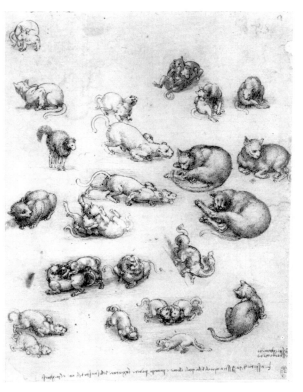

5. Francesco Melzi: *Head of a Man in Profile.*
Milan, Ambrosiana

6. Leonardo, perhaps retouched by Melzi:
Sketches of Cats. Royal Library, 12363

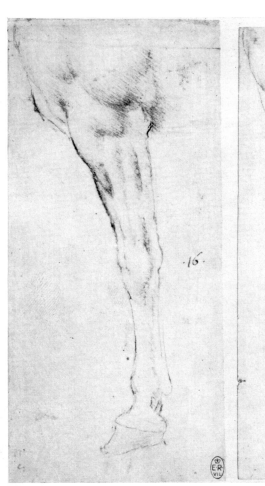

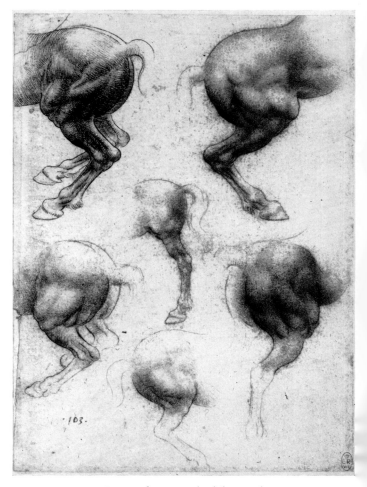

7. Leonardo: *Near Fore-leg of a Horse.*
Royal Library, 12301

8. Melzi after Leonardo: *Near
Fore-leg of a Horse.* Copy of Fig. 7.
Royal Library, detail of 12302

9. Leonardo retouched by Melzi:
Six Studies of the Hindquarters of a Horse. Royal Library, 12333

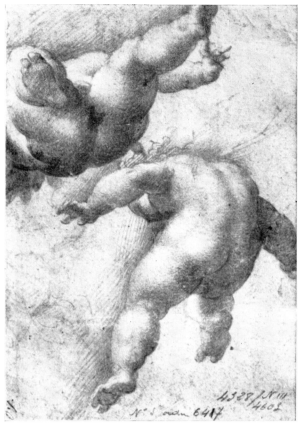

1. Parmigianino: *Studies of Two Putti* (red chalk).
Paris, Louvre

2. Parmigianino: *The Holy Family with Angels* (red chalk).
Paris, Louvre (*verso* of Fig. 1)

3. Parmigianino: *Study of a Servant* (red chalk).
Budapest, Museum of Fine Arts

4. Parmigianino: *Studies of two Women* (red chalk).
Budapest, Museum of Fine Arts (*verso* of Fig. 3)

5. Parmigianino: *Studies for a Preaching of the Baptist* (pen and wash, white heightening). London, British Museum

6. Parmigianino: *Studies for a Saint Jerome* (red chalk, pen and wash). London, British Museum (*verso* of Fig. 5)

7. Rosaspina after Parmigianino: *Saint Jerome*. Etching

8. Parmigianino: *Study of a Man holding an Ass* (pen and brown ink, pink prepared paper, white heightening). Private Collection

2. Bronzino: *St. John the Baptist kissing the Christ Child.* Florence, Uffizi

1. Bronzino: *The Christ Child recognizing his Destiny of the Cross.* London, National Gallery

3. Bronzino: *Venus disarming Cupid*. London, National Gallery

4. Bronzino: Detail of *La Fraude* from *Venus disarming Cupid*. London, National Gallery

5. Attributed to Pontormo: *Venus and Cupid*. Florence, Accademia

7. Anonymous 16th-century Italian engraving: *Venus disarming Cupid*

6. Engraving by J. Saenredam after Goltzius: *Venus and Cupid*

1. General View of the Oratorio of S. Giovanni Decollato, Rome

2. Michelangelo: *Christ*. Rome,
S. Maria sopra Minerva

3. Francesco Salviati: Detail from
The Beheading of S. John the Baptist.
Rome, Palazzo della Cancelleria

4. Study after Michelangelo's *Christ* in S. Maria sopra
Minerva, black and red chalk, 32·3 by 19·8 cm.
Florence, Uffizi, no. 215 Santarelli

5. Francesco Salviati: *S. Andrew*. Rome, Oratorio of S. Giovanni Decollato

6. Francesco Salviati: *S. Bartholomew*. Rome, Oratorio of S. Giovanni Decollato

2. Vitruv: *Forum*, ed. 1533

3. *Antikes Gastmahl, aus Borghinis Papieren.* Florenz, Biblioteca Nazionale

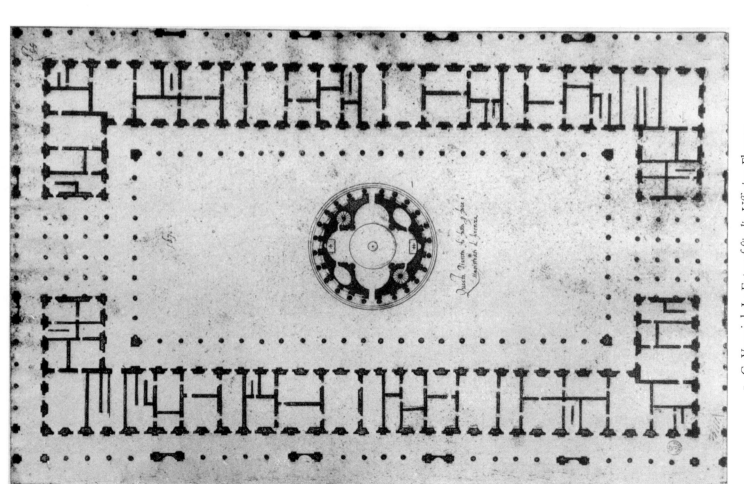

1. G. Vasari d. J.: *Entwurf für die Uffizien.* Florenz

5. Studiolo des Francesco I, Lünette. Florenz, Palazzo Vecchio

6. *Jahreszeitensarkophag.* Stich von Bartoli (nach Hanfmann)

4. *Knieende Stifterin*, aus Borghinis *Papieren.* Florenz, Biblioteca Nazionale

1. Giovanni Antonio Pordenone: *God the Father and Cherubs*. Cortemaggiore, SS. Annunziata, Pallavicino Chapel (photo Fiorentini)

2. Pordenone: *The Immaculata with the Fathers of the Church*. Naples, Capodimonte (photo Anderson)

3. Pordenone: *The Apostles*. Piacenza, S. Maria di Campagna, Chapel of St. Catherine (photo Manzotti)

4. Pordenone: *The Disputation of St. Catherine*. Piacenza, S. Maria di Campagna, Chapel of St. Catherine (photo Manzotti)

5. Pordenone: *The Assumption of the Virgin*. Piacenza, S. Maria di Campagna, Chapel of the Virgin (photo Manzotti)

6. Pordenone: *God in Glory, Seers, and Saints*. Piacenza, S. Maria di Campagna, detail of main dome (photo Manzotti)

7. Giulio Campi: *God the Father and Cherubs*. Cremona, SS. Margherita e Pelagia, presbytery (photo Negri)

1. *The Domestication of Cupid*, here attributed to Niccolò dell' Abbate. Present whereabouts unknown

2. Titian: *The Allegory of Alfonso d'Avalos*. Paris, Louvre

3. *Vesta*. Woodcut from Vincenzo Cartari, *Imagini de gli dei*, 1615, p. 523

4. *Temple of Vesta*. Woodcut from Vincenzo Cartari, *Imagini de gli dei*, 1615, p. 200

5. *Allegorical Figure*. Woodcut from Vincenzo Cartari, *Imagini de gli dei*, 1615, p. 527

6. Titian: *The Blindfolding of Cupid*. Rome, Borghese Gallery

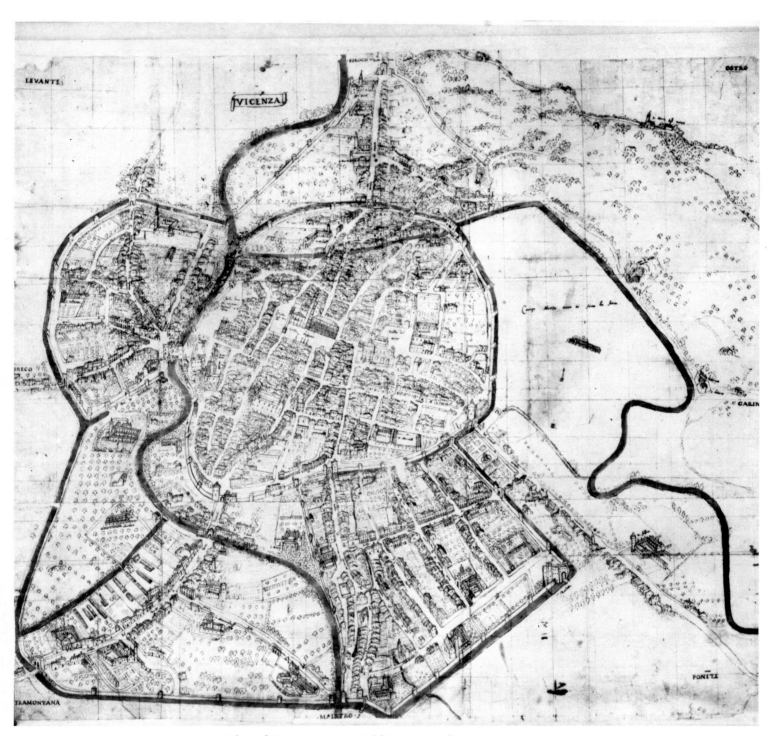

1. Plan of Vicenza. Rome, Biblioteca Angelica, B. 22. 11, int. 81

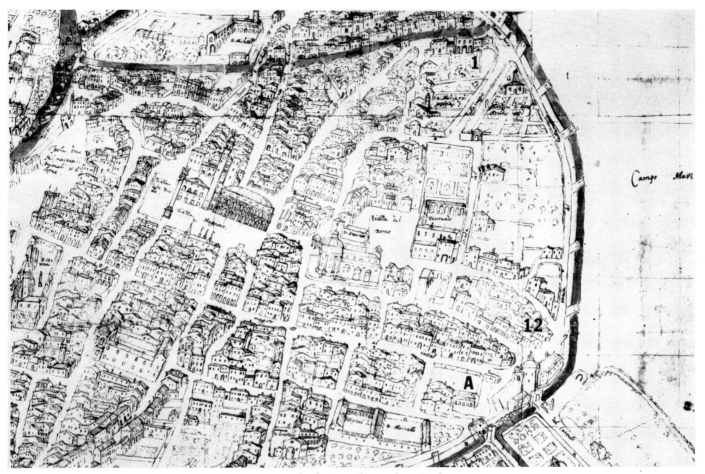

2. Detail of Fig. 1 (central section)

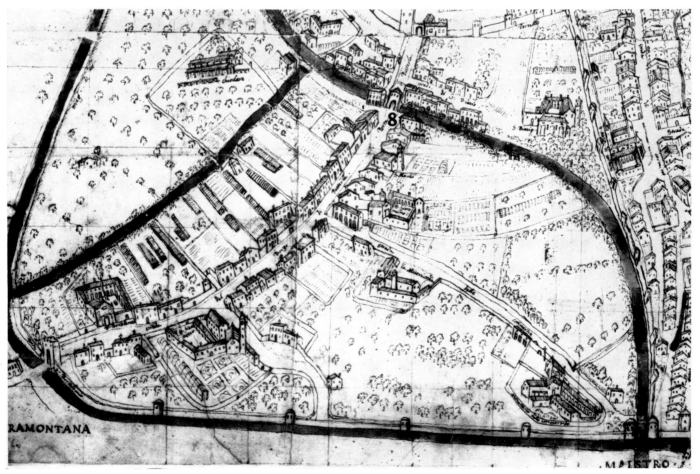

3. Detail of Fig. 1 (northern quarter)

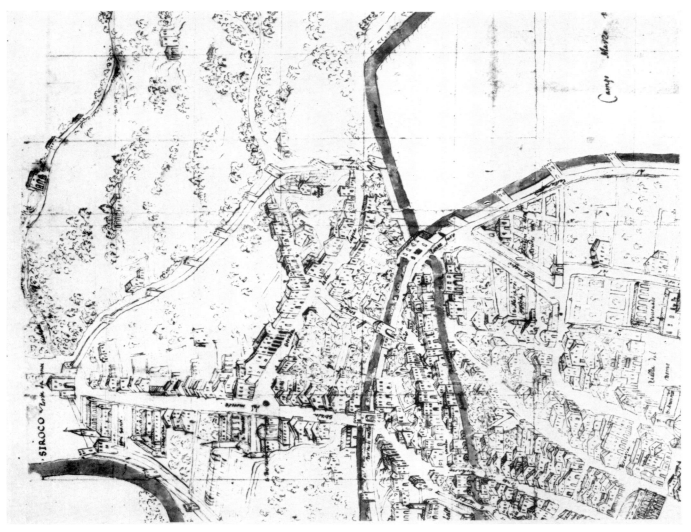

5. Detail of Fig. 1 (southern quarter)

4. Detail of Fig. 1 (eastern quarter)

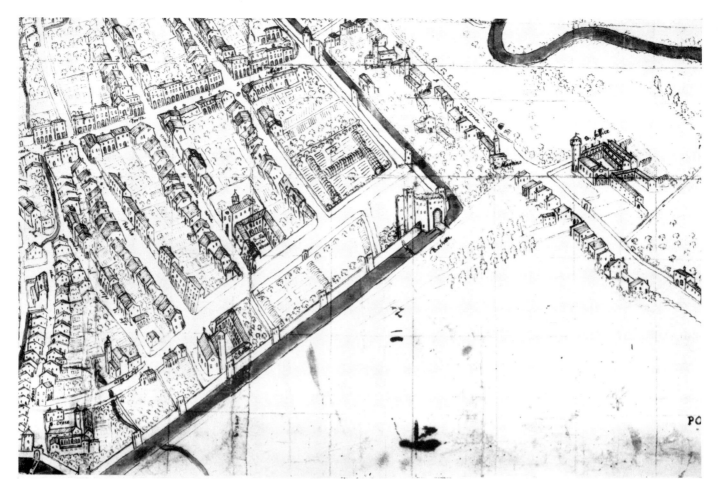

6. Detail of Fig. 1 (western quarter)

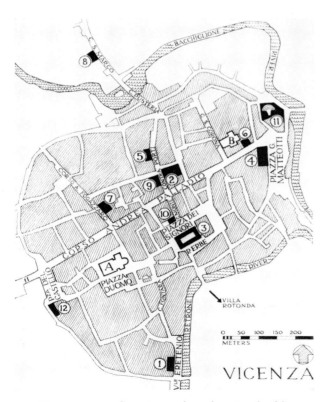

7. Vicenza, central section today, showing buildings
by Palladio

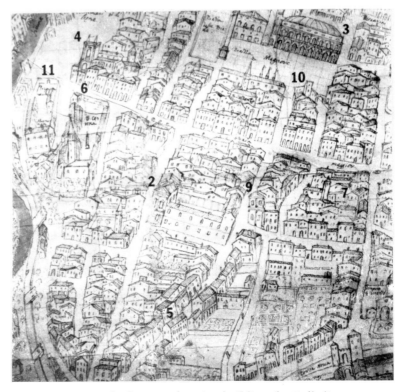

8. Detail of Fig. 1, showing buildings by Palladio

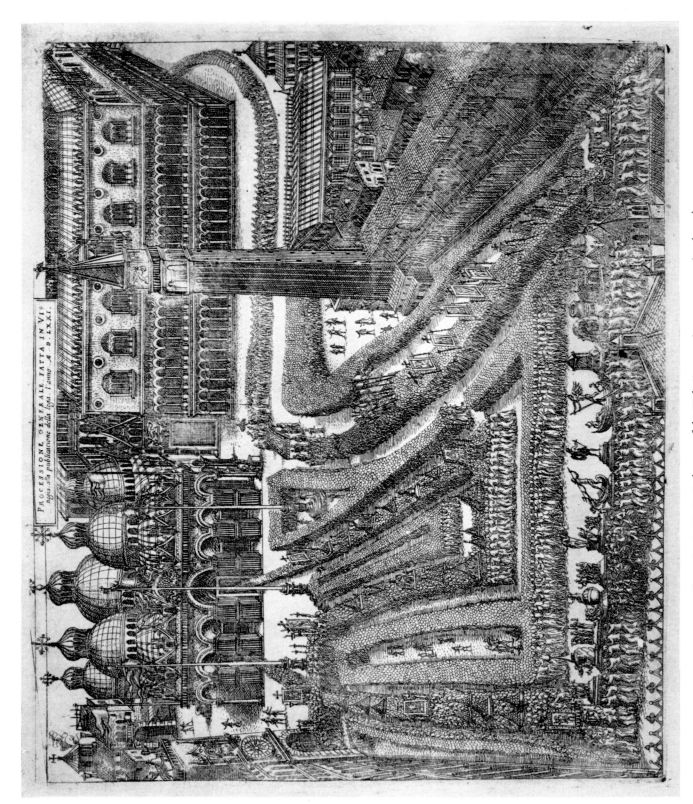

1. *Procession in Venice in honour of the Holy League.* Anonymous print (1571)

1. Antonello Freri: *Tomb of Angelo Balsamo* (detail), 1507, showing a *Sea-Thiasos*. Messina, Museo Nazionale

2. Giuliano da Sangallo: *Tomb of Nera Sassetti* (detail).
Florence, SS. Trinita

3. Bartholo Berrecci: *Royal Funerary Chapel*, 1517–33, Altar Wall.
Cracow Cathedral

4. *Royal Funerary Chapel*, Lunette of Altar Wall. Cracow Cathedral

5. Detail of centre of Fig. 4

6. *Royal Funerary Chapel*, Detail of Lunette of South Wall.
Cracow Cathedral

Wooden Figure of St. Roch, here attributed to Juan de Juni. Florence, SS. Annunziata
(photo Brogi)

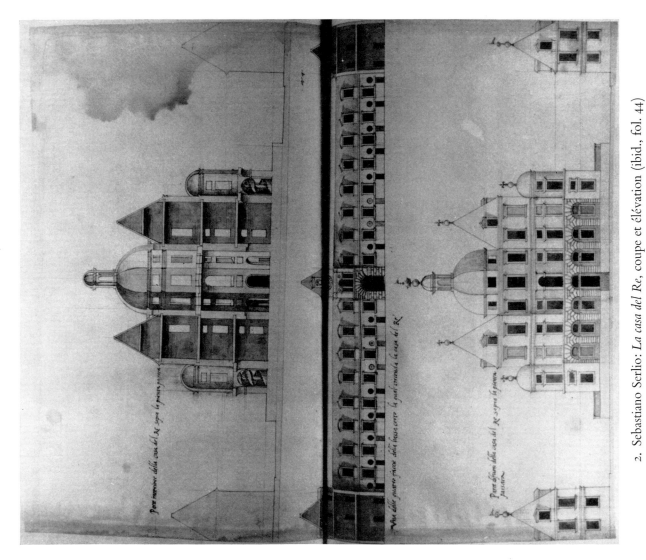

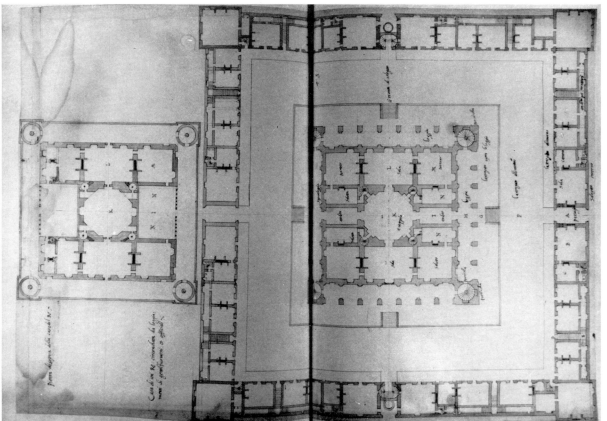

2. Sebastiano Serlio: *La casa del Re, coupe et élévation* (ibid., fol. 44)

1. Sebastiano Serlio: *Pianta . . . della casa del Re* (MS., Livre VI, fol. 43, Avery Architectural Library, Columbia University, New York)

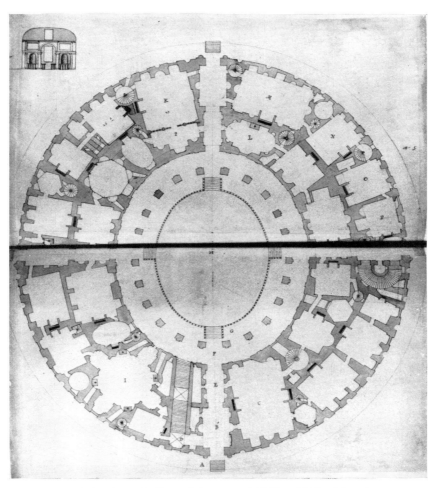

3. Sebastiano Serlio: *Château-amphithéâtre* (ibid., fol. 45)

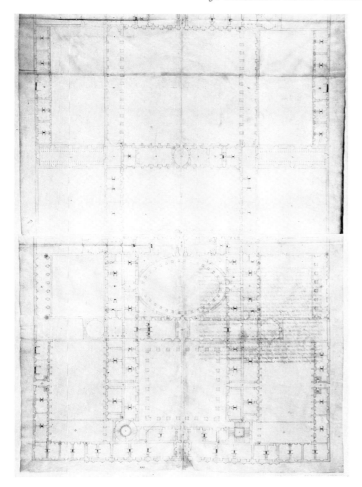

4. Sebastiano Serlio: *Palais à suite de cours* (MS., Livre VI, fof. 64, Staatsbibliotek, Munich, cod. icon. 189)

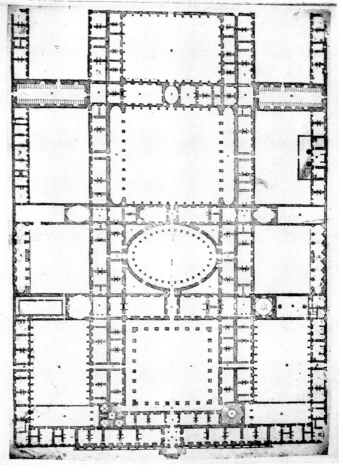

5. Gravure anonyme, *Plan de palais à suite de cours* (Institut de France, MS. 1043, fol. 15)

1. *La Cène*, 1515 (Panneau central du *Retable de l'Eucharistie*). Autun, Musée

2. *Abraham et Melchissedech*, 1515 (Volet du *Retable de l'Eucharistie*). Autun, Musée

3. *Les Saintes Femmes au Tombeau*. Cluny, Hospice

4. *Le Christ au Jardin des Oliviers*; *La Déploration du Christ*; *La Résurrection*, 1527. Châtillon-sur-Chalaronne, Hôtel de Ville

5–6. *La Montée au Calvaire*; *La Mise au Tombeau*, 1523 (Volets du *Retable de Nicolas Chichon et Jacquemette de la Botte*). Bourg-en-Bresse, Église Notre-Dame

7. *Sainte Barbe et un chanoine donateur*; *Adoration de l'Enfant*; *Sainte Catherine*, 1520. Saint-Pantaléon (Saône-et-Loire), Église

8–9. *Sainte Catherine*; *Sainte Barbe* (Volets de triptyque). Budapest, Musée des Beaux-Arts

1. Jean Clouet: *Inconnu au Pétrarque*, c. 1535. Hampton Court.
By gracious permission of H.M. the Queen

2. François Clouet (dans l'atelier de Jean): *François Premier*, c. 1535. Paris, Louvre

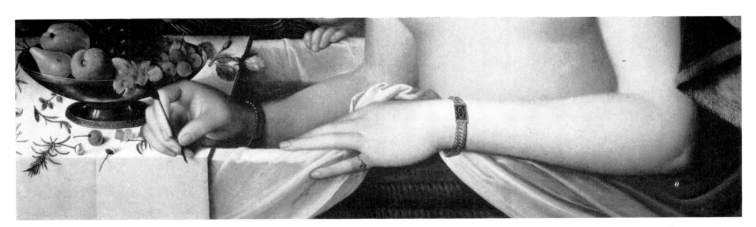

3. François Clouet: *La Dame au Bain* (détail des mains), c. 1570? Washington, National Gallery of Art, Kress Collection
(reproduced by courtesy of the Gallery)

4. Jean Clouet: *Inconnu* (crayon), c. 1520.
Chantilly, Musée Condé (photo Giraudon)

5. Jean Clouet: *Charlotte de France*, c. 1523–4.
Chicago, Collection Mrs. J. Epstein
(photo Art Institute of Chicago)

6. Jean Clouet: *Claude de Guise*, c. 1525–30. Florence, Palais Pitti
(photo Gabinetto Fotografico)

7. Jean Clouet: *Inconnu* (crayon), c. 1535–40.
Chantilly, Musée Condé

8. Jean Clouet: *L'Homme aux pièces d'or*, 1522. St. Louis, Mo., City Art Museum (photo The Museum)

1. Guillaume Dumée: *Figures dans un paysage*. Musée de Besançon

2. Guillaume Dumée: *Olinde et Sophronie délivrés du bûcher*.
Étude pour le Cabinet de la Reine du Musée du Louvre.
Paris, École des Beaux-Arts

3. Gabriel Honnet: *Sophronie s'accusant devant Aladin*.
Étude pour le Cabinet de la Reine. Cabinet des Dessins,
Musée du Louvre

4. Guillaume Dumée: *Clorinde demandant la grâce d'Olinde et de Sophronie*. Étude pour le Cabinet de la Reine au Louvre. Paris, École des Beaux-Arts

5. D'après Guillaume Dumée: *Olinde et Sophronie*. Étude pour le Cabinet de la Reine au Louvre. Bibliothèque Municipale de Rouen

6. Attr. à Guillaume Dumée: *Le Prévôt des marchands et les Échevins de la Ville de Paris*
(provenant de l'Hôtel de Ville, Paris). Musée Carnavalet, Paris

7. Guillaume Dumée d'après Toussaint Dubreuil: *Le Repas* (détail).
Musée du Louvre (provenant du château de Saint Germain)

2. Marcantonio Raimondi: *The Fall of Man* (engraving after Raphael)

1. Rubens: *The Fall of Man*. London, Private Collection

3. Rubens: *Lucretia* (copied from Marcantonio Raimondi's engraving after Raphael). London, Private Collection

4. Rubens: *Pan and Syrinx* (adapted from an engraving after Raphael). London, British Museum

5. Rubens and Jan Brueghel: *Pan and Syrinx*. London, Private Collection

6. Rubens: *Christ in Glory* (after Raphael's *Disputa*). Turin, Royal Library

7. Rubens: *Male Nude*
(after Raphael's *Fire in the Borgo*).
London, British Museum

8. Rubens: *The Vision of Ezekiel* (after Raphael).
Florence, Museo Horne

9. Rubens: *Group of Apostles* (after Raphael's
Transfiguration). Paris, Louvre

10. Rubens: *Harpy*. London, British Museum

11. Rubens: *River God* (after Raphael's *Council of the Gods*). New York, Pierpont Morgan Library

12. Rubens: *The Story of Cupid and Psyche*. Mertoun House, the Duke of Sutherland

13. Detail of Fig. 12

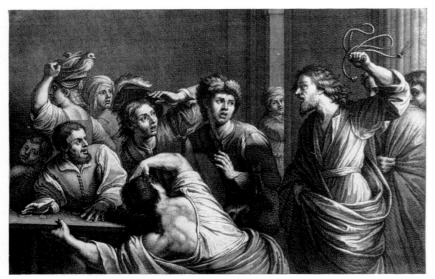

1. *Christ driving the Money Changers out of the Temple*. Engraving by Jean Haussart after a destroyed Manfredi formerly in the Mazarin and French Royal Collections

2. David Teniers the Younger: Detail from *The Gallery of the Archduke Leopold Wilhelm* showing a lost Manfredi *Capture of Christ*. Munich, Bayerische Staatsgemäldesammlungen

3–4. Manfredi(?): *Autumn, Winter*. London, Nicolson Collection

5. A follower of Manfredi (? French): *Summer and Autumn*. Rome, Private Collection

6. Manfredi: *The Tribute Money*. Florence, Uffizi

7. Manfredi: *Christ among the Doctors*. Florence, Uffizi

8. A follower of Manfredi (? French): *Gamblers*. England, Private Collection

9. Manfredi (?): *The Crowning with Thorns*. Formerly Baronesse Rengers-Van Pallandt Collection, Belgium

1. Pietro da Cortona: *Kopfstudie*, um 1630.
Neu-York, Privatbesitz

2. Pietro da Cortona: *Krieger und Gefangene*, um 1640.
Neu-York, Privatbesitz

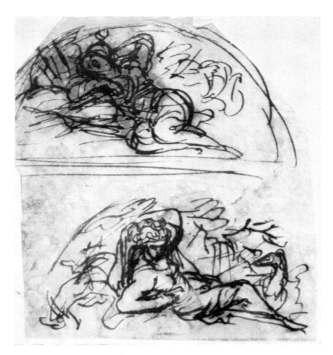

3. Pietro da Cortona: *Sitzende Figuren*, um 1640.
Neu-York, Privatbesitz

4. Pietro da Cortona: *Diana*, um 1643.
Neu-York, Privatbesitz

5. Pietro da Cortona: *Justinian*, um 1646. Florenz, Uffizien

6. Ciro Ferri: *Justinian*, 1659. Neu–York, Privatbesitz

7. Ciro Ferri: *David und Abigail*, 1665. Neu-York, Privatbesitz

8. Ciro Ferri: *David und Abigail*, 1666. Bergamo, S. Maria Maggiore

1. G. M. Morandi: Detail of *Portrait of Mario de' Fiori*.
Ariccia, Palazzo Chigi

2. Morandi: Modello for *St. François de Sales preaching*.
Private Collection

3. Morandi: Modello for *The Death of the Virgin*. Rome, Borghese Gallery

4. Morandi: *Cardinal Denhoff*. New York art market

5. Morandi: *SS. Valentine and Hilary*.
Viterbo, Duomo

6. Morandi: *Christ on the Cross*. Rome, Galleria Nazionale

1. David Beck: *Queen Christina*, 1655–56.
Gothenburg, Historical Museum

2. Unknown Artist: *Queen Christina*.
Engraved frontispiece to Gualdo Priorato's
Historia . . . di Christina di Svezia, 1656

3. Francesco Maria Nocchieri: *Queen Christina*, 1656.
Rome, Museo del Campidoglio

4. Unknown Roman Sculptor: *Queen Christina*, c. 1660.
Brunswick, Herzog-Anton-Ulrich Museum

5. Unknown Sculptor: *Queen Christina*, c. 1660–65.
German Private Collection

6. Abraham Wuchters: *Queen Christina* (detail),
1660–61. Siena, Count Piccolomini

7. Ferdinand Voet: *Queen Christina* (detail), c. 1669.
Florence, Uffizi

8. Michael Dahl: *Queen Christina*, c. 1687.
Grimsthorpe Castle

9. Giulio Cartari: *Queen Christina*, c. 1680. San Ildefonso, Palace of La Granja

10. Unknown Sculptor (Jean Théodon?): *Queen Christina*, c. 1687–88. Stockholm, Nationalmuseum

11–12. Ferdinand de Saint Urbain: *Medal of Queen Christina*, c. 1687–88

13. *Cast* from the Death Mask of Queen Christina made by Giovanni Giardini for her Tomb, 1689

1. Nicolas Poussin: *Tancred and Erminia*. Leningrad, Hermitage

2. Poussin: *Tancred and Erminia*. Birmingham University, The Barber Institute of Fine Arts

3. Poussin: *Bacchanal* (Drawing). Paris, Louvre

4. Poussin: *Childhood of Bacchus*. Chantilly, Musée Condé

5. Poussin: *Rinaldo and Armida*. Moscow, Pushkin Museum of Fine Arts

6. *Sepuchral Stele*. Greece, fifth century B.C. Rome, Villa Albani

7. Poussin, detail of Fig. 1

1. Pier Francesco Mola: *Erminia and Tancred*. San Francisco, M. H. De Young Museum, Kress Collection
(by courtesy of the Museum)

2. Pier Francesco Mola: *Erminia as a Shepherdess*. Paris, Palais du Sénat (photo Vizzavona)

3. Guercino: *Erminia and Tancred*. Rome, Doria Gallery (photo Alinari)

4. Drawing of a Roman sarcophagus: *The Last Homecoming of Meleager* (detail). Florence, Uffizi

5. Pietro da Cortona: *Erminia and Tancred*. England, Corsham Court, Lord Methuen

Claude Lorrain: *Pastoral Landscape* (LV 22), 1638. English Private Collection

3. Claude Lorrain: *Pastoral Landscape (Liber Veritatis drawing 23)*, 1638. London, British Museum

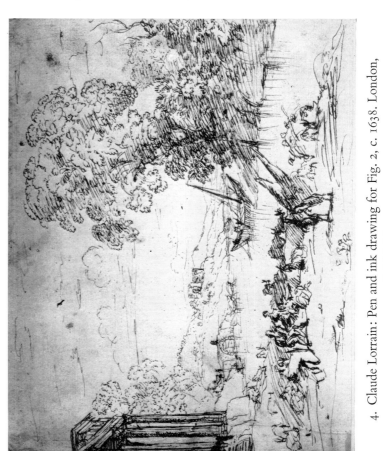

4. Claude Lorrain: Pen and ink drawing for Fig. 2, c. 1638. London, British Museum

2. Claude Lorrain: *Pastoral Landscape* (variant of LV 23), c. 1638. Collection, The Earl of Halifax

5. Detail of Fig. 1

6. Detail of Fig. 1

7. Claude Lorrain: *Harbour Scene* (*Liber Veritatis* drawing 19), 1637/38. London, British Museum

8. Claude Lorrain: *Harbour Scene* (variant of LV 19), c. 1637/38. Windsor Castle, H.M. The Queen.
Reproduced by gracious permission

9. Claude Lorrain: *Harbour Scene* (LV 19), 1637/38. English Private Collection

1. Matthieu Le Nain: *Portrait d'homme*. Le Puy, Musée Crozatier

2. D'après(?) Matthieu Le Nain:
Portrait de jeune homme (miniature), 1645.
Londres, Victoria and Albert Museum

3. Matthieu Le Nain:
Tête de fillette (détail du *Jardinier*).
Cologne, Wallraf-Richartz Museum

4. Attribué à Matthieu Le Nain: *Portrait d'homme*. Stockholm, Musée National

5. Matthieu Le Nain: *Portrait d'homme* (détail du *Jardinier*). Cologne, Wallraf-Richartz Museum

6. Matthieu Le Nain: *Portrait d'homme* (détail des *Joueurs de tric-trac*). Paris, Louvre

Sebastien de Pontaut
Seigneur de Beaulieu

7. D'après Matthieu Le Nain(?): *Portrait de Sébastien de Pontault, sieur de Beaulieu*. Gravure de Gérard Edelinck

1. Carlo Fontana: *Design for the Catafalque* for the Memorial Service for Pedro II, King of Portugal, in Rome, 1707. Windsor Castle, Royal Library. Reproduced by gracious permission of H.M. The Queen

2. Bernardo Vittone: Copy of the preceding design. Paris, Musée des Arts Décoratifs

3. Vittone: Engraving of a *Catafalque* from the *Istruzioni diverse*, 1766

4. Fontana: Another design for the same *Catafalque* as in Fig. 1. Windsor Castle, Royal Library. Reproduced by gracious permission of H.M. The Queen

5. Vittone: *Sheet of Studies*. After Fontana.
Paris, Musée des Arts Décoratifs

6. Vittone: *Design for the 'coretti'* to the side of the high altar of the Oratory of the Decollazione di S. Giovanni Battista, 1728. Paris, Musée des Arts Décoratifs

7. Vittone: *Sheet of Studies*. After Fontana. Paris, Musée des Arts Décoratifs

8. Vittone: *Design for the Altar* in the Santuario di Sant' Ignazio, Monte Bastia, near Lanzo, 1727? Paris, Musée des Arts Décoratifs

9. Vittone, engraving in the *Istruzioni diverse* based on the preceding design

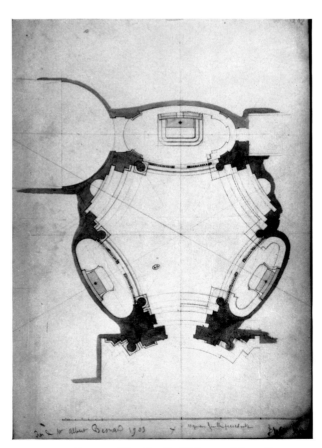

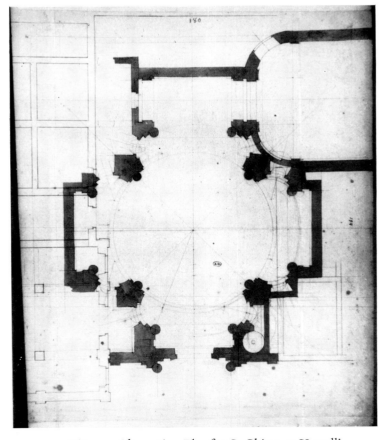

10. Vittone: *Plan* for S. Chiara at Vercelli. Paris, Musée des Arts Décoratifs.

11. Vittone: Alternative *Plan* for S. Chiara at Vercelli. Paris, Musée des Arts Décoratifs

12. Vittone: *Sheet of Studies*. Paris, Musée des Arts Décoratifs

13. Vittone: *Sheet of Studies*. Paris, Musée des Arts Décoratifs

14. Vittone: *Design for a Tabernacle*. Paris, Musée des Arts Décoratifs

15. Vittone: Alternative *Design for a Tabernacle*. Paris, Musée des Arts Décoratifs

THE WRITINGS OF ANTHONY BLUNT

COMPILED BY ELSA SCHEERER

T

THE WRITINGS OF ANTHONY BLUNT
COMPILED BY ELSA SCHEERER

BOOKS

The Drawings of Nicolas Poussin (in collaboration with W. Friedlaender). Warburg Institute, London, 1939–.

Artistic Theory in Italy. Clarendon Press, Oxford, 1940; 1956; paperback, 1962.

François Mansart. Warburg Institute, London, 1941.

The French Drawings in the Collection of H.M. The King at Windsor Castle. Phaidon Press, London, 1945.

The Nation's Pictures (in collaboration with M. D. Whinney). Chatto & Windus, London, 1950.

Rouault's 'Miserere'. Trianon Press, Paris, 1951.

Nicolas Poussin: The Adoration of the Golden Calf. Gallery Books, London, 1951.

Art and Architecture in France 1500–1700. Pelican History of Art. London, 1953; 1957.

The Drawings of G. B. Castiglione and Stefano della Bella in the Collection of H.M. The Queen at Windsor Castle. Phaidon Press, London, 1954.

Venetian Drawings of the XVII and XVIII Centuries in the Collection of H.M. The Queen at Windsor Castle (in collaboration with E. Croft-Murray). Phaidon Press, London, 1957.

Philibert de L'Orme. A. Zwemmer Ltd., London, 1958.

The Art of William Blake. Columbia University Press, 1959. Oxford University Press, 1960.

The Roman Drawings of the XVII and XVIII Centuries in the Collection of H.M. The Queen at Windsor Castle (in collaboration with H. L. Cooke). Phaidon Press, 1960.

Exposition Nicolas Poussin (Catalogue). Musées Nationaux, Paris, 1960.

Picasso: the formative years (in collaboration with P. Pool). Studio Books, London, 1962.

Poussin: lettres et propos sur l'art. Hermann, Paris, 1964.

Nicolas Poussin (The Masters, 7). London, 1965.

Seurat. Phaidon Press, London, 1965.

Nicolas Poussin. 2 vols. Bollingen Foundation, New York, 1967; *Catalogue raisonné.* Phaidon Press, London, 1966.

Picasso's 'Guernica'. Oxford University Press, London, 1967.

ARTICLES

1924

'Some Aspects of Modern Art', *The Heretick*, I, March 1924.

'Art and Morality', *The Heretick*, II, June 1924.

1926

'The Aesthetics of a Bromide', *The Marlburian*, LXI, 870, 23.vi.1926.

'De Cubismo', *The Marlburian*, LXI, 870, 23.vi.1926.

1933

'Riviera Styles', *The Spectator*, 29.ix.1933.

'Rhine and Danube', *The Spectator*, 24.xi.1933.

1934

'Doctrinal Advertisement', *The Spectator*, 5.i.1934.

'Odd Thoughts at Paestum', *The Spectator*, 9.ii.1934.

'Nature and Design', *The Listener*, 11.iv.1934.

'The Beaver and the Silk-worm', *The Spectator*, 2.xi.1934.

'Bosch and Bruegel', *The Spectator*, 30.xi.1934.

1934–35

'Time and Place in the Arts – I', *The Listener*, 27.xii.1934; II, *The Listener*, 2.i.1935.

1935

'The Art of Diego Rivera', *The Listener*, 17.iv.1935.

'Academies – I', *The Spectator*, 9.viii.1935; II, *The Spectator*, 16.viii.1935.

'Scientific Picture Galleries', *The Spectator*, 6.ix.1935.

'A Neo-Classical City', *The Spectator*, 20.ix.1935.

'The New English Art Club', *The Spectator*, 8.xi.1935.

'Rococo', *The Spectator*, 6.xii.1935.

1936

'Rationalist and Anti-rationalist Art', *Left Review*, June 1936.

'Dalou and his Workers' Monument', *Left Review*, October 1936.

1937

'The "Realism" Quarrel', *Left Review*, April 1937.

'Art under Capitalism and Socialism', *The Mind in Chains; Socialism and the Cultural Revolution*, ed. by C. Day Lewis, London, 1937, pp. 103 ff.

1937–38

'The *Hypnerotomachia Poliphili* in 17th century France', *Journal of the Warburg Institute*, I, 1937–38, pp. 117 ff.

'The Criminal-King in a 19th century Novel', *Journal of the Warburg Institute*, I, 1937–38, pp. 248 f.

'Poussin's Notes on Painting', *Journal of the Warburg Institute*, I, 1937–38, pp. 344 ff.

1938

'A newly discovered Poussin', *Apollo*, XXVII, 1938, pp. 197 ff.

'Holidays nearer Home', *The Spectator*, 15.iv.1938.

'Cross-Section of Art in England Today', *The Listener*, 16.vi.1938.

'How I look at Modern Painting', *The Listener*, 14.vii.1938.

'Two Artists and the Outside World', *The Listener*, 28.vii.1938.

'Standards – I', *The Spectator*, 9.iv.1938; II, *The Spectator*, 16.iv.1938; III, *The Spectator*, 23.ix.1938.

1938–39

'Blake's *Ancient of Days*', *Journal of the Warburg Institute*, II, 1938–39, pp. 53 ff.

'Blake's *Glad Day*', *Journal of the Warburg Institute*, II, 1938–1939, pp. 65 ff.

'God and Prince in Bach's Cantatas', *Journal of the Warburg Institute*, II, 1938–39, pp. 178 ff.

'An Echo of the "Paragone" in Shakespeare', *Journal of the Warburg Institute*, II, 1938–39, pp. 260 ff.

'The Triclinium in religious Art', *Journal of the Warburg Institute*, II, 1938–39, pp. 271 ff.

'Allusion and Abstraction in Modern Painting', *Student Forum*, 7.vi.1939.

1939–40

'El Greco's *Dream of Philip II*: An Allegory of the Holy League', *Journal of the Warburg and Courtauld Institutes*, III, 1939–40, pp. 58 ff.

'A Poussin-Castiglione Problem', *Journal of the Warburg and Courtauld Institutes*, III, 1939–40, pp. 142 ff.

1941

'Walter Richard Sickert', *Britain To-day*, LXIII, 1941.

1943

'Philippe de Champaigne's Portraits of the Échevins of Paris', *Burlington Magazine*, LXXXII/LXXXIII, 1943, pp. 83 ff.

'Jean Lemaire: Painter of Architectural Fantasies', *Burlington Magazine*, LXXXII/LXXXIII, 1943, pp. 241 ff.

'Blake's Pictorial Imagination', *Journal of the Warburg and Courtauld Institutes*, VI, 1943, pp. 190 ff.

'Blake's Brazen Serpent', *Journal of the Warburg and Courtauld Institutes*, VI, 1943, pp. 225 ff.

1944

'The early Work of Charles Lebrun – I and II', *Burlington Magazine*, LXXXIV/LXXXV, 1944, pp. 165 ff., 186 ff.

'The heroic and the ideal Landscape in the Work of Nicolas Poussin', *Journal of the Warburg and Courtauld Institutes*, VII, 1944, pp. 154 ff.

1945

'The *Joueur de Vielle* of Georges de la Tour', *Burlington Magazine*, LXXXVI/LXXXVII, 1945, pp. 108 ff.

'Two newly discovered Landscapes by Nicolas Poussin', *Burlington Magazine*, LXXXVI/LXXXVII, 1945, pp. 186 ff.

'The Château de Balleroy' (in collaboration with C. Gould), *Burlington Magazine*, LXXXVI/LXXXVII, 1945, pp. 248 ff.

'The Drawings of Giovanni Benedetto Castiglione', *Journal of the Warburg and Courtauld Institutes*, VIII, 1945, pp. 161 ff.

1946

'Paintings by Sebastiano and Marco Ricci in the Royal Collection', *Burlington Magazine*, LXXXVIII, 1946, pp. 263 ff.

'Some Portraits by Simon Vouet', *Burlington Magazine*, LXXXVIII, 1946, pp. 268 ff.

'The King's Pictures', *The Listener*, 7.xi.1946.

1947

'Sebastiano and Marco Ricci: A Footnote', *Burlington Magazine*, LXXXIX, 1947, pp. 101 f.

'Poussin Studies I: Self-Portraits', *Burlington Magazine*, LXXXIX, 1947, pp. 219 ff.

'Poussin Studies II: Three early Works', *Burlington Magazine*, LXXXIX, 1947, pp. 266 ff.

'The *Annunciation* by Nicolas Poussin', *Bulletin de la Société Poussin*, I, 1947, pp. 18 ff.

'Two Exhibitions of Seventeenth-Century Art', *The Listener*, 10.vii.1947.

1948

'Poussin Studies III: The Poussins at Dulwich', *Burlington Magazine*, XC, 1948, pp. 4 ff.

'Dipinti veneziani del XVII e del XVIII secolo nelle collezioni reali d'Inghilterra', *Arte Veneta*, II, 1948, pp. 127 ff.

'The Dulwich Pictures: Nicolas Poussin', *Leeds Art Calendar*, I, 1948, pp. 11 ff., and II, pp. 12 f., 18 f.

1949

'Nicolas Poussin', *Burlington Magazine*, XCI, 1949, pp. 355 f.

'Mannerism in Architecture', *Journal of the Royal Institute of British Architects*, LVI, 1949, pp. 195 ff.

'The Great Habsburg Art Collectors', *The Listener*, 21.vii. 1949.

'Landscape in French Art', *The Listener*, 15.xii.1949.

1950

'Poussin Studies IV: Two rediscovered late Works', *Burlington Magazine*, XCII, 1950, pp. 39 ff.

'Poussin Studies V: "The Silver Birch Master" ', *Burlington Magazine*, XCII, 1950, pp. 69 ff.

'Diderot and French Landscape Painting: An imaginary Letter', *The Listener*, 12.i.1950.

'The Ordeal of Cézanne', *Art News*, 4.xi.1950.

'Matisse and Picasso: Sculpture and Pottery', *The Listener*, 14.xii.1950.

1951

'Poussin Studies VI: Poussin's decoration of the Long Gallery in the Louvre', *Burlington Magazine*, XCIII, 1951, pp. 369 ff., and XCIV, 1952, p. 31.

'The École de Paris and the Royal Academy', *The New Statesman*, 20.i.1951.

'The École de Paris in Retrospect', *The Listener*, 22.ii.1951.

1952

'French Drawings from Fouquet to Gauguin', *The Listener*, 7.ii.1952.

'Roger Fry', *The Spectator*, 11.iv.1952.

1953

'The Royal Collection of Paintings', *Country Life*, Coronation Number, 1953.

'Picasso in Rome', *The Listener*, 9.vii.1953.

1954

'The Teaching of Art History and the Museum Profession', *Museums Journal*, LIV, 1954, pp. 159 ff.

1955

'The Courtauld Collection', *Art et Style*, October 1955.

'Die Sammlung Samuel Courtauld', *Die Weltkunst*, 15. xii.1955.

1957

'The Précieux and French Art', *Fritz Saxl: a volume of Memorial Essays from his Friends in England*, 1957, pp. 326 ff.

1958

'Poussin Studies VII: Poussins in Neapolitan and Sicilian Collections', *Burlington Magazine*, C, 1958, pp. 101 f.

'A neo-Palladian Programme executed by Visentini and Zuccarelli for Consul Smith', *Burlington Magazine*, C, 1958, pp. 283 f.

'The Palazzo Barberini: the Contributions of Maderno, Bernini, and Pietro da Cortona', *Journal of the Warburg and Courtauld Institutes*, XXI, 1958, pp. 256 ff.

'The Legend of Raphael in Italy and France', *Italian Studies*, XIII, 1958.

'Poussin dans les musées de province', *La Revue des Arts*, VIII, 1958, pp. 5 ff.

'Un bilan poussinesque', *Arts*, 2–8.x.1958, p. 13.

1959

'Poussin Studies VIII: A Series of Anchorite subjects commissioned by Philip IV from Poussin, Claude and others", *Burlington Magazine*, CI, 1959, pp. 389 f.

'Poussin Studies IX: Additions to the Work of Jean Lemaire', *Burlington Magazine*, CI, 1959, pp. 440 ff.

'Illusionist Decoration in Central Italian Painting of the Renaissance', *Journal of the Royal Society of Arts*, April 1959.

'The new Courtauld Institute Galleries', *The Studio*, CLVIII, 1959, pp. 1 ff.

1960

'Poussin Studies X: Karel Philips Spierincks, the first Imitator of Poussin's *Bacchanals*', *Burlington Magazine*, CII, 1960, pp. 308 ff.

'Poussin Studies XI: Some Addenda to the Poussin Number', *Burlington Magazine*, CII, 1960, pp. 396 ff.

'Two unpublished Drawings by Lemercier for the Pavillon de l'Horloge', *Burlington Magazine*, CII, 1960, pp. 447 f.

'A "Veduta" by Angelo Maria Costa', *Burlington Magazine*, CII, 1960, p. 529.

'État présent des études sur Poussin', *Actes du Colloque International Nicolas Poussin*, I, 1960, pp. xx ff.

'La première période romaine de Poussin', *Actes du Colloque International Nicolas Poussin*, I, 1960, pp. 163 ff.

'Poussin et les cérémonies religieuses antiques', *La Revue des Arts*, II, 1960, pp. 56 ff.

'Two unpublished Plans of the Farnese Palace', *Metropolitan Museum of Art Bulletin*, XIX, No. 1, 1960, pp. 15 ff.

1961

'A Copy after Giordano by Hubert Robert', *Burlington Magazine*, CIII, 1961, p. 433.

'A mythological Painting by Poussin', *Burlington Magazine*, CIII, 1961, p. 437.

'Poussin and his Circle at Rouen', *Burlington Magazine*, CIII, 1961, pp. 351 ff.

'Poussin Studies XII: The Hovingham Master', *Burlington Magazine*, CIII, 1961, pp. 454 ff.

1962

'Mantegna's *Triumph of Caesar* at Hampton Court: Report on Work in Progress', *Burlington Magazine*, CIV, 1962, p. 322.

'Poussin Studies XIII: Early Falsifications of Poussin', *Burlington Magazine*, CIV, 1962, pp. 486 ff.

'Some Corrections and Additions to M. Wildenstein's' *Graveurs de Poussin au XVIIᵉ siècle*' (in collaboration with M. Davies), *Gazette des Beaux-Arts*, 1962, II, pp. 205 ff.

'The Royal Collection of Paintings', *Apollo*, LXXVI, 1962, pp. 443 ff.

'The History of Art', *The Listener*, 4.v.1962.

1963

'Baroque and Antiquity: Introduction', *Studies in Western Art*, III. *Latin and American Art, and the Baroque Period in Europe* (Acts of the Twentieth International Congress of the History of Art), 1963, pp. 3 ff.

1964

'The Project of restoring Mantegna's *Triumph of Caesar*', *Burlington Magazine*, CVI, 1964, pp. 126 ff.

'Simone Martini at the Hôtel de Sully', *Burlington Magazine*, CVI, 1964, p. 129.

'Poussin Studies XIV: Poussin's *Crucifixion*', *Burlington Magazine*, CVI, 1964, pp. 450 ff.

'Un tableau d'Eustache Le Sueur', *Art de France*, IV, 1964, pp. 293 ff.

1965

'Poussin and his Roman Patrons', *Walter Friedlaender zum 90. Geburtstag*, Berlin, 1965, pp. 58 ff.

'Thomas Gambier Parry: a great art Collector', *Apollo*, LXXXI, 1965, pp. 288 ff.

'Poussin: A Tercentenary', *Guardian*, 18.xi.1965.

1966

'Poussin and Aesop', *Journal of the Warburg and Courtauld Institutes*, XXIX, 1966, pp. 436 ff.

'The first illuminated Books', *Blake. A Collection of Critical Essays*, ed. N. Frye (Twentieth Century Views), Englewood Cliffs, N.J., 1966, pp. 127 ff.

'The Variety of Poussin', *Granta*, 5.iii.1966.

1967

'Two Drawings for Sepulchral Monuments by Bernini', *Essays in the History of Art presented to Rudolf Wittkower*, London, 1967, pp. 230 ff.

'The Renaissance outside Italy', *Encyclopedia of World Art*, XII, pp. 121 ff. (McGraw-Hill Publishing Co. Ltd.), 1967.

'Don Vincenzo Vittoria', *Burlington Magazine*, CIX, 1967, pp. 31 f.

'The History of Thomas Gambier Parry's Collection', *Burlington Magazine*, CIX, 1967 ,pp. 112 ff.

'Seventeenth and eighteenth-century Pictures in the Gambier-Parry Collection', *Burlington Magazine*, CIX, 1967, p. 177.

REVIEWS

1928

'Self-consciousness in Modern Art', *The Venture*, No. 1, November 1928, p. 46.

1929

'Fonthill Abbey', *The Venture*, No. 2, February 1929, p. 75.

'17th Century Dutch Painting', *Cambridge Review*, 1.iii.1929.

'Johann Michael Fischer and the Bavarian Rococo', *The Venture*, No. 3, June 1929, p. 128.

'Seurat', *Cambridge Review*, 5.vi.1929.

'Bruegel', *The Venture*, No. 4, November 1929, p. 160.

1930

'Design from Giotto to Michelangelo', *The Venture*, No. 5, February 1930, p. 226.

'Cambridgeshire Children in Pictures', *Nation and Athenaeum*, 24.v.1930.

'Cubism', *The Venture*, No. 6, June 1930, p. 256.

'Popular Histories of Art': *A miniature History of European Art*. By R. H. Wilenski. *Cambridge Review*, 13.vi.1930.

1932

'Mr. Sacheverell Sitwell and Baroque Art', *Cambridge Review*, 5.ii. and 12.ii.1932.

'French Painting':

A Short History of French Painting. By Eric G. Underwood.

An Outline of French Painting. By R. H. Wilenski.

The French Pictures. A Letter to Harriet. By Raymond Mortimer.

An Account of French Painting. By Clive Bell.

An Introduction to French Painting. By Alan Clutton-Brock. *Cambridge Review*, 4.iii.1932.

'Quatro Cento': *The Quattro Cento. Part I: Florence and Verona.* By Adrian Stokes. *The Spectator,* 30.vii.1932.

'The Picasso Exhibition in Paris', *The Spectator,* 13.viii.1932.

'Ludwig and Louis', *The Spectator,* 1.x.1932.

The Horse in Art. By Lida L. Fleitmann. *The Spectator,* 8.x.1932.

'Plagiarism and Vulgarity', *The Spectator,* 15.x.1932.

'Art', *The Spectator,* 22.x.1932.

The Meaning of Modern Sculpture. By R. H. Wilenski. *Cambridge Review,* 28.x.1932.

'Living Sculpture': *Sculpture and the Living Model.* By Eric Gill. *The Spectator,* 29.x.1932.

'A Sculptor's Water-colours', *The Spectator,* 4.xi.1932.

Rubens: Painter and Diplomat. By Émile Cammaerts. *Cambridge Review,* 4.xi.1932.

'Mr. Nash and Others', *The Spectator,* 11.xi.1932.

'The Original English Painter', *The Spectator,* 25.xi.1932.

'Old Masters in Painting and Sculpture', *The Spectator,* 2.xii.1932.

Sir William Orpen, Artist and Man. By P. G. Konody and Sidney Dark. *The Spectator,* 23.xii.1932.

'Old Master Drawings', *The Spectator,* 23.xii.1932.

1933

'Drawing and Engraving':

Peter Paul Rubens. By Martin Freeman.

Phil May. By James Thorpe.

The Art and Life of Byam Shaw. By Rex Vicat Cole.

Thirty Personalities and a Self-Portrait. By Wyndham Lewis.

Wood-engraving and Woodcuts. By Clare Leighton.

Making an Etching. By Levon West.

The Spectator, 6.i.1933.

'Death at the Academy', *The Spectator,* 13.i.1933.

'The Royal Academy Exhibition – II', *The Spectator,* 20.i.1933.

'The Elizabethan Exhibition', *The Spectator,* 3.ii.1933.

'Style and Criticism': *Characteristics of French Art.* By Roger Fry. *The Spectator,* 10.ii.1933.

'Meissen or Nymphenburg?': *Porcelain as an Art and a Mirror of Fashion.* By Robert Schmidt. Trs. by W. A. Thorpe. *The Spectator,* 17.ii.1933.

'The Three Louis', *The Spectator,* 24.ii.1933.

'Prints at the British Museum', *The Spectator,* 10.iii.1933.

'Tchelitchew: Form and Content', *The Spectator,* 17.iii.1933.

'Austerity in Paint', *The Spectator,* 31.iii.1933.

Jacob Epstein. By L. B. Powell. *The Spectator,* 14.iv.1933.

'Post-Cubism', *The Spectator,* 28.iv.1933.

Appreciation of Architecture. By Robert Byron. *The Spectator,* 28.iv.1933.

'The Royal Academy', *The Spectator,* 5.v.1933.

'Sculpture: Primitive and Neo-Primitive', *The Spectator,* 10.v.1933.

'Chinese Painting': *A History of Early Chinese Painting.* By Osvald Sirén. *The Spectator,* 9.vi.1933.

The Art of Henri Matisse. By Albert C. Barnes and Violette de Mazia. *The Spectator,* 16.vi.1933.

'Exceptional Paintings', *The Spectator,* 23.vi.1933.

'Shapes and Objects', *The Spectator,* 30.vi.1933.

'Mr. Sickert and Mr. Fry', *The Spectator,* 14.vii.1933.

John Ruskin. By R. H. Wilenski. *The Spectator,* 14.vii.1933.

'The Art of Picasso', *The Listener,* 26.vii.1933.

'The Pre-Raphaelites and Life', *The Spectator,* 28.vii.1933.

Raphael. By Sir Charles Holmes. *The Spectator,* 28.vii.1933.

'Tiepolo out of Context', *The Spectator,* 4.viii.1933.

Beauty looks after Herself. By Eric Gill. *The Spectator,* 18.viii.1933.

'A Baroque Portrait Group', *The Spectator,* 18.viii.1933.

'French Art': *Commemorative Catalogue of the Exhibition of French Art.* Ed. by W. G. Constable. *The Spectator,* 1.ix.1933.

'The Renoir Exhibition in Paris', *The Spectator,* 22.ix.1933.

1934

'English Art':

A Short History of English Painting. By Eric Underwood.

A Short History of English Sculpture. By Eric Underwood.

An Introduction to English Painting. By John Rothenstein.

A Short History of Painting in England. By Miles F. de Montmorency.

English Watercolours. By Laurence Binyon. *The Spectator,* 5.i.1934.

Modern Sculpture. By Herbert Maryon. *The Spectator,* 5.i.1934.

'More about English Art':

English Painting. By R. H. Wilenski.

An Outline of English Painting. By R. H. Wilenski.

A Short Account of British Painting. By Charles Johnson.

British Painting. By C. H. Collins-Baker and M. R. James. *The Spectator,* 12.i.1934.

'The English Tradition in Painting', *The Spectator,* 12.i.1934.

'The Pre-Raphaelites', *The Spectator,* 19.i.1934.

English Pottery and Porcelain. By W. B. Honey.

Modern Drawings. By Campbell Dodgson. *The Spectator,* 19.i.1934.

'English Landscape', *The Spectator,* 26.i.1934.

The Ukiyoye Primitives. By Yone Noguchi. *The Spectator,* 2.ii.1934.

'Artists and Materials', *The Spectator,* 2.ii.1934.

'French Landscape', *The Spectator*, 9.ii.1934.

Claude Monet and his Garden. By Stephen Gwynn.

François Boucher and the Beauvais Tapestries. By Maurice Block. *The Spectator*, 9.ii.1934.

'Cathédrale engloutie': *Stones of Rimini.* By Adrian Stokes. *The Spectator*, 23.ii.1934.

'Contemporary Classics', *The Spectator*, 2.iii.1934.

'Side Shows', *The Spectator*, 9.iii.1934.

'Porcelain and Rococo', *The Spectator*, 16.iii.1934.

Russian Mediaeval Architecture. By David Roden Buxton. *The Spectator*, 16.iii.1934.

'The Prefaces of Baedeker', *The Spectator*, 30.iii.1934.

'Art from Above': *Enjoying Pictures.* By Clive Bell. *The Spectator*, 30.iii.1934.

Mexican Painting. By R. Montenegro.

Temple Church Monuments. By Mrs. A. Esdaile. *The Spectator*, 30.iii.1934.

Byzantine Architecture. By J. Arnott Hamilton. *The Spectator*, 13.iv.1934.

From Moscow to Samarkand. By Y. Z. *The Spectator*, 27.iv.1934.

'Greek Art and the Artist of Today': *L'Art en Grèce.* By Christian Zervos. *The Spectator*, 8.vi.1934.

'El Greco's "Laocoon" ', *The Spectator*, 28.ix.1934.

'Our Heritage', *The Spectator*, 5.x.1934.

'A Cubist Father', *The Spectator*, 5.x.1934.

'German Pretensions in Art', *The Spectator*, 5.x.1934.

The Tuileries. By G. Lenôtre. *The Spectator*, 5.x.1934.

'Romantic Landscape', *The Spectator*, 12.x.1934.

'Professor Roger Fry", *Cambridge Review*, 19.x.1934.

'English Painting', *The Spectator*, 19.x.1934.

'The Crafts Delivered', *The Spectator*, 26.x.1934.

'French Dictionaries':

Harraps Standard French and English Dictionary. Ed. by J. E. Mansion.

The Concise Oxford French Dictionary. Compiled by A. and M. Chevalley.

Shorter Commercial and Financial French Dictionary. By J. O. Kettridge. *The Spectator*, 26.x.1934.

Introduction to Cambridge. By S. C. Roberts. *The Spectator*, 2.xi.1934.

The Craft of Forgery. By Henry Rhodes.

The Study of Art. By R. H. Wilenski.

The David Collection. By R. L. Hobson.

Modern Publicity. Ed. by F. A. Mercer. *The Spectator*, 9.xi.1934.

'Midland Art Treasures', *The Spectator*, 16.xi.1934.

'England *v.* America', *Cambridge Review*, 16.xi.1934.

'Photographic Art', *The Spectator*, 7.xii.1934.

'Decoration and Observation', *The Spectator*, 14.xii.1934.

'English Architecture', *The Spectator*, 21.xii.1934.

'Modern Architecture':

Architecture Here and Now. By Clough Williams-Ellis and John Summerson.

Building to the Skies. By Alfred C. Bossom. *The Spectator*, 28.xii.1934.

'Life and Art in Photograph':

The Italian Renaissance. Ed. by A. K. Wickham.

The Polar Regions. Ed. by J. M. Scott.

A Book of Dogs. Chatto & Windus. *The Spectator*, 28.xii.1934.

1935

Westminster Abbey. By A. L. N. Russell.

Famous London Churches. By C. B. Mortlock. *The Spectator*, 4.i.1935.

'Great and Queer', *The Spectator*, 4.i.1935.

'Art and the Machine':

Art and Industry. By Herbert Read.

Regency Furniture, 1795-1820. By M. Jourdain. *The Spectator*, 4.i.1935.

'Flash in the Pan', *The Spectator*, 11.i.1935.

'Late Renoirs', *The Spectator*, 18.i.1935.

'Mannerism and Cubism', *The Spectator*, 25.i.1935.

Picture Making. By Charles Sims. *The Spectator*, 25.i.1935.

'Art and Society': *Dresden China.* By W. B. Honey. *The Spectator*, 25.i.1935.

'Baroque and Modern': *Henry Moore.* By Herbert Read. *The Spectator*, 1.ii.1935.

'Savage Art', *The Spectator*, 8.ii.1935.

'Candlelight', *The Spectator*, 1.iii.1935.

The Commemorative Catalogue of the Exhibition of British Art. *The Spectator*, 1.iii.1935.

'Epstein and Religious Art', *The Spectator*, 15.iii.1935.

'Michel-Ange Manqué': *The Master: A Study of Michelangelo.* By J. Howard Whitehouse and Colin Rocke. *The Spectator*, 15.iii.1935.

English Illustration: The 'Nineties. By James Thorpe. *The Spectator*, 15.iii.1935.

'Chinese Painting', *The Spectator*, 22.iii.1935.

'Miscellany', *The Spectator*, 29,iii.1935.

Carolingian Art. By Roger Hinks. *The Spectator*, 29.iii.1935.

'Applied Arts', *The Spectator*, 5.iv.1935.

The Modern Movement in Art. By R. H. Wilenski.

Portrait of America. By Diego Rivera. *The Spectator*, 12.iv.1935.

'Pure Form': *A Note on Modern Painting.* By R. H. Wilenski. *The Spectator*, 19.iv.1935.

'Eighteenth-century Painting', *The Spectator*, 19.iv.1935.

'Georgian Painting', *The Spectator*, 3.v.1935.
'The Royal Academy', *The Spectator*, 10.v.1935.
The Medieval Carver. By M. D. Anderson. *The Spectator*, 10.v.1935.
'Selection', *The Spectator*, 17.v.1935.
The Modern Movement in Painting. By T. W. Earp. *The Spectator*, 17.v.1935.
'Leonardo da Vinci': *A Catalogue of the Drawings of Leonardo da Vinci in the Collection of His Majesty the King at Windsor Castle.* By Kenneth Clark. *The Spectator*, 24.v.1935.
'From Royalty to Savage', *The Spectator*, 31.v.1935.
'Nineteenth-Century Classics', *The Spectator*, 7.vi.1935.
'Old Masters', *The Spectator*, 21.vi.1935.
'Russian Art', *The Spectator*, 28.vi.1935.
L'art primitif; l'art médiéval. By Louis Réau. *The Burlington Magazine*, LXVII, 1935, p. 47.
'Flemish Painting', *The Spectator*, 12.vii.1935.
'Sumerian Art':
L'Art de la Mésopotamie. By Christian Zervos.
The Development of Sumerian Art. By C. Leonard Woolley. *The Spectator*, 12.vii.1935.
'Italian Art in Paris', *The Spectator*, 19.vii.1935.
'Titian in Venice', *The Spectator*, 26.vii.1935.
'Cézanne', *The Spectator*, 2.viii.1935.
The Artist and his Public. By Eric Newton.
The Cathedrals of Normandy. By Jocelyn Perkins. *The Spectator*, 2.viii.1935.
'Architectural Foundations': *The New Architecture and the Bauhaus.* By Walter Gropius. *The Spectator*, 2.viii.1935.
'Imperial Christian Art': *Byzantine Art.* By D. Talbot Rice. *The Spectator*, 9.viii.1935.
The Triumph of Caesar. By W. Ormsby Gore. *The Spectator*, 16.viii.1935.
'Holiday Shows', *The Spectator*, 23.viii.1935.
Neo-Platonism of the Italian Renaissance. By Nesca Rodd. *The Spectator*, 23.viii.1935.
'The Museums of London': *Brief Guide to the National Museums and Galleries of London. The Spectator*, 30.viii.1935.
'Soviet Art': *Art in the U.S.S.R.* Ed. by C. G. Holme. *The Spectator*, 27.ix.1935.
'Brussels Exhibitions', *The Spectator*, 4.x.1935.
'Sleepers, Awake!', *The Spectator*, 11.x.1935.
'Salvation from the West': *Modern Art.* By Thomas Craven. *The Spectator*, 11.x.1935.
Six Architects. By Sir Reginald Blomfield. *The Spectator*, 11.x.1935.
'Rouault', *The Spectator*, 18.x.1935.

Paul Cézanne. By Gerstle Mack.
The Autobiography of Montaigne. Selected by M. Lowenthal. *The Spectator*, 18.x.1935.
'Survivors', *The Spectator*, 25.x.1935.
The Empress Catherine and the Princess Dashkov. By H. Montgomery Hyde. *The Spectator*, 8.xi.1935.
Forty Drawings. By Horace Brodzky. *The Spectator*, 15.xi.1935.
'Art and Dictatorship', *The Spectator*, 22.xi.1935.
Handbook to English Medieval Sculpture. By Arthur Gardner. *The Spectator*, 22.xi.1935.
'Cocteau and Derain', *The Spectator*, 20.xii.1935.
The Life of Christ in the Old Italian Masters. By Edward Hutton. *The Spectator*, 27.xii.1935.

1936

'A Courbet Exhibition', *Burlington Magazine*, LXIX, 1936, pp. 36.ff.
'Watteau and his Contemporaries', *Burlington Magazine*, LXIX, 1936, pp. 230 ff.
'A new Picasso', *The Spectator*, 3.i.1936.
'New English Painting', *The Spectator*, 10.i.1936.
'Chinoiserie', *The Spectator*, 17.i.1936.
'An Impure Impressionist', *The Spectator*, 31.i.1936.
'These Minor Monuments', *The Spectator*, 7.ii.1936.
'Matisse and Others', *The Spectator*, 28.ii.1936.
'Gainsborough', *The Spectator*, 13.iii.1936.
'Bargains', *The Spectator*, 27.iii.1936.
'Monet', *The Spectator*, 10.iv.1936.
'Ingres at the National Gallery', *The Spectator*, 1.v.1936.
'Realism at the Academy', *The Spectator*, 8.v.1936.
'Degas and La Fresnaye', *The Spectator*, 15.v.1936.
'From the Nineteenth to the Twentieth', *The Spectator*, 22.v.1936.
'Ladislas Peri', *The Spectator*, 5.vi.1936.
'Picasso', *The Spectator*, 12.vi.1936.
'Superrealism in London', *The Spectator*, 19.vi.1936.
'Daumier and Courbet', *The Spectator*, 26.vi.1936.
'Another Surrealist', *The Spectator*, 10.vii.1936.
'Decoration and Realism', *The Spectator*, 17.vii.1936.
'Cézanne and his Contemporaries', *The Spectator*, 24.vii.1936.
'The French nineteenth-century Exhibition at the New Burlington Galleries', *Beaux-Arts*, 1.x.1936.
'Painters are Men', *The Spectator*, 9.x.1936.
'Watteau', *The Spectator*, 30.x.1936.
'Matisse, Picasso and Braque at Rosenberg's', *Artist's News Sheet* (A.I.), November 1936.
'English Novelty', *The Spectator*, 27.xi.1936.
'French and Spanish', *The Spectator*, 11.xii.1936.

'A Socialist Decorator', *The Spectator*, 18.xii.1936.

Cézanne et Zola. By John Rewald. *Burlington Magazine*, LXIX, 1936, pp. 291 f.

'Below the Surface': *Masterpieces of French Painting.* A. Zwemmer Ltd. *The Spectator*, 3.i.1936.

Monuments and Men of Ancient Rome. By Grant Showerman.

English Drawings. By M. R. Ritchie.

The New Architectural Sculpture. By W. R. Agard. *The Spectator*, 24.i.1936.

Henry of Navarre. By Marcelle Vioux. *The Spectator*, 27.iii.1936.

'Artists' Memoirs':

Self and Partners. By Sir Charles Holmes.

Oil Paint and Grease Paint. By Dame Laura Knight. *The Spectator*, 3.iv.1936.

'Artist *v.* Critic': *The Painter's Eye.* By Edwin Glascow. *The Spectator*, 10.iv.1936.

Michelangelo the Man. By D. L. Finlayson. *The Spectator*, 8.v.1936.

'A Gentleman in Russia': *Murray's Handbook to Russia. Cambridge Review*, 5.vi.1936.

'Reynolds as Writer': *The Literary Career of Sir Joshua Reynolds.* By F. W. Hilles. *The Spectator*, 5.vi.1936.

Romanesque Architecture. By A. W. Clapham.

Ancient Monuments: Southern England. By W. Ormsby-Gore. *The Spectator*, 5.vi.1963.

'Humanist Savages': *Old Peruvian Art.* By H. V. Doering. *The Spectator*, 19.vi.1936.

'Richelieu': *The Cardinal Dictator.* By Auguste Bailly. *The Spectator*, 26.vi.1936.

'Progressive Art?': *Surrealism.* By Herbert Read. *Cambridge Review*, 27.xi.1936.

1937

'Lord Hastings at the Lefèvre Galleries', *Left Review*, January 1937.

'Academy Vanguard', *The Spectator*, 1.i.1937.

'Art from the Lumber Room', *The Spectator*, 8.i.1937.

'The English Home', *The Spectator*, 15.i.1937.

'The Ways of Abstraction', *The Spectator*, 22.i.1937.

'Seurat', *The Spectator*, 29.i.1937.

'The Reynolds Exhibition', *The Spectator*, 12.ii.1937.

The Life of Paul Gauguin. By Robert Burnett. *Left Review*, February 1937.

'The Art of the Few': *Art and Society.* By Herbert Read. *The Spectator*, 26.ii.1937.

'Spanish Art', *Cambridge Review*, 5.iii.1937.

'The French Again', *The Spectator*, 12.iii.1937.

'Jongkind and Rodin', *The Spectator*, 26.iii.1937.

'Bohemian Artists': *Bandits in a Landscape.* By W. Gaunt. *The Spectator*, 9.iv.1937.

'The New Realism in Sculpture', *Granta*, 21.iv.1937, and *Cambridge Review*, 23.iv.1937.

'La Semaine à Paris', *The Spectator*, 23.iv.1937.

Modern Plastic Art. By C. Giedion-Welcker. *The Spectator*, 30.iv.1937.

'The British Artists' Congress', *The Spectator*, 30.iv.1937.

The Loves of Goya. By Marion Chapman. *The Spectator*, 30.iv.1937.

Art and Society. By Herbert Read. *Christian Science Monitor*, 5.v.1937.

'The Royal Academy', *The Spectator*, 7.v.1937.

'A Nineteenth Century Anthology': *French Painting of the Nineteenth Century.* By S. Rocheblave. *The Spectator*, 14.v.1937.

'Imaginative Humour', *The Spectator*, 14.v.1937.

Baroque Painting in Rome. By Ellis K. Waterhouse. *Burlington Magazine*, LXXI, 1937, pp. 47 f., and *The Spectator*, 21.v.1937.

'Three Exhibitions', *The Spectator*, 21.v.1937.

'Picasso', *The Spectator*, May 1937.

'Modern Tapestries', *The Spectator*, 4.vi.1937.

'Art for All':

Vincent Van Gogh. By W. Uhde.

Rembrandt. By A. Bredius.

The Art of Ancient Egypt. By H. Ranke.

The Civilisation of the Renaissance. By J. Burckhardt. *The Spectator*, 11.vi.1937.

'Early Cubism and Surrealism', *The Spectator*, 25.vi.1937.

'State Sales', *The Spectator*, 2.vii.1937.

'Contemporary German Art', *The Spectator*, 8.vii.1937.

'Stage Designs', *The Spectator*, 16.vii.1937.

'Matisse and Rouault', *The Spectator*, 23.vii.1937.

'Art in Paris', *The Spectator*, 6.viii.1937.

Catalan Art. By Christian Zervos. *The Spectator*, 3.ix.1937.

'Tintoretto in Venice', *The Spectator*, September 1937.

'Modern Primitives', *The Spectator*, September 1937.

'Picasso Unfrocked', *The Spectator*, 8.x., 22.x., and 5.xi. 1937.

'Specialists', *The Spectator*, 22.x.1937.

'Dull Art', *The Spectator*, 29.x.1937.

Botticelli. By Lionello Venturi. *The Spectator*, 5.xi.1937.

'The London Group', *The Spectator*, 5.xi.1937.

'Balzac out of Love': *The Unpublished Correspondence of Honoré de Balzac and Madame Zulma Carraud. The Spectator*, 12.xi.1937.

'Picture Books':

Pieter Brueghel. By G. Glück.

El Greco. By M. Legendre and A. Hartmann.

French Painting in the Eighteenth Century. By S. Rocheblave. *The Spectator*, 19.xi.1937.

'East and West', *The Spectator*, 19.xi.1937.

'After Impressionism', *The Spectator*, 25.xi.1937.

'From Anarchy to Abstraction', *The Spectator*, 10.xii.1937.

'Art as Information', *The Spectator*, 17.xii.1937.

1938

'The Royal Academy Exhibition of Seventeenth Century Art', *Apollo*, XXVII, 1938, pp. 3 ff.

'Poussin's *Et in Arcadia Ego*', *Art Bulletin*, XX, 1938, pp. 96 ff.

'Seventeenth-Century Art at Burlington House', *The Spectator*, 7.i.1938.

'China and Children', *The Spectator*, 14.i.1938.

'Painting, Engineering and Mathematics', *The Spectator*, 21.i.1938.

'Baudelaire as Art-Critic', *The Spectator*, 11.ii.1938.

'Delacroix and the Romantics': *The Journal of Eugène Delacroix*. Transl. by Walter Pach. *The Spectator*, 18.ii.1938.

'Popular Art Books':

The Impressionists. By Wilhelm Uhde.

Cézanne. By Fritz Novotny.

The Disasters of War. By Francisco de Goya.

Art without Epoch. By Ludwig Goldscheider.

Degas. By Camille Mauclair.

Paul Nash. By Herbert Read. *The Spectator*, 25.ii.1938.

'The Eighteenth Century', *The Spectator*, 25.ii.1938.

'Sophistication and Naïveté', *The Spectator*, 11.iii.1938.

'The Art of the Future':

Portrait of Mexico. By Diego Rivera and Bertram Wolfe.

The New Architecture of Mexico. By Esther Born. *The Spectator*, 18.iii.1938.

'The Realists fall in', *The Spectator*, 25.iii.1938.

'English Art in Paris', *The Spectator*, 8.iv.1938.

'Neo-Classicism':

Annals of Thomas Banks. By C. F. Bell.

The Illustrations of William Blake for Thornton's Virgil. (Nonesuch Press). *The Spectator*, 15.iv.1938.

The Walpole Society Publications. Vols. 24, 25. *The Spectator*, 22.iv.1938.

'The National Gallery', *The Spectator*, 22.iv.1938.

'Mr. Wyndham Lewis' Portrait of Mr. T. S. Eliot', *The Spectator*, 29.iv.1938.

'Art: A Commonplace Academy', *The Spectator*, 6.v.1938.

'An Ordinary Painter' (Gustave Courbet), *The Spectator*, 13.v.1938.

'Augustus John', *The Spectator*, 27.v.1938.

'Furrin Art', *The Spectator*, 3.vi.1938.

'People in Concrete' (Laszlo Péri), *The Spectator*, 10.vi.1938.

'Tragedy in Art', *The Spectator*, 24.vi.1938.

'The Lesson of Still-Life', *The Spectator*, 1.vii.1938.

'Prints':

Six Centuries of Fine Prints. By Carl Zigrossen.

The English Print. By Basil Gray. *The Spectator*, 22.vii.1938.

German Baroque Sculpture. By S. Sitwell. *The Spectator*, 19.viii.1938.

'A Chinese Painter's Views on Art', *The Spectator*, 19.viii.1938.

Spanish Painting. By E. Harris. *The Spectator*, 26.viii.1938.

'A Bristol. Une Exposition d'art français du XVIIᵉ siècle', *Beaux-Arts*, 25.xi.1938.

'French Art in Bristol', *The Listener*, 1.xii.1938.

'Le Grand Siècle', *The Spectator*, 2.xii.1938.

'Guys and Lautrec', *The Spectator*, 9.xii.1938.

1939

'Three Views of Leonardo':

The Notebooks of Leonardo da Vinci. Ed. by Edward MacCurdy.

Leonardo da Vinci. The Tragic Pursuit of Perfection. By Antonina Vallentin.

The Romance of Leonardo da Vinci. By Dmitri Merejcovski. *The Spectator*, 24.iii.1939.

1946

The Creation of the Rococo. By Fiske Kimball. *Burlington Magazine*, LXXXVIII, 1946, pp. 128 f.

'Pictures from Paris Churches', *Burlington Magazine*, LXXXVIII, 1946, p. 200.

'French Seventeenth-Century Art', *Burlington Magazine*, LXXXVIII, 1946, p. 203.

1947

'French Seventeenth-Century Painting at Messrs. Wildenstein', *Burlington Magazine*, LXXXIX, 1947, p. 160.

1948

Claude Nicolas Ledoux. By Marcel Raval and J. C. Moreux. *The Architectural Review*, CIII, 1948, p. 274.

1949

The Old Architecture of Quebec. By Ramsey Traquair. *Burlington Magazine*, XCI, 1949, p. 208.

Georges de la Tour of Lorraine. By S. M. M. Furness. *Burlington Magazine*, XCI, 1949, p. 297.

Literary Sources of Art History: An Anthology from Theophilus to Goethe. Ed. by Elizabeth Gilmore Holt. *College Art Journal,* IX, No. 1, 1949, pp. 81 f.

The French Academies of the Sixteenth Century. By Frances A. Yates. *Times Literary Supplement,* 27.i.1949.

Histoire de l'architecture classique en France. Vol. II. By Louis Hautecœur. *Times Literary Supplement,* 22.vii.1949.

1950

Georges de la Tour. By F.-G. Pariset. *Burlington Magazine,* XCII, 1950, pp. 144 f.

Histoire de l'architecture en France. Vol. I. By L. Hautecœur. *Burlington Magazine,* XCII, 1950, pp, 207 f.

1951

Jean Goujon. By Pierre du Colombier. *Burlington Magazine,* XCIII, 1951, p. 97.

'Picasso Drawings at the I.C.A.', *Burlington Magazine,* XCIII, 1951, pp. 390 f.

1952

'Philippe de Champaigne at the Orangerie, Paris', *Burlington Magazine,* XCIV, 1952, pp. 172 ff.

'Delacroix at Wildenstein's', *Burlington Magazine,* XCIV, 1952, p. 268.

Le Château de Gaillon. By Elisabeth Chirol. *Burlington Magazine,* XCIV, 1952, p. 362.

1953

'Géricault at the Marlborough Gallery', *Burlington Magazine,* XCV, 1953, pp. 24 ff.

'Picasso in Rome and at Lyons', *Burlington Magazine,* XCV, 1953, pp. 331 f.

Matisse: His Art and his Public. By Alfred H. Barr. *Burlington Magazine,* XCV, 1953, pp. 399 f.

1954

Blake's Illustrations to the Divine Comedy. By Albert S. Roe. *Burlington Magazine,* XCVI, 1954, p. 389.

'The Treatment of Space in Ingres': *Ingres.* By Georges Wildenstein. *The Listener,* 11.iii.1954.

1956

'The Exhibition of Pietro da Cortona at Cortona', *Burlington Magazine,* XCVIII, 1956, pp. 415 ff.

Antoine Caron peintre à la cour des Valois. By Jean Ehrmann. *Burlington Magazine,* XCVIII, 1956, p. 418.

1957

Blake: Prophet against Empire. By David V. Erdman.

The Letters of William Blake. By Geoffrey Keynes.

William Blake's 'Songs of Innocence and Experience'. Facsimile. *Burlington Magazine,* XCIX, 1957, pp. 101 f.

L'Architecture française en Allemagne au XVIIIe siècle. By Pierre du Colombier. *Burlington Magazine,* XCIX, 1957, p. 426.

1958

Salons. Vol. I. By Diderot. Ed. by J. Seznec and Jean Adhémar. *Burlington Magazine,* C, 1958, pp. 101 f.

1959

Les Églises des Jésuites de l'Ancienne Assistance de France. By Pierre Moisy. *Burlington Magazine,* CI, 1959, p. 112.

'The Leadership of Poussin I: The Artist's Pictures come to America', *Art News,* New York, January 1959, pp. 30 ff.

1960

I Vermexio architetti ispano-siculi del secolo XVII. By Giuseppe Agnello. *Burlington Magazine,* CII, 1960, pp. 124 f.

Colloque Nicolas Poussin. Publié sous la direction de André Chastel. *Burlington Magazine,* CII, 1960, pp. 350 ff.

Inventaire général des dessins des musées de province – II. Toulouse, Musée Paul-Dupuy, dessins antérieurs à 1830. By Robert Mesuret. *Burlington Magazine,* CII, 1960, p. 502.

1961

Michele Sanmicheli. Catalogo a Cura di Piero Gazzola ordinatore della Mostra. Burlington Magazine, CIII, 1961, p. 152.

Jules Hardouin Mansart. By P. Bourget and G. Cattaui.

François d'Orbay. By Albert Laprade. *Burlington Magazine,* CIII, 1961, pp. 190 f.

Poussin-Studien. By Georg Kauffmann. *Burlington Magazine,* CIII, 1961, p. 285.

The Valois Tapestries. By Frances A. Yates. *Burlington Magazine,* CIII, 1961, p. 325.

Salons. Vol. II. By Diderot. Ed. by J. Seznec and Jean Adhémar. *Burlington Magazine,* CIII, 1961, p. 332.

'Poussin and his Circle in Rouen', *Burlington Magazine,* CIII, 1961, pp. 351 ff.

Picasso's Picassos. By David Douglas Duncan. *The Listener,* 30.xi.1961.

1963

Jacques Callot. Catalogue complet de son œuvre dessinée. By Daniel Ternois. *Burlington Magazine,* CV, 1963, pp. 214 f.

The Architecture of the Palazzo Borghese. By Howard Hibbard. *Burlington Magazine,* CV, 1963, pp. 566 f.

Johann Friedrich Eosander. Grundzüge einer Biographie. By Rudolf Biederstedt. *Journal of the British Archaeological Association,* XXVI, 1963, p. 87.

Patrons and Painters. A Study in the Relations between Italian Art and Society in the Age of the Baroque. By Francis Haskell. *The Spectator,* 5.vii.1963.

1964

Monastic Architecture in France from the Renaissance to the Revolution. By Joan Evans. *Burlington Magazine,* CVI, 1964, pp. 467 f.

1966

The Drawings of Raymond Lafage. By Nathan T. Whitman. *Raymond Lafage dessinateur.* By Jeanne Arvengas. *Burlington Magazine,* CVIII, 1966, p. 531.

OTHER WRITINGS

1934–35

The History and Theories of Painting in Italy and France 1400–1700, with special reference to Poussin. (Dissertation.) Cambridge, 1934–35.

1935

'A Letter from Cambridge', *The Spectator,* 1.iii.1935.
'A Letter from Cambridge', *The Spectator,* 7.vi.1935.
'A Letter from Cambridge', *The Spectator,* 15.xi.1935.

1936

'The May Term in Cambridge' (Letter). *The Spectator,* 5.vi.1936.

1937

'Picasso Unfrocked' (Letter). *The Spectator,* 22.x.1937.

1946–47

The King's Pictures (Introduction to the Catalogue and many entries). Royal Academy, London, 1946–47.

1948

The Blake Bicentenary Exhibition (Foreword to the Catalogue). Tate Gallery, London, 1948.

1949

Contemporary Paintings from Great Britain, the United States and France (Foreword to the Catalogue). Toronto Art Gallery, 1949.

1949–50

Landscape in French Art (Introduction to the Catalogue and entries for works from British collections). Royal Academy, London, 1949–50.

1950–51

Works by Holbein and other Masters of the 16th and 17th Centuries (Introduction to Catalogue and entries for the Seicento section). Royal Academy, London, 1950–51.

1954

'The Courtauld Institute' (Letter). *Burlington Magazine,* XCVI, 1954, p. 61.

'Samuel Courtauld.' Memoir in *The Courtauld Collection of Paintings, Drawings, Engravings and Sculpture.* By Douglas Cooper. (The Athlone Press) 1954.

1955

Nuno Gonçalves: The great Portuguese Painter of the 15th Century. By Reynaldo Dos Santos. (Foreword.) (The Phaidon Press) 1955.

1957

William Blake (1757–1827) (Introduction to the Catalogue). Tate Gallery, London, 1957.

1958

The Age of Louis XIV (Introduction to the Catalogue). Royal Academy, London, 1958.

'Venetian Drawings at Windsor Castle' (Letter). *Burlington Magazine,* C, 1958, p. 253.

1959

Nicolas Poussin (Foreword to the Catalogue). Minneapolis Institute of Art and Toledo Museum of Arts, 1959.

1960

'Poussin's Development: Questions of Method' (Letter). *Burlington Magazine,* CII, 1960, p. 489.

1961

'A mythological Painting by Poussin' (Letter). *Burlington Magazine,* CIII, 1961, p. 437.

1963

'Titian's *Perseus*' (Letter). *Burlington Magazine,* CV, 1963, p. 281.

1964

Goya: Engravings and Lithographs. By T. Harris. (Foreword.) (Cassirer, Oxford), 1964.

1964–65

'The Author: W. G. Constable', *Art Gallery of Toronto News and Notes*, IX, No. 3, September 1964, and *Canaletto Exhibition* Catalogue, Toronto, Ottawa, Montreal, November 1964–February 1965.

1966

'New Ways in History' (Letters). *The Times Literary Supplement*, 28.iv. and 5.v.1966.

1967

The Gambier-Parry Collection (catalogue), Courtauld Institute of Art, University of London, London, 1967.